Mute Dreams, Blind Owls, and Dispersed Knowledges

for Cliff Geertz
with warmest regards,
Mike

Mute Dreams,

Blind Owls, and

Dispersed Knowledges

PERSIAN POESIS IN THE

TRANSNATIONAL CIRCUITRY

MICHAEL M. J. FISCHER

Duke University Press

Durham & London

2004

© 2004 Duke University Press

All rights reserved

Printed in the United States of

America on acid-free paper ∞

Designed by C. H. Westmoreland

Typeset in Minion by

Keystone Typesetting, Inc.

Library of Congress Cataloging-in-

Publication Data appear on the

last printed page of this book.

Contents

By Way of Acknowledgments:
Divided Selves and Doubled Genealogies   vii

Prelude: After Epic, Writing, Painting, and Film   1

I.   Speaking After Zarathustra:
      Ritual, Epic, and Philosophical Forms of Reason

          Prologue   17
              1.   Yasna:
                    Performative Ritual, Narrative Mnemonic   25
              2.   *Shahnameh*:
                    Parable Logic   66
          Coda: Illuminationism:
                    Philosophical Allegory   131

II.   Seeing After Film:
      Textual and Cinematic Forms of Ethical Reason

              3.   Awaiting the Revolution:
                    Surrealism Persian Style   151
              4.   Filmic Judgment and Cultural Critique:
                    The Work of Art, Ethics, and Religion in Postrevolution
                    Iranian Cinema   222
              5.   War Again: Qandahar, 911—
                    Figure and Discourse in Iranian Cinematic Writing   259
          Coda: Balancing Acts (After 9/11)   355

Epilogue: Beyond "Mobile Armies of Metaphors":
             Scheherezade Films the Games   370

Notes   395
Bibliography   433
Index   449

By Way of Acknowledgments:

Divided Selves and Doubled Genealogies

In a world of divided selves, I count myself fortunate to have one of mine be indelibly Yazdi and even Qumi, Persian and Iranian. I still enjoy the snap of response when Iranians ask me how I know this or that about Iranian culture, and I reply usually, "Bacce Yazd-am" [I'm a child of Yazd; I'm from Yazd], and occasionally, "Va yek sol dar Qum zendigi mikardam dar mahalleh-ye Ayatullah Marashi-Najafi ruh-be-ruh-ye Hawza-ye Ayatullah Shariatmadari" [I lived for a year in Qum in Ayatullah Marashi-Najafi's neighborhood across from Ayatullah Shariatmadari's establishment]. Yazd was a divided city of marvels, good and bad, but a wondrous place for a twenty-something to be culturally imprinted amid the multiple communities of Zoroastrians, Shi'ites, Baha'is, and Jews. I arrived in 1969 and stayed for two and a half years, visiting periodically thereafter until 1977. It was an era in which there were still public drinking facilities on which were written "for Muslims only." But there were still twenty-three Zoroastrian villages, as well as a Zoroastrian city quarter; there were still twelve synagogues, all kept functioning at least in rotation; there were still active Zoroastrian-Baha'i and Muslim-Baha'i communities distinguishable only by women's dress; and aside from the regrettable but ethnographically informative activity of the anti-Baha'i organization, there were wonderful Shi'ite *rowza*s and *taziyeh*s, *zurkhana*s and bazaar life, libraries and antique stores, wind towers and ice houses, qanats and gardens, wooden looms and textile mills, almond baklava and refreshing faluda, silk brocades and, from Taft-e Yazd, the world's best pomegranates.

I had incredible teachers both foreign and Iranian. Among the foreigners, the small world of anthropologists, linguists, folklorists, art historians, archaeologists, and historians working in Iran produced some remarkable people. Linguists Bill Beeman, Jerry Clinton, Ed Davis, Don Stilo, and Wheeler Thackston Jr. provided role models of how to speak really elegant Persian, and if my Persian skills never reached any elegance, nonetheless their examples were constant encouragement, as was their support for my efforts at doing field linguistics on dialects (in my case, the central plateau dialect, Dari), and sociolinguistics, and exploring genre forms and literature. The archaeologists David Stronach, Bill Sumner, Carl Lamberg-Karlovsky, and McGuire Gibson provided me homes in Tehran at the British Institute for Persian Studies and the American Institute of Iranian Studies (as did David and Orick Peterson), and a visceral feeling for the exploration of ancient Iran. McGuire and I coaxed an unwilling University of Chicago Land Rover, with geography graduate student Michael Bonine and his wife, Marilyn, behind in a second Land Rover, across northern Iran and the circle route around Afghanistan from Herat to Lashgari-Bazaar and Qandahar, to Kabul, Jelalabad and up to Nuristan, through the Salang Pass into the Bamiyan Valley, around via Tashqurqan, Mazar-i Sharif, Balkh, Sherbarqan, Maimana, and back to Herat and Mashhad. The folklorists Margaret Mills, Charlotte Albright, and Mary-Ellen Page provided role models for eliciting how genre forms work in social context. Carol and Robert Hillenbrandt took me to Sultaneyieh and other Islamic sites to measure and map, photograph and deal with the hordes of friendly-hostile children who wanted to watch, crowd, and test out that ritual of tossing mud and small stones at strangers that was also portrayed in a few 1970s Iranian films. Richard Frye and Eden Naby were always genial hosts, sounding boards, and encouragers.

But it is, of course, my Iranian teachers to whom I am most indebted: leaders, priests, and laity of the Zoroastrian community both in Iran and India, teenagers and ayatullahs of the Shi'ite religious worlds in Yazd and Qum, film scholars and social scientists. Hamid Naficy made sure I got entry to the first North American Iranian film festival which he organized at the University of California, Los Angeles, and his work and friendship have served as a benchmark of serious scholarship on Iranian and transnational film (and television). I thank him as well for his feedback and suggestions on the first draft of this volume. Hamid also helped bring a series of Iranian films to the Museum of Fine Arts in Houston, which I thank along with the Greenway Theater for the special kindness of allowing me private viewings when I was out of town during their formal screenings. No such professional privileges or courtesies have been extended by the Boston Museum of Fine Arts, but I am nonetheless indebted to the annual Iranian film festivals brought to my current hometown of the past decade, initially curated by the Chicago Art Institute and later supported by the Ilex Foundation.[1] I thank Abbas Kiarostami; Bahman Qobadi (and his sister who stood in for him when the Bush Administration denied him a timely visa in 2002); Marziyeh Meshkini; Maysam and Hana Makhmalbaf; Tahmineh Milani and her husband, the architect and actor Muhammad Nikbin; Bahram Beza'i; and Maziar Bahari for their visits to Boston and responses to audience questions at the Harvard Film Archives and the Boston Museum of Fine Arts. Viewing these films over the years would not have been nearly as much fun without sharing them and discussing their references, allusions, codings, and poesis with Mazyar Lotfalian, Naghmeh Sohrabi, Mehdi Abedi, Fereydun Safizadeh, and Arlene Dalalfar, not to mention the wonderful Iranian community with whom we shared these events and who provided the laughter, gasps, and tears, as well as occasional explanations and interpretations. Naghmeh in particular has been an invaluable and exquisite translator for question-and-answer sessions with visiting Iranian filmmakers and actors at the Boston Museum of Fine Arts. Mazyar has been an intellectual companion and guide to the artistic and commentary scene of Iranians in America—being himself an actor in that scene—and a sounding board and resonator for my thoughts about the films of the last decade.

To my old friends from earlier Harvard days, Hossein Zia'i and Wheeler Thackston Jr., many, many thanks for the translations of Suhrawardi, without which the coda to part 1 would have been much impoverished. And, of course, part 1 as a whole is dedicated to all my neighbors and friends in the Zoroastrian suburb of Nasrabad-i Yazd, especially to Shariyar Damobed; Katkhoda Rustam "Pangar" Felfeli, who recited the Shahnameh for fun and moral edification; Banu Luti, who dictated women's work stories (Moshgel Goshah ["Difficulties Go Away"], Bibi Sehshambeh ["Lady Wednesday"], etc.)[2] to me in Dari and took me to (largely women's) rituals; and, in town, to Dastur Mehreban-i Mobed Siavush, who introduced me to high liturgy rituals that I relived again at Harvard with Dastur Feroze Kotwal, William Darrow, and James Boyd.

My delighted thanks to the two good readers for Duke University Press for their support and suggestions; to Joao Biehl, Joe Dumit, Beth Povinelli, Susann Wilkinson, and workshops at Harvard (organized by Omar Dewachi and Steve Caton) and at New York University (organized by Mazyar Lotfalian and Michael Gilsenan), for helpful thoughts about chapter 5; to Candis Callison for help with the illustrations; to my cousin Gal Kaminka for inviting me backstage in Fukuoka for the sixth annual RoboCup competitions that he helped organize (timed to be concurrent with the 2002 World Cup hosted jointly by Japan and Korea); and to his University of Southern California roommate, Jafar Adibi, who ignited the spark that led to the surprises of the cover photo and epilogue: the number of teams from Iran fielded at this high-tech meet. Again my delighted thanks to my editors Ken Wissoker and Pam Morrison for their expert care and for smoothing the process of putting the book into shape, and to Cherie Westmoreland for working my photographs into such a wonderful cover design.

Both I and Duke University Press acknowledge and thank Rosalind Williams, the Director of the Science, Technology, and Society Program, and Philip Khoury, the Dean of the Division of Humanities, Arts, and Social Sciences at MIT for a subvention toward the publication costs of this volume.

Chapter 3 originally appeared as "Toward a Third World Poetics: Seeing Through Short Stories and Film in the Iranian Culture Area," in *Knowledge and Society* 5 (1984): 171–241; chapter 4 originally appeared as "Filmic Judgment and Cultural Critique: The Work of Art, Ethics, and Religion in Iranian Cinema," in *Religion and Media*, ed. Hent de Vries and Samuel Weber (Stanford, Calif.: Stanford University Press, 2001); chapters 1 and 2 have been available in unpublished manuscript form since 1984.

As this book was being put to bed in June 2004, I had just returned from a three-week cultural exchange visit to Iran between students at the School of International Relations of the Ministry of Foreign Affairs of the Islamic Republic of Iran and students at the Fletcher School and Institute for Global Leadership at Tufts University. The satirical film *Marmaluk* (The Lizard), directed by Kamal Tabrizi (director of the earlier satirical *Leila Is with Me*), had recently come out and was the subject of universal discussion from President Khatami and Ayatullah Montazeri (both of whom enjoyed the satire) to every taxi driver, a confirmation of the role for film claimed in this book. It is about a man who escapes from prison disguised as a mullah and whose opinions are sought as if he were a mullah. The film was shown on the big screens only briefly and was then withdrawn. It was not banned, nor was it released, but was available on the street in VCD format. Neither banned nor not banned, said one of my new acquaintances, just like everything else in Iran. As the old folkloric introduction always says, *yeki bud, yeki nabud* (there was one, there was not one . . .).

Prelude: After Epic, Writing, Painting, and Film

Mute Dreams (*Gonge Khab Dideh*)

The idiom in Persian for the state of awakening after a dream, when one is still bewildered but beginning to decipher the images, is *gonge xab dideh*. Mohsen Makhmalbaf uses the idiom as the title for his three-volume collection of stories, interviews, and film criticism. The idiom also describes Abbas Kiarostami's sly assertions that the best films, and the kind of films he likes to make, are those that seem to put you to sleep, but that afterward you obsessively reconstruct, that stimulate you to rethink. There is even a mesmerizing and puzzling performance piece by Attila Pessayani titled *Gonge Xab Dideh*, which puts the idiom onstage and which, after a successful run in Tehran, premiered in New York City at Lincoln Center in July 2002.[1] The idiom, of course, comes from the couplet "Man gonge khab dideh o alam tamam kard. / Man ajez-am ze goftan-o khalq shenidanash" [I saw a mute dream and the whole world was deaf. / I am unable to say and people are unable to hear], a description of the prophets' experience of God's mercy and compassion, which they try to convey in human language but which all too often feels impossible to convey and is, in any case, received by others as if they were deaf.

"After Film" both evokes the reconstruction of meaning in which viewers engage after seeing a film and implies the need to understand film as a medium whose horizon of effects and potentials is being supplemented and enveloped by newer digital and multimedia environments (just as literary and oral performances have been repositioned by film, photography, video, and television). The latter process is due in part to the widening target audiences of the several media, which have shifted from being mainly domestic to being diasporic and transnational as well, such that these media now have multiple loci of address. Contemporary film audiences—whether domestic, diasporic or transnational—may feel the bewilderment (gonge khab dideh) and difficulty of deciphering the complex shifts among these layered loci of address, allusions, and implied knowledges as they are disseminated through the circuitry of what is sometimes called globalization and the postmodern conditions of knowledge.[2]

In the 1990s Iranian film became the most celebrated of national film traditions on the international circuits—initially in international festivals and traveling shows curated by museums of fine arts, but gradually distributed through commercial cinemas and video outlets—because of a poetics, a poesis, that speaks to the contemporary condition. It is a poesis that is deeply informed both by modernist traditions (many leading Iranian filmmakers attended film schools in Europe and the United States) and by Iran's own cosmopolitan traditions—a double play that parallels that of French New Wave in the 1950s and 1960s (and of Italian neorealism in the 1940s and 1950s, Eastern European film in the 1960s and 1970s, and Chinese Fifth Generation in the 1980s and 1990s). French New Wave played a part both in remaking postwar France through images of "fast cars, clean bodies: decolonization and the reordering of French culture," as Kristin Ross titled her 1995 book, and, reciprocally, in providing international images for rethinking Hollywood and the images of American modernity. So, too, films from Iran in the 1990s and early twenty-first century speak to their own domestic cultural politics and at the same time to more general ethical dilemmas in a world torn apart and pushed together. There is something about the minimalism, deliberate pacing, and subjectivities of these films that speaks to a world caught in the aftermath of religious tensors (stoicisms, purity logics, disciplinary moralisms) and to a world caught in the aftermath of wars received no longer stoically but through the recognition of post-traumatic stress syndrome and the increasing use of trauma as a metaphor of and for the current human condition.

One of the strong images that plays this double function, for example, from Makhmalbaf's film *Journey to Qandahar*: prostheses—plastic and wooden legs—dropping from the sky on parachutes to one-legged Afghans running on their crutches to catch these international relief offerings. The images of mine-devastated bodies and countries are global ones, not particularly Iranian ones; Makhmalbaf's image at the same time joins a series of strong images that form a hieroglyphics of reference in recent Iranian films. Some of these are evident already in the titles: *Shrapnels in Peace* being recycled as scrap metal, *Blackboard*s doubling as protection against helicopter gunships, *Rain* filling footprints, *Red Ribbons* marking off mined land, *The Time of the Drunken Horses* (mules) being used to cross borders by subsistence smugglers, cameras functioning as the inability to forget trauma and poverty (*Marriage of the Blessed*) and as alternative courts of appeal (*Close Up*). These images constitute an emergent new visual idiom and scopic regime. For American audiences, this emergent visual idiom provides both counterdiscourse (see what war does in the name of "collateral damage") and a profound commonality (we are all invested in the ideals of justice, cooperation, dealing with each life as precious, freedom, and ethical choice).

The uptake of Persian imagery into cosmopolitan circuits goes back to at least the pre-imperial worlds referred to in the Gathas of Zoroaster and acknowledged in classical Greek texts. The Persian Empire, with its Zoroastrian liturgical forms of legitimation, as Max Weber called the relation between imperium and religion, was the conceptual organizational alternative to the network of small Greek city-states. The dialectic between the two generated much thought about political forms, mercantile systems, iconic versus non-iconic religiosities, postal systems, epic poetry, and forms of knowledge and wisdom.[3] The Islamic conquest of Iran fixed its place as part of the monotheistic West, militating against further cultivating its roots and cognate structures with the Vedas, Buddhism, and Hinduism (or the anthropomorphic polytheisms of Greece and Rome). Persian cultural power expanded to the East again when, under the Mughul Empire in India, Persian became the court language, and artists, architects, and craftsmen were imported from the Perso-Islamic world. In Europe the figure of Zoroaster, if not a knowledge of Zoroastrianism, renewed ancient Iran's appeal as a dialectical Other in utopian critiques of Europe, from Mozart's *The Magic Flute* to Nietzsche's *Thus Spoke Zarathustra*.

In the twentieth century a new set of modernist initiatives wove Iranian creativity into world consciousness through new media, reaching new audiences. Folklore, new forms of poetry, new forms of short story, novels, and theater were, for reasons of language, addressed mainly to domestic audiences. But posters and film, by taking advantage of visual languages, were addressed also to international, diasporic, and transnational audiences. Posters of the 1977–1979 revolution, for instance, fused the artistic traditions of Islam with those of third-world revolutions, intermixing their distinctive palettes and icons. The revolution also deployed photographic and televisual reproductive and dissemination technologies to extend the impact of these iconographies and appeals across Iran and through diasporic networks of activists in Europe, America, South Asia, and the Middle East, and to address non-Iranian interlocutors in the lands of the Great and lesser Satans.[4]

In the early twentieth century modernist collections of folklore and their literary reworkings—in Europe, Japan, and elsewhere—became a tool of nation-building, of building children's character and attachments to locality, of moral production. Folklore and ethnography became contested arenas, naturalized as social charters for "primordial" sentiments and ways of organizing life, and fabricated for social reengineering.[5] The analytic study of oral recitations of national epics was put on a new footing through the work of Lord (1949) and Parry (1932) in the Balkans, in turn stimulating investigations of oral performances in context across the Middle East, Central Asia, South Asia, and elsewhere (e.g., Blackburn 1988; Blackburn et al. 1989; Caton 1990; Chadwick and Zhirmunsky 1969; Lyons 1995; Meeker 1979; Mills 1991; Slyomovics 1987).

The national epic of Iran and its precursors and sources in Zoroastrian tradition provided historically rich resources for such studies, both of oral and written performance in local contexts, be they medieval court patronage in the production of miniatures and manuscripts asserting claims of particular dynasties, or be they contemporary teahouse improvisations attuned to locals and their problems, tensions, or exploits. The Pahlavi monarchy attempted to attach itself, through its dynastic name as well as other symbols, to the two-and-a-half millennium tradition of monarchy rooted in the pre-Islamic Zoroastrian empires. Such multi-ethnic or multicultural empires provide a particular kind of political structure, incorporative of different ways of life. The Pahlavi monarchy invoked the tolerance of Cyrus the Great and his release of the Jews from the Babylonian Captivity, supported the practices of individualistic Sufism among its elites, and asserted its patronage and regulation of Shi'ite shrines and institutions. This last, of course, became contested ground from which the Islamic revolution of 1977–1979 arose (Fischer 1980a).

In this study, I examine three sets of media—oral, literary, visual—and their ethical resources and resonances. Herein are chapters on (1) two forms of *oral performance*, Zoroastrian high liturgy rituals and Firdausi's *Shahnameh*; (2) the modernist film and literary *narratives* that were important to the cultural politics of the 1960s and 1970s, a politics both responsive and hostile to the Kafkaesque surrealism of Sadeq Hedayat's 1939 masterwork novella, *The Blind Owl*; and (3) the production of a *figural hieroglyphics* in the films of the 1980s and 1990s in the aftermath of the Islamic revolution of 1977–1979, of the Iran-Iraq War in the 1980s, and of war in Kurdistan and Afghanistan in the 1980s and 1990s. All three sets of media, in quite different ways, depend on a kind of gonge khab dideh.

The rituals of Zoroastrianism are often quite obscure even to those who maintain them, but they do yield to decipherment of their gestural language. At their center is the achievement of a visionary and ecstatic poesis. Ancient rituals of this sort require from moderns an inquisitive attitude of recovery both toward the structural meanings of the ritual and also toward the legends and narratives attached to the ritual mnemonic. The ritual is an effort to capture, fix, and archive, yet also to provide tools leverage toward the poesis, structures of feeling, and performative visionary experiences of the ancients, or at least to renew the ecology of understanding and the understanding of cosmic ecology, thereby renewing the world itself.

By contrast, the *Shahnameh* has a narrative immediacy easy enough to follow. But among its various stories, too, is an intersignifying structure revealed only by comparative analysis, a mode of appreciation different from the pleasures of listening to each story in itself.

A dark, dreamlike, allegorical world characterizes the Persian surrealism initiated by Sadeq Hedayat, which draws not only on Persian imagery but also on European tropes and references, and comes to stark filmic expression in 1969 with *Gav* (The Cow), by the director Darius Mehrju'i and the scriptwriter-ethnographer-psychiatrist Gholam Husain Sa'edi. The New Wave films of the 1970s registered an innovative, politically charged world of repression and displacement. They were lodged in the cultural politics of resistance that saw itself as engagé. But these films were forcefully rejected by the religiosities of various class fractions (cleric, bazaar merchant, shopkeeper, urbanizing small town, newly educated) that ultimately collaborated to ensure that the coming revolution would be Islamic.

In contrast, a decade later a renewal of film not only continued the filmic discourses of the 1970s but began to develop further figural idioms. These new figural idioms operate less like texts: The montage and suturing tactics are to be deciphered not only semiotically. They operate virtually and hieroglyphically—virtual in Deleuze's sense of exploiting the multiple dimension of filmic potentials; of alternatively foregrounding soundtrack, music, silence, visuals, color, lectosigns or signs of inscription, noosigns or signs of interiority, chronosigns of varied temporalities; and of ramifying other channels of signification, sensuality, and paralogics as well as sense-making.

While these films hardly constitute a demotic popular form, they do return to the experiences of dispersed knowledges that the oral life-worlds of the epic taught to re-collect and re-interpret.

Dispersed Knowledges

for Pangar and the residents of Nasrabad-i Yazd;
for Dastur Mehreban-i Mobed Siavush of Yazd

In part 1, *Speaking After Zarathustra*, I am interested as an anthropologist in two kinds of oral performances as means of conservation and ethical fine tuning. In the centuries since Iran became dominantly Muslim, its Zoroastrian foundation has remained evident in such tokens as the names of the months, the celebration of Now Ruz (the New Year) on the vernal equinox (21 March), and in the national epic, Firdausi's *Shahnameh*. Ayatullah Khomeini tried to downplay the Now Ruz celebrations after the Islamic revolution of 1979, but that was one of the sites where his cultural revolution failed. Indeed, both he and Dr. Ali Shariati found themselves attacking the pre-Islamic heritage of Iran, while their language drew on the metaphors and symbols of that very heritage. The legacies of Zoroastrianism as maintained by the still-living Zoroastrian communities in Iran, India, and North America are different from the Zoroastrian legacies as understood through the *Shahnameh*. One of the goals of chapters 1 and 2 is to trace this difference. At the same time, both chapters trace a difference in the discursive modalities of ritual versus epic in Iran. Zoroastrianism and Judaism both had temple traditions that have long since been destroyed. Judaism—along with Islam—reacted by developing rich hermeneutic and theological debate traditions. Zoroastrianism took the other path, downplaying theological debate along with the rhetorical, grammatical, poetic, logic, legal, and philosophical critical apparatuses of scholasticism, turning instead to ritual, with its formal movements and gestural language, as the mnemonic around which legends and parables were maintained and to community cycles of feasts and philanthropic mutual support in order to withstand external pressures and pool resources for economic and social advancement in the periods when that was possible.[6]

The fragmentation of knowledge that ensued in the aftermath of the destruction of the Zoroastrian empire is said to have been re-collected by Firdausi from the carriers of the noble traditions: the *dehqan* (landowners) and *mobed*s (priests). Firdausi himself makes the point epistemologically general, rather than literal minded: "there is no lack of knowledge . . . but then it is dispersed amongst all the folk" (III: 369). If literacy is often said to facilitate analytic reason, development of the autonomous ego as an independent locus of judgment, and individuation of personhood and subjectivity apart from family and community (Foucault 1971; Goody 1977; Havelock 1986; Lévi-Strauss 1966; McLuhan and Fiore 1967; Ong 1982; Poster 1990), by contrast orality is said to be more embedded in multiplex social relations, in reason that plays on rich analogies and similitudes, and in parables that weave a subjectivity disciplined by and concerned with the common good. The writing down of epic operates betwixt and between these worlds. Although written down in canonic, verse form by Firdausi, the *Shahnameh* continues to be recited orally in contexts that adapt recitation to the specifics of local audiences (combining "prose" storytelling, verse recitation, and new versification). Even the text manuscripts constitute a set of variants adapted to their different patronage contexts. Thus even in its "canonic" form the epic is an organic, living body of variants.

Given the epic genre frame of kings and warriors, it is remarkable that the *Shahnameh* should conclude with powerful parables about the ultimate strength of wisdom over brawn, care of self and others over mere heroics and bravado. Gregory Nagy, in the foreword to Olga Davidson's recent book on reconstructing the composition of Firdausi's versified *Shahnameh* (1994), notes three important paradoxes that power the epic.

First, a key paradox, known throughout Indo-European mythic structure, is the relation between king and hero. The hero Rustam, who lives for 500 years across many kings' reigns, both challenges and upholds the idea of kinship: the king-hero relationship in the *Shahnameh* is a relationship like that of Achilles and Agamemnon in Homer, but the *Shahnameh* explores the many variants over the course of several dynasties. There is also a powerful parallel here, as Nagy indicates, with the role of the poet Firdausi to that of his patron, Sultan Mahmud of Ghazni, whom he both praises and criticizes. And so, too, the recited, living *Shahnameh* has functioned throughout the centuries to both celebrate Iranian nationalism and criticize the politics of the state. It has functioned, like Oedipus for Freud, to moderate (to tell again in public; to temper) father-son relations within the family and patrimonial relations of king and subject, state and society.

The second paradox, then, lies in the self-reflexiveness of the *Shahnameh*, the idea of the "book" working as a metaphor for oral tradition. Nagy invokes the idea of the *Shahnameh* as a collection of fragments, even at one point imaged as a set of mobeds physically holding fragments from which they recite and which in sequence become the *Shahnameh* recollected (remembered, gathered again). I am not persuaded, however, by Nagy's emphasis on the bookish nature of what remains an oral recitation tradition; I prefer Firdausi's verse: "there is no lack of knowledge . . . but then it is dispersed amongst all the folk." This, after all, remains true even under regimes of literacy and even more so today with print and electronic information overload.

Third, Nagy suggests a parallel between the paradox of the eternal fire in water (the mystical *farr*, which is the symbol of the legitimacy of righteous rule, kingship, and sovereignty), hidden and inaccessible at the bottom of a mystic lake which will be recovered some day by an eschatological hero, and the paradox of the poet's self-realization in a future moment, an idea which Nietzsche popularized in his *Also Sprach Zarathustra* (and which in a different way is evoked in the Gathas at the heart of the yasna ritual).

I dedicate chapter 2, on the parable logics of the *Shahnameh*, to Pangar, the Zoroastrian *katkhoda* or headman of Nasrabad-i Yazd, the suburb village of Yazd in which I lived for two years. Pangar was a wonderful reciter of the *Shahnameh*, not in a formal recitation setting, but simply as he was walking around the *kuches* (alleys) of Nasrabad on his daily tasks and to entertain and edify me. Similarly, I dedicate chapter 1, on the Zoroastrian high-liturgy yasna ritual, first to Dastur Mehreban-i Mobad Siyavush of Yazd, who first allowed me to watch a performance of the yasna; to Dastur Feroze Kotwal of Bombay, who taught me again and others at Harvard how this high-liturgy ritual is performed; and to Dastur Rustam Shahzadi of Tehran who encouraged my liturgical inquiries, encouraging me to go to Bombay and seek the advice particularly of Dastur Manuchehr Homji-Mehr. Dastur Mehreban-i Siayavush allowed and encouraged me to sit with him as he performed the ritual: unlike the Parsis of India, the Zoroastrians of Yazd allow genuine inquirers, particularly non-Muslims, into the fire temple.[7] Many years later Dastur Feroze Kotwal taught a seminar at Harvard on the yasna and a videotape was produced of the performance, albeit in a desacralized, nonritual context. Kotwal was much surprised that my notes on Dastur Mehreban's ritual performance formed as perfect a rendition as his own. My "reading" of the yasna is thus grounded in my ethnographic experience in the fire temples and Zoroastrian communities of Yazd, the teaching of Dastur Kotwal, the English translation of the *Gathas* by Stanley Insler, and the commentaries of J. J. Modi, Mary Boyce, James Boyd, and others.

So, too, my "reading" of the *Shahnameh* is informed by my ethnographic experiences in Iran. I have relied on the only full translation in English, the 1905 Warner and Warner translation, together with analyses based on contemporary *naqqals* or reciters by Shahrough Meskoub and Mary Ellen Page, analyses of patronage and allegories in manuscript miniatures by Sheila Blair and Oleg Grabar, William Hanaway's wonderful analysis of the Alexander Nameh and other medieval epics, Marsha Macguire and Dick Davis's work on the narrative of Firdausi, and Olga Davidson's analysis of the composition of the text of Firdausi. I had great pleasure in exploring the devices that structure the *Shahnameh*.

Among these pleasures are the recognition of three-generation units and doublings of erring fathers, heroic but still learning sons, and transcendent or responsible grandsons; of the threefold tests that heroes go through in these three-generation units; of archetypes in the first dynasty that become elaborated, clarified, and endowed with additional layers of parable meaning in later dynasties; of how these early genealogies in the *Shahnameh* are simplifications and transformations of Avestan legends, and more generally of how traces of ritual idiom get turned into narrative form (including the yasna itself in the story of the death of Afrasiyab); of the ambivalence of marriage alliances with foreigners; and of the parables that repeat and play on one another. The parables are occasions for naqqals to reflect on nationalism, kinship, heroism, honor, marriage strategies, religion, ethics, immediate versus ultimate rewards, parental-filial relations, anger, jealousy, ambition, zealotry, lust for power, obedience, loyalty, desire for long life, invulnerability, omnipotence. Among the stories are some which were further elaborated by later poets, writers, and reciters: Khosrow and Shirin, Rustam and Sohrab, Bozorgmehr figuring out the tactics and strategies of chess; Rustam's arguments with Sa'ad ibn Waqqas as a template for Persian versus Arab; the bridge built by Bazarnush as the mechanism of colonialism used against Iran in more recent times; and the stories of Noshiravan Adel as figurations of the rise of wisdom over martial brawn.

Blind Owls and "Journeys to Qandahar"

The telecommunications media (film, television, advertising, Internet) are helping to reorganize forms of reason, restructure social relations, and re-mobilize the figurability of personhood, subjectivities, and senses of self (Benjamin 1969; Castells 1996, 1997, 1998; Deleuze and Guattari 1980; Foucault 1971; Lyotard 1979; McLuhan and Fiore 1967; Ong 1982; Poster 1990; Žižek 1991). Telecommunications media encourage experimentation with alternative personas, ventriloquized audiences, and changing positions of enunciation to accommodate the flexibilities of identity, social organization, capital accumulation, and cultural reference demanded by the contemporary world (Poster 1990). The sensory surround of visual and multimedia channels plays on our optical unconscious (Benjamin 1969). Figural and rhetorical forms structure textual discourses in ways not always evident to authorial intention (DeMan 1971, 1979; Derrida 1967; Lyotard 1989). Sociolinguistic pragmatics invest communication with inescapable social relations of asymmetric power, status, and gender (Beeman 1986; Foucault 1979; Goffman 1959, 1961; Labov 1966, 1973). Film and digital logics (and their disseminations, topologies, and discursive powers) are quite different from those of traditional literacies. New visual and narrative forms reconfigure mythic, folkloristic, and ethnographic modalities.

In the beginning (of modernism in Iran) were new forms of poetry and short-story writing. The most prominent literary figure in the 1930s was the short-story and novella writer Sadeq Hedayat. Hedayat, like other modernists in Europe and Asia, was an avid folklore collector and refashioner. The images and stylistic compression of his stories—the dead discussing their lives as they hover above the Towers of Silence; the abandoned dog (*sag-e velgard*); and above all *The Blind Owl* (*Buf-e Kur*)—influenced a generation of writing and also, in the late 1960s, film scripts such as Dariyush Mehrju'i and Gholam-Hossein Saedi's 1969 film *Gav*. Other films of the New Wave began to develop a new filmic discourse: Masoud Kimiai's 1969 film *Qaisar* transformed the genre of B-grade revenge films; Mehrjui's *Agha-ye Halu* (Mr. Gullible, 1971) reworked the trope of innocent villager undone by and undoing the corruption among urban migrants; the wonderful soap operatic *Droshky-chi* (The Droshky Driver) explored cooperation and competition in overcrowded impoverished conditions; Parviz Kimiavi's 1973 film *Moghul-ha* (The Mongols) initiated a reflection about the media transformations of culture.

Buf-e Kur inaugurated a Persian style of surrealism that draws on but differs in emotional tone and philosophical consequences from French surrealism (and more so from Latin American magical realism). Engagé intellectuals (*roshan-fekran*, "enlightened thinkers") intended this surrealism as an aesthetic tonality, emotional mood, and allegorical resource for opposition and cultural critique, but to the intellectual leaders of the Islamic opposition it seemed empty nihilism. The incomprehension was mutual: the roshan-fekran could see in the writings and lectures of the religious leaders little more than atavistic repetition. And yet, I argue in chapter 3, common to both was a philosophical sensibility of stoic determination to struggle over the long term for social justice against overwhelming odds. Although the Islamic idiom carried the revolution, as film revived in the 1980s after a short hiatus, the film techniques of the 1970s New Wave provided the mirroring and tools with which to build a new cultural critique.

In chapter 4 I contrast two genealogies of Iranian film. One conceives of media technology as a foreign import and thus, whether carrying foreign or Persian content, as destructive of traditional modes of oral storytelling. Television, in particular, is considered destructive not only of oral performance forms but also of film understood as more artisanal and auteurial. The second genealogy understands media technology to have been assimilated into Iranian culture in the late nineteenth and early twentieth century and to now offer a mode of "writing with the camera" quite Persian forms of commentary, visualization, and calligraphies or hieroglyphics.

Film has become a parable and commentary discourse parallel to older poetry and epic traditions of ethical and moral reason. It is a space for and modality of judgment and critique. In a pair of provocative essays on religion and media, Jacques Derrida nominates the Muslim world as a site par excellence of dislocations and disseminations increasingly subordinated to a capital intensive, high-speed , transnational media industry; Islamic groups, when taking positions using the media to propagate their religiosities, are caught in a kind of autoimmune disease or frenzy that both extends their ideological reach and undoes it. In fact, Iranian film instead reveals that the commentary tradition is alive and well, that filmic discourse is evolving, and that the engagements of religion and media remain contestational, negotiating new chess moves in the regulatory structures both of government policy and financial channeling.

In chapter 5 I follow the extraordinary filmic discourse that has unfolded around the devastations of war on the borders of Iran in Khuzistan, Kurdistan, and now Afghanistan. I am particularly interested in the evolution of a new set of figural images and styles that both test and contest Deleuze's intuition of virtual rather than spatial filmic space-time and Lyotard's reworked Freudian dialectic of figural and discursive modalities disrupting one another: "figure dwells in discourse like a phantasm while discourse dwells in the figure like a dream. . . . Seeing interferes with hearing and speaking, as desire interferes with understanding" (Lyotard 1989, 33, 48). The heightened epistemological (dis)play and (dis)placement of "powers of the false" is productive of a new hieroglyphics. Working through these hieroglyphics (in the same way as Persians are used to deciphering poetry) is a political tool not only for undoing pieties, stereotypes, conventional understandings, and ideologies, but also for seeing in parallel stories set amid the after-effects of war in different locales the intersections of local, regional, and global processes, structures, and semiotics.

Thus although the title of Mohsen Makhmalbaf's 2001 film, *Kandahar*, is the name of the city in Afghanistan which in the 1990s was the seat of Mullah Omar and his Taliban religious fundamentalists, for Persian speakers the Persian title, *Safar-e Qandahar* (Journey to Kandahar), is also an idiom meaning a long journey, one from which one might not return. As the title of the film, the idiom functions as a metaphor for the course on which the devastations in Afghanistan by Marxist coup and revolutionary programs, Russian invasions, civil war, Taliban seizure of power, al-Qaeda base for terrorist training have set that society and the world at large. That the film was completed shortly before the U.S. invasion against the Taliban and al-Qaeda only makes it and its title even more resonant.

Set among ethnography, history, photojournalism, global satellite television, print journalism, and think-tank white papers, film provides alternative means of writing and composition. Where once one spoke of transitions from orality to literacy to electronic secondary literacy, one now begins to apperceive immersive virtual spaces wherein scenarios, n-dimensional matrices, iconic condensations, morphings and considerations of figurability, displacements, and secondary revisions work out alternative realisms (sur-, neo-, hyper-, magical) , entailing possible futures as well as alternative pasts that continue to interfere in their pluralizing ways with the present time.

After film come newer media forms. Multimedia, interactive, and immersive environments become performative spaces. One thinks of the fusion of Persian and rock musics and of the new generation of Iranian musicians who no longer dichotomize traditional and modern music forms, for example, the group O-Ham or the music in Makhmalbaf's film *Safar-i Qandahar* by Mohammad Reza Darvishi, who draws on his skills as an ethnomusicologist as well as a composer. One thinks of the calligraphic photography and video of Shirin Neshat (in which black-and-white figures of chadored women expose dense calligraphic script on face, feet, and hands); the powerful vocals of Susan Dehlim (both mystical and modernist visceral); the Persian television of California transmitted by satellite to Iran; the production of traditional *taziyeh* passion plays at Lincoln Center (with performers from Isfahan and with animal handlers from Chechnya); and in Fukuoka, Japan, the seven Iranian teams of high school and college students, male and female, competing in the sixth international RoboCup competitions in five leagues: small size, midsize, simulation, coaching, and rescue. The cover photograph to this volume shows one of these engineering students in chador, video camera in hand, filming the simulation league competition, with a RoboCup logo projected onto the chador from a spotlight on the Fukuoka sports dome. Cameras projected the competitions onto monitors for both large onsite crowd and remote viewing, allowed videocassette archiving for later team self-analysis, and made available potential transmission worldwide.

The chapters in this volume are companion pieces to essays on how the Qur'an is read and interpreted as a source of moral reason through parables and as a foundation for legal and political argument; on poster art, cartoons, and other "small media" as guerrilla cultural politics; on politically charged novels as eliciting enactments of what they describe (e.g., the Salman Rushdie affair); on debate traditions in the *madrasseh* or seminary system of Qum as demonstrating the richness of immanent critique from within tradition as well as the openness to engagement with the outside world; and on the theatricality of protest demonstrations from communal "riots" of the nineteenth century to those of the 1977–1979 Islamic revolution in Iran as consequential forms of symbolic politics. They are companion pieces to three book-length studies: an ethnography of Zoroastrianism in Iran and India set in comparison to Muslim, Bahai, and Jewish communities in the town of Yazd, *Zoroastrian Iran: From Myth to Praxis* (1973); an ethnography of the training of Muslim religious leaders in the seminary town of Qum, *Iran: From Religious Dispute to Revolution* (1980); and a volume organized around oral, literary, and visual media of Iran leading up to the revolution, *Debating Muslims: Cultural Dialogues in Postmodernity and Tradition* (1990).

I

Speaking After Zarathustra

RITUAL, EPIC, AND PHILOSOPHICAL

FORMS OF REASON

"I shall declare to you in verse, not in non-verse, in total inspiration."—ZOROASTER, *Yasna*

"There is no lack of knowledge, said the guide, But then it is dispersed 'mongst all the folk."—FIRDAUSI, *Shahnameh*

"The hoopoe is famous for his far-sightedness, while owls are blind by day."—SUHRAWARDI, "The Language of the Ants"

Katkhoda "Pangar" Felfeli at a wedding.
Banu Luti spinning yarns, spinning silk.
Both photos by author.

Prologue

"When our historical consciousness places itself within
historical horizons, this does not entail passing into alien worlds
unconnected in any way with our own, but together they constitute
the one great horizon that moves from within and . . . embraces the
historical depths of our self-consciousness."
—HANS-GEORG GADAMER, *Truth and Method*

Three paths to the ancient wisdom of Iran: ritual, epic, metaphor. Paths to three horizons of history. Coexistent paths for the present. Thus spake Zarathustra.

Epic is the easiest: telling stories. The great epic of Iran, the *Shahnameh* (Book of Kings) of Firdausi, completed in 1010 C.E., is to Iran what Homer is to Greece. Unlike the *Iliad*, which tells of but a few days in the ten-year war between the Achaeans and the Trojans, or the *Odyssey*, which recounts the homecoming of one central hero, the *Shahnameh* tells of the four mythical dynasties of Iran. The four dynasties reenact the fall of man in four steps—like the ages of gold, silver, bronze, and iron—away from the paradise of the gods. The story of the first dynasty, the Pishdadians (literally, "preliminary givens"), transforms the creation stories of Zoroastrianism into narrative form. The story of the second dynasty, the Kayanians (from *kai*, "king," "hero"), recounts the heroic age and the coming of an ethical world religion (Zoroastrianism, Islam) with its abuses as well as its rewards. The story of the third dynasty, the Ashkanians, together with Alexander the Great, who becomes assimilated to Iranian history not as despoiler-conqueror but as half-Iranian shah, is one of transition and romance. Finally there is the Sassanian dynasty, a historical dynasty, here mythicized as the apogee, culmination, and end of an age. The Sassanian dynasty contains the parables of good rulership built around the shah Nushiravan Adel (the Just) and his sage Bozorgmehr (great light), then declines toward the final defeat of Yazdigird the Third and of the Zoroastrian Empire (by the Muslim Arab invaders of the seventh century C.E.).

The parables are the key to the *Shahnameh*. For centuries now the stories of the *Shahnameh* have provided Iranians with multifaceted vehicles for contemplation, for exploring conflicts between fathers and sons, wisdom versus brawn, foreigners versus locals, fanaticism versus justice. The parables do not stand alone. Rather, the same conflicts are examined again and again with different characters and sometimes with the direct transitivity of generation: son in one story becomes father in the next, and what he did as son affects how he behaves as father. This extended parable or parabolic logic constitutes a structure of intersignification. That is, each story comments on prior and later ones. The beauty of this narrative structure is that one can tell the stories independently, or one can work them into more elaborate inter-signifying chains.

Firdausi's *Shahnameh* was composed in a period when Islam had already come to Iran. The legends of ancient Iran had been collected and preserved by a gentry class (the dehqan) and were used in tenth-century northeastern Iran at the Samanid court in particular—but even after the Samanids were conquered during Firdausi's lifetime by the ethnic Turk Mahmud of Ghazni—as a nationalist vehicle to assert claims of superiority and nonsubordination to the new Arabo-Islamic hegemony. Firdausi brilliantly played on this nationalism by writing the *Shahnameh* in the new literary vehicle of New Persian, keeping it as radically purged of Arabic loan words as possible. Firdausi and the dehqan were themselves no longer Zoroastrian, although there may have been Zoroastrians with whom they consulted.

So it is of interest to turn to Zoroastrianism itself and to see how it treats the same stories as those in the *Shahnameh*. There is a radical difference of spirit between Zoroastrianism—usually an optimistic world engaging creed—and Islam—often a more philosophical, world-weary creed. The Zoroastrian scripture, the Avesta, contains many of these stories. The Avesta is not recited in coffeehouses as a pastime, as was the *Shahnameh*; it is recited in ritual performances, of which one of the most central and important is the yasna, containing at its center the Gathas, the hymns composed by the prophet Zoroaster (Zarathustra, Zardosht).

Ritual is a radically different mode of thought than storytelling. The mythic texts and stories recited are often fragmentary, each fragment serving as a kind of gloss on a phase of the ritual rather than contributing to a coherence of the storyline. At the extreme, as Claude Lévi-Strauss notes,

> pure ritual . . . can be said to lose all contact with language, since it consists either of sacred formulae—incomprehensible for the uninitiated, or belonging to an archaic tongue that is no longer understood, or even of utterances devoid of any intrinsic meaning, such as are often used in magic—or of physical movements or of the selection and handling of various objects. . . . Gestures and objects serve *in loco verbi*; they are a substitute for words. Each is a global connotation of a system of ideas and representations; by their use, ritual condenses into concrete and uniform procedures which otherwise would have had to be discursive. . . . The performance of gestures and the manipulation of objects are devices which allow ritual to avoid speech. (*The Naked Man* 1971/1981, 671–72)

Ritual, Lévi-Strauss continues, uses the procedures of parceling and repetition as ways of reestablishing a sense of continuity which analytic thought and mythic categories break up.

> Ritual, by fragmenting operations and repeating them unwearingly in infinite detail, takes upon itself the laborious task of patching up holes and stopping gaps, and it thus encourages the illusion that it is possible to run counter to myth, and to move back from the discontinuous to the continuous. Its maniacal urge to discover the smallest constituent of units of lived experience by fragmentation and to multiply them by repetition, expresses the poignant need of a guarantee against any kind of break or interruption that might jeopardize the continuance of lived experience . . . . although the initial break with lived experience effected by mythic thought makes the task forever impossible. Hence the characteristic mixture of stubbornness and ineffectiveness which explains the desperate maniacal side of ritual. (Ibid., 674, 679)

This apprehension of a tension, or counterpoint, between ritual and myth (rather than a seamless connection) is arresting and may help us appreciate the gestural and formulaic repetitions of the yasna, which slow the pace of the text (as they do the ritual). However, one must know the entire ritual in order to see its structure; at the same time, one must scan for the narrative fragments and the production of the elixir *hom* (Vedic *soma*) and not lose sight of the forest for the trees.[1]

The point of the ritual is to achieve understanding and vision, which is accomplished through three means: the ritual gesture language of purification by parceling and separation, along with rhythmic, repetitive, chanted (both full and sotto voce) invocation of *mathras* (Vedic *mantra*); the ingestion of elixir (whether biochemically or psychologically, or merely ritualistic); and most important, by the stimulation of the mind into inspiration by the language of enigma, of poetic puzzles, of symbolic resonances. The parallels here with the oratorical contests of Vedic India and ancient Greece are remarkable: the *sadhamada* (symposia) or oratorical contests among Vedic priests were metaphorized as chariot races, as they are in the Gathas of Zoroaster; Plato in the *Phaedrus* and the *Republic* also compares the soul to a winged charioteer with a team of two horses, one clean-limbed, white, needing no whip, the other crooked, lumbering, ill-made, stiff-necked, black, eyes bloodshot, hairy-eared, deaf, and uncontrollable. By contemplating beauty, the soul is able to recall visions of the eternal forms of truth and reality, and by training itself in this art of "memory," says Plato, the soul can regain its wings and leave the corporeal world of incarnation behind.

The inspirational beauty of Zoroaster's Gathas—insofar as we can recover them from the obscurities of the text—and the other mythic and narrative fragments of the Avesta, together with their ritual and purity trappings are an enduring legacy of Zoroastrianism, maintained by the small surviving Zoroastrian community to the present. In the 1970s some twenty thousand Zoroastrians still lived in Iran, some ninety thousand in India (Parsis), and some thirty thousand in North America; the North American community has been growing ever since. The poetic-mythic core of Zoroastrianism is elaborated by the village and urban Zoroastrian communities of Iran not in a mystic direction but rather in an "ecological" one: an ethos of honesty and mutuality with one's fellow human beings and of active care for the elements and creatures of nature.[2] (This care of nature is tempered from a contemporary and comparative point of view by the elaborate division of creatures into those which are pure and good, and those which are the creatures of evil, as well as by a purity code not unlike, if a bit more elaborate than those of Shi'ite Islam and Judaism.) Among the villagers and urban residents of the oases in the central desert of Iran, a striking difference of ethos is often remarked between Zoroastrianism and the Islam that Shi'ism built around the passion of Husain and the Twelve Imams.

The mystic potentials in the mythos were developed primarily by Islamic thinkers, again with parallels in Neoplatonism in the West and the Upanishads in India. Beyond the mysticism itself, however, is the remarkable sensitivity to and skill with language, especially metaphor and symbol. Language often constrains and limits thought: it is a convention, a code, a system of difference which facilitates ordinary communication by making routine, repetitive, or probable certain kinds of implication, association, and logic. And yet, language has the capacity to point beyond itself, to show its own limitations, and to construct meaningful locutions not constrained by conventional logic. The tradition of linguistic philosophy developed in Iran by the so-called Illuminationist (*ishraqi*) philosophers or theosophists from Suhrawardi (d. 1191) on drew on the ancient lore of Iran and attempted to recover its visionary potential. What these philosophers did with the Zoroastrian heritage is quite different from what Zoroastrians themselves have preserved.

All three strands of thought through which pre-Islamic lore is carried into modern Iranian consciousness are rich in themselves. By paying attention to them individually, we gain access to separate horizons of history. The yasna is a codification of the third to ninth centuries and points further back in history. The *Shahnameh* is an early eleventh-century composition whose recensions also throw light on the eleventh through sixteenth centuries, and whose ideological ambiguity (especially the criticisms of the Zoroastrian hero Esfandiar as a proxy for criticizing the new Islamic overlords of Iran) continues to pervade Iranian nationalism. Illuminationist philosophy provides access to the development of a rich side of Islam from the twelfth through the nineteenth centuries. Once these horizons are understood in their own right, they contribute to an understanding of the rich tapestry of thought of contemporary Iranian culture.

Pre-Islamic figures stalk the discourse of modern Iran and are a deeply embedded component of Iranian nationalism. Even Ayatullah Ruhullah Musavi Khomeini, the leader of the Islamic revolution of 1979 who exercised the *velayat-i faqih* or supreme leadership of the Islamic Republic of Iran until his death, and Dr. Ali Shariati, the hero of the Islamic reformist youth of the 1970s, salted their speech with idioms and metaphors from the pre-Islamic heritage of Iran. Khomeini, in anger against the critics of the *ulama* (the Muslim clerics), used the tag line from Firdausi's *Shahnameh*: "*tofu bar to, ey charkh-i gardun, tofu!*" [spit on your face, oh heavens, spit!]. In the *Shahnameh* this curse is directed at the Muslim invaders and despoilers of Zoroastrian Iran. Shariati, who explicitly condemns the *Shahnameh*, nevertheless uses images from it: he speaks of Zahhaks (the great demon-king who usurps the throne) who in each age feeds on the brains of the youth, and he condemns the ritualism of the clergy as a *dakhma* (the Zoroastrian platforms for exposing the dead) mode of existence.[3]

References to the pre-Islamic Zoroastrian heritage of Iran can be like different readings of a common palimpsest text, appealing to different segments of society and offering different philosophical stances. A scholar like the late Ibrahim Pour-i Davoud might be at home in all three rhetorics and philosophical stances. A Zoroastrian is likely to be at home in two: his religious traditions and the *Shahnameh*. A literate Muslim is likely to be at home in a different two: the *Shahnameh* and Illuminationist philosophy. The ordinary Muslim is likely to be at home primarily in the *Shahnameh* stories. Western literary, philosophical, and musical traditions draw on excerpted fragments of these stories, such as Matthew Arnold's version of the Sohrab and Rustam story in nineteenth-century America or the fanciful reworkings of the Zoroaster legend by Mozart and Nietzsche.[4]

The ordering of the following chapters is historical, beginning with the yasna, but the reader, of course, is free to read in any order. The analysis of the yasna is intended to introduce the cosmology and symbolism of Zoroastrianism, as well as illustrate its ritual mode of religiosity and of conceptualizing the world. It is close to what Eva Hunt has called a pantheistic transformational symbolic system. Personifications of divine or cosmic elements and forces take on in this context their full force as poetic-mnemonic aids to the religious imagination. Victorian condescensions toward the "pagan," "primitive," or "religious" mind become naively inappropriate. Eva Hunt writes of the prehispanic Mesoamerican imagination,

> The merging and overlap of divine images did not simply reflect an ' "improvised" 'or ' "unfinished" ' religious pantheon. It was in fact the pantheon's very nature. Prehispanic religion . . . was truly pantheistic. Scholars have usually treated this issue in an over-simplified fashion, arguing, for example, that although prehispanic peoples were polytheistic there is clear evidence that they also conceived of a single unique god (for instance, Hunab Ku). This evidence has been treated as if it shows these groups to have been in some sort of transitional stage between polytheism and a more "advanced" religion, monotheism. This view is "evolutionism" at its most naive. In fact Mesoamerican cultures were neither polytheistic nor monotheistic. In their view, as in those of all pantheistic cultures, reality, nature, and experience were nothing but multiple manifestations of a single unity of being. God was both the one and the many. Thus the deities were but . . . multiple personifications, . . . partial unfoldings into perceptible experience. The partition of this experience into discrete units such as god A or god B is an artifice of iconography and analysis. . . . [D]ivine reality was multiple, fluid, encompassing the whole, its aspects were changing images. . . .

For didactic, artistic, and ritual purposes, however, these fluid images were carved in stone, painted into frescoes, described in prayer. It is here, at this reduced level of visualization, that the transient images of a sacralized universe became "gods," with names attached to them, with anthropomorphic attributes, and so on. (1977, 55–61)

For example, she writes, "the god of wind could be pictorially represented with some of the body features, face painting, or paraphernalia of the gods of death to indicate the idea of the wind in his "'angered'" form as hurricane or tornado" (55).

The Zoroastrian pantheon is both similar and different from that of prehispanic Mesoamerica. There is a more dualist struggle of the forces of good and evil, and the pantheon is less visually objectified. But the seven aspects of the godhead (*amshaspands*) and their helpers (*yazatas, hamkars*) have a similar fluidity, and there are taxonomies of several varieties (directions, elements, astronomy, life forms, etc.) which create rich multivalent symbols.

The pressure of Islam in Iran and of Christianity in British India encouraged Zoroastrians to reformulate explanations in terms closer to the dogmas of those "monotheistic" religions. Those apologia often seem superficial once the richness maintained in the ritual tradition and devotional discourse of Zoroastrianism is explored. There is an enormously appealing ethos which finds its groundings in Zoroastrian rituals: evil, deceit, and impurity are loose in the world; hence the forces of purity, honesty, and good must constantly be renewed and strengthened. By so acting, human beings can maintain the purity of the world.

Only a few traces of the rhetoric of Zoroastrian ritual remain in the *Shahnameh*. One of the most lovely is in the final episode of the reign of Shah Kai Khosrow, where the evil Afrasiyab is destroyed in a narrative version of ritual action familiar from the yasna. The binding of Zahhak by Faridun and the use of Homa (Humai) to transfer the seed of royalty from the last Kayanians (Bahman) to the Sassanians are other such traces. Narrative has here become dominant and is handled in each dynasty as a different mode of appropriating the Iranian past. Thus, the account of the first dynasty, Pishdadian, is a renarration of creation *myths*; the account of the Kayanian dynasty is a linked set of *parables* about the foibles of man; the account of the Ashkanians and Alexander focuses on *romance* and stories about the marvels of the world; finally, the account of the historical Sassanians points to *wisdom* as superior to military brawn. The *Shahnameh* carries both a sense of the pessimistically rebellious attitude of a dominated culture, especially in Firdausi's asides, and also the more heroic, straightforward optimism of its Zoroastrian legacy.

These two attitudes are performed in two popular settings for recitation. In the coffeehouse, naqqals (reciters) elaborate the philosophical tags supplied by Firdausi, supplementing them with the poetry of Hafez and others and with the parables of Shi'ism. In the *zurkhaneh*, the traditional gymnasia, maintained today by the artisanal classes and found in or near the bazaars, the *Shahnameh* is recited to the martial beat of the *tambak* drum. The tone here is more vigorous than philosophical, but the zurkhaneh is also under Islamic auspices: its patron saint is Ali, the son-in-law of the Prophet Muhammad, and not only the *Shahnameh* but also other Islamic texts are used to accompany the exercises of the *pahlavans* (athletes, heroes).[5]

Henri Corbin has argued to the delight of many upper-class Iranians that Illuminationist philosophy, from Suhrawardi (d. 587/1191) to the Shaikhis of the nineteenth century, used a theosophical interpretation of ancient Iranian wisdom and symbolism as a way of syncretizing Platonic and Islamic ideas about the hidden Imam (Corbin 1946, 1960/1977). Only insofar as the linguistic philosophy—metaphor, symbolism, and the limits of language—embedded in these discussions draw on Zoroastrian imagery, a minor aspect of this tradition, is Illuminationist philosophy considered here.

It is rewarding, in each instance of reappropriated Zoroastrian imagery, to explore its historical horizons, the rhetorical idiom which provide its coherence and ability to survive to the present, and its place in contemporary usage. The greatest rewards, however, are simply in trying to make more accessible and engaging a rich cultural heritage to which world civilization is deeply indebted for its religious imagery, literary stories, and philosophical modes of reflection.

1 Yasna: Performative Ritual, Narrative Mnemonic

"I shall declare to you in verse, not in non-verse, in total inspiration."—ZOROASTER, *Yasna*

There is a story that after years of fruitless proselytizing Zoroaster complains to God that only one man has converted. God replies that it does not much matter if Zoroaster makes converts, for at the end all will convert except Evil himself (Zahhak, Ahriman), who cannot. For Zoroaster this is unsatisfactory. The world of man is at stake. Why should men live in misery when they could achieve the restoration? And so in the Gathas he urges God and man to cooperate.

Understanding religion in modern times depends increasingly on an attitude of recovery: of unraveling ancient and half-forgotten meanings; of piecing together clues embedded in language, ritual, and customs that are now more emotionally than intellectually compelling; of (re)constructing an intellectual persuasiveness, informed in large part by appreciations for the historical growth of traditions. Such an attitude, once the exclusive realm of scholars within a given tradition, is of growing concern both among the nonreligious, who must come to terms with the political realities represented by religious movements, communities, and individuals, and among members of religious traditions, who must defend or clarify (even if only to themselves) the emotional core of their identities. No community is more open to this modern attitude, or feels more in need of it, than the Zoroastrian one.

An anecdote. Although, understood superficially, this anecdote might fall into the genre of the joke about the half-forgotten ritual still performed only by one native and six intently observant anthropologists, it actually instead testifies to the importance of ritual in preserving a tradition so that meanings decayed in one era can be recovered in a later one.

21 January 1971. Dastur Mehreban-i Mobed Siavush had invited me to observe his performance of the *yasht* (*yasht-i visperad*, a yasna ritual extended by twenty-four short sections of recitation) on the first day of the *gahambar* (a five-day holiday occurring every two months). This ritual may only be performed during the first daylight watch (*havangah*, sunrise to noon) and is begun with the first light after dawn. So I arose at five A.M. and made my way to the fire temple. Dastur Mehreban allowed me to sit in the room where the high liturgies are performed (the *yazishn-gah*) outside the *pavis* or water channels (from *paw* or *paki*, meaning "clean" or "pure") which enclose and separate the pure ritual space. He complained that, although it normally required two priests, he had to perform the three-hour ritual alone because there were so few priests.[1]

After the ceremony, he told me that he had learned to perform the rituals from his father and that he was the only one of the locally resident priests (only six remained in Yazd proper, with one more in Sharifabad forty kilometers away) who really knew them. As a young man he had gone to Tehran to engage in trade, but his father had asked him to return and take up the priesthood because there was no one else. So he had returned, studied with his father, and been examined by the old dastur, Mehreban-i Tirandaz. On various occasions, he had suggested to the other priests that they should meet regularly to discuss and learn the proper ways, but they were uninterested.

He was content to have me just sit and observe but afterward asked what I had learned from what I had seen. I replied that I had just wanted to see what was done, I had taken detailed notes, and now I would have to consult the books and ask him and others about the meaning. He confirmed a few meanings I had learned from reading Jivanji Jamshedji Modi's classic *The Religious Ceremonies and Customs of the Parsees*.[2] But he demurred, claiming to know very little about symbolic and theological meanings.[3] The person to ask was Rustam Shahzadi in Tehran, or better yet, I should go to Bombay.[4] He discouraged me from consulting Khodadad-i Shahriar Nerosangi, his rival in Sharifabad.[5] Khodadad was, Dastur Mehreban asserted, full of superstitions and his insistence that Muslims be excluded from partaking in the gahambar was wrong.[6] If you read the Avesta, he continued, Zoroaster says that if someone does you an evil turn, that is no reason for you to compound the evil. Moreover, many of Khodadad's superstitions were not even Zoroastrian ones, but Muslim ones.[7] Later in the morning, when I returned from the fire temple and told my Zoroastrian neighbors what I had seen, I was surprised to find that many of them were extremely hazy about the ritual, even about the fact that it was regularly performed on the first day of the gahambar on behalf of the community and not merely on an individual's request to produce the elixir *haoma* as a prophylactic against illness or for a departed soul.

Almost ten years later, the Parsi priest Dastur Firuz Kotwal conducted a semester-long seminar at Harvard on the yasna.[8] When I mentioned my 1971 experience, Dastur Kotwal expressed skepticism both about the efficacy of performing the ritual with one priest and about whether the Yazd community could be expected to have maintained a correct ritual procedure at all. This goaded me to look up my field notes and compare them item by item with what Dastur Kotwal had shown us. I was delighted to find the two ritual procedures were identical: a vindication of Dastur Mehreban's efforts, as well as of my hopeful response to his query. Dastur Kotwal's open-minded demonstrations and teachings a decade later brought alive the detective game of recovering the meanings encoded in the yasna as no reading of J. J. Modi or other scholarly descriptions could.

Exploring the meanings of the yasna (worship, sacrifice), the basic high-liturgy ritual of Zoroastrianism, can provide one of the most direct entries into the religion. Although the present text for this ritual was codified only in the Sassanian period—a codification of seventy-two chapters from various portions of the partially preserved twenty-one *nasks* (books) of the Avesta (Kotwal and Boyd 1982)—and although the ritual itself may have been slowly expanded in both Achaemenian and Sassanian times, nonetheless the yasna has a dramatic unity and coherence which make it a key link to the most ancient past, as well as a mnemonic framework for the elaboration of Zoroastrian cosmology and eschatology.[9] Until the Avesta was written down in the Sassanian period, the ritual served as the occasion for practicing and preserving the texts orally. Since Sassanian times, a few elements—animal sacrifice with a libation of fat to the fire, and the participation of eight priests—have dropped out: their places, however, are preserved in the text and so can be reconstructed.[10] A few other minor changes—substitution of metal twigs for vegetable ones in the *barsom* (see below), substitution of a metal mortar and pestle for stone ones, introduction of a stone seat for the officiating priest, substitution of a metal sieve for one of bull's hair, introduction of German silver or brass fire-holders—are also marked.

In the yasna, God (Ohrmazd or Ahura Mazda), with the aid of the archangel Sorush, manipulates the elements of the universe in order to create a pure world and to provide means of communication between the world of men and the spiritual world. There is an evocation of the conversion of King Vishtaspa (or Gushtasp) by the prophet Zoroaster and of the ritual duties of each Zoroastrian. And there is a recitation of the Gathas, the oldest portion of the Zoroastrian scriptures, attributed to Zoroaster or his immediate disciples.[11]

There are two means by which one can recover the meaning of the yasna. First, since ritual action provides the dramatic unity and coherence of the yasna as a whole, once the basic framework of ritual and symbolic elements are identified, it is then possible to utilize the yasna as a mnemonic for multiple bits of Zoroastrian lore. One cannot, however, begin with such bits and expect them to reveal the coherence of the ritual. That the creation story, cosmology, mythic composition of the prophet, or the eschatological drama are being reenacted can only be a post facto judgment. Each of these can be attached to the yasna to deepen its symbolic resonance; the yasna can in turn become a mnemonic for them. But none of them can account for the entire ordering of the ritual. To begin with, it is clear that the text is an assemblage of disparate pieces. Some parts are in the dialects of Avestan and are chanted in full voice (*goshadeh*, "open voice"); much of the text is in Pazand, the Pahlavi (Middle Persian) of the Sassanian period, and is chanted sotto voce in a mumbled undertone (*basta*, with "closed" lips). The seventeen gathas are ordered by metrical form, and they are not arranged continuously but enclose eight other chapters. And so on. In other words, it is to the ritual structure rather than to the text, the folklore, or the philosophical elaborations that one must first turn. Why else, after all, should the priests have chosen the ritual form as the preservative medium?[12]

The second means of recovery involves the central narrative portions of the text, particularly the *Gathas* of Zoroaster, but also the yashts (hymns; odes) to Hom, to the fire, and to the waters. The poetic language used is what Willard Johnson, writing about the *Rig Vedas*, has called the language of enigma, of verbal puzzles. Priests in Vedic India prepared for their ritual tasks by composing and trying to respond to such poems in oratorical contests (sadhamada; viz. Greek, *symposia*), metaphorized as chariot races. The poetic puzzles are *bráhmans* (with the accent on the first syllable, as opposed to *brahmán*, priest), a term which includes hymns and mantras and which refers particularly to the powers of these forms. In these "chariot races," the most formidable brahmans are entered by those whose speech is prepared with poetic inspiration (*kratva*).[13] Their patron is Agni, fire, the inner light of divine inspiration. The effort was to gain a nimbleness of mind, an extraordinary consciousness, an ability to grasp what is normally unseen. Gaining such vision was metaphorized as Vac revealing her beauty, like a bride desiring her husband. Not only were these brahmans verbally composed, but they were often figures utilizing sound repetitions (*yamaka*) and the protective rhythm of meter to move one forward through the searing fires of approaching divine insight.[14] Inspiration was aided by, and metaphorized as, the elixir soma.

Among the many images in the Vedas which are resonant with the Gathic texts are those of the cow as the vision of a harmonious, beneficent world; the rising sun as an initiatory experience; the changing moon becoming whole as insight; the sun and moon as the creative powers (*maya*) chasing one another, one rising while the other wanes, like two children playing or like the priests going round the sacrificial altar; the wandering of the sun as the perpetual search for inspiration; chariots as figures of divinities and horses as figures of divine speed; and the seven priests who yoke the wheeled chariot of the sacrifice (*yagna*). Regarding the ritual of worship (yagna), the Vedas pose the following brahman.

> I ask you: what is the farthest end (limit) of the earth?
> I ask: where is the navel of the world?
> I ask you: what is the semen of the powerful horse?
> I ask: what is the highest sky of speech?

To which the following answers, respectively, are provided: the altar (fire, inspiration); sacrifice (the ritual); soma (the elixir); the priest (in a state of inspiration). There is, as well, Dirghatama's (Deep Gloom) account of failure in a sadhamada poetry contest, in which he describes the setting of the fire before him, the preparing of the sacrifice, and yet his despair at being unable to achieve inspiration; so he prays for the gift of understanding.

In later times, the poetic chariot races were standardized into a ritual disputation form, the *brahmodya*. In later times, as well, the this-worldly ethic of the Vedas was transformed into an ascetic other-worldly ethic of the Upanishads. The famous imagery, for instance, of the two competing birds in the fig tree became inverted. In the earlier period, the victor is the bird who eats of the fig and thereby participates in transcending inspiration; but in the Upanishads, the eating bird is condemned to mere worldly existence, while the abstinent bird achieves the nonexistential, transcendent state.

In following the translation of Zoroaster's Gathas by Stanley Insler, it becomes clear that they are superbly constructed compositions, analogous to the brahmans insofar as they depend on an abstract play with metaphors. All too often in previous attempts at translation these metaphors have been taken literally, thereby destroying their coherence.

Ritual Setting

The ritual is performed by two priests: the *zot* and his assistant, the *raspi*. In Sassanian times, when there were numerous priests available, supported with ample funds, eight priests took part.[15] The zot performs the role of Ohrmazd, seated cross-legged on a platform, with his back to the north, the side of the demons. The raspi plays the role of all the other seven priests, stationing himself in the position of the priest who had special responsibility for the fire; he represents Sorush, guardian of both the material world and especially of the transfer of souls after death between this world and the next. In order to perform the ritual, both priests must undergo a severe purification: the nine-day long *bareshnum*. Once in their roles, they are elevated beyond the world of men: there are stories both of the Sassanian king Khosrow Ano-shiravan (r. 531–579 C.E.) and of a senior nineteenth-century priest in India, both of whom having entered a fire temple while a yasna was in progress were offended by the failure of the zot to acknowledge their presence, until reminded that to do so would transgress the spiritual state and activity of the yasna performance.[16]

The performance takes place in a sacred space, six paces long by four paces wide, marked off from the ordinary world by furrows (*pavi*): each time the priest enters or leaves the pavi, he unties and reties the sacred girdle (*kusti*) around his waist, reciting the appropriate *baj* or Avestan framing mantra (*mathra*). Every Zoroastrian should wear the kusti and many deliberate acts, particularly those involving changes in states of purity, involve the untying and retying of the kusti. The kusti is a white, woven wool band of seventy-two threads. The number seventy-two is associated with the seventy-two chapters of the yasna, as well as with the seventy-two names of God/Ohrmazd in the Ohrmazd yasht. The seventy-two threads of the kusti are grouped into six units of twelve, corresponding to the six cardinal directions, the six gaham-bars, and the six amshaspands. Ritual actions at the beginning and the end of the yasna are directly imitative of tying the kusti.

The pavi (sacred space) contains three main stone stands. At the south end is the stone platform on which stands the *afringanyu* (metal fire vase). The vase itself is empty and acts simply as a stand for a concave lid (*sarposh*) containing the fire. The consecrated fire, as Kotwal and Boyd (1982, 41) put it, is not merely a symbol of divinity but with its *nur* (glow) and *khvar-rah* (divine glory) is a pure (*paw*) material presence (*getig*) of the spiritual (*menog*) dimension. And it is in this sense that the Avesta refers to the sacred

Yasna ritual setting, main fire temple, Yazd. *Photo by author.*

fire as the "son of Ahura Mazda or God" (e.g., Atash Nyayis: 4–6). Sacred
fires come into existence through an elaborate process of taking fire from
multiple sources, placing over each source fire a ladle with holes and sandalwood and allowing the sandalwood to catch fire, then combining these pu-
rifications of the source fires in a further series of purifying steps. Two small
stone stands are to the west of the fire and hold sandalwood (*esm*) and
frankincense (*bui*) to be offered to the fire. Nearby is a tray with larger
sandalwood chips, tongs for picking up chips or sparks which fall from the
fire and must be returned to it, and a ladle for offering the sandalwood and
frankincense to the fire.[17] In the middle of the pavi is a stone ritual table with
implements for the ceremony. At the north end is the stone platform for the
zot (an innovation of unclear antiquity).[18] The zot is said to sit with his back
to the direction of the demons, the land of winter, of cold and darkness. This
association of north with evil is reaffirmed in the purification ritual, *sishu*,
where the celebrant moves from the north (hell, impurity) to the south. In
the epic traditions of ancient Iran, as well, the Turanians, archrivals of the
Iranians, were to the north. But the north-south symbolism is probably also
more abstractly and complexly cosmological: there is a rough agreement
with the ancient Chinese correlation of the five elements with directions: fire-

TABLE 1. Amshaspands (Aspects of Divinity)

Avestan	Pahlavi	Persian	Gloss	Symbol
Vohu Manu	Vohuman	Bahman	good thinking	ghee, *waras* (hairs)
Asha Vahista	Artavahist	Urdibehesht	truth	fire
Khshathra Vairya	Shahrivar	Shahrivar	sovereignty	metal
Armaiti	Spendarmat	Esfand[armuz]	piety	earth
Haurvatat		Khurdad	completeness	water
Ameretat		Mordad	immortality	plants
Ahura Mazda	Ohrmazd		wise lord	man

south; earth-center; water-north; metal-west; and plants-east. So, too, in the yasna, the fire is to the south and water to the north. In the Pahlavi traditions of the Bundahishn, north is less associated with demons (who belong more to the direction "down") than with Ohrmazd, the paradise of Yima (the Var) where the seeds of resurrection are stored, the pole around which the celestial bodies revolve, the land of the midnight sun or eternal light. In the yasna, the zot in the role of God/Ohrmazd sits to the north facing south.[19]

On the ritual table (*urwis, alat-gah*) are the following items: two small metal cups holding libations of (1) hom juice and (2) consecrated water; (3) a dish containing three, five, or seven tail hairs (*waras tashte*) of a white, uncastrated, consecrated bull without blemish, tied around a ring; (4) a metal dish holding three hom twigs and a pomegranate twig; (5) a mortar of stone or (nowadays) metal; (6) a metal dish containing the round unleavened wheat wafer (*dron, luwog*) with three markings (to differentiate it from the similar but unmarked wafers called *frasast*) and a pat of ghee; (7) a metal dish with consecrated milk mixed with consecrated water (*zohr*) called the *jivam tashte* and a metal stick (*barsom tay*) called the *jivam tay* laid across it;[20] (8) a covered metal dish of filtered reserve hom juice in case the other hom becomes vitiated; (9) a pair of metal moon or crescent shaped holders (*mah-rui, barsom-dan*) with twenty-one barsom twigs (originally tree twigs but now of brass or silver) laid across their top, bound thrice with a date-palm leaf, "kusti."[21] To the west of the ritual table and zot-gah is a large container of water (*kundi*), filled to the brim, in which are kept the pestle and the nine-holed strainer. Next to the kundi is a vase or pitcher for carrying and pouring water. This ritual set up is the result of the preliminary *paragna* ritual performed by the raspi of the yasna to obtain the consecrated ingredients for the yasna.[22]

All the amshaspands, the six aspects of divinity (seven, counting the encompassing godhead itself, Ahura Mazda or Spenta Mainu) are represented in the ritual by their traditional symbols.

The Ritual Drama

The ritual is a three-part drama.[23] The opening act contains a preparation of the ritual implements and a preliminary sharing of food (the dron wafer) with the divine. The central act contains the manufacturing of hom, the physical ritual product which remains after the completion of the ritual. It also contains the recitation of the Gathas of Zoroaster: seventeen hymns in five groups (hence popularly known as the Five Gathas of Zoroaster) preserved in a language in places obviously corrupted and no longer quite clear but nonetheless striking in poetic structure and lyric quality. The final act is a libation to the waters, the symbol of haurvatat, the aspect of divinity signifying completion of the divine vision and thus prosperity and well-being.

It is dawn when the yasna begins: only during the first watch of the day (the *Havan-gah*) may it be performed. The sun, symbol of divine light, understanding, and truth, and a medium of purification, drawing the spiritual upward, is rising over the eastern horizon. The zot priest, facing east, dressed in white trousers, tunic, and cap, pulls down the white face veil (*padan*) over his nose and mouth (that no spittle or breath inadvertently defiles the fire or ritual work).[24] He places his palms together and recites one of the oldest Gathic prayers, Ashem Vohu, in praise of *asha*, truth (symbolized by fire and by the sun). He bows his head to his palms in a gesture of respect, then enters the pavi or sacred arena from the west at the position of the Atarvaksh (the priestly caretaker of the fire). He places some sandalwood on the fire.

Invocation and Barsom Yasht

The zot proceeds north to the water, where he consecrates his right hand by pouring water over it. He takes the dish of dron and ghee from an auxiliary pot and places it on the ritual table (alat-gah). He then reconsecrates both hands, the left first by holding the pitcher at the neck with his right hand, pouring water over the left, while chanting an Avestan formula, "May it please Ahura Mazda." The consecrated left hand can now be placed inside the pitcher and so holding it (since the outside is less pure) pour water over the right hand. Meanwhile the raspi enters the pavi with the same preliminaries (reciting Ashem Vohu, facing east), but he goes around to the east side of the fire (facing west). The zot, his left hand still holding the pitcher from the inside, comes to face the raspi, the fire between them. Raspi and zot change places. The zot chants the dedication (*takshnun*) of the fire and then consecrates the fire stand by pouring water with his left hand and washing with his right; he moves clockwise, starting on the east side, and recites three times the Ashem Vohu.

It is said in the Hom Yasht (yasna [hereafter Y.] 9–11) that Zoroaster was serving the fire (in some interpretations, consecrating the fire stand) when Hom first came to him. The clockwise movement is said to model the diurnal cycle, beginning with the rising sun in the east.

The zot returns the pitcher to its place and then walks, palms together (that they touch no object) counterclockwise around the ritual setting (so as to avoid the north) to the east side of the zot-gah. He stands first with the right foot on the zot-gah, and as he recites praise for the angel or spiritual quality in whose name the ritual is being performed, he stands upon the zot-gah, hands open, reciting in an undertone. The raspi (in the position of the Atarvakash on the west side of the fire, facing east) feeds the fire. The zot, placing his right big toe on his left foot (a sign of humility according to Modi, of the oneness of God, according to Kotwal), and the raspi recite in unison facing each other, an explicit sign of their necessary complementarity (as that between God and man). Indeed, sixteen times during the yasna, the zot and raspi exchange baj, reestablishing *paiwand* (ritual union) and reinforced strength for facing evil or ritual tasks.[25]

The first chapter of the yasna (table 2), recited during the above ritual gestures, contains twenty-three verses. The first nineteen are dedicatory formulas, each beginning, "I announce and will complete my yasna (worship) to" Ahura Mazda, the amshaspands, the various other spiritual entities of creation, the divisions of time (seasons, days) and space (the ritual order), the *fravashis* (souls) of saints and fertile women. Verses 20–22 are expiatory formulas to the same entities, "If I have offended thee / all ye lords, whether by thought or word or deed, whether by act of will or without intent or wish, I earnestly make up the deficiency in praise to thee." The final verse is a credal formula, "I confess myself a Mazda worshipper of Zoroaster's order, a foe to the *daevas.*"

TABLE 2. Outline of the Yasna Structure

Yasna chapter

1–2	Invocation & Barsom Yasht	water, vegetable
3–8	Dron Ritual	water, vegetable, animal
9–59	Hom Ritual	
9–11	Hom Yasht	
12–59	Fshusho Mathra	
19–21	Bayan Yasht	
22–27	Homast	
28–54	Staota Yasnya	
28–34	Gathas	
35–41	Yasna Haptanhaiti	man and message
43–53	Gathas	
56–57	Srosh Yasht	divine messenger
60–61	Blessings on the House & Deprecations of Ahriman	
62	Atash Niyash	fire
63–72	Ab Zohr	
65	Aban Niyash	water, divine completion
71	Conversation with Frashaostra	
72	Binding of Ahriman	

Thereupon follows chapter two, the Barsom Yasht (or ode to the barsom). The zot leans down to put a few drops of water from the big pot with his right hand on the barsom, then picks up the barsom with his left hand. Throughout the ritual the barsom will be held with the left hand, while the right performs most of the ritual. Now with both hands, the zot touches the barsom to each of its two holders, back and forth, two times each, while chanting the Ashem Vohu three times. The raspi responds. Repetition: touch barsom to each holder three times, moisten with water, touch holders three times, moisten two times, touch holders eight times.

The barsom was once a major sign of Zoroastrianism. Firdausi tells the story of Yazdigird III, who, fleeing before the Arab invaders, sought refuge in the house of a miller. When served dinner, Yazdigird asked for the barsom so that he could perform the grace before meals, thereby giving away his identity, so he was slain by the general Mahui Suri. In Firdausi's epic, the form of the mealtime grace involving the barsom is associated with the higher social estates, with the gentry, and with the heroes (pahlavans). Thus, the miller did not himself have a barsom and had to send out to search for one. This elaborate form of the grace before meals is called the Dron Yasht and in modern times is performed by priests in the fire temple. Any meal, however, is the consuming of the creations of Hordad and Amurdad, and should be treated as a priest treats a sacred ceremony. The act of eating, therefore, is surrounded by a baj, in its most elaborate form involving the barsom, in its simplest form involving an opening blessing, then silence during the meal, and a closing blessing to end the meal. The concept of the baj (from Old Persian *wak* or *waj*, "word," "speech") is a formula (mantra, mathra) which precedes, accompanies, or follows an action once an initial baj has been recited; nothing may be spoken until the concluding baj.

The barsom is mentioned not only in the *Shahnameh* but also by Strabo (bk. 15, chap. 3, sec. 14) and, J. J. Modi thinks (probably correctly), in Ezekiel 8.16–17, in each instance as a defining feature of Zoroastrianism.[26] The *Shahnameh* describes how Shah Khosrow Parviz had a priest open a banquet with the barsom ceremony, which caused Nyatus, the Christian ambassador from Rome, to leave the table. The barsom seems to be the equivalent of the *kusha* of the Vedic priests, the sacred grass they spread as a god-seat (sustenance for the divine cow/vision) or more directly also the sticks they held during the soma libation. Modi draws attention to the parallel of the Roman *flamines* (fire priests) who also held twigs of a particular tree.

The barsom represents the vegetable creation and is freshened with sacred water periodically, as rain freshens the earth. Originally, tree twigs, the barsom, are tied together with a kusti of date-palm leaf. In yasna 13, the knots of this kusti will be retied as a way of girding up for the central portion of the ritual. In yasna 59 the knots will be loosened to mark the end of this special unit of the ritual. And at the end of the entire yasna, in yasna 72, as many knots as possible will be tied in a binding of the evil forces of Ahriman. The date palm is an emblem of immortality, an emblem widespread in the ancient Middle Eastern world: the Chaldean tree of life; the Assyrian symbol of fertility; the Egyptian emblem of the soul's immortality associated with the god Throth, who superintended man's life; the Hebraic emblem of righteousness used in the feast of tabernacles (see also Ps. 92.12); as well as a standard Greco-Roman emblem of honor, royalty, and righteousness.

The text of the Barsom Yasht (Y.2) repeats more or less the list of objects of worship from yasna 1, this time suggesting that the worshipper should approach them through the sacred water (*zaothra*, zohr) and barsom "bound with its girdle and spread with sanctity."

Dron Ritual

The zot now seats himself cross-legged, sets the barsom on its holders, and places two fingers on them. Between each short chapter of the yasna, from chapters 2 to 8 (the Sarosh Darun or consecration of the bread in honor of Srosh), the zot moistens the barsom with his right hand. These six chapters have variant formulas of invocation: "I desire to approach" the spiritual and ritual entities; "these [ritual items] do we present"; "I offer." Yasna 5 (identical with yasna 37) is a statement of worship of Ahura Mazda as creator.

The ritual tasting of the dron or wheat wafer with ghee now begins.[27] During yasna 7, the raspi feeds the fire twice. The zot moistens the barsom with his right hand between chapters 7 and 8. In both chapters there is an exchange of baj between zot and raspi, strengthening their paiwand or mutual power: the raspi salutes the zot with both hands to the forehead, and the zot returns the salute with his right hand to his forehead. The raspi feeds the fire a third time, then goes counterclockwise to stand to the east side of the zot. The zot takes the dron with his right hand; with his left sleeve he pushes up the veil over his mouth. He kisses the dron, then breaks off a piece, dips it in ghee, and tosses it into his mouth. The remainder of the dron he hands with its dish to the raspi, who returns it to the auxiliary pot whence it came. The raspi returns to his post. After the completion of the yasna, the dron will be sent to the house of the sponsor of the ritual. It is a blessing and sharing of the dron with the divine through the medium of the zot.

The eighth chapter, recited during the dron ritual, is composed again of formulas of dedication to the spiritual entities, invocations of their aid for men who wish to practice the righteous ways of Mazdayasnianism, invocations to Ahura Mazda to render such men sovereign over creation and to strip the wicked of power, and finally assertions of intent to rouse the leaders of men to carefully follow the precepts and rituals of Mazdayasnianism. A touch of dramatic heightening is given by the dialogue between zot and raspi as the dron is about to be tasted.

Zot: I offer, with piety, these things, this dron, water, hom.
Raspi (*feeds the fire and responds*): Oh ye righteous men, partake of the
    consecrated food.
Zot (*partakes*).

Hom Ritual

The hom ritual is the inspiration of the zot with previously prepared hom, the making of new hom, and the recitation of the gathas. Again we begin with consecrations and preparations, the sign of a new ritual segment. The zot washes one of the cups, then uses it to pour water on the ritual table: three pourings, refill, repeated four times (i.e., twelve pourings in four groups of three) while reciting four Ashem Vohu (with its threefold iteration of the value of asha, truth). The work space is thus readied. The raspi now purifies his right hand. The zot gives him the cup with the hom. He carries it to the fire, feeds the fire, and then carries the hom counterclockwise to the east side of the zot, holding it close to the barsom while the zot finishes reciting chapters 9 to 11, the Hom Yasht, again moistening the barsom between each chapter.

Hom Yasht (Y.9–11). This yasht, the first of the dramatic dialogues in the yasna, is an ode to the powers of hom (Avestan [hereafter Av.] *haoma*, the *soma* of the Indic tradition), an intoxicant it describes as unlike other intoxicants: it does not induce fury ("rapine of the bloody spear," [Y.10.8]) but friendship; victory over tyrants, demons, thieves, murderers, liars, sorcerers through forewarning more than through brute force (e.g., Y. 9.21); and healing and vitality. There is also a foreshadowing of the theme of the Gathas that divine gifts such as hom depend on a mutuality between God and man: "hom grows while he is praised, and the man who praises him becomes victorious" (Y.10:6). Above all, haoma endows wit, perhaps what the Greeks would have called *metis*, the quickness of mind which can upset power relations based purely on might. All other *madha* (intoxicants) are accompanied by the demon Aeshma (wrath) with the bloody club; but the madha of haoma makes one nimble (Y.10:8).[28]

Exactly what substance hom originally might have been has recently been the subject of renewed interest. Ilya Gershevitch (1974) has argued in favor of a modified version of the hallucinogenic mushroom (*Amanita muscaria*, the fly agaric) theory proposed by R. Gordon Wasson. The fly agaric belongs to the cultures of the forest lands north of the Central Asian steppes: Siberian shamans used it. As the Iranians and Indians migrated south across the steppes, they had to find substitutes. In recent times Zoroastrians have made hom from the ephedra plant native to eastern Iran and Baluchistan. Apologists, seeking scientific justifications, claim that this plant has mild curative chemical properties much like those of aspirin.[29] In the Avesta one finds hom being described as tall, good smelling, yellow-green (*zari*), tasty, and having spreading branches which grow in the mountains; these descriptions do not fit the fly agaric, whose cap is red, and as a mushroom is neither tall nor has spreading branches.

In the Vedas, soma is described not only as a stimulant of warriors and of Indra but also as a hallucinogen (ingesting quantities of which would lead to immobility). Soma's father is Parjanya, god of thunder: folk beliefs associate the sprouting of mushrooms with thunder, and the mushroom cap is iconographically a good thunderbolt handle in form. Gershevitch attributes the persistence of these confusions in the myths of Indra between the effects of stimulants and hallucinogens to the distance of the Indians from their Central Asian origins. The Iranians, however, were closer to those origins; the Saka nomads to the north of Iran had hom, as did perhaps a number of steppe nomadic groups, including the Turanians. The Iranians therefore devalued the warrior legends associated with the elixir, demoting Indra to a minor figure.[30] Indeed the Zoroastrian texts refer to the immobilizing power of hom. In the Hom Yasht (Y.11.7) there is a reference to the fettering of the Turanian king, Frangrasyan (Afrasiyab in Firdausi's *Shahnameh*). When Haosravah (Khosrow in Firdausi) pursued Frangrasyan to avenge his killing of the Iranian hero and Haosravah's father, Siyavush, Frangrasyan took refuge in an underground fortress and thought to invoke the deity Hom to give him strength. (Mushrooms grow underground.) But Hom took the side of Haosravah, binding Frangrasyan in a stupor. (Gershevitch notes that reindeer have been so stupefied after eating fly agaric that they can be tied and taken alive.) The Hom Yasht also refers to the dethroning of Keresani by Hom because Keresani had become too fond of power, too self-centered, and thus too tyrannical (Y.9.24). The reference here may be to the story of how Frangrasyan's brother Keresavazadah attempted to cheat Haosravah in a horse race, but how Haosravah was able to bind him instead.[31]

The ephedra plant, used in recent centuries as hom, is a woody, branching plant, with twigs that are jointed like fingers. It is used by Pathans and others as a general curative. When it flowers it becomes a golden bush (*zari* in the Avestan description). Gershevitch suggests that because the fly agaric is the only known hallucinogen which passes through the urine with unreduced potency, migrating Iranians might have used the ephedra's diuretic as a criterion when seeking a substitute. In the tenth-century pharmacology of

Abu Mansur Muwaffaq, the "*hom* of the Magi" (*haum ul majus*) is identified as a diuretic resembling asmin (*maraniya*), hot and dry in the second degree, good for rheumatism, mucous fever, and promoting menstruation.

More important than identifying the original hom substance is the poetic and ritual force of the Hom Yasht. It begins in a narrative dialogue: at the Havan-gah, Hom came to Zoroaster as he was serving the fire and singing the Gathas. Zoroaster asks questions of him, and Hom responds. First Zoroaster asks who Hom is, and Hom responds that he is the one who drives death afar, that Zoroaster should pray to him and prepare him for the taste. Zoroaster asks who first prepared hom in this material world, who was second, third, and fourth. Hom responds. In each case, the preparer's reward was a son, an offspring who was able to accomplish important things. Vivanghvant had been the first to prepare hom; his son, Yima, the first king, made herds and men flourish in an age when there was neither cold nor heat, aging nor death, nor envy. Athwya was the second to prepare hom; his son was Thraetaona, the slayer of the three-headed evil monster, Dahaka (or Zahhak). Third was Thrita, father of two sons: Urvakhshaqa, a great judge and institutor of order; and Keresaspa, a great hero and fighter against the demons. Finally there was Pouroushaspa, the father of Zoroaster. Zoroaster was the first reciter of the Ahuna Vairya mantra and so was able to dispel the demons.

As the Hom Yasht continues, Zoroaster calls on Hom for inspiration, strength, victory, healing, and prosperity in his battles against haters, demons (*daevas*), sorcerers, tyrants, evil princes and priests (*kavis* and *karpans*), and wolves. The rhetorical form of the yasht comprises blessings, praises, invocations, and warnings on how to treat hom properly. If misused, the three pure creatures—cow, horse, and hom—bring the curses of childlessness, evil fame, and slander. An odd locution in yasna 11 speaks of hom's portion including an "offering, tongue and left eye" (Y.1.4–5): perhaps this is acted out in the raspi's holding the hom cup to the left of the zot as he recites the Hom Yasht.[32]

Inspiration of the Elixir. Toward the end of yasna 11, at verse 9, the zot takes the hom cup from the raspi with his right hand, reciting a formula that who is one becomes two, that what is two becomes three, four five, five six, six seven—a formula perhaps of the increasing strength gained through hom. (It is just before this that in the Visperad ritual, the zot calls for each of the eight priests and the raspi answers for them.) The raspi turns to his post. The zot recites three Ashem Vohu. He raises his face veil with his left arm and while the raspi recites an Ashem Vohu, the zot takes a swallow; this is repeated thrice. This hom had been prepared by the raspi in the paragna ritual done prior to the yasna. Its ingestion is to bring the zot into a higher state of participation in the divine processes, preparing him for the task of making hom.

The zot cleans the hom cup with ashes from the fire given him by the raspi, then washes it in water, and replaces it on the ritual table. In an undertone both priests recite an Ashem Vohu and name both the sponsor and the yazata (spiritual entity) in whose honor the ritual is being performed. The zot repurifies the workspace by pouring out water in the four directions (moving clockwise as in the opening consecration of the fire stand) while reciting four Ashem Vohu. He then turns the cup upside down next to the barsom.

Fshusho Mathra (Y.12–59). The central portion of the ritual is marked by the regirding of the barsom, just as before and after a deliberate task, a Zoroastrian reties his kusti; at the end (Y.59) the barsom knots will be again loosened. Keeping the fingers of his left hand on the barsom as he does throughout, the zot with his right hand ties knots on the date-palm leaf bindings of the barsom, and recites the *frastuyi* or "praise of religion" chapters (Y.12–14). Yasna 12 contains the credal statement, "I am a Mazdayasnian and profess the Mazdayasnianism of Zoroaster, and praise good words, good thoughts, and good deeds." (Shorter versions occurred at the end of the Hom Yasht [Y.11.16–17], as well as in the opening chapter [Y.1.23].) Yasna 13 is a set of invocatory formulas ("I address my invocations to"), ending with an affirmation of belief in the mantra Ahuna Vairya; yasna 14 is a set of dedicatory formulas ("I will come to you as praiser, priest, invoker, sacrificer, reciter"), ending in an exchange of baj between zot and raspi. Four times the zot recites the Gathic mantra Ahuna Vairya—an invocation of Ahura Mazda as truth, judge, sovereign, and protector of the humble. The new knots are hooked over the crescent horns of the barsom-holder. The invocatory and dedicatory formulas continue through yasna 15 and 16.

The ingredients and implements for hom production are readied. The hom cup is turned upright. The natay (metal twig) lying across the milk dish is picked up, and the milk poured into the cup and then back into the dish. With the natay, the zot laves the barsom with milk six times. He readies the mortar, placing it upside down in the kundi (pot of water). Again with the natay, he laves the barsom eight times with the milk (a total of fourteen lavings, like the preliminary acts in yasna 1 as the zot prepared to seat himself). He lifts the pomegranate twig and hom cup, holding them next to the barsom, pouring some drops onto the barsom, and then setting them down.

Bayan Yasht (Y.19–21). This yasht follows, containing the commentaries on the three ancient mantras—Ahuna Vairya, Ashem Vohu, and Yinhe Hatam (a reworked version of chapter 51, verse 22). The commentary on Ahuna Vairya is the most interesting. It begins with a dialogue in which Zoroaster asks Ahura Mazda to repeat the mantra. In the course of Ahura Mazda's reply, he comments that this mantra correctly recited is worth one hundred other prayers, and even incorrectly recited is worth ten other prayers; it is a prayer whose recitation will assure the soul's transport over the Chinvat Bridge to heaven. There is reference as well to the four social estates (priests, warriors, agriculturalists, and artisans) and to five levels of political organization (household, village, tribe, province, Zoroastrian realm); Ragha (the city of Rayy) is named as the center of the Zoroastrian realm (i.e., a Sassanian interpolation, as is the reference to four social estates).

Homast: Extracting the Hom Juice (Parahom) *(Y.22–27).* With this invocation, the homast, the pounding and extracting of the hom juice, may begin. Structured invocatory formulas (Y.22–27) end with the ringing assertions, "This [ritual] is to strengthen Ahura Mazda and to smite *Angra blainyo* [Ahriman]." The mortar is taken from the pot of consecrated water and is rung three times against the stone table, warning the demons. It is set upright and ready. Into it are put the four ingredients: hom twigs, milk, pomegranate twig, and consecrated water (zohr). The raspi readies an offering for the fire. The zot takes the strainer (with nine holes) from the kundi and places it on a cup. The raspi feeds the fire. The raspi requests the zot to speak the will of Ohrmazd (Y.26.11), and the zot responds, "May he who knows by asha . . ."; that is, the spirit speaks through the office of righteous judging. In the later texts, this is said to have been the words Zoroaster spoke at his birth. The zot takes the pestle from the water pot and runs it around the lip of the pot, pounds it three times on the ritual table (base, head, base), and rings it against the mortar with three whole notes and nine rapid rings, undertoning in Pazand, "May Ahriman be defeated a hundred thousand times."

The pounding of the hom mixture now begins, rhythmically alternating with the ringing: three poundings and a ringing sequence, to represent (so suggests the *Dadistan*) Zoroaster and the three future redeemers, or *sayao-*

*shant*s. The ringing sequence is a beat of 1,2; 1,2; 1,2,3,4, with increasingly rapid beats, ending 1, 2 or 1,2,3,4. After the first three pounding and ringing sequences, three drops of consecrated water are added while reciting *Ashem Vohu*. The pestle is rolled counterclockwise around the lip of the mortar with the index finger extended along it eleven times. The pestle is then used to fish out the solid residue from the mortar and this is touched to the barsom, milk, hom cup, and ritual table (earth). The residue is returned to the mortar. Another sequence of pounding and ringing follows. Then the contents of the mortar are poured through the strainer into the hom cup. The residue is put back into the mortar; a bit is poured from the hom cup into the mortar for further squeezings. The hom cup is touched to the barsom and a drop is poured on the barsom. The cup is set down and covered with the strainer.

Ahunavaiti Gathas (Y.28–34). With the first squeezing of the hom juice, the first group of the Gathas of Zoroaster are recited. Each of these hymns is structured differently. They all work with an economy of abstract symbols and mantric formulas, as well as the fundamental conceit of the mutual interdependence of god and man. Only through their mutual support can either survive. It is to heal a world fallen into deceit and ruin that this "yoking" of divine and human is directed. Among the mantric formulas are plays with the arrangement of the names of the amshaspands, the six attributes or aspects of the godhead. Among the symbols is the cow, representing the beneficent vision of a good world, peaceful and joyous, composed of asha (truth), *vohu manu* (good thinking and determination), *khshathra* (just rule), *armaiti* (piety), *haurvatat* (completeness), and *amaratat* (immortality)—in other words, *daena* (vision, conception) whence the Persian word for religion: *din*. The immortal forces of god are also called the bulls of heaven. Righteous men are called plants (through which the cow grows fat), cultivators, cattle breeders, draft oxen of truth, and swift steeds of good thinking. Pasturage thus functions dually as the substance on which the cow feeds and the vision of paradise to which the cow is brought by her human caretakers.

The first gatha (Y.28), beginning "With hands outstretched," is a series of entreaties addressed to Ahura Mazda and two of his most important forces— truth and good thinking—to recognize the awakening of the virtuous spirit in Zoroaster and his desire to lead men according to the vision of a world governed by truth and good thinking; and to evoke compassion in Ahura Mazda to aid and instruct him. Zoroaster promises a dual mode of action: worship of god and enactment of good. He acknowledges a final judgment and appeals to god in the name of himself, his patron King Vishtaspa, and noble follower Frashaoshtra.

During the next two gathas, all ritual action comes to a halt as Zoroaster's poetry pours forth. Yasna 29, "To you the soul of the cow lamented," is perhaps the most dramatic of the hymns.

VERSE 1. The cow laments, why was she created if she is to remain oppressed by the cruel forces of deceit? Why has no human being come to protect her?

2. Virtuous spirit, who bears responsibility for the cow's existence, asks truth if the cow's judgment is accurate.

3. Asha (truth) acknowledges the correctness of the complaint and says no mortal protector has yet been found.

6. Ahura Mazda tells this to the cow but reassures her that a human protector will be found and promises milk and butter (i.e., strength and prosperity).

7. Good thinking (vohu manu) says Zoroaster is the one who can aid the cow.

9. The cow complains that Zoroaster lacks power.

4. Zoroaster refers to the Wise Lord keeping his promises (verse 6). (Now that he has been named and partly accepted by the cow, Zoroaster can speak in his own voice.)

5. Zoroaster supplicates on both his own behalf and that of the cow for power to help him.

10–11. Zoroaster supplicates first for both strength and for power to rule in harmony with truth and good thinking; later he supplicates for the same but without reference to strength or power. He promises to Ahura Mazda the gifts of piety (armaiti) and obedience (saraosho) if Ahura Mazda intercedes; these are unique gifts men can give god, the power of god being only as strong as the belief men place in him.

Yasna 30 is a hymn or instruction concerning the consequences of choosing good and evil. The first two verses are addressed to Zoroaster's adherents; the next two attempt to persuade the Wise Lord to aid Zoroaster to increase his followership and heal the world of the afflictions of deceit; and the final verse tells his followers there is no other possibility to save themselves. It is a hymn rich in the metaphors of the Gathic poetry (swift steeds of good thinking, draft oxen of truth, yoking with truth, the community of the fertile cow, the increase of plants, water for the cow). Even more striking is the urgency of Zoroaster's effort to get both god and man to cooperate, to convince them to act jointly for their mutual good.

After these two arresting hymns, the production of hom continues: there are three more squeezings, accompanying each of the next three Gathas. The raspi adds two sticks of wood to the fire. The natay is used to anoint the barsom with milk six times. The barsom is moistened with water. The mortar is pounded and rung: seven whole notes and then a long rapid ringing. There follows another laving of the barsom with milk using the natay. More zohr is added to the mortar. Another pounding and ringing: 1,2, 1,2,3, rapid ringing, 1,2. Hom juice is poured from the mortar through the strainer into the hom cup. Again the barsom is moistened with water. The mortar is pounded and rung loudly and long: 1,2, 1,2, 1,2, 1, 1,2, 1,2, 1,2,3,4,5,6,7,8 . . . , very rapid 1,2,3. The barsom is laved with milk using the natay. A few more drops of zohr go into the mortar. Pounding and ringing 1,2, 1,2,3, rapid ringing, 1,2. Hom juice is poured from the mortar through the strainer into the hom cup. Again the barsom is moistened with water. Again a pounding and ringing: 1,2, 1,2, 1,2, 1,2,3, 1,2, 1,2, 1,2,3,4, rapid ringing. And the fourth and final squeezings are poured through the strainer into the hom cup. Zohr is put in the mortar and poured through the strainer into the hom cup. The mortar is turned upside down. The residue is taken from the strainer and tossed onto the floor. When it dries, the raspi will feed it to the fire (in Y.62). The zot laves the barsom with milk using the natay.

By this point the first six Gathas have been recited. Yasna 31 begins with verses addressed alternating to the immortal forces and to the adherents of the Prophet, and explores the nature of the divine, its moral principle, and its mutuality with man. Yasna 32 begins by condemning the old gods who chose deceitful ways and brought the world into ruin; it refers to the sins of Yama, the evil karpan priests, and the deceitful kavi princes; it invokes the judgment of hell for sinners and heaven for followers of the Wise Lord and asks the latter for more support. Yasna 33 speaks of worshipping the Wise Lord who provided the means of healing the world.

Finally, yasna 34 is a promise to Ahura Mazda that the faithful will strengthen his power through worship and enactment of the vision, followed by a challenge: if you have the power, then lend it to us in this struggle, for many oppose us, retreat from us, and are threatened; so tell us thy directives and wishes, be they for praise or for worship; instruct us how to bring about the realization of good. With this resonant plea, the raspi, having washed his right hand, takes the hom cup to the fire. He feeds the fire. (The offering of fat to the fire used to occur at this point.) Then, carrying the hom counterclock-wise to the east of the zot, he returns it to him.

   Reenacting the Creation of Zoroaster. The zot places the hom cup on top of the upside-down mortar and places on the very top the milk dish. A kind of human icon is thus constructed, which for some brings to mind the legends of the divine creation of the prophet Zoroaster[33]: his *tan gohr*, or material substance, is represented by the mortar, in which are fused his two spiritual components, his khwarrah as represented by the milk and his frawahar as represented by the hom. The legends say that these components of Zoroaster were formed at the first creation, six thousand years before his birth. The khwarrah is part of the realm of infinite light which descended into the womb of Zoroaster's grandmother as she bore Dugdav, Zoroaster's mother. The baby girl was born radiant, and soothsayers predicted that the moral order would proceed from this light. The demons, or *divs*, attempted to destroy this radiance by bringing wintry travails, plague and disease, and rapacious enemies to the village. Dugdav was accused of sorcery, and to save her, her father sent her to the house of Patiritarasp, whose son Purushasp she married. Meanwhile, vohu manu (good thinking) and Urdibehesht or asha (truth) fashioned Zoroaster's frawahar from the realm of infinite light in the form of a column of hom. They gave the hom to two birds whose offspring had been devoured by snakes (creatures of Ahriman) and who placed it in their nest. When the snakes again attacked, the frawahar of Zoroaster killed them. Eventually Purushasp was directed by vohu manu and urdibehesht to the River Daiti on whose banks he saw the hom in a tree and was enabled to reap it.

   The third element, Zoroaster's tan gohr, is meanwhile conveyed by Ahura Mazda to the world via water and plants, that is, hordad and amurdad. A cloud releases spermlike rain in an amount that would be produced by two bulls, the reaction of the divine forces to the prior destruction of the world by Ahriman: in the second quarter of creation (the years 3,000 to 6,000) Ahri-man had salted the waters, withered the plants, broken the sky, sullied the fire, and slain the first bull and the first man. Amurdad subsequently collects the plant matter (hom from the cosmic tree, a source of immortality and renovation), pounds it, and scatters it in the clouds. The rain renovates the plants, and Purushasp is instructed to bring six white, yellow-eared cows to graze. Purushasp drinks of the milk of the cows, has Dugdav milk them into a four-sided pot, and mixes milk with hom, consecrating it to Ahura Mazda, following which he and Dugdav drink it. The demons, led by Ceshmag the

Unwise, attempt but fail to prevent the copulation of Purushasp and Dugdav and the conception of Zoroaster.

Thus the production of hom is said to reenact the creation of Zoroaster, the vehicle of the divine vision, from the elements: hom, water, and milk. In the telling of the legends, emphasis is placed on the fact that nothing is injured in divine creation: God drew the form of his prophet from milk which relieved the pain of the cow's full udders. In one version, the cow eats dried leaves so that there is not even killing of vegetation. Zoroaster, as related above (in the Hom Yasht), is not the only or first son produced by the making of hom. The symbolism of these legends and of the Gathas are consistent: the use of the cow, its sustenance, and its products are metaphors for the transitivity between the divine conception and human good action.

There are four elements involved in the production of hom which are also linked to the legends of Zoroaster securing his first converts at the court of King Vishtaspa. Vishtaspa asks for four wishes and is granted one for himself, the other three for his sons, Peshotan and Esfandiar, and his advisor, Jamaspa. Via an intoxicating elixir (wine, hom), Vishtaspa is granted a vision of the next world. Via milk, Peshotan is granted immortality until resurrection. Via pomegranate juice, Esfandiar is granted invulnerability to attack. And via fine aroma (the sandalwood and frankincense offerings of *esm-buy*), Jamaspa is granted the ability to see into the future.

By attaching legendary and folkloric meanings to the ritual, the ritual is enhanced and its mnemonic utility increased; but these meanings clearly are not exactly tailored to the ritual actions. It is the stylized ritual which contains its own logic and coherence. The bringing together of the production of hom and the recitation of the Gathas is fundamental, accompanied as it is by the alternation of loud percussion to smite the demons and cessation of ritual action to concentrate on the beneficent vision of the Gathas and the oldest Gathic mantras.

Yasna Haptanhaiti (Y.35–41). The Yasna Haptanhaiti ("worship of seven chapters") is accompanied by no ritual. It is a collection of Gathic mantras which are preceded and followed by Zoroaster's Gathas. It's positional centrality, fenced and protected by the Gathas, themselves already accorded ritual centrality and protection, signals something quite important and confirms the historian of religion's suspicion that here resides a key exercise in the construction of the Zoroastrian conception of the godhead. Of note among the invocations to Ahura Mazda, the fire, the soul of the animal world, the fravashis, and the waters is the oldest usage of the term *amsha spenta* for the aspects of the godhead (Y.39.3). Furthermore, Mary Boyce suggests (1975a, 51), this set of texts is so archaic that it reveals pre-Zoroastrian elements being fused into their Zoroastrian form. Ahura Mazda is addressed here as husband to the waters, an epithet applied to him nowhere else and reserved in the Vedas for Varuna. Ahura Mazda is also called here "harm to him whom you may destine for harm," again an unusual epithet and again one in the Vedas reserved for Varuna or for Mitra (Av. Mithra). Boyce finds here evidence of a triadic set of god terms. Only three divine figures in the Iranian tradition are ever given the title Ahura (lord): Ahura Mazda (what *mazda* means is still not fully deciphered, but in the Haptanhaiti it means "memory" [Y.40:1] and otherwise is conventionally glossed "wisdom"); Mithra (covenant, contract, social bond), who is associated with fire and the sun, coming eventually to displace Hvar as the sun; and Apam Napat (Son of the Waters) who is probably the Vedic Varuna.

In the Vedas Mitra-Varuna form such an intimate pair that they became paradigmatic of any binary unit (night and day, left and right hand, in-drawn and outgoing breath) and often were invoked as a compound (*dvandva*), Mitravaruna, yet they also have distinct personalities. Varuna ("child of the waters" is a common epithet) established heaven and earth. Dominion (*ksatra*) is his in particular, and he is the punitive judge. Mitra is the more purely benevolent side of social covenants and bonds between friends, citizens, trade partners, marital partners, and treaty partners. Above Mitra-Varuna there is an unnamed Ashura (Av. Ahura).

In the Iranian tradition this triad is slightly modified. It is Varuna who seems to lose his name and some of his prominence, being called by one of his epithets "son of the waters" (Apam Napat). Mithra takes on some of the sterner judging attributes and becomes more prominent. Covenants are sworn by Mithra in the presence of fire, and several forms of ordeal by fire are used to enforce social order. Pouring molten lead on the accused's breast in fact becomes the mechanism of purification at the Last Judgment. Ordeal by sulfurous mixtures ("burning brimstone") has become the Persian idiom for swearing an oath (*sogand khordan*). Mithra is also in charge of the morning watch. Three times a day, one is supposed to recite the "Hymn to the Sun" (Khorshid Niyayesh) and each time this is to be followed by the prayer to Mithra (Mir Niyayesh). In time the veneration of Mithra overshadowed that of the sun (Hvar), and in modern Persian the sun is called *mihr* (from Mithra).

Varuna's position is somewhat more curious. No name Varuna exists in the Iranian tradition, only Apam Napat. And for Apam Napat there is no hymn, no day of the month name, nor is any yasna dedicated to him alone. Nonetheless, Apam Napat is one of the thirty yazatas invoked in every ritual. When water is invoked in the yasna, so is Apam Napat (e.g., Y.1.5). Apam Napat is in charge of the afternoon and is one of the three to be called Ahura. Apam Napat is called "high Lord" (Burz, Burj) who watches over the waters and the *khwarrah* (Middle Persian *farrah*). The khwarrah, which represents royalty and rule, accompanies Mithra across the sky and when kings disgrace themselves flies away in the form of a bird or runs away in the form of a ram.

Although today there is no ritual action during the Haptanhaiti, Boyce speculates that once it may have accompanied offerings to fire (mithra) and water (Apam Napat). Today the Hapanhaiti is explicitly in honor of Ahura Mazda, yet with the two possibly telltale epithets of Mithra and Apam Napat which indicate a more archaic triadic arrangement. The usage of *amsha spenta* here, Boyce speculates, may indicate a shift from a triadic structure to its doubling, the six-fold "godhead" of the *amshaspands*.

Attached to the Haptanhaiti, and concluding it, is an eighth chapter (Y.42) called the Haptan Yasht, which is often recited by the laity as a separate yasht, or prayer unit.

The Gathas Continued. The Gathas here continue to display a variety of poetic forms. Yasna 43 takes the form of an entreaty to Ahura Mazda, describing the prophet's understanding of the workings of the virtuous spirit in both god and man, how the prophet had awakened to this understanding, and how Ahura Mazda's encouragement had helped him overcome his doubts about mankind's ability to bring about the beneficent vision. The prophet-poet acknowledges the reward and punishment in judgment of men's deeds, he swears allegiance to Ahura Mazda and to serving the fire of truth, and he entreats Ahura Mazda to provide help in achieving the common goals of god and mankind. The following Gatha (Y.44) is a rhetorically powerful hymn, each line addressed to Ahura Mazda and beginning, "This I ask Thee." In it Zoroaster speaks of his adherents as ten mares with their stallions and a camel, a play on the suffixes -*aspa* (horse: Vishtaspa, Jamaspa), and -*ushtra* (camel: Frashaoshtra and Zarathustra). Yasna 45, in a similar formulaic style, is addressed to Zoroaster's adherents, beginning each time, "I shall speak."

"To what land to flee" (Y.46) is perhaps second only to the cow's lament of yasna 29 in dramatic intensity. In the first part Zoroaster speaks of his rejection by men, his need to seek refuge and help, and his condemnation of the evil priests and princes. In the second part he glories in the virtuous spirit which has arisen in his followers: Friyana the Turanian, Vishtaspa and his advisors (the brothers Frashaostra and Jamaspa), and the Haecataspa branch of his own Spitama family. He conveys his vision to Jamaspa, he says, through the inspired transports of poetry. This poetry utilizes the metaphors: bulls of heaven (immortal forces), draft oxen of truth (god and man yoked together), and a fertile cow (this worldly predicate) and a steer (divine and human agents) as the future prize.

The first verse of yasna 47 has been analyzed by Gernot Windfuhr (1976) as a mode of word-order play known in Muslim rhetoric as *lozum*. It contains the names of all six amshaspands plus two forms of God's name (Ahura Mazda and Spenta Mainu), plus the formula "good words, good thoughts, good deeds." Yasna 48 (like Y.31) is alternatively addressed to god and to man, and suggests that the plants (the faithful) on which the cow (the beneficent vision) grazes are nourished by good thinking and that saviors (saoshyant) are those who act in the knowledge of Ahura Mazda's teachings.

Yasna 49 continues the alternating rhythm, describing the truthful, then the deceitful. Zoroaster first laments that he has been falsely accused and pleads for the Wise Lord's intervention; he describes the deceitful who spread falsehood and affirms his faith that truth will win out. Again he characterizes the deceitful and contrasts the ability of men who realize the possibility of a better world to bring it about; he pleads for the Wise Lord's aid to the latter. He asks rhetorically if there are any men who are dedicated to the Wise Lord, then draws attention to Frashaoshtra and Jamaspa asking aid for his alliance with them. He then characterizes the contrasting fates awaiting the deceitful and the truthful, and he swears to honor the forces of the Wise Lord if they in turn will intercede to help bring about the rule of truth and good thinking. The imagery of this Gatha is largely pastoral: the faithful are referred to as both cattle breeders and cultivators (of plants, as in the preceding Gatha), but it is particularly the dialectic of bringing the cow to pasturage (through piety) and the cow thereby producing milk and butter (strength, prosperity, and peace) which is elaborated. Yasna 50 praises the Wise Lord as the creator of truth and good thinking, which alone can advance the human condition. Again there is an alternating rhythm. The question as to whether or not there is any other path is answered with an affirmation of truth and good thinking being the only way. A promise to worship and obey is yoked with an entreaty for wisdom and truth to grow among men. Affirmation of alliance with Ahura Mazda is yoked to a request for aid. Ahura Mazda's visible creative accomplishments (the sun and moon) are acknowledged as signs of subtler moral visions. Among the poetic usages in this Gatha are the swiftest steed required for the race with deceit, footprints of milk as marks of strength derived from worship, and the healing of the world of deceit and decay. Yasna 51 continues the mood, describing the vision of rule by good thinking and truth, contrasting deceitful and truthful men, praising the supporters of Zoroaster, and declaring as a fair exchange the rule of truth and good thinking for the worship of men.

The Hashmam, or praise of the dawn (Y.52), intervenes before the final Gatha and is a general verse of praise.

Said to have been composed by Zoroaster on the occasion of his daughter Pourucista's marriage, the final Gatha (Y.53) is called the "wedding sermon" because it is an admonition to brides and grooms, suggesting a yoking like that of Ahura Mazda and the faithful among human beings. The Gathic prayer that follows, the Airyema Ishyo (Desiring Aireyema [Y.54])—and that concludes the Staota Yesnya (words of praise and worship) of chapters 28 to 54—is part of the Zoroastrian wedding service. The Airyema Ishyo, said in yasna 3 to be the best mantra against sickness, will be recited on Judgment Day by the saoshyants. Airyema (companion) in the Vedas is one of the lesser divinities (a set of six, seven, eight, or twelve adityas) who accompany Mitra-Varuna and is also one of two lesser Vedic divinities that reappear in Zoroastrianism. Baga (he who distributes) is the other and apparently was the titular focus of eastern Iran's autumn festival, the Bagakana, as Mithra in western Iran was celebrated in the Mithrakana, later Mehregan. Interestingly, the Airyema Ishyo not only prays for the sacred reward of performing the ritual but notes that the ritual is a legacy of a more ancient world.

A lovely ode to the Gathas follows (Y.55), calling the Gathas "our guardians and defenders and spiritual food." To them are dedicated "all our landed riches, and our persons, together with our very bones and tissues, our forms and forces, our consciousness, our soul, and fravashi." From the Gathas are sought rewards for the world beyond the present after the parting of our consciousness and body; also power, health and healing, and progress and growth in this world. Accompanying the claim that the Gathas were produced by Ahura Mazda is a plea that they might appear easily to the enlightened. The final verses, like the Airyema Ishyo, exalt the "praises of the yasna" and acknowledge that they are a legacy of the ancient world. Yasna 55 concludes, "And we worship each part of the praises of the yasna, and their recitation as it is heard, even their memorized recital, and their chanting, and their offering."

Srosh Yasht (Y.56–57). An invocation to Srosh is an ideal transition to the final movement of the ritual. Srosh, although not one of the amshaspands, is said often to participate in their councils; he is associated in the Gathas with khshathra; in the later Pahlavi texts he is called "salar-i zaman-i Ohrmazd," leader of the creation of God. He is a major mediator between this world and the next, particularly as a guide to the soul at death. In yasna 57 he is said to live on the mountain which reaches the other world (Haraiti Bareza), to have been the first reciter of the Gathas, the first to use the barsom, and the first wielder of the mantric weapons: the Ahuna Vairya prayer, the Haptanhaiti, and the Fshusho Mathra. Because Srosh is the guide to the soul of the newly deceased and was the first reciter of the Gathas, the Gathas are recited when a corpse is carried to the towers of silence.

Yasnas 56 and 57 are both odes to Srosh. The former is thought to be from the lost Hadokht Nask (the twentieth of the original twenty-one books of the Avesta). The latter serves the laity as their primary nighttime prayer.

Blessings and Deprecations (Y.60–61). The zot now laves the barsom with milk using the natay. Yasnas 58 and 59 having concluded the Fshusho Mathra (Y.12–59) of beneficent mantras, the knots of the barsom bundle which were tied in yasna 13 are now loosened.

Blessings on the house of the celebrant are sought in yasna 60. A kind of Avestan prayer for health (*tan dorosti*), yasna 60 plays an important role in the Afringan ceremonies (blessings done by priests in a ritual setting in individual homes).

Then Ahriman and his deceitful hordes of evil are deprecated in the resounding call of yasna 61: "Let us peal forth the *Ahuna vairya* in our liturgy between the heaven and the earth, and let us send forth the *Asha Vahista* in our prayer the same, and the *Yinhe hatam*. And let us send forth in our liturgies between heaven and earth the pious man for blessings, for the encounter with, and for the displacement of Angra Mainyu with his creatures . . . for he is filled with death." The zot lifts the cup of consecrated water, sets it down with a resolute ring, and places it before the mortar. He inserts the natay halfway into the barsom bundle and removes the dish of milk covering the hom cup, placing the dish too on the table.

Atash Niyash: The Litany to the Fire (Y.62). The Atash Niyash is always recited standing. The zot takes a second natay which has been lying at the base of the barsom holders. He rises to his feet on his stand (zot-gah), holding the barsom bundle in his left hand, the single natay in his right. He faces the fire, palms together. Zot and raspi recite the Atash Niyash in unison. The zot sits.

The Atash Niyash possesses a certain poetic elegance. Like the Gathas, an abstract dialectical conceit is constructed with material metaphors. The fire should be well nourished with wood, perfume, and fat so that it will be aflame, glowing, and able to ignite progress and heroic renovation. Such an active fire is called a "swift-driving charioteer." He who nourishes the fire receives glory, booty, growing understanding, nimbleness of tongue, virility, sure-footed offspring, alertness, influence, and the ability to nurture and to rescue others from oppression. If the fire of the righteous spirit be nourished, it will grow from smoldering ember to flame to swift-driving charioteer, a victorious warrior sweeping darkness and evil before him.

Ab Zohr: Libation to the Waters (Y.63–72). The final portion of the ritual is the libation to the waters. The Ab Zohr may also be undertaken at any time to purify the waters and to atone for pollution; households perform it twice a year in Urdibehesht and Azar, as well as during the marriage ceremony.[34] As part of the final act of the yasna, the zot begins by reciting the Ashem Vohu. Still holding the natay, he pours three drops of hom over the barsom bundle into the cup of consecrated water (zohr). He taps the hom on the mortar and touches it to the barsom in his left hand four times, then replaces the hom cup on the mortar and the natay across the base of the barsom holders. Taking the natay from the barsom bundle, he uses it to anoint the bundle with milk; he then replaces it in the bundle. He turns the barsom holders on their side, laying the single remaining natay across them. They are thus retired.

The Aban Niyash (litany to the waters [Y. 65]) is now recited. The zot picks up the hom cup with his left hand, and with his right turns the mortar upright, tapping it four times on the ritual table. Into the mortar he pours hom, zohr, and milk, mixing the water and hom by pouring them back and forth in their two small cups. The zot takes one cup of the mixture in his right hand, and holding the barsom in his left, stands by the east side of the zot-gah, facing west, to recite the Aban Niyash. (The water pot is to the west side; water represents Havartat, completion, the opposite of the rising sun in the east). The raspi stands beside him palms together.

The Aban Yasht invokes the waters as healing, nurturing, purifying the male seed, sanctifying the female womb, and regulating the flow of breast milk. Personified with the name Ardvi Sura Anahita, the spiritual powers of water are located as descending from the cosmic mountain, Hukairya, which reaches into the heavens, and as flowing thence into the cosmic sea, Vouru-kasha, before dispersing throughout the seven climes. The healing powers of

Ardvi Sura Anahita are invoked for the righteous; her destructive torrential side is directed against evildoers.

The zot sits. He taps the zohr cup against the mortar, then touches it to the barsom five times. He pours a drop on the barsom. He taps the mortar again six times (in Y.66, which says, "I offer this potion with hom and solid offering to Ahura Mazda, the amshaspands, Srosha, and the fire"). Yasna 67 has no ritual; it repeats the invocations of yasna 33. A second litany to the waters follows in yasna 68: addressing the Ahuran daughter (water), it offers the potion of hom and milk to make the waters flow, the plants sprout, and the human vital juices potent, "for healing, for progress, for growth, for ceremonial merit, for renown, for equanimity, and for that victory which makes the settlements advance" (Y.68.1). During yasna 68, the zot covers the mortar again with the milk dish. He mixes the contents of the hom and zohr cups again by pouring their contents back and forth. He taps the full cup from mortar to barsom four times and pours a little into the milk dish on the mortar, repeating this three times. After pouring all into the mortar, he dips in one cup to fill it and pours the contents back and forth between the two cups. He covers the mortar with the milk dish turned upside down. The zot gets off the zot-gah, faces east with the raspi still by his side. They turn south, then west.

Yasna 69 is composed of fragments; yasna 70 is an invocation to the amshaspands, Ahura Mazda, Zoroaster, Srosha, Mithra, Rashnu, and the Masnayasnian religion.

Conversation with Frashaostra and the Binding of Ahriman (Y.71–72). The zot seats himself again for the final two chapters. The raspi walks clockwise around to purify his left hand. The zot recites the conversation of Zoroaster first with his disciple Frashaostra and then with Ahura Mazda (Y.71), then taps the cup four times against the barsom and mortar. Frashaostra asks Zoroaster what the ritual recital is. Zoroaster answers with a long list of objects of worship. Ahura Mazda then asks Zoroaster if he will pronounce these words at the end of his life. If he does so, Ahura Mazda promises, he will keep Zoroaster's soul from hell. Zoroaster replies that all shall be as Ahura Mazda desires. The raspi returns counterclockwise to the zot's east side. The zot recites the rout of Ahriman and his hordes (Y.72, and as in Y.61), meanwhile tying as many knots as he can on the barsom, thus binding Ahriman and his hordes of thieves, bearers of falsehood, magicians, and heretics. The zot then hands the barsom bundle to the raspi. They both face the south (zot still seated) and recite in unison. The zot then says an Ashem Vohu.

The zot rises now from his seat and greets the raspi with a handshake, taking the latter's hand between his palms. Holding hands they go to the southeast corner. There facing east, palms together, they recite in unison, nod to the north, bow, exit from the sacred area, touch hand to forehead and earth, untie and retie their kustis. The zot returns into the pavi, proceeding first to purify his left hand. He then takes the covered mortar from the ritual table, offers sandalwood to the fire, and exits again to the southeast. Both priests proceed to a well or stream to infuse the zohr into the waters of the earth. Facing east they recite the Avestan mantras for the waters, the sun, vegetation, and prosperity.

The ritual is now complete, and the sponsor and others may drink of the newly produced hom.

In the 1971 yasht-i visperad, hom was of primary interest to the laity. An old woman came for some hom, arriving just before the end of the ritual. The hom was considered a prophylactic and aid against all illnesses. (Yasnas may be dedicated to haoma against illness and plague. They may also, according to the medieval Rivayats, be dedicated for victory in war, possibly drawing on the story of Haosravah's victory over Fanrasyan. They can be dedicated for good harvests and for sons who will become famous, drawing on the story of the sons given as rewards to the four fathers who first prepared haoma [Boyce 1975a, 97].) As to the ritual itself, for most Iranian Zoroastrians this and the other liturgies seemed largely meaningless motions, although some might recognize and appreciate sections of the text, especially the more narrative units, that are used in other ritual contexts, such as the Gathas, the Aban Yasht and the Atash Yashto. The associated legends—the four wishes of Gushtasp associated with wine/hom, pomegranate, milk, and fragrance; the stories of the cosmic eras of the world; the divine composition of Zoroaster—were, of course, widely known and frequently retold. But toward the ritual and its text, the honest, if interested, puzzlement of Dastur Mehreban was widespread among the community.

The ritual acts compose a kind of stylized language: tying and loosening knots, ringing, moistening the barsom, anointing the barsom with milk, consecrations in water, directional movement, combining elements—all these constitute a vocabulary, each item of which is appropriate to certain contexts and not to others. This ritual vocabulary, furthermore, is arranged into a series of scenes, each with a beginning, middle, and end, and the scenes are arranged in a coherent sequence: consecration and preparation; the making of the elixir (hom) and achieving of the transcendent vision of Zoroaster;

completion, rededication, and strengthening of the good elements of the universe.

The verbal imagery constitutes a consistent poesis, and one can discern some contrasting historical layers in their deployments. Popular Zoroastrian, particularly Parsi, literature and speech often draw on martial metaphors, which notably are not part of the idiom of the yasna or the Gathas. This popular imagery talks of the Zoroastrian as a soldier in the battle of Good against Evil. Therefore, it is often said that (in contrast to the keening and wailing of Muslim mourners, both family and professional mourners) one does not cry at the death of a true Zoroastrian because having fought the good fight, he or she will have a beautiful reward in the next world. Perhaps such language is a coloration from Muslim idioms (the martyr in the holy war goes directly to heaven), or in India from the influence of the metaphors of kshatria warriors even in the soteriologies of nonviolence, as in the Jain imageries of being descended from kshatrias or being warriors on the path of overcoming the temptations of this world. As used by Zoroastrians these martial metaphors are innocuous enough.

But the idiom of the yasna and the Gathas, while it includes fighting the demons and evil, dominantly deploys a set of pastoral metaphors, and not, or not just, in the literal sense of having to do directly with cows or stock and herdsmen (sheep not cows were and are the primary stock in Central Asia, even if *gav* can be used as a generic term for livestock). Rather, this poetic idiom deploys a marvelous dialectical and abstract idiom in which what is at issue is the relationship between sustenance, strength, and result. If man forgets God, the cosmos figured through the amshaspands and the good decay. Inversely, without a sense of the cosmic struggle, of goals beyond immediate or instrumental needs, man has no clarity of purpose. The cow, then, is that vision husbanded by man. The result of the husbandry are the beneficent products (milk and butter). Man is a plant which provides the sustenance for the cow, for the strength of the vision. As metaphors for relations of transitivity and mutuality, cow, plant, steed, milk, water, and so on make sense as a set; as literal terms they do not.

Having discerned the metaphorical coherence of the Gathas and the yasna, one may then as subordinate observations attempt to also discern clues to the historical layering of the imagery. Mary Boyce suggests that in the Gathas "whereas cattle imagery recurs again and again . . . there is not a single simile there drawn from tilling the soil—no mention of plough or corn, seedtime or harvest, though such things are much spoken of in the Younger Avesta." In the Vendidad (3.30), Ahura Mazda tells Zoroaster that "the core of the Mazda-worshipping religion" is sowing grain: "He who sows grain, sows righteousness (*asha*)" (Boyce 1975a, 14). There is, Boyce suggests, a tracing of the transformation from pastoralism to agriculture of the Iranian peoples as they moved from the Central Asian steppes to the Iranian plateau. The earliest evidence of Iranians on the plateau is around 1700 B.C., when warriors are still termed *rathaeshtar* (chariot riders). By the first millennium, warriors (in the Younger Avesta, the compositions after the oldest stratum of the Gathas) are being termed *bashar* (horsemen), the term which eventually in Persian comes to mean "person."

To complete and round out the understanding of the yasna as a key to the cosmology of Zoroastrianism, a fuller unpacking of the metaphorical code, attached to and enacted by the yasna ritual, can be briefly reviewed under three headings: the creation scheme; divinity and the amshaspands; and the legends of Zoroaster.

The Creation Scheme

There are four (in some versions three) eras of the world, each lasting three millennia. In the first era all was in a disembodied spiritual state: the menog (Persian, *minoo*). In the second era things took material and sentient form: getig (Persian, *guiti*). Substantiation is not bad, but it is vulnerable. It was in this period that Evil (Angra Mainyu, Ahriman) broke the stone sky, salted the waters, withered the plants, sullied the fire with smoke, and slew the first bull and the first man. It is the gods of this period that Zoroaster in his *Gathas* accuses of having chosen badly, of having followed the paths of deceit, and so of having brought the world to ruin. Their priests are the evil karpans. But the principle of immortality (Amertad) retrieved the seed of the bull and of man, purifying them in the sun, and took the plant hom and pounded it and scattered it in the clouds and rain so that the world could renew itself. Zoroaster is born at the beginning of the third era, at the midpoint of man's existence and of the world. His conceptual seed has been available since the first menog times, and his being or substantiation is itself a recapitulation of the cosmic story. His vision is a realization of the path of truth and good thinking: that the world can be healed and restored with the help of man. With man's aid God (Ahura Mazda) can accomplish this healing, and Zoroaster calls on God to aid man so that the latter can strengthen God. As related in the epigram to this chapter, Zoroaster complained to God that after ten years of fruitless proselytizing only one man had converted. For God it matters little, but says Zoroaster, the world of man is at stake: why should men live in misery, when they could achieve the restoration? And so the Gathas are urgent attempts to persuade both God and man to cooperate. After Zoroaster there will be three more sayoshants, or saviors, all born of his seed, and in their own way again cosmic recapitulations. Zoroaster's seed is preserved in the bottom of Lake Kasoya. The final saoshyant will be conceived by a maiden bathing in this lake (Y.13.62).[35]

The Legends of Zoroaster

Although Zoroastrians know varying amounts of folklore about Zoroaster, he is not of any particular centrality to belief or concern. There is refreshingly little tendency to elevate him as an object of worship or veneration in the Islamic or Christian manner.[36] People are quite content that he be a shadowy innovator and founder.

A superb attempt to trace the gradual elaboration of legends about him has been made by William Darrow (1981). The materials in Avestan about Zoroaster are relatively few but already speak of his divine creation proceeding from the menog to getig, his conferences with Ahura Mazda and the amshaspands, his visionary travels to heaven and hell and the *hamastagen* between, his commentaries on yasnas 26, 34, and 33 while emerging from the womb, his riddling debates and frustration of Angra Mainyu's temptations, his listing of the holy weapons with which he will smite evil, and his use of the Ahunvar prayer to frustrate the demon Buiti. Darrow suggests that in the Sassanian-Hellenistic period biographical elaborations of the Zoroaster figure were increasingly used as vehicles to introduce doctrine (on sacrifice, purity, eschatology), to incorporate the apocalyptic motifs of that period, to provide historicized commentaries on the yasna, and to Westernize the legend (moving events from the Balkh area to Rayy and Azarbaijan). This process accelerated in the Islamic period: most of the legendary corpus was collected in the ninth-century Denkart and Zatspram, and further pressed into an Islamic mould in the thirteenth-century Zardusht Nameh, complete with the emphasis on the bringing of a book. (Compare the pressure on Jews in the Islamic environment to elevate Moses into "the" Jewish prophet.) More recently, in India there has been an iconographic pressure to visualize Zoroaster as a Christlike figure.

The date of Zoroaster has been the subject of much speculation. The "traditional date"—258 years before Alexander—seems to be a Parthian con-

flation of the beginning of Zoroastrianism with the beginning of the Achaemenian period. If the 258-year figure refers to Zoroaster's birth, thirty years
later (228 years before the Seleucid era) would mark the beginning of Zoroaster's prophetic activities. This latter figure corresponds to 539 B.C., when
Cyrus the Great conquered Babylon and established the Perso-Babylonian
Empire of the Achaemenids.[37] For a time, scholars supported such a sixth- or
seventh-century B.C.E. dating, with linguistic arguments drawing parallels
between the language of the Rig Veda and the Avesta. But earlier dates have
also been proposed, and a new consensus seems now to support the (also
speculative) date of 1080–1500 B.C.E. There is a traditional date involved here,
too, a Khwarezmian tradition reported by al-Biruni, which dates Zoroaster
four generations (120 years) after Siyavush, in turn dated 888 years before
Alexander (i.e., before the Seleucid era); that is 1080 B.C.E. Interestingly,
Xanthos of Lydia says Zoroaster appeared 600 years before Xerxes's invasion
of Greece in 480 B.C.; this also works out to 1080 B.C.E. Again scholars can
find linguistic justifications to support this date. Some Parsis, of course,
would push Zoroaster's date back to 6000 B.C.E, but this seems to be simply a
reflex of the eschatological world-age doctrine and not a historical dating.[38]
Even here, then, the traditions of Zoroaster would demonstrate a mythic
rather than historical function.

The creation of Zoroaster has already been recounted down to his conception. His arrival and role had long been prophesied by the primeval ox; by the
first man, Yima; and by the hero Faridun. During Zoroaster's gestation in
Dugdav's womb, the divs caused her to fall ill and tried to tempt her into the
hands of an evil witch-doctor, but she was warned by Ahura Mazda and the
amshaspands, and directed to cure herself by washing her hands (purification), building a fire on which she cooked meat and cow's fat to eat, or in
another version (in the Denkart) by rubbing her hands with butter and
burning fuel and incense. The image here is of the ritual sacrifice: purification, sustenance shared between man (food) and God (aroma). In the fifth
month, according to the thirteenth-century Zardusht Nameh, Dugdav has a
vision in which clouds blot out the sun and wild animals tear open her
womb. She cries out, but Zoroaster says nothing can happen since God
protects him. A radiant mountain drives off the cloud, and from it emerges a
youth with a divine book and a luminescent branch capable of destroying
Ahriman. The youth scatters the wild animals and replaces the fetus of Zoroaster in the womb. Three days before the birth, the village becomes luminous.
The divs try to attack but are kept away by fires. The customs of keeping fires
lit in the house of a pregnant woman and lamps lit for three nights after a

birth are related to this story. There is a taboo against breaking the connection (paiwand) between fire and the newborn infant by stepping between them, in order that divs not find an opportunity to attack.

Zoroaster's birth is, of course, accompanied by miraculous signs, of which the most famous is that he laughs instead of crying as do most infants. The laughter is motivated according to a delightful parody of Iranian politesse: in the Zatspram, Ahriman chooses among the divs looking for an opportunity to attack, ultimately sending his lieutenant Akoman. Ohrmazd counters by sending Vohuman. The two meet at the door. Vohuman politely defers precedence in entering to Akoman. Akoman declines, less out of equal civility than out of a perverse refusal to do anything his rival tells him. Vohuman thus enters and shuts Akoman out. Zoroaster laughs. The Denkart provides a less playful, more eschatological version: Akoman shows the infant the sad end of man's bodily life, bringing him to tears; but then Vohuman shows him the happiness of the next world, bringing him joy and mirth.

Equally miraculous is the story of Zoroaster pronouncing Gathic texts as he emerges from the womb and as he materializes from the menog into the getig, as encoded in the yasna ritual (Y.26.11), where in form the raspi is to zot as Zoroaster is to Ohrmazd, and in content the zot plays the role of Zoroaster as material vehicle for the divine message.

Next come the trials of the infant in the house of his distant relative, the false *karap*-priest, Durasrob (both families are descended from Manuchehr): Durasrob's hand withers when he tries to crush the infant's hand; Zoroaster does not burn when placed on a blazing pyre; placed in the path of stampeded oxen and horses, the lead animal each time stands over the baby and protects him from the herd; when Zoroaster is placed in the den of a she-wolf whose cubs have been slain to anger her, the wolf's jaw is frozen, and Vohuman and Sorush bring a ewe for the infant to suckle until Dugdav can retrieve Zoroaster. Darrow points out that these five trials form a well-structured cycle: the initial and final trials concern opposite evil forms (human, male; animal, female) and frame the middle three stories in which representatives of the good creation (fire, oxen, horses; possibly: khwarrah, tan gohr, and frawahr) cannot be perverted. One might add that the frame stories concern as well the perverse forms of force (khshathra) and sustenance (milk, vohu manu). In any case, the themes of the laughing infant (Moses), the failure to burn (Ibrahim), the failure to expose a child (Oedipus, Romulus and Remus) are standard mythic devices, as are structured cycles of trials (Rustam and Esfandiar, Hercules, Dede Korkut).

Several more stories involving unsuccessful attempts by Durasrob and his eldest son, Bradrokesh, to pervert or destroy Zoroaster are related during the course of Zoroaster's childhood. Other stories of Zoroaster's youth show his discernment of deceit and uncleanness; his generosity toward cattle, a pregnant bitch, and the poor; his search for knowledge; and his piety.

At the age of thirty, Zoroaster receives his formative prophetic vision. He is on a journey into the land of *airyana vaejah* (the Ur-land of the Aryans). There is a miraculous crossing of a watery barrier (a pavi). On the forty-fifth day of the New Year (the first seasonal gahambar), Zoroaster dreams that mankind is gathered in the north under the leadership of his cousin and first convert, Maidyomah; in a later variant, he dreams of an army of the faithful from the south defeating an army of the enemy from the east. Five days later, at dawn on the final day of the Maidyoizaramaya gahambar, Zoroaster goes to the River Daiti to get pure water for making hom. The Daiti has four branches of increasing depth, representing, according to the Zatspram, Zoroaster and his three successor sons, the depth of the waters signifying the deepening spread of the good religion. In the deepest, Zoroaster encounters Vohuman in human form. Their exchange is in the Gathas (Y.43.7–10), Vohuman asking Zoroaster who he is and for what he strives, Zoroaster replying, "for righteousness." Vohuman then ascends with Zoroaster to the assembly of Ahura Mazda and the amshaspands in the menog, and there Zoroaster is shown a vision of heaven and hell. (This is the version in the thirteenth-century, Islam-influenced Zardusht Nameh; in the earlier versions, he is taken up the River Madan.) Zoroaster questions Ahura Mazda in a kind of catechism: What are the three best things? Good words, good thoughts, good deeds. What is to be worshipped? The brightness of God's glory. A proof for dualism, a vision of heaven and hell, and three ordeals: Zoroaster goes through a fire in three steps (good words, good thoughts, good deeds); molten metal is poured on his chest (the trial of the final days which destroys evil and eternalizes the righteous); and he heals a chest wound by the laying on of his own hands. Finally Zoroaster receives the Avesta and is instructed to recite it before Vishtaspa.

Over the next ten years, Zoroaster confers with the amshaspands in seven conferences at seven locations and is instructed in the care of that portion of creation that each amshaspand represents. His preaching during this period is unsuccessful; he makes but one convert, Maidyomah, and complains to Ahura Mazda.

Finally, the turning point comes: the king Kai Vishtaspa converts. Among the minor motifs is the initial jailing of Zoroaster through the deceit of jealous sages who plant impure objects in his room. The harshness of prison has become a folk allegory for the austerities of the nine-night purification cere-mony (Boyce 1977, 117–18). Zoroaster vindicates himself and cures Vishtaspa's prize black horse, extracting in return four promises: that Vishtaspa believe in Zoroaster's mission, that Vishtaspa instruct his son Esfandiar to fight for the new religion, that Vishtaspa have the queen instruct the women in the new religion, and that the deceitful sages be punished. Among the other motifs are the various proofs Zoroaster is asked to provide: the planting of his staff, which grows into a cypress; causing divine fires to descend; revealing the thoughts of Vishtaspa; performing cures. The cypress-tree story (although not in the Zoroastrian texts) has become the folk explanation for the great cypress that is the symbolic center of Iranian Zoroastrian villages and is usually next to the fire temple. It is perhaps the cosmic tree, Gaokarana, which grows in the Vourukasha Sea and which contains white hom. It certainly represents Amertat, renewal and immortality.

The major motif of the conversion story is, of course, the four wishes of Vishtaspa and their realization via elixir (wine/hom), milk, pomegranate, and incense to, respectively, Vishtaspa (a vision of his place in the world to come), Peshotan (immortality), Esfandiar (invulnerability), and Jamaspa (foreseeing the future). These four elements become central to any Zoroas-trian ritual, not only the inner or high liturgies.

Zoroaster lives thirty-five more years until he is killed at age seventy-seven by Tur-i Brados, the middle son of Durasrob, while praying during the invasion of Iran by the Turanian army of Arjasp. A popular, clearly Islam-influenced version has it that as he was stabbed in the back, he threw up his rosary (*tasbi*), and it hit and killed his assassin. Where it landed, or alter-natively where Zoroaster was buried, there grew a mighty cypress tree. It was this cypress that the Caliph Harun ar-Rashid ordered cut to build his great palace in Baghdad, the sacrilegious felling of the sacred tree causing Harun's downfall. The tree is popularly said to have been on the site later used by Muslims for the grave and shrine of the Eighth Imam, Imam Reza, in Mash-had. It is for this reason, say village Zoroastrians, that they sometimes go on pilgrimage to Mashhad, not on account of Imam Reza. Others say the death and cypress were in Tus, a small town near Mashhad, associated with Firdausi.

It is the epic traditions of Iran, codified by Firdausi in his *Shahnameh*, which expand and frame the tale of Zoroaster, Gushtasp, Esfandiar, and Jamasp, and the series of wars between the righteous Iranians and the deceit-ful Turanians. The epic traditions constitute a major component in Iranian identity, of Muslim as well as Zoroastrian Iranians. A hint of the fluidity of

TABLE 3. Seating Arrangement of the Amshaspands

ahura mazda = spenta mainu

1. vohu manah   4. spenta armaiti

2. asha vahishta   5. haurvatat

3. khshathra vairya   6. amaratat

sraosha

these traditions prior to their written codification has already been indicated in the passage on Zoroaster's date. Mythic elaborations tie Islamic legends to the Iranian ones through a marriage between the House of the last Zoroastrian king and the House of the Prophet of Islam. Later elaborations in mystical Islamic philosophy have even provoked the (inaccurate) characterization of Shi'ism as essentially Zoroastrianism in Islamic dress.[39] There is a grain of truth to this characterization, but there is a far more important distinctiveness to the living Zoroastrian communities, which cannot be matched in any of the several styles of Shi'ite religious or social behavior. For those of us who have had the privilege of experiencing it in its Iranian village setting, it is something very special and precious.

The Amshaspands

The principles composing the godhead are often badly translated into English. They are often hypostasized by meaningless glosses and left to function as empty pieties. Or they are analogized as angels. By keeping in mind their proper names, their ordering, and their interrelationships, one can easily appreciate a simple yet profound poetry of the moral order. In the Bundahishn a seating arrangement before the throne of Ahura Mazda is described (table 3). Ahura Mazda sits as zot and with the aid of Sorush as raspi manipulates the elements of the universe to create a pure world and means of communication between men and the spiritual existence. Three of the six amshaspands are female in gender (spenta armaiti, haurvatat, and amaratat); three are neuter (masculine). Haurvatat and amaratat almost always occur paired; in the Gathas they are rarely instrumental in the manner of the first four principles but are rather predicates, results: completion and eternality (immortality). Vohu manu and asha vahista (fire) frequently also occur to-

TABLE 4. Lozum Arrangement of Yasna 47.1

ahura mazda		spenta armaiti
	1. vohu manu	
	2. asha	
	5. haurvatat	
	6. amaratat	
	3. khshathra	
	4. armaiti	spenta armaiti

gether; in the Gathas they are frequently addressed by Zoroaster and appear to represent different aspects of the intellectual process: asha, truth, is associated with strength, a kind of black or white ruthless judgment; vohu manu, good thinking, appears to be more flexible, more strategy and process oriented, more visionary and associated with the growth of reason and understanding. In yasna 29 the drama of the cow's lament, for instance, spenta mainu (the virtuous spirit) asks asha if the cow's complaint is justified; asha replies decisively in the affirmative. It is good thinking who points out a solution, naming Zoroaster as the cow's human protector. The cow complains that Zoroaster has little power, and Zoroaster himself then prays for strength and just rule (khshathra). In the final lines Zoroaster concentrates on the need for truth and good thinking, making power a subordinate concern, and concludes that if asha and vohu manu are made available to men, men can provide God with the unique gifts of piety (armaiti) and obedience (saraosho). Armaiti is (like haurvatat and amaratat) a consequence of good thinking and truth (vohu manu and asha); the piety and worship of God by men is a recognition of the path provided by God to men for healing the world and for simultaneously putting truth and good thinking into use. There is always this duality to worship: ritual and worldly action are mirror images, necessary complements. So, too, the amshaspands are mantric terms, formulaic utterances, but also moral principles to be activated. Armaiti is thus the most mediating of the six principles, both instrumental and consequence. In yasna 45:4, vohu manu is said to have been fathered by Ahura Mazda via his daughter, armaiti.

Windfuhr sees in yasna 47.1 a lozum arrangement: the six amshaspands are paired off in two ways. The first and fourth (vohu manu and armaiti) go together as volitional and mental (good thought), and they enclose the sequence. The second and fifth (asha and haurvatat) go together as decisive and final (good words). The third and sixth (khshathra and amaratat) go together as powers of renewal and action (good deeds). Good words, good thoughts, good deeds is the Zoroastrian golden rule, also contained in yasna 47.1. (Windfuhr suggests a rough parallel with the stoic set: justice, bravery, self-control.) This pairing order of male and female principles is juxtaposed to the more usual pairs in a kind of double acrostic (table 4).

Each of the six represent an aspect of creation for which there is a seasonal celebration (gahambar) and a calendrical position. The order of creation is: sky, said to have been of stone crystal, and in later texts coming to be represented by metal (Shahrivar, khshathra); water (hordad, haurvatat); earth (Spendarmad, armaiti); plants (amurdad, amaratat); animals (Bahman, vohu manu); man (Ohrmazd, Ahura Mazda); fire (ardibehesht, asha vahista). Fire, in this scheme, is the separate and encompassing seventh; in the scheme of the aspects of the godhead, it is Ahura Mazda who is the encompassing term. Six months take their names from the amshaspands and two more from symbols of the amshaspands (water and fire). In between are four month names taken from the Indo-Iranian and Babylonian pantheons: Mithra, Tishtrya, Fravashi, Dathus.

2   *Shahnameh*: Parable Logic

" 'There is no lack of knowledge,' said the guide.
'But then it is dispersed 'mongst all the folk.' "
—FIRDAUSI, *Shahnameh*

"This intersignification process . . . the whole bulk of
'sayings' plus 'deeds' (ordinary, extraordinary, miraculous)
is connected . . . with . . . the narrative . . . in terms of mutual
interpretation, of symbolic interference."—PAUL RICOEUR,
"Biblical Hermeneutics," *Semeia*

At least as powerful a source and vehicle for the Zoroastrian and pre-Islamic lore of Iran as the Avesta (and the rituals and traditions of Zoroastrians) are the epic traditions codified by Firdausi in the *Shahnameh* (Book of Kings), completed in 1010 C.E. For most Muslim Iranians this is the primary vehicle and source; for Zoroastrians it is secondary and in many ways contrasts with their own traditions.

Such contrasts range from the obvious to the more subtle. Among the obvious are the valuations of Shah Gushtasp and Alexander the Great. To Zoroastrians, Gushtasp is the exemplar of great and valiant rule, the first important convert of Zoroaster, and the protector of the faith; in the *Shahnameh*, Gushtasp is a self-centered, power-hungry usurper of his father's throne. To Zoroastrians, Alexander the Great is an unequivocal figure of evil, a despoiler of Iran; in the *Shahnameh* and in later romance epics (e.g., the *Darab Nameh* and the *Eskandar Nameh*) Alexander is incorporated into the line of legitimate shahs, a mythic royal figure of half-Iranian blood who explores the limits of the world even to the vicinity of the fountain of youth.[1] A third example is Kai Kaus. The Vendidad treats him as an immortal, who like Jamshid and Faridun through hubris loses divine grace. Firdausi treats him instead as a man easily led astray by passion, wrongheadedness, and evil counsel. While the transformation from hubris to fickleness might be one of degree, it marks a difference between the logic of the mythic and that of the parable. Either way, Firdausi uses Kai Kaus as a clue to his poetic design for the Kayanian dynasty, which he initiates with Kai Kaus.

More subtle but pervasive are the philosophical frames or commentaries provided by Firdausi, which have little resonance in the Zoroastrian texts and which are characteristic of the delight in ambiguity and double-meaning in texts produced by people under cultural domination. In the prologue, for instance, Firdausi warns the reader,

> Deem not these legends lying fantasy . . .
> For most accord with sense, or anyway
> contain a moral,

and suggests a valuation of the present relative to the legendary time,

> The famed successful heroes of old time,
> What men were doing in those days that we
> Inherit such a world of misery. (1.108)[2]

Again, regarding the fallen shah and cultural hero Jamshid, Firdausi writes,

> What better shah was ever on the throne
> And yet what profit could he call his own. . . .
> The world will keep its secrets though for food
> It give thee sweets and honeycomb. . . .
> 'Twill play with thee, a pretty game indeed
> Anon, and cause thy wretched heart to bleed.
> My heart is weary of this Wayside Inn:
> Oh God! release me soon from the toil therein. (1.140)

Such world-weary stance is much elaborated in Muslim Iran but almost not at all among Zoroastrians. To be sure, Firdausi has more optimistic comments as well.

No good or evil will endure but still
Good furnisheth the better monument
. . . thy monument on earth
Will be the reputation left behind.
And therefore deem it not of little worth.
No angel was the glorious Faridun,
Not musk and ambergris; he strove to win
By justice and beneficence the boon
of greatness: be a Faridun therein. (1.170)

But again even here: "Lo! where is Faridun the valiant now, / Who took away from old Zahhak the crown?" (1.170).

The concern with royal legitimacy and martial heroism throughout the *Shahnameh* likewise has little resonance in contemporary Zoroastrianism but is an important reflex of the preoccupations of the eleventh through fourteenth centuries, when the Turkic Ghaznavids and the Mongol Il-Khanids were attempting to establish their legitimacy as rulers of Iran. What remains of martial heroism among Zoroastrians is a pervasive use of the metaphor of righteous individuals acting as warriors on the side of Ahura Mazda (Ohrmazd), which underpins the ethic of honesty, forthrightness, and battle with all deceit. This contrasts strikingly with the Muslim Iranian sense of martial heroism, which is taken much more literally and applied to questions of honor (*namus*) and holy warfare (*jihad*); furthermore, for Muslim Iranians (perhaps thanks to an engagement with Hellenism), deceit and cunning wit are important weapons.[3]

The value of the *Shahnameh* for the present study lies in three arenas: its power as purveyor of pre-Islamic lore in Islamic Iran, much of this power deriving from the parables (and parabolic logic) embedded in the dynastic framework; its exemplification of the ambiguities of Iranian nationalism in dealing with Turkic, Semitic, and Roman (and, by analogy, all foreign) cultural influences; and its status as a prototype for studies of codification of an oral tradition.

Firdausi considered himself a collector and versifier: he did not invent the stories himself. More interesting, a hundred years later, Nizam-i 'Arudi of Samarkand claimed that when Firdausi had completed his thirty-five-year-long effort, he dictated it to 'Ali Dilam, who wrote it out in its presumably final, polished form; Firdausi then took a reciter, Abu Dulaf, to present the poem at the court of Mahmud of Ghazni. The seven-volume manuscript was not given to the shah, for when Firdausi left Ghazni chagrined at the small

monetary appreciation he had received, he took the epic with him. Consequently, despite the existence of a written text, the epic continued to be transmitted in oral form. As revealed by studies of epic recitations, initiated by
Milman Parry and Albert Lord, bards do not memorize verbatim but invent
and reinvent, guided by storylines, formulas, and verse mnemonics. From the
start, then, Firdausi's epic was subject to the textual variations of oral transmission. One can see such variation quite clearly in contemporary recitations of the *Shahnameh*, studied by Mary Ellen Page (1977). Bards (*naqqal*)
may attempt to memorize Firdausi, but they work from prose abridgements
(*tumar*, "scrolls"), many of which contain stories and variations not found in
Firdausi. Moreover, it has been suggested that this sort of variation has always
existed and is reflected in extant versions of the manuscript.

Firdausi's original manuscript (the seven volumes purportedly transcribed by 'Ali Dilam) has long disappeared, if it ever existed. Grabar and
Blair (1980) point out that there is no evidence of a manuscript of the epic
until 1276–1277; then, suddenly, within seventy-five years, eleven manuscripts appeared, all but one illustrated. There is considerable textual variation among these manuscripts, with not just verses but entire stories added
or dropped. This suggests a vital oral tradition, a Persian *qur'an* (recitation)
rather than, say, a Persian bible (text). Fourteenth-century manuscript illustrations, as studied by Grabar and his students (Grabar and Blair 1980;
Simpson 1979), confirm both the lack of strict codification and the idea that
the motive for written texts emerged in part from Il-Khanid attempts to
establish legitimacy for their rule. Insofar as there is a standard text, it is the
version written in 1425–1426 C.E. for the Timurid prince Baysunghur. In
recent years, a team of Soviet philologists under E. E. Bertels has compiled a
critical edition based on the oldest copy (1276–1277 C.E.), with comparative
readings from five other copies from the thirteenth to fifteenth centuries.

The history of non-Iranian dynasties striving to establish claims to legitimate rule and cultural acceptability is central to the dynamic tension built
into Iranian thinking about nationalism. This tension reveals itself in at least
four places: in Firdausi's motives; in the agenda behind Il-Khanid patronage
of the fourteenth-century illustrated manuscripts; in the use made of the
Shahnameh in 'Ala' al-Din 'Ata-Malik Juvaini's 1290 *Tarikh-i Jahangusha*
(History of the World Conqueror); and in contemporary recitations.

Firdausi belonged to a class of gentry (dehqan) invested in preserving the
Persian national tradition. Such gentry would have provided the patronage
of, audience for, and interest in bards of knightly heroism. Indeed, Firdausi's
first patron, Abu Mansur, employed men with distinctly Persian names,

Shahnameh miniature: Firdausi and the Court Poets of Ghazni.

possibly Zoroastrians who would have still known Pahlavi, to help with the task of collecting traditions. Firdausi's third patron, Abu'l Abbas Fazl bin Ahmad, had served the Samanids, the dynasty centered on Balkh where the New Persian literary tradition was born; it was he, as chief minister to Mahmud of Ghazni, who changed the bureaucratic language for state documents from Arabic to Persian.

This linguistic development was a catalyst for the release of Islam from its Arabocentric parochialism. Mahmud of Ghazni, to whom Firdausi somewhat opportunistically and unsatisfactorily attempted to dedicate the *Shahnameh*, had the power to end Arab hegemony and to restore a new Persian world empire. Mahmud, however, proved less receptive to the *Shahnameh* than Firdausi had hoped, perhaps, as Theodor Nöldeke suggests (1979), because he was a Turk and son of an upstart slave, and so might have felt uncomfortable with a poem that emphasized the legitimacy of kings and the evilness of Turks. He was, moreover, a fervent Sunni and anti-Shi'ite. Indeed, as Nöldeke notes, the Iranian Buyids who controlled western Iran at that time would have had a better claim to be successors of the ancient kings of Iran; despite being Iranian and Shi'ite, however, the Buyids ruled in the name of the Arab caliph. Mahmud later changed his mind about Firdausi, attempting to reward him more handsomely, but the poet died before he could receive the tribute.

Firdausi, in any case, is the greatest of a long line of collectors of the epic stories. Such collection in the form of written texts seems to have begun in the Parthian period, with a struggle by the Zoroastrian priests and others to preserve their language and culture against the seductions of Hellenism (much like the struggle of Jews in Hellenistic Palestine). The Parthian king Valkash (Vologeses I, r. 50–78 C.E.) ordered his brother, Tiridates, apparently a Zoroastrian priest, to collect the scriptures (Warner and Warner 1905, intro., chap. 2). There are also two brief epic texts: *Zariadres and Zarer* and *Vis-o-Rus*. After the restoration of a culturally Iranian empire under Ardashir (r. 226–240 C.E.), founder of the Sassanian dynasty, the scriptures were collected more systematically, together with Pahlavi (Middle Persian) glosses (the Pazend or Zend Avesta), analogous to the Jewish *targums*. The canon of twenty-one nasks, or books, was closed around 330 C.E., with perhaps a few minor additions appearing as late as the sixth century. We know of at least two epic collections in the sixth and seventh centuries as well, one focusing on the hero Zarer, the other on Ardashir. In the 1425 *Shahnameh* manuscript of Baysanghir (grandson of Timur), the preface tells that the epic stories were also collected under the Sassanian shah Nushiravan and that the last Sassanian shah, Yazdegird (r. 623–652), employed a dehqan, Daneshwar (Learned), to put them in chronological order, the *Khwadaq Namag*, said to have been translated into Arabic by Ibn Maqal. The preface also says that after the Arab invasion, the Caliph Omar had the tales translated into Arabic, that some of the manuscripts made their way to Abyssinia, and that others were taken to India, where they were transcribed into Persian and updated through the end of the Sassanian era. It was this Indian version, according to the preface, that the Samanids entrusted to the poet Dakiki to versify and on which Firdausi later drew. Al-Biruni (d. 1048) claimed to know of six *Shahnameh*s in Arabic (none of which survive).

Firdausi acknowledged the thousand verses of Dakiki, who was murdered before completing his poem, as his inspiration. Firdausi incorporated Dakiki's verses intact. As has been often pointed out, it is striking that Firdausi should have not reversified Dakiki, and there may have been a good political reason: Dakiki's verses are the story of the prophet Zoroaster. By adopting Dakiki's words, Firdausi avoided making a personal statement about Zoroastrianism and thus dodged criticism by Muslim purists. Consequently, the poem retained a degree of anti-Islamic innuendo, which many Iranian readers enjoy pointing out.

Language is another medium of the *Shahnameh*'s nationalism, Firdausi having striven to purge his poem of Arabic loan words and to write in unadulterated Persian. (Firdausi himself, it seems, knew no Pahlavi and little Arabic.) To this day, among Iranians, the *Shahnameh* stands as the exemplar of pure Persian. In its language, religion, and royal-heroic dual structure, the *Shahnameh* serves as an agonistic, subversive, ongoing critique of the corruptions of the present.

If the composition of Firdausi's text reflects the cultural dynamics of the gentry in the eleventh century, the production of showpiece manuscripts with miniature illustrations in the fourteenth century may reflect the evolution of such dynamics. The nine illustrated manuscripts produced in the first four decades of the fourteenth century seem to fall into three groups. Four were produced under the patronage of the Inju court, the rulers of Shiraz (1330–1352) under the Il-Khanids; all are stylistically similar, are dated, and include some statement identifying their scribes or patrons. Four smaller-format manuscripts, again forming a stylistic set, are thought to have been produced in Baghdad around 1300. And one, the most lavish and with the largest format, the so-called Demotte manuscript, was purportedly produced in 1335 in Tabriz.

The subjects chosen for illustration in the fifty-eight extant miniatures of the Demotte *Shahnameh* (the manuscript appears to be unfinished with more miniatures planned) suggest that the manuscript was prepared for the vizier Ghiyath al-Din around 1335, when after the death without heir of Abu Sa'id, Ghiyath al-Din arranged for Arpa to succeed to the throne. This analysis, by Grabar and Blair (1980), begins by noting that the Demotte miniatures reflect five primary themes: enthronement; fantastic creatures encountered in battle, hunting, or travel (i.e., tests and trials); funerals which portray a variety of fourteenth-century death customs;[4] scenes depicting the discovery of a legitimate right to the throne;[5] and women who establish or thwart claims to the throne.[6] The concern with legitimacy, of course, corresponds to the predicament of the Mongols: they have an investment in depicting legitimate shahs who, like themselves, did not come to the throne through simple hereditary inheritance. That blood and birth neither ensure nor are the only grounds for legitimacy is one of the *Shahnameh* motifs—thus the illustrations of Alexander the Great as an Iranian shah; the accession of the upstart Ardashir, founder of the Sassanian dynasty; and the elevation of Zav to the throne by the hero Zal.

But more interesting than this general concern with legitimacy may be the references in the miniatures to the intrigues of the reign of Abu Sa'id (r. 1316–1335). Grabar and Blair (1980) suggest that the pictures of Zal's love for Rudaba, Zal's letters to Rudaba, the upstart Shah Ardashir's seduction of Gulnar (Shah Ardavan's harem favorite), Adavan's daughter's attempt to poison her husband and the new shah (Ardashir)—all these may be allusions to the career of Baghdad Khatun, whose father, the vizier Amir Chupan, was murdered by Shah Abu Sa'id so that he could take her from her husband and marry her himself, which he did; Khatun was caught corresponding with her former husband in a conspiracy against her new husband, was later accused of killing Abu Sa'id by poison, and was eventually executed for a subsequent plot. A similarly veiled allusion appears in miniatures that depict the sons of Mahbud being accused of bringing poisoned food to Nushiravan, an allusion, presumably, to the charge that Rashid al-Din had poisoned Shah Uljaytu by having his son deliver a fatal cup of wine. Or, again, the miniatures that portray the two coffins of Rustam and Zavara or the presentation of Iraj's head to Faridun may allude to the fate of Amir Chupan and his son, who were executed and whose coffins were carried across Iran to Medina; another of his sons was killed in Egypt, his head sent back to Iran. The illustration of Zal appointing Zav to the throne parallels Ghiyath al-Din's selection of Arpa; Ghiyath al-Din might also have read himself into the figure of Prime Minister Bozorg-i Mehr that appears in two of the miniatures, with the king in one and receiving reward in the other.

The Demotte manuscript, then, can be read both in terms of Il-Khanid interests in legitimacy and in terms of Ghiyath al-Din's efforts to secure the legitimate transition of the throne from Abu Sa'id to Arpa.

Circumstantial evidence suggests that the four smaller-format *Shahnameh* manuscripts were produced in Baghdad around 1300, their production being concerned less with claims to legitimacy per se than with a public demand for written versions of the text; a generation for whom allusions to the *Shahnameh* were second nature feared that the next generation was losing such familiarity and that without written texts the epic might die. Simpson's analysis (1979) both of the texts and of 226 miniatures in three of the four manuscripts reveals significant variation in the texts and suggests that the production procedure was to transcribe an oral recitation while leaving spaces for illustration at semiregular intervals. In this way, variant repertoires could be preserved, each manuscript would be a unique object for the patron, and the differing illustrations could attract a larger readership. The primary patron for these four manuscripts, Simpson suggests, might have been Ghazan Khan (r. 1295–1304 C.E.), the seventh and the most learned of the Il-Khanids, who wintered in Baghdad, spoke seven languages, and sponsored Rashid al-Din's *Jami' al-Twarikh* (Collection of History).

A key element in Simpson's argument is the use of quotations from the *Shahnameh* by 'Ala' al-Din 'Ata-Malik Juvaini in his 1290 C.E. *Tarikh-i Jahangusha* (History of the World Conqueror). Juvaini was of a Persian family from Khorasan which had served the Seljuks, the Khwarazm Shahs, and the Mongols. He accompanied Arghun Khan to Mongolia twice and served as an advisor to Hulagu in his campaign against the Ismailis of Alamut (where he was instrumental in saving the Ismaili library) and in the siege and capture of Baghdad (ending the Abassid Caliphate). He became governor of Baghdad in 1259; his brother, Shams al-Din, served as governor of Tabriz. Juvaini's *Tarikh-i Jahangusha* is filled with literary quotations. The largest number come from the Qur'an, but the second-largest number (some fifty direct quotations) are from the *Shahnameh*. The latter are often used to convey opinions which might be imprudent in the prose of his own composition. Moreover, Simpson suggests, full appreciation of the force of their meaning in the context of the *Tarikh-i Jahangusha* required an audience which knew the *Shahnameh* well enough to identify the location from which the verses were taken. The Mongol overlords would not have been such an audience, but there was a learned stratum of Persian officials and intellectuals who would have known the *Shahnameh* as second nature. This was the generation of the poet Sa'di and the philosopher Nasir al-Din Tusi. Juvaini, in other words, could use the *Shahnameh* to introduce a nuance of critique, just as Firdausi had used the verses of Dakiki. In his introduction Juvaini explicitly bemoans the destruction of Iranian cultural and educational institutions during the course of the Mongol invasions and laments the rise of a new generation of officials who consider Uighur to be the language of learning. Later, in relating how Ghengiz Khan heard that Khwarazm Shah Jalal ad-Din' was arming defensively against the Mongols, Juvaini goes so far as to quote the *Shahnameh* line "Tidings came to Afrasiyab [the Turanian or Turkic archenemy of the Iranians] that Sohrab [one of the great Iranian heroes] had cast a boat upon the waters"; and again, praising Jalal ad-Din, he quotes, "The knight of the world, the son of Dastan, the son of Sam, will not lightly put his head in the snare." There is a wonderful subtlety here, for should the

Il-Khanids object to being identified with the enemy Afrasiyab, Juvaini and his Persian nationalist allies could protect themselves by pointing out that Afrasiyab had some Iranian blood, being descended from the great Iranian liberator, Faridun. That the Il-Khanids were Turanian could not be denied, but via the *Shahnameh*'s genealogical interconnections between the House of Turan and Iran, they could be incorporated as kin who through defense of Iran and proper conduct could become legitimate rulers. Kai Khosrow, a grandson of Afrasiyab and one of the greatest Iranian kings in the *Shahnameh*, could serve as an archetype. Thus might the intricate net of implication draw the Il-Khanids toward the sensibilities of their subjects.

Such double "readings" of the *Shahnameh*, glorifying the ancient heroes while making contemporary points, can be seen as well in the way modern naqqals recite the epic. A typical performance of approximately an hour and a half, begins with a Quranic invocation ("Bismillah . . ." [In the name of God . . .]) and a selection of poetry, often from Sa'di, Hafiz, or Nizami. The epic then begins. A verse may be recited as a lead-in, then recapitulation of the story from the day before or as preparation for the present selection. The story is then declaimed in prose, interspersed with poetry from the *Shahnameh* text, and peppered with digressions: drawing attention to particular features, providing background explanations, and making didactic analogies (*masal*).

Thus, in telling the story of the hero Rustam rescuing the king Kai Kaus, then thrashing the king to make him realize his foolishness (it works: Kai Kaus sees the error of his ways), a Shiraz naqqal comments: "Islam, sir, is founded on three things: . . . [a] the disposition and manner and character of the Prophet, [b] the wealth of Khadijeh [the first wife of Muhammad], and [c] finally, even the sayings of the Arabs themselves affirm, the sword—the sword and strong arm—of Ali. If Ali was right and honorable to use the sword for Islam, then Rustam was right in using his strength for Iran" (qtd. in Page 1977). The same naqqal tells of the villainy of Afrasiyab, first usurping his father's throne and then ignoring his father's desire to be buried in Iran near his own grandfather (Faridun). The naqqal here introduces a hadith from the Sixth Imam that Ali appeared in a dream ordering that a heretic not be buried in the Muslim cemetery (*vadi os-salam* [valley of peace]). The next night, again Ali appeared in a dream, but now ordered the cemetery to be opened to the heretic's corpse. Asked about the discrepancy, Ali admitted to first refusing the heretic's funeral party, but since they had gotten lost and had gone to Karbala where the dust of Husain blew over the corpse, God had forgiven the heretic. So, too, concluded the naqqal, Pashang (Afrasiyab's father) had sinned against Iran, but by returning even after death to the realm of his grandfather, there was a chance for forgiveness.

By comparing the oral versions, the tumar, and Firdausi's text, one can see a variety of Islamicizing changes, such as the preceding masal, but also other kinds of shifts and reworkings, such as the modified deployment of devices like marriage and genealogical ties. In the ancient myths the puzzles of creation are regularly metaphorized as a differentiating process of marriage: an undifferentiated stage of existence divides into a male and female who marry and generate offspring, a process roughly analogous to cellular meiosis or mitosis. Thus the primal human being, Gaiumart, is killed by Ahriman and undergoes a three-generation meiosis: first he divides into the male and female pair Mashya and Mashyoi, who bear a son, Siyamak; Siyamak and Nashak, his female side, bear the pair Fravak and Fravakain, who in turn produce the fifteen pairs who populate the seven climes. One of these pairs is Hushang and Guzhang who originate the oldest mythic dynasty of Iranian kings. Hushang and his great grandsons, Tahmuras and Jamshid, are the culture heroes who introduce civilized skills to mankind. The whole process then repeats itself. Jamshid loses divine grace; Zahhak, as Ahriman's proxy, seizes power, as well as the sisters of Jamshid; Faridun later overthrows Zahhak, claiming descent from Jamshid, and bears by Jamshid's two sisters three sons—Tur, Iraj, and Salm—who establish the royal houses of the east, center, and west. Jealous that Iraj has inherited dominion of Iran (the center), Tur and Salm kill him, and thus begin the feuds which weave the story of the *Shahnameh*.[7]

Firdausi perhaps understood this technique well enough, for it is he who puts the second repetition into this clear form. He abandons the first series of meiosis, simplifying it into a linear genealogy: Gaiumart is made the first king of the Pishdadians (literally, "the original dispensation" or "the preliminary givens"). He is succeeded by his grandson Hushang, his great-grandson Tahmuras, and his great-great-grandson Jamshid. Then there is the usurpation by Zahhak from the Arab lands of Baghdad. Faridun liberates Iran and reestablishes the line of Jamshid. Though his son, Iraj, is slain, the line carries on with Iraj's grandson, Manuchihr. One more important genealogical line is introduced in the reign of Manuchihr: that of the house of Zabul, the line of the great heroes who protect the kings of Iran (Sam, Zal, and Rustam). This seems to be an independent Scythian epic grafted onto the main epic traditions and a reflection of the migration of a Scythian branch to Zabul in southeastern Iran, or so scholars speculate. Indeed this genealogical line does not appear in the Avestan texts, although some of the names and mythic elements associated with it do, such as the magic bird Simorgh. Oral variants attach this genealogical line to the royal one in the same way that pre-nineteenth-century government was divided between the Persian bureaucracy (*sultanat*) and the Turkic military command (*sepahsalari*). There are thus three or four genealogical threads with which to weave marriages, wars, and feuds: the house of Iran, Zabul, and the enemy (first Zahhak to the west, later Turan to the north and east).

In Islamic-period texts, genealogical devices replace the meiotic-mythic ones. In the oral versions of today's naqqals, no use seems to be made of the meiotic-mythic marriages except in one brother-sister marriage, that of the children of Noah, whose line leads to the first Iranian king, Kayomars (Gaiumart); that is, the story is fitted to the Western biblical-qur'anic creation frame.[8] Several parent-child marriages are utilized, but these are all viewed as evil incest rather than as mythic devices.[9] Thus, Zahhak marries both his father's wife and his own daughter, and Bahman marries his daughter Homa against the warnings of the prophet Zakaraya (another biblical-qur'anic signifier), causing the end of the recitation cycle, which occurs, among contemporary naqqals in Shiraz, with a Bahman story considerably more elaborate than Firdausi's laconic line that Bahman fell ill and died. In the expanded version, Bahman destroys the house of Zabul (in revenge for the death of Esfandiar), thus destroying not only the protectors of the throne but also the house which could marry the other lines and continue weaving the story fabric. Then, while Bahman builds a castle for his wife-daughter, a dragon blocks the access road. In true heroic style, Bahman hosts a feast of warriors and boasts of the dragon-killing exploits of his grandfather Gushtasp and his father, Esfandiar, proclaiming that he too will take up the tradition. A young hero first, and without permission, attempts to face the dragon but does not succeed, setting a contrast to display Bahman's genuine bravery. Bahman challenges the dragon, but because of his sins he has lost heroic grace and is sucked into the dragon's mouth. The hero Azarbarzin, darkly contemplating Bahman's destruction of Zabul, allows him to die before slaying the dragon. In Firdausi, by contrast, the marriage of Bahman with his daughter Homa is instead a signaling device that links both the next cycle of Alexander stories and the succeeding Sassanian dynasty.[10] Homa's brother, disinherited, leaves, quietly marries a high-born lady, has a child, and dies. This child's descendants will eventually found the new dynasty. In the meanwhile, Homa's son Darab introduces the Alexander story and the Ashkanian (Parthian) interregnum.

If contemporary naqqals deal only with the first third of the legends

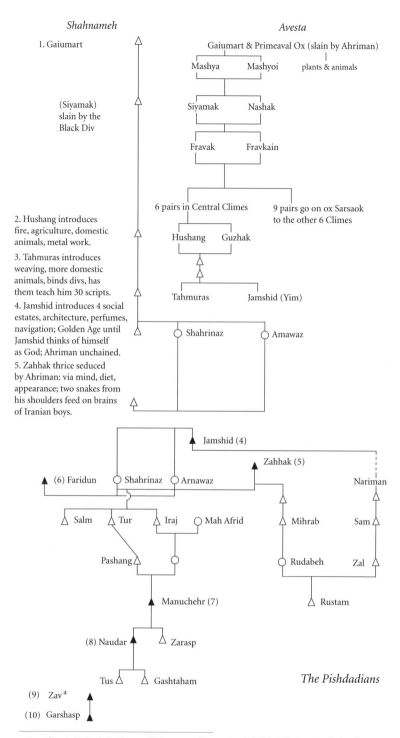

Shahnameh   _Avesta_

1. Gaiumart

Gaiumart & Primeaval Ox (slain by Ahriman)

plants & animals

Mashya   Mashyoi

(Siyamak)
slain by the
Black Div

Siyamak   Nashak

Fravak   Fravkain

6 pairs in Central Climes   9 pairs go on ox Sarsaok
to the other 6 Climes

2. Hushang introduces
fire, agriculture, domestic
animals, metal work.

Hushang   Guzhak

3. Tahmuras introduces
weaving, more domestic
animals, binds divs, has
them teach him 30 scripts.

Tahmuras   Jamshid (Yim)

4. Jamshid introduces 4 social
estates, architecture, perfumes,
navigation; Golden Age until
Jamshid thinks of himself
as God; Ahriman unchained.

Shahrinaz   Amawaz

5. Zahhak thrice seduced
by Ahriman: via mind, diet,
appearance; two snakes from
his shoulders feed on brains
of Iranian boys.

Jamshid (4)

Zahhak (5)

(6) Faridun   Shahrinaz   Arnawaz   Nariman

Salm   Tur   Iraj   Mah Afrid   Mihrab   Sam

Pashang   Rudabeh   Zal

Manuchehr (7)   Rustam

(8) Naudar   Zarasp

Tus   Gashtaham   _The Pishdadians_

(9)   Zav [a]

(10)   Garshasp

---

a. According to Firdausi, Zav is son of Tahmasp, and is appointed shah by Zal, since Naudar's rule was unjust and
he lost the royal grace. His bypassed son, Tus, displays his jealousy on three occasions during the reign of Kai Kaus,
but is generally a loyal hero and general for Iran. According to the Bundahishn, Zav is a grandson of Naudar.

related by Firdausi, there is nonetheless plenty of material for them to elaborate, reflect on, and comment on. Some hint of the philosophical style of the naqqals is provided in the work of Shahrokh Meskoub, who dedicates his book *Moqaddama'i bar Rostam o Esfandiyar* (Introduction to Rustam and Esfandiar) to them and who wants to preserve both their work and their tone. The tragedy of Rustam and Esfandiar provides the climax to the second of the four dynasties of the *Shahnameh*: the Kayanians. The Pishdadians, the first or original dynasty or dispensation, are the culture heroes, their stories setting the epic stage by introducing the cast of heroes and laying out the basic conflicts between good and evil (men and demons, Iran and Zahhak), between east, west, and center (Tur, Salm, and Iraj; or China-Turkestan, Arabia-Rome, and Iran). The Kayanians, then, represent the heroic age and the age in which the new faith is adopted by the Iranian royal house. The Kayanian heroic age is the story of the prophet Zoroaster, of the kings Lohrasp, Gushtasp, and Bahman, and of the heroes Rustam and Esfandiar. The new faith nominally is Zoroastrianism, but it is as well a stalking horse for Islam. From this latter sense, the portrayal of the flaws of the champions of the new faith emerge as subtle yet powerful Iranian nationalist statements. The reworking of Zoroastrian characters becomes less a slap at Iran's pre-Islamic faith and more an indictment of, or at minimum a wariness toward, Islamic fanaticism. Within this frame, the dilemmas of Rustam (the heroic embodiment of the old virtues) and Esfandiar (the champion of the new faith) are crafted into a finely balanced tragedy. It is this tragic sense which Meskoub draws out.

After allowing Meskoub to help introduce the parable structure of the Kayanian period, which is already foreshadowed and set up in the second half of the Pishdadian period, I will return to the doublings and inversions of the structure of the tales, which cause the stories of the *Shahnameh* to compose an arena of "intersignification"—that is, multiple parallels provide vehicles by which reciters can make the stories comment on one another.

The tale of Rustam and Esfandiar, Meskoub notes, is of two apotheoses of heroism whose flaws and humanity are nevertheless revealed. Esfandiar received the gift of invulnerability; his epithet is Ruintan (the bronze bodied). Yet like other such figures (Achilles, Siegfried, Krishna) he has a weak spot, in this case his eyes. Although the Avestan tradition endows his invulnerability through eating pomegranates, the tradition Firdausi uses has him baptized in bronze: he closes his eyes as the molten metal pours over him. Pouring of molten metal is a motif from the Last Judgment and so reinforces Esfandiar's eschatological role. But his eyes remain vulnerable. It is ironic that a baptism to free one from fear should be partially vitiated by that fear (closing the eyes). "Tars, baradar, marg ast" [Fear, brother, is death], runs the Persian tag. But the all-too-human point of the metaphor is that it is his spiritual sight which is vulnerable, not his martial skill. Esfandiar is the champion of the new faith, winning wars against those who would destroy it, such as Arjasp, the leader of the Turanians. Esfandiar builds fire temples and converts nations. He also, however, has burning desire to replace his father, Gushtasp, as king, justified in his eyes by his greater ability to defend and spread the faith. After all, Gushtasp left the country vulnerable to Arjasp's second attack, in which Zoroaster and eighty priests were slain. Esfandiar's underlying character flaw, then, is his single-minded obsessiveness, his inability to compromise—in a word, his fanaticism. His intent is good, but his means and strategies become warped.

Esfandiar's character flaw develops in counterpoint to, and repetition of, his father's own obsessive fatal character flaws. Gushtasp had forced his own father, Lohrasp, from the throne. Lohrasp had seen himself as a caretaker king, saving the throne for the legitimate collateral line temporarily without an adult heir. Gushtasp went to Rome, proved himself in a few minor heroic trials, married a daughter of the Caesar (Nahid), and in alliance with his father-in-law challenged Iran. Lohrasp, feeling it an unbearable disgrace for father and son to fight, abdicated the throne to Gushtasp, spent his retirement as an ascetic, and was eventually killed along with Zoroaster. Having won the throne with the aid of Iran's enemies, Gushtasp kept it through deceit and prevarication. Thus, being incapable of defending Iran or the new religion, he has constantly to depend on his son Esfandiar. Gushtasp's bad conscience at usurping his father's throne fixates on and amplifies his fear that Esfandiar will do the same, and worse, to him.

In a famous scene, Gushtasp assembles the notables and asks them what they think about a son who wants not only his father's throne but also his death. The scene is thought by Iranians to resonate with a number of later historical shahs: Harun ar-Rashid, who threatened his son with blinding; Shah Abbas Safavi, who blinded his son; Nadir Shah, who blinded his eldest son, Reza Qoli Mirza, after accusing him falsely before the notables; Fath Ali Shah Qajar, who sent his son Abbas Mirza to war without proper munitions. The Nadir Shah parallel is told as an exact replay of the Gushtasp scene; the others are more approximate, but all are predicated on suspicions of the sons plotting against their fathers.

In a major test, his first defensive war to protect Iran, Gushtasp loses his brother Zarir, several sons, as well as many of his chief heroes. In desperation, Gushtasp offers his daughter, Humai, to the man who avenges Zarir. He vows to give the throne to his son Esfandiar and the army command to his other son Peshotan if Iran emerges victorious. But when the war is won under the leadership of Esfandiar, Gushtasp prevaricates. He sends Esfandiar first to convert the nations, then imprisons him on a trumped-up charge of plotting regicide and usurpation of the throne. Arjasp attacks again and surrounds Gushtasp, forcing him to send again for Esfandiar. (In the course of chasing Arjasp, Esfandiar undergoes his seven heroic tasks.) Again promises are broken, and Esfandiar after the war is set new tasks before he can gain the throne. The last of these is to bring Rustam in chains before Gushtasp on flimsy charges of attempting to set Zabul independent of Iran.

Esfandiar's mother, his brother Peshotan, and even a camel blocking his way (the forces of nature), all try to dissuade him from a path that can only lead to a tragic end—parallel to the animal which tries to block Imam Ali from going to his martyrdom (Fischer 1980a, 17)—but Esfandiar is driven to fulfill his father's request. He is driven both by a desire to have Gushtasp acknowledge him as deserving of the throne, feeling a moral imperative not to push Gushtasp aside as Gushtasp had done to Lohrasp, and by a conviction that he could better serve the religion, as Gushtasp was obviously partially enthralled by Ahriman's demons. Gushtasp, however, views Esfandiar as being just like himself: merely power hungry. An insoluble dynamic between father and son is thus set up. Given this dynamic, Esfandiar acquits himself reasonably well in his confrontation with Rustam.

Rustam, meanwhile, although by far purer in motive and conduct than Esfandiar, also has flaws in his lineage. Claiming descent on one side from Jamshid through the line of Iran's greatest heroes, Rustam is descended through his mother from Zahhak. Furthermore, touches of tragic hubris dog the paternal line. Jamshid, for instance, had lost the royal grace by claiming quasi divine status. In the more recent past, Rustam's grandfather Sam had feared his albino son, Zal, to be an Ahrimanic mutation and had left him to die by exposure. Zal was raised (and forever protected) by the mythical meat-eating bird, the Simorgh, described in the Bundahishn as flying like a bird, possessing teeth like a dog, and dwelling in holes like a muskrat; each year it shakes the tree of vegetation to scatter seeds for the coming year.[11] Sam had eventually welcomed back the adult Zal. Perhaps consistent with his lack of fathering and his carrion-eating childhood (as Ahrimanic flaws), Zal fell in love with Rudabeh, daughter of Mihrab, the ruler of Herat and a descendant of Zahhak.

Both Sam and the shah, Manuchehr, consulted astrologers about Zal's proposed marriage and foresaw no evil, but rather that it would produce

Iran's mightiest hero and defender (Rustam). Mihrab also became a loyal vassal of Iran. In time, Rustam had a child, Sohrab, who cried whenever Rustam held him. Fearing he might crush the child in anger, Rustam leaves an identification medallion and departs. Mother and child suffer a difficult and eventful life between the clash of Turanian and Iranian forces. Sohrab grows up and falls in love with Afrasiyab's daughter; Afrasiyab demands Rustam's head as a brideprice. Finding out his true paternity, which had been kept secret, Sohrab proposes to dethrone Shah Kai Kaus, put Rustam on the throne, then attack Turan and dethrone Afrasiyab. The story is a favorite of modern naqqals who expand the details and subplots far beyond what can be found in Firdausi. The tragic denouement comes with Rustam facing Sohrab in single-handed combat and slaying him before discovering his identity.

The Sohrab story is one of a series of father-son parables that occur within a larger set of morality tales which compose the Kayanian dynasty and set the stage for the Rustam-Esfandiar story. The challenge of telling the Sohrab-Rustam story lies in finely balancing the elements of the tragic failure of father and son to recognize one another. Rustam initially considers whether the descriptions of this young champion might not be of his son but dismisses the possibility, calculating that Sohrab ought still to be much too young to be a warrior of note. Sohrab, in turn, is provided by his mother with a guide to point out his father. This guide, Zhanda Razm, Sohrab's maternal uncle, accidentally stumbles on Rustam, who has slipped into the Turkoman camp in the dark to scout out his rival. Zhanda Razm challenges the figure in the shadows to show himself, and Rustam kills him lest he be discovered and captured. Sohrab then questions the captured Iranian *pahlavan* (champion) Hajjir about the pahlavans of Iran arrayed on the battlefield, but Hajjir hides Rustam's identity, claiming he is in Zabulistan, fearing that the young Sohrab might well best the aging Rustam in single combat and that such a disaster would demoralize Iran. Sohrab several times asks Rustam point-blank whether he is not the famous Rustam, and Rustam denies it. Sohrab throws the older warrior but lets him rise when he calls for two out of three throws. Rustam then throws Sohrab and stabs him. Only then does Sohrab display Rustam's amulet, and the father recognizes the son.

Sohrab charges Rustam with lack of love (abandonment as an infant now recapitulated in adulthood).

> If thou art indeed Rustam, thou hast slain me
> In wanton malice, for I made advances,
> But naught that I could do would stir thy love. (2.174)

Rustam is too distraught with remorse to counter charge Sohrab, but Tahmina, Sohrab's mother, grieves.

> Before he drew his dagger . . . why didst not thou
> Show him the token thy mother gave thee?
> Why didst thou not declare thyself to him?
> Thy mother told thee how to know thy sire. (2.185)

She blames herself: "Why went I not with thee? . . . He would have known me." Her sense of guilt is compound: she had kept her son's progress from Rustam lest she lose the son to the father; she further had had to hide the son's identity from Afrasiyab, Rustam's enemy (Southgate 1974). Rustam attempts to get the king, Kai Kaus, to provide Sohrab with a life-saving elixir, but the king fears that Rustam and Sohrab, both alive and in tandem, would pose a threat to his throne. After all, Sohrab had threatened to dethrone him, and in a fit of anger at the sovereign's errant demands, Rustam once had cried, "My might and my successes are from God, not from the shah. . . . I am not his slave, but God's" (3.143). In fact, this retort had occurred in response to Shah Kai Kaus's rebukes that Rustam had not responded more quickly when Sohrab, leading Afrasiyab's forces, had attacked the White Castle of Iran and taken Hajjir prisoner.

Firdausi makes two comments on this tale, first on the advantage-seeking but often self-deceiving stratagems of men.

> O world! thy doings are a mystery
> The fish in the streams, wild asses on the plain,
> And beasts of burden know their young again,
> But toil and lust forbid a man to know
> The difference between a child and foe! (2.163)

Then Firdausi has Bahram comfort Tahmina, saying that this world is but a way station and that summons to depart for the next world come from God, so one ought not to fix one's heart too deeply on the events of the world.

The rhetorical elegance of the tale lies in its delicate dialectical ironies: Rustam literally pierces the heart (or liver, in Persian idiom) of Sohrab, but it is his own which is truly pierced, in that he must live with the emotional agony; Sohrab seeks his sire, the fount of his life, but instead finds his grave; Rustam's lack of paternal love is counterpoised to Sohrab's lack of filial trust; and both are guilty of seeking in the stratagems of combat what should have been openly proclaimed in identifying words. In the telling, various keys may be struck: royal (Sohrab sinned by presuming to dethrone a legitimate Iranian king), nationalist (Sohrab is the flawed outcome of a marriage with a non-Iranian, from a father who himself is of flawed lineage), or oedipal (murderous impulses of fathers against sons who normally replace them).

In *The Crowned Cannibals* (1977) Reza Baraheni takes up the oedipal key, speculatively and with passionate, politically focused anger locating some of the repressive psychopolitical dynamics of contemporary Iran in this ancient mythic pattern. Instead of a Freudian desire for the death of the father, Baraheni speculates, this psychic history is focused on the reciprocal pattern of a father's' unconscious desire to repress and even prevent his son's developing autonomy, a desire that the father then enacts in reality. Instead of Oedipus and Jocasta, then, the model of and for the "masculine history" of Iran lies in the stories of Rustam and Sohrab, Gushtasp and Esfandiar, and, perhaps, Sam and Zal.

In Firdausi's telling, Sohrab's story is most immediately a prologue to the even greater tragedy of Siyavush, who becomes Rustam's ersatz son, a kind of replacement for Sohrab. Siyavush, the son of Kai Kaus and a Turanian princess, is raised by Rustam. He returns to the royal court as a young man. In an elegant episode, similar to the story of Joseph and Potiphar's wife, Siyavush resists the seductions of Kai Kaus's Yemenite wife, Sudabeh. To prove his loyalty to the king, Siyavush leads an army against an incursion by Afrasiyab. He puts the invaders to flight and negotiates a treaty with Afrasiyab. When Kaus rejects the treaty, distrusting the Turanian word, Siyavush feels his honor in danger: if he fights on against Afrasiyab without cause and against his own word, he will incur the wrath of God as well as shame in the eyes of men; if he delivers the army into the hands of his replacement and returns to court, Sudabeh will continue her intrigues against him and say he could not face the enemy. So Siyavush defects to join forces with Afrasiyab. He displays his tact and diplomacy in a polo game (doublet to the battlefield). He is befriended first by the sage and general Piran and then increasingly by Afrasiyab, both of whom give daughters to him. The jealousy of Garsiwaz, brother of Afrasiyab and, although not commented on, Siyavush's maternal grandfather, is roused; he intrigues against Siyavush and persuades Afrasiyab to turn against him. Ultimately Garsiwaz slays Siyavush. (The relation between Garsiwaz and Siyavush is thus an inverted doublet to the relation between Afrasiyab and Kai Khosrow: in the former the grandfather is the murderer; in the latter revenge is consummated by the grandson.)

Revenge for Siyavush becomes the primary motive for a major section of the *Shahnameh*: for the reigns of both Kai Kaus and Kai Khosrow and especially for Rustam. Mourning for Siyavush may, in fact, have been a major annual ritual in ancient Central Asia, the original form of what in Islamic Iran became the mourning for Husain, the grandson of the Prophet Muhammad and the martyr of Karbala. Kai Khosrow, the son of Siyavush by Farangis (daughter of Afrasiyab), escapes his father's fate at the Turanian court through the protection of Piran, who warned him to play mad, one of the great comic riddle scenes of the epic.

In this scene, Afrasiyab looks at the heroic physique of the young man and blanches. Piran quakes with fear that the ruse will not work. Afrasiyab recovers and asks, "Oh you, young shepherd [a metaphor for the royal role?], what do you know of the days and the nights? What do you do with the flocks of sheep, count goats and lambs [leaders and followers?]?" Kai Khosrow responds not to the words at face value but to the implicit challenge: "How do you mean hunting? I have no arrow, bow or string." Afrasiyab asks about his *amuzegar*, his teacher (God?). Kai Khosrow parries, "Where'er there is a leopard, the hearts of valiant warriors are rent" (i.e., "Beware, for I am well trained"). Afrasiyab asks about his parents, Iran, and the comforts of home. Kai Khosrow again responds in code: "The rending lion is not o'er powered by a fighting dog" (i.e., according to the hero's code of honor one only fights equals: a lion or hero or shah cannot be defeated by a dog). Afrasiyab suggests that the young man will return to Iran to be near the king of the brave. Kai Khosrow replies, "Two nights ago a horseman passed me on the hills and plains" (Siyavush or perhaps Siyavush's *cause* may be the horseman). Afrasiyab, thoroughly outwitted, laughs, becomes "as happy as a flower," and says with condescending glee, "You will not learn wisdom, you cannot learn to revenge your enemies." Kai Khosrow replies, "There is no cream upon the milk [i.e., no nutrition, no fat content]; I fain would drive the shepherds from the plain [i.e., he should take over since the present royalty—either Afrasiyab or the fickle Kai Kaus—is not productive]" (2.32).

Dismissed by Afrasiyab, Kai Khosrow is located and brought to Iran by Giv. After a trial of skill between Kai Khosrow and Fariborz, the son of Kai Kaus, which Kai Khosrow wins, he is made joint sovereign with Kai Kaus and swears to Kai Kaus and to Rustam that he will avenge Siyavush. His long reign (nearly a fifth of the *Shahnameh*'s length) is composed of four military campaigns and ends with the final slaying of the brothers Afrasiyab and Garsiwaz. This final episode is perhaps the most Zoroastrian scene in the entire epic. Kai Khosrow's task of cleansing the earth of the agent of Ahriman now finished, he appoints Lohrasp, from a collateral princely line, to reign, then withdraws to read the Avesta and pray and to eventually ascend from the mountaintop into heaven.

The four campaigns of Kai Khosrow's reign provide a frame for the substantive play of the stories. In the first campaign, sibling rivalries are sorted out. There are three such sibling rivalries to be clarified. First, there is still a legacy from the Pishdadian dynasty: Tus, hero and son of Naudar, the eighth Pishdadian, is not completely reconciled to the eclipse of his line in favor of the Kayanians. When Kai Khosrow is brought back to Iran and Kai Kaus wishes to share the throne with him, it is Tus who puts forward Fariborz, the son of Kai Kaus, as the more appropriate heir. So Kai Kaus sets a test between his son and grandson to see who has inherited the royal grace. The test is to capture the div-controlled fort of Bahram near Ardabil. Fariborz fails; Kai Khosrow succeeds. Tus is then placed in command of the Iranian army in the first of the four campaigns against Turan to avenge Siyavush. Kai Khosrow instructs Tus not to take the shorter route through Kalat because that is where Kai Khosrow's half brother, Farud, lives. Tus disobeys. Farud attempts to welcome the Iranians and to join the avengers, but Tus, feeling already twice bypassed, fears Farud will eclipse his own authority and become the de facto leader and symbolic embodiment of the mission. Tus thus insists on not recognizing this kinsman to his liege, but on seeing only an enemy Turanian, whom he orders slain.

Farud's death is developed by Firdausi as, again, an elegant minor tragedy. Farud tries to signal Tus not to trifle with him and attempts to defend himself without causing an irreparable breach with the Iranian forces. Tus sends first his son-in-law and then his son to kill Farud. Farud slays each of them in the hopes that Tus will desist. Gradually the greater heroes of Iran are sent against Farud, and he responds by shooting their horses but avoiding them. The young hero Bizhan eventually continues on foot after his horse is shot and mortally wounds Farud, who manages to return to his castle and destroy it and all within before dying himself. Piran, Farud's father and Kai Khosrow's erstwhile protector, attacks the Iranian forces and decimates them. Tus is sent home in disgrace. Fariborz sues for a truce. Tus, thanks to the intervention of Rustam, is eventually restored to grace with the argument that having lost a son and son-in-law, he had understandably lost as well his reason.

The second campaign is a frame for displaying Rustam's skills as champion of righteous vengeance against the Ahrimanic deceits of Turan. Tus fails again in battle, but Rustam comes to the rescue, routing the Turanians. As Piran used the cover of night for successful, and morally righteous, attack in the first campaign, so Rustam uses a night attack in the second campaign. But the military campaign this time is only a frame for two stories: how Rustam fought and killed the div Akwan (i.e., Akem Manu, "Evil Thought," one of the aspects of Ahriman), and how Rustam saved Bizhan from the pit into which Afrasiyab had him thrown. There is also the cautionary love story of Bizhan and the daughter of Afrasiyab, Manizha, which prefigures the story of Esfandiar rescuing Humai and Bid Afrid.[12]

The third campaign is built around single combats of the twelve Rooks (as in chess) or champions of Turan and Iran. Iran wins all of the individual contests. The hero Gudarz is in charge of this campaign for the Iranians, and his opponent is the worthy, tragic figure Piran, whose defeat signals the end of all traces of good in Turan.

The fourth campaign is led by Kai Khosrow himself. The Turanians are engaged four times, and each time Afrasiyab escapes, finally fleeing across the sea. In pursuit, Kai Khosrow makes a royal procession through the world—to China, which acknowledges his sovereignty, and to Makran, whose king must be defeated—before setting out from Makran to cross the sea. Kai Khosrow fails to track down Afrasiyab and returns home.

The final episodes of Kai Khosrow's reign and the final defeat of Afrasiyab are the most dramatic and the most Zoroastrian. First of all, Kai Khosrow prays,

> This feeble slave of Thine hath evermore
> Some trouble in possession of his soul.
> The world—its mountains, deserts, wastes and waters—
> Will I thresh out to find Afrasiyab
> Because he walketh not Thy Way, O Judge!
> . . . guide me to that doer of ill deeds,
> For though I am but an unworthy slave
> I am the Maker's worshipper. . . .
> If thou art pleased with him, O righteous Judge!
> Divert my thoughts from any further strife
> Quench in my heart the fire of my revenge
> And make my purpose conform with Thine. (4.253–54)

He reads the Avesta. He and his grandfather, Kai Kaus, go to the great fire temple of Azargashasp to bathe, to worship God, and to stand before the fire, that God might show them Afrasiyab's hiding place. Afrasiyab, meanwhile, has taken refuge in a cave, and is discovered by the hermit, Hom, who lassoes him with his kusti. Afrasiyab manages to escape and dives into Lake Khanjast (Urumiah). Hom devises a stratagem to catch the wily Afrasiyab: he has Gudarz and Giv and the two shahs bring Garsiwarz (Afrasiyab's brother) from prison to the shores of the lake. When Afrasiyab hears Garsiwarz's voice and comes to the surface to look, Hom lassoes him. Kai Khosrow formally accuses Afrasiyab of the murders of his own brother Ighriras, of the shah Naudar, and of Siyavush. He then executes the two evil brothers. The two shahs return to the fire temple to give thanks and praise God.

This story is but a narrative version of the legends from the yasna having to do with the elixir hom, the cosmic Lake Vourukasha (in which the savior's seed is stored), and Haosravah's victory over Frangrasyan (Afrasiyab) and Keresavazda (Garsiwarz). (Afrasiyab built an underground palace where he offered sacrifice to obtain the glory of Iran. Three times he is said in the Avestan legends to have tried to seize it by force. Homa finally captured/paralyzed him and delivered him to Haosravah (Kai Khosrow), who slew him.) Having cleansed the earth of Ahriman, Khosrow ascends to heaven, and as the Avestan prayer hopes for all, "Mayest thou be freed of sickness and die king Haosravah."

Now, back to Rustam and Esfandiar. Kai Khosrow appointed Lohrasp as successor. Lohrasp was pushed aside by his son Gushtasp, the shah converted by Zoroaster. Gushtasp's son, Esfandiar, wants to become shah because he thinks he can further the faith more effectively than his father, but he wants his father's blessing; he does not want to push his father aside. Gushtasp sets him the task of first bringing Rustam to court in chains. Given Rustam's own lineage and his personal tragedy with Sohrab, as well as the loss of his foster son, Siyavush, it is clear that Rustam, when facing Esfandiar, has suffered his share of tragedy; furthermore, his loyalty to the throne is unswerving, and his sense of right and wrong is tempered like fine steel.

Esfandiar and Rustam each engage in efforts to avoid fighting the other, but their efforts are tragically opposed. First, Esfandiar sends his son Bahman to try to talk Rustam into putting himself in chains, and in return Esfandiar will intercede with Gushtasp. Bahman spoils the effort by trying to roll a boulder onto Rustam, who simply kicks it aside. Bahman and Rustam share a meal, and Rustam signals his strength by eating a prodigious amount.[13] He sends back an answer to Esfandiar that while he will gladly appear before Gushtasp, he will not come in chains.

Esfandiar now goes to Rustam himself. He praises Rustam and attempts to persuade him that he is so great that even if he allows his hands to be bound, no shame will fall on him, for all will recognize that it is a ploy. Rustam stalemates this with his own praise of Esfandiar, the invulnerable, whom no one can best. Esfandiar tries again with praise: lucky the one on whose side you fight, for not even fate (*ruzegar*) can oppose you, that is, please help me, don't force me to fight you. Rustam begins to raise the stakes by praying for Esfandiar in the manner of older pahlavans (athletes, heroes) in the gymnasia (zurkhaneh) praying for younger ones; in other words, he invokes the code of honor in which a younger pahlavan never actually forces an older one's back to the mat. It is a statement of equality to fight, and they are unequal. Esfandiar denies that he has come to fight. Rustam knows better (there was the episode with Bahman) and so tests Esfandiar by inviting him to share a meal. Esfandiar declines: it would be dishonorable to fight those with whom one breaks bread. Rustam invites himself to Esfandiar's table.[14] Esfandiar cannot refuse but attempts in various ways to slight Rustam so that he will withdraw, first trying to seat him to his left instead of to his more honorable right, where he places Bahman; then chiding his presumption that his men could challenge the king's troops without severe consequences; and finally speaking of the shame of Rustam's ancestry, that Zal was born of a demon (div) and that his greatness stemmed solely from serving Esfandiar's family.[15] Rustam responds to the second by asking Esfandiar to leave their men out of it: if there is to be a contest, it should be between the two of them alone. Rustam responds to the ancestry slur by acknowledging his descent from Zahhak and warning Esfandiar of false pride in ancestry: it is what you do, not who you are. Kings can be corrupt or weak, as exemplified by Gushtasp. Moreover, he points out, Esfandiar also has foreign blood: his mother was Caesar's daughter, and Caesar descended from Salm, a fratricide. Esfandiar then toasts Rustam and attempts to squeeze his hand; but it is Rustam who turns Esfandiar's hand to pulp. Esfandiar is finally forced to admit his purpose.

It is Rustam's turn to try to find a way out for Esfandiar, for he recognizes that if Esfandiar persists, he, Rustam, has only a choice of evils. He must protect his heroic essence: it would be dishonorable to simply flee, but the other choices are also unpalatable. He must protect his followers and the people of Zabul: he cannot allow himself to be bound as a common criminal, nor killed, for his people would need to avenge their honor and would be slaughtered by the king's troops. On the other hand, should he kill Esfandiar, his name would become infamous for killing a young heir to the throne and defender of the faith. He tells Esfandiar that Gushtasp is toying with him: there will always be yet another task. He offers to go unbound with Esfandiar to Gushtasp, and if the king orders him bound or killed, then he will allow

Esfandiar to execute the order, implying in this offer the unlikelihood that Gushtasp would be willing to chance the consequences of such a dishonorable royal order and that hence Esfandiar's mission cannot be but a cruel hoax. He attempts to prolong the debate, that Esfandiar might weary and withdraw. All to no avail.

Clearly one of the joys of the naqqal is to draw out the fine balance between these two heroes, who respect each other, whose heroic boasting is not bloodthirsty or empty but who attempt to persuade and are moreover willing to face a tragic death with dignity. The battle is joined. Rustam cannot kill Esfandiar and is himself finally wounded. Zal calls the Simorgh to cure Rustam and his horse, Rakhsh. The Simorgh (a supernatural counterpoint to Esfandiar's invulnerability) reveals to Rustam Esfandiar's vulnerability and gives him a special tamarisk arrow, but the Simurgh also affirms the dreadful fate to be suffered by he who kills Esfandiar—doom in both this world and the next. Again Rustam considers ways out: would it not be better to flee and suffer a lesser dishonor, rather than the larger dishonor of infamy? But it is too late for such a course: his followers and people are at risk. Courageously he returns to the battle and slays Esfandiar.

Esfandiar now rises to the occasion. As his corporeal eyes lose life, his spiritual ones open. He abandons the glazed vision of fame and religious zealotry. He has the courage to face the truth and tell Rustam of Gushtasp's hand in the scheme to devastate Rustam's court at Zabul and province of Sistan with the intent of making such an example of royal power that docility and discipline would be adopted by all his subjects. Finally, he asks a favor of Rustam. The court seer, Jamasp, has said that Esfandiar's son, Bahman, will become shah, and he asks Rustam to be a guardian to this son. There is an Islamic saying that states that the end of one's life helps define one's memory: one can live a good life but irredeemably spoil it with one bad act; but one can also live a wild life and redeem it with a final good act.[16]

The moral of the tale, as Meskoub sees it, is that men should strive to be like Rustam: to have no expectations from fate but to maintain their dignity and sense of right and wrong and to allow the chips to fall where they may. And men should also strive to be like Esfandiar: to recognize the truth, no matter how bitter, and to have the courage to prefer an honest enemy and to trust such an honest man even with the guardianship of one's son. If one cannot win in life, then one should face death in such a manner as to win through it.

A slightly different interpretation is suggested by Marcia Maguire (1974, 1978), who very usefully compares how Esfandiar's career is constructed by

Firdausi as a doublet to that of Rustam's, changed only by the difference, albeit basic, that Esfandiar is a hero in the service of religion, while Rustam is a more archaic-style hero.[17] Maguire overestimates the degree to which Rustam in his confrontation with Esfandiar represents an anachronism, a hero attempting to operate in a world no longer heroic. Nonetheless, her detailed comparison of the two heroes is an extremely valuable illumination of the epic's structuring techniques, and read in a slightly different context may serve to summarize Firdausi's treatment of the second dynasty, the Kayanians, in relation to both the first and third ones.

Maguire correctly perceives Esfandiar and Rustam as partial doublets, focusing both on their seven trials and on their roles as rescuers of besieged Iranian armies and captured Iranian figures. She points out how Firdausi identifies them with each other through the use of the same set of heroic epithets not applied to others: *piltan* (elephant bodied), *tahmtan* (powerful), and *tajbakhsh* (king maker). Rustam kills a raging elephant as a child; with fine irony, Esfandiar's mother calls him a raging elephant when he insists on fighting Rustam.

The primary methodological deficiency in Maguire's account is to not place the Esfandiar-Rustam doublet into the larger context of the structure of the Kayanian dynasty. The need to differentiate Esfandiar and Rustam as religious versus areligious thereby disappears and moots the inconsistencies such a hypothesis generates, for example, how Rustam constantly calls on God, and the fact that the Avesta and fire temples are crucial to the reign of Kai Khosrow long before Esfandiar. Instead, Rustam and Esfandiar are cast as but one of a series of doublings which provide a parable structure of inter-significance among all the major characters of the dynasty. A closer look at the seven trials of Rustam and Esfandiar shows them to be similar but not identical, fitting into a pattern with Gushtasp's three trials as well. Finally the observation about the importance of the *Avesta* and fire temples in the reign of Kai Khosrow forces attention to the minimal elaboration given the story of the arrival of Zoroaster and reinforces the notion that Zoroaster's reform is incorporated into the misuse of religion as an ideological weapon by Gushtasp and Esfandiar, that is, as a critique of the deployment under Arab rule of Islamic domination over Iran.

I will now attempt to schematize and summarize the Kayanian dynasty by first looking at the framework provided by the twelve male figures and ten sovereigns composing the Kayanians.

Kai Kubad is simply a formal introductory figure.[18] Zal sends for him to fill the vacant Iranian throne, and Rustam fetches him.[19] The theme of the

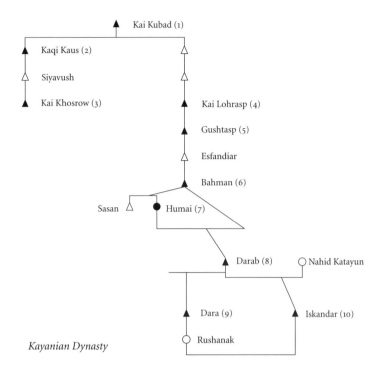

Kai Kubad (1)

Kaqi Kaus (2)

Siyavush

Kai Khosrow (3)

Kai Lohrasp (4)

Gushtasp (5)

Esfandiar

Bahman (6)

Sasan   Humai (7)

Darab (8)   Nahid Katayun

Dara (9)   Iskandar (10)

Rushanak

Kayanian Dynasty

relationship between the House of Zabul or Sistan (Zal and Rustam) and the House of Iran is reaffirmed as basic to the survival of the dynasty. Indeed, this relationship is formally analogous to that asserted by Zoroaster in the Gathas between God and man: one of mutual aid to secure the success and happiness of Iran. Kai Kubad is of further importance only as a linkage figure between the two collateral lines of the dynasty: that of Kai Kaus, Siyavush, Kai Khosrow; and that of Gushtasp, Esfandiar, Bahman.

These three-generation units form the first significant doubling, each structured as (1) an erring father/king, (2) a tragically heroic son/prince, and (3) a transcendent grandson. The three units summarized in table 5 are only the central cases, but other father-son and grandfather-grandson examples play on similar problematics and all function as a system of "intersignification," as commentaries one on another.

Kai Kaus and Gushtasp are paired figures: each commits a series of three errors. Firdausi subtly transforms the Kai Kaus of the Avesta from one of the immortals (like Jamshid) who through hubris lose the divine grace into a man easily led astray by passion, wrongheadedness, and evil counsel.[20] It is loss of grace through hubris that Kai Kaus's grandson Kai Khosrow fears after

TABLE 5. Three-Generation Units

Erring Father/King	Kai Kaus	Gushtasp	Rustam
(Marriage with)	(Turan)	(Rum)	(Samanghan)
Heroic Son/Prince	Siyavush (−)	Esfandiar (+)	Sohrab (+) Faramarz (−)
Transcendent Grandson	Kai Khosrow (+)	Bahman (−)	Bizhan (+)

Responsible for his own death (+) or not (−). Ascends to heaven (+) or not (−).

having cleansed the world of Afrasiyab's evil and having completed his vows of revenge; hence he abdicates and withdraws into worship of God. (Lohrasp similarly abdicates and withdraws into worship of God to avoid the sins of fathers fighting with sons. Lohrasp otherwise functions like Kai Kubad as merely an introductory figure, a king who sees himself as a caretaker, placed on the throne thanks to a divine vision of Kai Khosrow, the latter then having to convince the House of Zabul to accept Lohrasp.)[21] There is thus a reference and resonance in these Kayanian stories to the stories of the preceding Pishdadian dynasty.

Kai Kaus's three errors occur in the realm of the divs (he allows himself to be seduced into invading their realm in Mazandaran and is captured), in the realm of men (he campaigns into Yemen, desires and marries a princess, and is imprisoned, leaving Iran open to Turanian and Arab invasions), and in the realm of the angels (he is seduced by Satan or Iblis's agents into fashioning a throne carried by eagles to capture the heavens) (table 6). Each time he must be rescued by Rustam. Each time he repents of his foolishness. After the third of these rescues, Rustam goes with seven companions to hunt across the border in Turan; the party is noticed and attacked but easily defends itself. (Might one speculate that the mythic code here is that just as Rustam is protected by the seven amshaspands; Iranian sovereignty in turn is protected by the House of Zabul?)

Gushtasp's three errors are injustices against his father (Lohrasp), his son (Esfandiar), and the protector of the throne (Rustam). Each of these are followed by deaths among Gushtasp's many sons. In anger against his father's desire to keep the throne for an heir of Kai Khosrow, Gushtasp goes to Rum (either Rome or Greece: the ruler is called Caesar, but the personages are Greek, the most important figure later in the story being Alexander). There Gushtasp wins a princess and a political alliance and threatens Iran. Lohrasp yields the throne. Zoroaster comes and the royal house converts. Arjasp, the

TABLE 6. Kai Kaus and Gushtasp's Regimes

	Kai Kaus	Gushtasp
3 errors	*world of*	*injustices against*
	1. divinities: 7 trials of Rustam	1. father: 3 trials of Gushtasp; marriage/conspiracy with Rome
	2. men: marriage with Yemen	2. son: 7 trials of Esfandiar
	3. angels: Rustam's hunt	3. Rustam
Father-son parables: loss of sons		
	Sohrab and Rustam	Esfandiar and Rustam
	Siyavush	(death of Rustam)
Grandson succeeds		
	joint rule with Kai Khosrow	abdicates to Bahman

new Turanian king, begins a new war, rejecting demands for either tribute or conversion. Gushtasp loses many sons in the war, and Esfandiar must save the military situation. Esfandiar is promised the throne for this, but his succession is continuously postponed. When Esfandiar is falsely accused, Gushtasp uses the excuse to imprison him, at least until he is once again needed to save the military situation after many more sons have died. Again the promise of the throne is put off, first until Esfandiar saves the captured Hom and Bid Afrid (involving his seven trials), and finally until he brings Rustam to the king in chains. This last is the injustice to Rustam. This time instead of losing many sons, Gushtasp loses just the most important son: Esfandiar. Typically, Gushtasp bemoans this loss as a poisoning of his life, not as something for which he should shoulder responsibility.

While Gushtasp and Kai Kaus are structural doubles, they also contrast: Kai Kaus is fickle and ultimately repents, and his reign ends gloriously in tandem with his grandson. Gushtasp never changes. He uses treason and threat to gain the throne, deceit and prevarication to keep it. He takes credit for the deeds of Esfandiar as his son but refuses responsibility for what happens to him.

Shahrough Meskoub asks why this best of kings in the Avesta becomes the worst of kings in the *Shahnameh*, and proposes as an explanation that under the Sassanians, just before the Arab invasion, Zoroastrianism had become a state religion, empty and dead, used as a mobilizing tool against Rome, emptying the country economically and spiritually. Kingship was, with increasing shrillness, claimed to be a kind of earthly divinity. (Shapur I claimed to be descended from the gods; Anushiravan claimed to be created in the image of God; Khosrow Parviz claimed to be a god among men, precisely the hubris which caused Jamshid's fall and which Kai Khosrow feared.) The key Avestan figure of the alliance between kinship and religion was Gushtasp, and so Gushtasp had to absorb the hostility of the people against the abuses of the state religion. The Muslim historian Tabari, for instance, asserted that Gushtasp built a stone house to lock up the Avesta, to restrict access to the caste of priests, a device of hierarchy and control which was to be increasingly oppressive. If Meskoub is correct, it would also explain why Zoroaster is such a relatively unimportant figure in the *Shahnameh*: he is assimilated to the abuses of Gushtasp, religion used as a tool of control. Gushtasp indeed sends Esfandiar out to convert the world, to make them pay tribute, and in his eulogy for Esfandiar, Gushtasp says he was a hero of the religion of which he, Gushtasp, is king. Four centuries after the oppressions of the Sassanians had begun to fade from memory, the figure of Gushtasp could as well stand for a more contemporary religious oppression, that of an excessively Arabicized Islam.

In any case, the theme of loss of sons is central to both Gushtasp and Kai Kaus's reigns in the *Shahnameh*. Framed by Kai Kaus's three errors and subsequent reparation by sharing the throne with his grandson, the righteous Kai Khosrow, are the two much beloved and retold stories of Sohrab and Siyavush. Both of these stories intertwine the life and lineage of Rustam with the royal Iranian lineage. Siyavush is wronged by Kai Kaus as Esfandiar is by Gushtasp.

The theme of problematic marriages with outsiders is also prominent throughout (table 7). Gushtasp sired Esfandiar by a Rumian princess, an alliance repeated at the end of the Kayanian dynasty of which Alexander is the issue. Kai Kaus sired Siyavush by a Turanian princess; and, a second marriage out, with the Yemenite princess, Sudabeh, causes many of Siyavush's problems. Rustam sired Sohrab by a princess of the Samanghan marshes between Iran and Turan. It is as if each of these stories of marriage and fatherhood is a commentary on the others, exploring the different permutations and possible results. Siyavush is a blameless hero, wronged by his father, by his mother's father, and by his wife's father, and he is martyred. His legacy lives on in the vengeance pursued by his son, foster father (Rustam), and father. Esfandiar is a blameworthy hero who repents and thus burnishes his heroic

TABLE 7. Marriage Alliances

Offspring	Father	Mother
Manuchehr	Turanian	Iranian (half slave)
Rustam	Iranian (Sistani)	Arab
Siyavush	Iranian	Turanian
Kai Khosrow	Iranian	Turanian
Esfandiar	Iranian	Roman (Rumi)
Alexander	Iranian	Greek (Rumi)

status. He is somewhat sordidly avenged by his son. Sohrab is in part to blame and dies tragically. Farimarz, another son of Rustam, while blameless and heroic, is less paradigmatically tragic, becoming a victim to the crossfire of feud. The marriage which produces Rustam's slayer, his half brother Shaghad's alliance with the king of Kabul, parallels Gushtasp's marriage with Rum but is also an inversion of the marriage which produced Rustam. Zal, Rustam's father, married a daughter of the king of Herat, but instead of that marriage leading to problems for Iran, as did Gushtasp's marriage alliance with Rome, Zal brought Herat into the Iranian alliance system.

All these parallels, variations, and inversions, in other words, do not constitute categorical marriage norms and transgressions, but are rather parables, to be played with, considered from every possible angle, inexhaustible material for new reciters and interpreters. This continues with the third generation, in which injuries are reversed, problems settled, legacies transmitted. Kai Khosrow kills the evil grandfathers Afrasiyab and Garsiwaz. Bahman inherits some of Esfandiar's faults but also passes on the seed three ways: through his daughter-wife Humai (Homa) he has both an immediate heir and an affine link by which to incorporate Alexander; through another wife he has a delayed link to the future Sassanian dynasty. Bizhan, a grandson of Rustam, inherits Siyavush's armor and heroism and follows Kai Khosrow out of this world, ascending without death. Farimarz remains in the world to avenge Rustam's death but is himself slain by Bahman to avenge Esfandiar's death. Thus ends the house of Zabul.

A closer look at the seven trials of Rustam and Esfandiar, and the three trials of Gushtasp is warranted here. Maguire (1974, 1978) suggests that Esfandiar's motives of religious zeal and ambition to succeed his father provide his trials a logic and a progression between plot units that is missing in the more ad hoc trials of Rustam. Esfandiar travels with an army; he has foreknowledge thanks to a Turanian prisoner/guide. Rustam travels alone, possesses no foreknowledge, and seems to stumble into his successes almost by chance. Indeed, Rustam falls asleep, and his horse, Rakhsh, defeats the lion in the first trial. Again Rustam falls asleep, and this time when Rakhsh attempts to warn him of preternatural danger, he is initially angry at the horse for waking him and only discovers that he is dealing with a witch by exclaiming God's name in his anger. Esfandiar, by contrast, is quite prepared for the witch: he feeds her wine to redden her face and has Zoroaster's steel chain with which to make her reveal her true fetid hag form.

My own reading of Rustam's trials grants him more credit and perceives more interconnections in the plotting from stage to stage. In fact, in each trial Rustam learns something useful for winning the next trial. In the first he learns the importance of vigilance, and so stations Rakhsh on guard. In the second he is not irrationally angry at Rakhsh for wakening him, but he cannot see his enemy until God reveals the witch to human sight. He thus learns the need to pray to God, which he does religiously, and so is able to slay the dragon and bind the witch. From his experience with the witch, he learns not to trust surface appearances, and so is able to use ingenuity to capture Ulad who will supply the local knowledge necessary for the final two trials to free Kai Kaus from the div Arzhang and to gain the liver of the White Div so as to restore sight to the Iranian captives (this knowledge he gets from the now freed Kaus).

If, instead of trying to evaluate the heroes as religious or transcendent-goal oriented, one analyzes each set of trials, one finds a tripartite structure (table 8). There is perhaps a more symmetrical structure to Esfandiar's trials, with the most dangerous trial being the middle one, the witch, where both ingenuity and magical power can be turned to evil and need to be fought. But in both Esfandiar's and Rustam's trials there is progressive learning and need for skill, from the simplest challenges, which require only strength or vigilance, to a need for combined skill, ingenuity, God's help, and solid knowledge from experience. Only with all of these does one have the mature, seasoned, and successful hero. Gushtasp's trials follow the same pattern, but simplified.

In terms of symbolism, it is worth at least asking whether the set "wolf, dragon, man" might not refer to Turan, the Arabs, and either Rum or internal foes. The symbol of the wolf and the affix *gorg* (wolf) as a component in personal names are pervasive in the descriptions of the Turanians. Zahhak is often called a dragon. In terms of moral message, the uses and failures of such

TABLE 8. Trial Sets: Rustam, Esfandiar, Gushtasp

Rustam's Trials

	Content	*Form*	*Requisites*
Nature	lion	animal	vigilance
	desert/ram	signs of nature	prayer
World gone evil	dragon	animal transformation	God's grace and skill
	witch	human transformation	prayer and skill
	Ulad	human being	ingenuity (distrust appearances)
Restoration	Div Arzhang	bodily imprisonment of Kaus	knowledge
	White Div	spiritual blinding	knowledge

Esfandiar's trials

Nature	wolves	animals	strength
	lions		
Supernatural	dragon	animal transformation	ingenuity
	witch	human transformation	prophet's chain and ingenuity
	Simurgh	animal transformation	ingenuity
Nature and man	climate	elements	God (beyond ingenuity)
	river and man	man	persuasion, knowledge

Gushtasp's trials

Nature	wolf
Supernatural	dragon
Man	Ilyas

mature, seasoned heroism and leadership are further reflected on in a number of battle scenes, most clearly perhaps in the confrontation between Piran and Gudarz in the Battle of the Twelve Rooks (Kai Khosrow's third campaign against Turan). Both the Turanian sage Piran and the veteran Iranian hero Gudarz attempt to carefully outmaneuver the other; each is preempted by hotheaded younger heroes. The clear problematic is that leadership depends on a careful balance between exhilarating risk and prudent skill.

TABLE 9. Comparison of Kai Khosrow and Bahman Reigns

Kai Khosrow's Reign	Bahman's Reign
revenge: four campaigns against Turan	revenge: imprisons Zal, hangs Farimarz
Hom captures Afrasiyab	Homa bears Darab
ascent to heaven	submerged dynasty: Sasan

The Kayanian dynasty ends with a complicated succession, but one that still parallels the ending under Kai Khosrow of the struggles with Afrasiyab (see table 9). The themes and stories of the Kayanian dynasty have parallels not only among themselves but also in the preceding Pishdadian dynasty. The Pisdadian versions can now be seen as the key archetypes.

The Pishdadian dynasty falls into two parts. There is first Firdausi's linear genealogization of the myths of creation and the culture heroes. In the original Avestan myths Gaiumart and the Primeval Ox are slain by Ahriman, and through their process of dying, human beings and plants and animals are generated. Siyamak is midway in the meiotic process that eventually produces the first king, Hushang. Firdausi turns this into a simple three-generation unit, one quite parallel to the aforementioned three-generation units, with their middle generation heroes slain by the forces of evil. (It is thus Siyamak, rather than Gaiumart himself, who is slain by the Black Div.) In this case, it is not until the fourth generation, as represented by Tahmuras, that revenge is pursued: Tahmuras is known as the "binder of divs" and forces them to teach him thirty different scripts. Firdausi only tells part of the Avestan myth that Tahmuras bound Ahriman with spells and rode him like a horse. In the Avestan tale Ahriman seduces Tahmuras's wife into telling Tahmuras's secrets and thus is able to throw Tahmuras and swallow him. Tahmuras's brother, Jamshid (Yima, a figure with many important legends in both Iranian and Indian traditions), drags Tahmuras from the entrails of the fiend, thus restoring the culture of the world, but not before Tahmuras dies.[22] Yima is the first to be offered a covenant with God and is told to build a mystic underground fortress, the Var, in preparation for the final resurrection. It is perhaps because of the building of the Var that Firdausi says Jamshid brought architecture to human beings. Jamshid is the archetype of the hero-king who loses grace: under his rule there is a Golden Age, until he begins to think of himself as God.[23]

The stories in the first part of the Pishdadian dynasty are simplifications and transformations of the more complicated Avestan legends. They provide the first archetypes, however, of structures that will be repeated, clarified, and endowed with increasingly parabolic meaning throughout the next sixteen reigns. Jamshid, as loser of the sovereign grace (*khvarr*), is the archetype for Naudar, the eighth Pisdadian, who is unjust, whose subjects therefore revolt, and whose reign must be put in order by the hero Sam; for Kai Kaus, the second Kayanian, who is thrice led astray and must be saved by Rustam; and for Kai Khosrow, who having created a Golden Age fears the fate of Jamshid. If there is a sequence here, it is one of learning: the danger becomes progressively less severe.

The marvelous, unforgettable story of Zahhak is the archetype both for the three errors of Kai Kaus and of Gushtasp and for the threefold structure of the trials (victories over evil) of Rustam, Esfandiar, and Gushtasp. Zahhak, the son of a bedouin chief or Arab king, is thrice seduced by Ahriman. The order of the seductions—first in his mind, then through his diet, and finally in his appearance and public face—is the inverse of the order of learning to overcome evil in the trials. First the young Zahhak is tempted by secrets, the classic satanic teaser: "I know something powerful that no one else knows, and I'll tell you, if you agree to my conditions." The condition is patricide: Zahhak must kill his father. The sweetener to the condition is that Zahhak succeeds to the throne. The second seduction has eschatological resonances and parallels the killing of Gaiumart. In exchange for world empire, Zahhak takes on a new cook recommended by Ahriman. Until that time, men did not kill to eat but were vegetarian. Ahriman, as the new cook, slowly seduces the king, first with partridges and pheasants, then with lamb and fowl, and finally with veal and saffron with rose water, musk, and well-aged wine. In the Avesta demons tempt Mashya-Mashyoi (the first meiotic incarnation of the dying-regenerating Gaiumart) away from living on water to feed first on plants, then milk, then meat. It is both the life cycle and the resurrection motif: as human beings begin to die, they first desist from eating meat, then milk, and finally take only water; so, too, at the end of time, men will desist from meat, eating only vegetables and milk, then will undergo a period of existing only on water, and finally, for ten years before the saoshyants (saviors) arrive, will need no sustenance at all. Meat-eating is a sign of vigorous mortal life and as such is furthest removed from death and resurrection, a sign of this world as opposed to the next. (The symbolism repeats itself in the legends of the meat-eating, magical bird, the Simorgh, which serves as a protector to Zal and Rustam.) The third seduction, finally, comes when

Shahnameh miniature: Binding of Zahhak.

Ahriman, perhaps in a mock gesture of respect, kisses Zahhak on both shoulders: two serpents grow from the shoulders and daily must be fed the brains of two Iranian youths.

If one can label these three seductions as mind, body, and deference, status, or power, do they not fit in reverse order both the errors of Kai Kaus (wanting sovereignty over the land of divs in Mazandaran; contracting marriage for procreation with Yemen; wishing for control of the heavens) and those of Gushtasp (usurping the public power of the throne; his misuse of his

بیا ورد ضحاک را چون نوند
بکوه دماوند کردس بند
از و نام ضحاک چون خاک شد
جهان از بد او همه پاک شد

British World War II propaganda poster: Binding Hitler/Zahhak. *Courtesy World War II Collection, Manuscripts and Archives, Yale University.*

son as extension of himself; the violations of the ideals of loyalty and sovereignty upheld by Rustam). The trials involve first, nature, second, the transformations of beings, and third, changing the minds of men. Good and Evil thus become parts of triadic structures that generate an increasing dimensional, nuanced, and psychologically detailed pedagogical schema.[24]

Zahhak's descent into becoming the archetype of evil is followed by the archetype of Iranian nationalist struggle for freedom. Two figures are pivotal:

the blacksmith Kaveh, who designs the Kayanian flag out of a leather apron decorated in a brocade of *Rum*, a jeweled pattern on a golden ground; and the prince Faridun, who claims descent from Jamshid and who overthrows Zahhak and binds him to Mt. Demavand until the end of time, when Zahhak will burst his chains and fight one last time. A legend of the origin of the Kurds is associated with this heroic tale: the twins Irma'il and Karma'il become royal cooks and manage to mix sheep brains with human brains, thus saving one lad each day, and composing a secret army of them; these saved men are the ancestors of the Kurds.

Kaveh sues for justice: only one of his eighteen sons is left alive and now has also been taken for the serpent's meals. Zahhak agrees this is unjust and releases the boy but fails to gain the old man's gratitude. Kaveh raises an army against Zahhak to help Faridun. Meanwhile, Zahhak has had a vision of his end at the hands of Faridun and attempts to search out the boy before he matures. Zahhak kills the boy's father. The miraculous cow Birmaya cares for Faridun. Faridun escapes, is raised by a sage on the mountain for a time, then demands to know his ancestry from his mother. Asking her to pray, he marches on Baghdad to overthrow Zahhak.

Faridun is the archetype of the great Iranian heroes. He has a miraculous childhood (Zal will be raised by the Simorgh; Rustam kills a raging elephant as a child). He has a heroic set of tools: a giant ox mace and magic taught him by the archangel Sorush. (So, too, Sam's mace of one blow will be passed down to Rustam, who also has a lasso of sixty coils, prayer, and the aid of the Simorgh at both death and on the battlefield against Esfandiar. Esfandiar likewise has a "mace like Sam's" and the prophet's chain. Bizhan uses the mail and helmet of Siyavush.) As in the yasna, Faridun does not attempt to cut off Zahhak's head but rather to bind him.[25]

The reign of Faridun begins the second half of the Pishdadian dynasty. This second half constitutes a repetition of the first half, but transformed into the archetypical idiom which will be used through the end of the Kayanian period. In terms of surface content, it establishes the feuding between Iran and Turan, and Iran and Rum, which will last throughout the *Shahnameh* in several cycles: Tur, Afrasiyab, and Arjasp lead Turan in cycles of competition with Iran; then the story of Alexander initiates a series of confrontations with the West. In more structural terms, Faridun-Iraj-Manuchehr constitutes the paradigmatic three-generation unit.

This unit includes a threefold testing, a slaying of the favored heroic son, righteous settling of scores by the grandson, and transmittal of sovereignty from grandfather to grandson. Faridun's three sons are matched with three

British World War II propaganda poster: Hitler/Zahhak, with Mussolini and Hirohito depicted as snake heads on his shoulders being fed the brains of Iranian youths. *Courtesy World War II Collection, Manuscripts and Archives, Yale University.*

Yemenite princesses (foreshadowing Kai Kaus's marriage with Yemen, whose issue is Siyavush). The lads are provided with knowledge and magic by Faridun to pass the first preliminary test by their prospective father-in-law. A more serious test occurs as they return with their brides. To test his sons, Faridun suddenly appears in the form of a dragon (paralleling the dragon as a middle term in the series of trials undergone by Rustam and Esfandiar). The eldest son flees, seeking safety. The second son stands firm to do battle but does so rashly, without proper preparation or prudence. The youngest son boasts of being Faridun's son, warns the dragon off lest it be killed, and stands his ground. It is, says Firdausi, a prudent mix of ingenuity and fight. Faridun names his sons and divides the world among them: Rum goes to Salm; China and Turan go to Tur; Iran and Arabia go to the youngest, Iraj. The third and most severe test now follows: dealing with their lots in public life. Tur and Salm are jealous of and murderous toward Iraj; Iraj, in an effort to placate and soothe them, gives up his crown.

> Strife is unlovely in religious men.
> Why set your hopes so much upon this world?
> How ill it used Jamshid who passed away
> At last, and lost the crown and throne and girdle? (1.196)[26]
>
> . . . . .
>
> Canst thou approve and reconcile these twain—
> To be a murderer and live thyself?
>
> . . . . .
>
> Wouldst thou have the world? Thou hast it. Shed not blood.
> Provoke not God, the Ruler of the World. (1.201)

The brothers, blinded with jealous rage, cannot listen, and they kill Iraj. After his death, a slave girl, Mah Afrid, bears Iraj a daughter. This daughter marries Pashang (a son of Tur, who at the end of his life wishes to be buried in Iran, a desire rejected by his son Afrasiyab). This daughter of Iraj bears Manuchehr (son of Manu). Manuchehr, prefiguring Kai Khosrow, with his great grandfather's support avenges his father, killing the evil brothers Tur and Salm, as well as their ally Kakwi, a grandson of Zahhak. Faridun then crowns Manuchehr and retires to austerities and grief over his three sons.

> "My days are changed and darkened by these three,
> Who were my heart's delight and grief withal,
> Thus slain before me miserably, in hatred,
> And as my foes would wish. Such ills befell them
> Through their perversity and evil deeds;
> They disobeyed me and the world frowned on them."
> His heart was full, his face all tears till death.
> Though Faridun is gone, there is his name

Still left through all the years that have passed by;
He was my son! all excellence and fame—
One who found profit in adversity. (1.232–33)

Faridun introduces the theme of passing on the throne while still alive (as will Kai Kaus, Kai Khosrow, and Gushtasp), of retiring to austerities (as will Kai Khosrow and Lohrasp), and of introducing the reflections on filial extensions of self.

The parallels between the Faridun story unit and the later Kayanian units are numerous, almost open-ended. Iraj and Siyavush are each *causus belli* of major Iranian campaigns against Turan. Kai Khosrow and Manuchehr are both half Turanian; both complete their tasks, establish a prosperous realm, and retire. The comparative matrix now expands (figure 10). If there is a sequencing, it appears that the initiatory generation of the unit is slowly transformed from a blameless, characterless, mythic figure (Gaiumart, Hushang) into an increasingly fallible human being. Gushtasp is a sadly comic or perverse inversion of Faridun. The second- and third-generation figures become increasingly responsible figures. Siyavush and Kai Khosrow are still too good to be true, while Esfandiar and Bahman are all too human.

What one makes of all these parallels and structural reverberations is very much up to the reciter. Shahrough Meskoub's work (1964) is but one living example of how the epic tradition constitutes a philosophical idiom in the form of parables through which one can reflect on not only nationalism, kingship, heroism, honor, marriage strategies, religion, ethics, ultimate versus immediate reward or punishment, and parental-filial relations, but also on the passions, the results of anger, jealousy, ambition, zealotry, lust for power, obedience, and loyalty, as well as on hubris and the hypostatizations of desires for immortality, invulnerability, omnipotence, and the like. It is a parabolic (parable) logic, not a normative or propositional one: one cannot say the *Shahnameh* expresses Iranian suspicion of marriage (or other relations) with foreigners or supports an ideology of hereditary monarchy. Rather these and alternative strategies are opened by the *Shahnameh* stories to discussion, debate, and criticism.

Parables by their very nature are never self-explanatory. They are always hermeneutically unfinished, polyvalent structures whose meaning can take on different valences, resonances, and communicative force in different tellings. They conjoin descriptiveness of ordinary life or conventional tropes (heroes battling dragons, miraculous childhoods) with surprise and paradox,

father		Gaiumart		[Hushang		Faridun		Kai Kaus
slain son		Siyamak		Tahmuras		Iraj		Siyavush
restoring grandson		Hushang/ Tahmuras		Jamshid]		Manuchihr		Kai Khosrow

Three-Generation Units: Pisdadian & Kayanian

some of which is provided by expectations from other similar stories, some of which is provided by local circumstances and contemporary allusions. (Thus, as Meskoub puts it, even Rustam, the paragon of strength and heroism, and Esfandiar Ruintan, "the Invulnerable," taste the bitterness of defeat, powerlessness, and death.) The linked parables, playing structural relations one way, then another, are tools for learning to analyze the interpersonal narratives we live by, for understanding that stories can be played out in alternative ways. They become rich allegories and resources for cultural critique, all the richer because they are transitive multigenerational, with legacies that have consequences for other actors, and involve alliances, challenge and response, wit and quickness of mind. Recited, retold, dramatized in live contexts, the parables of the *Shahnameh* traditions can and do continue to inform and stalk the present.

In this world of intersignification, the *Shahnameh* is derived from but not identical to the legends in the Zoroastrian religious corpus. This reminder is not to insist on a radical separation but rather to draw attention to the historical, rhetorical, and philosophical shifts and changes registered in the ways of telling these tales, both across communal lines and also within the *Shahnameh* itself as one moves from dynasty to dynasty. One can see the process of transformation most clearly in the changes from the Avestan creation myths to Firdausi's genealogical account in the first half of the Pishdadian dynasty, and then further from the first half to the second half of that dynasty. Other traces—the story of Kai Khosrow and Homa; the several invocations of Homa in the reigns of Kai Khosrow, Gushtasp, and Bahman; the underground Var, built by Jamshid and besieged by Afrasiyab; Lake Vourukasha, where Afrasiyab sought refuge, and perhaps in the motif of the baby Darab set afloat *dar ab* (in the water); the loss of farr, or divinely blessed sovereignty, by Jamshid, Kai Kaus, and Kai Khosrow; the binding of

Ahriman/Zahhak by Tahmuras, Faridun, and Homa; the kusti as a device for binding evil, as represented by Rustam's lasso, Esfandiar's chain given to him by Zoroaster, Homa's kamerband with which he twice caught Afrasiyab—reflect clearly a ritual idiom which has been personified and replotted into narrative form.

The last two dynasties of the *Shahnameh* can be dealt with relatively briefly. Not only do contemporary bards pay them little attention, but Firdausi himself treats them with relative brevity. The legends of Alexander seem to have been more popular in the tenth to sixteenth centuries than they are today, although some of them continue in the form of oral folklore.

The figure of Alexander is richly embroidered around the pursuit of esoteric knowledge: he is not only tutored by Aristotle, in the Syriac Pseudo-Callisthenes version he is the son of an Egyptian magician-king;[27] in many versions his mother exudes a mysterious "bad odor" (invoked by some in etymologies for his name);[28] he is universally portrayed as a seeker of knowledge, going through the world questioning, learning, and eventually being endowed with wisdom and even prophecy.[29] In the Qur'an he is presented as a renewer of religion, and in the Syriac version of the Pseudo-Callisthenes he is a second Esfandiar, commissioned by God to overthrow a false religion. His story is one of engagement not only with Greek philosophy but with Hindu wisdom. An underlying theme of this pursuit of wisdom and esoteric lore, particularly in the tenth century, is the relation between kinship and wisdom: does kingship carry a divine grace? On what is the legitimacy of kings based?

In the tenth century *adab* literature, which taught the norms of gentility, and the *Mirrors for Princes*, which taught statecraft, Alexander and Ardashir, founder of the Sassanian dynasty, were stock figures for discussions of good versus bad kings. The historian Bayhaqi (who served in the chanceries of six Ghaznavid amirs from 416–441 A.H./1025–1048 C.E.) initially suggests that both Alexander and Ardashir performed miracles, but he later distinguishes between prophets and kings, and between kings who are just (*padshahan*) and tyrants (*mutaghalliban*). His is a technique of quietly raising issues in one place and leaving the reader to draw conclusions about the careers of historical kings he describes elsewhere with polite praise. Between Alexander and Ardashir, Bayhaqi prefers the Persian, "contrast[ing] the meteoric rise and fall of Alexander, followed as it was by the reign of the *muluk-i tava'if*, the lesser kings, that is, the Parthians, with the long line of just rulers who followed Ardashir" (Waldman 1980, 81).

In Firdausi, too, there is a contrast between the relatively brief account of Alexander's meteoric rise and fall, followed by an even briefer treatment of the Ashkanians, on the one hand, and the lengthy narrative of the Sassanian dynasty on the other hand. But in Firdausi the Sassanians are troubled and problematic throughout. Firdausi deals in depth with only three of the twenty-nine Sassanian kings, and the dynasty is a paradigmatic case of dramatic establishment followed by long decay, with only intermittent flashes of reinvigoration. Alexander, by contrast, serves as a kind of doublet to Esfandiar, albeit one in which knowledge supercedes martial brawn and that concludes with a certain astuteness of forethought. The dying shah, Dara, asks Alexander to marry his daughter, Roshanak (Roxana), so that

> Thou mayest see born to her a youthful prince
> Who will revive the name Esfandiar,
> Relume the altar of Zardusht, take up
> The Zandavesta, heed the presages,
> The feast of Sada and the Fanes of Fire,
> With glorious Nauruz, Urmuzd, and Mihr
> And lave his soul and face in wisdom's stream,
> Restore the customs of Luhrasp and follow
> The doctrine of Gushtasp, maintain both high
> And low in their degree, illumine the Faith,
> And see good days. (6.55)

It is, of course, Alexander himself, rather than a son, who bears some similarities to Esfandiar. Like Esfandiar and Kai Khosrow, Alexander travels the world, albeit more to search for knowledge than to convert (like Esfandiar) or than as a royal procession (like Kai Khosrow), though it is that, too.

Firdausi's account of Alexander may be divided into five parts: his extraordinary accession to the throne of Iran; his battle of wits with two kings of India; his establishment of the Quraish, the tribe of Mohammad, in control of Mecca and Arabia; some further battles of wit in pursuit of the queen of Andalusia; and the events surrounding his death, including his travels toward the fountain of youth, his building of a wall against Gog and Magog, and the omens of death.

The accession story is composed of his struggles with his half brother, the shah Dara. Their common father, Darab had, after defeating Rum, taken a daughter of Caesar as a wife but had sent her back before she bore Alexander. The motif of a princess with bad breath, bad odor, or a poisonous kiss is invoked but not elaborated by Firdausi. When Dara becomes shah, Alexander refuses to send tribute, thus setting the conditions for military confrontation. Disguised as his own ambassador, Alexander visits the Persian court to scout his rival, but his royal bearing is recognized, and he slips away. Alexander claims to want only the right to travel through the Iranian realm, not to take the throne (though his angry refusal to pay tribute to some extent contradicts this claim). Battle ensues, and Dara is defeated three times and flees to Kirman. Dara writes a letter of surrender, and again Alexander claims to want only the right of passage. During a fourth battle, Dara is treacherously slain by two of his ministers. Alexander arrives in time to receive Dara's final words and his daughter.

In the sixteenth-century Darab Nama, this daughter, therein called Buran Dokht, believes that Alexander paid the assassins, so she takes up arms against him. Alexander is unable to defeat or capture her in battle, until one day he comes upon her bathing in a stream. Alexander marries her before proceeding on his travels to India, Yemen, and Mecca, converting all to Islam along the way. In the process of being Islamicized, William Hanaway points out (1970), Alexander loses many of his heroic qualities, becoming indecisive, disinclined to fight, distrustful of advisors, and easily led astray by charlatans. Buran Dokht becomes a kind of alter ego to compensate for these deficiencies; she has to constantly extricate him from imminent defeat and disaster. Hanaway makes a case for seeing this protective goddess of both Alexander and Iran as the pre-Islamic Anahita, invoked in the Zoroastrian Aban Yasht and elsewhere as the protectress of the fertilizing and purifying waters for the cosmos in general and for human procreation in particular: "Ardvi Sura Anahita . . . who makes the seed of all males pure, who makes the wombs of all females pure . . . who makes all females bring forth in safety . . . who purifies the milk in female breasts . . . the whole of the waters that run along the earth" (I.2). She also instructs Iranian heroes that they may smite the daevas, the minions of Ahriman. It is therefore significant that Alexander should capture her not in battle but as she bathes in the waters. If Hanaway is correct, and he provides many supporting details, this is another magnificent narrative transformation of a ritual idiom such as that found in the story of Kai Khosrow. The story of Buran Dokht, in any case, is one of the finest examples of a warrior woman in the heroic literature.[30]

Having become shah of Iran, Alexander proceeds to India. There, King Kaid has ten dreams. His sages decipher these as images of the consequences of bad kingship and interpret the whole series of dreams as a warning not to fight Alexander. They advise King Kaid to tame Alexander with four gifts: a princess in marriage, a sage, a physician, and a cup which never is empty. Alexander accepts the gifts after testing them.

The testing of the sage is a classic of its genre. Alexander sends the sage a bowl of ghee (I am already full of knowledge, what need have I of you?). The sage adds a thousand needles (there is room for improvement and for sharpened wits). Alexander melts the needles into a plate (the cares of my office blunt my finer faculties). The sage polishes the plate and turns it into a mirror (I can amend that and give you access to wisdom). Alexander exposes the mirror to the dampness of the night: it dulls and rusts (the improvement will not last). The sage repolishes it and adds a preservative against rust (the sage denies that wisdom is not enduring).[31]

A second Indian King, Fur, engages Alexander in battle, and Alexander uses his wits: he fashions a naptha-filled iron horse that explodes into flame and stampedes Fur's elephants. A parallel sequence, in which Alexander pits his wit against a dragon who swallows naptha- and bane-filled ox skins, occurs when Alexander goes to the West in pursuit of Queen Kaidafa of Andalusia (a female doublet to King Kaid).[32] Between these two stories is the one in which Alexander liberates Arabia from the tyranny of Khuza, the successor to the unjust Qahtan, a descendant of Shem, and puts the Quraish in charge.

The final movement of Firdausi's Alexander story is framed by four omens of his impending death: two corpses and a talking tree warn him, and a stillborn monster-child appears as the final signal. After the first warning, Alexander travels to the city of women (Amazons with their left breasts removed), to the city of men, and then with Khizr (an Islamic figure like the Zoroastrian Sorush and the Jewish Elias, who move back and forth between heaven and earth) into the Vale of Gloom in search of the fountain of youth. Khizr makes it to the fountain, but Alexander loses him in the gloom. Alexander builds a molten-metal–covered wall to protect civilization against the monsters Yajuj and Majuj (Gog and Magog), perhaps an eschatological reference to the molten metal at the end of time which will purify the earth of evil, but if so, a reference not developed further. After the third omen (the talking tree which is male during the day and female at night), Alexander undertakes one last circuit of the world, making a truce with China, reconquering Sind and Yemen, and coming to rest in Mesopotamia at Babel, where he finds the treasure of Kai Khosrow. He writes to Aristotle, who advises that he not appoint a single successor but that in order to protect Rum he divide his empire among the Iranian princes. The omen of the stillborn child occurs. Alexander writes to his mother with instructions for Roshanak's posthumous child. Having arranged the affairs of state and family, Alexander dies. His coffin is taken to Alexandria.

The Alexander story in the *Shahnameh* functions as a marvelous interlude between the heroic Kayanians and the more recent historical Sassanians, elevating for a moment the questions of wisdom and wit to a place of primacy in considerations of royal success. These questions are addressed with increasing frequency toward the end of the Kayanian reign and in the stories of such figures as Bozorgmehr during the Sassanian dynasty, but as they appear in the story of Alexander, they can be disentangled, for a moment, from the complicating themes of legitimate lineage, parental-filial relations, and solidarities between king and people.

Between the life of Alexander and the founding of the Sassanian dynasty by Ardashir Papakan, there were, historically, five centuries, the period of the "tribal kings," the Parthians.[33] These centuries are condensed by Firdausi, who speaks only of the submerged lineage of Sasan (son of Bahram) whose descendants, all named Sasan, worked as camel drivers and shepherds. The last of the Sasans (the fourth by the count of the *Shahnameh*) works for Papak (or Babak), a vassal of King Ardavan. Papak, in a dream, recognizes Sasan's identity and sponsors his son, Ardashir, at the court of Ardavan. Ardashir outshines Ardavan's sons, causing jealousy and eventually mutiny among the troops. Ardashir fights for the throne and wins it.

The story is then retold in a more mythic style which establishes Ardashir as a demon-slayer, that is, as legitimate: divinely graced, righteous royalty, not merely a warrior able to seize a throne. This is the story of the Worm and Haftwad, a story that begins like many a woman's work story, resonates with the Kayanians, and ends with an eschatological motif.[34]

Haftwad's daughter is spinning. She bites into an apple, sees a worm, and saves it. Miraculously, her spinning output is doubled. She cares for the worm and is rewarded with growing wealth. When the governor attempts to tax this wealth, Haftwad revolts, overthrows the governor, and begins to create his own mini-state. Ardashir, who meanwhile has seized the throne of Ardavan, is brought into conflict with this expanding mini-state and is initially defeated. Like Esfandiar and Rustam before him, Ardashir disguises himself as a merchant to gain access to the city of the worm (Kerman).[35] Once inside the city's defenses, he feeds Haftwad and his men wine, then destroys the worm by feeding it molten metal (the eschatological motif again).

Now comes the Sassanian dynasty, the last great Iranian empire before Islam. Firdausi's portrayal is a grand saga of the apogee, culmination, and end of an age. There is first a recapitulation of Kayanian themes in a three-generation unit, beginning with the founder, Ardashir. Ten kings quickly follow, with little more comment than their births and deaths; only one of these, Shapur 'Zul Aktaf, the ninth Sassanian, is developed slightly, as a minor parody of Alexander. Then comes the reign of Bahram Gur, the fourteenth Sassanian: a synoptic paradigm of good kingship. A three-generation unit now introduces the centerpiece of the dynasty: the final restoration of the pre-Islamic glory in the reign of the sage-king, Nushiravan. His reign ends with a dream in which Muhammad and the replacement of the Zoroastrian world is foreseen. A closing three-generation unit traces the tragic decline of the Sassanian Empire. And then, after three kings and two queens pass quickly with barely more than a mention, the dynasty ends with the defeat, flight, and assassination of Yazdegird III.

Ardashir's reign as the first Sassanian monarch centers on the marriage-descent motifs of the Kayanian cycle: outmarriage yielding royal strength, generational transitions, and the manifest obviousness of royal grace. In securing himself the throne, Ardashir takes his predecessor Ardavan's daughter as his wife. She schemes with her brother and attempts to poison Ardashir. Noticing her nervousness, he has four fowl eat from the poisoned cup which he has spilled. They die. Ardashir orders her executed despite her pregnancy, but his prime minister secretly rescues her, castrating himself to demonstrate that it is not for his own bed that he saves her. Seven years later, when Ardashir bemoans the lack of an heir, the prime minister produces his son, Shapur (literally, "son of the shah"). Ardashir orders him to play polo with other boys to see if he can recognize the boy without assistance: he does. Meanwhile, plagued by war, Ardashir sends a messenger to the wise King Kaid of India to have his fortune told. The reply does not please Ardashir: all will be well if your seed mingles with that of Mirak. Mirak had seized Ardashir's palace while he was campaigning against Haftwad, and Ardashir had had to interrupt the external campaign to return and recapture his own capital. Ardashir has the realm searched for Mirak's daughter with the intent of killing her, but she is well hidden, disguised as a village girl. One day the young Shapur, on a hunt, comes to the village and sees her drawing water. His men have not the strength to lift water from this well, and he himself does so only with difficulty, but she—the warrior-woman motif again—can do it easily. Shapur weds her. Their child, Urmuzd, is hidden from Ardashir until one day he appears on a polo field and noticeably outshines the other boys. Kaid's prophecy has come true: Ardashir's reign prospers domestically, the

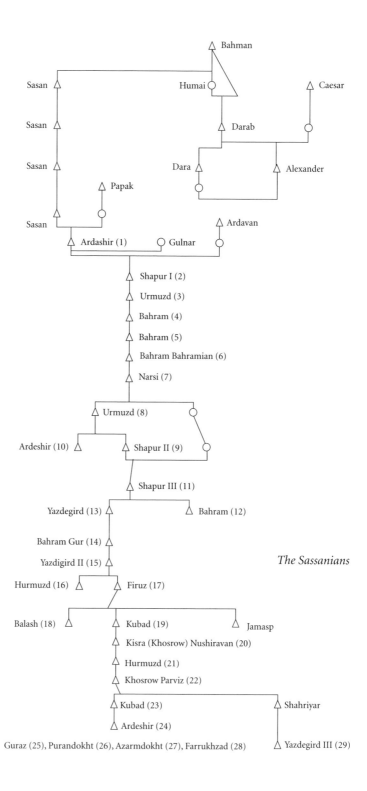

The Sassanians

forces of Rum are defeated, and the Ruman general Bazarnush builds a bridge at Shushtar (a bridge that later becomes elaborated into a parable of the mechanism of Western colonialism).[36]

Among the next ten reigns, only that of Shapur II ('Zul Aktaf) is developed. It is the reign in which Mani comes to Iran from China. Charged with the heresy of painting God and worshiping icons, he is flayed, stuffed with straw, and hung on the city walls. More intriguing is the preceding and inverse story of how Shapur goes to Rum disguised as a merchant, is recognized, arrested, sewn up inside an ass skin, and released by an Iranian servant girl who stretches the skin with warm milk. Ardashir then calls for barsom, the Avesta, and a high priest and with his troops retakes the city of Ctesiphon from Rum. The story is a veritable inversion of the one in which Alexander uses naptha- and bane-filled ox skins to slay the dragon. The figure of the Iranian female who rescues Shapur with warm milk perhaps refers to the Anahita motif. In any case, the ritual elements of milk, barsom, and Avesta are explicit. Thus strengthened, Shapur is victorious and founds several cities with the prisoners he takes.

The narrative of the first great Sassanian reign—the fourteenth, that of Bahram Gur—provides a kind of synopsis of good rulership, with parables of justice at its center and a repetitive structure of seeming disregard for Iran exploded by dramatic rescues and demonstrations of concern. The first of these repetitive structures is provided by Bahram's youth and assertion of rights to the throne. He is raised and educated at the Yemenite court of Munzir, suckled first by two Persian and two Arab nurses, then taught by three sages, respectively, penmanship, the arts of the hunt, and royal administration. At the age of eighteen he chooses two horses and two Rumi damsels. One of the latter, Azada (freedom) accompanies him on a hunt and eggs him on to nigh-impossible tasks; he kills her in anger and learns never to mix women with the hunt. He returns to his father's court in Iran but is unhappy there; he ignores protocol (he falls asleep at a state banquet), is imprisoned, and manages to escape back to Yemen. When Bahram's father, Yazdegird I, dies (amid divine signs), the Iranians, who had judged Yazdegird to be evil, reject his son and elect Khosrow king.[37] Bahram marches on Iran, argues that he, too, had suffered at Yazdegird's hands. A test between Bahram and Khosrow is arranged: a crown is placed between two lions. Khosrow demurs, saying that if Bahram can retrieve the crown, he can have it. Bahram bathes, prays, smites the lions with an ox-headed mace, and is hailed king. His first act is to remit taxes.

There then follow a series of six parables of wise rule. When Bahram travels in disguise among his subjects, a poor water carrier hosts him elaborately, while a rich man gives him no hospitality, so Bahram gives the latter's wealth to the former. Bahram outlaws wine drinking because the good Kirwi's eyes were plucked out by a crow while he lay drunk; but he allows wine in moderation after it helps a shoemaker to consummate his marriage and to ride a lion. Bahram next experiments with egalitarianism, telling villagers that they are all chiefs; when anarchy and ruin results, he appoints one man to rule, and prosperity is restored. At the house of a merchant, Bahram is treated poorly, but an apprentice treats him well, and again Bahram reverses their fortunes. Falling ill after slaying a dragon, Bahram is cared for by a peasant woman; his thoughts turn dark, and the woman's cow goes dry; he repents for his dark thoughts, and the cow gives milk. Finally, Bahram confiscates and redistributes the wealth of a rich shepherd who is so miserly that he himself lives without decent clothing, food, or housing.

> I should by rights attach this man. He hath not
> Amassed these hoards by thievery and bloodshed,
> Hath not incited others to do wrong,
> But he hath been ungrateful and not had
> The fear of God within him, hath kept ward
> O'er all this treasure to the detriment
> By such amassing, both of heart and soul. . . .
> . . . . .
> A buried gem is nothing but a stone
> Affording no one either food or raiment. (7.73–74)

The themes of good rule are clear: reciprocity and mutual concern among all citizens (parables 1, 4, and 6); moderation in taboos and rules (2); the need for a certain amount of hierarchy or lines of authority (3); the vigor and mental health of the king (5).

Interdigitated between these parables are accounts of Bahram's numerous marriages and one of his love of the hunt. These are seen by both Iranians and foreigners as signs that he is too wrapped up in sport and women to protect the realm.[38] China and Rum prepare to invade. Bahram prepares a small force against China, which the sages mistake again as a sign of lack of serious concern. Humai and the sages ask quarter from China, fearing Bahram will not protect them. But, as in his youth, Bahram comes through victoriously, defeating the forces of China and reestablishing the clear (and mystical) boundary between Iran and Turan. This is followed by other evidences of good rule: officials are instructed to treat subjects well; challenging questions from Rum are elegantly answered.

A third time, Bahram appears to leave Iran. He travels in disguise as his own ambassador to the court of Shangul in India. There he proves himself in wrestling and archery and in trials against a wolf and a dragon, finally winning the daughter of the king (shades of the trials of Gushtasp, Rustam, and Esfandiar). Shangul eventually suspects the visitor is royalty, but Bahram escapes. The two kings make a treaty of friendship, and Shangul visits Iran. Again, on his resumption of royal care, Bahram remits taxes.

The reign ends with a story of how Bahram brought the Gypsies to Iran and a just-so story of how they came to live on the margins of society. The people complain that the rich drink wine to minstrelsy, while they have no such enjoyments. So Bahram asks Shangul to send ten thousand Gypsies. Bahram supplies them with wheat and oxen, thinking they will become peasants. The Gypsies instead merely eat the wheat and oxen, and so are thereafter condemned to live by their wits and music, like the dog and wolf on the margins of society.

Now comes the climactic center of the Sassanian dynasty: the story of Nushiravan "the Just," framed by two three-generation units. The preliminary three-generation unit includes the Mazdakite efforts at religious reform, the fall of the Rustam-like hero Sufarai, and ill omens of famine, eclipse, and war. The first of the three shahs is Firuz (the seventeenth Sassanian), whose reign begins with drought, eclipse of the sun, and a war. To deal with the drought, Firuz lifts taxes and distributes the state stores of grain. But he also breaks the boundary agreement with Turan that was reestablished by Bahram Gur; he therefore is defeated and killed. Firuz's son Balash is young and incompetent, but the great hero Sufarai assumes the duties of regent and marches on Turan to free prisoners of war, especially Balash's brother, Kubad, and the high priest Ardashir. Sufarai puts Kubad on the throne. Kubad hears popular slander against himself in favor of Sufarai (that is, that Sufarai is the real king and power, and Kubad but a puppet king, king in name only). Kubad calls on the hero Shapur of Rai to bind Sufarai. Unlike Rustam, Sufarai allows himself to be bound and brought before the king. Though the populace begins to rise against this injustice, Kubad is persuaded by his jealousy and by ill advice to kill Sufarai. The people revolt, seize Kubad, hand him over to Sufarai's son Rizmihr, and install Jamasp as king. Rizmihr, however, proves loyal to Kubad and helps him regain the throne. Famine and drought recur, but Kubad now has a minister, Mazdak, who introduces salutary reforms.

Mazdak converts Kubad with two parables. If a man is bitten by a snake and a second man possesses an antidote but refuses to give it to the stricken man, what, asks Mazdak, should the judgment on the second man be? Kubad judges him a murderer. If a man is bound and starving and a second man possesses bread but refuses it to the starving man, what is the judgment? Again Kubad declares the second man a murderer. So Mazdak opens the royal granaries to the people. When he explains what he has done, Kubad is persuaded and embarks on an egalitarian rule. Firdausi gives little more detail about Mazdak, but it appears that the reforms endanger the power base of the nobles and the priests, thus leading to a resistance movement, led by Kubad's son, Kisra "Nushiravan." Mazdak gambles on winning a public confrontation, accusing Kisra before the king of not following the faith and of immorality. A public debate is organized, and Kisra victoriously defends the old faith of Zoroaster against Mazdak's innovations, and he accuses Mazdak of instituting a communism of property and women which will create anarchy in relations of authority, deny fathers and sons the means to recognize one another, and deny the means for discerning good men from evil ones. Mazdak is hanged. Kisra (the Arabic form of Khosrow) is given the title "Nushiravan" or restorer: he is, for the pre-Islamic world order, a final Kai Khosrow.

Nushiravan's reign begins by putting the realm in order, bringing to court the great sage-minister Bozorgmehr (great light), and with a court intrigue. The central portion of his reign has to do with wisdom, with alternatives to fighting—marriage, chess, backgammon—and with the fables of Bidpai (or Kalila and Dimma). A second court intrigue involving the fall and restoration of Bozorgmehr precedes the preparations for the succession.

After assuming the throne, reorganizing the administration and taxation, settling border disputes, building a wall against Turan, and suppressing a claim to the throne by a son who thinks Nushiravan has died, Nushiravan dreams that a boar sits on his throne and drinks from the royal cup. The very young Bozorgmehr, still studying in Marv, is able to decipher the dream and is installed at court. (The dream exposes a youth who, disguised as a maid, has followed his beloved into the royal harem: both the harem girl and the youth are executed.) Bozorgmehr is then tested and shows his brilliance in a series of seven banquets. At the first banquet, Bozorgmehr merely displays his wit in a string of twenty-six proverbs and in his praises of the king. Beginning in the second banquet, Bozorgmehr is tested by the sages on fate and fortune, on status and position, on the virtues of the sages, and on the faults of kings. The middle three banquets continue with discourses on wisdom and knowledge (including the five characteristics of the sage and the seven of the fool), and on the nature of royal justice and virtue. The sixth banquet is a jousting with riddles: what is the thing whose increase will harm, whose decrease will strengthen? Eating. What are the heart's three blemishes which men retain though they need them not? Self-consciousness, envy, and slander. Finally, in the climactic banquet, the king orders Bozorgmehr to speak the truth about him, Nushiravan. Bozorgmehr responds with an elegant discourse on the proper role of the shah and the duty to obey a good shah: "The service of the monarch of the world / Is, saith the sage, the path way of the Faith." Carefully tucked into the speech are cautions about arbitrary powers.

> When a king
> Hath God's grace on his face, the world's heart laugheth
> For joy.
> Although the shah should be a mount of fire
> Still would his servants find existence good,
> For if such fire burn at the time of wrath
> It will shine the more when gratified.
> The shah at whiles is milk and honey, whiles
> A biting bane. His acts are like the sea
> . . . . .
> One getteth from the sea a pinch of sand,
> Another hath the pearl within the shell. (7.312–13)

Firdausi's text is a flexible vessel awaiting interpretive delivery: it could be spoken as pure sycophancy, but it could also be given a sharp double edge ("when a king"), a veiled warning to keep one's distance from such a fickle, arbitrary power ("one getteth . . . a pinch of sand").

Following this warning comes a tale of court intrigue, this one a threat to the king averted, one that reads like an inverted variant of the Jewish Purim story of the evil vizier Haman and the good vizier Mordecai, and perhaps the Purim story is a response to this one recorded in Firdausi.[39] The chamberlain, Zuran, is jealous of the prime minister, Mahbud, who had secured Nushiravan's succession and whose wife is trusted with preparing the royal food, delivered daily by his two sons. Zuran has bound to him through debt a Jew who knows sorcery, who can poison milk by viewing it from a distance. (The notion of evil eye is divided here into its parts: the Jew is stigmatized with the mechanism, but Zuran possesses envy, the necessary motive force.) As the sons of Mahbud bring the royal food one day, Zuran asks to have a look; they lift the cover, and the Jew views it from afar. Zuran then warns the king that the food is poisoned. The shah orders the sons of Mahbud to taste the food: they die. The shah then hangs his loyal minister. Years later Zuran drops a clue about what happened, the story comes out, and he and the Jew are also hanged.

The central portion of Nushiravan's reign is devoted to alternatives to bloody warfare. This commences when the Khan of China decides it the better part of valor not to fight Nushiravan but to offer a daughter in marriage. He attempts to hide his prized daughter and offer another instead, but the wise envoy of the shah, Nastuh, recognizes the princess and insists on her. All peripheral wars cease. Nushiravan gives prayers of thanks at the Azargashasp fire temple, barsom in hand, and endows the temple and priests. A council with Bozorgmehr is treated to discourses on the ten demons of Ahriman and the ways of wisdom.

The king of India sends the game of chess to Nushiravan with the challenge: if you can figure out how to play this game, we will pay tribute; otherwise you pay us tribute. The Indian envoy gives away several clues.

> To find out footman, elephant, and host
> Rukh, horse, and how to move wazir and king
> . . . . .
> An emblem of the art of war and thou
> Wilt see, when thou hast found it out, the tactics
> The plan, and order of a battlefield. (7.385–86)

Bozorgmehr follows the clues and displays the game.

> The sage then fashioned him a battlefield,
> Whereon he gave the kings the central place,
> And drew their forces up to left and right
> The footmen eager for the fray in front.
> Beside the king his prudent minister
> Was posted to advise him in the fight.
> The warrior-rukhs impetuous on their steeds
> Were at the wings and fought on right and left.
> Adjoining these the battle chargers stood,
> So that the great king proved the Raja's match.
> And then the elephants of war arrayed
> On either side both eager for the fight. (7.388)

Shahnameh miniature: Nushiravan Receives an Embassy from Hind.

Bozorgmehr then sends to the king of India a more abstract version of such game—backgammon (*takht-e nard*)—as a counter challenge.[40]

The story of the invention of chess is then told. A king dies, leaving a young son. The widow marries the deceased's brother and has a second son. The brother dies, and the two boys pester the mother about who will succeed to the throne. She refuses to choose, fearing the other will be filled with revenge. The sages are consulted, but each advises according to which son is his patron. Warriors line up behind their patron, and war seems inevitable. The elder son attempts compromise: joint rule or division of wealth. The younger refuses. The sage of the elder son foresees that the younger brother will soon die and advises his liege to stall for time. They propose building a special battlefield away from civilization and sharply bounded by a sea or moat. The younger brother agrees, and when all is prepared, battle is joined. The younger brother, in the midst of battle, dies in his saddle without having been wounded. When the warriors return, the mother accuses the elder son of murder and prepares to kill herself on the younger son's funeral pyre. The son denies fratricide and, by threatening to cast himself on the pyre as well, forces her to listen to how the younger prince died. To help her visualize, the sages construct a chess set, sharply bounded as if by a sea, and show how the prince died checkmated not stabbed. The mother studies the chess game day and night, using it as a way of working out her grief, "to medicine her sufferings" (7.423). Chess thus is both the analogue of war with strategy at its center and a teaching device against adversity, emotional and strategic.

The pursuit of wisdom continues. Nushiravan sends the physician Barzwi to India in search of a drug said to make the dead speak. After years of searching, Barzwi encounters a sage who points him in the right direction.

> The noble heart must hear to understand.
> The herb then is the sage, the mountain knowledge
> As bring ever distant from the throng;
> The corpse the man whose knowledge is to seek
> . . . . .
> In sooth 'tis knowledge that doth make men live
> . . . . .
> Kalila is the herb, and understanding
> The mountain. In the monarch's treasury
> On making quest there, thou wilt find a book
> Of knowledge that will point thee out the way. (7.427)

Accordingly, Barzwi visits the library of the king, each day reading and memorizing a section of the text, then secretly writing it down in letters to Nushiravan. Thus came the parables of Kalila and Dimma to Iran, and Bozorgmehr copied them out. Later, says Firdausi, the caliph Mamun had them translated into Arabic. Then the Samanid prince Nasr (r. 914–43 C.E.) and his prime minister, Abu'l Fasl, translated them into Persian, and the poet Rudaki versified them.

Nushiravan thus possesses the tools of wisdom—chess and fables—but has not yet assimilated them. There follows a second tale of court intrigue, this one demonstrating Bozorgmehr's earlier cautions on the fickleness of royal power. (It is a tale which in a variant women's work story is central to village life.)[41] One day while the shah naps with his head in Bozorgmehr's lap, his jeweled amulet falls off, and a bird picks up the jewels. Bozorgmehr recognizes in this an ill omen for himself. The shah wakes, notices Bozorgmehr biting his lip, and jumps to the conclusion that Bozorgmehr has not merely stolen the amulet but plans evil. Bozorgmehr is imprisoned and there behaves in a fashion which perhaps has become paradigmatic of Iranians who feel themselves unjustly imprisoned by the state: when the shah inquires about his repentance, Bozorgmehr replies, "My station both in public and in private / Far bettereth the monarch of the world's" (8.6). Such answers infuriate the shah, who has Bozorgmehr tortured, but to no avail. Eventually, when the shah needs him to respond to a challenge from Caesar, Bozorgmehr is released. As in the chess story, Caesar has sent a riddle box: if you guess what is inside, we will pay tribute; otherwise, leave us alone. Bozogmehr prays and interprets as omens the first three women who pass by: the first is married and has a child; the second is married but childless; the third is unmarried and childless. Bozorgmehr divines that the box contains a pierced pearl, a half-pierced pearl, and an unpierced pearl.

With the rehabilitation of Bozorgmehr comes also the maturing of Nushiravan's wisdom. It is the shah now who is questioned by the sages and who provides wise answers. Nushiravan writes a letter of advice for his son Hormuzd and has the sages test Hormuzd's worthiness to succeed. After a war with a young, successor Caesar, Nushiravan dreams of Muhammad under a brilliant, rising sun. Bozorgmehr predicts the end of the Zoroastrian era.

The decay of the Zoroastrian imperial order is portrayed through a final three-generation unit: Hormuzd (578–590 C.E.), Khosrow Parviz (590–628 C.E.), and Kubad (February–September 628 C.E.). The contrast with the preceding three-generation unit is instructive. In the earlier set each generation committed a fundamental sin: Firuz broke the boundary treaty; Kubad destroyed the generation's hero; and Nushiravan dealt ruthlessly with Mazdak. Yet, on balance, these three shahs were good and redeemed themselves. In the present set bad begins to outweigh good. Firdausi tells three stories about the first two reigns, each of which is a repetition or variant of previous themes, used here to demonstrate the pervasive decay. He uses the story of Kubad's reign to level an explicit set of charges against the occupants of the throne and their weak defense. The three themes are the royal (mis)use of wise men; the sordid decay of relations between king and hero; and the dilemmas of royal marriage alliances.

Although it is said that Hormuzd ruled well for ten years before turning evil, Firdausi begins with the way Hormuzd eliminated his father's advisors. The condemned sages become, like Bozorgmehr, paragons of dignified resistance, upholding Zoroastrian ritual and devotion to truth. When the scribe Izid Gushasp is imprisoned, the high priest Zardusht (Zoroaster) visits, although frightened for his own life, and the two men share a ritual meal with barsom in hand.

> Then the board was spread
> Before those holy men who next began
> To mutter prayers with sacred twigs in hand. (7.82–83)

The visit is reported to the shah. Izid Gushasp is slain. Zardusht is invited to the palace and offered poisoned food. Realizing what is happening, yet unable to refuse, the priest eats, hurries home, and tries antidotes, then tells the royal messenger who has come to check on him that the king is cursed. Next, the king asks the loyal advisor Bahram Azarmihan to publicly condemn the sage Simah Barzin. Bahram Azarmihan does so and in a dramatic flourish responds to Simah Barzin's challenge to specify an instance of disloyalty; with fine irony, Bahram Azarmihan recalls that when Nushiravan had asked the sages whether Hormuzd was worthy of the throne despite his half-Turanian blood, most had voted against Hormuzd, but Simah Barzin had lobbied successfully in his favor. Now Simah Barzin must suffer the consequence. Hormuzd has Simah Barzin slain and Bahram Azarmihan imprisoned. Bahram Azarmihan sends word to the king that he knows what can secure the king's happiness. Brought a final time before the king, he reveals where a letter from Nushiravan is hidden. The letter, in Nushiravan's hand, predicts that Hormuzd will rule righteously for ten years but that two evil years will cause his fall. Hormuzd has Bahram Azarmihan killed; but then he tries to reform and indeed rules righteously for ten years.

Firdausi does not dwell on the ten righteous years, illustrating those years only briefly with the story of how Hormuzd, reacting to the trampling of a farmer's field by the favorite horse of his young son, Khosrow Parviz, has the horse's ears and tail docked despite the boy's bitter protests and pays the farmer tenfold for his crop. Firdausi then turns almost immediately to the story of the hero Bahram Chubin, scion of the Arsacid house at Rai.[42] Enemies rise up against Iran on all sides. The aged Nastuh, who had fetched Nushiravan's bride from China, comes to Hormuzd to recount the predictions of Chinese astrologers that a hero would come to save Iran. Nastuh promptly dies, but a hero matching his description is found in Rai: Bahram Chubin.

Chubin is given command of the army, but as he departs, Hormuzd has second thoughts, fearing that Bahram will revolt and claim the throne. Chubin disobeys the order to return, saying it is ill luck for an army, once on the move, to return. In a few small incidents Bahram Chubin shows himself just: he hangs before his troops a soldier who has taken an old woman's hay without paying. But a larger incident of protocol reveals the imprudence of both Chubin and the king. After the defeat of the forces of King Sawa, the slain king's son, Parmuda, requests special quarter from Hormuzd. Bahram Chubin demands that Parmuda treat him as a superior. Parmuda refuses and is supported by Hormuzd, who sends Chubin women's clothes instead of a robe of honor. Chubin dons the clothes before his troops, and they are affronted as well. Chubin then sends bent swords to the king, who sends them back broken. Chubin issues coins in the name of Khosrow Parviz; the prince, under suspicion of sedition, flees Iran. Amid the intrigue, Hormuzd is blinded by the brothers Bandwi and Gushtaham, allies of Bahram Chubin.

Khosrow Parviz (who has reconciled with his father) and Bahram Chubin are thus rivals for the throne. Khosrow Parviz calls on Chubin to behave like a loyal pahlavan, to be like Rustam. Bahram Chubin invokes his royal Arsacid lineage and asserts that the Sassanians are usurpers who do not rule properly. There are a series of battles. Khosrow Parviz is put to flight and secures an alliance, both military and marital, with Rum. He is nevertheless defeated twice more. He flees up a blind canyon and prays to God for deliverance; the archangel Sorush, clad in green, miraculously appears and lifts him up the cliff face.[43]

This is a turning point, and in the next battle Chubin is routed. A pause in the story before the final demise of Chubin provides a reassertion of the Zoroastrian order. A banquet is held by Khosrow Parviz, complete with barsom. The Christian ally from Rum, Niyatus, leaves the table in anger, saying he will not participate in paganism, that all prayers should be to Christ. Mariyam, the wife of Khosrow Parviz from Rum, mediates. Meanwhile, Bahram Chubin has sought refuge at the court of China. There he displays his prowess, slays Makatura, a greedy vassal of the Chinese emperor, and prepares to invade Iran. When his envoy to China finds that the Khan's ears are closed to reason, Khosrow Parviz pays Makatura's brother to kill and revenge himself on Bahram Chubin. There follow a few more mopping-up incidents: the assassination of the brothers who blinded Hormuzd; Khosrow Parviz's marriage to Bahram Chubin's sister, Gurdya, one of the great woman-warriors of the *Shahnameh*, whom he makes governor of Rai; and the birth of an heir, Shirwi or Kubad.[44]

Shirwi's horoscope is not optimistic, but Khosrow Parviz puts the kingdom in order and reasserts the dignity of the imperium. Thus, when Caesar sends gifts to the celebrations for Shirwi's birth, asking at the same time for the return of the Cross, Khosrow Parviz reciprocates the compliments but does not accommodate the request.[45]

> About the Cross of Christ: a well based Faith
> Hath reason for its guide. Concerning those
> Who, as thou say'st, are sad because their Prophet
> Was crucified yet call Him " 'Son of God', "
> And say that on the Cross He laughed, if He
> Was son He hath but gone back to his Father;[46]
> Be not concerned about some rotten wood.
> If foolish utterances proceed from Caesar
> His letter will be laughed at by the old.
> . . . . .
> And if I send it from Iran to Rum
> The land will laugh at me. (8.374)

The challenge of Bahram Chubin settled, Firdausi turns to the story of Khosrow and Shirin. A century later, in the hands of the poet Nizami, this was to become the classic Persian love story.[47] But in the hands of Firdausi it is a much more ambiguous parable of marriage alliances. Khosrow and Shirin had been sweethearts but had parted when Khosrow fled Iran and during the period when he fought Bahram Chubin for the throne. One day, on his way to hunt, he sees her on the roof of a house along his way: she calls to him, and he takes her into his harem. The sages mourn, fearing the evil that comes from an evil mother, citing Zahhak and Alexander. Khosrow tries to allay their fears by having a bowl of blood cleaned and refilled with wine: Shirin's bad reputation exists only because she once was his lover; by taking her into the harem, he feels, her status will be clarified and cleansed. Things prove not quite so neat: Shirin subsequently poisons Mariyam and after a year succeeds to the position of chief wife.

After reconstructing the ancient throne of Faridun, elevating the young minstrel Barbad, and building a great palace at Ma'adain, Khosrow begins to turn evil.[48] A disloyal retainer uses the unrest in the empire to invite Caesar to attack; Khosrow is able to finesse this challenge.[49] But a loyal retainer, Farrokhzad, leads an insurrection in the name of Shirwi (Kubad), dethrones Khosrow, and exiles him in the old capital of Ctesiphon.

There follows the drawing up of formal charges against Khosrow: parricide and regicide; illegitimate accumulation of wealth from the oppression of the people; keeping troops away from Iran for long periods; refusal to restore the Cross; the slaying of his mother's brothers; imprisonment of his son; and intimidation of chiefs and vassals. Khosrow defends himself: his father had been roused by slander against him, and so he had had to flee Iran, during which time his father was blinded by his mother's brothers; after the long, well-known fight with Bahram Chubin was settled, vengeance for his father demanded the death of the mother's brothers. As for the imprisonment of Shirwi, Khosrow characterizes it as protective custody: no harm was done, and its prudence was reinforced by the evil horoscope attending Shirwi's birth. All others who were imprisoned were evil-doers, and by setting them free, Shirwi is endangering Iran. He casts the matter of the Cross as a trivial consideration: many important gifts had been sent to Rum; what is the big deal about a rotting piece of wood. Finally, regarding the economic charge, he claims that taxation was necessary to defend the realm and to have the means for royal redistribution.

> A pauper shah will be unjust, and he
> Whose hand is empty hath no strength or worth.
> Without the means of largesse, he by all
> Will be declared a fraud and not a shah. (9.21)

The defense is effective: the envoys are abashed, and Shirwi wonders if he has done wrong toward his father. The chiefs of the realm, however, fearing the young shah will repent, insist on Khosrow's death as well as those of his other sons. It is done. Kubad asks Shirin to be his queen (after initially reviling her); she leads him on, has him grant her great wealth, which she gives to the poor and religious institutions, and then she kills herself in Khosrow's mausoleum. Kubad in turn is poisoned.

Five reigns follow in rapid succession and confusion. Finally, a grandson of Khosrow Parviz takes the throne as the last Sassanian shah: Yazdegird III (632–653 C.E.). The commander of the Iranian army, Rustam, is aware that the stars bode ill for Iran and the Sassanian dynasty, but he heroically challenges the commander of the Arab Muslim forces, Sa'ad ibn Waqqas: who are you? What do you want? Acknowledge the shah! Then follow the *Shahnameh*'s famous lines.

> The Arabs, from drinking camels' milk and eating lizards
> Have reached a pitch whereat the Persian throne
> Is coveted! Shame, shame on circling heaven! (9.79)

Sa'ad ibn Waqqas challenges the effete and civilized ways of Iran, and calls on Rustam to accept the faith of Muhammad.

> We hold the sword and spear to be our mates:
> Brave warriors make no mention of brocade,
> Of gold and silver or of food and slumber.
> Ye have no part in manhood but are like
> To women with your colors, scents, and forms.
> Your prowess is in donning broidery
> Adorning roofs and decorating doors. (9.80)

Rustam deems it better to suffer an honorable death than to give up his faith. He leads his troops into battle and is defeated and slain.

Yazdegird III flees to Khorasan in hopes of gathering a new force there. Mahwi of Sur conspires with Bizhan to attack Yazdegird at Marv. A battle ensues, and the shah flees, seeking refuge in a mill. When the miller discovers him, Yazdegird asks for food and for barsom that he may eat with full ritual form. The miller goes out to look for barsom and thereby gives the shah away. The sages attempt to dissuade Mahwi from killing Yazdegird, but he has shown his hand publicly and is too far committed to draw back. Bizhan commits the actual deed, then goes mad and slays himself. Thus, sadly, ends the *Book of Kings*.

The *Shahnameh* of Firdausi stops here, but the legendary and parabolic elaborations do not. For Zoroastrians, the legends of Yazdegird III are but beginnings for their life after the Arab invasion. To this day their calendar is dated from the reign of Yazdegird III. The legends of the Parsi migration to India open with the flight of Yazdegird's family and entourage to Khorasan (and beyond, to China in some versions); the legends of the Zoroastrian shrines around Yazd also begin with the flight of Yazdegird's family. For Muslims as well there are continuation legends, the most important being those of Bibi Shahbanu, the wife of Imam Husain and the daughter of Yazde-

Shahnameh miniature: Simorgh Carries Zal to Her Nest (by
Hazine, 2153, folio 23a, Tabriz, ca. 1370). Topkapi Palace
Museum, Bilkent University, Ankara, Turkey.

gird III, which tie together the House of the Prophet and the Twelve Imams
with the legitimate line of Iranian kings.

Modern scholars often search the *Shahnameh*'s narrative of the Sassanian
dynasty for references to history. Such a search, together with the work of
early Muslim historians, provides one kind of collection of information on a

period poorly documented.[50] While there is nothing wrong with this kind of search, it is clear that even in this, the most historically sensitive of the four dynasties in the *Shahnameh*, there is a parabolic rather than historical structure. Firdausi has elegantly represented the climax and decline of an age and has crafted his storytelling to that end. His devices are familiar from earlier portions of the epic; their employment shows as well the continuous process of movement from the more mythic and heroic earlier dynasties to the more recent, more fallible, and more human kings. As the decline of the Zoroastrian imperium is traced, a countervailing moral structure is taught, encouraging wisdom over martial brawn. The theme of the search for wisdom is elaborated by later poets who take up and retell in new ways some of the stories in the *Shahnameh*. Nizami does this with the tale of Khosrow and Shirin and with the story of Alexander; Farid-ud-din Attar (d. 627/1230) does so with the story of the marvelous Simorgh.

Among the familiar devices used by Firdausi are the three-generation units, the ambivalence of foreign marriages, the traces of ritual idiom, and the use of repetitions or doublets from earlier in the epic and from within the dynasty to make comparative distinctions.[51] But most important are the parables, for it is the detachable parable which perhaps most clearly lodges in the popular memory: the two most important from the Sassanian dynasty are the story how Bozorgmehr figures out chess and backgammon and the tale of Khosrow and Shirin. But other stories were also later elaborated into parables: the bridge built by Bazarnush, for example, as a parable of colonial mechanisms used against Iran; or the elaborations on the story of the confrontation between Rustam and Sa'ad ibn Waqqas sometimes stressing the ignorant and uncivilized Arabs, sometimes stressing the overcivilized, effete, and oppressively inegalitarian Persians.[52]

In all of this—the movement away from the ancient Indo-Iranian ritual idiom; the saga of decline and decadence from the heroic age and from the purity and perfection of the cosmic elements into a world of impurity, deceit, and unruly passions; the world-weary commentary and the search for mystic philosophies which transcend the mundane, fallen world—it is clear that one is progressively dealing not with a Zoroastrian ethos but with an Islamicized version of it. There are points of contact between the two moral traditions—the stories and Iranian nationalism—but each develops the stories differently and values the key characters differently. Each contributes threads to the complex fabric of Iranian culture, lying sedimented as well in the stories and parables that have disseminated into world culture far beyond the ritual and mystical borders of Iran.

Coda   Illuminationism:

Philosophical Allegory

"The hoopoe is famous for his sharp-sightedness, while owls are blind by day."—SUHRAWARDI, *The Language of Ants*

"[In spring] the hoopoe becomes a Simurgh whose shrill cry awakens those who are asleep. . . . All knowledge emanates and is derived from his shrill cry. . . . His food is fire."
—SUHRAWARDI, *The Simurgh's Shrill Cry*

"The spiritual luminaries, the wellsprings of kingly splendor and wisdom that Zoroaster told of, and . . . the good and blessed king Kay-Khusraw unexpectedly beheld in a flash. All the sages of Persia were agreed. . . . For them, even water possessed an archetype in the heavenly kingdom which they named 'Khordad.' That of trees they named 'Mordad,' and that of fire 'Ordibehesht.' These are the lights to which Empedocles and others [Hermes Trismegistus, Agathadaemon, Socrates, and Plato] alluded."
—SUHRAWARDI, *The Philosophy of Illumination*

Calligraphic bird and line drawing of Walter Benjamin as Paul Klee's *Angelus Novus*. Bird from Farid Ud-Din Attar, *The Conference of the Birds* (New York: Continuum, 2000), 153. Line drawing by Lloyd Spencer, Faculty of Media, Trinity and All Saints College, University of Leeds, www.tasc.ac.uk.

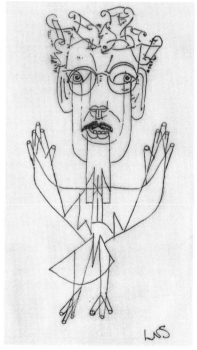

The systematic mystical philosophy called illuminationism (*ishraqi*) or science of lights (*'ilm al-anwar*), elaborated by Suhrawardi and his successors in Arabic and Persian philosophical and allegorical genres, forms a third deployment of the ancient Zoroastrian symbols and metaphors, after those of the Persian epic *Shahnameh*, and of the Avestan and Pahlavi, or middle Persian, Zoroastrian rituals and scriptures.

My interest in the tradition of illuminationism (*hikmat-i israqi*) in the present context is threefold: (1) the use of metaphorical poetics and recipro- cally its teaching of interpretive attentiveness which still informs the domes- tic and diasporic Iranian audiences of contemporary Iranian films and artis- tic productions; (2) the discussion of political legitimacy which negotiates between the terms of the Zoroastrian tradition mystical *farrah* or *khvarnah* and Islamic doctrines of *imamat* and illuminationist *hikmat* and *hokumat*, a negotiation in which even Khomeini found himself not always unscathed; and (3) the discussion of the degree to which philosophy is largely a game of its own invention (ontology, metaphysics, existence/being, essences, and so on, what Suhrawardi calls "beings of reason" [*i'tibarat 'aqliya*]) or has some- thing of more general interest to offer about knowledge (epistemology) and authority (legitimacy).

Suhrawardi cast his effort only partly in terms of a recovery of ancient Iranian wisdom as symbolized in the amshaspands, the rituals addressed to the divine light (the sun, the sacred fires in the fire temples), the stewardship by kings such as Kai Khosrow and sages such as Bozorgmehr (great light) of divine incandescent charisma of sovereign legitimacy (*khvarnah, farrah*). The cup of Jamshid and Jamasp inherited by Kai Khosrow, which allows foresight into the future and the mysteries of the cosmos, is emblematic. But Suhra- wardi combined this Iranian symbolism of light/knowledge/wisdom versus dark/ignorance with a Neoplatonic theory of creation through emanations from the light of lights (*nur al-anwar*, God); with an Islamic doctrine of the *nur* (divine light) out of which the 124,000 prophets and the twelve Shi'ite Imams are created and which still resides with the occulted Twelfth Imam; and with a systematic concern with rational philosophical reason. This sys- tematic mystical philosophy has had enormous influence in literature and the arts as well as in philosophy, and remains important in Iran (and else- where in the Islamic world) to this day. Suhrawardi points to the accounts of such pre-Aristotelian Greek philosophers as Hermes Trismegistus, Pythago- ras, Empedocles, Agathadaemon, Socrates, and Plato as evidentiary testi- monies and confirmations of the experiences and rational reconstructions that he himself experienced and worked out, articulated through Platonic

Ideas, Shi'ite notions of an occulted Imam, and *nayranj* (special, occult, even sorceric) powers of sages, viziers, and philosopher-kings from Egypt and Greece to India.[1]

Suhrawardi attempted to work out an epistemology grounded in experiential self-knowledge and apperception of something like what Kant later would call innate or a priori ideas, or in the language of Suhrawardi's times, Platonic forms. Such an epistemology must begin, Suhrawardi argues, with Peripatetic (Aristotelian) rational or discursive philosophy (*hikmat bathiyya*). It needs ascetic discipline. And it uses linguistic and analytic tools to separate the metaphysical self (I-ness) from its worldly "accidents" (the physical, socialized, conventionalized individual)—what Maimonides would later call a guide to detachment or a guide for the perplexed that could be of use also in the government and stewardship of this world.[2]

In the ordinary Sufi metaphors that have become familiar world wide, one might gloss Suhrawardi's goals, approximately, to be (1) to release the soul (often metaphorized as a bird, frequently the falcon) from its material cage (the body, but also more generally the constraints of time, space, and passion), and to provide an account of and self-knowledge of consciousness and its abilities to achieve insight and wisdom; (2) to elicit from language a comprehension of a third world of archetypes or images which mediate between the sensory material world and the intelligible world of thought; and (3) to construct didactic devices to help novices to transcend both the material world and the constraints of language.

But while other great mystical teachers of the age—Sana'i, Attar, and Rumi—used a variety of poetic and narrative genres (the heroic *mathnawi*, the amatory *ghazal*, and the *hikayat*, or anecdotal illustrative tale), Suhrawardi is distinguished by his insistence on the importance of rational philosophical groundings as well as esoteric vision and insight. He wrote, in Arabic, four philosophical texts intended to be read as a cycle, beginning with discursive philosophy (hikmat bathiyya) and ending with intuitive philosophy (*hikmat dhawqiyya*). In technical philosophical terms, the goal of his texts is to provide an intuitionist foundation for the logical reconstruction of Peripatetic philosophy, the guiding principle being that to know something is to obtain an experience of it, that whether or not one can analyze that something further, there is something essential about the responses evoked in human beings (including visions), about Platonic forms or archetypes of those experiences, and about the metaphysics of such entities as the self. In addition to the cycle of four philosophical texts, Suhrawardi also wrote shorter epitomes of his philosophy in both Arabic and Persian, as well as eleven allegorical tales in Persian and Arabic.

For some commentators the defining characteristic of Suhrawardi's philosophical texts is their rationalism (Ha'eri 1992; Walbridge and Ziai 1999; Walbridge 2000); for others the mystical poesis (Corbin 1946; S. H. Nasr 1964); and for yet others both are necessarily critical and complementary (Thackston 1982; Aminrazavi 1993, 1997).

Shihabuddin Abu al-Futuh Yahya ibn Habash ibn Amirak al-Suhrawardi, Shaikh al-Ishraq (Master of Illumination), or Suhrawardi al Maqtul (the executed) (A.H. 549–587/1154–1191 C.E.) was born in Suhraward, a village near Zanjan in northwestern Iran, spent his twenties in Anatolia, and eventually settled in Allepo in northern Syria, where he became a mentor to the governor, Malik al-Zahir, a son of Saladin. He was executed at the order of Saladin, who, having overthrown the Ismaili Fatimids of Egypt and having fought the Ismaili "Assassins," felt he could take no chances on the strategic city of Aleppo falling under the sway of yet another advocate of a philosopher-king and Ismaili-like charismatic shaikh. Because Suhrawardi taught an esoteric doctrine, he needed a living transmitter/successor to pass on his teachings, but his execution foreclosed this possibility. His three searches—for illumination, for patronage, and for transmission—all had an afterlife. An important commentary on his work was written in the thirteenth century by Shahrazuri, and this was further elaborated by Qutbuddin Shirazi (d. 1311 C.E.), a scientist and student of Nasiruddin Tusi. In the seventeenth century there was a revival of illuminationism under Mir Damad (d. 1040/1631) and his important critic and student, Mullah Sadra (d. 1641). There was also a revival of sorts and an interest in Zoroastrian lore in Mughal India at roughly the same time.[3]

Interpretive Attentiveness: From Zoroastrian Imagery to
the Metaphysics of Light

Among the simpler of the transformed, inverted, pre-Islamic metaphoric figures used by Suhrawardi are the cow, falcon, steed, and Simorgh. The cow—the beneficent vision of the Avesta—becomes the carnal soul that must be killed/sacrificed to achieve inspiration: it's horns represent greed and desire, two chains to the material world. The falcon, or bird of the soul, no longer represents the indwelling of transforming grace in this world but the spiritual essence seeking release and abandonment of this world. The steed, as well, is no longer a metaphor for righteous effort in this world but for escaping it. Suhrawardi compares the initiatory experience of mystical visions to be like being on a galloping horse and imagining "that one is rushing out of the body leaving it behind in its place." Elsewhere he calls this the "steed of yearning" for transcendence.

The Simorgh, like the falcon, has been transformed into the call of transcendence rather than a transformative power within the corporeal world. Suhrawardi retells the Rustam and Esfandiar story. The Simorgh—which saved the infant Zal (in this version by finding a gazelle to provide milk) and which lives in the Tuba tree (a Qur'anic interpolation: *tuba*, "blessedness," hence a cosmic tree of Paradise)—is so luminous that it dazzles any eye which looks at even its reflection in a mirror. Rustam, in this version, polishes his mail and helmet, and the mail of his horse, to a mirrorlike quality. When Esfandiar faces Rustam, the rays of the Simorgh reflecting off the mail so dazzle him that he imagines he is injured in both eyes and falls from his horse. The two-feathered shaft of the special arrow given Rustam by the Simorgh in the *Shahnameh*, says Suhrawardi, must be the two wings of the Simorgh.

In spring, the time of rebirth and awakening, the hoopoe flies to Mount Qaf, the home of the Simorgh, and itself becomes a Simorgh. The shadow of the luminous wings of the Simorgh cure; its cry arouses the sleeping and provides knowledge to the few who listen. In his short treatise "The Shrill Cry of the *Simorgh*" Suhrawardi compares the first mystical stirrings to pleasurably dazzling lights: flares (*tawali*) or rays (*lawa'ih*) of the sun. When the lights of transcendence are no longer fleeting but linger instead, Suhrawardi calls it the *sakina* (compare Hebrew *shekhina*).

The polished iron of Rustam's breastplate which causes Esfandiar's downfall and the opening of his spiritual eyes is but one of a series of perfectly polished and transparent bodies—mirrors, still water, the dream world of the imagination—that act as revelations in the material world of the beings in the third world of archetypes (*'alam-i mithal*). The seventeenth-century commentator on Suhrawardi, 'Abd al-Razzaq Lahiji (d. 1072/1662), described this third interworld as a reality which is objective and extramental, and whose objects possess shape and extent but not material substance. That Islamic Peripatetic philosophers and scholastic theologians deny the possibility for extended form to exist without matter, Lahiji asserts, constitutes their basic rift with the theosophists. The interposed third world of the theosophists was part of a gradation between matter and spirit. The nineteenth-century

Shaikh Ahmad Ahsa'i (d. 1241/1926), founder of the Shaikhis, argued that the doctrine of bodily resurrection required such a mediate interworld or, in following Ibn 'Arabi, four interpenetrating worlds. To insist on such a possibility provides for a richer mystical object for didactic contemplation.

The tradition initiated by Suhrawardi remained a lively one through the nineteenth century. Shaikh Ahmad Ahsa'i and his successor, the Qajar prince Shaikh Haj Muhammad Karim Khan Kermani (d. 1299/1870), followed Suhrawardi in drawing on Zoroastrian imagery. Ahsa'i spoke of the third interworld as Hurqalya, claiming this to be a Syriac term used by Sabeans and Mandeans for a homologue of the paradise of archetypes gathered by Yima. Yima was instructed to build a Var, a hold in which to preserve the seeds or archetypes for the world of resurrection.

Henri Corbin (1960/1990), in his influential account of this tradition, locates the Var in the land of the midnight sun, where light never goes out and which is administered by Khizr, the Islamic spiritual figure who moves back and forth between this world and the spiritual one. Corbin explains that this places the cosmic orient (the place of the dawning of light and wisdom) in the north. Note that this does not accord with the Zoroastrian ritual tradition, which associates the north with Ahriman.

Kirmani elaborated a mystic vision of Zoroaster in which he witnesses the decline of seven empires—represented, as in the Book of Daniel, as seven metals—but then is consoled by Ahura Mazda (Ohrmazd) with the vision of a resurrection led by the eschatological hero Bahram Varjovand (possessor of the Var). Kermani identifies Bahram Varjovand with the Twelfth Imam of Shi'ism and works out other correspondences between Shi'ite, Zoroastrian, Ptolomaic, and Neoplatonist schemes.

Suhrawardi himself called the interworld of archetypes "Esfandarmaz." It contains guardians of the natural species corresponding to both the amshaspands and to Platonic Ideas: thus Urdibihisht stands for fire, Khurdad for water, Murdad for plants, Shahrivar for minerals, and Esfandarmaz for love. In Corbin's synthetic interpretation Suhrawardi and his followers struggled to recreate a Mazdean *imago terrae* in which, through a medium of analogic reason or mental dramaturgy, the cosmos was created and can be brought back to perfection or recreated by the liturgy of the amshaspands, that is, the yasna. The Islamic illuminationists, however, did not try to recover the physical liturgy of the yasna, but instead attempted to puzzle out ways in which their souls could be purified to participate in the higher spheres of spiritual wisdom. It is a harmonics of cycles, correspondences, transformations, and tropisms toward the spiritual light.

Corbin sketches a visionary geography in which the original khvarrah (light, energy) prefigures the eschatological *frashkart* (restoration). The earth is set out in the shape of a mandala, with six lands surrounding the central seventh, Iran-vaj (Iran-origin), where Ohrmazd celebrates the creation liturgies, where Yima creates the Var, where Zoroaster arrives on Noruz (the New Year) of a new millennium, and where the final saoshyant will usher in the resurrection. On this earth mandala, mountains rise up so that the earth is separated from the heavens. From the top of Mount Hukairya, the waters of Ardvi Sura Anahita pour down onto the earth, watering the white haoma of immortality, the tree which contains all seeds, cures for all illnesses, and in which the Simorgh dwells. Mount Ushidarena, the first peak to catch the dawn light, channels the waters of Advi Sura Anahita into the cosmic sea, Vourukasha, which surrounds the earth. Mount Chakad-i Daitik is the peak of judgment, where the soul crosses the Chinvat Bridge into the next world and into one of the seven heavens. Beyond the encircling mountains and the cosmic sea are the emerald cities of Jabarsa and Jabalqa where no clothing is needed, where the diet is vegetarian, and where there is no sexual differentiation. (Jabarsa, according to Suhrawardi, is a mystical state achieved by Aristotle.) When Zoroaster arrived in Iran-vaj, he went to the River Daiti, where he had been born, and there was met by Bahman/Vohu Manu to be taken into the presence of the amshaspands. He was told to take off his dress and material body, and to don a garment of musk. Musk in the sacred botany is associated with Armaiti, who is correlated by the Neoplatonists with *sophia* (wisdom), the daughter of Yahweh, the craftswoman of creation, the maid to whom all youths betroth themselves in their search of knowledge. Not only is there a sacred botany, through which the art of gardening acquires liturgical meaning, but an alchemy of metals. When Gayomart dies, seven metals emerge from his body, with gold from his soul and seed. Spenta Armaiti gathers this gold, and from it emerges the plant which forms the first couple Mahryag-Mahriyanag. At the end of time, Armaiti will enter Lake Kansaoya and will conceive from the golden khvarrah seed the sayaoshant. Corbin finds traces of this underlying harmonic scheme throughout the history of illuminationist theosophical thought.

The use of Zoroastrian imagery does not really depend so much on the specifics of this visionary geographic cosmology which Corbin tries to reconstruct and systematize. More important is the metaphysics of light which Suhrawardi substitutes for Ibn Sina's (Aristotelian) metaphysics of being and which provides an interlanguage between an epistemology of the self, a metaphysics said to be rationally grounded, and justifications for an increasingly tenuous language of political and religious-institutional legitimacy. The metaphysics of light, of course, fits nicely with the Zoroastrian use of fire/sun/light as the sign of divinity and goodness to which one addresses prayers throughout the day, facing the sun at dawn and dusk, as well as feeding and facing the sacred fires of the hearth, the village fire temple, and higher-level sacred fires constructed through elaborate rituals of purifying the various fires of both nature and human affairs via sandalwood into purified composite fires. Conversely, in the Zoroastrian scheme, darkness signifies evil and the realm of Ahriman. The world is a mixture of good and evil, and thus constitutes the field of ethical battle, whose outcome should be a purification and restoration of the completeness of the good and vanquishing of Ahriman.

Suhrawardi claims that wisdom or esoteric understanding is both prepared for and confirmed by rational disciplines. In the twelfth century the canonic philosophical disciplines were four: logic, physics, mathematics, and metaphysics (logic:math :: physics:metaphysics). Suhrawardi critiqued and modified this fourfold canon of the Aristotelians and Islamic Peripatetics (*'ilm-i mashsha'i*). While he did not provide accounts of mathematics nor include physics in his mature opus, *Hikmat al-Ishraq* (The Philosophy of Illumination), he took, for instance, the work of the great Islamic Peripatetic philosopher and physician Ibn Sina (Avicenna) and substituted *light* for the Greek *being* as the key metaphysical term. Light, after all, he says, is the necessary condition for things to be observed by a sound eye and is the most apparent of phenomena because all else is recognized by it. Walbridge argues that Suhrawardi simplified the regnant physical theories of vision and sound to a satirical degree in order to point out that no matter what the physics of vision or sound might be, perception is something else altogether, a matter of consciousness. "What makes vision actual is the consciousness of the thing seen by a self-conscious subject" (Walbridge 2000, 160). Likewise, one does not experience vibrating air, one experiences sound—something which cannot be defined to a deaf person or explained in terms of other senses (ibid., 162). Consciousness requires *ilm-i hudur*, knowledge by presence.

A linguistic analysis, an epistemology, a practice of self-knowledge, and a metaphysical ontology follow. When one says, "I know something," one is linguistically claiming to know oneself. The discursive "I" of such statements can be shown to be different from the body. Immaterial and immutable, it is a metaphysical "I." For this "I" to know itself requires the mode of cognition Suhrawardi calls *al-ilm al-huduri* or "knowledge by presence." Attributes of the self include its worldly desires and attachments. For the essential self to reveal itself, these "secondary qualities" or "accidental attributes" must be removed like removing veils that darken and obscure the essential self (*dhat*). These four steps are like stages on a journey: realization, separation, destruction of the accidental qualities (worldly desires, attachments), and annihilation of the individual ego so its I-ness (*ana'iyyatuka*) can be revealed to itself.

This "annihilation" is achieved through asceticism. Indeed, Suhrawardi says that one must fast for forty days, eat little, avoid meat, and practice asceticism before embarking on his hikmat-i israqi. Regarding his own understanding, he notes that it came to him first through mystical exercises and was only later reinforced by logical proofs and confirmed by parallel experiences expressed symbolically in the writings and teachings of the ancients. Without attaining a certain level of mystical initiation, he continues, it would be best to stick to discursive rational philosophy and Peripatetic teachings. But it is clear that of the three forms of cognition—logic, sense impressions, and innate ideas or direct apprehension—the first two are not self-sufficient and always require some a priori grounding or starting point (innate ideas).

One of the most attractive features of Suhrawardi's philosophy is its insistence that "beings of reason" (*i'tibarat 'aqliya*)—that is, metaphysical entities—while they designate valid mental distinctions, do not entail corresponding existence of real distinctions in concrete things (Walbridge and Ziai 1999, xxi). It is a remarkable admission that philosophy is largely engaged in artifacts of its own creation. But it is also a reason for the move toward an illuminationist practice or discipline as a mode of knowledge that supplements and supercedes that of rational discursive philosophy. Like Kant, and along the lines of the fully rationalized philosophies of the European Enlightenment (drawing still on the tropes of light, vision, self-evident experience), Suhrawardi believes that knowledge is based on not just the senses, and not just on definitions and logic, but also on self-evident a priori ideas or Platonic Forms. These last are to be found through a physical and philosophical purging of the self down to its essence, a kind of phenomenology of reduction. (European phenomenologists such as Husserl do not make asceticism part of formal training, though many were in their personal lifestyles relatively ascetic, and the speculations of Merleau-Ponty on the body and the embodied mind might have led them back in this direction.)

If the revealing of essence is a kind of unveiling of darkness and obscurity into light and self-consciousness, then Suhrawardi suggests there are four classes of being which according to the axes of light/dark and dependent/ independent can be mapped in a two by two logic box (see table 10). All

TABLE 10. Four Classes of Being (Suhrawardi)

	Light	Dark
Independent	self-sufficient and self-conscious	dusky and material bodies
Dependent	accidental light	dark accidents

conscious beings are immaterial light, differing from one another by their intensities. The most intense is the Light of Lights (nur al-anwar), the first cause, what Ibn Sina calls the necessary existent God.

Divinely inspired rulers, whether in this world or in occultation (like the Twelfth Imam), must show signs of divine grace: they link the world of pure being/light from which all emanates and the world of sense perception. They reside in the eighth clime, a separate realm located between the purely intelligible and the purely sensual. Rulers on earth can attain receptivity for this grace through the practices and disciplines of hikmat-i israqi. Conversely doing wrong can cause the loss of this royal grace, the ancient khvarnah, *kharra-yi kiayani*. Possession of this grace allows the exercise of healing powers.

Hikmat/Hokumat (Wisdom, Rule) in a World with Unseen (*Gha'ib*) Connections

It is fascinating that when Ayatullah Ruhullah Khomeini attempted to formulate arguments for legitimate political rule by clerics in his lectures on "Hokumat-i Islami, Velayat-i Faqih" (Islamic Government, Guardianship by the Juriconsult), he could not do so on the analysis of the hadith and *sunnat* literature by which he tried to make his case (Khomeini 1971; Fischer and Abedi 1990, chap. 2); he instead had to fall back on the presumptive intent of the Prophet and the Imams (and through them the presumptive intent of the divine message as transcribed in human language in the Qur'an). Khomeini himself wrote mystical poetry and, after the Islamic revolution of 1977–1979 in Iran, engaged in televised mystical interpretations of the Qur'an. While he himself did not dare to claim to be an enlightened philosopher-king or to justify his political leadership in other than rational and political arguments, popular imagery played ambivalently on the title "Imam," used in the Arabic-speaking Shi'ite world as an equivalent to the titles *mujtahed* and *ayatullah* among Persian-speaking Shi'ites, and the separate usage of "Imam" to refer to the twelve divinely inspired Imams descended from Muhammad's daughter, Fatimeh, and son-in-law of the Prophet Ali. The Twelfth Imam, who has withdrawn from this world in occultation and will return at the end of time. A mujtahed is one who has been educated to the level at which he has been given formal permission (*ejazeh*) to decide questions of Islamic law and right conduct without appeal to a more learned scholar. An ayatullah (sign of God) is a mujtahed who has also taken on an administrative leadership role, collecting religious taxes for communal use. Although considered less learned than other leading ayatullahs, Khomeini in the 1970s took on political charismatic leadership and effectively used the Persian idiom of seeking long-term values over short-term politics: the revolution, he once famously commented, was not fought to raise the price of watermelons.

The cry of the 1977–1979 revolution was *adelat* (justice), that is, a society based on values of social justice. Social justice, notes the illuminationist philosopher Qutb al-Din Shirazi (d. 1311), stands in a feedback relation with the legitimacy of governments. He recounts that the Sassanian kings held special courts in which people could bring suit against the king. The king would bind himself with oaths to judge these cases fairly. But Yazdegird III abandoned this practice, and the Sassanian dynasty soon disintegrated. Standard metaphors and symbols express this relationship: the word for leadership, *riyasah*, is connected to *ras* (head); the king as head of the body politic must see to the needs of the body, which in turn supports the head. When kings in the *Shahnameh* and Avesta act unjustly, they eventually lose the royal farr or khvarnah, and are deposed.

The mystics add three observations to this common sense: (1) there is a parallel relationship between the cultivation of true knowledge to rule the self and cultivation of wisdom to rule a society (praxis, discipline, ordeal); (2) knowledge, foresight, insight, and judgment all depend on relations unseen, hidden, or occulted (*gha'ib*); (3) use of knowledge-power therefore often operates in a fraught field where the effects can tip in either a healing or a devastating direction (causing accusations of sorcery; powerful viziers meeting a tragic demise, whether justly or unjustly accused).

Suhrawardi retells the tradition of the royal khvarnah or *kharra-yi kiayani* (royal light, divine glory) as something that anyone who obtains wisdom (*hikmah*) can receive. While Suhrawardi distinguishes the kharra that can be bestowed on anyone from the royal kharra-yi kiayani, there are many forms of intellect and illumination. By purifying the self and becoming open to wisdom and divine light, one gains the insight to rule with justice, as well as the power to predict the future, control the elements of the earth, cure the sick, make wild beasts obey, create natural events such as earthquakes, make things (food, sounds, shapes) appear at will, and talk with the unseen. There are physical ascetic practices for purification but also philosophical ones (as in the analysis of "I-ness"). The receiving of divine glory radiates in persons as divine light (*farra-yi izadi*) and empowers miraculous acts. The opening of the inner eye of wisdom allows one to participate in the "eighth clime" (*al-iqlim al-thamin*) that interzone of the 'alam al-mithal or *'alam al-khayal* (*mundus imaginalis*). Suhrawardi also invokes the doctrine of the *qutb* (hidden pole) whose presence in each age keeps the world from ruin. In institutional Iranian Ithna Ashari (twelver) Shi'ism, this figure is the Imam Zaman, the Imam of the age, currently the occulted Twelfth Imam, and accords with the nur doctrine, a myth that a special divine ray of light created Muhammad, 'Ali, Fatima, Hasan, and Husain, and also created all of the other 124,000 prophets, each breathed into human form at appropriate points in history, often making for miraculous births (Fischer 1980, 25–26). During the Islamic revolution of 1977–1979 popular discourse toyed with the theologically hubristic but nonetheless exciting possibility that Khomeini might be the Imam Zaman. In noninstitutional Sufi mysticism such a qutb is unlikely to be identified with a temporal ruler. His cosmic function does not depend on his presence being recognized. Still, Suhrawardi notes the possibility held out by the ancient royal farr that, should the state be in the hands of the qutb, the age will be luminous.

Those who achieve wisdom go under many names: brethren of abstraction (*ikhwan al-tajrid*), perfect souls (*al nufus al-kamila*), ascetics (*ashab al-riyadat*), wayfarers (*ashab al suluk*), visionaries (*ashab al-mushadah*), possessors of the command (*ashab al-amr*), people of insight (*ikhwan al-basirah*), pure souls (*rawshan ravanan, ravan pakan*), brethren of truth (*baradaran-i haqiqat*), creators of images (*ashab al-baraya*). Toward the edge of the transgressive is the term *ta'allah* for intuitive or illuminationist philosophy as opposed to discursive (*bahth*) or rational philosophy. *Ta'allah* means to become a god and is the term used to translate Greek notions of divinization (Walbridge 2000, 204). Sovereignty, Suhrawardi says, belongs to one who is *muta'allih* (divinized). Another term for the divine sage is *hakim ilahi*, and one begins to sense the potential of an ecstatic, charged, demonic/divine personage on the edge of what is tolerated by jurists, or in this case by Saladin and rival jurists in Aleppo.

Dealing with the unseen world (*gha'ib*) is a major theme in Persian storytelling as well as theology, probing the hubris of all human attempts to know what is coming. Figuring out what to do requires a knowledge of often hidden, occulted, unseen causes, effects, interactions, implications, embeddednesses, leverages of power and wit. This is the subject of many morality stories in popular folklore as well as in written collections such as the tales Sheherezade tells in *The Thousand and One Nights* to fend off her death at the hand of King Shahriyar, each tale internally depending on all sorts of unanticipated connections. In Shi'ism, gha'ib refers to a series of inner truths: a God who is not visible, a Twelfth Imam who is in occultation, a personal inner faith, and the special light (nur) that created the Prophet and the Imams.

In Suhrawardi's *hikmat-i israqi* of the powers attainable by the sages those of the creator of images (*khaliq al-baraya*) are among the more interesting. The 'alam i-mithal or world of images is an interzone between the physical world and the immaterial world of mind. "It is the plane of ghosts, of the forms in mirrors, dreams, and worlds of wonder beyond our own" (Walbridge 2000, 26). Walbridge continues: "It is obviously useful as a way of accommodating the miraculous and the eschatological, as well as odds and ends not conveniently fitting into the Aristotelian scheme of forms-in-matter. Suhrawardi does not systematically develop the concept, but his followers did. (It has nothing to do with the Platonic Forms, which are entirely different in function and ontological level.)" (ibid.). There is a connection to reincarnation: Suhrawardi says that souls of the imperfect might be reincarnated in the bodies of animals and thus purified, and this he says might occur in the world of image rather than in the physical world, or perhaps in both (ibid.). Fazlur Rahman indicates that Mullah Sadra held a slightly different perspective: at resurrection, he felt, lower animals will be resurrected not as individuals but as species, reverting to "what Plato called the World of Ideas and what the ancient Persian sages called the 'Guardians' (or Masters, Lords) of dead images, i.e., material bodies (*arbab al-asnam*)" (1975, 262). If sages have powers of creating appearances that can outwit enemies or be used perhaps to teach those who can be taught, this would provide ambiguous powers of the occult (liable to accusations of sorcery), powers such as those used in the fights between Rustam and Esfandiar and the demons, and an important weapon of transparency of the Jam-e Jamshid. In the Zoroastrian cosmological battle between good and evil, between the forces of light and darkness, the end comes with a victory of Good. Suhrawardi suggests that cosmic cycles caused by the motion of the celestial spheres and lights, no matter how complicated, must eventually return to their original positions and then repeat, a kind of eternal return. "The same individual will not return, though an exact duplicate of that individual will come into being. This is also the explanation of providence. Things cannot be other than they are since the existing universe reflects the rational order existing among the celestial lights" (Walbridge 2000, 26).

Safir-i Simurgh (The Shrill Cry of the Simorgh)

Whether or not one wishes to play in the language games of philosophical ontology and metaphysics, the battles of wit using "the language of the birds," ants, porcupines, scorpions, salamanders, and so on remain among the most seductive, playful, and popular of the Persian oral and literary arts, honed between the eleventh-century Firdausi and the twentieth century.

Firdausi gives us one of these contests in the story of Alexander testing the Indian sage sent him by the local King Kaid. Alexander sends a bowl of ghee (i.e., I am already full of knowledge, what need have I of you?). The sage adds a thousand needles (i.e., there is room for improvement and for sharpened wits). Alexander melts the needles into a plate (the cares of my office blunt my finer faculties). The sage polishes the plate and turns it into a mirror (I can amend that and give you access to wisdom). Alexander exposes the mirror to the dampness of the night where it dulls and rusts (the improvements will not last). The sage repolishes it and adds a preservative against rust (the sage denies that wisdom is not enduring). A parallel story used by the Parsi Zoroastrians describes their flight from Iran to India after the defeat of the Sassanians. They petitioned the local ruler of Sanjan on the coast of Gujurat to allow them to settle. He sent back a brim full glass of milk. They sent back the glass with sugar added (we will add sweetness but otherwise cause no displacement or disturbance); in a variant version it is a gold ring that adds value but no displacement or disturbance.

Suhrawardi offers in parallel style the *Treatise on Birds* (*Risala al-Tayr*), metaphors for the path of asceticism and wisdom. "Guard yourselves in the manner of a porcupine. . . . Shed your skins like a snake and go like an ant that no one may hear your footsteps. Be like a scorpion with your weapon always held behind you, for the devil approaches from behind. . . . Like a salamander be in the midst of fire so no harm can come upon you tomorrow" (Thackston 1982, 21). In other words, shed your ego like a snake sloughs off its skin, walk the path of truth quietly like an ant who makes no noise, and be like the salamander. The salamander is the symbol of gold in alchemy, and

Simorgh and mullahs: the renewal of Turkey.

gold is the sign of divine intellect; folklore has it that should a salamander survive a fire it is hardened to every further attack, which is reminiscent of the Qur'anic story of Abraham surviving the fire. *The Treatise on Birds*, Suhrawardi's Persian translation and reworking of the text by Ibn Sina, is an allegory of birds flying freely and being caught in a hunter's trap (the prison of the world or the body), then trying to free themselves and return to their liberated state. Some manage to partially free themselves, but the protagonist knows not how and begs for help from the others (one can in principle achieve liberation by oneself, but to remove all the bonds requires the guidance of a master). The birds set out on their path and stop to rest, then need a voice to urge them not to get distracted by beautiful rest areas along the way (attaining a degree of grace makes it easier to hear the call and find the way further).

Illuminationist texts, like the Upanishads of India, turned much of the imagery of Zoroastrianism and the cognate Vedas upside down. Experiments with symbolic poetic forms increasingly led to a play with indirect and reversible meanings, with a duality of surface absurdity or blasphemy, but intelligible underlying metaphor and allegory. Such duality easily lent itself to spiritual cover for vulgar and heterodox play with ludic or subversive intent. This play could consist of simple clichés or more sophisticated turns of metaphor: praise of wine, women, and song became standard metaphors for the elixir of inspiration and sensitivity to the intelligible sounds of the natural universe; the relation of lover-beloved for that of worshipper to God; and the transience of things of this world for moral and ethical counsel. A more sophisticated use of vulgarity was the psychological assertion that to gain control over one's faculties one needs to engage in ascetic practices, tests, and ordeals, in order thereby to break the seductive spells of desires, conventions, and social pressures which prevent full use of one's spiritual capacities. This poetic and argumentative strategy was put to use both in individualist rejections of social convention (the *darvish*) and in more "socialist" assertions of egalitarianism, including movements of young men (*futuwwat*) invested in initiation ceremonies (*kumerbandan*) with kusti-like cummerbunds. The songlike quality of poetry was recognized for its intoxicating powers, which can prepare one for ecstasy, communion with the divine, and intensify one's innermost divine spark. The linguistic play of poetry provides serious challenges to the mind, literary license, and deniability should there be accusations of subversiveness. The most challenging uses of poetic duality and symbolic play were quite ingenious, even revelatory, probings of the etymological-metaphorical and grammatical structure of language and human understanding. To probe that which lies beyond the ken or descriptive powers of language, one might use logic to show how language can mislead, or conversely one might use the mysteries of linguistic metaphors and figures to confound logic itself.

II

Seeing After Film

TEXTUAL AND CINEMATIC FORMS

OF ETHICAL REASON

3   Awaiting the Revolution: Surrealism Persian Style

"Surrealism is a bourgeois disaffection . . . [a]n aesthetic that yearns to be a politics."—SUSAN SONTAG, *On Photography*

At the end of the nineteenth century, two notions of culture vied: that of high culture, or culture as what was best in civilization; and that of culture as that which constituted the collective understanding of a society. During the first half of the twentieth century, anthropologists elaborated and refined the latter concept. It passed into general discourse and democratized views about the role of ideas in society. Phenomena that would have been dismissed by conservative proponents of high culture—popular culture, religious idioms, socially grounded ideologies, contestatory styles, the thought of peasants or of migrants—were incorporated into a dynamic understanding of societies as composed of competing groups, strata, and classes. During the second half of the twentieth century, as the substantive purview of anthropologists shifted increasingly from small-scale societies toward the great agrarian civilizations and toward industrial and information-age societies, their notions of culture had to accommodate, in an explicit fashion, competing rhetorics within complex societies. As a result, new formulations of culture emerged, midwifed in part by cross-disciplinary exchanges between anthropologists, literary critics of the several poststructuralist schools, other social scientists, and scholars of cultural studies, gender studies, and postcolonial studies, among others.

Various cultural materials have provoked contemporary efforts to reformulate the notion of culture. Short stories and films can be viewed by proponents of high culture as expressions of the best a civilization has to offer: the finely crafted products of trained, educated professionals. Short stories and films can also be described in terms of anthropological concepts of culture as vehicles of expression of a particular stratum of society: the intelligentsia, a stratum within the bourgeoisie, a particularly ambivalent stratum, one that often has difficulties reconciling its social origins with its aspirations, and one whose boundaries are not necessarily contained by geography or nationalism. Short stories and films are not merely expressive of the intelligentsia, however; they also inform their audiences—often in ways inaccessible through other media and certainly through standard social-science techniques—about the society in which their authors live.

Short stories and films, thus, are emblematic of a fundamental issue in contemporary efforts at formulating a theory of culture: the issue of "transparency." Culture is not transparent: one cannot take short stories and films at face value; authors do not always understand all of the things they have transmitted through their texts. Short stories and films do not directly mirror or describe society; not only are they creative and re-creative fictions, but they and all modes of representation are always mediated—by conventions, by borrowed techniques, by multilevel structures of communication. One needs a method or series of methods for "reading" cultural products/texts.

The first methodological injunction is conventionally unexceptionable: one must always attempt to place cultural products in their social context. I will attempt to discuss something about the audience reception of the stories and films, about the traditional symbols they use and the modern corpus of symbols they have created, as well as about the authors and their techniques. Important here are some tentative suggestions about surrealist techniques and how they differ in an Iranian context from European or Latin American ones.

More provocatively, I argue for a technique of close reading and for attention to ambiguous possibilities of the text. Various readings of a film or short story are always possible. The task of the anthropologist is to define the range of possible readings and to explain the appeal of different readings for different audiences. This is not merely a matter of method or of depth of understanding. Rather, there is no other way of understanding another culture. For example, it is not very useful to attempt to formulate categorical differences between Iranian and American notions of manhood or to formulate rules by which an American could learn to behave in an Iranian fashion. Efforts at such formulations tend to be superficial and trivial, if not ethnocentric, invidious, stereotypic, and racist. What is known about the differences between Iranian and American notions of manhood is present in the texts of the short stories and films. The process of understanding is one of engaging/reading the texts, acknowledging the ambiguities they pose, both for their authors and for Iranian and non-Iranian readers, and the alternative implications they suggest. Instead, then, of coming to the conclusion that Easterners are worried about female modesty, male honor, and duties of revenge, one comes to appreciate the sense of the tragic and of the interconnectedness of social acts that are coded in stories of revenge, and to recognize a humanist logic not far from our own, albeit constructed and embedded differently. There is no denying cultural differences; the challenge is to draw attention to productive methods for eliciting them and following out their implications. Categorical definitions are rarely useful; the rewards of cultural comprehension and of cross-cultural conversation emerge in the process.

It is important to set several restrictions for new formulations of a theory of culture on the basis of engagement with short stories and films seen as products of a complex society in which there are competing readings and rhetorics. A theory of culture must not be constrained by national boundaries, by notions of unchanging symbolic lexicons, or by assumptions of single, unified symbol systems for each society. These restrictions are more challenging in practice than in the abstract, as is clear in the case of Iran and its cultural extensions into both the Indian subcontinent and the Middle East.

During the 1960s and 1970s the Iranian intelligentsia saw itself as the articulate vanguard of social criticism and opposition to both the shah's resistance to democratization and the clergy's obscurantism. Calling itself "enlightened thinkers" (roshan fekran), this intelligentsia, along with many foreign observers, evaluated the literature it produced according to whether or not it was politically engagé. After the revolution of 1977–1979, which established the Islamic Republic of Iran, these same critics and observers flagellated themselves for having been misled and thus dismissed much of the literature they had once hailed as timid, as lacking in revolutionary content, and as divorced from the pulse of the masses. This literature, however, can be resurrected as a powerful and artistically impressive discourse that illuminates the strains and contradictions of a liminal stratum that existed between the first world, from which it drew many of its techniques, and the third world, from which it drew childhood memories and amid which it tried to anchor its existence.

Surrealism figures prominently in my reading of this literature. As has been noted before (Bradbury and McFarlane 1976), modernism and surrealism have spread to many countries, yet each cultural setting has left its own distinctive imprint. Surrealism in France has a political programmatic edge; surrealism in Latin America luxuriates in the fantastic. In Iran surrealism generates an emotional tone which can provide access to a pervasive philosophical structuring of Iranian culture, one that plays on a tragic sense of the universe parallel to, but in a much different idiom than, the tragic sense elaborated in Iranian Shi'ism. Throughout Europe both surrealism and modernism operate on the assumption that the world has become technological and dehumanized. Iranian and Middle Eastern modernism—including, for instance, the Sudanese novel *Season of Migration to the North* by Tayeb Salih and the Pakistani film *Towers of Silence* by Jamil Dehlavi—inhabits a different context, reacting against a rigidified, fundamentalist, and patriarchal universe, a much more traditionalist enemy than that faced by European modernism.

The films and short stories produced in twentieth-century Iran formed a mode of philosophical discourse—parallel to earlier theological, mystic parable, and epic discourses—through which at least one stratum of Iranian society could debate and attempt to work through its existential problems. It is a discourse both in the sense that authors read one another and their texts comment on prior texts in this mode, and in the sense that these authors use a distinctive, surrealist style. Surrealism's juxtaposition and collage techniques—decoupage, montage, dissemination—model the modern juxtaposition of social experiences that once could only rarely meet; they present the contradictory yet emotionally powerful ties among which modern individuals must select groundings for self-identity and action; and they provide brief considerations of alternative combinations. Surrealist techniques would seem ideally suited to exploring modern dilemmas found in parts of the Middle Eastern world, more so than postmodern techniques, which have lost the sense of a traditionalist enemy. Modernist writings can open windows into Iranian society but must not be mistaken as speaking for the entire society: not only did many sectors of Iranian society object to these writings, but they had their own, quite different ways of expressing their dilemmas. Similarly, while modernist writings are informative about Iranian society, readers must not mistake fictive devices for documentary representations. The internationally acclaimed film *Gav* (The Cow) has often been described as a portrayal of village poverty, superstition, wariness of outsiders, and fatalism, but the film is much less an ethnography of village life than it is a study of pathological mourning which intimates much about both the philosophical structure of Iranian culture and the handling of emotion. Modernist discourse is not a simple and transparent one, but it is profoundly revealing. It is, moreover, a discourse similar to discourses of intelligentsias elsewhere in the modern world, both in the so-called first world and, perhaps much more interestingly, in the third world.

An investigation of these modernist discourses provides a valuable challenge (or reality check) to theories of culture which limit themselves to national or geographic boundaries; to theories of culture which posit a stable, relatively unchanging, symbolic lexicon as the core of identity; and to theories of culture which assume a unified symbol system and mode of discourse for each society. One is forced to recognize and contend with a more dynamic notion of symbolic discourse, wherein symbols are in a constant process of shedding and taking on new identifications or meanings. This process is subject to some manipulation by what the literary critic Harold Bloom would call individual "strong poets," but it is also subject to broad social and historical currents of acceptability. Authors such as Egyptian playwright Tawfiq al-Hakim or the novelist Naqib Mahfuz, who wrote wonderful revisions of ancient Greek mythologies and pharaonic heritage for a modern Middle Eastern world, found this possible in the 1930s and 1940s but quite unacceptable and intolerable in the 1960s and 1970s, when they had to turn to more Islamic settings and frameworks lest they lose their audiences. Similar patterns affected Iran and other parts of the Middle East (see Laroui 1976; Fischer 1982). One is forced to deal with societies in which there are multiple, often competing and mutually antagonistic, discourses. There are perhaps affinities here with what the literary critic Mikhail Bakhtin called the dialogic: multiple languages coexisting within a novel. Culture, for the modern anthropologist, is a kind of novel: a compendious mode containing a variety of styles. But the anthropologist is always insistent on searching out "elective affinities" between discourses, styles, or rhetorics and social groups, situations, and positions. Competitions between rhetorics often provide powerful indexes of social and class competition.

Given this approach to culture, a third-world or postcolonial poetics is not to be sought only in the products of the intelligentsia. On the contrary, their products must be juxtaposed with those of other strata, and the points of contact and disagreement traced out. While cultures are not unified symbolic structures, their parts are not disassociated structures. This chapter forms part of a larger project to map out in some ethnographic detail the competing rhetorics in Iran and by so doing to contribute to a theory of culture that is dynamic, illuminates historical and political-economic reality, and is sensitive to the hermeneutics of cultural rhetorics as seen from the inside. I have elsewhere examined the several Islamic rhetorics of Shi'ism: the more privatized philosophical and mystical understandings of the modern upper classes; the dramatically and social-ethically organized "fundamentalist" understandings which appeal to the urban petite bourgeoisie and the rural migrants into the cities; and the modernist or reformist compromises which appeal to the newly literate masses of young Iranians from traditional homes (Fischer 1980,

1982). Other chapters in the present volume examine the nationalist, pre-Islamic heritage of Iran as filtered directly through the Zoroastrian community; as filtered quite differently through the Iranian national epic, the *Shahnameh* of Firdausi; and as filtered through illuminationist philosophy.

What in the artistic discourse of the intelligentsia of the 1970s models and displays something about the culture in which they worked, that is, about others than themselves in the culture, and what reflects more about their own dilemmas? Three prefaces explore questions about audience (much of the modernist discourse was rejected by the traditional and Islamic classes and strata); about the authors and their social stratum; and about generational changes, the broad social and cultural currents which influenced the cultural texts. The chapter then analyzes a series of short stories and films, focusing in turn on the intelligentsia's dilemmas of locating themselves (1) between East and West (and as a sub-issue, between Zoroastrianism and Islam, the central ambivalence of Iranian nationalism), (b) between past and present (the alienation of modernity as refracted by the constraints of third-world positioning: political tyranny, economic distortion, religious straightjacketing, and psychic repression), and (c) between popular local culture and the modern world system, to both of which the intelligentsia and, in different ways, the other strata of society belong.

The text for the first of these three dilemmas is a film, *Towers of Silence*, that is built around the enabling metaphor of a mixed marriage between a Zoroastrian mother and a Muslim father. The film takes as its central subjects the confusions resulting from the contradictory intertwining of Muslim and Zoroastrian (or pre-Islamic heritage); the inability to escape into modernity (represented in the film by the widow of the offspring of the mixed marriage moving to New York with her son) and be free from the legacy of the past (she passes on obsessions and nightmares to the infant which ultimately bring him back to the land of his origin); and the inability to change the corrupt present by revolution. The film is marginal to the discourse of Iranian intellectuals strictly defined, but it introduces themes which obsess them in a more subtle and submerged way. This should become clear in the subsequent discussion about the central and initiating text of Iranian modernism, Sadegh Hedayat's *The Blind Owl*, which contrasts the diseased present to that more noble period of early Islam in Iran, culminating in Firdausi's epic *Shahnameh*, when Iranians actively revolted against the impositions of Islam. This is a far more involuted and difficult text than *Towers of Silence*, but it, too, is a parable of a convoluted psyche, an effort to exorcise through writing, an effort to liberate the self from the contradictory claims of the past. Hedayat, in this text and in his other short stories, created a lexicon of images which were played with by subsequent writers, thereby constituting a discourse.

In the 1960s this discourse expanded into the medium of film. Here again, ethnographic portraiture—local color, depictions of the past or of the rural—constitutes neither muckraking realism, nor utopian gestures toward a lost sense of community. Rather, such portraiture becomes projective screens on which problems can be defamiliarized and explored through powerful surrealism. They pose strange, nightmarish, or comic puzzles to the viewer, despite being dressed in realistic settings that generate a sense of familiarity with locality and tradition. The films thereby consider the dilemmas of urbanization, of claims on honor, and the handling of emotion, all issues facing the popular classes of Iran, but all with deeper philosophical and cultural import for the intelligentsia as well. The final film discussed, *Gav*, illustrates especially well how the modernist discourse of the intelligentsia and the more popular religious idioms paralleled each other but remained mutually unintelligible and mutually repugnant. Just as the modernists viewed the religious idioms as pessimistic, dead repetitions and failed to appreciate the positive power which would explode into a revolutionary movement, so, too, did the religious classes view the modernist idiom as nihilistic and fail to understand the effort of modernism to raise consciousness and explode from within the deadening and repressive force of convention and traditional repetition. Yet both drew on a pervasive Iranian philosophical sadness which could contribute a stoical sense of determination and strength, as well as a humane gentleness.

Prefaces

A story is only an outlet for frustrated aspirations, for aspirations which the storyteller conceives in accordance with a limited stock of spiritual resources inherited from previous generations.
—SADEGH HEDAYAT, *The Blind Owl*

Audiences: Class Lines

The position of the bourgeoisie and the intelligentsia come into focus more clearly when viewed first from "below" and from provincial cities. Two such cities provided homes for me in 1969–1971 and in 1975: Yazd and Qum (Fischer 1973, 1980). I begin in Yazd. The date was October 5 or, by the Iranian calendar, 13 Mehr 1969.

Defiant was how the womenfolk dressed to go to the movies. It was the opening night of a new film at Cinema Soheil. I was going with several families of the bureaucratic elite: heads of agencies. One of the men was a grandson of a famous nineteenth-century reformist minister. Another had served in a number of cities and was due to be promoted to a more important post in Ahwaz. They were not natives of Yazd. To some of the locals, they may have represented the intrusion of the state and its ideology of modernization. Locals were allowed to serve in positions no higher than deputy head of an agency, in accordance with the age-old bureaucratic principle: there must be in command a circulating elite, loyal only to the central government, without local loyalties or power bases. The state was also visibly manifest in the broad streets, which had been cut through the old twisting alleys, a surgery begun in the 1930s with some of the newer streets as yet unhealed, bizarrely lined by houses literally sliced in half such that one drove past their interiors instead of their exteriors. The state was apparent as well in the new bank buildings, the modernist railroad station (a track-laying machine brought the line through Yazd on 9 December 1970), the schools, the airport, and the statue of Mohammad Reza Shah Pahlavi on the main traffic circle, which had replaced some pretty trees and reflecting pools.

This bureaucratic elite felt embattled. Although considering themselves to be on the side of the future and of reason, and although often arrogant and patronizing toward social inferiors, few of this elite ever lost the sense of hard-fought progress against ignorance, superstition, poverty, and social inertia. Nor did they forget that they were a privileged minority. For example, the wives and daughters of the elite appeared unveiled at private receptions and parties, but dared to appear unveiled among the ordinary public only when they went in groups to the movies, protected by their menfolk. The idealism, despair, and naiveté of the bureaucratic and intellectual elite of the Pahlavi era can be appreciated only when one understands that the elite felt ethical growth and political responsibility had been perverted by both the clerics and the monarchy. Academic accounts of this despair rarely capture the sense of entrapment the elite felt at all levels—economic, political, psychological—instead minimizing it as a transitional phenomenon and dismissing it in the language of progress, modernization, and backwardness. Short stories and films, by contrast, capture and illustrate this despair in its rich complexity. In the metropole of Tehran, the despair often became diffuse and globalized, but in provincial towns such as Yazd the despair was more often focused on the conflict between past and future. There was, however, continuous cross-fertilization between the more particularistic provincial concerns and the more generalizing metropolitan perspectives, located first in the migrations of ambitious provincials to the metropole and of the circulating elite back to the provinces, second in the changing socioeconomic bases of provincial towns, and third in the expressive media of film and short stories, which circulated among audiences in both settings.

It is sociologically important to remember, however, that appeal of these genres was demarcated by social boundaries. No serious study of audience reactions to either short stories or films was conducted during the 1970s. But the clergy was conspicuously hostile to films in general, and large segments of the literate, religiously oriented intelligentsia were offended by such modernist writers as Sadegh Hedayat, not only for his antagonism toward traditionalist Islam but also for his nihilistic pessimism. Moreover, this religious reaction intensified in the 1970s, not only in Iran but throughout the Middle East; as the Moroccan social historian Abdallah Laroui (1976) pointed out, to avoid losing their audiences, writers in the 1970s had to return to Islamic themes, abandoning the pre-Islamic themes they had explored since the 1930s (see also Fischer 1982).

In Yazd hostility to the cinema was chronicled in the events surrounding the closing of the first cinema, which had been opened by a Zoroastrian in the 1930s. In the 1970s there were two functioning cinemas; a third had failed, and many Yazdis complimented themselves on not wasting time at the movies. The primary patrons of the cinema, they claimed, were non-Yazdis working in Yazd. Cinema Soheil was owned by a Zoroastrian and a Bahai, but a Muslim manager fronted for them; Cinema Mahtab was Muslim owned. Someone composed a ditty contrasting Cinema Soheil with the new Barkhorda Mosque located nearby.

> Yeki sakht masjid, yeki cinema
> Yeki gasht gom-ra, yeki rahnema
> To khod dideye aql-ra baz kon
> Tafavot bebin az koja ta koja.
> [One built a mosque, one a cinema.
> One leads astray, one guides.
> You yourself, open the eye of your reason,
> Observe the difference from whence to where.]

Haj Mohammad Husain Barkhorda was persuaded to build a mosque, rather than the hospital he had intended, as an architectural counter to the growth of a sinful part of town: the two cinemas and two cafes that served beer and arak.[1] Nonetheless, as a simple sociological survey conducted in 1974 indicated, 70 percent of Yazd's high school students chose movies as their favorite pastime (Naficy 1981, 283). Movie prices were kept low by government regulation to provide a popular entertainment outlet.

In the even more clerically dominated town of Qum the first cinema opened only in 1970 and then not in the center of town near the shrine, but across the river. The cinema burned down in 1975, possibly due to arson, and there was no hurry to rebuild it. A few religious leaders, recognizing the power of the cinema and the impossibility of denying it to the youth, urged that an alternative religious cinema be created. The popular preacher Shaikh Mohammad-Taghi Falsafi is said to have proposed this in the late 1950s or early 1960s in a public speech from the *minbar* addressed to the leading cleric of the day, Ayatullah Sayyid Husain Borujerdi. A similar debate occurred with the introduction of television. (Falsafi is fondly remembered for a double entendre riddle: what is it that rises at night and sleeps during the day in Qum as well as elsewhere? The television antenna.) By the time of the 1977–1979 revolution, control over television programming was a top priority of the religious revolutionary leadership.

In the decade 1968–1978, four hundred eighty feature films were produced in Iran (Naficy 1981, 345). Many of these were *film-i abgushti*, in American idiom "Grade B" (*ab-gusht* is the common man's stew, and these films archetypically have a scene in which the protagonist eats *ab-gusht*). But the best of the films, the "New Wave," included a number of internationally acclaimed films, beginning perhaps in 1969 with Daryoush Mehrju'i's *Gav* (The Cow), based on a "story for film" by the renowned short-story writer Gholam Husain Sa'edi. There are multiple connections between short stories and films: the latter became a kind of extension of the artistic revolution that had begun with short stories. Each provided an important arena of discussion and reflection for the new modern classes—about themselves, about their relation to other classes, and about their cultural roots.

Producers: Liminal Bourgeoisie

Betwixt and between: east and west, tradition and modernity, popular culture and elite forms of literacy, Islam and post-faith morality, anti-bourgeois (self-)critique and modernization goals in education, in individual freedom, and in political participation—such liminality is the locus of the Iranian writers and filmmakers of the Pahlavi period, and of intellectuals elsewhere in the Islamic world. It is a familiar position that modernist intellectuals have endured and used with tremendous élan throughout the modern world. It is worth recalling the general characteristics of modern intellectuals before turning to the specific contributions of Iranian and Middle Eastern writers. Writers since at least Karl Marx and Friedrich Nietzsche have pointed to this social locus as one productive of a special insight, an ability to look to two sides of a divide and through juxtaposition compare and evaluate. Literature produced in this locus has the potential both to provide illuminating cultural descriptions and to explore the tensions and problems of the contemporary historical conjuncture.

Writers (and large portions of the intelligentsia in general) find themselves to be an ambivalent stratum of the bourgeoisie. Educated and committed to bourgeois occupations and lifestyles, they also aspire to participate in older elite culture as well as in the emerging technological culture. Yet they have family and childhood ties with nonelite culture and the popular classes. The gradual decline, moreover, of aristocratic patronage for "high art" has led to dependence on middle-class audiences, to shifts in standards of artistic evaluation, and often to economic insecurity or the inability to live by art alone. This can seem like a process of quasi proletarianization, generating feelings of marginality and alienation. The writers' dilemma is compounded by their sense that the work they would prefer to do will appeal to none of their potential audiences; they are obliged to produce either what Peter Jelavich (1982) has termed "historicist elite bourgeois culture" (re-creations of the architecture, interior design, painting, and writing of previous ages) or "Trivialliteratur" (vaudeville, commercialized pop music, pulp novels), the "popular bourgeois" culture that is noncritical, nonparticipatory, and relatively banal. In the United States, the artists' dilemma is conventionally portrayed as the choice between producing art or mass culture. Art, here, is defined as work that stimulates consciousness or critical reflection, although work so represented in fact often merely serves as a commodity for status-seeking patrons. Mass culture is said to deaden critical consciousness and to encourage a false sense of community; it limits communication to the lowest common denominator and plays on infantilizing emotions that can be manipulated for commercial or political ends.[2]

In Iran the writers' dilemma in the 1970s was not yet so much a choice between art and industrially produced mass culture, as a negotiation between the demands of art and popular culture. Writers used popular culture, drawing on folk traditions and communal forms, not only for grounded renewals of art but also for artistic critiques of contemporary society.[3] In Gholam

Husain Sa'edi's portrayals of village life or Sadegh Hedayat's evocations of pre- and early Islamic Iran, the past and the rural are not cast as utopian alternatives to the present but used instead as projective screens on which problems can be defamiliarized and explored in a powerful, fictive surrealism.[4] At the same time, by using realistic settings, these fictive challenges to the imagination reinforce a sense of familiarity with and participation in locality, tradition, and the lives of the popular classes. The resulting art thus appears engagé, with the artist (the narrative voice in the story) and the people often identified or similarly portrayed as victims/opponents of bourgeois society.

This is not to say that many writers may not have genuine engagé motives or explicit political objectives, but only to separate out artistic technique as itself deserving of analysis. When one identifies the elements of artistic technique, one is no longer surprised, as so many Iranian and Western scholars have been, to find that Persian writers of the Pahlavi period proved more reformist than radical and to be relatively distant from the populist currents which achieved hegemony through the 1977–1979 revolution.[5] It is perhaps ironic that while many modernist intellectuals adopt an antibourgeois posture, they are condemned to be appreciated primarily by bourgeois audiences. But this is ironic only given aspirations or illusions of being spokesmen for the people. Otherwise, their role is a critical and crucial one: serving as a vehicle of self-critique for the dominant bourgeois class, throwing into relief not only the areas of power and economic victimization of the popular classes, but also the bourgeoisie's devilish exchange of material comfort for poverty of the soul. These modernist intellectuals provide the outsider with a wonderful window into their society as long as the outsider does not confuse their writing with the voice of the entire society.

The degree to which the ambivalent liminality of the writers of the Pahlavi period is displayed in their personal lives—writing about villagers and *bazaaris* while pursuing aggressively cosmopolitan and individualistic lifestyles themselves—remains a rich and almost untouched psychological and cultural mine, clues to which are scattered in several autobiographical sketches as well as in a few literary narratives which take as their theme the situation of Western-trained Iranians. For the present, it may suffice to mention two important Iranian polemicists who focused public attention on the negative aspects of this liminality. In the 1970s Dr. Ali Shariati popularized the French term *assimilé*, describing the consequences of the intelligentsia's alienation from its cultural roots. Shariati endorsed the views Jean-Paul Sartre expressed in his introduction to Franz Fanon's *The Wretched of the Earth*: the brightest third-world students are brought to the colonialist metropoles, emptied of their cultural values and knowledge, filled up with Western notions, then returned to their own societies as seeds for the consumption requirements of Western capitalism. A decade earlier, Jalal Al-i Ahmad had popularized the term coined by Ahmad Farid, *gharbzadegi* (West-struckness), which then entered the Persian political vocabulary.

Both Shariati and Al-i Ahmad argued that Islam had provided some protection against colonialism, avoiding some of the problems of what to them was "pagan" Africa. Shariati was to become identified with the strong faith that Islam could continue to provide a creative cultural armor for a modern technological Iran, a faith that helped fuel the 1977–1979 revolution (Fischer 1980, 154–56, 165–70). Al-i Ahmad argued in *Gharbzadegi*, a long essay published in sections between 1962 and 1964, that the educational system as well as other modern institutions of Iran were staffed by *gharbzadeh* Iranians serving the needs of Western technological domination:[6] the cinemas were merely piggy banks into which Iranians dropped coins each week to enrich Metro Goldwyn Mayer stockholders; the army consumed half the national budget allegedly to defend the borders while those very borders remained open to the invasions of profit-seeking companies; democratic political facades were designed merely to gain financial credit; women were enfranchised by a system in which voting was a farce, and they were unveiled so as to spur Western cosmetic and clothing industries, thus becoming pawns in a world in which they had no economic independence and hence no real freedom of action. Al-i Ahmad described the cities as flea markets for Western goods, edged by cancerous slums. He called for socialization of land, nationalization of industry, administration of the opinion-making media by an elected council of writers and intellectuals, and local production of the new machine technology.

Gharbzadegi condemned the mechanical age altogether, not merely the cultural alienation of intellectuals and colonialism (which Al-i Ahmad calls a two-headed, cholera-like disease: one head being the objective forces of the West, the other being "ourselves who are West-struck"). Al-i Ahmad sees fascism as the final product of the machine age: fascist parties play on the emotional derangement of human beings regimented to suit the needs of machines. Signs of the degradation of humanity include the ready-made heroes of Hollywood films and the fact that the fabrication of space heroes should center on astronauts stuffed like laboratory rabbits into nose cones while the scientists who made it all possible remain anonymous. He ends with an apocalyptic flourish, invoking Camus, Ionesco, Ingmar Bergman, Sartre, and

Nabokov: Camus's *The Plague* and Ionesco's *Rhinoceros* he "chooses" (his word) to interpret as the cholera-plague of machine domination in both East and West. Fictional endings in Sartre (Erostrate firing into a crowd), Nabakov (driving a car into a crowd), and Camus (Meursault killing a man) he sees as a sign of the End, of Resurrection: they have given up on human activity; after the age of faith comes the time of punishment; the machine demon will drop the bomb; as the Qur'an says, "The hour of Judgment is nigh and the moon is cleft asunder" (Sureh 54.1).

Not only in the essay *Gharbzadegi* but also in his career trajectory, Al-i Ahmad is an excellent illustration of the liminality of writers. Born into a religious family (his father, elder brother, and two brothers-in-law were clerics), he became a Marxist, and much of his fiction suffers from efforts at social realism, which tend to be only lightly fictionalized social commentaries, as in his novella, *The School Principal*. A follower of Khalil Maliki in the Mosaddeq era, he broke with the Moscow-linked Tudeh Party, tagging it *Hezb-i Tuti*, the "Parrot Party"; toward the end of his life (he died in 1969), he turned back increasingly to Islam. Like Shariati, whom he tried to have invited to join the Writers' Association of Iran in 1968, "against the opposition of many of the members" (Milani 1982), he called for a renewal of Islamic and Iranian culture. This call was informed by and cast in the metaphors and references of Western discourse, as was Shariati's.

The Writers' Association's opposition to Shariati was perhaps a marker of the historical changes cresting during the 1970s, and it raises questions about the relation between writing styles or themes and social forces. The writers of the sixties and seventies, though often trained in the West or holding college degrees in English literature and thus being conversant with the artistic currents of the contemporary period outside Iran, were nevertheless members of a society which had not entered fully into the mass-society formation in which America and much of Europe found themselves. Modernism, rather than postmodernism, therefore, seemed the more natural vehicle for Iranian writers. Postmodernism reflects the over-bombardment of advertising and communication which makes available such a plethora of detailed information that it exceeds the capacity to distinguish disinformation; postmodern writers therefore seek in their fiction to represent the dilemmas of constructing humane interaction or even a mere sense of plot or rationale amid total, random, or absurd access to information, and their attitude toward writing becomes one of intellectual play.[7] Modernism, by contrast, revels in the juxtaposition of what traditionally could not have come together—African masks in Parisian salons, Japanese haiku on American Indian reservations—and plays with subjective experience via dreams, autonomous writing, childhood regressions, and primitive thought interpreted as access to unrepressed humanity. But there is still a world of order which defines the juxtaposition of fragments and against which the modernist collage can act as a critique.

Over the past century there were changes within Iranian modernist styles paralleling the quite dramatic changes in political mood. Long before the 1977–1979 revolution, it was remarked in the Middle East in general that there had been a change since the 1930s, when it had been possible to speak of Islam as a force keeping the Muslim world backward. This had been the era of Ataturk in Turkey; of Taha Husain, Tawfiq al-Hakim, and the early Naqib Mahfuz in Egypt; and, in Iran, of Mohammad Ali Jamalzadeh, Sadegh Hedayat, Ahmad Kasravi, Ali Akbar Davar, and other modernists in the government, as well as Reza Shah. By the 1970s, intellectuals and politicians could not afford to take such positions, partly because the inundation of the cities with rural migrants had created a politicized mass with religious groundings. Writers turned from probes of pre-Islamic glories, which only isolated them from the general public, and turned instead to the local rural and lower-class urban environments out of which the current society was being forged. And so, for instance, the Marxist Al-i Ahmad became increasingly religious in tone, and the religious writer Shariati became the cynosure of attention.

This shift should not be dismissed as a pandering to the mob or the market, or as an indicator that writers are merely reflections of social currents. Rather one is presented with an increasingly vivid set of portraits of social practices and circumstances that are implicit moral critiques both of the elite and modern bourgeois urban milieu and of the strictures and moral turpitude of traditional ways.

Two basic questions must be asked about the modernist literature of the Pahlavi period. One, given that literature provides an inventory of social customs, practices, conflicts, what picture of Pahlavi society is portrayed: of peasants, of the bazaar, of Shi'ism, of Zoroastrianism, of self- or super-ego construction, of masques of interaction, of the possibilities of politics and of creativity? Two, given that art can transcend local conditions, although it illuminates and is grounded in local particularities, does this literature provide enduring prisms for philosophical play in the same manner that theological discourse, mystic parables, and epic poetry have done in the past? That is, is there a discourse or systematic rhetoric here, one which responds to the condition of bourgeois liminality and modern social transformation?

Generations: Themes and Styles

One might speak of two artistic revolutions during the twentieth century in Iran, one in the written media of poetry and prose, and a second in the visual medium of film. The first began roughly with fin de siècle agitations for a constitutional revolution.[8] Poetry was invested with political themes and social criticism; to do this poets broke the centuries-old bonds of genre forms and stylized language.[9] Then prose broke its bonds: in 1921 Sayyid Mohammad Ali Jamalzadeh issued a collection of short stories with a call for the use of simple colloquial language and for the use of fiction as a vehicle for social criticism. Gradually, over the next half century, the short story became a major artistic medium.[10]

Both poets and short-story writers made a self-conscious attempt to establish a new mode of discourse. In the aesthetically less-successful efforts this discourse often resulted in purely political or sociological commentary. In the aesthetically more-successful efforts writers found new means of formulating images through which changes in Persian life could be comprehended and integrated. Such works achieved a poetic power which might (or might not) also carry a political message but which was nuanced and worthy of sustained contemplation, portraying the dynamics of Persian social interaction and thereby providing insight rather than mere complaint.

The debate about a new mode of discourse is not itself a new theme of Persian literature. The twentieth-century prose innovator Jamalzadeh invoked, somewhat recklessly, a couplet from the tenth-century poet Farrokhi Sistani, which out of context sounds progressive.

Fasaneh gozasht kohan shod
hadith Eskendar
Sokhan navar ke no-ra
halavati ast digar
[Old myths have worn out
the story of Alexander.
Word strings which are new
are henceforth sweeter.]

But it was Farrokhi's contemporary, Firdausi, with his attempt to write a pure Persian poetry without Arabic loanwords, who pioneered something new, rather than Farrokhi, who was condemned by Persian nationalists for his sycophancy toward Mahmud of Ghazni. So, too, in the contemporary debate, mere imitations of Western forms have limited audiences. Interest and power accrues rather to those who can draw on the past in novel ways to renew the spirit. Hence the power in the poetry of Mehdi Akhavan Sales, for instance, whose poem "Khaneh Hashtom va Adamak" (The Eight Trials [of Rustam] and the Doll) combines a modern verse style, ancient mythical figures as analogues for contemporary dilemmas, and the emotional recall and music of the old coffeehouse reciters of the *Shahnameh*. Sadegh Hedayat's prose has a similar power. Literary power depends on deeply embedded, often tacit, layers of allusion as well as on novel forms. In the contemporary debate Islamic traditionalists condemn not only foreign borrowings but also efforts to examine non-Islamic currents in Iranian identity. Denials of both sources of creativity can only lead to desiccation and brittle decay, against which the roshan fekran (intelligentsia) revolted.

The second artistic revolution—film—extended the artistic endeavor of the revolution in the written media, offering a greater capacity for dynamic portrayal and greater potential for reaching wider audiences. More directly and efficiently than short stories, film can show how people learn and adjust, how through interaction both actor and situation can be transformed. Film does this with a visual simulation of realism and immediacy that can be less demanding on the audience's critical abilities while at the same time more lavish with persuasive detail. A new wave of sophisticated Iranian films began in the late 1960s with *Showhar-i Ahu Khanum* (Ahu's Husband [1969]), *Gav* (The Cow [1969]), *Qaisar* (1969), *Agha-ye Halu* (Mr. Gullible [1970]), *Tangsir* (1972), *Moghul-ha* (The Mongols [1973]), *Shazdeh Ehtejab* (Prince Ehtejab [1974]), and *Dayereh Mina* (The Cycle [1974]).

Readings

Two "texts," a film and a novella, introduce well the Iranian vocabulary of surrealist modernism and themes of East versus West, past and present, and the artistic enterprise. Not only is the novella, *The Blind Owl* by Sadegh Hedayat, one of the most well-known of modern Persian literary works and perhaps the most analyzed and discussed, but it is also central to the modernist endeavor in Iran both in its technique and in its imagery. Published originally in Calcutta, it draws on Indian imagery and Western narrative techniques, thus standing as a challenge to those Iranians (and foreigners) who would restrict Iranian culture to Iran's political boundaries. The film,

Towers of Silence by Jamil Dehlavi, a Pakistani, while peripheral to the artistic discourse of Iran in the strict sense, parallels that discourse in style and problematic. Moreover, it presents the dialectic between Zoroastrian and Muslim in a particularly clear manner and poses the questions of East versus West better than any Persian literary work to date—and perhaps as well as any modern work in the Middle East. Both substantive issues pervade Iranian writing in subtle and indirect ways. This film serves, from the periphery of Persian culture, as an illumination of issues which were more difficult to express directly in the center.[11]

East and West: *Towers of Silence*

Signs ought to present themselves only in two extreme forms: either openly intellectual and so remote that they are reduced to an algebra as in the Chinese theater, where a flag on its own signifies a regiment; or deeply rooted, invented, so to speak, on each occasion, revealing an internal, hidden fact, and indicative of a moment in time, no longer of a concept.—ROLAND BARTHES, "The Romans in Films," in *Mythologies*

When the past and the rural in modernist story and film are used as projective screens on which problems can be defamiliarized and explored in powerful, fictive surrealisms, this device is often a double play: while there is an intellectual casting of strange, nightmarish puzzles, realistic settings within these puzzles generate a sense of familiarity with locality and tradition. The techniques of surrealism are best understood in light of allegedly realist issues, such as the relation of the modern educated man, or the Westernized man, to his traditional setting.

The primary form of such questions has been the essay rather than film or story. Essays by Frantz Fanon (1961/1968), Albert Memmi (1957/1976), Octave Mannoni (1950/1956), Abdallah Laroui (1974/1976), as well as the Iranians Ali Shariati (1978, 1979) and Jalal Al-i Ahmad (1961b, 1982) have framed a series of questions about alienation, formation of colonial or dominated mentalities, and the dynamics of cultural settings on styles of resistance by the oppressed. A few novels have lightly fictionalized these discussions, but few works of art have molded them into a sufficiently powerful enough form to take on a life of their own in the imagination.[12] One such work of art, in the film medium, does manage to present such an imaginative puzzle about the relation between East and West, fused, as is so often the case, with the relation between past and present and with the religious competitions of the Middle East.

Towers of Silence (1975) takes as its central subject the confusion resulting from the contradictory intertwining of Zoroastrian and Muslim; the inability to escape into modernity from the legacy of the past; and the inability to change the corrupt present through revolution. The play of Zoroastrian and Muslim integrates the film within the concerns of Persian cultural dilemmas. Historically, the northern parts of the Indian subcontinent have been intimately interrelated with Iran, not only by the migration of Zoroastrians and others from Iran but also by the strong cultural role of Persian language and culture under the Mughuls. However, the influence of the Persian cultural arena on Pakistan matters less here than the nature of the themes and techniques of the film.

Towers of Silence is structured through the consciousness of a young woman, now wife to a goateed New Yorker, widow of a son of a mixed marriage—a Zoroastrian mother who had died when he was five and a Muslim revolutionary father who had been shot by soldiers a few years later—and mother to the infant son of the latter. It is the dead lover who dominates the film through her memories and through her fears for his child. The psychic dilemma of this dashing, mustachioed young man is portrayed as a dual oedipal one: he rejects his father's Islamic dogmas, yet is condemned to repeat his father's fruitless revolutionary life and violent death; he searches for his mother (the same actress plays his mother dressed in white and his lover dressed in black), yet he attempts, unsuccessfully, to use her tradition to protect his criminal or political activities. Neither rejection of the past nor repetition of it, neither revolution nor religion are portrayed as escapes from the corruption of human life. The only signs of purity and renewal of hope are in the eternal cycle of nature, from the cry of the newborn infant to the cry of the vultures who clean away the impure remains of humanity to the vast waves of the sea which bring pregnant turtles to lay their eggs on land and wash away the dead and decaying of the earth. And yet, fears the young widow in New York, her infant son does not start afresh and free from his father's legacy.

The film's surrealistic juxtapositions—drawing on powerful scenes of funeral rites, love, childhood, political conflict, religious dogma—create in the viewer the same confusion of selecting groundings for self-identity and action that confront the individual in contemporary Iranian or Pakistani society. The individual is confronted with emotionally powerful and clear ties, which may be contradictory among themselves or only partially integrated into any holistic conception of self and purpose. Such is the modern dilemma, which film and short story, as brief considerations of alternative combinations, are well suited to explore.

The film may be divided into three movements: (1) New York and the young woman's memories and fantasies while making love, rushing home to her infant, and writing her memoirs; (2) a surrealistic interval internal to her memories, which are less products of her direct experience than of her dead lover's memories as he told them to her; (3) a conclusion constructed out of a tragic fortune told for her child and of her memories of his father's death.

Close Reading

In art as in science there is no delight without the detail, and it is on the details that I have tried to fix the reader's attention.
—VLADIMIR NABOKOV, *Speak, Memory*

Credits. We hear the clicking of the printing presses. We see a dustjacket rolling through them. The dustjacket pictures a veiled woman: a chadri veil with an open mesh so we can make out her nose and eyes. The title on the dustjacket is that of the film, *Towers of Silence*. In the background, we now hear, is the soft chant of the Avesta, the Zoroastrian scripture. As the picture shifts to birds high in the air, the woman's voice muses, "The vultures sweep earthwards to perform their funereal duties, solemn high priests of Ahura Mazda, engendering the purification of the world." A dedication—"To my father"—appears on the screen while the woman's voice continues: "No one knows where they come from or where they go to next. In the towers of silence the vultures gnaw on your soul. The little dog with four eyes was made to slit the face of your mother." There appears the profile of a woman's face framed in a black sari, worn Muslim style, with the hair covered. The woman's voice concludes, "And the evil spirit was exorcised." (Note the incongruities already juxtaposed: maternal voice, paternal dedication; Muslim photo, Zoroastrian title.)

Movement 1, Scene 1. [Zoroastrian funeral rites.] We see the face of a bearded Zoroastrian priest. A small boy peers in the window. The priest sits cross-legged by the corpse of the woman whose profile we have just seen. The boy watches. A second priest enters holding a four-eyed dog (with white spots above the eyes), bringing it to view the corpse (to affirm its death, to see into the other world and scare off the demons of impurity, the *droj-nesa*): this is the *sag-did* funerary rite. The corpse is then carried on a metal stretcher (metal does not transmit impurity) by four bearers connected to one another by *peyvands* ("connectors" made of the kusti, or sacred girdle of seventy-two threads) so that no individual faces the impurity of a corpse alone. Eight men follow behind in pairs. The boy follows.

Scene 2. Vultures converge on the tower of silence. The boy follows them. He tries the door to the round tower of silence. It is locked. He looks up at the birds sitting on a nearby tree. As a woman's voice sings a wordless, wailing tune, the boy climbs the tree to look over the wall into the round enclosure. The woman (his mother), naked, is laid out amid bones and a skull covered with ants. A young mustachioed man (the boy as an adult) approaches her in a dreamlike slow motion. He is naked; they embrace, and he begins to kiss her, she to caress his head. Suddenly there is a piercing cry of the vultures, which turns into the cry of a baby. The woman looks up, opening her eyes, and the camera moves back from the close-up of the lovers' heads, revealing them in bed. The man is an older, goateed male. She rises to go to the infant. Above the cradle hangs a toy white dove (contrasting with the black vultures). The man goes to the bathroom to wash his face. She enters. There is silence. She says, "I am sorry." He relents, comes to embrace her, and says, "I want you to treat this child as if it were my own." (Thus far, most of the major characters have been introduced in their merging and diverging aspects: the two children, the two husbands, the two women.)

Scene 3. The woman, now in her black sari, approaches the tower of silence. There is Indian instrumental music (sitar and tabla). A jeep is parked by the tower, and a dwarf with malformed feet stands in the tower's doorway. Birds fly overhead. A lizard or chameleon is on a tree. (The chameleon, perhaps, confirms to the viewer that the merging, diverging ambivalences of the characters are intentional; after all, all the women are played by the same actress. Perhaps, as well, the chameleon refers to the age-old Iranian dismissive tag for Arabs and Muslims: lizard-eaters. The tree, in any case, is a repetition of the tree on which the boy was climbing.) As the woman walks past the jeep, she sees crates in the back. The dwarf motions her away from the tower of silence. A male voice says, "It is forbidden to enter. It's an abandoned tower of silence, sacred burial ground for Zoroastrians." She approaches the young man leaning against the jeep and asks, "Is this where corpses are left to be devoured by vultures? It's grotesque." He replies, "You speak in ignorance. The vultures are divine ministers who strip the flesh. The skeleton is dried by the sun and thrown into a well, where it gradually crumbles into dust. Rich and poor meet on a level of equality after death. My mother was laid to rest here." The young man takes her for a ride in the jeep.

Scene 4. There is a cry of vultures, a flashed image of a baby in a playpen, a vulture perched on its railing. The woman, now dressed in white, looks up at the birds in the sky above a New York street. In a panic she hails a cab. There is a driving tabla beat with sitar music. An image flashes: driving in the jeep through a flock of large vultures. In the cab the woman bites her thumb with anxiety. She jumps out of the cab and runs into a building, up spiral stairs (perhaps tracing the roundness of a tower of silence), dropping her bag in her hurry, past a round window through which she peers down, again seeing the vulture perched on the child's playpen. She rushes down to the room below. The baby smiles and waves—there is no vulture. She picks the baby up. The music subsides.

Scene 5. Back to Karachi: the young man and woman continue driving in the jeep through a lower-class area on the outskirts of town. She says, "Tell me about your childhood." He obliges, saying, "I was born here. My father was in the army. He was a Muslim. My mother was from a Zoroastrian family. They fell in love. It was quite a scandal. Zoroastrians don't tolerate marriage outside their own community. A few years after I was born, they divorced, and she went back to her parents. She died when I was five. After that I went to live with my father for a while. One day he disappeared." They come to the seashore; birds fly over a ruined building. They walk toward a small house and enter it. "This is where I saw my father for the last time." The walls facing the sea are curved (perhaps like those of a tower of silence), while the walls away from the sea have corners (perhaps symbolizing the crookedness of life versus the purifying infinity of death). They kiss.

Scene 6. The young man runs through a tunnel toward some stairs, his back to the camera. The birds are flying in the sky. A black-and-white feather floats in the air across the screen. The woman's hand caresses the young man with the feather; he is lying face down. As she moves the feather from his arms toward his shoulder one sees a bullet-hole/inkwell in his left shoulder. She dips the quill into it and writes on his shoulder, "the bird." The camera zooms in on the writing, then recedes. She is now writing on a piece of paper at a desk in a study: "The bird sings with its fingertips." The older goateed man enters in a dark suit and takes the pen from her. She picks up her sheaf of papers; he grabs them and tosses them away.

Movement 2, Scene 7. Back at the beach, outside the house by the sea, the young man begins to explain Zoroastrianism to her. "In the beginning there existed twin spirits who represented good and evil. Both possess creative power. Ahura Mazda is life and light, and Ahriman darkness and death. Although nature is divided and rent asunder by two conflicting principles,

"The bird sings
with its fingertips"
Memory: wife-mother
with quill (*Towers
of Silence*)

man is free to choose and will bring about the ultimate triumph of good and the overthrow and annihilation of evil." Suddenly two soldiers kick in the door of the little house. The boy and his father are inside, the father seated and writing, the boy watching. The soldiers say to the father, "You are under arrest." The father seizes a gun and tries to shoot but is instead shot. The boy squats by his father, who still holds the gun in his hand, then rises and runs away toward the sea, along the rocks (a partial repetition of the running in scene 6 and later in scene 18).

Scene 8. Sunset. The moon. A sea turtle comes out of the sea and slowly crawls up the sand to lay her eggs. The boy watches. She returns to the sea. The boy digs up ten eggs. He picks up one and squeezes it: it breaks. A dark liquid (blood, ink) runs out. The moon clouds over.

Scene 9. Nighttime rendezvous. In the little house the young man rises from the cot and takes a lantern out into the night to the jeep. A second vehicle arrives. The deformed dwarf and another man get out. The young man goes to the back of the jeep, opens a crate, takes out a machine gun, and carries it to them. He returns to the woman in the house. She is wrapped in a white sheet. She turns out the lantern.

Scene 10. Dawn. The woman stands by a window. The young man sleeps on the cot, a fly crawling on his arm, another on his forehead. The little boy looks at a fly he has in a small wooden cage. He also has a jar of flies. He takes the cage to the wash basin, fills the basin with water, and puts the cage in. His father enters, looks at what the boy is doing, says nothing, proceeds to the toilet, and urinates. He leaves without a word and without flushing. The boy goes to look at the toilet. It is crawling with ants. Crowd noise. The image is flashed of the skull covered with ants in the tower of silence. A dog barks hysterically. A black dog, foaming at the mouth, is outside the window of the house by the sea and barks at the woman. The young man awakens; quietly and deliberately, in slow motion, he gets a gun from the same shelf from which his father had picked up a gun and shoots the dog.

Scene 11. The camera moves to the dog; it is no longer the dark, scruffy, rabid dog but a well-kept white one which writhes in agony. The camera follows the path of the bullet back from whence it came: it is now the father holding the gun, not the young man. By his side is the little boy with a look of dismay. The father leads the boy away. The father and boy are seated on a carpet facing each other, each with a Qur'an on a book-holder before him, each wearing a white cap. The father chants beautifully in Arabic the Ayeh Julud (Skins Verse) from Sureh 4.55: "Surely those who disbelieve in Our signs—We shall certainly roast them at a fire; as often as their skins are wholly burned, We shall give them in exchange other skins, that they may taste the chastisement" (Arberry translation, 1964, 80). The father then says to the boy, "You grieve for a rabid dog. The Prophet has said the saliva of the dog is unclean. Allah sends dogs to hell." The boy takes off his hat, closes his Qur'an, gives it back to his father, and runs out.

(The revulsion of the half-Zoroastrian boy is the inverse of the revulsion of the young Muslim woman in scene 3; what is purification to one is abomination to the other. Note also, however, the further aptness of the Ayeh Julud to the theme of repetition as becomes clearer when, in the final scene, the soldiers change only their uniforms, with son repeating father, with the association of the cry of the vulture and that of the child at both the beginning and the end of the film. Repetition is an ambiguous motif, colored to some extent by the viewer's own background, something the ayeh perhaps also helps elicit. Preliminary observations among Iranian viewers indicate that Muslim believers, initially at least, tend to reject the film as another of the profoundly fatalistic works of art produced by those who have lost their faith and confidence in Islam; the motif of repetition for them is strongly negative: change is only skin deep, contemporary existence is hell. More secular viewers and those more attuned to Zoroastrian values see the theme of repetition as the positive perennial struggle that each generation and each individual must choose in the fight against evil. As the young man says in scene 7, "Although nature is divided and rent asunder by two conflicting principles, man is free to choose and will bring about the ultimate triumph of good and the overthrow and annihilation of evil.")

Scene 12. Carrying the white dog in his arms, the boy exits the gates of his father's city house and follows the road out of town, bringing the dog to the desert vultures. A wailing, wordless, female vocal repeats the sound background of scene 2, when the boy climbs the tree; but this time it is softer. The boy passes the same kind of cactus plants as were by the tower of silence in scene 2. The vultures are almost in formation to receive his offering. They are feasting on a carcass of a cow. A human skull lies on the ground, further reinforcing the correspondence with the tower of silence. The woman in black sari walks among the vultures. They scramble to perform their duty of stripping the polluting and decaying flesh. The woman raises her arms straight out, like a vulture in flight. The birds rise from their task and take flight, leaving behind the clean skeleton of a cow. A dog walks in the background.

Scene 13. The seashore: the woman in black sari stands by the ruins. A black-and-white calf lies dead on the shore. A wave washes over it, removes it, and leaves the beach clean. In the background, in a lively cantillation, a male voice sings, "Allah-hu, Allah" [God is great, God].

Movement 3, Scene 14. A dwarf, not the one with the deformed legs, stops the jeep with the young man and woman. He points along the seashore. The young man nods. The dwarf runs ahead. As the jeep proceeds along the road, the woman looks at herself in the rearview mirror.

Scene 15. A woman's voice murmurs in an echo-chamber, slowly becoming more distinct: "I see a distant land. Something hidden. Something unresolved. Time. Confused. The tapestry of dreams." Tarot-style cards appear on the screen, marked "Knight of the Swords," "The Tower," "Death," "The Hanged Man." The speaker is revealed to be a fortune-teller, and she now says distinctly, "I see successive revolutions perpetuating a corrupt system. There is a dark man struggling against the dark forces of oppression. I see for him a violent death. You bore his child. I see him returning to his place of birth. I hear the rush of wings." The baby cries; he lies on the fortune-teller's table. His mother kisses a book. The fortune-teller lays out her gruesome cards of men tied to stakes.

Scene 16. As the jeep drives through the street on the outskirts of town toward a village, the male cantillation repeats, "Allah-hu, Allah." There is a crowd in the village. The young man gets out, followed by the woman, now in the chadri veil. They go to a storage shed. The dwarf shows the young man an ammunition shell. The image flashes to munitions machinery. We hear the sound of presses (like the printing presses in the credits) stamping out bullets.

Scene 17. They drive back into town in the jeep to a munitions factory. The young man gets out and says, "Wait for me. There are instructions I have to give the workers." There are more images and sounds of the munitions presses. Solo tabla percussion accompanies the young man as he walks through a storage yard and past the machinery making bullets. Suddenly two soldiers (the same two from scene 7) step before him and say, "You are under arrest." The young man knocks them out with two quick karate chops. Then he calmly takes a gun from one of their hands and shoots them.

Scene 18. The sitar and tabla music wells up in a wild beat (as in scene 4). The deformed dwarf runs up the steps to the tower of silence. The young man drives the jeep with the corpses in the rear. He gets out at the tower of silence, finds the door unlocked. Inside, the dwarf lies dead next to some wooden crates (like those in scene 9), the machine gun by his side; he has been shot in the right shoulder. The young man returns to the jeep to unload the dead soldiers. The woman looks behind him; he turns. The two soldiers appear, this time in darker uniforms. He runs across the dunes. The soldiers shoot. The woman in black sari appears before him with open arms. He is shot in the left shoulder (as in scene 6). Cries of vultures; the cry of the infant; image of the infant palms clasped together; Avestan chant Ashem Vohu.

The film is structured through repetitions, juxtapositions, traditional symbols, color coding, and shifting memories. The young woman's consciousness and the symbolism unify the film, textured by the interplay of her own remembered experiences, memories related to her by her dead mate, and her fears for her child. The color codings, black and white, resonate with death and life, evil and good, but they are binary structuring devices rather than simple signs: the young woman in Karachi is dressed in black in relation to her mustachioed lover, but she is white in relation to her goateed New York mate; the same actress plays the mustachioed young man's mother dressed in white and his lover dressed in black. So, too, black and white establish or reinforce the relationship between the rabid dog and the white dog; the light of day versus the dark of nocturnal revolutionary activity; the white eggs, moon, and skeletons versus the black ink, blood, vultures, ants, and flies; motherhood and renewal versus death and nightmarish repetition.

Ink and blood, memory and heredity, link the generations. The film opens with the presses (ink) and the veiled woman (psychic repression). Woman is the carrier of both repression and renewal: she represents motherhood; it is she who moves to New York; and it is her memories and memoir-writing which are recounted. The film opens with death (a funeral) and ends with birth (the cry of the infant). So, too, the middle section of the film opens with sunset and death and ends with purification. Life and death are always associated: there is continuity, continuous struggle. Ink and blood, art and life, are also fluids of alternating and competitive importance for constituting the future. A hadith of the Prophet says, "The ink of the scholars is superior to the blood of the martyrs."

Among the structuring symbols of the film are the animals. The dog—a sacred companion and ritual helper to Zoroastrians, an object of impurity to Muslims—is a traditional symbol, which Dehlavi (like Sadegh Hedayat) uses to critique Islamic dogma.[13] The dog appears first in its role in the Zoroastrian funeral rite. The boy's father's cruel killing of a white (pure) dog because "the Prophet said the saliva of a dog is unclean and Allah sends dogs to hell" causes the boy to reject his Islamic training and contrasts with his later (in the film, earlier) mercy-killing of a rabid dog.[14] The boy takes the corpse of the white dog into the desert for the vultures, and there, too, a dog is ritually present. In Zoroastrian ritual the dog is able to see into the other world, to determine when life has finally left the dying man, and to keep the demons of impurity at bay.

The vulture, too, is a traditional symbol. Zoroastrians have no use for bodily remains, considering them to be the most impure things in the world; they believe it an act of generosity and purification to donate the remains to the vulture. By eating the dead, the vultures recycle dead matter into living matter, cleansing the earth of impure, decaying matter and perpetuating the cycle of cosmic continuity. For Muslims, great quantities of water are purifying, and Dehlavi, with minor liberties, uses the sea (rather than fresh water) as an Islamic image of cleansing (the chant of "Allah-hu, Allah" accompanies the image of the sea washing away the corpse of a calf). Dehlavi fuses the

Zoroastrian and Muslim images of cleanliness by juxtaposition: the boy brings the white dog to the vultures who rise up from the skeleton of a cow; then we see the dead calf washed by the sea.

The birds sitting in the tree in scenes 2 and 3 also play on the motif of the two birds of paradise in the tree of life. In the early (Rig Vedic) Indian tradition the bird who eats the tree's fruit achieves transcendence; the later traditions of the Upanishads it is the bird who abstains who achieves transcendence. Zoroastrian tradition is always closest to the Rig Vedic tradition. One ascends the tree of life in hopes of "breaking through the sky" and achieving transcendental understanding. By eating this worldly shell, the vultures release the soul for its journey (often imagined in Zoroastrian texts and Persian poetry as the flight of the bird). Transcendence is achieved also through memory: the young woman writes with a bird feather, "The bird sings with its fingertips."

According to Zoroastrianism, small insects, ants, and flies are unclean, although as long as they are alive, they are generally regarded with indifference; larger insects, beetles, wasps, and tarantulas are killed intentionally as they are considered creatures of Ahriman. According to Islam, insects are clean (they have no gushing blood) and are even cleansing (they are among the *motahharat*, or cleansing agents, in the section on *enteqal*, or transformation, in Islamic purity codifications: should a Muslim praying in a mosque kill a mosquito on his arm and his own blood appear as a result, he need not renew his ablution because that blood is clean). In the film, ants and flies are thus ambivalently associated with corpses, urine, torture, and nocturnal revolutionary action. The young boy contains and kills flies, and the scene with his father in the bathroom foreshadows his rejection of the latter's Islamic doctrine. Ants are associated with the skulls in the tower of silence and with the flies crawling on the young man who is sleeping after his nocturnal gun running. The association of crowd noise with ants signals the masses, valuing them negatively. Young Pakistani viewers interpret the father with his fancy house as an ousted member of a previous coup, and the film as a saga of corrupt elite politics in which the son, too, is fatally caught.

The lizard/chameleon also plays a dual function. While representing Firdausi's famous tag "lizard-eating Arab," the chameleon expresses the transformations of son/man, mother/lover, modern New York/traditional Karachi, rejection/repetition. It is a surrealist symbol par excellence (ambivalences, transformations), but it retains its warning of evil: lizards belong with snakes as creatures of Ahriman. The chameleon thus introduces the dark, underground, doomed revolutionary motif.

The turtle is another ambivalent traditional figure. It lives between land and sea (dual-habitated: Persian, *dozist*; Arabic, *zu-hayatin*); it abandons its eggs. In the didactic fables of childhood it stands for endurance and patience (tortoise versus hare) and humility (in a variant story the turtle beats the overly proud reindeer who gets his antlers caught). But the turtle shell is also a cursed result of unclean dealings or stinginess. In one tale a little girl aiding her mother making dough is caught cracking her lice on the side of the bread bowl; her mother in anger picks up the bowl and dumps the sticky dough onto the little girl's back and curses her, "May you remain like this." A variant has the little girl refusing a request for bread from Imam Ali, and so he curses her.

In the film the turtle scene is powerful and visually lyrical. Its meaning is established by its position in the film, following as it does the scene in which the young man explains Zoroastrian ethics to his lover at the house by the sea. "In the beginning there existed twin spirits, good and evil. . . . [M]an is free to choose." A flashback shows two soldiers shooting the father and the boy's dash to the sea, juxtaposing death, renewal of youth, the cleansing sea. Then comes the turtle scene: sunset (death), the moon (reflected light, the son as a reflection of the father), the sea turtle emerges to lay her eggs (renewal), the boy digs up the eggs and breaks one, ink/blood runs out, the moon clouds over (ensnared in life's corruption). There follows a scene of the young man engaged in revolutionary activity; as he sleeps after his nighttime (dark, corrupt) foray, he is covered with flies. A flashback shows him as a boy playing with flies, his father's urination crawling with ants, the skull in the tower of silence crawling with ants. A bark (chasing away evil?) awakens the young man, and he shoots the rabid dog. A flashback juxtaposes the father killing the white dog, the revulsion of the boy, and his purifying rite of disposing the corpse (cleansing, renewal).

This use of juxtaposition to create a chain of meaningful association and movement works throughout the film. The scene in which the father dies at the hands of the soldiers also involves a view of him writing at a table. The preceding scene is the striking one of the woman using the surrealist feather/quill to caress (remember) the young man, then to dip into the inkwell of his bullet wound and write, "the bird." This is followed by a view of her in New York writing, "The bird sings with its fingertips" (vultures cleanse with claws and beaks; quills record/sing with their inked tips). The ink/blood imagery is the unifying thread, appearing again at the end of the film when the young man is shot in the left shoulder.

The theme of repetition, the struggle between inability to escape the legacy of the past and the hope of renewal through a new generation brings the film to a close. The goateed man attempts to stop the woman from recording, from obsessing about the past. At the beginning of the film he says, "I want you to treat this child as if he were my own." Later he attempts to destroy her memoirs, perhaps so that the child might have a chance at a new uncomplicated life in the New World. This is an unrealistic hope. The psychic fears have been shown to be strong: the woman's panicked rush to the child in the crib to save him from the vulture. She holds the infant in her arms—an image repeated after the turtle and the dog sequences—and has his fortune told. "Men struggle against repression, but successive revolutions perpetuate a corrupt system. I see a young man struggling who meets a violent death. You bore his child. I see him returning to his place of birth."

This surrealist black-and-white film does not end on a note of despair. On the contrary, it ends with the cries of the vultures (cleansing), the child (hope), and the sound of the *Avesta* (the call for a struggle on behalf of goodness, truth, and justice). But it is a cautious, realistic tone, full of a contemporary sense of confusion and ambiguity. The ability to combine and juxtapose the tenacious, yet odd and conflicting fragments of the past is one of the marks of the modern consciousness captured in contemporary film (and short story).

Past and Present, Art and Psyche: *The Blind Owl*

This secret self-ravishment, this artistic cruelty, this lust to impose form on oneself . . . cauterizing into oneself a will, a criticism . . . this uncanny, weirdly enjoyable labor of a voluntarily divided soul making itself suffer . . . this whole, active 'bad conscience' . . . is the true womb of all ideal and imaginative experience.—FRIEDRICH NIETZSCHE, *On the Genealogy of Morals*

One of the key texts of modern Persian literature is Sadegh Hedayat's *The Blind Owl* (1937), a short novella so powerful it is said to have triggered a series of suicides when it was published.[15] In technique and theme it clearly belongs to the same universe of discourse as Dehlavi's film. It is, however, much richer and, on reflection, more positive. It is, perhaps, also more easily misunderstood, particularly by those many Iranians who find it merely pessimistic and despair inducing. Hedayat eventually committed suicide himself (in 1951 in Paris), acting out in life the killing of many of his literary protagonists. All of these deaths may be read as calls to action, as a rousing from the sloth and living death of his contemporaries. Many of his literary colleagues finally understood this, and much of prerevolutionary Persian literature not only resonated with the imagery of Hedayat's stories but continued to use his device of portraying Iran as diseased, a drugged dream, a progressive decay which can and must be thrown off.

It is the quest for the key to health and beauty, for which Hedayat probes in Iran's cultural heritage, that makes his work positive, inspired and inspiring. If one considers the entire corpus of his writing—his collection of folklore, his use of folklore in his stories, his essays on ancient Iran, his bitter satires of current decay—one sees the lover, not a suicide. The unprepared reader may be alarmed by Hedayat's searing, painful plumbing into the depths of the Iranian soul. And yet, despite his hostility to Arabs, Hedayat constructs his stories from a remarkably cosmopolitan range of technique and imagery, revealing an Iranian self-confidence and openness to the world which displays the beauty of Iranian culture, in striking contrast to the diseased, insecure chauvinism of those who would deny the value of anything nonnative or non-Islamic. This latter path, says the work of Hedayat, leads to isolation, narcissistic obsession, and spiritual death.

The engagé writer Jalal Al-i Ahmad detected the positive message of Hedayat. Hedayat was for him a child of the Constitutional Revolution—an era of euphoria and new beginnings—whose hopes for a new Iran had been dashed first by the dictatorship of the 1930s and then by the restored dictatorship in the post–World War II period, both eras portrayed by the engagé writers as times of tyranny, misery, corruption, and deceitful dealings. Al-i Ahmad, while recognizing the dialogic nature of *The Blind Owl*—a conversation with the self in search of recollections and meaningful introspections—nonetheless draws attention to details which reflect, rather superficially, the tyranny and deceitfulness of the times: drunken policemen come and go, people turn from serious social engagement to introversion, characters are unable to be forthright and therefore hide behind multiple masks. For Al-i Ahmad, Hedayat's descriptions thus constitute a protest against political tyranny and obscurantist religion. (The narrator in *The Blind Owl* repeatedly finds religion of little use, childish, at best recreational for the healthy but not for the spiritually ill.) This is a valid, if superficial, reading of *The Blind Owl*.[16]

The Blind Owl is a finely crafted story, and by turning to its techniques one may better appreciate Hedayat's positive message. The novella parallels Dehlavi's *Towers of Silence* in a number of telling ways; it is almost as if Dehlavi, like so many Iranians, was attempting a commentary on, update of, or dialogue with Hedayat. Both employ similar surrealist techniques of juxtaposition, repetition, alternation between two time settings, and merging/splitting of leading male and female characters. They use similar narrative vehicles of searching for absent parents and of flawed marriages (a mixed marriage ending in divorce in one case; quasi incestuous marriages in the other). They similarly engage violence (revolution in one case; murder in the other) and death (vultures in one case; blister flies and maggots in the other). They even share a few symbols: ink/blood as poisoned/exorcising links between generations; the dog as able to see into the other world; cosmic trees of life; birds of the soul; mirrors (the woman in Dehlavi's film frequently looks at her own image in the rearview [retrospective] mirror of the jeep; Hedayat's narrator has a mirror in his room and sees his wife's eyes as accusatory mirrors).

Hedayat's story, like Dehlavi's, is symbolic on several levels. In the most obvious sense, Hedayat treats writing as therapy, as clarification, as making sense: a man kills his wife and must somehow retell the story in order to relieve his obsessive guilt. The Persian genre is *dard-e del* (pain of the heart), that is, telling the tale to a trusted confidant in order to relieve the psychological pressure. A Persian proverb says that talking is the bloodletting of the heart or soul and that remaining silent will surely lead to insanity (*dard-e del hajamat-i del ast*). As in Dehlavi's story, so also in Hedayat's the sins of the current generation are not original: the murderer's mother was loved by both his father and his father's brother; he himself was forced by old codes of honor to marry his father's sister's daughter, with whom he had been suckled (those who suckle together may not marry, for that would be incest). The first layer of meaning, then, points to the exorcism of an obsession, to writing in order to regain sanity, to establishing a narrative sequence and thus coherence out of confusion. As with Dehlavi's tale, the reader/viewer does this along with Hedayat's protagonist.

The second level is oedipal both in its sexual metaphorization and, perhaps more significantly, in its struggle for self-knowledge and mastery over the dark forces of the psyche or soul. The story is of a boy/man or repressed Middle Eastern male who cannot seem to establish a healthy sexual relationship with a live woman and so regresses into fantasies of revenge against the castrating bitch/whore. Only as a corpse, a lifeless object, or with closed (spiritless) eyes does the woman surrender to the repressed male, and he seems able to possess her only through a violence which destroys the beloved. There are fleeting exceptions: when he succeeds in drawing her portrait, for instance, and when he acknowledges her intelligence; but these are insubstantial and provocatively frustrating satisfactions. Hedayat's protagonist hides behind male codes of purity and honor as justifications for his failures and dilemmas.

For Freud, and for Hedayat as well, the oedipal metaphor does not simply express repressed impulses to slay the father and marry the mother which generate distortions in and obstructions to relations with same-generation women; it also symbolizes the courage of deep self-knowledge required to disarm destructive and recurring impulses. In the Greek myth Jocasta lacks this courage and perishes, while courageous Oedipus purges himself and survives, even finding peace. The oedipal dynamic—whether in the Greek myth, in Freud's clinical observations, or in musings about sexually segregated societies—turns on the fortitude needed to woo and conquer Psyche, the soul. Freud used Oedipus as the master metaphor for the process of self-discovery, of psychoanalysis; he used the myth of Eros and Psyche as the master metaphor for the nature of the struggle of the rational self (the "I" or ego or narrator) with seemingly impersonal impulses (the "it" or id).[17] So, too, Hedayat's Eros, the young lover, struggles with the turbulent portions of himself in order to tame the witch and woo the beauty of the soul. This is an ongoing effort, not something that can be won at the end of the story.

Third, Hedayat's story is of a lover of Iran despairing over Iran's cultural decay, searching like an alley dog among the refuse for valuable tidbits. Hedayat uses the past to critique the present. Although decay and misery existed in the past as well, the past's beauty can flicker into life (like the narrator's fantasy about his wife's corpse); whereas in the present even the potential carriers and reworkers of culture (the narrator himself) are undergoing decomposition. Hedayat wants to encourage potential culture carriers to activate themselves. The narrator is able to capture his wife's beauty and spirit as her corpse flickers to life; capturing her in a drawing on paper gives him power; and the creative, evocative painting can produce an emotional effect, can generate a kind of life. It is the failure of the narrator to sustain this creativity which Hedayat bemoans. The cry of *The Blind Owl* (that ambivalent bird which warns Persians of death) seems to be: wake up, disentangle this nightmarish condition, establish a coherent relation with one's childhood and cultural origins of self, so that one can deal in a healthy manner with others (of the opposite sex, of other-world cultures). This third reading constitutes an elegant reworking by Hedayat of nineteenth-century debates and fictive parables on the nature of art, on its ability to capture or distill experience, on the trade-offs made by different arts between spontaneity and durability of effect, on the ability of art to transform consciousness, and on the issue of whether art generated in times of evil can itself be unpoisoned.

Close Reading

Some fictions, [the Genie] asserted, were so much more valuable than fact that in rare instances their beauty made them real.

—JOHN BARTH, "Dunyazadiad," in *Chimera*

In *The Blind Owl* three brief commentaries frame two major narratives. In the opening commentary, the narrator diagnoses the dis-ease which has obsessed and corroded his mind. It is a disease which cannot be comprehended by reference merely to everyday consciousness. It is a reverberation from the past, from the deep experiences of generations through history. Expanding one's awareness to encompass this past experience is deeply upsetting: it isolates one from ordinary folk, and it alienates one from the comfortableness of conventional everyday thought. Once such awareness has been glimpsed, however fleetingly, it is impossible to forget: it becomes like a poison, an obsessive search to re-achieve, for it is a beauty, a transcending of the experience-limited self to a completion or union, a searing passion. One can try to forget, to return to contentment with conventional understanding, to dull oneself by mechanically applying oneself to work or by imbibing wine and opium—but these bring only temporary respite. The alienation and isolation destroy one's sympathy with one's fellow human beings: their obliviousness to what one has glimpsed becomes a kind of torture; their universe becomes as elusive and unreal as the shadows of the past. To retain some sanity, some means of control, the narrator determines to write down his experience, to establish the sequence of events, to know himself, and perhaps thereby to exorcise or tame his disease.

The first narration is set roughly at the time of Hedayat's writing. A clue to the temporal setting appears in the triple repetition of two geran and one abbasi as coins of payment, contrasting with the more ancient two dirham and four peshiz as used in the second narration.[18] The narrator describes first his upsetting vision and then the sequence of its appearance and haunting repetition.

The vision is described not as a flash of sunlight (unequivocal goodness) but as the flash of a falling star (a Persian image for the dubious side of fate) and as an ambivalent woman whose radiance illuminates her glory and the narrator's wretchedness.[19] A few passages later she is described as having an "air of mingled gaiety and sadness [which] set her apart from ordinary mankind."[20] Her eyes in particular sear into the narrator, eyes which frighten and attract "as though they had looked upon terrible transcendental things" (9), eyes later described as mirrors, albeit reproachful mirrors, to the narrator's soul. It is as if she is his fate, that cross-gender personification of one's deeds which accompanies one in the afterlife to heaven or hell. The narrator speaks of her as passion-kindling, as if "torn from her husband's embrace," as "a female mandrake . . . torn apart from its mate" (21), and as familiar as if "my soul had lived side by side with hers . . . and had sprung from the same root" (11).

It has been two months and four days since the narrator had this vision, and since then he has been unable to continue his occupation of painting pen cases. His vision was not of a woman alone but of a tableau, indeed the very tableau that he daily used to replicate on pen cases, now abruptly transformed from the crude, lifeless stereotypic pen-case conventions. The tableau is composed of two human figures, male and female, old and young, each with a symbol of flora: the old man sits beneath a cypress tree; the young woman holds a morning glory. Steam separates them. This is, of course, the standard Persian miniature: an old man enjoying his heavenly houri. The morning glory is associated throughout the text with graves and death: she is of the ethereal next world. The cypress is a standard iconograph for youth, vigor, life. The stream separates this world and the next. But the tableau is also enriched with Hindu symbolism: the old man is described as an Indian fakir, like the narrator, an individual apart from society (in India he would be sitting under a Bo tree, pursuing enlightenment and escape from this world's travails); the girl is described as a Hindu temple dancer, a Shaivite lingam-temple dancer who like Parvati and Kali, the wives of Shiva, is associated with death and destruction but who through the force of her dance can overcome death and the endless cycle of rebirth.

The initial vision is itself a double-vision occurring inside and outside the narrator's room. It occurs on the thirteenth day of Noruz (the Persian New Year), when people vacate home and city to picnic; those who fail to vacate are said to be subject to attack by evil spirits, and so perhaps it is for Hedayat's narrator. The narrator's uncle, described as the old fakir and resembling both the narrator and his father, comes into the room. As the narrator fetches a bottle of wine—wine left by his parents and specifically by his father, wine from the time of his birth—he glimpses through a ventilation shaft the tableau outside. A hair-raising sinister laugh from the old man terrorizes the narrator, and the vision disappears. Even the aperture disappears. For two months and four days the narrator searches for some material trace of his vision: he circles the house, he takes obsessive walks like a murderer returning to the scene of his crime, like a decapitated chicken, or like a hungry dog sniffing and rooting through the "sweepings, burning sand, horse-bones, and refuse heaps" for tasty morsels (15).

Finally, there is a nocturnal repetition, a nightmare. The narrator returns from one of his obsessive walks to find the woman by the door. She enters and lies down upon his bed. He fetches the wine left by his father, returning only to discover that she is dead: she has surrendered to him, but with her eyes closed. He forces some of the wine between her clenched teeth, tries to warm her with his body, but finds her "mouth was acrid and bitter and tasted like the stub end of a cucumber" (21). Yet his initial reaction is one of elation, of communion with the universe, of inspiration to try to capture her spirit on paper before her corpse decays. As a painter, after all, he is accustomed to depicting dead bodies and objects. Over and over again he attempts to capture that emotional power. Finally her cheeks take on a crimson color like that of the meat in butcher shops and her eyes open; for a brief instant his painting succeeds and she is in his power.

As dawn begins to break, though, he needs to dispose of the corpse. He dismembers the body and packs it into a suitcase. The old fakir with the sinister laugh turns into a hearse driver with a team of two skeleton-thin black horses. The narrator rides in the back with the suitcase on his chest. They proceed toward the shrine of Shah Abdol'Azim on the outskirts of the ancient town of Rayy, coming upon a scene that is the negative of the miniature tableau: a dead tree by a dry stream. There they dig a grave and uncover an ancient jar; they exchange the suitcase and the jar. During their return, the narrator holds the jar to his chest; on it is a portrait of the woman identical to the one in his own painting. The painter of the jar must have been a kindred soul, an "ancient partner in sorrow." He sets his painting side by side with the jar, stokes up his brazier, and smokes his stock of opium. The weight on his chest leaves him, and he soars "freely in pursuit of my thoughts, which had grown ample, ingenious and infinitely precise" (41). Gradually, he regresses backward through his life, into childhood memories, then into darkness, as if suspended from a hook in a well-shaft. He falls, forgotten memories flash by, and finally there is oblivion. When he comes to, he finds himself in a small room in a peculiar yet natural position.

The second brief commentary intervenes. He has awoken at twilight in a new but familiar world. He is feverish and giddy, and his hands are bloody, yet he feels animated and restless. He does not fear arrest: when the police come, he can drink the poisoned wine. What is important is to write, "to expel the demon," to "vent onto paper the horrors of my mind" (45). And so the second narration begins.

The effort to write is likened to squeezing "every drop of juice from my life as from a cluster of grapes and to pour the juice—the wine rather—drop by drop like the [healing] water of Karbala [consecrated with martyr's blood] down the parched throat of my shadow" (46).[21] Although it stems from an alienating condition, writing is invigorating, at minimum a dance of the macabre, a dance against death, a purgative. The narrator speaks of having been transformed from a wasted, sickly young man into a bent old man. He sees his shadow multiplied everywhere; he is everyman; and yet he sees himself set apart from the ordinary rabble, their categories of time, truth, and reality no longer having meaning for him. One's life is nothing but a fiction, a story, and countless such stories have been repeated ad infinitum. What truth they contain is uncertain, but they are essential components of human life and constitute the legacy of generation to generation.

He likens his room to a tomb, a place of frigid darkness and smells of decay from things and people past. Still, there has always been an eternal flame burning in him. The room has a double vista: a mirror inside reveals his circumscribed existence and his ravaged face; two windows open outside onto the great bustling city of Rayy. Through the window he can see a butcher shop and an old odds-and-ends man who once was a potter and still retains one jar from his youth. The narrator likens himself to a decomposing corpse.

The doublet to his tomb is the room in which took place the trial by cobra whence his uncle emerged old and white with a sinister laugh. Outside that room is the vivacious lingam-temple dancer, the narrator's mother, who has left him a bottle of wine. This wine is described in terms parallel to those the narrator uses to describe his writing: "Perhaps she also had pressed out her life like a cluster of grapes" (59). His uncle and father were twins; both loved the temple dancer, who chose between them (after giving birth to the narrator) through a trial by cobra. Before the trial she danced for them, moving with the seductive and sinuous movements of the snake. The boy was then given to his father's sister to raise and was suckled by the same nanny as the latter's daughter.

This story of illegitimate love corresponds to one that takes place in the next generation: the marriage of the narrator and his cousin. Despite knowing that those suckled together cannot marry, the narrator nevertheless committed such a prohibited, incestuous marriage. The relationship is deeply ambivalent. On the one hand, he claims to have married her because she looked like her mother and later admits to having been smitten by her as if "she had poured into my soul some poison" (64) (like father, like twin, like son). On the other hand, he claims to have been forced into the marriage to preserve her honor: she had kissed him at her mother's deathbed, and her father, an old bent man with a sinister laugh, had witnessed it.

The parallels and identifications here are extraordinarily dense: like mother, like wife, of course, but the narrator also sees in his wife a resemblance to himself. It is as if, on the one hand, there is still only the one Persian miniature of the man and his houri: like father, like twin, like son, like father's sister's husband or wife's father; like mother, like wife, like wife's mother or father's sister or adoptive mother. Between male and female is a seductive power of questionable legitimacy, a powerful metaphor for the relation between this world and the next: defiance of death by love, the dance of the cobra (Kali-Parvati dances with cobras around her neck), the poisonous wine.[22] A houri remains young and ethereal, but man ages with experience, knowledge, and enlightenment, becoming the hoary sadhu with the mocking laugh. Yet, on the other hand, it is as if male and female are but mirror images of the self: wife resembles husband; they are like entwined mandrake roots, suckled together, offspring of siblings. In the first narration the woman is the corpse, is dismembered like the crimson sheep carcasses, and her eyes reflect the pain of transcendental knowledge. In the second narration the roles are reversed: it is the narrator who likens himself to a corpse, entombed, slowly decomposing, dismembered like the crimson sheep's carcass, unsure if his arm does not act apart from his body. It is he who becomes the visionary with the hoary voice/laugh of the past, of experience.

If the first narration is of an upsetting vision, the second narration is of frustration. For two months and four days, or perhaps it is two years and four months, the narrator and his bride have slept apart, he claims. She would, he fantasizes, sleep with the rabble—a tripe peddler, an interpreter of the law, a cooked-meat vendor, the police superintendent, a shady mufti, a philosopher—but not with him. If in the first narration the plot or action or sequencing is a quest to recapture a flash of inspiration, in the second narration the plot is one of regression into childhood memories and passivity, then gradual maturation toward action. The narrator takes to his bed, regressing into childhood memories and listening to the stories of his nurse, idle prattle, stories retold endlessly through the generations, constantly renewed, renewing, the stuff of humanity. His wife continues to torture him; she even becomes pregnant.

The action of the second narration occurs over four days and nights, revealing a temporal structure from passivity to action. On the first day the narrator is passive and he attempts to flee; that night he has nightmares in which he is a passive victim. On the second day the narrator attempts to confront his fears; that night he has more violent nightmares but is an active agent. On the third day he forms a resolve and his illness/crisis breaks; that night he acts but fails. Finally, on the fourth day he interacts with others, an open exposure of hatreds; and that night he completes an action. (Perhaps the duality of day and night, fantasy and nightmare, is the referent of the refrain "*two* months and four days" since it is stated explicitly that the duration—month, day, or year—is, as in a dream, indeterminate.)

On the first of these four days, then, the narrator decides to flee. He has a childish regressive reaction, attempting to flee his misery, he says, rather like a dog or a bird who, knowing it is to die, goes off alone. He walks through the city among the rabble—all identical, their faces expressing greed for money and sex, constructed "only of a mouth and a wad of guts hanging from it, the whole terminating in a set of genitals" (73)—then beyond the city into the drying sun and intoxicating smells of childhood and sweet old wine. He compares the walk through the city to exploring an empty house, wandering from room to room, finally confronting the bitch, his wife, in the last room. He now comes to the River Suran at the foot of a stony and barren hill with a cypress tree on the riverbank (the same setting of the first narration, in which the corpse is buried and the jar uncovered). He sits and recalls that childhood day on the thirteenth of Noruz when he and his future bride were playing and she fell into the river. She was pulled out, stripped, and dried; the narrator illicitly peeked at her nudity. In this reverie the narrator walks back to town and finds himself in front of his father-in-law's house. He finds his wife's younger brother there, as alike to her as two halves of an apple (an expression also used in reference to the twins in the first narration). This brother calls her "Mummy" for want of a real mother; the narrator kisses the boy on his half-open mouth. The result we already know: the father is watching and emits a horrible laugh which makes hair stand on end and the lips taste like the stub end of a cucumber, acrid and bitter.

He escapes to his own house, but along the way he observes that his shadow has no head, a sign of impending death. Getting a nosebleed from fear, he collapses into bed, where he slips into a nightmare: drunken policemen are hanging the old odds-and-ends man from a gallows in Mohammadiyya Square; his mother-in-law is dragging him toward the gallows, shouting, "String this one up, too." He wakes in a sweat. He notices the water jug is balanced precariously on the shelf; when he attempts to secure it, it falls and shatters. His agitation lessens, the dawn comes, his nurse enters, the signs of life of the day filter in through the window.

On the second day the narrator stays in bed listening to the nanny's stories, but they fail to bring the usual peace. The narrator observes that "there are people whose death agonies begin at the age of twenty, while others die only at the very end, calmly and peacefully like a lamp in which all the oil has been consumed" (84). He thus expresses the Iranian folk belief that those who are too much enmeshed in the attachments of this world are extracted only painfully, like a rusty nail being extracted from a board with screeches and difficulty (a vivid and commonly used metaphor). It is an ironic self-comment by the narrator: he feels himself being extracted from life painfully; his attachments to life are to true living, not to the empty conventional motions of the rabble-men who populate the present era. Release from this false life is not a simple matter of an individual's death. As Hindus and Buddhists say, relief from the cycle of generations is more difficult to achieve. For Hedayat's narrator, the challenge is not so much to achieve individual salvation as to aim for a social one, an effort to reclaim the beauty of Iranian culture from the generational cycles of decay, of living death. By noon the narrator's agitation has increased, and he upsets the bowl of soup which his nanny brings. The doctor arrives with a new supply of opium. With the opium again freeing his spirit, he sees his position clearly. From this state of mind, he remarks on his nurse's efforts at religious cures on his behalf—prayers, fortune-tellers, begging alms on the last Wednesday of the year. Religion, he comments, amounts to "childish things of which the best that could be said was that they provided a kind of recreation for healthy, success-ful people" (89), that is, for the rabble. For his illness, for his particular form of fear of death, such things are useless. "Was not I myself the result of a long succession of past generations which had bequeathed their experiences to me? Did not the past exist within me?" (88). He is in this sense a living corpse, embodying the past, alienated from the rabble, existing between death and life. It is only a matter of perception as to which is death: the life of the present rabble or the narrator's glimpse of the past and sense of the cycle of generations.

Night comes and along with it the images of transition between this world and the next or transcendent world. The call of the muezzin sounds like the cry of a woman in childbirth or like a dog howling (as she gives birth to the next life; as it looks into the next world). Voices of the drunken policemen sing (the first of four repetitions), "Come, let us go and drink wine; Let us drink the wine of the Kingdom of Rayy. If we do not drink now, when should we drink?" (91)—a play, perhaps, on an old Omar Khayyam quatrain.[23] The narrator shrinks in momentary terror. He sees frightening figures in the lengthening shadows, one of which reminds him of the butcher. Experiencing nausea and vertigo, he returns to bed.

The nightmare again has him walking through a town: the people are all dead, standing motionless, with drops of blood from their mouths congealed on their coats, and when touched their heads fall off. This happens when he attempts to take the knife from the hands of the odds-and-ends man and when he tries to give a cake to his wife's little brother. He wakes with a shriek.

The third day dawns. This is a day of stronger resolution: he is dying, he should take the wife-bitch with him, so he takes out a knife. (It is a bone-handled knife, the same knife that the butcher had used in the previous night's dream and that the narrator had used in the first narration. There is but one knife, just as there is but one Persian miniature.) Sometimes conscious, sometimes drugged with opium, he contemplates; his illness crisis breaks, and when night comes he tries to act. He begins by reflecting on his fears of death, noting that his primary fear is that the atoms of his body might later be incorporated into the bodies of rabble-men. He attempts to withdraw deep into himself, into solitude, like a sadhu escaping society. He longs for nonbeing, for a death with no afterlife. He comments on death, on the drive for procreation as an attempt to deny death, on death as a savior from the deceptions of life, on the voice of death that frequently draws one so deep into thought that one loses consciousness of time and place and has to make an effort "to perceive and recognize again the phenomenal world in which men live" (101). He reviews his fears, both of the bodily signs of death and of the anxieties "lest the feather in my pillow should turn into dagger-blades . . . the paws of the dog outside the butcher shop should ring like horses' hooves [as they bring carcasses to the butcher or draw hearses] . . . lest the worms in the footpath by the tank in our courtyard should turn into Indian serpents" (101). He reflects on the flow of life that persists behind the various masks men wear and on the meagerness of the shadow his body casts in the bathhouse (the insubstantiality of his life's contributions). He meditates on the tableau on the pen case.

While he stokes up his opium brazier and pipe, thoughts of the odds-and-ends man remind him of his option to commit suicide with the poison/wine. Talking to himself, he suddenly sees the nanny staring at him, and he laughs. Unimpressed, she merely takes his opium away. He murmurs the words of the song, "Come, let us go and drink wine." Suddenly fear strikes him, and he feels his illness crisis coming on. The crisis is triggered in part by a view of the odds-and-ends man out the window, in part by the memory that his nurse had told him that the odds-and-ends man had visited his wife. Fearing cuckoldry, he had gone to buy the jar from the old man, but when he offered to pay two dirham and four peshiz, the old man laughed, striking the narrator with shame (the same shame he had felt twice before, both on hearing the laugh of the old man: first, when he kissed his future wife by her mother's deathbed; second, when he kissed her brother). Yet he tells himself cuckoldry at the hands of this old man would not be like that at the hands of the rabble-men: the old man had a mission to show people the discarded things of life. "What a stubborn life was in them and what significance there was in their forms!" (108–9). Indeed, the old man with his ailments and misery was "a kind of small scale exhibition organized by God for the edification of mankind . . . a sample and a personification of the whole creation" (109).

The crisis comes, triggered by the sound of a kettledrum: he flushes, becomes short of breath, and collapses. Miraculously, the bitch enters. At first she is disenchanted; the narrator views her merely as a lump of butcher's meat, and his response to her drives her out. Then she returns and he kisses her legs; they taste acrid and bitter like the stub end of a cucumber. He is carried away by the experience both of her nearness and of the revelation that she might have some feeling for him. When he comes to, she is gone. He sits by a lamp, letting the soot cover his face, and contemplates the myriad faces his visage could assume: the old man, the butcher, his wife—he could see them all in himself. Was he not "the custodian of the heritage," were not "the expressions of my face the result of a mysterious sequence of impulses, of my ancestor's temptations, lusts, and despairs?" (114). The grotesque humor of all these images causes him to laugh, a "harsh, grating, horrible laugh which made the hairs on my body stand on end" (115). This time the nanny is suitably horrified not only by the laugh but also by his cough and the clot of bloody phlegm that emerges.

Night comes and so does sleep. The narrator is awakened by a band of drunken policemen singing the song, "Come, let us go and drink wine. . . ." He remembers his resolution, dresses in a cross between the attire of the butcher and that of the odds-and-ends man, and goes to his wife's room. His resolution is stiffened by the image of the butcher saying "Bismillah" before cutting up the meat. Someone sneezes and laughs; he hesitates and runs, throwing his knife onto the roof of the house. (Persian superstition cautions one to postpone what one is about to do if someone sneezes.) He has, however, brought back his wife's nightgown.

The fourth day dawns, and lo, on the breakfast tray is his knife, brought back to him by nanny, who had bought it from the odds-and-ends man. This is the day for completion. Nanny speaks of massaging the pregnant belly of the bitch and notes the bitch's claims that she got pregnant in the baths. The narrator responds, sarcastically, that no doubt the child will look like the old man. The bitch's brother enters saying to the narrator, "Mummy says the doctor said you are going to die and it'll be good riddance for us. How do people die?" (122). His mother had said, moreover, that had she not had a miscarriage (the night before) the whole house would have belonged to them. The narrator laughs his hollow, grating laugh. He reflects on the soulless Turkoman faces of the brother and sister, "so appropriate to a people engaged in an unremitting battle with life, a people which regards any action as permissible if it helps it to go on living. Nature had shaped this brother and sister over many generations." Terrified by the narrator's laugh, the boy runs out of the room. The narrator feels transcendent, "a miniature God, I had transcended the mean, paltry needs of mankind and felt within me the flux of eternity" (123).

As night gathers, the narrator senses that his shadow has become more real than himself, that all the others are but shadows of himself, and that his shadow has become like a screech owl. "The odds-and-ends man, the butcher, nanny and the bitch, my wife, were shadows of me, shadows in the midst of which I was imprisoned. I had become like a screech-owl, but my cries caught in my throat and I spat them out in the form of clots of blood" (123). The screech-owl shadow leans forward and reads intently every word the narrator writes.

Night closes in: again the narrator feels he is in a tomb, a weight on his chest, the stammerings of death in his ear. This time he does not fall asleep but hears the drunken policemen singing, "Come, let us go and drink wine. . . ." Suddenly, he feels a superhuman force, and he gets up and goes to his wife's room. She is expectant and calls him in. He disrobes and gets into bed holding the knife. They embrace. "No, I sprang upon her like a savage, hungry beast," and her body opened and enclosed me within itself like a cobra coiling around its prey," and "her legs somehow locked behind mine like those of a mandrake." Without warning, she bites through his lip. As he struggles, he involuntarily jerks his hand, feeling the knife sink into her flesh. She releases him with a shriek; her body instantly turns cold. The narrator bursts into a cough, a hollow grating laugh, which terrifies him. He returns to his room and views himself in the mirror. He has become the odds-and-ends man, with white hair and beard "like those of a man who has come out alive from a room in which he has been shut up along with a cobra" (127).

In the third and final commentary the narrator comes to himself, having spent his energy in his frenzied nocturnal effort at self-exorcism. It is cock's crow, a misty morn, the charcoal in the brazier burned to cold ash. His mind, too, feels emptied like the ashes. He looks for the jar he had received from the hearse driver and sees instead a bent old man holding the jar at the door. The man laughs and runs off. The narrator attempts to chase but cannot catch him. He returns and inspects himself: bloody, blister-flies circling, maggots on his coat, and a dead weight (his own body) pressing on his chest (soul).

Perhaps it is the story of a murderer after all; perhaps it is still the murderer in all of us who remain unconscious of our role in the flow of generations and who are carried along by our unconscious drives and conventional programs; perhaps it is the sentient man (not a rabble-man) attempting to deal with the retreating mystery of the generations, doing violence to it as he fails to capture its entirety.[24]

The juxtaposition of Dehlavi's *Towers of Silence* and Hedayat's *The Blind Owl* helps to bring to the fore differences between the media of prose and film, as well as perhaps a difference in philosophical stance. Deep analysis does not ordinarily occur in a single viewing of a film. The momentum of the film is part of the experience. In *Towers of Silence* it induces a feeling of partial confusion analogous to the experience of the identity search of the main characters. Yet, by the same token, the pieces must be reasonably clear and simple. The main characters know well the elements of which their lives are constructed; at issue are coherence, the possibilities of choice, and the causal nexus. With Hedayat's book, by contrast, the reader is free to flip back and forth, collating and cross-referencing, a freedom that allows greater complexity without loss of coherence.

The consideration of technique leads, however, to a philosophical appreciation of Hedayat's surrealism. Hedayat is not merely a modernist exploring a new syntax of art which can accommodate contemporary experiences: the emptiness of assertions that there are absolute truths; the dangers of assertions that society rather than the individual is the custodian of human values; the recognition that the senses often transmit misleading information and that language often distorts as it communicates; the juxtaposition of habits acquired in traditionally disparate modes of life; the deadening constraints placed on the spirit by religion, family, and work; the recognition that psychic logic is different than the logic of reason and that the inner and outer modes of thinking interpenetrate in human life in a way that cannot be severed or hierarchized without severe damage. Above all, Hedayat is not a

Dadaist, a nihilist who sees life as nothing but a cruel joke, an endless and gruesome hall of mirrors, of inversions, repetitions, and parallels. Rather, much like André Breton, Hedayat deploys surrealist techniques to explode a world grown dead through convention, through religious rigidity, and through political corruption.[25]

Surrealism, both as a specific movement and as a more general set of modernist techniques, has spread throughout the world. Yet there is a cultural specificity to its employment, and Hedayat's surrealism, while drawing on his experiences in France, is ingrained in an Iranian context. Surrealism and modernism in France work on the assumption that the world has become technological and dehumanized. Iranian modernism instead reacts against a rigidified, fundamentalist, and patriarchal universe, a much more traditionalist enemy than European modernism faced.

It is worth calling attention to the period of the past which Hedayat uses to critique the present. He does not look to pre-Islamic Iran for his less-corrupted images, but to the early Islamic or medieval period. In this, Hedayat only partly foreshadows Ali Shariati's bitter polemics in the 1970s against the rigidification and formulation of a hegemonic Islamic orthodoxy from the Safavid period (1501–1722 C.E.) on. Shariati remained an Islamic chauvinist, urging a return to a more original, more flexible, more ethical, and purer "Alavi" Shi'ite Islam. By contrast, it was not so much to Islam in the early medieval period that Hedayat draws attention, even though in that era of expansion Islam was intellectually open and could incorporate influences from both the West and the East. Rather Hedayat looks to the period of active Persian revolts against Islam—of Babak, Mazyar, and Afshin; of the Barmakis; of Tahir "Zulyaminein"—which found its most lasting expression in the *Shahnameh*.[26] It is the dialectical or oppositional stance to a hegemonic Islam that makes the early medieval period more relevant to the present than pre-Islamic Iran.

Indeed, although taken from Perso-Islamic civilization, the central image of *The Blind Owl*—the Persian miniature of an old man and his houri—is given a special twist by Hedayat. Meditation on what meanings can be invested in this stereotypic art form—a component of the third level, artistic reading—opens up a rich psychological and cultural exploration, incorporating Hindu and Buddhist symbols, and as Michael Beard (1982) suggests, running the tableau through a full cycle of transformations from the old man as representative of the self to representative of the other, from the woman as representative of the ethereal virgin to representative of the castrating whore. But it is not just a meditation on possibilities; were the novel entitled *Persian*

Miniature, its meaning would change. The blind owl, the owl of death, is an ambiguous omen: perched on a house it means destruction; perched on a ruin it means renewed prosperity (Lashgari 1982, 48). The blind owl is the narrator's shadow. They live in a house on the edge of the new city over the ruins of the old city. *The Blind Owl* is thus a call to cease conventional reproductions, to come alive again through the associative, recombinant faculty of the mind.

Underscoring this interpretation is that the tableau of the old man and his houri appear in other Hedayat stories, the most relevant to the consideration of the past as critique of the present being "Akharin Labkhand" (The Last Smile), a portrayal of the Barmaki revolt. The Barmakis were Iranians (originally a family of Buddhist priests in Balkh) who attempted to infiltrate what they considered an alien Arab Islamic bureaucracy and to destroy it from the inside. Their goals were to reestablish the ancient Noubahar Fire Temple and to reintroduce Buddhism. Responsible for the deaths of the Fifth, Sixth, and Seventh Shi'ite Imams, the Barmakis were eventually exposed and massacred. In Hedayat's story the narrator descends into a basement to meditate and drink wine in front of a fire and a statue of the Buddha. A girl is with him. He receives a letter, which she surreptitiously reads. (She is a secret agent for the Caliph.) The narrator is found dead the next morning, sitting like a Buddha.

In at least six other stories, Hedayat utilizes the tableau of an old man and a young woman; he also experiments throughout his fiction with many of the images in *The Blind Owl*, making *The Blind Owl* a kind of encapsulation of his body of work. In "Dash Akol," an old man falls in love with his young ward but cannot bring himself to change his protective relationship to her; when another man seeks her hand, Dash Akol turns his feelings inward, becomes drunk, fights the suitor, and dies. In "Sayeh-ye Moghul," Shahrokh, the Iranian patriot, attempts to revenge the slaying of his fiancé, Golshad. He is injured and takes refuge in a tree, where he perishes in the winter snows while meditating on his happy memories of Golshad. In the spring peasants find his skeleton; the head seems to be hideously laughing (a laughter which resounds through *The Blind Owl*).

The laughter is, of course, the shrill laugh of Silenus, the wise companion of Dionysus, as he responds to King Midas's question, What is the best and most desirable of all things to man? "Not to be born, not to be, to be nothing. But the second best for you is to die soon" (Sophocles, *Oedipus at Colonus*, line 1224). Hedayat's interpretation and response seems to be that of Nietzsche, that art was to overcome this terror "in the face of the titanic powers of nature, the Moira [fate] enthroned inexorably over all knowledge, the vulture of the great lover of mankind, Prometheus, the terrible fate of the wise Oedipus, the family curse of the Atridae which drove Orestes to matricide; . . . all this was again and again overcome by the Greeks with the aid of the Olympian *middle world* of art; or at any rate it was veiled and withdrawn from sight" (1872/1967, sec. 3). It is this philosophical use of art that both Nietzsche and Hedayat seem to value, a philosophical play with the notion of "appearance" (existence, illusion as a transfiguring into perfection, deceitful illusion as mere appearance; viz. the German *Schein* and *Erscheinung*, the Sanskrit *maya*). Nietzsche cites Schopenhauer's criterion of the philosophical ability: "the occasional ability to view men and things as mere phantoms or dream images" (ibid., sec. 1), to explore the ambiguous and interpenetrating relations between the incompletely intelligible everyday world, the perfections of ideas and imaginings, and the deceits and corruptions of illusions, appearances.

Nietzsche is only part of a nineteenth-century tradition of parables and debates about the nature of art, a tradition on which Hedayat seems clearly to draw and which comprises the third, artistic, level of understanding *The Blind Owl*. The whole spectrum of arts, from dance/music to painting/writing, are examined in *The Blind Owl*. The latter arts are the most awkward, being tied to representation, the medium almost inevitably distorting and deadening the object. The former—represented often by Salomé (e.g., in Flaubert, Mallarmé, Yeats, Huysmans, and Moreau) and by Begum Dasi in Hedayat's story *The Blind Owl*—convey experience directly: one speaks, for instance, of the music of the celestial spheres; in the Hindu imagery used by Hedayat the dance of Shiva and his wives is so powerful that it can overcome death and the endless cycle of rebirth. The paradox lies in the fact that dance and music are ephemeral; writing is more permanent. But it is only through writing, through the words of the narrator's confession, that one can know of Begum Dasi's dance.

As Michael Beard (1982) puts it, writing can indicate a world outside itself; the degraded material at hand in the world of alienation and distortion nonetheless represents a way out of itself. The plastic arts stand in between, and in *The Blind Owl* Hedayat plays with a contrast between lacquer-box pen cases—rectangular and enclosing the pen (in its alienating, deadening body/tomb), on which are painted crude stereotypical miniatures—and a clay vase or jar—round (circling like a dance, open for holding flowers) on which is painted a portrait of the woman. (Omar Khayyam, too, metaphorically juxtaposes a jar and a woman, and Hedayat's narrator says, "I squeezed the warm moist sand. . . . [I]t felt like the firm flesh of a girl" [77].)[27] The object of love, the sensuousness of vitality, stands in complementary opposition to the lover, the word, and the pen.

Deirdre Lashgari (1982) rephrases the parable of the arts in more activist terms: if art is the process of distilling experience into "wine," and if the experience is evil, will the wine not be poisoned? Hedayat uses precisely this imagery: the old wine poisoned with cobra venom left to the narrator as his parent's legacy. The narrator speculates on the power of art not merely to achieve consciousness (as when he captures his wife's spirit in a drawing), but also to transcend/escape the travails of consciousness: "if it were possible for my being to dissolve in one drop of ink, in one bar of music, in one ray of colored light . . . then I should have attained my desire" (42). This imagery echoes that in which an easy death is compared to an oil lamp gently using up oil, in contrast with the difficult death of one who is too attached to the material world, whose soul must be extracted with pain and screeching. Lashgari invokes the traditional dialectic between the alienation and pain of the material world and the peace of the ideal. The poisoning of the ethereal, beautiful unattainable girl in the first part of the story illustrates what happens when the ideal comes into contact with poisonous reality; inversely, in the second part of the story, the wife at home in the material world is shown to be trafficking with butchers and drunken policemen. But Hedayat's point, as Lashgari acknowledges, is not a simple devaluation of the material world. Rather, the narrator commits murder as the only response open to an artist when his art/ideal has been systematically distorted by the powers that be; it is an attempt to force the reader to react and help take responsibility for creative action.

The Blind Owl ultimately is posed as a puzzle, both an intellectual puzzle for the reader to pick apart and a moral puzzle. (Think of the grotesque old man as Hedayat himself laughing at those of us enthralled with his story, at our struggles to define the beauty we cannot quite possess, and at how our frustrations lead us to the verge of dismissing/destroying his novella as perverse, meaningless, or destructive.) The intellectual puzzle leads to delightful parallels with modernist writers such as Rilke and Kafka, who influenced Hedayat, and with many others with whom the parallels, or the participation in a common discourse, are striking.[28] Reading Hedayat's work requires collating and cross-referencing images, descriptions, and fragments of action. In the process the reader is forced to consider in multiple ways an inventory of traditional Persian cultural elements, which provide not only the associative layering that makes Hedayat's work richly Persian but also clues that suggest that his ultimate perspective is affirmative, is not dismissive of life or history as merely bloody repetition.[29]

Popular Culture and Elite Literacy

A text is henceforth no longer a finished corpus of writing . . .
but a differential network, a fabric of traces referring endlessly to
something other than itself, to other differential traces.
—JACQUES DERRIDA

It would be possible at this point to illustrate, by analyzing such stories as "The Lead Soldier" by Bozorg Alavi and "Man in a Cage" by Sadegh Chubak, how the techniques and imagery used by Hedayat reverberate through much of modernist Persian literature (Fischer 1973, 378–89).[30] Not only is there in this sense a tradition and a discourse, with each author commenting, as it were, on his predecessors' efforts to capture a sense of Iran on paper, but it is interesting that this discourse should appeal to committed socialists such as Alavi and to authors like Chubak who rejected simple political readings of their work. In all of these cases, one reads for the grounded Persian imagery, the folklore, historical references, the ethnography. One is as interested in these specifically Persian elements as in the discourse pattern of the intelligentsia.

The films that follow—two comedies about villagers coming to Tehran; two genre films about honor and modesty in lower-class urban neighborhoods; and a film about a peculiar, archetypical, village—offer more substantive portrayals of the lives of the popular classes, although again not in documentary terms but through artistic vehicles.

Comic Pains of Urbanization

Agha-ye Halu (Mr. Gullible)

Chaplin, in conformity with Brecht's idea, shows the public its blindness by at the same time presenting a man who is blind and what is in front of him. To see someone who does not see is the best way to be intensely aware of what he does not see: thus at a Punch and Judy show, it is the children who announce to Punch what he pretends not to see.
—ROLAND BARTHES, "The Poor and the Proletariat"

This comic film by Ali Nassirian began life as a television play in 1342/1963. The two-scene television play is set entirely in a coffeehouse in the Pasqualleh neighborhood of south Tehran. There are three main characters: the rural bumpkin, Halu (empty head); the *rind* or innkeeper; and the prostitute. Two minor characters complete the triangle of each scene: a skilled panhandler of many masks (beggar, diviner, knife seller); and Dash Habib, the bullying neighborhood protector. There are also three silent, background figures: a waiter and two musicians (stringed *saz* and *zarb* drum).

Comedy is said to depend upon types, and this is a classic comic cast. The central pair are the classic wit and fool, *eiron* and *alazon*, sophisticate and naif, city slicker and country hick. But rind, *dash*, and prostitute are also types. A term popularized largely through the poetry of Hafez, *rind* is one in a series having to do with ambiguous cleverness.[31] In Hafez, as also in Jalaludin Rumi, the rind is associated with wine drinking, free spirits, and with true understanding beyond conventional social constraints or formal religious rules. For others the rind is merely a drunkard, skilled thief, or ruffian, deceiving, cunning, and quick to see how to take advantage of a situation. *Dash* lies midway between the immoral *aubash* (young street toughs) and the selfless, usually aged, darvish concerned more with spiritual values than material attachments. The dash is typically a mature man who exercises his strength in a paternal, protective role for the women, children, and weak of his neighborhood (see Bateson et al. 1977).

Friendship and love are focal themes of the television play. The first scene turns male friendship inside-out for inspection. Halu arrives oddly dressed (so reads the stage instruction): in a baggy, old-fashioned, striped brown suit, flowered tie, dark yellow shoes, green chapeau, drooping black mustache, holding yellow worry beads. The first two lines alert the audience to the parody on *ta'arof* that will follow—*ta'arof* refers to forms of polite discourse in Persian which allow social intercourse to occur while jockeying for status, conflicts of interest, or uncertainty of commitment continue below the surface. The rind says, "Please come in, this is a simple darvish hut" [*befarmaid, kolbeh-ye darvish e*], but instead of politely standing aside and allowing the guest to enter first, he turns and walks ahead. Halu responds with an inappropriately stilted form of thanks: *salamat bashid*. Initially, Halu draws the audience's superior smiles: clearly a hick out of place, attempting to speak a bookish Persian partly to hide his provincial accent, using a stilted and high-flown linguistic register to which he is unaccustomed and which is inappropriate to the situation. Slowly, however, he begins to pick up some of the rind's style of repartee. During the evening, he is taken for a ride by the rind, who offers him drinks as if in hospitality (Halu does not realize that he is being charged and that the language of friendship and hospitality is but a ruse to run up his tab); by a beggar to whom the rind encourages Halu to give alms; by a diviner whose fortune-telling he is induced to engage; and by a knife seller from whom he is encouraged to buy. Halu thinks these three look suspiciously alike, but the rind assures him that they are different men and that each is worthy of Halu's patronage. As the scene ends, audience sympathy is clearly with Halu, the representative now of everyman's experience of being duped by sweet-talking shills and ruses.

In the second scene, Halu has accepted an invitation to spend the night. In the bedroom he finds the prostitute, "daughter" of Fathullah Khan, the rind. At first, the audience may think that Halu does not realize what she is, and there is a certain humor in his humble approach to yet another inappropriate situation. But midway through the scene, it becomes clear that Halu knows full well that she is a prostitute and is nonetheless proposing marriage, on the condition that she wash herself with the "water of repentance" (ab-i towbeh). (There is special religious merit in marrying such a woman if she repents by following a particular ceremonial form.)[32] Halu is no longer simply the object of our sympathy, a man ill-used by commercialized social relations (paying for "friendship" and "love"); he is now a symbol of moral goodness, the unvarnished mirror reflecting back our corruptions. The prostitute recognizes this and is touched, but she is caught: she is the dash's girl, and he enters like a bull to kick Halu out. As Halu exits, he confronts each character with his or her corruption: he gives to the dash the knife he had purchased and for which he has no use; he pays the rind but asks if he is not the one who "eats the bread of the day" (blows with the wind); he asks the prostitute if she is the one who is willing to sell herself but not become his honest wife; and he hires the musicians ("don't worry, I'll pay you") to play for him, saying "for friendship I would put my existence on a plate and give it you."[33]

Halu has come to Tehran, as he tells the rind in the first scene, to find a wife, which is not an uncommon move for provincials, attempting to "marry up," to find a city woman. Halu appears instead to have fallen into the urban sewer, yet it is he who rises through the narrative sequence from provincial naïf to moral measure. There is a moral punch to his redemption.

In the film version, the coffeehouse scenes do not appear until the second half. The first half of the film is a kind of doubling of the theme's emplotment to more social settings, and of course the film is able to document visually the frenetic urban chaos as it must seem to a newly arrived provincial: there are delightful ethnographic portraits of leave-taking in the village, the familial discourse among strangers on the bus, the crowded confusion and lack of politeness at the Tehran bus station, the trauma of crossing busy streets, the shock of seeing immodest magazine pictures displayed on newsstands and undergarments in shop windows, the invasion of noise in the hotel room (from the street, from the love-making next door), the use of public baths after a nocturnal wet dream, the homosexual clerk in a fancy boutique, the mixture of busy rudeness and exaggerated solicitousness at a tailor's shop, flirtation with a chadored woman, and the nondescript storefront offices of middlemen (real-estate brokers in this case). This is perhaps the best part of the film.

The first half of the film becomes focused on an attempt to involve Halu in a shady real-estate deal, a foreshadowing or doubling of what will happen in the coffeehouse. Halu resists the real-estate brokers and is beaten for his pains, just as he resists corruption in the coffeehouse and is there beaten by the dash. The real estate segment is heavy handed, the least-well-acted or emplotted portion of the film, serving primarily as a device to draw Halu through the streets of Tehran (he has come to town with the name of the real-estate broker), and the beating is merely a crude way of jettisoning this part of the plot when it is no longer needed. In the meantime, by wandering through the streets and going into shops, Halu has encountered Mehri, the prostitute, and, not knowing that she is a prostitute, has fallen in love with her. She takes him to the coffeehouse, where the actors involved in the real-estate segment of the film reappear.

From this point the film generally follows the script of the television play, but with several significant alterations, the most important being that at the end Halu is merely beaten and kicked out, with none of the redemption of his character that occurs in the play. Instead, the final scene shows him back on the bus, leaving Tehran. He remarks to his seat mate that traveling is a good thing, that it makes a person fully cooked (*adam-ra pokhteh mikonad*), that is, it turns one from a raw innocent into a more seasoned being. The overall effect is melodrama rather than the comic moral punch of the television script.

At the time the film was first released, viewers took it as a metaphor of the corruption of Iran by modernization and westernization, a point made most delightfully in the opening credits of the film: Victorian curlicues and cherubs serve as a frame in which the destructible gentle protagonist is stripped of his clothes frame by frame until he is left covering his bare chest with his arms, dressed only in his pajama bottoms (worn by traditional folk under their trousers; at home, one removes the trousers and lounges in the pajamas); and the credits end with a large hat—the Reza Shah–imposed Western headgear—plopping down on him. This opening sets a comic tone, preparing the viewer for the story of the rural hick who attempts to use high-flown proper Persian forms in the hustle-bustle of a modern, impolite city with predictable consequences.

Inevitably, Halu's trip works out badly and ends with him leaving Tehran somewhat changed and wiser. In the meantime, dramatically, he has left behind in the coffeehouse a symbol of his past: the little book in which he wrote bits of poetry and proverbs, which he had once loved to read and recite, and which he had used as a defensive veil against harsh reality. The Persian character's otherworldly, self-blinkering refuge in poetic reverie is thus jettisoned. But, in the end, the melodramatic flaws of the film almost turn this comic and self-ironic tone into another traditional cultural form, into an expansion of the widely known, though false, hadith.[34]

Imam Jafar Sadeq (the Sixth Imam) said to Mofazal, his student and trusted transmitter of hadith: To the north of Tehran there is a black mountain called Alborz. At the foot of this mountain there will be built a city called Tehran. Its palaces will be like those of paradise. Its women will be like the black-eyed houris of paradise. And if you want to keep your faith, run from this city, jump from stone to stone as a fox runs from the hunter.

Doroshkeh-chi *(The Droshky Driver)*

To a joke, then, I owe my first gleam of complete consciousness—which again has recapitulatory implications, since the first creatures on earth to become aware of time were also the first creatures to smile.
—VLADIMIR NABOKOV, *Speak, Memory*

Agha-ye Halu embodies one form of comedy. Roland Barthes's notes on Charlie Chaplin's *Modern Times* stress the revolutionary power of portraying the pre-revolutionary, the worker blinded by hunger, oblivious to and even frightened of strikes or collective action. The aesthetic power lies in showing the public its blindness. So, too, *Agha-ye Halu* attempts to show Iranians their loss of moral brotherliness in the process of change in which they have become locked.

There is a second form of comedy, using a more familial setting, which for ethnographic purposes is perhaps one of the best vehicles for displaying and reviewing norms and customs. In the film *Doroshkeh-chi* by Nosratullah Karimi, a widow, Zina, and her widower brother-in-law, Baba, wish to resume a twenty-five-year-old courtship and marry. Zina's son, Morteza, objects to Baba usurping his father's place; Zina's brother, Akbar, objects to Baba himself. Twenty-five years before, Akbar had objected to Baba because he was only a droshky driver; he objects to Baba, however, because he wants Morteza to marry his daughter, not Baba's daughter. Since Zina's husband and Baba jointly owned the house, the two half-families live separately together in the house.

This contradiction of intimacy (cousinship, sharing the toilet) and yet distance (rules of modesty) sets up a series of situations in which Persian behavioral rules break down. The main conflict (between Morteza and Baba) is sustained by the inability of any of the actors to achieve his initial desires without the cooperation of the others. Morteza has sufficient power to prevent the marriage of Zina and Baba: they want his blessing, but toward the end of the film they fear even to embrace in his presence, since he has tried to poison them all. On the other hand, Morteza cannot prevent Baba from usurping his father's place in the affections of Zina and his younger brother, Hasan. Akbar uses Morteza's antagonism to Baba to try to wean him away from Baba's daughter in the hopes that Morteza will contract a marriage alliance with his own daughter. Through daily interaction, however, Morteza is finally broken of his paternal fixation, and after the climactic crisis of nearly poisoning and then incinerating them all in a fire, he pushes Zina and Baba back into each other's arms. All ends happily, but he is changed, they are changed, and a new family solidarity replaces those disrupted at the beginning of the film by his father's death.

The plot is contrived and soap-operatic; what gives the film its humor and warmth, as well as its ethnographic value, are its depictions of a funeral, a circumcision, and courtship and modesty rules. The film opens at the funeral, with a group of mourning women sitting on the ground wrapped in black chadors. The characters are introduced, and the authenticity of Morteza's grief and passion is established not only by his open weeping and how he throws himself about, but also by how his generosity ends squabbling over how much to pay the Qur'an reader. Akbar's daughter's level of intelligence is also established during Morteza's grief displays, when she throws a glass of water in his face to calm him. At the funeral dinner, in a comic aside, an old man instructs his neighbor to forget the water and wolf down the meat before it disappears. The competition between the dead man's brother (Baba) and the widow's brother (Akbar) is established: Baba says he has acquired two sons; Akbar replies that when Morteza wants to marry, it should be to his *dai* (mother's brother) that he should come.

The circumcision of Hasan, the deceased's younger son, provides an inter-lude midway through the film and is portrayed with all the humor and terror of the event.[35] Hasan wanders around the courtyard where the women are preparing for the festivities, crying and pleading that he is afraid. His dai's wife tells him, "You will become a man, you will get a wife and have children." All the women treat it as a joyful event. Baba arrives with the musicians and circumciser. Their unannounced arrival throws the unchadored women into a scramble for their chadors. Akbar's wife, in an absolutely hilarious (albeit stock-comic) move sends the audience into an uproar when in her haste to cover her hair, she throws her skirt up over her head. Hasan, in desperation, runs. He is chased by Morteza and the mechanic Mahmud. They catch him and carry him, struggling, to the evilly grinning circumcisor, who is sharpen-ing his razor. Baba intervenes, orders them to let Hasan go, advises Hasan not to be afraid, and takes him under his own wing. Hasan bravely protests that if it must be done, he will do it himself, and he suddenly breaks away, running up onto the roof and threatening to throw himself off. Morteza prepares to catch him if he falls. In backing away from the menacing adults who now are primarily worried that he will fall off the roof, Hasan does just that, but is caught by Morteza, who carries him, kicking again, to be circumcised. Despite his squirming and screaming, the circumcision proceeds. His fore-skin is handed to the waiting women, who receive it with jubilation.

A picnic follows. When Baba and Morteza bring out some arak and turn their backs for some "men's talk," Hasan perks up at the phrase and asks if he can join. Baba shoos him away, saying he is yet a child. Hasan objects that any child who is circumcised becomes a man, which causes general laughter. Zina mediates by saying that Morteza is also a child and will always be a child to her. Hasan regains the upper hand by calling her comment sour grapes and asks if she too has been circumcised. Then the musicians come, and it is time for dancing. Baba solves the problem of modesty by having the musicians turn their backs to the celebrants. His daughter then drops her chador and dances. She and Morteza flirt; Zina and Baba flirt. The couples wander off, including the mechanic and his girl, leaving Hasan the odd one out; he runs from pair to pair, only to be shooed away.

Rules of courtship and modesty provide a primary source of humor throughout the film. Just after the funeral scenes, Baba and Zina ride in his droshky; responding to her protest that it is too soon to talk of their love, he pulls out his riding crop, on which he has notched each passing day, and informs her that the statutory three-month, eleven-day waiting period is over. He takes Zina to a cinema, but young men brush up against her in the line, which leads to a confrontation, so the couple leaves; the younger pair (Morteza and Baba's daughter) have meanwhile joined the line farther back. Each couple is unknown to the other, as they keep their activities secret from each other. There are problems with sleeping arrangements in the shared house. Morteza wants to sleep in the courtyard, but his mother shoos him up to the roof, that being the place for men. His cousin comes up to neck with him there. Baba leads Zina up the steps to take a peek, at the same time using the narrowness of the staircase as an excuse for their own embraces. Each male attempts to be vigilant about the modesty of his women: Morteza pulls his mother's chador over her at the picnic when he notices her flirting with Baba; Baba in a humorous reversal demands at one point that his daughter speak up and not whisper to Morteza, rebuking her to tears. There is further hilarity and pathos when Morteza builds a wall across the courtyard, dividing the house into two parts. Still, noise, sugar, and toilet all have to be shared, which provides the means for irritating the other side and for the surreptitious meetings of the lovers.

The best set piece in the sexual comedy takes place in Akbar's house, where he attempts to interest Morteza in his daughter and has her bring tea. This is a brilliantly performed comic scene in which the girl's mother places a glass of tea on a tray in her daughter's hands and forces her to smile. The girl does not make it out of the kitchen before dropping the first glass. She makes it to the men with the second glass, but drops it on Morteza's foot. She is wearing a white chador wrapped round her waist and over her head, thus revealed from waist to face in hopes of gaining her prospective suitor's approval.

The climax and turning points of the film come in two subplots. First Morteza and Akbar take Baba off to get drunk with some girls and have Zina witness this; Zina is successfully alienated from Baba, until later, via a heated exchange between Morteza and Akbar, she learns that it was a put-up job. Meanwhile, Hasan, finding Baba utterly demoralized and defeated, in remorse rouses him by saying that whenever he does bad, then tries to make it up by being helpful, following after people, being repentant, and so on, he is eventually forgiven. In ethnographic terms the scene does show a typical setting for male sport outside Tehran: the carpet covered *takht* (a wood platform) set over a mountain stream, with a bottle of arak, fruit, and some food. In the second climactic scene Morteza once and for all works out his hostility toward Baba's usurpation of Zina's and Hasan's affections. The scene is a bit overdone, more like a parody of grade-B films of honor and revenge in which the revenger goes to a coffeehouse to tank up on arak, then in a warrior frenzy commits his fatal defense of honor. In this case Morteza poisons the ab-gusht (a stew), but when he sees his beloved preparing to eat, he attempts to kick the spoon from her hand and succeeds instead in kicking over the fire and setting the house ablaze. In the struggle to save everyone, Morteza's passion is extinguished, and at the end he pushes Baba and Zina gently into each other's arms.

In ethnographic terms, this film displays many rules, rites, customs, and concerns of the popular classes. But to what extent are these portrayals distorted by the artistic devices through which they are displayed? With the exception of the contrivances of the general comic story line and the overly cinematic, clichéd climax scenes, the set pieces on the funeral (including the meal), the circumcision, the presentation of a daughter to a suitor by having her serve tea, and so on, successfully model typical fears and actions and conflict; family comedy, then, seems to be a reasonably naturalistic domesticating vehicle. Hasan's circumcision contains the elements people typically describe that rite to contain and in particular captures the ambiguity between becoming a man and remaining a child. Masculinity, after all, is worked out over a long period and cannot be effected instantaneously by a rite; at best, the rite helps dramatize and set up the tension which then needs working out. Morteza in the film is engaged in working out a later stage of the process, one concerned with the tension between rules of honor and happiness. His warrior fantasies (arak and revenge) may even be seen as adolescent reference frames, debased perhaps by going to too many movies of the sort described in the next section.

Tragic Defenses of Honor: *Qaisar*

Cans't thou approve and reconcile these twain—
To be a murderer and live thyself?
—FIRDAUSI, *Shahnameh*

One of the popular genres of film in Iran, perhaps the functional equivalent to the American Western, is the story of an attack on a man's *namus* (his women; that form of male honor vulnerable through the purity of women) and his tragic duty to carry out vengeance.[36] It is tragic because honor once besmirched cannot be completely restored and because murder even in defense of honor destroys one's social world, one's legal standing, and one's religious purity. Nonetheless, it is a moral and heroic obligation which cannot be ignored, on pain of losing all dignity for self and family. The associations in these films are heroic, Islamic, judicial, and masculine, the virtues of masculinity being encoded in the following series: aubash (street tough, immoral), *javanmard* (youth, moral), dash (maturity, moral, physical strength), pahlavan (heroic strength and morality), darvish (aged, spiritual strength, loss of physical power). This series is part of the mental reference frame for males both as they pass through adolescence and as they consider how to play roles of authority, be they bureaucrat, factory boss, or professor.

The 1969 film *Qaisar* by Mas'ud Kimia'i is widely regarded to be the finest of the genre, a film that transcends the ordinary genre level and achieves its own artistic merit. As with *The Blind Owl*, viewers divide in their reception of the film. Middle-class viewers claim to distance themselves, regarding the film as an argument against vengeance and as a portrayal of life "as it really exists" among the lower classes of south Tehran. Among adolescents in the town of Abadan, on the other hand, the chivalrous and heroic elements were not devalued. For several weeks after the film was released, youths placed knives in their shoes in symbolic identification with Qaisar. As one of them told me, "It is the state's job to take care of such matters, but everyone approved of Qaisar's settling the score before the police took over."

The elegance of the film *Qaisar* lies in the symbolic intensity it achieves through harmonizing the heroic, Islamic, judicial, and masculine associational frames. There is first the dramatic tension: will the affront to namus be successfully avenged before the state judicial system intervenes? Qaisar's sister Fatima has been raped by the brother of her best friend, and the film opens with her committing suicide with a razor in the bathroom. Farman, Qaisar's elder brother is killed in the first attempt at revenge. Qaisar succeeds in carrying out the vengeance but is stabbed by his final quarry and is shot by the police before they capture him. Farman (command) says in response to the argument that revenge will only cause further killings: it is a question of namus, it cannot be avoided. Qaisar, too, immediately recognizes that his sister's death is also his own social death: "I have no more work in this world," he says. He cannot run away; through vengeance he is made unclean (*najes*); he cannot marry. The logic of the drama, secondly, is intensified by structuring the action within a small social universe which completely falls apart: the rapist is the brother of the victim's best friend; another brother is a business associate of Qaisar's fiancé's father and a fellow butcher like Farman. As the death of Fatima means the death of her brothers, so their death means the death of their mother. Even the one interfamilial bond, Qaisar's engagement, is ruptured: he goes to a shrine (*imam zadeh*) and prays, "I know I am sinning; I cannot marry a pure girl; please make her reconciled and give her happiness."

Shoe (*Qaisar*)

The heroic associations are amplified by references to the epic *Shahna-meh*. The film opens with the credits given against tattoos of old kings and knights, an eagle with talons spread, an eagle lifting a cherub, and a cherub holding a knife to the throat of an eagle. Pictures of pahlavans (epic heroes, athletes of the traditional zurkhaneh, or gymnasium) are constantly on the walls shadowing Qaisar (Caesar) like his fravashi, or soul. Each time he sights a quarry, he bends down and pulls up his shoe backs (casual Persian walking is done with turned-down backs), the martial tambak drum and chain percussion of the zurkhaneh well up, and he makes the kill in the straightforward, no-nonsense Zoroastrian mode of battling evil. After he kills the first of his quarries, his mother's brother raises a copy of Firdausi's *Shahnameh* and asks desperately if the accounts are not now balanced, and Qaisar grimly says no: two more brothers to go.

Heroism in this day and age (Qaisar is an oil-field worker, has come home from Abadan) is no simple epic matter, and Islamic associations are used to reinforce the tragic implications. There are several retreats to imam zadehs for moral guidance and for acknowledging the tragic moral imperatives involving one in sin and impurity. (Ali, the First Imam, is also the patron of the zurkhaneh, and one of his famous sermons is a rigorous demand placed on the modesty and chastity of women.)[37] It is apt that the raped girl is named Fatima, the daughter of the Prophet and symbol of the Islamic community's namus. Her dishonor and the vengeance it requires makes Qaisar najes. If, in a sense, the arak which Qaisar drinks before going to find Mansur (the rapist and the final of his three targets) is the Islamically forbidden (*haram*) intoxicant of the pre-Islamic warrior, it is aptly symbolic of the dissolution of this micro *umma* (Islamic community) both because it breaks Islamic rules and because in Muslim mystical imagery intoxicants transport one out of this corrupt world.

A second film in this genre, Sayyid Motalebi's *Miadgah-i Hashem* (The Meeting Place of Hashem) carries forward some of the debate initiated in *Qaisar*, but lacks its epic elevation. In Motalebi's film, although the aggrieved husband, Qadam, defines the issue as namus, he is determined to take the rapist/murderer to the police alive. This is a duty incumbent on him, not the police: he reports the crime to the police but suppresses the identifying clues. However, he feels, it is not incumbent on him to exact a literal blood price. In this interpretation he is opposed by his brother-in-law and his son, as well as by the companions and parents of the perpetrator. In other words, he is doing what is legally correct but against social pressure from all sides. Again, the social universe is a small, interrelated one: the rapist is the son of the Qadam's best friend (Hashem) and former sweetheart whom, out of friendship, he had left to Hashem to wed. Again, religious imagery is used: Qadam dresses in a black shirt of Moharram; Hashem tells his wife to take down the decorations for a religious meeting (*rowza*) because the house has become unclean. But the tragic contours of the plot are less clean. Three subsidiary moral issues are introduced. First, there is the respect Middle Easterners pay to passion. The rapist, for instance, excuses himself by recounting that he had only meant to tease the woman but that when she clawed him he had lost his head. This is paired with the rage that possesses the dead woman's brother on hearing this excuse, a rage that leads him to nearly kill the boy on the spot. Second, there is blood compensation, as represented by Hashem's offer to exchange everything he owns for his son's life and thus continuation of his line, his son being his only child and the only he will ever have. Third, there is the bond of friendship, which, while not stronger than the trust of namus, may override the bond of love. Sacrificing love for the happiness of a friend, as Qadam had for Hashem, is an ancient theme, the locus classicus being the love of both Khosrow and Farhad for Shirin, which Sayyid Motalebi has used more fully in yet another film of this same genre, *Kuche Mardha*.[38] In *Mihadgahe Hashem* all these moral claims ultimately prove too complex for the plot to handle, and an artificial ending is contrived by having the young rapist fall off a roof and die.

The genre of honor and revenge plays out themes of javanmardi (male chivalry) and dash behavior (paternal protectiveness, ranging from the truly moral to the bullying) with varying degrees of sophistication, maudlin passion, ethnographic reality, and religious or epic symbolism. The psychological and social themes of uncontrollable passion, friendship for better or worse, compulsion of moral duty and justice all seem to revolve around a search for stability in a changing world where religious and epic rules are of uncertain application, and even simple rules of propriety seem confused. Above all, a film like *Qaisar* and, to a lesser extent, films like *Miadgah-i Hashem* and *Kuche Mardha* illustrate the ways in which deeply rooted cultural terms (the *Shahnameh*, zurkhaneh, Khosrow and Shirin) help formulate popular conceptions of male behavior. What remains partially open to question is to what extent these reflect the thought of the social classes of the bazaar or to what extent these conceptions of masculinity use figures from the bazaar as imaginative vehicles for thought.

Village Gravity: *Gav* (The Cow)

God loves not those who are joyous.
— QUR'AN, Sureh 28.76

God wrote but one poem; a masterpiece
God's poem is sadness, sadness seated in the heart,
that's all.
— NADER NADERPOUR

The 1969 film *Gav* (The Cow) is one of the first and probably still the most internationally famous of Persian New Wave films. Based on a story and screenplay by Gholam Husain Sa'edi,[39] it starkly and enigmatically presents an archetypical village through an episodic series of black-and-white images. It is the story of a poor village in which a cow dies and its owner goes mad with grief, much to the dismay of the villagers. Sa'edi, as well as being a writer, is a psychiatrist and has provided the best ethnography to date of the *zar* possession cults along the Persian Gulf. In *Gav*, he presents a case of pathological mourning in a way that illuminates much about the philosophical structure of Persian culture, transcending the rural setting of the story, "the harsh realism of its ethnographic portraiture that allegedly caused it to be banned for a time" (Naficy 1981); it also transcends being a film whose alleged value lies in "graphically representing village life, superstitions, fatalism, and wariness of the world beyond itself" (Hillmann 1982b, 16).

It is a story or film like an onion, as Iranians might say, with even deeper layers or wombs of meaning (*chand batn*). Three sets of ambiguity are posed as artistic guides that draw us toward the deeper levels. First, the central event of the film is the death of Mashd Hasan's cow (Mashhadi is a title gained by going on pilgrimage to Mashhad, the shrine of the Eighth Imam, the most important shrine in Iran), but it is not clear if this was the work of an insider or of the three shadowing and threatening outside figures called "Prussi" in the screenplay and "Baluria" in the film. The three outsiders do enter the village and Mashd Hasan's barn, but they are surprised to find Mashd Hasan acting like a cow rather than the cow herself. They, moreover, are cornered by the villagers and are driven out, an indication that the villagers can act, that they are not totally paralyzed by fatalism and fear. Earlier in the dark of the night, Hassani had given a chicken to Mashd Reyhan; she laughingly asked if it belonged to the Prussi, and he said yes. Mashd Islam's cart also seems to be on the move that night; further, Mashd Islam's goat and Hassani both stick their heads through holes in the adobe walls to look about. The cow at this point is still alive. Indeed, we never see the killing of the cow, so we remain as mystified as the villagers, who suggest various possible causes: the evil eye (something social and internal to the village), a snake (external natural causes), and the Baluria (external social causes).

In an earlier play, "Short A, Long A," Sa'edi describes a group of neighbors in a Tehran neighborhood threatened by thieves; each neighbor displays hesitation and unwillingness to act individually or collectively, a theme that also appears in his play "Club Wielders of Varazil" (Chub Dastan-i Varazil). Is this also the theme of *Gav*? In *Gav* the story is complicated by the teasing that villagers inflict on one another. Mashd Hasan's concern for his cow and the villagers' fear of the three strangers are the subject of ambivalent concern and joking. The son of Mashd Safar jeers at the fears of the men and the brave but empty words of Mashd Jabar, who claims that he is ready to take revenge on the Baluria for the loss of three lambs and asserts that the village must take collective action. Is it coincidental that the son of Mashd Safar has been teasing the village idiot at the time of this exchange? There is teasing but also genuine concern for one another. After the village headman stops the son of Mashd Safar and the children from teasing the village idiot, the son of Mashd Safar shortly proves to be more protective of the idiot; he also, while exposing the hollowness of the men's brave words, makes practical suggestions to Mashd Hasan for protecting the cow. A parallel figure is the old lady, Nana Khanom, who swings her walking stick at the idiot as he runs from his tormentors—she misses, falls down, and everyone laughs—but she, too, is genuinely concerned when the cow dies.

A second ambiguity—less central to the plot but critical to the mood of the film—is the use of funeral and wedding images. While funeral images dominate, there is a constant alternation with the lighter side of life, the sense of ongoing renewal. The film occurs over a four-day period. On Monday, while the menfolk worry about the three threatening Baluria, the children engage in a raucous procession around the village pond, burning three scarecrows. That night is the nocturnal meeting of Hasani and Mashd Reyhan (lovers perhaps). In the early morning, Mashd Hasan leaves for the village of Mishnoo to see if he can find a stud bull to breed his cow. The village headman urges Mashd Baba to come to a funeral (the *majlis tarhim, majlis tazakor, khatm,* or *porseh,* the gathering after a burial to give condolences) and not to let a little dispute appear like a *pedar koshtigi* (killing a man's father, that is, an unredeemable damage to friendship). Later in the morning the cow dies. In the evening the women take out the religious standards (*alam*), which are somewhat similar in shape to the scarecrows, for a funeral procession to the mosque outside the village. Early the next morning, Mashd Hasan returns. Amid the commotion of his reaction to the cow's death, a young couple agree to betroth. That night, the Baluria come and are repulsed. Mashd Hasan's insanity grows. Thursday afternoon, as is customary, people go to the graveyard. The men discuss taking Mashd Hasan to a doctor in town. While they attempt to do this, preparations for a wedding are in progress, and so the film ends.

The alternation is key: do the scarecrows stand for the Baluria, and the invasion by the Baluria for Mashd Hasan's insanity? Is the funeral in effect for the cow, for the failure of the scarecrows to keep away the dark Baluria? Does the wedding in some way stand in for the bovine mating? Is there some identification between the idiot and the madness of Mashd Hasan?

The third ambiguity, and the primary surrealist feature, is the transformation of Mashd Hasan into a cow. In the opening scenes of the film, Mashd Hasan happily brings the cow home from pasture. He washes the cow in a pond, talks to it, drinks water with it. After sighting the Baluria, he decides to sleep in the barn. He plays with the cow, getting down on all fours, putting grass in his mouth, imitating the cow, and laughing. In the morning he leaves the cow safely at home while he departs the village. When he returns the following morning, his first concern is whether the cow has been watered, and he goes to fetch a pail of water. Although a villager attempts to break the news to him gently, saying the cow is lost, he begins to crack: my cow does not wander, she is out in the pasture and will return, he says. That night Mashd Hasan begins to bellow and rush about in the barn. The next morning he is found at the fodder stall chewing grass. He insists he is the cow of Mashd Hasan. Someone asks where his horns are, and he begins to bang his head against the wall; the villagers quickly capitulate. They try telling him the cow has died and they have buried it. That night the Baluria are surprised to find Mashd Hasan in the barn; they are chased away by the villagers. An old woman attempts to exorcise Mashd Hasan with pins, prayers, and sprinklings. Thursday afternoon at the graveyard, the men decide to take Mashd Hasan to a doctor in town. They try first to lead him out gently, but he becomes violent. They tie him up and attempt to drag him out. It begins to rain. The Baluria watch from a distance. Mashd Hasan resists and is beaten by the villagers with the desperate scream, "You animal!" The men look at one another in despair. Mashd Hasan bolts and slips, rolling down a hill face first into a puddle. As the wedding preparations continue, the men harness a horse and cart to take Mashd Hasan away. Such is the stuff of possession and insanity. Mashd Hasan becomes a cow—not one with four feet and a tail, but one whose visage, behavior, and articulation take on definite bovine features. It is a portrait of a certain form of depression, of a grief that has gone awry.

The three ambiguous signpostings constructed by the filmmakers seem to point in certain directions. The loss of a cow is a serious matter in a poor village, and one can understand on the most literal level the obsession of Mashd Hasan. The cow is his existence, his essence.[40] A cow does not only provide milk for the village; if it works in the fields it may also be worth an extra fifth of the harvest, doubling its owner's income.[41] The cow represents many things, from the fertile goodness of Zoroastrian legend and ritual to the political conundrums of modernization (including what one Iranian commentator called his countrymen's "fear psychosis").[42] Through this film, the cow joins a series of animal figures in modern Persian literature—including Hedayat's abandoned dog (*sag-e velgard*) and Samad Behrangi's "little black fish"—who challenge Iranians to think about the nature of their social ties and to evaluate both internal and external sources of illness, decay, fear, and alienation.[43]

With regard to how Sa'edi, in particular, deals with the themes of fear, grieving, teasing, and perhaps repression of anger, it is useful to recall that Sa'edi originally included the story "Gav" in a 1964 collection, *The Mourners of Bayal*. The three ambiguities of the story itself provide further clues. First, who killed the cow and what is the role of the Baluria? There is a real outside danger represented by the Baluria—they do enter the village—of which all the villagers are aware. And yet, they seem also to represent the shadows of paranoia, the excessive fears that build up in Mashd Hasan and help trigger his displaced grief. Second, the alternation of wedding and funeral images suggests that healthy life has ways of dealing with tragedy, death, and sadness. Indeed, the villagers attempt to gently channel and release Mashd Hasan's

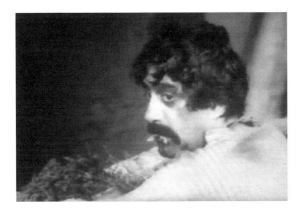

Still from *Gav*

grief. When the cow dies, their first concern is how to handle Mashd Hasan. Perhaps, one villager says, they should not tell him the cow has died. But, retorts another, he will see the cow is not there. So they bury the cow. Mashd Hasan returns the next morning, and they try to break the news slowly and gently. When one cannot grieve, people fear heart attack: news of grief should not come as a shock, and once received must be released. At the end of the film, the villagers are still looking for ways to allow release for Mashd Hasan. They ask if the doctor in town will be able to talk Mashd Hasan out of his denial and displacement, allowing him to unblock his fixated fantasy of being the cow and move instead into a simple, mature, realistic sadness.

Third and most important, the theme of sadness is not merely an appropriate reaction to loss. Sadness in Muslim Iran is a central philosophical attitude, instilled through childhood teasing, cultivated through poetry as a companion to the soul, and elaborated in religion through hadith, prayer, and *rawza*.[44] Sadness is associated with depth of understanding, with thoughtfulness, with maturity, with awareness of the true nature of reality. There are, of course, levels of sadness, ranging from the trivial to the most profound.[45] The philosophical sadness associated with the thoughtful character is neither a wallowing nor a nihilistic sadness, but a balanced realism. As a hadith of Imam Ali puts it: if you are too happy, go to the graveyard; if you are overly sad, you should also go to the graveyard. Two character types are often contrasted: *adam-e sangin* (the weighty or serious person) who rarely laughs, and even when he smiles, smiles a bitter smile; *adam-e sabok*, who laughs and jokes and is a lightweight, a fool. Laughter, too, has its modalities. The grin of a fool is *nush-khand* (from *nush*, a root having to do with drinking); the ironic smile of a philosphical sort is *nish-khand* (*nish*, "bitter"). The rind in

Agha-ye Halu is thus *saboki*, always joking, urging enjoyment of the moment, and Halu chastises him at the end for blowing with the wind ("eating the bread of the day"). The dash in *Agha-ye Halu*, and the typical dash, is *sangin*, gruff and unsmiling (consider Hedayat's "Dash Akol" or the tragic dash figures in the honor and revenge genre). Sadness and the sangin character represent a mature realism and ability to control one's feelings. In *Gav saboki* is represented most extremely by the idiot who, like Mashd Hasan, is tormented (although by children, not grief) and whose emotions blow with the moment from fear and anger to laughter without any control or long-term comprehension.

Emotional control is taught through teasing. (The idiot is teased but cannot learn.) Children are teased to the breaking point, beyond what they can bear, until they burst into tears. Teasing tempers character like steel, as does adversity. One thinks of the proverbial *shagerd-e ahangar* (the blacksmith's apprentice, who is given tasks even when nothing needs doing to instill discipline) and of the *adam-i ab o atesh dideh* (the person who has been tempered by water and fire). The great figures of Shi'ism are those who have endured beyond the ordinary and who control their feelings of aggression and rage (*kazm-i gheys*): Moses, Noah, Mohammad, Ali (and in recent times, Khomeini) are all characterized in these terms.[46] Control can be taught, but it depends as well on one's personal essence (*gowhar*) or sensitivity (*hassasiyat*): perhaps, after all, Mashd Hasan's essence is that of a cow, more base and animal than tempered, manly, spiritual, and human.

The sensitive person is one who fully recognizes the tragic dimensions of reality and who can turn such comprehension into a refuge, who can use sadness as a companion, a "patient stone" (*sang-e sabur*), a tool for dard-e del, for poetic steeling, for stoical strength. ("Agar kuh-e gham nabud, panahi nadash-tam," says a Yazdi poet: "If I did not have this mountain of sadness, I would have no place for refuge.") One does dard-e del with a sympathetic listener, which is usually not a person, but a mountain, a light, a shrine, a well, the Qur'an.[47] Such sadness is not a weakness but a source of strength. It is for this reason, perhaps, that at times of personal tragedy, people cannot express their grief in their own voice but must find a poetic simile, an expression used by someone respected for his comprehension, who can serve thus as an anchor, as a mode of secure channeled release, a reassurance.[48] Mashd Hasan has failed to find such a *zaban-e hal* (a tongue [apt to, facilitating] the state [of release, reconciliation, peace, sadness]), or has found only a perverse one. *Gav* is not a clinical portrait of madness from grief. It is, after all, a fiction, a fabulation, utilizing ambiguity and surrealist techniques to present both an intellectual puzzle and to create a mood.[49] The intellectual puzzle contains elements of village ethnography and, no doubt, political innuendo, but it is primarily about Mashd Hasan's mourning madness and more generally about ways of handling emotions such as grief. The mood engendered is somber but not without humor or the encouragement gained by seeing a comic character who does it wrong. The film ultimately is more about the warmth of village love and the distance demanded by its teasing atmosphere than about evil. It leaves you with a rueful smile: nish-khand rather than nush-khand, a sangin smile.

Conclusions

> The warped floor of the lair and soundconducting walls thereof, to say nothing of the uprights and imposts, were persianly literatured with burst love letters, tell tale stories.—JAMES JOYCE, *Finnegan's Wake*

A difference seems to exist between the creative writing—mainly poetry but also historical novels, satires, vignettes—of the turn of the century in Iran and that of midcentury. The former was more explicitly political and imbued with positivist hope. The writing of midcentury was moodier, more pessimistic, but also more artistic, more thought provoking. It is as if the earlier writing were produced by aristocrats and individuals who thought they could change the world; and as if the later writing were by middle-class, salaried folks, more skilled in their scribal craft, but considerably less convinced that the world could be radically changed. The style of such scribal folk would be, and was, both to pose puzzles for intellectual play and to generate doubt, skepticism, and wariness toward the status quo. Politically, this could feel engagé, even revolutionary; it could contribute powerfully to the preparation of the middle classes for the revolution which began in 1977–1978. And yet, it could also seem, particularly after the revolution, if not tame, then only mildly reformist, a sharpening of the mind rather than of politics, a renaissance of elegant Persian miniatures in a new idiom.

What does one learn about Iran from this idiom? This chapter has directed attention to (1) the artistic structure, the fact that the stories and films are not unmediated portraitures; (2) the possibility that the short stories and films in Iran have been class-linked media or that different strata in society "read" the stories differently; and (3) the utility of the stories as illuminations of Iranian society both through bits of ethnographic portraiture and "indexically" through tacit clues.

The first of these is the least problematic, for literary criticism allows one to rise above the banality of classifying Persian films and stories merely by subject and theme. Much of modern Persian writing utilizes modernist techniques (surrealist ones, stream-of-consciousness, formalism, comic inversion) and thus contributes to world literature a particularly Persian perspective, as well as contributing to creative and cognitive idioms in Iran. Modernist techniques had an elective affinity with the sociocultural position of the secular intelligentsia, in contrast to postmodernist techniques, which seem to be the experimental idiom of the contemporary American intelligentsia—a phenomenon that relates to the nature of the traditionalist social environment against which the Iranian intelligentsia defined itself, as well as the third-world position of Iran in relation to the West.

The second issue—the class-linked nature of this idiom—requires more testing and thought. While is not at all clear that the stories examined here represent Iranian society in terms all Iranians would recognize and affirm, it is equally unclear that these stories can be reduced to a middle-class perspective. True, religious folk regard the film medium with suspicion, and they react negatively to Sadegh Hedayat. True, schoolboys react to *Qaisar* differently than do middle-class folks; what the former seem to affirm as valuable (though they may not act on those models), the latter seem to reject as archaic patterns of the past still maintained in the lower classes (although middle-class professors and factory managers often like to think of themselves as behaving in the manner of a dash, pahlavan, or darvish).

This ambiguity is intertwined with the third set of questions, regarding how artistic vehicles display, portray, and model Iranian society. For each story or film, one can inventory the ethnographic customs, rules, typical situations, conflicts, formulations, symbols, and the like. More subtle are the indirect ways in which the stories reveal tacit understandings of Iranian culture. The film *Gav* is not particularly useful as an ethnographic document about village life, despite Hillmann and Naficy's labeling; it is far more useful as a support for the cognitive style of moody self-reflection one finds as well in Hedayat and other writers such as Bozorg Alavi and Sadegh Chubak. What ostensibly are films about the popular classes turn out to be more illuminating as explorations about character, varieties and stages of manhood, emotions, and styles of social interaction—subjectivities that often transcend class boundaries. Sadness is a sign of depth for both the religious skeptic Hedayat and for the Shi'ite believer, each rejecting the version of the other as too pessimistic and soul-destroying.

This mutual incomprehensibility is an important datum of social conflict, a reminder that understanding cultural rhetorics is not a transparent matter even for members of the same society, and an interesting hint of the powerful life-affirming possibilities of critiques formulated in tragic terms. Again, the parallel with French surrealism is worth considering. Surrealism presented itself as destroying, exploding from within the deep, irrational, psychic interior and violating sedate and deadening middle-class complacency. The point of this destructiveness was to recapture creativity. Similarly, the Persian cultural idiom for centuries has stressed the tragic view of reality as a defense of the soul against the corruptions and evils of the world. The modernist intelligentsia employed surrealist techniques to intensify this attitude, to waken it from the slumber of convention, and thereby perhaps to irritate and anger people into action. That the religious classes could not see this, that they saw only the negativity, the merciless critique of superstition and religion, of obedience to tradition and to oppressive authorities is but the mirror image of the intelligentsia's inability to see the employment of passion plays and sermons about the martyrdom of Imam Husain thirteen centuries ago as anything but obscurantist, repetitive, and inhibitive of critical thought, when in fact they helped mobilize a revolution.

Just as the tragic view need not lack life-affirming power, it also need not lack humor. In his 1967 novel, *The Patient Stone* (*Sang-i Sabur* [an object to which one tells one's sorrows, dard-e del]), Sadegh Chubak not only experiments with using five points of view and the stream-of-consciousness techniques of soliloquy, interior monologue, and interior dialogue (two selves of the same character), but also with a carnivalesque world-upside-down vision.[50] Ahmad Agha, the dominant narrative voice, establishes a comprehension of the present world as having just undergone a cosmic quake, his metaphor for the disruptive forces loose in the world. He, like the narrator in *The Blind Owl* and the woman in *Towers of Silence*, writes to establish his rootedness, to record his loneliness and that of those around him. He bemoans the loss of past writing, which might have provided a sense of rootedness, and fears his own efforts will also become lost: "Where are the Sassanian writings? Where's Rudaki's 'Kalileh and Demneh?' Where are Beyhaqi's works? . . . I ask you, didn't this country have anything? Did the Achaemenians, and the Parthians, and the Sassanians come from under bush? No books, no art, no economy, no religion, no army, no stories, no poetry, no buildings, nothing? . . . Who destroyed it all? Bastards. The Arabs didn't bring us anything. Whatever we had they destroyed. To hell with it. . . . I won't be a writer either. Only a bird with a crooked beak can eat figs, you know" (quoted in Ghanoonparvar 1979, 157). What is left of the past must be re-understood: the heroic wars of the epics, of course, were only bloody massacres; the legendary justice of ancient kings (Anushiravan the Just in particular) were empty facades.[51] Chubak joins Ahmad Agha in this inverted visioning, creating characters who are not what they seem: the doctor who kills his patients, the cleric who is a pimp, the prostitute named Jewel, the rejected child named Goldenlocks, the ugly woman with the name of the Queen of Sheba, and so on.

All this re-visioning culminates in a countercosmogony and an undoing of the monster, God, by the primal man and woman through the ingenuity of the golden-haired Satan. (The terms used for these characters are those from ancient Iran: Zurvan, Ahriman, Mashya, and Mashyaneh; the plot, inverted, is from the Bible and Qur'an.) At the end, God melts away amid earthquakes and falling stars, leaving man and woman under the tree of knowledge, facing an uncertain future as the sun boils up out of the ground with bloody flames. (This is an inverted image of the biblical day of resurrection, when God will roll open the upper firmament like a scroll, removing the tent of the skin of Leviathan from the sun and requiting the wicked: "Behold the day cometh, it burneth as a furnace; and all the proud, and all that work wickedness shall be stubble" [Mal. 3.19, Ps. 19.5].)

The repetitions and distorted mirrorings of the surrealist technique recur in *The Patient Stone* but perhaps with a sense of dynamism and possibility for reordering provided by the carnivalesque apocalyptic. The depiction of isolation and loneliness is a result of the cosmic quake, the historical shaking of Iran from its roots, the turning of things inside out, and disconnecting individuals one from another. The search for connectedness to others and to the past are themes that reverberate throughout the stories and films of Iran. The questions are puzzling: of course, we are Muslim, but we are culturally older than that; why are our oldest roots so strong and yet so ill defined? What is it about our past that continues to motivate us with powers deep below our conscious awareness? What is the relation between our cultural past and the forces of the contemporary world?

What is so powerful about the way modern Persian stories and films explore these questions is their multiple answers, intertwined like Chinese or Turkish puzzle rings. There is the imponderable absurdity of the given, of fate, or as Ahmad Agha puts it, the cosmic quakes. There are the historical layerings of culture, the external invasions which have been both destructive and provisioning (the Turanians, Alexander, the Arabs, the Mongols, the West, the new technological Mongols like television, as Parviz Kimiavi put it in his 1973 film *The Mongols*). And, most sensitive, there are the internal dynamics, both those of decay ("cankers that eat the soul," as Hedayat's famous opening line of *The Blind Owl* puts it) and those of strength and pride, which may find Islamic dress and metaphors but which also seem often to be rooted in Iran's older Zoroastrian identity.

All these techniques, metaphors, and stories force a re-visioning of the world on the reader. The revisioning may be pessimistic or tragic, but it is not complacent or accepting of the powers that be. For the anthropologist, they provide a rich challenge to construct cultural interpretations sensitive to class differences, to intertexuality among cultures and across historical horizons, and to "tacit" understandings acted out or narrated but not fully conscious. Cultural interpretation must rely on a richness of procedure—of reading and engagement—equal to the subtlety and intelligence of the producers of the culture.

4 Filmic Judgment and Cultural Critique:

The Work of Art, Ethics, and Religion in

Postrevolution Iranian Cinema

Truth in Painting

In the display window of Al-Hadi Bookstore in London I notice a volume of Iranian revolutionary posters, collected on the occasion of the sixth anniversary of the revolution (A'li 1985).[1] I enter and ask to see it, ask its price. The shop assistant takes it out to show me, but says it is not for sale, it's a shill, a device to bring customers like me into the shop. You know, he says, I'm an Iraqi; Iranians are supposed to be my enemy (the Iran-Iraq War is still not resolved); but look, I just have to show you, whatever the Iranians turn their hand to has high aesthetic production values.

So, too, with Iranian films. In the 1970s there was a small New Wave of Iranian films. With the revolution, cinema was among the key cultural tools identified as worth controlling. For a short period, production declined and turned propagandistic. But even the production of war films during the Iran-Iraq War had distinctive characteristics, rarely demonizing the enemy, drawing instead on the moral themes of the Karbala story, of self-reliance, overcoming fear, and coping with the tearing of the social fabric among soldiers under stress and between the front and the society behind the lines (Sohrabi 1994; Varzi 2002, 137, 267). By the mid-1980s New Wave filmmaking had revived, and by the 1990s Iranian films were among the most highly regarded in international film festivals around the world.

On the Questions of Globalatinization and the "End of Commentary"

Emile Durkheim at the end of *Elementary Forms of Religious Life* suggests that science and religion do not stand in a relation of replacement but that there is always a shifting dialectical relation between what societies take as scientifically knowable and the puzzles at the limits of reason that generate religious responses (1912, 431). Religion's return to center stage in the age of teletechnologies raises questions about the interaction between media and the forms of religion. In two rich and provocative essays Jacques Derrida (1998, 2001) focuses attention on the transformative powers of teletechnologies, with which religions have double relations, both utilizing them and being undone by them. Stressing the power of capital and the concentration of media power, Derrida speaks of a "new war of religion" which "inscribes its seismic turbulence directly upon the fiduciary globality of the techno-scientific, of the economic, of the political and of the juridical. It brings into play the latter's concepts of the political and of international right, of nationality, of the subjectivity of the citizenry, of the sovereignty of states" (Derrida 1998, 20). He invokes the Muslim world as a site par excellence of telecommunicative dissemination and of displacements of locality and tradition, warning that "the surge <defurlement> of 'Islam' will be neither understood nor answered as long as . . . one settles for an internal explanation (interior to the history of faith, of religion, of languages and cultures as such), as long as one does not define the passageways between this interior and all the apparently exterior dimensions (technoscientific, tele-biotechnological, which is to say also political and socioeconomic, etc.)" (1998, 20).

The "forms" of religion that are transformed by teletechnologies are various, and Derrida detours first through an array of impossibilities and paradoxes of meaning ("at the limits of reason") as generative of religion and religiosities. Further, he suggests, teletechnological media and Christianity are currently allied and hegemonic in making all visible, incarnate, "brought to you live and direct" (thus, "globalatinization" [*mondialatinisation*]), in contrast to Islam and Judaism, which refuse this iconicity and this presencing, insisting on infinite commentary, because God is never directly self-revealing. Yet, as other religions attempt to use teletechnologies they are drawn into this logic of globalatinization, of making visible/present and of long-distance spectralization. Such use of teletechnologies can operate with a "terrible logic of autoimmunity" (Derrida 1998, 13), undoing the propaganda of such religions even as it extends their reach. And so Derrida asks if globalatinization is the end of commentary in the Islamic and Judaic sense, while at the same time observing that globalatinization, while it seems ultrapowerful and hegemonic at the moment, is also in the process of exhausting itself. In the meantime, those who use teletechnologies in a frenzy of outbidding for attention, for profits, for followers, generate a "maddening instability among positions" and the "madness" of "absolute anachrony of our times" (12–13). (Derrida's primary examples are from television: evangelical Protestant television in the United States, making miracles present, and Roman Catholic televisual reports on the travels of the Pope, also imaging the transcendence of the dying/suffering body. He notes that Islamic and Jewish television in contrast tends to be of talking heads, discussion.)

Samuel Weber (2001) expands the discussion by invoking Walter Benjamin's initial understanding of the mediality of language as *Mitteilbarkeit*, im-part-ability, the possibility of a medium to divide and distribute itself, to im-part itself, its capacity of "come-going," of arrive-leaving, of withdrawing. Also relevant to the discussion is Levinas's figure of religion as *adieu/a Dieu* (a goodbye to dogma or received orthodoxy that initiates movement toward God or the Other). Hent de Vries (1998, 2) points to the profound sedimentation of religious idiom in language that counters any easy ability to count religion as obsolete. But he emphasizes that Derrida thinks of the return to religion not as a return to what is already there, but rather as a movement after respiratory interruptions (ibid., 4) that inspires a renewal of spirit; along those lines, de Vries continues, teletechnologies are interruptive and novel in their political-economy configurations of nationalism and sovereignty issues, expansive capitalist and transnationalist mechanisms, and their technoscientific formats. Moreover, de Vries notes, again citing Derrida, successful religious performatives seem always to be *perverformative*: "Any religious utterance, act or gesture, stands in the shadow of—more or less, but never totally avoidable—perversion, parody and kitsch, of blasphemy and idolatry" (ibid., 11).

What Place Iranian Cinema
on the Stage of Globalatinization?

A reader's hypothesis: nowhere today is teletechnology more revelatory (*Offenbarung*) or useful as access to revealability (*Offenbarkeit*) than in films about and within the moral, ethical, and religious struggles of Iran.[2] Of course, one needs to read filmic technologies and telecommunications as Levinas understands the Book: "I understand Judaism as the possibility of giving the Bible a context, of keeping this book readable" (qtd. in Derrida 1998, 55). One needs in other words not to speculate from too much afar, nor to grant too much too quickly to the forces of abstraction, capital, and specularization, but rather to engage ethnographically with the directors, producers, distributors, and audiences, with their understandings, references, and allusions. It is not at all clear that globalatinization is the end of commentary or that the forces of capital and concentration of media ownership merely suck all onto a Christian-defined terrain or performativity, though it may well be that the Muslim world today is a site par excellence of telecommunicative dissemination and of displacements of locality and tradition.

Some forms of Derrida's worries were expressed twenty years ago by the leaders of the several factions of the Islamic revolution of 1977–1979, not only in the call to take cultural control of television and cinema, but more generally in Ayatullah S. Muhammad-Kazem Shariatmadari's warnings that should Islam become an instrument of the state, should clerics become government functionaries and official politicians engaging in the daily negotiations of power, should clerics completely control the media, Islam in Iran would become corrupt and destroy its own moral authority.[3] To Derrida's catalog of quintessentially televisual religious projections one might add the demonstrations of the Islamic revolution staged for the camera, especially at the time of the seizure of the U.S. embassy, which stopped on cue when the cameras were turned off. Perhaps the audiocassettes used by Ayatullah S. Ruhullah Khomeini from Paris in his campaign to oust the shah also fit the mold of globalatinization insofar as their geopolitical context was against the power of the Great Satan of the West. Television, radio, audiocassettes, sermons, pamphlets, and the dramatic poster campaigns of the revolution marked a kind of messianic space in which globalatinization and Islamic discourse agonistically generated multiple hybridizations of form and content, and in which a population was caught up in a heightened experiential regime in which conflicting background assumptions became available for world-historical productivity, not only within Iran but, as the slogan of the times had it, also for the "export of the revolution." (Recall even the effort to export the revolution to African Americans, crystallized in a dramatic Islamic Republic postage stamp fusing together the image of Malcolm X and that of Bilal, the first *mu'ezzin* [caller to prayer] of Islam.)

Throughout the twentieth century, film was one of the most powerful media, fostering a crosscultural comparative understanding among peoples of the globe, borrowing and modifying genres, styles, consumption aspirations, sensibilities, affect, and recognition of difference. While crosscultural referencing and awareness may be part of globalatinization—and part of what Walter Benjamin referred to as a loss of the naive parochial sense of original aura, a kind of captioning or reflexive indexing of art's social provenance—it need be neither a homogenizing process nor a wild frenzy of unstable positions driven merely by efforts to stake claims in the market. It can also work to establish niches in diasporic and transnational circuits.

Persian and Arabic have several words for religion: *mazhab* is the sect, legal school, or organized religious affiliation; *iman* faith; *deen* the noun for religion in general. *Dawa* (invitation), religious missionary work, is the call to deen. Insofar as cinema "picturizes" (as the colorful South Asian English verb puts it) and provides a sound system for deen (not just the call to prayer, but other religious sounds in poetry, in music, and in debating, arguing, deliberating voices), it performs calls to response and responsibility; it calls for community but also stages the struggles for ethical decision making against unthinking custom or tradition; it calls for translatability across languages and cultures and regions and class divisions; and it calls for ethical response to dramas of life, to the Other, and to the changing terrains of the moral and the ethical.

What is moral has to do with the social; the ethical is individual decision making: both are under pressure of change. It would be well to have windows and voices that open into the discussions and debates within the moral terrains of Iran and other Islamic worlds. The key terms of the Islamic revolution in Iran, after all, had to do with justice (adelat), a central component of deen, not just religion in the institutional sense (mazhab). Filmic judgment is a terrain, despite the state-constrained production facilities of the Islamic Republic of Iran, in which ethical as well as religious issues have been dramatized in ways that, while often deploying genre formats and cinematic borrowings and conventions, escape the stereotypic, that constitute an evolving moral discourse parallel to older poetic, qur'anic, epic, literary, or theatrical ones.

Constraints on film production exist not only in terms of censorship but also in terms of audience demand. The number of theaters in Iran has declined to 287, from 417 before the revolution, and there is now an effort to build more cinemas to support the industry. Meanwhile, however, spectatorship for Iranian films has been declining, and some would argue that the state has supported films for export, rather than films for domestic consumption, in order to pay the costs of production. A conference was convened in

December 1998 in Tehran to consider the dilemmas of audience and film production ("International Film" 1999, 14). At least four strands overlap in discussions about audience: (1) the vulnerability of all national cinemas to Hollywood or global cinema; (2) the struggle of the Islamic state—much like the earlier Hollywood Hayes code in the United States—to set moral boundaries, which, while restrictive, functions at times like the rules of a sonnet, that is as a creative game that can generate some excellent results; (3) the struggle between art cinema and commercial cinema even within a vigorous national cinema industry (as India and Hong Kong illustrate most dramatically, as does the United States with its independent film industry); (4) the place of production for the niche of international connoisseurs or for a diasporic audience. While such considerations pose problems for claims about the efficacy of this medium in the public sphere, they hardly constitute grounds for dismissal. In the late 1990s, newspapers were clearly the primary medium for cultural struggles in the Iranian domestic political arena—but film, is in any case, rarely a directly instrumental medium. Nor is to recognize the cultural work of Persian films to disregard the role of Hollywood and other global film influences in the construction of fantasy within Iran, or even their roles within Persian films as interlocutors or vehicles for refashioning in local idiom.

For the Perso-Islamic world, the religious terrain of moral parabolic reason has included for centuries not just the Qur'an and its commentaries, nor just the passion of Karbala (the exemplary stories used in sermons from the martyrdom of the First Imam), but also the *Shahnameh*, its recitations in the zurkhanehs, the codes of pahlavans and javanmardi, the poetry of Hafez and of Rumi, and the codes of being a darvish (being unattached to the politesse and hypocrisies of the social world). Who, including clerics, would make a major decision in life without a quick divination (if only in jest) by opening Hafez or Rumi? Efforts in the most fundamentalist days of the Islamic Republic to downplay the Persian New Year, which is of Zoroastrian origin, have never succeeded.

But even taking the Qur'an itself, it is worth remembering the hermeneutic richness that contests interpretations in the political arena in ways rarely reported by Western journalism (except insofar as journalists have reported on clerics who have defended the moral authority of Islam against what they felt were the political interpretations of the state). If, as is often asserted, Islam and the diasporic Muslim world are important to speculations about the social dynamics of globalization in the twenty-first century, one should understand their oral, textual, and telemedia modalities, which operate both in parallel and as counterpoint to globalatinization. Derrida's call not to ignore the exterior forces influencing internal accounts of Islam is well taken, but at the same time one must not ignore the internal resources Islam brings to the global stage: one needs to thicken the cultural accounting, as well as pay attention to the vectors of globalization. At the core of Islam is the recitation of the Qur'an, an oral form ill captured by its textual transcript (*mushaf*). When one listens to recitations of Sura 96, considered the earliest revelation to Muhammad, it becomes clear that it is made up of different fragments. The rhythm or musicality changes, and the content indicates differences between the times the fragments occurred (in the cave during Muhammad's withdrawal from Mecca; in Mecca on Muhammad's return from the cave). In these two fragments from the time of withdrawal and the time of his return to Mecca, several distinctive features of the Qur'an are already evident: (1) there is a dual order: the first revelation chronologically does not come first sequentially (the suras, or "chapters of verses," are ordered roughly by length, from longest to shortest); (2) the narrative unit is the fragment, not the sura; (3) meaning is conveyed by the sound and would be much more difficult to establish by the text alone ("taught by the pen; taught man, that he knew not" [96, 1–5]); (4) meaning is further established by a knowledge of the occasions or allusions of the fragments, without which the text is inscrutable, legible but unintelligible; (5) the fragments are of various genres, including dialogs with staged voices (between God and Abraham, Moses and Khidr, God and Satan, Moses and Pharaoh), implicit dialogs in which Muhammad has been asked a question by Jews or unbelievers ("Say to them *qul!*"), and addresses from God to Muhammad and through him to Muslims; (6) only by recapturing the divine sound, as well as one can, is one able to approach the presence of God and apprehend His divine words—as human speech is inadequate to the divine, so is the written text a poor transcript of the divine tablet (*lawh mahfuz, Umm al-Kitab*) of the seventh heaven.

So, too, cinema is writing with light and sound, involving multiple codes of signification. Cinematic discourse is constructed through films that cite one another, creating thereby a commentary tradition, an ethical discursive arena parallel to older poetic, qur'anic, epic, parable and theatrical forms. Iran's cinema addresses domestic, diasporic, and international audiences. And so one returns to at least a heuristic readers' hypothesis: nowhere today is teletechnology more revelatory or useful as access to revealability than in the films about and within the moral, ethical, and religious struggles of places undergoing sharp cultural struggle such as Iran, the Balkans (Emir Kustarica's *Underground*, Milcho Machevski's *Before the Rain*), and India. In India some commercial filmmakers are attempting to comment on such contemporary problems as religious communal riots (Mani Rathnam's *Bombay*), Kashmir (Vinod Chopra's *Mission Kashmir*), and caste violence (Sheikur Kapur's *Phoolan Devi*). Furthermore, many films now incorporate relations with the Indian diaspora, effectively turning Bollywood into a transnational form, with many Hindi films making more money on their diasporic audiences than on their domestic ones. While Iranian films do not have the same money-making draw, their dissemination to the diaspora via curated film festivals and video is not insignificant.

Filmic Judgment and Cultural Critique

The phrase "filmic judgment and cultural critique" forms a double-voiced invocation. It refers in part to one of the key films of postrevolutionary Iran, *Close Up* (*Kloz up*, *Nega'i Nazdik*) by Abbas Kiarostami (1990), which like Michelangelo Antonioni's *Blow Up* has as one of its themes the paradox that when one investigates something carefully, one tends to find further complexities, not simple clarifications. While "blow up" refers to the enlargement of a photograph until the image becomes too grainy to decipher, *Close Up* refers to its filmic medium, as a starting point from which to contemplate cinema as an alternative space to the court system for critical reflection and judgment about social and cultural matters.

Based on a true incident, *Close Up* is the story of a man who tried to pass himself off as the filmmaker Mohsen Makhmalbaf. He is arrested and brought before an Islamic court. The film is framed in part through the story of the journalist who broke the story and that of the documentary filming of the court trial, with director Kiarostami's voice on the soundtrack. It is a kind of psychodrama, in which a poor man unable to support his family experiences fragile moments of dignity and self-esteem by getting people to believe he is the famous director. It is like a narcotic, a kind of gambling or deep play, in which he is aware that he is not able to manage the pose, yet is drawn back again and again to experience those moments of power. But it is not just a psychological story of dignity and self-esteem; it is also a social drama of Iranian society. In explaining himself, the man says that he posed as Makhmalbaf, not just any director, because Makhmalbaf's films are about people like himself, that they are the kinds of films he would see again and again because they put people like himself on screen. The Islamic judge attempts to get the

Wide-angle of judge
Sabzian and Kiarostami
close-up (*Close Up*)

plaintiffs, a family who felt they had been taken in by the fraudulent pose, to settle with the defendant; in this respect, it is a realistic portrayal of the work of an Islamic court, more accurate than the violent images of Islamic revolutionary courts that the Western press is fond of purveying.[4] In the courtroom, Kiarostami says to the defendant that there are two cameras, one focused on the courtroom proceedings as such, the other aimed at the defendant, and it is to the latter that the defendant should speak those things which may not be admissible in court but which he would like to be used to explain himself. The camera here is literally posed as an alternative court. Filmic judgment.

Filmic judgment stands here also as a general set of anthropological questions: the questions about how filmic media and telemedia over the course of the twentieth century have changed the ways we perceive and judge; the shifting dia-logical, dialogic, and crosscultural texture of ethical, moral, and religious discourses; and the theatrical, performative, and political shapes of discursive power in public spheres that reflect, diffract, and contest institutional forms and conventions.

As an anthropologist, I am interested in film first as a vehicle of ethnography, as a kind of register, a descriptive medium, of cultural patterns, of patterned social dynamics, of the present tense, and of the hybridities or the transnational negotiations of globalizing and localizing cultural processes. By "present tense" I mean the common intuition that there is something about film, even if often illusory, that gives an impression of being able to present the complexities of the present moment with an immediacy that is difficult to achieve through writing, in part of course because filmic media can present complexity through multiple means: musical, soundtrack, visual, and verbal. When Walter Benjamin (1969) spoke of a new mode of perception that cinema taught through "distracted" scanning of multiple sensory channels, he suggested that it created an absent-minded consciousness; but I would like to suggest that the subjectivities created are a more complex dialectic between absent-mindedness and self-reflective consciousness, each side of this dialectic being itself a complex set of negotiations, especially under conditions of rapid and politically explicit social and cultural upheaval.

As an anthropologist, I am also interested in film as a complex vehicle of cultural critique. At minimum, film over the course of the twentieth century fostered a comparative perspective. Popular consciousness moved from the peep show or distanced views of the exotic Other to cinema or closer views.[5] Film has become, as has the novel since the nineteenth century, a space for externalizing cultural and social patterns, dramas, dilemmas, and processes so that a society can see itself and reflect on itself. This raises both philosophical questions about the reconstruction of consciousness and sociological questions about the reconstruction of public spheres and the social functions of film.

Beginning with the nineteenth-century discovery that the brain does not just register perceptions but analyzes and reconstructs, consciousness has had an important history. Like the brain, so too the various apparatuses of perceptual prostheses like the camera and projector. Like sociocultural understandings, so too the cinema is understood, as Walter Benjamin (1969) put it, as a gymnasium of the senses, wherein one is constantly checking one's reactions and understandings against those of others. Regarding cinema and telecommunication, let me telegraph with a few theoretical touchstones of the past century. First, Walter Benjamin suggested in the 1930s that film was a key technology of modernity, a place where people learned to deal with the shock of the new, learning a new mode of apperception, which he called "distraction," meaning the ability to scan and sample, to rapidly integrate fragmentary new information coming through multiple sensory channels (Benjamin 1969). At issue in any effort to think of the ways film functions as cultural critique is an inquiry into a double-sided relation: on the one hand is film's "absent-minded" functioning on the level of daydream or fantasy or even at the level of subliminal absorption of images and information that are barely registered but are later processed and integrated; on the other hand is its mirroring cultural work of making explicit, external, and available for conscious critique the patterns underlying everyday life that otherwise flow past in less-available forms. Second, Paul Virilio (1989) in the post–World War II era counts film not just as a technology of speed but even more as a technology of "degrangement," detaching populations from their localities, drawing them to the economic promises of the great cities, but also mobilizing them for war, marking them for destruction. Third, Slavoj Žižek (1991), playing out late-twentieth-century psychological and Lacanian psychoanalytic perspectives, argues that film plays on processes of seduction not so much by picturing the objects of desire themselves as by staging the circuits of desire, the unending substitutions of desire, the circuits of obsession. Fourth, Wilhelm Würzer (1999) provides a more cognitivist claim that the pleasure of film lies in the challenge of actually seeing the order of representation exposed, of watching displacements, detours of judgment, de-framings of power. Fifth, Gilles Deleuze (1983, 1985) suggests not only that cinema is a kind of nomadic war machine, the camera able to move about in a deterritorialized fashion, seizing and remobilizing cultural bits for its own strategic purposes, but also that there has been an important break between pre–World War II films ("classical") and post–World War II films.

Post–World War II film, Deleuze suggests, uses a different time-space image beginning with Italian neorealism and French New Wave, in which objects are more carefully observed than in classical realism. Optical and sound elements, for instance, often take on autonomous existence, and many other sign systems can also be foregrounded: chronosigns, lectosigns (modes of inscription), noosigns (interior mental associations). Time-space becomes virtual rather than spatial, such that these various dimensions of signification can be foregrounded and interrelated in a variety of ways. At issue here is not merely an epistemological but also a political shift. Epistemologically speaking, more precision leads to a less-easy realism, and what is usually being investigated in the postwar world are the powers of the false. This is, perhaps, what contemporary Polish filmmakers and critics call *odkłamanie* (*od*, negative particle + *kłamanie*, "lies"), countering the lies, myths, and conventional assumptions on which communist society was constructed. The hopes and fears of the contemporary society are also constructed on shifting sands of partial truths that need countering. The shock of the cinema, says Deleuze, can no longer be the forms of thought like Serge Eisenstein's montage techniques of the prewar era, because since then, both fascist and mass commercial art have appropriated modernist forms. The shock of the cinema rather, as Ackbar Abbas (1992) felicitously puts it, is to show that we are not yet thinking, to point to what is out of the frame, to what is not present. Abbas's interpretation is suggestive of Lacan's understanding of the fantasies that motivate our neurotic behaviors, when through labile dreams or memories past events take on great significance in the absence of a therapist who can suggest that these are but dream figures and thus help us integrate them and defuse their overweening power. Such psychodynamic or psychological readings of films can add to their interpretive richness. However, even without the psychological register, what is out of the frame often becomes as powerful a visual motivation "for the camera," or for the viewer's curious eye, as is deferral of resolution in good narrative and storytelling.

Midrash 1

Mark Tansey's "The End of Painting" provides a parallel puzzle: it pictures an American cowboy shooting an image of himself in a framed mirror projected on a movie screen. As Mark Taylor comments, "the image is resolutely illusionistic, and implicitly narrative, functioning like a koan, simultaneously provoking and shattering reflection" (1999).

If, then, we can in a preliminary way say that the new forms of consciousness or perception fostered by film have something to do with speed, multiple channels of information, scanning and sampling tactics, nonlinear attention, and pleasure in juxtaposing forms that shape and change informational perspectives or meaning, we can in similar preliminary fashion telegraph a series of anthropological-sociological functions of film that constitute the reconstruction of sociocultural consciousness. Studies of Hollywood in the 1920s point out how film performs future-oriented cognitive work, allowing immigrant working-class populations to think through new lifestyles. Larry May (1980) notes that one third to half of the scriptwriters were young women, and the scripts reflected their interest in portraying new roles for women in balancing family and careers. Others have noted similar patterns, as Betty Friedan (1963) did for stories in women's magazines, contrasting the support for career women evident in the 1930s with the insistence on shifting women back into the household in the 1950s.[6]

Film has also been a vehicle for working through past social traumas: Pierre Sorlin's studies of European film industries show how films about World War I took more than a decade to emerge (there was a similar lag in American production of films about Vietnam), but then how the films of France and England thematized fears of espionage in democratic societies while those of Germany and Italy had different obsessions (Sorlin 1991). He also saw national differences among World War II films, each country downplaying the help received from others and deepening the suspicions of others; at the same time, World War II films introduced cruelty and sadism in a new way and were deeply pessimistic about the partisans of the resistance (who are usually killed). Films also help create national publics: Antonia Lant (1991) looks at the ways in which gender definitions create a British style of realism in contrast to American films in order to mobilize national identity and a national public during World War II. Films introduced comparative perspectives to local populations all over the globe, serving as ethnographic writing machines, registering description (location, footage, modeling behavior, emotion, customs), registering hybrid forms in the present tense, and translating domestic differences within states trying to constitute themselves as coherent nations. The Iranian film *Bashu* does this in a particularly dramatic way.

Among the most visually striking of the postrevolutionary films, Bahram Beza'i's *Bashu, the Little Stranger* is an antiwar film about a little boy in southern Iran whose parents die in a fireball of Iraqi bombs and who climbs on a truck to escape, emerging a day or two later in the totally different linguistic and physical environment of Gilan in northern Iran. A peasant woman takes him in and protects him against the xenophobia of the villagers, having in the process to come to terms with his different language and the fact that his dark complexion will not wash off. It is a film about racial and cultural differences within Iran, as well as about the difficulties of the home front during the war with many of the menfolk away. Although banned until the end of the Iran-Iraq War, *Bashu* is a powerful way for Iranians to view themselves. At the first North American Iranian film festival where it was shown, *Bashu* elicited tears and cheers from a staunchly antirevolutionary

Iranian audience, which suddenly found itself confronted with evidence that not all that was happening in Iran was bad.

Although in some respects film is already becoming an archaic cultural form for thinking through the modalities of transnational cultural change — computer-mediated communication and digital media, it might be argued, provide the leading edge—in other respects, it continues to evolve as a central medium, along with television, for cultural negotiations over the local and the global, for working through comparative perspectives in different national settings, and for the reconstruction of society and public spheres after social traumas of civil war, revolution, state collapse, earthquake, and other massive social disruptions. Like advertising, film operates as one of the key modalities of insertions into popular culture, amplifying, refracting, leveraging, and modifying the *sensus communis* (operating most effectively in Walter Benjamin's absent-minded modality), but also with interruptive possibilities for response, reaction, talking back, and reflective critique.

The Work of Interruption in Prerevolutionary and Postrevolutionary Iranian Cinema

Indeed, the work of interruption is dramatic in the punctuations of cinema burnings, censorship, and political contestation over the freedom of cinematic production and the commentary generated thereby—in Iran, and in many other countries undergoing the reshaping of the public sphere (for example, India, China). The work of interruption is ethical in the Levinasian sense: interrupting both spontaneity (unthinkingness) and totalizing (aestheticizing). Interruptive articulation: both articulating pieces of noncontinuous, even noncommensurable, discourses and stuttering, hesitant, halting efforts toward articulate speech, finding in articulations of both sorts an immanent form of cultural critique.

Three types of interruptive activity can be distinguished in pre- and postrevolutionary Iranian cinema: the politics of cinema-going in prerevolutionary Iran; cinema burnings as part of the struggle for control over its means of production during the revolution proper and its aftermath in the dynamics of demand and availability of theaters and kinds of films; and the disruptions caused by the reception of films which struck a public nerve, thus polarizing audiences.

Frame 1: The Politics of Cinemagoing
in Prerevolutionary Iran

Flashback to 1969, an opening night at Cinema Soheil in Yazd (described in chapter 3) and recall the emotional tonalities of cinemagoing: "Defiant was how the womenfolk dressed. . . . This bureaucratic elite felt embattled. . . . The wives and daughters appeared unveiled at private receptions and parties, but dared to appear unveiled among the ordinary folk only when they went in groups to the movies protected by their menfolk." Recall the hostility to the cinema by many of the locals, the building of a mosque across the street explicitly to challenge such entertainment. Remember the modernist streets cutting through the old urban fabric. Recall the ambivalence of the modernist, nonlocally recruited, bureaucratic elite, which saw itself optimistically fighting ignorance, superstition, poverty, and social inertia, and in this endeavor felt pessimistically trapped in strongly conservative provincial worlds—trapped economically, politically, and psychologically. It is this despair and entrapment, from a perspective of a would-be modernism, that the New Wave films used as an artistic palette.

No film did this more powerfully than *Gav*, directed by Darius Mehrju'i, which initiated the New Wave in 1969. Based on a story and screenplay by the psychiatrist, ethnographer, and writer Gholam Husain Sa'edi, this rustic noir film seemed pregnant with political meaning and anticipation, despite being primarily a finely crafted intellectual puzzle about mourning, the handling of emotion, and philosophical realism or melancholia. The film was structured by three sets of ambiguity: over blame or causation (who or what killed Mashd Hasan's cow: a social internal cause, an external natural one, an external social one?); over health and dealing with tragedy (is this pathological mourning or destruction of the political economy down to bare life?); over the cultivation of inner strength versus passivity (could there be resistance to the state in which people found themselves?).

The year 1969 marked a decade before the revolution. The interruptive work at the time was the delicate move and counter-move between modernists introducing the cinema—defiantly protecting unveiled women in public space as one symbolism among many, including the arrival of train tracks, cheap intercity bus travel, and an airport—and, on the other side, the building of a mosque across the street from the cinema as an architectural counter-symbolism that was part of a long history of agitation against the cinema.

Frame 2: The Revolution

19 August 1978, Abadan (southern Iran). On the twenty-fifth anniversary of the restoration of the monarchy in 1953, a stunning tragedy was perpetrated. Four hundred people died in a fire in the Rex Cinema. It is a turning point in the revolutionary process of 1977–1979. Although five cinema theaters had been burned during the month of Ramadan, which had begun on 5 August, to protest the importation of foreign films purveying sex and Western materialism, this time people blamed the Shah's secret police: the cinema was in a working-class section that did not cater to foreigners or elites; the film being shown was Iranian, not foreign; the fire department was noticeably slow to respond, and the equipment would not function when it did arrive; and the police prevented citizen rescue efforts.

Control over cinema, over the means of production of a powerful cultural tool, was one of the goals of the 1977–1979 revolution. Some of the more avant-garde of the New Wave of Iranian films, although portraying themselves as politically engagé critiques of the Shah's tyranny, were rejected by the religious and popular classes as effete and nihilistic. Audience members purportedly received films like Parviz Kimiavi's *Moghul-ha* (1973) by tearing up the cinema seats, outraged not because they reviled the film's content but because they were frustrated at not understanding the film's techniques. Kulturkampf existed not only between the state and dissidents; more tragically for the course of the revolution, Kulturkampf divided the elite strata and the religious/popular strata, who had different aesthetics and could not understand each other's form of discourse. The latter criticized the avant-garde elite for nihilism, while the elite in turn accused the religious and popular classes of "repetition" of old religious stories.

Moghul-ha (The Mongols) is a melancholy, if humorous, meditation on the unstoppable corrosion of Persian culture by Western technology, making Persian culture at best archaic. It is about television's destruction not only of oral culture but also of film. It opens with scenes of the filmmaker studying a foreign, French technology: turning the pages of a history of cinema, showing the various early forms of creating moving images. French technology is combined with Persian content: the filmmaker's wife reads from Juvaini's "History of the Mongols" as the filmmaker matches images of running Turkomen actors in traditional garb with the Muybridge stills of moving imagery. An old man asked about the past, about the Mongols, looks into a mirror. The film is composed in classic modernist montage fashion out of fragments of Persian visual icons—the illiterate Turkomen, a darvish, ruins of old mud forts, a caravanserai, windmills, the recitation of the epic *Shahnameh*—and contemporary references—a microwave relay tower, an intercom buzzer on a wrought-iron gate, reference to European films. In the end the filmmaker is not only not understood by his actors ("Cinema chi-eh?" [What is cinema?]) who just want to go home, but he himself is beheaded in a microwave tower figured as guillotine, his head rolling off as a film canister.

Frame 3: Postrevolutionary Films that Touch a Social Nerve

The mid-to-late 1980s. Mohsen Makhmalbaf's films *The Peddler* (1986) and *The Marriage of the Blessed* (1988) were received by many in Iran as sharp criticisms of the Islamic revolution from one who had previously been the head of the Center for the Arts of the Organization for the Propagation of Islam. Makhmalbaf was reported to have objected to the peace Khomeini concluded with Iraq as a mockery of the sacrifices Khomeini had until then demanded until, of selling out a generation of young men who had given their lives in the war to fight via Karbala on to Jerusalem.

Marriage of the Blessed is the story of a war photographer who is traumatized and sent to an insane asylum. He is rescued by his fiancée, and they spend their time in Tehran photographing the social ills that the revolution promised but failed to solve. The camera here functions analogously to its role in Kiarostami's *Close Up*.

The Peddler is a stylistically innovative film, a triptych, three interlinked stories. The first, set in the slums of south Tehran, is inspired by an Albert Moravia short story and tells of a couple who have three children crippled by malnourishment. The wife is pregnant, and the husband begs her to abandon the child in the hospital so that it can have a decent life. She is unable to leave the child, so they try to find other places to abandon it, places where they can watch to ensure it is adopted by someone who will care for it. It is a series of heartbreaking failures, with some horrific scenes of an orphanage where they refuse to leave the child.

The second segment seems to be a take-off on *Psycho*, but is about a young man who takes care of his old mother. Made crazy by mechanical culture, he is obsessively driven by clocks and the routines of housekeeping. In one hilarious scene he is unable to cross a busy street near the central Tehran bazaar. Toward the end of this segment he is abducted in a car, robbed, and tossed out onto the street.

The third segment shot in film-noir style takes place in the bazaar and a

Camera as speed
and nomadic war
machine
Cinema, chi-e?
[What is cinema?]
(*Moghul-ha*)

coffeehouse inhabited by the underworld and Afghan refugees. It is the story
of a man who is intimidated by his mafia bosses and therefore dies a pointless
and animal-like death, suffering this death multiple times in his imagination
long before he actually dies. Characters from all three segments of the film
come together: the underworld of the third segment is made up of the
abductors of the young man in the second segment, and the poor couple of
the first segment scavenge from the grocery bag the man drops as he is
abducted. Makhmalbaf himself argued at the time that the film was developing a distinctively Islamic filmic rhetoric about birth, middle life, and death,
coded with color and light symbolism (divine blue frames an opening shot of
a fetus as well as the final shots of merging into death), and that it was
misread if taken as a social critique. But the richness of the footage and the

Filmic Judgment and Cultural Critique   239

testimony of his impersonator in *Close Up* suggest that the social critique does not go unnoticed by Iranian audiences, or by his fellow filmmakers.

The Late 1990s

In 1997 two films stirred up audiences in Iran. Abbas Kiarostami's film *A Taste of Cherry* (1997) pushed the envelope of Iranian morality in a story about a man who offers others money to bury him after he commits suicide. Dariush Mehrju'i's film *Leila* polarized Iranian audiences, touching a raw social nerve by telling the story of an infertile wife pressured by her mother-in-law to help her husband find a second wife and of the series of unhappy consequences that follow for all involved.

Abbas Kiarostami's Palm d'Or-winning *A Taste of Cherry* is a parable about the choice to live (or not), about the duty to respect and aid the desire or call of others, and about ways of transcending this world literally, socially, mystically, or through the art of film. We never learn much about the character, Badii, who poses these challenges. Though he seems well-to-do and carries a mien of melancholy, in fact we learn little about him or his motivations. Rather than a psychological or character portrait, he seems rather to provide a philosophical function, a projective screen, and a kind of open signifier or token that carries questions for the way the other characters are challenged to react to the need or desire of a fellow human being. There are three men to whom Badii offers money to bury him after he commits suicide by taking sleeping pills, and they provide three different ethical and practical responses. In the course of these requests and responses, Badii himself is gradually transformed into a less isolated person.

A Kurdish peasant boy, only two months in the army, runs away from the dilemma and from the manner in which Badii approaches him: it is a fear reaction. An Afghan *talabeh* (seminary student), visiting a fellow Afghan security guard at a construction site, invokes Islamic rules and refuses to help but considers the request more sympathetically and seriously than the Kurdish lad could. Finally, an older Azeri Turkish–speaking taxidermist who needs money for his daughter's operation tries to dissuade Badii with humor and tries to call his bluff, but promises to help him.

There are various possible allusions in *A Taste of Cherry* to Sadegh Hedayat's *The Blind Owl* (being eaten up from the inside, the use of shadows and icons of this world and the next), and to Dariush Mehrju'i's film *Gav* (shadows, noir, isolation versus community). The Kurd, Afghan, and Azeri Turk evoke the strong communal life of Iran's ethnic minorities in contrast to the anomie of the middle-class Tehrani (Badii). The film is visually filled with the unfinished: building sites, the guard who makes tea which is never drunk. The film is also filled with icons from Kiarostami's earlier films—the tree of life, the curving road, the Landrover—and with icons of Iranian culture—the moon clouding over (from the *Qur'an*), the vultures, and the dog (who sees into the next world and whimpers or barks at the demons of impurity and death). The Kurd, Afghan, and Azeri Turk also evoke key institutions: the army, religion, and education (the taxidermist's university and natural science museum laboratory).

The ambiguous ending of the film—vital to keeping it alive as a parable—is said to have proved unsettling to the censors. One widely circulated story about the film's release, which, whether accurate or not, adds to the film's richness of intepretation in its public sphere work, is that the censors banned the film until a video coda was added. For the censors (and many viewers) the suggestion that the suicide might have been completed or allowed in the film to be a viable option was too un-Islamic to allow. In one interview, Kiarostami tells a different, but perhaps not contradictory, story, that by a fluke in Italy the film played without the video epilogue and was so popular that the distributors continued showing it that way. Kiarostami says that he wanted to have it playing in the same market with alternative endings, but the distributors would not pursue the experiment (Saeed-Vafa and Rosenbaum 2003, 29). In an earlier interview (Sterritt 2000), Kiarostami says, "Committing suicide is forbidden in Islam, of course, and is not even spoken of. But some religious people have liked the film because they felt that, just as you said, it shows a quest to connect with something more heavenly, something above physical life. The scene at the end, where you see cherry blossoms and beautiful things after he's died, has that message—that he has opened the door to heaven. It wasn't a hellish thing he did, it was a heavenly transition." He continues slyly, "There was controversy about the movie, but after I talked with the authorities, they accepted the fact that this is not a movie about a suicide—it's about the choice we have in life, to end it whenever we want. We have a door we can open at any time, but we choose to stay, and the fact that we have this choice is, I think, God's kindness: God is kind because he has given us this choice. They were satisfied with that explanation. A sentence from [the Roman-French philosopher E. M. Cioran] helped me a lot: 'Without the possibility of suicide, I would have killed myself long ago.' The movie is about the possibility of living, and how we have the choice to live. Life isn't forced on us. That is the main theme of the movie." Moreover, he points out that a truly well-made film will elude the censors. In Iran one does have to be sensitive to censorship, "and it has influenced my work to a certain extent. However, my films have escaped the sharp censorship scissors . . . probably because the censors did not quite understand what they should censor in them! A movie is good, I think, when the censor does not understand what should be censored. If a film is made so a censor cuts some parts of it, then those parts should have been cut, because he understood them!"

This is a point about Kiarostami's aspirations for a poetic cinema, one that in principle, like good poetry, draws one back again and again for multiple viewings or readings and is not something that is simply grasped, assimilated, and put away in one sitting. It is in this sense that Kiarostami says in the same interview, "I think movies and art should take us away from daily life, should take us to another state, even though daily life is where this flight is launched from. This is what gives us comfort and peace. The time for Scheherezade and the King—the storytelling time—is over." But it is not just a simple traditional mysticism of escape from or rejection of this world. On the contrary, it is a deep play with what is *ghayeb* (a master term of popular Persian understanding of both Shi'ism and the world in general), what is "hidden," as the truth or the Hidden Imam exists in occultation or withdrawal from manifest obviousness. Again Kiarostami from the same interview: "I want to tap the hidden information that's within yourself and that you probably didn't even know existed inside you. We have a saying in Persian, when somebody is looking at something with real intensity: 'He had two eyes and he borrowed two more.' Those two borrowed eyes are what I want to capture—the eyes that will be borrowed by the viewer to see what's outside the scene he's looking at. To see what is there and also what is not there."

A Taste of Cherry ends ambiguously (both with and without the video epilogue). The gamble Badii plays with himself is a kind of Russian roulette in which he needs a helper to have a clear outcome: to shake him awake if he is not going to die and to bury him if he is dead. In either case, the music track at the end plays Louis Armstrong's instrumental version of "St. James Infirmary," acknowledging that death always awaits (Saeed-Vafa and Rosenblum, 2003: 28).

Through the course of the film, Badii becomes less isolated and more able to talk to people: in the opening scenes his questioning of a man in a telephone booth is preemptory, then a bit more humane with a rag-picker, but still too prying for the solider boy, who is frightened off. With the talabeh, he has become a bit more other-oriented ("I know you will think, but . . .") albeit still too instrumental ("I don't want your tongue or your mind, only your hands"). With the Azeri Turk, he seems to have connected through the older man's recognition of his pain and anxiety, and this time it is the Azeri who takes the lead in questioning and engaging him. The older man tells of how close he once came to suicide and how the taste of a mulberry and the sound of children's voices made him change his mind. A taste of cherry is the metaphor for this attachment to life. In the final movements of the film, Badii runs back to reassure himself that the taxidermist will be with him, accompany him to the Chinvat Bridge (to the next world), will not abandon him, will be there, because he is not sure what he wants the outcome to be. It is a gamble: he wants God to decide and someone to wake him if he is to live. The scene of the cherry blossoms can be understood literally as Badii having died, or it can be a symbol of the contemplative possibility that allows us to choose life, or again as a symbol of transcending this world of tribulations philosophically or through such poetic art as this film. The video epilogue shows us the scene of the burial site, but it is now the green scene of the shooting of this film. There are marching soliders on the meadow below (from the segment with the soldier boy), a cameraman appears, then a man with a tripod, and then Kiarostami with a walkie-talkie ordering the marchers to sit. Homayun Ershad, the actor who played Badii, walks up the hill and offers Kiarostami a cigarette.

While in reviews much of the debate about the meaning of the film has focused on the endings, beginnings are equally important. The opening scene of *A Taste of Cherry* is a brilliant invocation of the ambiguity that reigns throughout: we see Badii in his car slowly cruising the streets of Tehran looking at groups of men. He might be looking for a laborer or two. Many of the men standing around are looking for work and offer themselves to him (Kargar? Worker? How many? Will you have two?). He might be looking for a sexual pickup. He might be looking for a friend. The ambiguity toward the end of the film in a way is more traditionally coded: in his apartment when he is presumably getting the sleeping pills, we see him only from the street as a shadow through the window blinds. In the real world, as it were, he is but a shade, and it is only through the detours and refusals in the diegetic storytelling that his life continues. That the interlocutor who is willing to help him is a taxidermist, who works to preserve dead quails for the purpose of teaching students a skill for living, is not insignificant. As he drives to the burial site, there is rain and lightning; the lights of an approaching car can be seen in the dark. Through the flashes of light we see his eyes open, then close, and the screen goes dark with only the sound of rain continuing. Everyday life is phantasmagoric and hard to negotiate, and in this understanding, the film

Car-seat
view of life:
laborers
Shadow of
life, tree
of life
(*A Taste of
Cherry*)

plays again with the thematics of *Gav* and *The Blind Owl*, and with the thematics of the painting on the pen case in the latter.

Midrash 2

It is not accidental that the most interesting filmic traditions for an exploration of contemporary religion should come from societies disrupted by social violence and nigh Lyotardian differands of moral perspective. The question of art, ethics, and religion after the Holocaust is a central topos for the late twentieth and early twenty-first centuries.

In the haggadah for Passover, one of the central stories has to do with the questions of the four children: the wise one, the evil one, the simple one, and the one too young to be able to ask his or her own questions. On the philological level, the four children are a mnemonic for the impera-tive, slightly reformulated four times in Deuteronomy and Exodus, to retell the story of the liberations from slavery and from idolatry. On the conven-tional homiletic level, the imperative of retelling (which falls ethically on all, whether or not one's ancestors actually were among those enslaved) is parsed psychologically: some ask to understand, some ask questions to start an argument, some are too simple to ask much, and some do not know how to formulate a question. Exoduses are many in Jewish history, and that history animates the telling for many families whose own lives have been marked by such involuntary displacements and resettlements. The word *simple* for the third child is *tam*, which also is the mystical state of union with God. This tip or trace has led me in recent years in my own retelling to invoke a historicized layering: the question about ceremonies concerns the Exodus from Egypt, through which much of the ritual structure of Jewish tradition was formu-lated; the question about rules and statutes and judgments concerns the Babylonian captivity and the period in which the two talmuds were written, establishing the constitutive hermeneutic tradition and active modality of Jewish intellectual self-understanding and renewal; the question represented by *tam* concerns the expulsion from Spain and the dissemination of the cosmopolitanism of Jewish creativity as well as the flowering of the mystical tradition to which this usage of *tam* belongs; most important, the child who is too young to ask represents the inability of post-Holocaust theology, phi-losophy, and art to know how to formulate the question.

It is here, perhaps, that the queries of Theodor Adorno, Paul Celan, and Emmanuel Levinas about the ethical dilemmas of art reside, and where the modality of film has come to supplement the previous modalities of ethi-cal discourse traditionally represented by mythology, epic poetry, the plays of Shakespeare, and post-Romantic poetry. Film can work here, not as image or direct representation (idolatry of the biblical idiom, the nonethical of Levinas), but as an *écriture* that deploys its modalities of semiosis, cam-era angling, and reframing to bring the imaginaries of the self and the possi-bilities for response into question, into conversation (the infinite commen-tary of midrashic work), and into a call across cultures and across local mythologizing.

The Work of Ethics in Filming Iran

In the decade before the Islamic revolution of 1977–1979, Iran had already developed an extraordinary film industry. In chapter 3 I explored some of these films (along with some of the associated short-story literature) as an access to the class-stratified cultural politics of Iran, arguing that the filmic and modernist literature had become a discourse parallel to earlier epic-parable, oral storytelling, poetry, and religious discourses built around the Karbala story of the martyrdom of the Third Imam, Husain. This new discourse was built around a kind of surrealist vocabulary initiated by Sadegh Hedayat, the short story and novella writer of the 1930s and 1940s. Like the older discourses, this one served contemporary society as a vehicle for parables that help with moral evaluations of life's dilemmas. It was, however, a discourse understood only by parts of society, and thus for an anthropologist provided access to competing cultural rhetorics. Much of the cultural politics of the 1970s was about Westernization, modernization, and technology being out of local control, being a means of subordinating Iran to the needs of the industrial West. There was a mutual disdain between the religious classes, who dismissed this newer filmic and literary discourse as nihilistic, and the intelligentsia, who dismissed the religious classes as merely repeating archaisms. There was, nonetheless, a common underlying philosophical structure of melancholia leading to stoicism and determination. Today we ask if this *Kulturkampf* was but a step toward what Derrida calls globalatinization or if the richness in these local appropriations and commentary modalities continues.

Came the Islamic revolution of 1977–1979, and there was a short hiatus in filmmaking. But within four or five years, filmmaking reappeared. Some films were pure propaganda, either stolid productions of old religious stories or, increasingly, films directed at the rural youth to encourage them to "volunteer" for the war against Iraq in the irregular forces called the Baseej. Naghmeh Sohrabi (1994) points out that the better of these films, quite remarkably unlike U.S. war films, do not demonize the enemy—in fact, they rarely portray an enemy—but instead focus on an almost Sufi-like aesthetic of self-sacrifice, of overcoming fear, of mutual support and care between commander and soldier, and of the alienation between the commitment of soldiers and the lack of commitment on the home front. War films continue as a genre to be produced and are disseminated through television. Many of these films were made by people who served on the front. Filmmakers such as

Makhmalbaf and Hatamikia got their start in the war movies section of Qanun Islami Filmsazi, a largely documentary unit of the Jihad-e Sazandegi (Corps for Reconstruction), under filmmaker Morteza Avini (Varzi 2002). By the mid-1980s, many films seemed to continue the traditions of the pre-revolution New Wave, transformed however into a more popular genre, eschewing the fetishized sexuality of either the Hollywood-male-gaze variety or the indigenous honor-revenge ab-gusht (a workingman's stew) or grade-B variety, yet capable of searing social criticism.

Two directors of the postrevolutionary period define some of its key parameters. Mohsen Makhmalbaf, who began as head of the Organization for the Propagation of Islam's Center for the Arts but allegedly went to jail briefly for voicing criticism of Khomeini when the old man finally agreed to a cease-fire with Saddam Hussein, saying that Khomeini had sold out the youth, had made the bloodshed of a generation meaningless, had given in to the man his generation had been taught to think of as a satan for whom there could be no accommodation. Makhmalbaf has made an astonishing variety of films, many of which are defining moments in the construction of the filmic discourse of postrevolutionary Iran, including *The Peddler*, *Marriage of the Blessed*, *Once Upon a Time, Cinema*, *Boycott*, *A Time of Love*, and *Bread and Vase*. Of note in his filmmaking trajectory, according to his own account, is that he moved from more instrumental uses of film to becoming increasingly involved with the techniques and possibilities of filmmaking as a rich medium of expression in itself.

The other is Abbas Kiarostami who headed the Qanun film unit before the revolution, producing films by Bahram Beyza'i and Amir Naderi, as well as his own. Kiarostami employs a kind of cinema verité style but with an economy of form that turns the everyday into parable. He often draws on the lives of children, uses nonprofessionals as actors, includes ambient sound, and deploys exquisite spare shots of living spaces and nearby landscapes. A tradition of making films for and about children has existed since prerevolutionary times, and it had become fashionable by the end of the 1990s to say that films about children had become a staid genre form. And yet, there is something powerful about viewing the complexity of adult life through the eyes and metaphors of childhood, of ways of solving problems, finding one's place in institutions, and negotiating relationships—and Kiarostami does it particularly well. Other directors such as Dariush Mehrju'i and Bahram Beza'i were New Wave directors before the revolution and have stayed on and reemerged as key figures in the postrevolutionary filmic discourse.

It is a filmic *discourse* in the sense that films build on and refer to one another, constitute an intertextual fabric. This filmic discourse is highly self-conscious of its own medium, often incorporating commentary on the film-making into the film. Most important, it is a cultural discourse in the sense that it constitutes a parabolic medium for discussions of ethical behavior, not in the fashion of dogma, preachments, or explicit religious invocations, but rather in the fashion of posing dilemmas and working through their possibil-ities, constraints, and implications (parallel to the ways in which the poetry of Firdausi, Hafez, Sa'edi, and Rumi were and continue to be used). Often these films are politically, but also morally, controversial. One could argue that film has resurfaced as a key cultural idiom against the dogmatism of the conservative leaders of the state such as Hojat ul-Islam, Ali Khamenei, Kho-meini's successor in the office of velayat-i faqih. It is important to remember that the current President of Iran, Muhammad Khatami, was for many years the liberal protector of the film industry in his role as minister of culture, and that his election to the presidency was based on a campaign to build a liberal civil society.

Like *Close Up*, another well-known film by Kiarostami, *And Life Goes On* (*Zendigi va Digar Hic* [literally, "life and nothing else"]) also begins from real life. The director and his son drive through the devastation of the earthquake which hit northern Iran in search of a boy who had starred in an earlier film of Kiarostami's. One mostly sees people stoically attempting to clean up shattered buildings, helping one another when they can, but often only able to be of partial help. The final scene is a kind of hieroglyph of this theme: two boys who have been given a lift by Kiarostami get out of the car and tell Kiarostami that the next hill is very steep and that he will have to take a running start to make it. We see a long shot of the switchback road down one hill and up the next. Kiarostami's car does not make it up the hill, and he backs down to the bottom. A man carrying a gas canister stops to help him push-start the car, and Kiarostami guns the engine and makes the turn up the hill. Near the top he stops and waits for the man to catch up, gives him a lift, and they disappear together.

Both these films comment on the difficulties of life in Iran under the Islamic revolution. They are among the many threads of the intertextual filmic discourse of a corpus of socially conscious films in the postrevolu-tionary era. Two other threads in this intertextual discourse are Mohsen Makhmalbaf's *The Peddler* and *Marriage of the Blessed*. A third Makhmalbaf film, *Once Upon a Time, Cinema* (1992), when read against *Moghul-ha*, Par-viz Kimaivi's prerevolutionary film about the invasion of television, provides a way of contrasting the place of film in the postrevolutionary and prerevolu-

The future (Atiyeh) waits to see herself in the promise of cinema
(*Once Upon a Time, Cinema*)

tionary eras. The Makhmalbaf film has a social critique subtext: it is widely seen by Iranians as a protest against the clerics' desire to control the cinema industry. Both *Once Upon a Time, Cinema* and *Moghul-ha* present genealogies for cinema in Iran. *Moghul-ha* portrays television as a foreign technology that is corrosive to Persian culture, particularly to oral cultural forms, but also to Persian film.

By contrast, Makhmalbaf's genealogy of film in Iran reflects a good-humored self-assurance that Iran is able to incorporate new technologies without losing cultural focus. It opens with the importation of camera technology by a Qajar prince and a reprise of footage from turn-of-the-century Tehran. The film is then composed of famous scenes from the entire history of Persian filmmaking. The opening premise is of a Charlie Chaplin–like cinematographer whose beloved is Atiyeh (the future): he promises not to forget her, to remain true to the promise of cinema. In a spoof of the guillotine scene from *Moghul-ha*, he survives a death sentence by the Qajar prince for filming things too intimate to the royal court. Later, he makes a fool of the shah by turning him into a bovine (allowing him to act the part, a spoof on Dariyush Mehrju'i's *Gav*), thereby warning the rulers of Iran (clerics or shahs) not to meddle in things they do not fully understand lest they undo themselves. The film ends in color with a sequence of clips from postrevolutionary films, all scenes of people embracing, including a signature zigzag run up a hill to a cypress tree from Kiarostami's film *Where Is My Friend's House?* similar to the final scene of *And Life Goes On*. It is this last sequence of clips in color, as it were, that is the fulfillment of the promise not to forget the promise of using film for social good.

Everyday and Extraordinary Islamic Ethics

Four final "film clips" will serve to indicate some of the range of this post-revolutionary filmic discourse, in which religion is inserted in the background but remains motivationally central, in which class and gender issues are foregrounded in a film by one of Iran's women directors, and in which derangements from the Iran-Iraq War are figured as part of contemporary social problems. Global connections intrude everywhere, and one can question, perhaps, if the moral abstractions in some of these plots may be responses to globalatinization, as if called forth in a world of unstable reference points as displacements and assertions of principle in new social contexts.

Ali Reza Davudnezad's 1992 film *Niaz* (Need) is a morality play, which along the way portrays the hard work of sewing, construction labor, shoemaking, printing, and blacksmithing. Two boys, Reza and Ali, need jobs to help support their desperately poor families in South Tehran. Both are brought to a print shop where there is but one job opening. For a trial period they are each given half a job. They initially act as rivals and hold fights after work, which are broken up by passersby; but the rivalry is even more intense between others on their behalf. Mansur, the neighbor who is trying to help Reza, ruins Ali's work. One day Reza does not come to work, and Mansur uses the opportunity to reveal to Ali his motives for undermining Ali's work, telling the boy that Reza has to care for a sick mother. Ali visits Reza, and seeing that Reza's circumstances are even poorer than his own, he quits the print job. The film opens with a scene of the graveyard where Ali's father is buried, and throughout the film Ali tries to live up to the idealized values of the father. In the final scene, Ali is working in a blacksmith's shop, making metal standards for the religious processions of Muharram. In these *alamiyat* (standards, signs) the message of the film is embodied.

Rokhshan Bani-Etemad's 1995 film *Ru-sari Abi* (The Blue Veiled) is a tale of oppressive class-based abstractions of morality, propriety, and honor, countered in an older man's search for giving and receiving human help. It is the story of a widower (played by the great actor Ezattollah Entezami), owner of a tomato growing and processing company, who through his own intense loneliness is sensitized to the loneliness of his employees. He hires and eventually takes as a mistress a woman from the slums, thereby violating the sense of propriety and honor (*abruh*) of his daughters, who invoke the cultural stereotype of widowers vulnerable to seduction by women who want their money. The tension between father and daughters results in a heart attack and a confrontation, and eventually the widower declares his former self dead. The film ends with a boundary—a train crossing a road, the poor mistress and her siblings approaching on foot from one side, the widower in his car approaching from the other—breached.

Ebrahim Hatamikia's 1997 film *Ajans Shishe-i* (The Glass Agency), a brilliant reworking of Sidney Lumet's *Dog Day Afternoon* (1975), treats war veterans not just as heroes or victims but as capable of mobilizing their war-based derangements in the service of ethical and moral intentions that nonetheless violate social norms, in the process exposing the ethical and moral ambiguities of normality. As in *Niaz*, much of the religious content is in the detailing, while the ethical content appears in the negotiations of the plot. Hajji is an ex-commando leader who recognizes his ailing wartime group member, Abbas, now thin and sick with neurological problems from the 1984 Iraq offensive, Karbala 5. A third member of their commando team, a doctor, performs a series of tests—reflex tapping, X-rays, CAT scan, spinal tap—and establishes that Abbas has shrapnel in his neck requiring delicate surgery best done by an Iranian specialist in London. The Fund for Disabled Soldiers is disorganized and bureaucratic, with long delays, and though they finally agree to pay for the surgery, the payment does not arrive at the travel agency as arranged. Desperate, Hajji takes the travel agency and its clients hostage, and the film turns into a psychological thriller, with members of the old commando unit arriving on motorcycles to help out their mates, the state's antiterrorist team, including another member of Hajji's old commando team, arriving with both force and talk, and of course CNN and BBC camera crews. Both inside and outside characters take many different positions, ranging from the travel agent who dismisses Hajji's sacrifice in the war ("I didn't ask you to fight for me"), to those who mock Hajji when he prays ("Prayers done in seized property are not acceptable"), to those who admire the former buddies for their loyalty to each other, to the antiterrorist team member who joins Hajji in prayer but with whom Hajji knows he cannot negotiate because there is too great a bond of trust between the two of them. There are references to both Karbala and the Persian New Year, with a Hajji Firuz, the clown figure of the season, among the travel-agency customers and

Filmic Judgment and Cultural Critique   251

an old man who recites from Firdausi's *Shahnameh*. Hajji tries to use old storytelling parables ("Yeki bud, yeki nabud . . ." [Once there was, once there wasn't . . .]) to further explain his intentions to the hostages. Throughout, personal loyalties aften conflict with position taking: the young antiterrorist policeman who was a commando with Hajji finds himself torn; when the police cut the electricity and phone lines, Hajji allows hostages to call out on a cell phone (yet another opportunity for different opinions to be aired as the hostages explain what they think is happening); and Abbas wants only to go home but will not abandon Hajji.

Like Makhmalbaf's *Marriage of the Blessed*, *Ajans Shishe-i* evinces not only a thematic of purity/martyrdom struggling against the corruption of the world but also a critique of the reforms that the Islamic revolution failed to bring. (When a hostage says, "Who knows how much money you made out of the war," Hajji snaps back, "I was a farmer before the war and had a tractor; after the war, I returned to my farm except now without a tractor and without medical insurance.") At issue, both in the diegetic story and just off-screen in reality, is the struggle between the work of remembering the heroism of the Iran-Iraq War and its mobilization around the morals and ethics of Karbala, versus the normalization of everyday and bureaucratic life. The ethical struggle is complicated by potential misuses of abstract morality on both the sides of normalcy and of mobilization, with the ethics of what is appropriate to do revealed in ephemeral flashes of insight and action; in negotiation, trust, and willingness to sacrifice self; and in a brinkmanship of using imaginative threats while trying not to do harm. The film was a succès de scandale, causing much debate from both right and left about its portrayal of veterans.

In Kiarostami's *The Wind Will Carry Us* (1999), the ethics of voyeurism and of the relation between the rural working classes and the middle classes (including ethnographers, journalists, filmmakers, and film audiences) are juxtaposed to the ethics of kinship, friendship, and communal relations. Behzad ("well-born," also the name of a famous Persian miniaturist, 1450–1536 C.E.) goes with a crew of two to a village in western Iran in hopes of filming a strange funeral rite when an old lady dies. The title is from a poem by Farough Farokhzad, which resonates throughout the film, not only for the unpredictability of fate, life, and death but also for the love, mutual aid, exchange, patronage, and pedagogical relations that sustain or destroy communities. All these are explored in the relations between Behzad and Farzad, the young boy (grandson of the old lady) who serves as Behzad's guide and eyes and ears in the village, between Behzad and the village school-

teacher, and between Behzad, the young lovers Zeinab and Yusuf, and Zeinab's mother, who at the opening of the film directs Behzad to the village.

The film's signature comic scene, remembered and quoted by anyone who
has seen it, is of the repeated cell phone calls that Behzad receives, which
cause him each time to run to his car and race up a zig-zag road to a tree of
life (both signature Kiarostami icons) growing in a cemetery at the top of a
hill, where the reception of the electromagnetic spectrum is unimpeded.
Here a somewhat comic situation develops: Yusuf is digging a well; Behzad
watches a dung beetle, but then flips a poor turtle onto its back in a fit of
pique at a phone call from his funder, Mrs. Goodarzi, who wants to shut his
project down if there is no ritual to be filmed. We are but dust, industriously
working like Sisyphus, only to have our efforts as likely as not be blown away
by the wind. The well hole collapses on Yusuf and the turtle marching across
a gravestone is flipped onto its back. After Behzad leaves, the turtle rights
itself and continues on its way. The turtle, denizen of two worlds, in this case
mediates between the underworld (of reptiles and gravestones) and the world
of electromagnetic reception on the hilltop. The graveyard itself of course is
also a mediator between the underworld and the world beyond, visually
indicated by its position on a hilltop.

The discourse about the next world, the unseen world of hidden causes,
uncertainty, fate, and the complexity of human moral interactions and consequences, is central. Kiarostami points out in an interview (Starrett 2000)
that there are eleven persons in the film whose presence is felt but who are
not seen. These include the young couple whose future is uncertain, Yusuf
and Zeinab (we never see their faces), the old lady who may or may not be
dying, Farzad's mother, and the two women who constantly call Behzad on
the cell phone: his mother, who wants him to return for a family funeral, and
Mrs. Goodarzi, who wants to shut down the fruitless wait for the old lady to
die. Behzad's crew is also impatient at the endless waiting and accuse him of
not planning well, but as in many Persian parables, the point is that the best-
laid plans of men cannot control for hidden complexities and causes, and to
gamble too heavily on such planning is hubris if not impious usurpation of
the role of God.

But it is not just a pleasant Persian meditation on the unseen world: the
film has a biting edge because of the nature of the funeral rites and the impact of the political and cultural economy represented by Behzad and we as
viewers on the fate of the village.

In a dark milking room Behzad recites Farokhzad's poem to Zeinab, a
sixteen-year-old village girl, as she milks a cow for him: "In my night, the

wind comes to meet the leaves." It is, he glosses, about lovers, as when you go to see Yusuf at the well. The poem is also about despair, the red and anxious moon, clouds like mourning women awaiting the rain, the trembling night, and "worries that spin about you and me, . . . lay your hands on mine, your lips on mine, the wind will carry us." There is a charged potential of seduction in the heavily symbolic scene as Behzad recites to encourage the girl to dream beyond her fifth-grade education and circumscribed village existence. The girl asks how long Farokhzad had studied, and Behzad answers, with the white lie of paternalist encouragement: "only four or five classes, but it is not how much you study, rather it is the experiences you have that enable poetry." It is the mother who sends Behzad into the womb of the milking shed with her nubile daughter, and it is the lover, Yusuf, who directs him to Zeinab for milk. Zeinab preserves her modesty in the milking shed, refusing to tell her name or show her face; and when asked how much the milk is, she first politely says they are happy to give it as a gift, but when he seems to not understand the *ta'rof* (politeness form) and says thank you as if accepting a gift, she says he can pay her mother. The mother in turn takes the money, but then runs after him and returns it, saying they are honored, thereby articulating first that their relation is a formal market one but then reestablishing a non-intimate relation of village hospitality to guests. This delicate balance is important, one of several moments of moral education in the film (for Behzad and the audience) to reorient Behzad toward engaging in the exchange relations of life, gift exchanges and obligations of humanity.

Farokhzad's poem is also quoted by an under-employed rural doctor as he gives Behzad a ride on his motorbike through a golden field of ripening wheat. Summoned when the sides of Yusuf's hole collapsed on him, the doctor tells Behzad that there is nothing wrong with the old lady except old age, and there are worse illnesses. Death for instance: death is when you close your eyes and can no longer see God's kindness. Behzad counters that the other world is said to be beautiful, but Doc replies: who has come back? "She is beautiful as a houri, but wine is better; prefer the present: even a drum sounds melodius from afar." Third, Farokhzad's poem resonates with Behzad's apology to the young boy, Farzad, for having been angry at him, saying that men, like automobiles, sometimes just run out of steam, blow up, and need to rejuvenate. Farzad retorts that Behzad has not done any work to need rejuvenation, and Behzad replies that idleness and keeping oneself apart can also cause one to go crazy.

It is Farzad's grandmother who is dying and one of her sons (Farzad's mother's brother) comes to visit her but cannot stay, because he must return to his post as a border guard forty-five minutes away. Farzad's mother, who has been caring for the old lady, has been in a relation of *qahr* (not speaking) to her brother for years. But as the old lady begins to eat, revive, and ask about her family, the brother asks his sister if he is a bad son; she replies in relief (perhaps due to a vow that if her mother recovered she would again speak to the brother) that he is not a bad son, just seized (*gereft*) by other concerns. Their other two brothers, living in Ahwaz and Khoramshahr, have not even visited. In parallel fashion, Behzad asks Farzad if he is a bad person; while this is a gambit to repair relations (*qahr* on the part of the boy), Behzad is also thinking about his own refusal of his mother's request to return to Tehran for a local funeral there. Implicit is the question: What is he doing in an alien village waiting for a funeral with which he has no connection except an exploitative one, when he should be home for a funeral with which he has family ties.

Behzad ("well-born") and Farzad ("happily born") are a pair, as are Zeinab and Yusuf. Farzad also has a surname, Sohrabi. As in the Sohrab-Rustam relation, the village lad's life is being put at risk by the media and economic invasions of the adult, middle-class, urban worlds of Behzad. Yusuf (Joseph, who is tossed into a well by his brothers but by diligence and fate ends as vizier to the pharaoh of Egypt) and Zeinab (the strong female of the family of the Prophet who provided leadership after the martyrdom of the Third Imam until the Fourth Imam could assume his role) are both, at least temporarily, "buried alive" (like Hedayat's narrator in *The Blind Owl*), one in a collapsed well, the other in the cavelike milking room. It is striking that only Yusuf and Zeinab have Islamic names: all the other names are Zoroastrian or Persian, of which the most signal is Mrs. Goodarzi, a Zoroastrian-sounding name, the funder or patroness in Tehran who constantly calls Behzad to find out why his work is not completed and suggests that he must return if there is no imminent funeral. One member of his crew anxious to get back to Tehran is Keyvan ("world"). The only other kind of name is Tajdowlat ("crown of government," a Qajar-sounding title), the name of the feisty woman teahouse owner who is constantly sparring with the patriarchal-talking old men who are her customers.

Balancing the destructive elements of voyeurism and economic relations from Tehran in this play of symbols seems to be the discourse of Islamic backwardness and parochialism versus Persian civilization and cosmopolitanism, familiar since at least Firdausi's *Shahnameh*. The communal goodness of the village and of nature's cycles is represented by the lactating cow, the golden wheat fields, and the pregnant woman (Farzad's aunt, who gives housing to the filmmakers and delivers a tenth child, returning to work the following morning); against this backdrop Farokhzad's poem is recited by the doctor, the filmmaker, and perhaps recognized by one more familiar figure, the schoolteacher.

When Yusuf is buried in the collapse of the hole he is digging, Behzad is galvanized out of his social isolation and into social action. He rushes to round up villagers to help, gives schoolboys a ride, and most importantly lends his car to the villagers to take Yusuf to the hospital. He then must not only ask for a ride back to the village on the doctor's scooter, but now asks the doctor to look in on the old woman, offering to fetch her pain medicine from town. For a moment one thinks that Behzad has changed, that he adds to his motivations a concern for the local people. More likely, it turns out, he wants to seize the opportunity that a different funeral will happen first. Kevyan and his other crewman, however, have already left the village.

This film is given a biting ethical edge in a conversation between Behzad and the schoolteacher, which also reveals why the funeral rite cannot be captured as a film of something exotically folkloric. Behzad stops to give a lift to the schoolteacher, who walks with a crutch. The schoolteacher asks what Behzad is doing in the village and considers first the villager's speculation that the Tehrani is looking for treasure in the graveyard. Behzad smiles at the femur on the dashboard, which Yusuf had unearthed and Behzad carried around as a talisman. (It was after Yusuf, trying to be helpful, had offered to lend Behzad his shovel, and Behzad had said that would not help with his dilemma, although he sardonically muttered *sotto voce* that one blow with the shovel could solve the problem.) The schoolteacher continues slyly: have you come for the ceremony? Behzad immediately guesses that Farzad has revealed the nature of his quest; so he asks the schoolteacher what he thinks of the ceremony. The teacher replies that it is painful, doubly so, for he has watched his own mother scar her face twice, the second time at the funeral of the local factory boss. The funeral of the factory boss was so painful because people are desperate for jobs, which are being cut; and they feel obliged to compete in debasement and dramatic demonstrations of their loyalty to the factory owners so that they can be among the few allowed to keep their jobs. As the teacher alights, Behzad asks that he not be too hard on the exams (Farzad has been obsessing about the upcoming examinations). The teacher smiles, assures Behzad he will be compassionate, and then asks Behzad not to reveal their conversation to Farzad (that Farzad couldn't keep Behzad's secret; that there is a corrupt, adult underside to the community's funeral rituals). The teacher seems to have that easy confidence of people who operate in two worlds, neither hostile toward the outsider-voyeur nor defensive about local practices.

In the end, Behzad slips quietly out of the village under the cover of early dawn, despite hearing the weeping at the old woman's house. One thinks that he now wants to respect the villagers and not be only an external voyeur. But just then his professional eye catches the funerary procession of women, and he whips out his camera to snap a series of quick shots, then waves guiltily. Only one woman fixes him (us) with a steely stare; the others ignore the camera. As he leaves the village, he tosses the femur into a stream and watches it float by goats eating grass: fertility, continuity, nature's recycling of death into life. There is a difference between Behzad the miniaturist and Behzad the filmmaker in patronage, content, class relations, and historical horizon, but the fate of Sohrab, Yusuf, and Zeinab remains perennial. Excuse me, there's a call from Mrs. Goodarzi.

Conclusions

Filmic discourse in Iran has six dimensions: (1) Cinema in Iran constitutes a discourse in the technical sense of being both intertextual (one film referring to others) and a moral resource for parables; it is not, either for filmmakers or for audiences, merely mindless and disconnected entertainment. (2) There is a style to this discourse and filmmaking that one could call post-traumatic realism, drawing on earlier Italian neorealist and East European absurdist-surrealist styles, which focuses on the everyday, on the problems and repair of society, and on the problematic cultural codes inherited from the past. (3) There is a transformed concern with desire and seduction, no longer in terms of the sexuality of Hollywood or of the honor-revenge of prerevolution ab-gushti films, but rather with the ends to which desire ought to be directed. Both *Close Up* and *Once Upon a Time, Cinema* illustrate the circuits of desire and obsession in Iranian society and suggest how they might be mediated and redirected through film. (4) Traces of the master narratives of the moral discourses of traditional Iran remain, such as the Karbala master narrative of Shi'ism. These are often not foregrounded but provide background context. In *Niaz*, one of the more interesting of the war-propaganda period films, the final scene is of Ali blacksmithing the alamiyat to be carried in the religious processions of Ashura, a visual allusion or trace that invokes the entire moral apparatus of the Karbala story. (5) The films themselves provide an explicit discourse about the role of cinema in the public sphere: both *Close Up* and

Once Upon a Time, Cinema take as a primary theme the proper uses of cinema, as does *Marriage of the Blessed*; the disjunctive collaging effects and symbolic codings of *The Peddler* also draw attention to the medium. The oeuvres of both Abbas Kiarostami and Mohsen Makhmalbaf now include films about making the other films in the oeuvre (Kiarostami's *Through the Olive Tree*; see also Abolfazl Jalili's *A True Story* [1996]). In *Boycott* and *A Time of Innocence* Makhmalbaf even restages events from earlier in his life and in the history of the revolution, using the actual characters from those times as coaches for nonprofessional actors in the restaging for the films. (6) Through their international circulation, these films have a chance to enact a cultural ambassadorship of a kind which can cut across more stereotypical print and television journalism and provide some access where language blocks readership of complex novels, stories, or essays that circulate within Persian-speaking worlds.

The Islamic Revolution in Iran was fought, and continues to be fought, on many fronts. Film is among the most revelatory, critiquing, contesting, and negotiating the religious and ethical ideals of Islam and the Islamic revolution arguably more effectively than the philosophers or religious scholars to whom most in the West turn for pronouncements on what Islam is or means for Muslim populations. Film performs a kind of "art captioning" to Iranian social life, externalizing the complexities of subjectivities formed in the interplay between various pedagogies and technologies, of which those of globalatinization and televisual formats form but one, if powerful, set. These religious and ethical modalities are lodged in a few discrete alamiyat at the end of *Niaz*; in moral dilemmas (*A Taste of Cherry*); in clashes of moralities (*Leila, A Time of Love*); in explorations of integrity (*Close Up, Boycott*) and moral duty (*Bashu*); or in explorations of social policy (*The Peddler, The Marriage of the Blessed*). They are often examined through the parabolic lives of children, in the use of nonprofessional actors, and in the dilemmas of the everyday, the everyday as an anthropological and philosophical workspace with multiple registers or cultural resource levels, filled with hybrid symbols, metaphors, parables, fantasies, desires, and other tools with which to fashion responsiveness and write life anew, renew life. If abstraction all too often is an evil in dogma and religious violence, and if the abstractive dynamics of an unregulated global market could sweep national cinemas into very marginal corners, the commentary elicited by a filmic discursive medium of storytelling through a mosaic of detail and tropic redeployments can re-enlighten and reorient ethics and religion, both deen and mazhab.

5 War Again: Qandahar, 911—Figure and Discourse in Iranian Cinematic Writing

The problem with narrative film is that people from all walks of life come out of watching it with the same story. Non-narrative film allows people to use their own mind, frames and experiences, and they walk out with experiences they have created from watching the film. . . . I like films that have lasting power where you come out and immediately or much later begin to reconstruct what happened. I like to put you to sleep, let you have a nap, but afterwards make you stay up at night thinking.
—ABBAS KIAROSTAMI, Harvard Film Archives, 7 June 2000

Men go to war in a kind of madness, then afterwards the madness leaves them, the war disappears, but women are left to cope with the mines and their aftereffects.—SAMIRA MAKHMALBAF, in Meysam Makhmalbaf's *How Samira Made* The Blackboard

Some 12,000 girls, still under burka and having been denied access to school for the past seven years, had come to the Ministry of Education to register their names and attend school in Herat. We asked a group of those very burka-covered girls to accompany us to the site of the school and lay the cornerstone of their school. A friend of mine called me by my name, and one of the girls recognized me from under her burka. She told the others. They all talked about *Kandahar*, though none of them had actually seen it. They had only heard of its story from Persian-speaking radio broadcasts.—MOHSEN MAKHMALBAF, *The Guardian*, 11 January 2002

On behalf of Iran and the new generation and hope in my homeland . . . the young generation who struggle for democracy and a better
life in Iran.— SAMIRA MAKHMALBAF, accepting the Cannes Prix
du jury for *The Blackboard*

Iranian cinema over the past twenty years, especially those films that portray
life in the aftermath of war, challenge contemporary social and cultural
theories, especially political theories, by providing alternative lenses with
which to view the muddled debates between so-called political realists and
those who insist that the political real leaks through, disrupts, or overflows
the freeze frames of political theory.

What One Sees Is Not All that Is Happening

Whether in literature or political science—or, as Mohsen Makhmalbaf notes,
in film—realism is an artifact of a reductive process of framing, zooming,
naming, categorizing, or enumerating (body counts, weapons counts). In
politics or political science realism is a reduction to momentarily fixed opposing forces. Its procedure is like any diagramming effort, selecting some
material while excluding, making invisible, other data deemed for the moment irrelevant. As Mohsen Makhmalbaf says, "With a wide angle lens we
can create a Sabzian [the protagonist of *Close Up*] who dissolves into his
social background and becomes a statistical sample; or with a telephoto lens
we can separate him from the background so that he stands out. Which is
realism? Through color, lens, frame, picture size, story line, acting, we create
a reality different from the rest, and thus preserve our own interpretation"
(1990).

The real, of course, as Jacques Lacan and Slavoj Žižek point out, "is never
directly 'itself'; it presents itself only via its incomplete-failed symbolization,
and spectral apparitions emerge in this very gap" (Žižek 1994, 21).[1] This gap is
where film often enacts its most haunting power: "mute dreams"; the rain-
filled footprint in Majid Majidi's *Baran*; the femur floating downstream in
Abbas Kiarostami's *The Wind Will Carry Us*; and many other graphic images
in Persian films and stories.[2] In part this spectral supplementarity and un-

freezability of the real is captured in the parables of Moses and Khizr, whose best-laid plans are undone by the unseen workings of what man can only symbolize as "divine providence," thus dramatizing the limitations of reason, as well as man's hubris. This is the comedic parable of Kamal Tabrizi's film *Leila Is With Me* (1996), which is set during the Iran-Iraq War; it offers the counterpoint stories of a photographer who, fleeing the front, inadvertently ends up there and of a young boy who is determined to get there to achieve martyrdom but is held back on the grounds that it is not yet his turn, and both thereby fulfill their divine purposes.[3]

One alternative to freeze-frame realism is respect for virtual hyperrealities (in Deleuze's sense of *virtual*, that is, multiplying the possible alternative dimensions of description or measurement that can be foregrounded), sometimes also called "situated knowledge," "perspectivalism," or "relativism" in the sense of paying attention to internal fractures and partial divisions. Makhmalbaf is fond of quoting Mawlana Rumi: "Truth is a mirror that falls from the hand of God and shatters into pieces. Everyone picks up a piece and believes that the piece contains the whole truth, even though the truth is left sown about in each fragment" (Makhmalbaf 1990). Film and ethnographic methods provide some of the most powerful tools for acknowledging the limits of generalizations, photographic representations, slogans, and motivations. Both film and ethnographic methods, especially in conjunction, provide the means for paying attention to the subtle leverage points of power: rhetorical shifts, attached fantasies and specters, alternative genealogies, kinships, and friendships.

Virtual hyperrealities, perspectivalism, situated knowledge, or relativism do not end in the paralysis of decision making. On the contrary, they engage the Other on many grounds, weaving relations, opening alternative routes to negotiated ends. This is not merely an argument against the reductionism of Samuel Huntington's 1996 thesis of clash of civilizations, although it is that as well. Huntington's destructive stereotyping contributes to a mutually self-reinforcing alliance with reactionary culturalist claims among fundamentalists around the world. Mobilizing and inflaming religious ideology makes positions increasingly nonnegotiable, which is why religious symbolic language is such a dangerous demagogic tool (as illustrated by the boomerang effect the United States experienced after its cynically opportunistic use of Islamic fundamentalists against the Russians in Afghanistan—although that indictment of U.S. policy is insufficient).[4] The counterargument to Huntington is that religions have many internal countervailing traditions. One should therefore never yield to religious demagoguery on the grounds that matters of belief cannot be countered, for there are always critiques from the inside that can provide alliances for social justice and accountable governments (goals for which civil society in the United States also increasingly needs allies). More practically, one should never allow conflicts to degenerate into last stands on religious grounds.

Cosmopolitan cultures need protection in places endangered by the disintegration of states, particularly in the postcolonial world—and Islamic societies are not the only examples of such. Michael Ignatieff (2001) argues that the backlash against United States hegemony and military power is not that it has become imperial, but that it has allowed the world outside the enclaves of rapid first-world-style growth (including first-world enclaves within third-world states) to disintegrate. He distinguishes between those problems to which realist politics may be attuned, which states can effectively address, and those problems in zones of state disintegration where military force has little or only temporary purchase. This is an internationalist argument, not just an argument for nation-state building: it points to the need for a weave of international and transnational institutions and regulatory structures that can support the construction of civil society, the production of public goods, investment in human resources, and protection against the ravages of uncontrolled market globalization.

Film is among the most supple of media both for internal domestic cultural critiques and for the building of cross-cultural, transnational understandings. It is no accident that Richard Powers should devote a novel, *Plowing the Dark* (2000), to the dystopian similarities between a virtual-reality cave at the University of Illinois and the psychology of a kidnapped, blindfolded American in a Beirut basement, connected by the (un)seen of art and the Gulf War.[5] Abbas Kiarostami transmutes the electronic cave into the filmic cube of sensory surround: "Sound is more important than image. . . . Of the cube of life, on screen you see one dimension, the other five dimensions are added through sound. . . . Sound reminds the viewer that what one sees is not all that is happening. . . . Sound allows us to give volume to the film" (Harvard Film Archives, 7 June 2000).

What one sees is not all that is happening. As Deleuze puts it, the images and signs in post–World War II film experimentation—Italian neorealism around 1948, French New Wave around 1958, German New Cinema around 1968—are organized by fabulation, a falsifying narration defined not by representation but by simulacra whose qualities are "powers of the false" (Deleuze 1985, Abbas 1992). Powers of the false can be read politically, as in the odkłamanie form of cultural critique used in Polish films of the 1990s: undoing myths, political ideologies, or assumptions of common sense, not necessarily claiming to reveal *the* truth, but showing the falsities of the conventional assumptions and ideological structures we live by, showing the palimpsest layerings of historical constructions that provide staying power to these "falsities" (Fischer 1997). Powers of the false can also be read psychoanalytically in the manner that Jean-François Lyotard adapts from Freud: the figural as a libidinal series of condensations, displacements, and secondary revisions of the rational and symbolic. Or as Walter Benjamin, also drawing on Freud, had earlier written, "A different nature opens itself to the camera than to the naked eye. . . . The camera introduces us to the optical unconscious" (1928/1979, 245).

Deleuze organized his thoughts on these waves of film experimentation around a distinction between movement-image and time-image. Movement-image, which deployed montage and various techniques of juxtaposing and suturing images, still drew on an analogy with writing as print-technology and syntax. The syntax was still traditional narrative: plot, character, family-romance, national allegory. Time-image by contrast uses a more abstract, virtual syntax, a kind of serialism rather than traditional montage, and, most important, draws attention to the powers of the false, to what is beyond the frame or screen, to "what is not being seen," to the figural, the optical unconscious, and the interplay—dissonant as well as harmonic—carried by different sensory dimensions. These include dialogue, soundtrack, and music tracks, as well as different visual sign systems representing psychological or psychodynamic interiority, class or socioeconomic markers, iconic referents to other films, and cultural or philosophical metacommentary (such as mystical referents in Iranian films that index both conventional religion or conversely anticonventional, antireligious, noninstitutional purity).

The notion of hieroglyph that had so intrigued the early-twentieth-century modernists (Sergei Eisenstein, Sigmund Freud, Ezra Pound) has been radicalized. In the understanding of early-twentieth-century modernists, the hieroglyph analogy was still taken from print technology (pictographs) and from drama (Noh theater, Brecht). The idea of hieroglyph invoked a polyvalent representation of sound, association, and elemental recombinations, but as transcription of what was absent and could only be indicated. In the second half of the twentieth century, filmic and digital technologies enabled more manipulations of the multisensory dimensions of apperception, new forms of visibilities, both for effects of realism and for effects of various kinds of cultural, psychological, or figural abstraction.

Deleuze credited Michel Foucault with the idea that epistemic shifts are "marked by the emplacement of audiovisual regimes: changing articulations of the visible with respect to the expressible—modes of seeing and modes of saying—that organize knowledge, power, and subjectivity in distinct historical eras" (Rodowick 2001, 172). These shifts are sometimes schematized as pre– versus post–World War II (Deleuze), and other times as precamera, camera, and post–World War II or electronic media (Benjamin, Adorno).

In Adorno's formulation—before virtual reality and computer technologies—"artworks recall the theologumenon that in the redeemed world everything would be as it is and yet wholly other" ([1970] 1997, 6). Art can stand in a negative dialectical relation to the empirical world and thus can function as facilitating cultural critique, rather than as just negative criticism or wish fulfillment.[6]

Iranian film has participated in these shifts since 1969, beginning with Darius Mehrju'i's *The Cow* and recommencing again in the mid-1980s after the 1977–1979 Revolution. The frame of war's aftereffects underscores the oft-noted similarities between Italian neorealism and strands of these Iranian films. Some of the imagery goes back at least to World War I and Freud's (and W. R. Rivers's) reassessments of psychoanalysis in the face of shell shock and amputations (Dawes 2002, 147). There is a passage in Makhmalbaf's *Marriage of the Blessed* in which a soldier under bombardment stumbles and falls, discovers a hand on his face, and caresses it as comfort; he opens his eyes and sees that it is a severed hand. In his essay "The Uncanny" Freud cites as examples of the uncanny being lost in a fog and encounters with "dismembered limbs, a severed head, a hand cut off at the wrist" (1953, 17:237, 244). At the time when waves of village boys recruited into the Baseej were being sent across minefields on the Iraq-Iran border, comparisons were frequently made to the massive casualties of World War I and to the grim trade-off between preserving hardware such as tanks and risking the lives of disposable youths.

The return of these phenomenological experiences, defining moments, captured in both narrative and film, are now processed also as palimpsests and mutations of time under changing conditions. They are repetitions with a difference, a slippage, a twist, a reconfiguration, with new connections, new harmonics. Commenting on Deleuze, Rodowick suggests that the innovations of Italian neorealism, French New Wave, or New German Cinema "all derive from the experience of physical, social, and psychological reconstruction of societies devastated during the Second World war. . . . As images of empty and wasted spaces surged in everyday life, postwar cinema discovered 'a dispersive and lacunary reality' that motivated ambiguous and undeciphered images. . . . The protagonists of New Wave films thus define a nomadism where the characters of the time-image wander errantly and observe in emptied and disconnected spaces. . . . [such nomadism] unhinges images and sounds into disconnected series and episodic sequences" (2001, 174–75). Deleuze emphasizes a more abstract concept: the feeling or perception of the intolerable, the unbearable, and of exhaustion. Iranian film (with one or two exceptions) has not moved into quite the dissociative but everyday bourgeois spaces of French New Wave, retaining instead a firm grounding in the impoverishment of socioeconomic life as well as the richness of cultural resonances, more like east European film in this respect.

Iranian films weave into these experiments Iran's own rich cultural traditions. The following films do not merely provide commentary on the aftereffects of war but also create a dialogue between the logics of the parable and the figural, between discourse and figure. Is the figural more libidinal or more imagistic? This remains an open question, part of the work of interpretation, of the open texture of the interpretation of culture, that also involves the work of ethical and political consideration in rapidly changing worlds where traditional modes of ethical and political struggle are not always applicable to emergent forms of life.

War Again: Civil, Regional, Global

The Iranian film to watch in 2001 was Mohsen Makhmalbaf's *Safar-e Qandahar* (Journey to Qandahar [English title: *Kandahar*]); *safar-e Qandahar* is idiomatic for a "long journey" sometimes without return. Even President George W. Bush said he wanted to see it shortly before he began the bombing campaign. Images from the film began to circulate by word of mouth, radio, and print reviews long before the film was available in cinemas. These images crystallized what the world knew of Afghanistan of the late 1990s. They were colorful, surreal images of prostheses and veils, isolation and poverty. They were images of the country said to be the most landmined in the world, torn apart by internal strife, itself the aftermath of regional and proxy global warfare. But they were images not devoid of hope. The veils that covered women were colorful, and hid more than women. The film technique was not at first to everyone's taste; "flawed," "flat performances," "not enough plot," "underdeveloped characters," said many when asked to react immediately, but after thinking about it and trying to articulate what they understood, many acknowledged they liked the film better and better. But like/dislike is the wrong category for a film that intends to awaken affect and aid and to do so in ways that strike into our figural (un)conscious well beyond the ineffective modalities of tear-jerking melodrama or the now mind-numbing documentaries of children in distress. That women should be at the center of this film is also not incidental to a father, husband, and collaborator of women filmmakers joining a small but important lineage of women directors in Iran.

Other Kinds of Visuals and Sounds Interrupt

9.11. "In an emergency, call 911." Dateline: September 11, 2001: al-Qaeda operatives fly a fuel-loaded Boeing 676-200 passenger plane into New York's World Trade Center's north tower. Twenty minutes later, *securing maximum live television publicity*, a second plane, exceeding the design limit of speed at that altitude, banks into the south tower.[7] A third plane dives into the Pentagon. A fourth crashes into the ground in Pennsylvania, diverted from its target by passengers wrestling the hijackers. They have been alerted by *cellphone communications* that this is not just an "ordinary" hijacking which can end well. The slow collapse of the World Trade Center towers takes long enough to allow many thousands to escape, but nearly three thousand are trapped and die. The buildings collapse as *Hollywood films* have shown in special effects many times before. The collapse performs as designed by the building's architects, who had tried to plan ahead for possible damaging events: straight down to avoid much damage to surrounding buildings. In planning for worst case scenarios, the architects had considered the possibility of a small plane accidentally hitting a tower (a B-25 bomber flew into the Empire State Building in 1945), but they had not anticipated a commercial airliner's enormous quantities of jet fuel, which led to the infernos that melted both buildings' steel supports. Amateur *videocameras* captured the huge, tornado-like balls of dust that rushed through the streets of lower Manhattan covering everything in ash, dirt, and an acrid smell on an otherwise sunny, crystal-clear-blue-sky day.

Other Kinds of Airdrops and Journeys Interrupt

In response, after issuing ultimatums to the Taliban government in Afghanistan to hand over Osama bin Laden, Ayman al-Zawahiri, and other al-Qaeda leaders, the United States, with support from the British, the ground forces of the anti-Taliban Northern Alliance, and a coalition of facilitating nations (including Iran, Pakistan, Uzbekistan, Tajikistan, Russia, China, and NATO member countries) began a bombing and ground military campaign which chased the Taliban from power and al-Qaeda from its training camps and garrisons.

War Again

Iran fought a bloody eight-year war against Iraq in the 1980s. Iraq's strongman, Saddam Hussein, miscalculated that the 1977–1979 Revolution in Iran might have so weakened Iran that it would not be able to resist his claim to islands in the Persian Gulf and the province of Khuzistan itself, oil-rich, with Arabic-speakers, and a strategic littoral that has sometimes constrained Iraq's freedom of access to the Gulf and Indian Ocean. The 1980s war devastated the port cities and petroleum industries of Khoramshahr and Ahwaz. A number of Iranian films deal with the trauma and the aftermath, notably Amir Naderi's *The Runner* (1985), Bahram Beza'i's *Bashu, The Little Stranger* (1986; banned until 1989), Kianush Ayyari's *Beyond the Fire* (1987) and *The Abadanis* (1993), Mohsen Makhmalbaf's *Marriage of the Blessed* (1989), Khosrow Sina'i's *In the Alleys of Love* (1991), Ahmad-Reza Darvish's *Kimia* (1995), and Ebrahim Hatamikia's *The Glass Agency* (1997), *The Red Ribbon* (1999) and *Ertefae Past* (Low Heights [2002]), and Jafar Panahi's *Crimson and Gold* (2003). These films hardly ever focus on the Iraqi enemy or on the fighting itself (Sohrabi 1995; see also Naficy 2001b and Varzi 2002 on the remarkable units of warfront filmmakers).[8] At issue is internal strength of character, reconstruction of a torn social fabric, and recognizing and tolerating ethnic, linguistic, and cultural diversity.

The Kurdistan border with Iraq in the late 1990s, during the aftermath not only of the Iran-Iraq War but also Iraq's internal war against the Kurds, also became the subject of several remarkable films, notably Bahman Qobadi's *The Time of the Drunken Horses* (2000), his preparatory documentary *Life in Fog* (1997), and his *Marooned in Iraq* (2002); Samira Makhmalbaf's *The Blackboard* (1999) and the documentary by her brother, Meysam Makhmalbaf, *How Samira Made* The Blackboard (2000); Darius Mehrju'i's *Bemani* (2002), and Fariborz Kamkari's *Black Tape: A Tehran Diary (The Videotape Fariborz Kamkari Found in the Garbage)* (2000). As Samira Makhmalbaf made clear in her speech at Cannes, and as her sister Hannah, brother Meysam, and stepmother Marziyeh Meshkini made clear when they spoke at the Boston Museum of Fine Arts in 2001, the battle is a dual one: on behalf of Kurds but also on behalf of democracy and liberty for all Iranians.[9]

And now, Afghanistan. Afghan refugees had been pouring into Iran ever since the Russians invaded Afghanistan in 1979, and on meeting resistance in the late eighties, among other tactics, conducted campaigns to drive people from villages into cities. More refugees came after the Russians left, and internal civil struggles for control further devastated the country. The difficulties Afghan refugees faced in Iran figured in several Iranian films: Makhmalbaf's *The Peddler* (1986) and *The Cyclist* (1987), Abbas Kiarostami's *A Taste of Cherry* (1997), Ebrahim Hatamikia's *The Red Ribbon* (1999), Hassan Yektapanah's *Jomeh* (2001), Majid Majidi's *Baran* (2001), and Abolfazl Jalili's *Delbaram* (2001). But Makhmalbaf notes that, prior to *Safar-e Qandahar* and the associated documentary *Afghan Alphabet* (2001), only his 1987 film, *The Cyclist*, had taken Afghanistan's plight as its subject matter, and then only indirectly. Even documentary footage of Afghanistan in the 1990s was very limited.[10] By 2003 several films had been shot in Afghanistan, including Samira Makhmalbaf's *Panj-e Asr* (At Five in the Afternoon [2003]); Hana Makhmalbaf's documentary *Joy of Madness* (2003), about the making of *Panj-e Asr*; *Osama* (2002), a striking debut film by Siddiq Barmak, the Afghan director trained at the Makhmalbaf Film House; and Payam Babak's *Silence between Two Thoughts* (2003), shot five kilometers from the Afghan border in eastern Iran, virtually in Afghanistan, about Afghanistan both figurally and really. *Qandahar* is a powerful montage of images. It is worth juxtaposing to an Italian documentary, filmed in the Panshir Valley, that has a similar studied avoidance of explicit political commentary and a similar commitment to disclosing to the world's film-watching eyes the devastation of these wars: Fabrizio Lazzaretti and Alberto Vendemmiati's *Jang* (War): *In the Land of the Mujahedin* (2000).

Both films were made before the U.S.-led military action against al-Qaeda and the Taliban, but both are eloquent protests against viewing the effects of war as merely "collateral damage." As Dr. Gino Strada says in *Jang*, "The war is tragic not just for death and wounds, but especially because war leads to broken relations between people. It takes a generation to repair, if at all; only five minutes to shoot a gun." This is both correct and too romantic. In many parts of the world, people are forced to live with people who have killed members of their families, to live with practicalities on the surface while dealing with submerged and traumatic histories.[11] Americans watched in amazement as Afghan victors allowed Afghan Taliban forces to switch sides, while non-Afghans (Pakistanis, Egyptians, Malaysians, Chechnyans, even an American and a few British and French citizens) were placed in prison camps. The American media was fond of characterizing Afghans, and particularly Pashtuns, as feuding tribals, organized in clans ruled by ruthless warlords. Not only did the American press pay little attention to the poetry of Pashtun and other Afghan lives—a feature that is given at least a little, if insufficient, play in the Italian documentary, wherein both young men and old compose ballads about their war experiences—but it also remained largely ignorant of (or silent about) the nonviolent Pashtun movement, led by Abdul Ghaffar Khan in alliance with Mahatma Gandhi in the 1930s and 1940s, against the creation of Pakistan, for which Abdul Ghaffar Khan was imprisoned for the rest of his life by the new Pakistani state.

The attacks against the New York World Trade Center towers raised the stakes for those concerned with the infrastructures of civil life, as had already been tested by Aum Shinrikyo in a 1995 Tokyo subway attack using sarin nerve gas. Such attacks had been building for some time; they did not come out of nowhere. Such attacks also do not always come from outside: as with the Tokyo attack, both the 1995 bombing of the Alfred P. Murrah Federal Building in Oklahoma City and the 2001 anthrax attack through the postal systems in Florida, Washington, and New York were as far as we currently know domestic terrorism. Previous attacks had failed, had been rehearsals, as it were: not merely had there been an attempt on the New York World Trade Center (with a car bomb as in Beirut and in Omaha), but a planned airplane attack on the Eiffel Tower by Algerian hijackers had been foiled in Marseilles, when the hijackers had demanded the plane be fueled with far more than was needed for the flight to Paris, alerting authorities to what was happening. Dangers of an anthrax attack via finely ground spores in envelopes had been demonstrated early in 2001 in two sets of Canadian scientific experiments, following a hoax letter; such threats had been received for years by abortion clinics. Precision coordination of attacks had been demonstrated in the 1998 bombings of the U.S. embassies in Kenya and Tanzania, as well as in foiled plans for earlier attacks at the turn of the (Christian) millennium (2000 C.E.).

Inside and out, like a Möbius strip, without clear boundaries: "We have to be mature and get used to the new chaos," Haruki Murakami advises. "We have to be patient with that chaos. There is no simple or clear solution for it. One of the most important things is sympathy and respect. In the war between our network and their network these can go a long way" (qtd. in Howard French, "Seeing a Clash of Social Networks: A Japanese Writer Analyzes Terrorists and Their Victims," *New York Times* 15 October 2001, sec. E, p. 5).[12] This need not mean fatalism. It can mean making the infrastructures of civil life more robust. The challenge is to create defenses without destroying civil society, civil rights, due process, and openness. It is, in any case, something Iranians and many others have been already living with.

It means both a self-strengthening and a responsiveness to others, which is a preoccupation of Persian cinematic discourse. A double-sided battle: inside and out. These are old themes of Persian moral discourse: *anderun/ birun* (interior, private, familial, women's parts of a house versus exterior male visiting rooms, public arenas beyond the house), *batin/zaher* (interiority, hidden, mystical meanings versus exterior, public, superficial facades), *darvishi/ta'arof* (simplicity, directness versus politeness codes), *darvishi/luti* (male ideal of abjuring the ways of the world and living by doing what is right versus male ideal of maintaining neighborhood order and protection with all the violence and corruption that that may require), *sabr* (patience, stoicism, determination to follow the path of justice even in a world of overwhelming injustice). Inside and out, like a Möbius strip, where the inside and outside are not always distinguishable.

Efforts to characterize organized terrorism as it has changed over the past few decades have proceeded along four main lines: psychological, socioeconomical, organizational, and technological. While all four are important avenues to explore, a tradition of novels—from Esfandiari's *Day of Sacrifice* (1959) about the apolitical adolescent dynamics of participation in political demonstrations, to Salar Abdoh's *The Poet Game* (2000) about the mixed motives of Islamist underworlds, and Mohsen Hamid's *Moth Smoke* (2000) about the decay of life in nuclear-charged, drug-disseminating, money-laundering, corrupt Pakistan—cautions, as does Murakami, that taken too categorically, these characterizations often miss their mark.[13]

There is a philosophical aesthetics, a way of ethical being in the world, that Persian tradition has cultivated for centuries, that endures in the filmic discourses of the present, one that in the national epic of Iran, the *Shahnameh*, is developed through parables about the ultimate strength of wisdom over brawn, of care for self and others over mere heroics and bravado. At the same time, film has become a dramatic medium with which to register generational change, from the filmmakers who began the Iranian New Wave in the period since Darius Mehrju'i's *Gav* (1969) awaiting the revolution, to the postrevolutionary filmmakers who demonstrated how to live beyond the slogans and in-fighting of the two decades of the revolution, and now to the young generation in their twenties and thirties, born after the revolution and trying to midwife the promise of President Khatami's call for freedom and civil society.

Shrapnels in Peace: War's Aftermath in Khuzistan

"With a wide angle lens we can create a Hussain Sabzian (with a wide angle lens) who dissolves into his social background and becomes a statistical sample; or with a telephoto lens we can separate him from the background so that he stands out. Which is realism? Through color, lens, frame, picture size, story line, acting, we create a reality different from the rest, and thus preserve our own interpretation. . . . Social realism in the Eastern bloc, neo-realism in Italy, magical realism in Latin America—all point to the fact that realism is not a singular."
—MOHSEN MAKHMALBAF, "Realism in the Whole of Realism: On the Pretext of Reviewing Abbas Kiarostami's *Close Up*," in *Ganj-e Khabdideh*

Khuzistan, the oil-producing province closest to Iraq, is the site of powerful images that began to be developed in the 1980s. Amir Naderi's 1984 *The Runner* (*Davandeh*) and Bahram Beza'i's *Bashu, The Little Stranger* are two of the best-known antiwar or humanist films of this period, the former more antiwar by indirection, the latter more explicitly. Both contain images that have become iconic in almost every documentary and retrospective of Iranian film: the image of the boy Amiru (Majid Niroumand) running, or beating on a barrel of water with a chunk of ice against raging flames; the image of a village woman (Susan Taslimi) rising up out of the fields holding the ends of her white headscarf, with eyes flashing, an image of a ferocious protectress. But it is perhaps with Kianoush Ayyari's 1987 *Beyond the Fire* that a haunting minimalist, hieroglyphic imagery begins to form, a style that is renewed in Hatamikia's *The Red Ribbon*, Marziyeh Meshkini's *The Day I Became A Woman* (2000), and Ali Shah-Hatami's *Shrapnels in Peace* (*Tarkesh-ha-ye Solh* [2001]), and is continued in Kurdistani and Afghanistani films by the Makhmalbaf Film House and by Bahman Qobadi.

Icons, Parables, and Hieroglyphs

In *The Runner* three strands of Amir Naderi's filmmaking style crystallize into parabolic concision: a concern with survival skills against tyranny and adversity, a delight in the energy of preteen youths along the Persian Gulf littoral, and a shift from neorealism toward hieroglyphic iconography or abstract cinematic writing. *Tangsir*, Naderi's 1973 adaptation of the novel by Sadegh Chubak, set in the port of Bushire, is the story of the legendary Zar

Still from
The Runner
Susan Taslimi
(*Bashu*)

Muhammad who at the turn of the twentieth century waged a one-man war against four swindlers and fueled a popular revolt against local tyranny. Politically charged in the allegorical mode of the 1970s, *Tangsir* is both a historical period piece and neorealism in color. In two short films he made around the same time, Naderi did studies of the life of boys along the beaches of Khuzistan: in one a gift from abroad, a harmonica, makes a boy leader of his group as his friends compete around him (*Harmonica*, 1974); in the other, a boy's daily chore of filling a bowl with ice seems charged with meaning (*Waiting*, 1975). Other Naderi films, in urban settings, focus on survival strategies of the poor: in *Requiem* (*Marseyeh*, 1978) a man released from prison finds his mother has died and learns to find a new community with two other street peddlers.

In *The Runner*, also shot along the sunny shores of Abadan, an illiterate thirteen year old lives aboard an abandoned boat. As in many Iranian films, life and cinema interact. Naderi found Majid Niroumand, the actor, through a newspaper photo of a boy who had won a race. Amiru, the character, runs after boats, planes, and trains. He desires to travel, to escape his life as a scavenger, selling what he collects for next to nothing. He picks up foreign magazines with pictures of planes and realizes that he must learn to read. Too old to go to school, he is admitted to a literacy class.

The images in *The Runner* came to be developed by the cinematic discourse of Iran: images of getting along with disabilities (a man on crutches, an old couple crossing a highway with difficulty, the woman, ill, bent, coughing, having to sit several times); microeconomies of scavenging or peddling (selling ice water, shining shoes); competition, vigilance, and fighting for one's rights; work sites and housing that are recycled turf (abandoned boats, abandoned buses, construction sites, under bridges); the joy of life, spirit of determination, and overcoming. This is an upbeat film, carried by the energy and playfulness of youth, sun, and seascapes. American music adds notes of desire: Nat King Cole's "Around the World in Eighty Days," Satchmo's "What a Wonderful World" and "What the World Needs Now." But the flames indirectly acknowledge and protest the war that, perhaps, has caused the marginality of Amiru's life outside family or village.

The flames become explicit in Beza'i's *Bashu*: the fires set off by Iraqi bombing envelope the boy's parents, and this becomes a traumatic memory that intervenes again and again.[14] Bashu climbs into a truck to escape and ends up in northern Iran, where his skin color and language make him an initially unintelligible exotic. He is taken in by a woman whose husband is not the only husband away at the warfront, leaving a hollow village of old men, women, and children. The film, when it was finally released, became a vehicle for Iranians to experience the cultural and racial diversity of their country, to break down their xenophobia and fear of difference.

Image Trauma: The Camera Cannot Forget

If *The Runner* and *Bashu* produced iconic images, hieroglyphs, that are instantly recognizable and citable, Mohsen Makhmalbaf's 1989 film *Arusi Khuban* ("Marriage of the Blessed," or perhaps "Marriage Made in Heaven," from the idiom "good marriages are made in heaven") began to explore the disturbances caused by images themselves. Hajji's mental disturbances are figured as a camera, his eyes the shutters that open and shut. The photographic (and filmic) record is the inability to forget. It is the reproduction and welling up of flashes of remembrance of past promises or truths that juxtapose themselves against present realities or hypocrisies. Hajji's camera, says a friend, is "the anxious, watchful eyes of the revolution."

The camera becomes a vehicle of filmic judgment. It is also a nomadic war machine in Gilles Deleuze's sense of making alternative dimensions of reality visible by de- and re-territorializing perspectives in ways the state or hegemonic common sense would wish to marginalize. It is a recording device with which society displays itself, often in a schizoid way by juxtaposing images that normally do not go together, or simply by focusing. The figure of the war photographer bridges two sets of Iranian films: on the one hand the war films proper of the 1980s, which focused on soldiers overcoming fear, on strengthening the self, on stoicism and dedication to justice (Sohrabi 1995); and on the other hand the films of the 1990s which turned to the moral issues of everyday life, of social justice, of character facing the challenges of temptation, and to cultural critique.

The war photographer is named Hajji Pakdel ("Hajji Pure Heart," Hajji being the title of one who has made the pilgrimage to Mecca). His birthday is Eid-e Qorban, the day of sacrifice, the celebration that concludes the rituals of the hajj. There is a suggestion thus that the true hajj and blood sacrifice (*qorbani*) is not so much to Mecca but through inner testings in the trauma of war, and that this hajj causes Hajji to obsessively pursue a photographic career of social justice. The trauma (inner hajj) and obsession (purity, justice) drive him back into the madness and vagabondage associated with the darvish, into an inner truth at odds with the corrupt outer world. While the film works in these traditional terms, it also is a powerful portrait of shell shock.

The film opens with images of Hajji in a mental ward for the shell-shocked intercut with flashbacks of the terror of being shelled on the battlefront. *Shell shock* is probably more accurate than the more recent term *post-traumatic stress disorder*, which Americans began to use after the Vietnam War. The Iran-Iraq War has often been compared tactically to World War I, and the disorientation caused by the pressure-explosions of shells is what Makhmalbaf, in interviews, has explicitly named as the cause of Hajji's psychic injuries. Cinematically, we shift between ward and front, and the camera is foregrounded by jump-cuts, often of the photographer's eyes opening and shutting, or of him aiming a camera at one scene that with a click is semiotically linked to a different one.

Hajji's physician says there is nothing wrong with him physically, aside from a foot injury that requires a leg cast. Over the course of the film his foot heals, and he moves from wheelchair to cane to walking freely. However, the doctor says, we do not know what to do for him psychologically, so it would be best if he were to be put back to work, get married, get involved with family and community. The suggestion is ironic, since the photographer's work is the cause of his problems. But it is not just the shell shock and trauma of wartime photojournalism that is at issue; far more central to the message of the film are the photographs that Hajji and his fiancée, Mehri (kindness, giving through love [*mehrya mahabat*]), take of social problems in Tehran on his release from the hospital. The photographer couple's documentation of urban social problems was received by many as a courageous early protest against the failures of the revolution to address the problems of the poor, which it had claimed to be its goal to solve. It was considered to be an even more bold protest against Ayatullah Ruhullah Khomeini's cease-fire with Iraq, which some felt made a mockery of the idealistic sacrifice of a generation of youths. The youth were suddenly seen as cannon fodder, disposable on the front and inassimilable in the cities at home. Indeed, the film was originally dedicated to the "*Baseej*, the martyrs of the front and strangers in the city," although the dedication was later removed. The Baseej were the cannon-fodder troops of village boys who had been indoctrinated into becoming martyrs and were used to cross minefields and overrun mortar positions, resulting in the kinds of casualties not seen since World War I.

Hajji's father-in-law-to-be would like his daughter to marry someone wealthy enough to support her in style. In the process of dealing with his daughter and future son-in-law as they photograph the social problems in Tehran, however, he discovers that his son-in-law's sanity might be a more important concern. Or rather, it is not just his sanity: the larger question is what is sane, moral, just, or right in postrevolutionary, postwar Iranian society. The failure of the revolution to solve the problems of poverty and justice in the capital are as much at issue as the trauma of having been in battle. The father of the bride is wealthy and therefore among those the groom holds responsible for immorality and for selling out both soldiers and the disadvantaged of society.

In the opening scene of the hospital, Hajji's eyes watch his fiancée; each time he blinks, she dissolves and disappears. His eyes are like a shutter opening and shutting. He is in a locked ward amid a bedlam of patients. One

Typewriter, troops, and tanks (*Marriage of the Blessed*)

man wears a round tin on his head and pretends to call in air cover: "Send angels!" Screaming patients are injected with sedatives. Tanks and an infantry line appear along a dirt ridge; airplanes appear overhead; the tiny figure of Hajji points his camera upward at the planes as bombs drop. The picture is knocked askew. Viewed from an angle are tanks, wounded bodies, a man waving a flag until he stumbles and falls. Hajji falls on his back. He caresses a hand that is on his face, opens his eyes, and sees it is a severed hand. An armless man writhes nearby. Repeat; shutter clicks; open and shut, open and shut.

Hajji leaves the hospital in the sidecar of Mehri's motorcycle, followed by her father's Mercedes. In the darkness the headlights illuminate three slogans from the revolution on whitewashed walls: "Crops belong to the farmer even if he is a usurper of the land" (a saying of Imam Sadeq); "We will bring the capitalists and feudalists to trial" (a saying of Ayatullah Khomeini); "We want the country to belong to the slum dwellers" (a slogan of the revolution). A film poster for the 1983 film *Diyar-e Ashegan* (Land of Lovers), an early war film about the conversion of a conscript into a dedicated Baseej by one who is martyred as he prays, is coming down and is replaced by a film poster for *Taaraaj*, a film about an opium addict who repents, informs on smugglers, and is killed with a reporter in a confrontation with the smugglers. As Hajji tries to take a picture of the *Taaraaj* poster, he screams as he has a flashback of bombing and fires. The shutter clicks. Past and present: revolutionary promise; contemporary corruption; purity of the fight on the warfront; hedonism on the home front.

Days of revolution
Shooting
postrevolution
poverty
(*Marriage of the
Blessed*)

When Hajji points the camera, he often sees pictures of the past. Taking a picture of his future father-in-law and his business partner holding tea glasses, he sees them through the viewfinder in an earlier scene drinking arak. Taking a picture of two Baseej, one now crippled, the shutter clicks; we see them as healthy and young on the front. As the soundtrack slows (past tense), he sees demonstrations with posters of Dr. Ali Shariati and Mortaza Motah- heri; when he looks again through the viewfinder in the present, the same streets are empty of political activism. Hajji and his fiancée take photos in the streets of the poor and needy, passing walls inscribed with revolutionary slogans. But Hajji's editor says, "This subject is getting old. We'll print sun- flowers instead."

The wedding theme is the classic one of poor boy gets rich girl. Her brother is retarded, a symbol of inbreeding and more generally of the strategy of in-marrying to keep wealth within the family. Mehri's father may feel that giving a daughter to the revolution (to a revolutionary idealist) is a way of currying favor with the new regime, and he assumes that the groom will become a member of his family rather than that his daughter will take wealth away.

In a traditional image and ritual symbolic gesture Mehri breaks open a pomegranate for Hajji (*xun-e anar*, or blood of the pomegranate, being a metaphor for fiancée, or blood of the heart). It is a doubly troubled image. First, as she breaks open the pomegranate to peel and seed it for Hajji, he has a flashback of his mother, a laundress who washed rich people's clothes, putting soap on her chapped hands, too poor to have soothing lotion, thus only aggravating the chapping. Second, as Mehri brings the bowl of pomegranate seeds to Hajji, her retarded brother suddenly releases doves, startling her, and she drops the bowl, the red of the pomegranate seeds spraying the air like spurts of blood. Hajji screams, hearing and seeing mortar shells exploding. Four times, Hajji sees Mehri coming and vanishing: each time she blurs and dissolves, he blinks to clear his eyes, and she reappears, like his camera shutter shutting and opening, the crash of the bowl like mortar fire, the red pomegranate spray triggering flashbacks of blood. It is a structuralist set piece: Mahm' Ali, the retarded brother, releases doves, symbols of peace, but Hajji sees war; Mahm' Ali is a mindless optimist, his sister a pragmatic optimist, Hajji a pessimist. The father wants to call off his daughter's marriage to this traumatized "crazy" man.

Mehri takes Hajji into his darkroom to help him therapeutically "review our memories," but first she removes his war photos from the walls. She holds up a lamp to pictures of their childhood to try to get him to forget the war. But when he sees a photograph of his mother, he says "Did you have to remind me that my mother is a laundress?" She tries to get him to think about their marriage, asking, "When did you ask for my hand?" He replies defensively, "My memory is all right. Are you testing it?" She turns on a film projector: a scene of chadored women studying in a classroom. She reminds him that he had brought the film to her as a gift, then tries to turn it off just as it begins to show starving children in Ethiopia. Hajji turns it back on: they are films he had made of drought in Africa, of the massacre of Palestinians at Shatila, of scenes from the Iranian revolution. It triggers war memories, and he faints. There is no getting away from Hajji's memories and associations. Mehri pleads with him, "Why must you take on the burdens of the world?" Cinema, photography, won't let us forget.

In the middle passage of the film, we watch Hajji at work taking pictures: in a studio; in the streets with Mehri; arguing with his magazine editor. In the studio a couple sits for a portrait, the woman unveiled and bald. Hajji looks through the lens at the image upside down, but despite these Islamic work-arounds (he is looking not at a woman but at an upside-down image through a mechanical device; she does not show her hair), he stalks out saying to his business partner: your client. In his arguments with the magazine editor, issues of censorship are raised, and when he gets a copy of the magazine, he finds that the only image they have used is of a sunflower. At stoplights, when beggars approach, he has flashbacks of wounded soldiers. Boys who want to clean the windshield of the car trigger flashbacks of starving children in Ethiopia.

The wedding itself of course does not go well and is something of a tragicomic set piece. Hajji invites veterans, many of whom are crippled. The butler at the entry announces, inappropriately, "Blessed be the souls of the dead." Classical music is played, which again is unsuitable for a wedding, but it is the only music approved by Islamic authorities. Hajji himself appears in military garb (*shalvar-i Amrika'i*, or American trousers) instead of wedding suit. He takes photographs: a little girl dancing barefoot triggers memories of Ethiopian children. An image of his father-in-law and his business partner drinking tea is almost identical to a photo of them drinking arak shown by the retarded brother. A fellow veteran makes a toast and lauds "Hajji with his camera [as] the eye of the revolution." Hajji is called to the micro-phone: "Those of you who wear two differently colored socks [i.e., are poor], welcome. Those of you who have cars of different colors [old, repainted, touched-up old cars], welcome. Those of you with two different kinds of wives [polygamy], welcome. The family went through much to put on this party: they had to sell watermelons at five rials more than the fair price. Eating what is forbidden is delicious [*harram-khori khosh mazast*]." Hajji tries to get the assembly to chant this last line, and then, set off by the sight of ropes of a wedding tent set up in case of rain, he goes into a *rawzeh* singsong, "Omar-i Sadr [the assassin of Imam Husain] came near the tents of Hus-ain. . . ." Hajji then chants, "Fire, fire, fire," his head spinning with flashbacks of war and the bowl of pomegranate seeds flying into the air. Hajji is carried off, but Mahm' Ali comes to the microphone to continue the chant.

Hajji is back in the mental ward, a repetition of the film's opening, with the man in the tin hat still calling in the angels for air cover and the other patients engaged in a disharmonious version of *sineh-zani* (the ritual rhythmic chest beating either in memory of the martyrdom of Imam Husain, or, during the war, a chanting of slogans to liberate Karbala in Iraq). But while some ritually beat their chests, others hold their hands in the air in surrender. Mehri visits and tries to bring Hajji back to reality. One night, however, Hajji escapes into the city. He sleeps like a homeless person in a vacant lot, and when a photographer snaps his picture, he sits up to shout, "Don't take my picture!" He calls Mehri from a phone booth to say goodbye. She rushes out to find him. She finally sees him in the middle of a traffic jam, no longer a revolutionary, a photographer, or a person with identity. He is now a vagrant (*velgard*), a spectacle observer (*tamasha-gari*), and himself an object of photography.

The final shots are of a sharply rat-a-tat-tat-ing typewriter against a battlefield. Has the recording machine of the war correspondent turned into a machine gun causing friendly fire damage to fellow Iranians? It is an image of the betrayal registered in many Baseej accounts of what they felt when they heard about the cease-fire. It is certainly an image of the corruption of the home front corroding the spirit and commitment of the warfront. It is also an image of two powerful historical and ethnographic writing machines. Perhaps it is one more image of Hajji's delirium: the sound of the typewriters in his editor's office causing battlefield flashbacks.

The final shot is an aerial view, looking north over the many small buildings of south Tehran toward the wealthy highrises. This is the battlefield of the Iranian revolution as it continues to unfold in Makhmalbaf's films as well as in the real struggles on the ground.

Marriage of the Blessed is of double interest in Iranian film history. Not only is it one of the first films to make Makhmalbaf's reputation, but he saw it as a pedagogic attempt to teach Iranian viewers how to see, read, and think cinematically. The montage technique of juxtaposition in order to establish a chain of significations and to initiate a kind of cinematic writing through images rather than through narrative or plot alone was something, he argued, that, outside of the Western-educated classes, did not come naturally to an Iranian aesthetic tradition steeped in orality. Even the Persian visual arts, he argued, used quite different tactics in miniatures, calligraphy, or geometric patterns.

Sounds and Furies:
Unhinging Melodramas, Acting Out Psychodramas

The themes of memory and filmic representation, ethics under modern technologies of death and life, and psychological and ethical brinkmanship are followed up in the 1990s by, respectively, Khosrow Sina'i's *In the Alleys of*

Love (1991), Ahmad-Reza Darvish's *Kimia* (1995), and Ebrahim Hatamikia's psychodrama-thriller, *The Glass Agency* (1997). If melodrama explores the struggles against and within hegemonic social moralities; psychodramas in the aftereffects of war engage unresolvable compulsions, obligations, and necessities.

Sounds. In the Alleys of Love, dedicated to the people of Abadan, opens with the sounds of the oil refinery's whistles, boys playing, the chanting of the *hussainiyeh dasteh*s, the drums and cymbals and horns of the *tekiyeh* band, and air-raid sirens; these sounds are accompanied by visual flashes of fires and of acres of broken and charred palm trees. The film is structured as an interwoven tapestry of genres: flashbacks, laments, filmic recreations, memories, and interrupted lives updated. Khosrow Sina'i graduated with a degree in film direction and screenwriting from the Academy of the Dramatic Arts in Vienna, as well as in the theory of music from the Vienna Conservatory. Primarily known as a documentary filmmaker, he has collaborated since 1973 with the National Iranian Television. The dominant theme music of *In the Alleys of Love* is the laments of the tekiyeh or hussainiyeh, the mourning for the martyrdom of Hussain, and a now ruined *tekiyeh* in Abadan figures among the filmic visuals. It is a thoroughly Iranian Shi'ite aesthetic, but the layering is not unlike Viennese or Central European memoirs. It strikes the melancholy reflexive notes not only of nostalgia but of the distortions of cinema's restagings.

A young man walks through a graveyard. He sits at the grave of a child-hood friend and says, "I have finally returned." Through flashbacks, we see the chaos of Iraqi bombings and the frenzied evacuation. Boys of families who refused to leave shout "Cowards!" at those who scramble to escape. Among the ruins is that of the movie theater, the Cinema Rex (alluding to the fire that killed four hundred in the days leading up to the revolution). The young man descends some steps to his father, who says the ruins of Abadan must be fixed up lest it become dust and blow away. The young man says, "We cannot live in this rubble. How can we start over?" The older man replies, "I do not know, but at least in one's own hometown one has some respect. Didn't you see how they came to the refugee camp and took Abadanis to act as extras in their films . . . clowning for the camera for a measly buck!" The young man wanders through the ruins and his memories: games with his childhood friends, the young girl he watched through sunglasses, the excitement of the tekiyeh chants, the cinema (accompanied by classical *santur* music). He finds an old man crooning to his geese, "That's my baby, see how we meet again, they say mountains may never meet, but men will, *baleh*

[yes]." The old man is Uncle Abolfazl Dahesh Tavakoli who tells of surviving homelessness, raising children, not allowing them to become construction workers, building lean-to shelters, having a daughter now in New York and two sons in Ahwaz, one more who died. A boy calls to Tavakoli, "Your ducks and turkeys, dogs and cats, what do you call them? What are their names?" Uncle Dahesh replies, "Meski, Emily, Domko, Bubu." A turkey squawks. Tavakoli soothes, "There are no more bombs, don't be scared, baba. Remember those days of bombs and shells!" The turkey squawks.

In the next scene a filmmaker visits the refugee camp to find extras for his film, which restages the chaos of the Abadan bombing and the agonies of leaving. The young man watches (remembers). The director tells them, "Show your feelings in your eyes." The young man remembers a party in England, before he returned to Abadan, with music and dance, drums, flutes, and tambourines, and a friend's warning, "You won't find any of this over there." As the dancers in London move to the garden outside, the screen is interspersed with shots of rubble in Abadan, and the music track turns to ululating women, small boys playing at war, and machine-gun fire. There are images of twisted pipes and rubble, men falling dead; sounds of machine-gun fire. Tavakoli says, "Listen, even the nightingale is back, calling us." He holds an exploded shell in his hand, "Dear God, what we all went through!" A two year old plays in an alley next to a man in a wheelchair in front of a blue door. "Your eyes were always glued to this blue door." The man in the wheelchair says, "Didn't you live in the next alley? Weren't there three or four of you? I heard one of you was martyred [*shahid shodeh*], God rest his soul [*khodah biamorzeh*]." The blue door is to the house of the girl the young man used to watch. Suddenly the door opens: a filled-out woman comes to retrieve the child; flashback to the young girl who says as they leave, "We will come back." Shaken, the young man next sees a boy with a basketball: his childhood friend. "I waited for you for such a long time." The boy dribbles the ball rhythmically. Tekiyeh music, mottled wall, trumpet, drums.

The tapestry of sounds, musics, genres, and constellations of symbols makes a contemplative weave. Uncle Dahesh Tavakoli, storyteller of oral-narrative traditions, plays with animals as symbols of life and renewal. The film director, too, uses people to restage their own lives, to remember, to montage together a plenitude of small stories. The emotion is most powerful in the small gestures, in the eyes: "Show your feelings in your eyes."

Sounds and Symbols. If Khosrow Sina'i's *In the Alleys of Love* foregrounds sound and music, memory and the restagings of cinematic representation, Ahmad-Reza Darvish's *Kimia* (1995) draws attention to the peopling of technologies in an age of breakdown and war. The film opens with technological and communications media: trumpets, car radios, martial music, a film canister, a reel-to-reel tape recorder, gunfire and bombs, Arabic music, "testing, testing," sirens, a microphone, a car's gear shift, more bombs, a man is hit, airplanes, cars being packed for evacuation, Reza's car has a dead battery, he tries to find a cable connection, he faces the camera. Relying on Shi'ite cues for the protagonist's moral compass, the film is melodramatic in generic form and structure; its interest lies in the weave between the technological and Shi'ite traditionalism.

A husband desperate to get his wife to the maternity hospital is strafed and separated from her; she dies on the operating table; the baby is taken to safety and adopted by the female doctor. When Reza, the husband comes back after nine years of having been a prisoner of war in Iraq, he tracks down his daughter, far from Khuzistan, in Mashhad, where, amid the symbolism of the shrine of the Eighth Imam and the flight of pigeons/doves, he eventually allows the woman doctor to continue to mother his child. Framed with technological means of life and death, basic passions and ethical values are at issue in a postwar world where the pieties of traditional social and ascetic ideals often must be renegotiated.

In the first part of the film, technologies break down and go wrong. In the hospital the respirator stops; the hospital has been hit and the power is cut off. The telephone the doctor uses to call her husband's clinic goes dead; his clinic has also been hit. The motorcycle and the car that Reza and his friend Morad use are strafed by airplanes, and the car explodes with Morad inside. In the second half of the film, technologies—trains, cars, phones, clocks—are of use only in properly peopled ways. The second half opens with a train disembarking prisoners of war from Iraq, including Reza. Although he finds his house bombed out, his parents gone, and the school in rubble (a clock still says twelve o'clock), he learns from the old schoolteacher that his daughter is in Mashhad. He borrows a car and drives there, where he finds Shokuh, the doctor: they stare at each other; she panics and flees. She jumps into her car to escape but nervously backs it into another—it is Reza's but she does not know that—and responsibly leaves a note on the windshield. He finds her again in the hospital (flashbacks of the Khuzistan bombing, the hospital operation under Brueghel-like conditions).

He follows her home, and they talk, but she lies, claiming that the power had failed and that both mother and fetus had died. Now trapped, she prepares to pack, drawing the blinds, not answering the phone, frightening the nine-year-old girl, Kimia. Shokuh's brother, an engineer, tries to negotiate with Reza, offering him money and arguing that the girl is better off with a caring mother. Reza has a hotel room looking onto the Shrine of the Eighth Imam; it is the same room he had shared with his wife on an earlier trip, perhaps their honeymoon. Meanwhile, Shokuh collapses and is hospitalized. Reza sees her with his daughter in the hospital. He has a dream of walking across the desert and coming on white doves on a *tel* or *tepeh* (mound, potential archaeological site); on the tepeh is a well, and when he looks into it he sees the face of his dead friend, Morad. Acting on the dream, he acknowledges the doctor's maternal love, leaving her a note and a toy train for Kimia. As he leaves, he visits the shrine and watches the pigeons/doves fly up in a sign of having done the right thing. The film ends with the image of a train going down a single track.

The film's earlier scenes—the chaos of escape from the air raids and tank incursions—are not unlike the scenes in *In the Alleys of Love*. Here, too, is an old father who cannot be moved or who slows the efforts of the more agile. Here, too, are images of destroyed schools. Symbols of life's renewal are also invested in biology: children of the next generation, geese and ducks, pigeons and doves, goldfish. When the school building is hit, a goldfish bowl explodes, and Morad rescues the goldfish, putting it into a well at high noon (the clock says twelve o'clock). A flashback of the well in his dream triggers Reza's reflections on the fragility of the gifts of life: Morad giving life back to both the goldfish and Reza; Miluheh, his wife, giving her life for Kimia; Shokuh offering maternal nurture for Kimia. Doves and trains represent, respectively, journeys of the soul and journeys on this earth. The film thus becomes a meditation on self-sacrifice on behalf of life, rather than a martyrdom of death (the war from which Reza returned).

Artistically speaking, this film is not of the same quality as many of the others discussed here, but it does illustrate features of an Iranian philosophical ethics of stoicism and spiritual release, which are carried even by a melodramatic form.

Dialogues and Furies. Hatamikia's 1997 brilliant and riveting thriller *The Glass Agency*, an homage to and reworking of Sidney Lumet's *Dog Day Afternoon* (1975), takes the aftereffects of war in the direction of psychodrama, weaving together shell shock and posttraumatic stress disorder with tight narrative plotting, and depicts the political clashes of ideology in a postwar society attempting to live life as if it were normal. Ex-commando leader Hajji takes hostage everyone in a travel agency in order to force the agency and the Fund for Disabled Soldiers to pay for the trip to and surgery in England for one of his former men whose life is threatened by shrapnel lodged in his neck

(shrapnels in peace!). The ethical struggle is complicated by potential misuses of abstract morality in both mobilization (in the war, in taking hostages)
and normalcy. It is a brinkmanship of using imaginative threats while intending no harm.

The ethics of what is appropriate action is revealed in ephemeral flashes of
insight, action, negotiation, trust, and willingness to sacrifice self. In one
brilliant scene, a comic set piece inside the travel agency, the various hostages
begin to argue about how the injustices affecting the injured veteran and
Hajji's efforts at repair relate to the claims of the war in defense of the
revolution, to the postwar society, and to their own rights to live their lives. A
second brilliant scene captures how the police and Hajji negotiate in a high-
stakes standoff. (Both of these set pieces mobilize social and political satire
more complexly than their counterparts in *Dog Day Afternoon*.)[15] Members
of Hajji's former commando unit are on both sides of the standoff: the lead
negotiator for the police and the state is one; others, hearing of the standoff,
arrive on motorcycles to offer Hajji reinforcements against the state. The
tension is sustained not only by the dynamics of the potentially lethal standoff but by the fact that the drama is not good versus evil, but negotiation and
compassion in a nexus of salutary goals complicated by passion, determination, idealism, and pragmatism.

Jafar Panahi's *Crimson, Gold* (2003, scripted by Abbas Kiarostami) provides a similar parable, this time a botched jewelry store robbery (caught on
the security camera). The would-be robber is a war veteran, significantly
named Husain, whose body is bloated by cortisone medication; he ekes out a
living as a pizza delivery man and petty thief. He comes across as stoic,
experienced (in contrast to Ali, his young future brother-in-law and accomplice in crime), and under extraordinary pressure from the daily indignities of
class, labor, and illness, which become crystallized in the humiliations he
experiences in an upscale jewelry store, where he wants to inquire about the
price of a piece of jewelry for his fiancée. During the course of the film, we
watch him attempt to make three pizza deliveries: the first is to an army officer,
whom he recognizes, and who at first does not recognize this apparition from
the diseased, disabled, impoverished working class; but before getting rid of
him with an additional tip, the officer acknowledges a quite different moral
horizon in the past when they had served together in the war and Husain was
injured and presumably thought dead ("You were such a saint, I thought you
had gone to heaven"). In the second pizza delivery, Husain is detained in the
driveway by a police stakeout of a raucous party. It is a set piece displaying the
intrusions of the fundamentalist police forces and showing Husain's prag-

matic humanism. Husain hands out free pizza slices to everyone stuck in the driveway: arrested partygoers, parents who have come to pick up their adult children, and also the young conscripts who are forced to man these nightly stakeouts. The third pizza delivery is to a neurotic son (returned from America) of the absentee owners of an outrageously fancy penthouse on the eighteenth floor. The young man, Pourang ("full of color, passion," "full of it"), invites him in, gives him the run of the penthouse, and treats him as someone to whom he can pour out his laments (a comic *dard-e del*) about the girl who has just left. As soon as she calls and he invites the girl back, Husain again becomes a nonentity. It is after this third delivery that Husain tries to rob the jewrely store where he had twice been snubbed. The movie opens with the chirp of a small bird against a black screen, and then the reprise of what the security camera captures of the robbery attempt. The bird is seen later in the film when Husain, after the second visit to the jewelry store, this time dressed up in suit and tie, wearily climbs up to his tiny, grim, unpainted room with a single bed and a bird cage. Cage, bird, Husain: the symbolic writing of traditional imagery is clear, as is the powderkeg of life as a damaged veteran.

Toward Hieroglyphic and Figural Logic:
Turtles, Red Ribbons, and Scrap Metal

"The dream-work is not a language; it is the effect on language
of a force exerted by the figural (as image or form)."
—JEAN-FRANÇOIS LYOTARD, *Discours, Figure*

With Kianoush Ayyari's 1987 *Beyond the Fire*, a different style seems to be (re)born. Beautifully shot, with close-up camera attention to details, it is painted in the sharp colors of the deserts behind Ahwaz and is enacted with comic-book stylization and plotting. Still, there is a parabolic and emotional seriousness that keeps one's attention and leaves indelible after-images and hieroglyphs. The color, detail, and spaghetti western, Krazy Kat, or hillbilly real McCoy stylized feuding contribute to the hieroglyphic legibility and after-images. The emotional struggle between brothers, between mother and sons, between milkmaid (and her brother and uncle) and the brothers provides a figural-libidinal feel. That the serious commentary is hieroglyphic and figural, rather than literal or direct, is made clear in the opening white-on-black writing: "Thanks to the workers of Number Three Refinery, Ahwaz, . . . to the Ahwaz gendarmerie, and to the contemplative values of cinema." We see oilfield gas flares and oil spurting from drilling rigs. It is spring 1973. A flare explodes into flames as the names of the actors scroll by. A jail-cell lock is unsnapped, plastic sandals drop out of the cell into the hall-way, and bare feet step into them. We see the feet and the boots of the guard. As the feet walk down the hall, the camera shifts to waist-high shot, and we see a bag being carried. At the guard desk, questions and answers follow: "Name?" "Nowzar." "Literate?" "Illiterate [*bi-savad*]." "Religion [*mazhab*]?" "Shi'a." "Single or married?" "Single." We see again the desert and oil rigs with flares in the distance.

A first hieroglyph is the feet stepping into the sandals, an instantly recognizable visual reference to *Qaisar*. A theme of revenge or justice is thus established, but the plastic sandals signal a lighter touch. *Beyond the Fire* is a kind of combined Cain and Abel, Krazy Kat story of fighting between two brothers set in the oilfields of southern Iran. The National Iranian Oil Company (NIOC) has taken over a village. The payment the NIOC gave for the brothers' house has been appropriated by Abdul Hamid, the elder of the brothers. Nowzar, the younger brother, had knifed Abdul Hamid to get his share of the payment. Set in 1973, the story is an allegory of the fratricidal strife set off by modernization and the enclave oil economy under the Shah, wherein some got rich and others were excluded; whether the allegory pertains as well to the postrevolutionary period is left to the viewer to determine. The brothers seem incapable of verbalizing their love; instead, as in the cartoon "Krazy Kat," they communicate their bond through ceaseless fighting and by doing things for one another. The new life of the oil industry displaces the old village life, turning villages into ruins, turning those who cannot get the new jobs into the rural analogues of slum dwellers, and forcing people into factions that fight over what is left of the old economy and the refuse of the new economy.

Nowzar is released from jail and sets off to find his perfidious brother, but his vengefulness possesses less melodramatic gravitas than *Qaisar*, and instead immediately assumes the quality of the kind of satirical obsessiveness, and even abstraction, that comic books or perhaps a Gothic or Faulknerian novel of the U.S. South or Southwest also promote. The resources over which the brothers have fought are minimal, and Abdul Hamid is now a lowly gatekeeper for a fenced-off piece of NIOC desert property who attempts to compensate by unsuccessfully styling himself the dandy with items from the PX that higher-paid employees have thrown away. He lives in a raw-wood shack, the door decorated with Marlborough cigarette covers. (Marlborough was the cigarette of choice in the prerevolutionary period, symbolic, like the harmonica and magazines in Naderi's films, of the good life in the guise of foreign goods.) Nowzar is the no-frills, no-concern-for-material-goods, emotional brother who is consumed with envy and rage at Abdul Hamid's taking of the money. Nowzar falls in love with Asiya, a mute village girl who sells milk to the workers. The mother of the feuding brothers lives in an old bus and screams, "Why do you two always fight? Leave me alone! I have no sons!" When Nowzar tries to bring her some pastries, she throws them out of the bus but will not let the old man with whom she shares the bus pick them up: they are hers, gifts from her son.

Many allusions can be read into the film's hieroglyphs, beginning with the Cain and Abel thematics of Dr. Ali Shariati's writings in the late 1970s, with the brothers standing for social classes in conflict. The oil flares are reminiscent of *The Runner* and *Bashu*, both also shot beautifully in the bright colors of Khuzistan. The abandoned bus turned into a squat is a nod to Makhmalbaf's *The Peddler*; the couple in that film also live in an abandoned bus and are unable to cope with their crippled offspring. There is even a reference to Mehrju'i's *The Cow*; a shot of Nowzar looking out the window of a village house echoes the shot of the peasant looking out the window in Mehrju'i's stylized village. There are also echoes of *Qaisar* both in the opening shot of Nowzar's bare feet stepping into his plastic sandals as he begins his quest for justice (and revenge), and in the shots of the bare feet of Asiya and her brother Saeed marching across the desert to the roll of a tambak drum. The melody of Johann Strauss's "The Blue Danube," on a tape tossed away by an oilworker, and that of the tambak interweave across the music tracks that accompany the interwoven sounds and images of the new oil economy and the old village economy.

After Nowzar's release from jail, he is dropped at a crossroads by a *kifayah*-wearing driver of a pickup truck. The driver expects to be paid, and Nowzar gives him a coin. The driver complains it is not enough. Nowzar replies, "It is all I have," and walks off, then runs back and thrusts in his watch. The driver, insulted, angrily throws the watch onto the ground. Nowzar walks away, ignoring the watch. The driver backs up. The camera angle is from the ground: the driver gets out, furtively dashes to pick up the watch, then drives off. The scene is emblematic both of the psychological theme of fratricidal fighting as communication and of the political theme of modernization, of the impoverishment of workers who often have to swallow pride and honor to take whatever economic scraps come their way. It is also a mini-scenario, condensation, or hieroglyph of the action of the film as a whole. A watch figures in both.

Nowzar finds his brother, harasses him, digs up the knife with which he had slashed Abdul Hamid's face, and watches from a hilltop over the oilfield like an outlaw. Abdul Hamid yells at Nowzar, throws money at him, and tells him to get a job. The milkmaid, Asiya, is afraid of Abdul Hamid and will not come closer than the gate. She makes her little brother, Saeed, deliver Abdul Hamid's milk. Saeed recognizes Nowzar as the better of the two brothers and facilitates his efforts to woo Asiya. To that end, Nowzar gets a job at the oil rig, buys gold bangles for her, and a watch for Saeed. Abdul Hamid is enraged and goes to Asiya's uncle to get the bangles and watch back. Only slowly does it dawn on him that these are not tactical maneuvers against him, but that Nowzar is trying to woo Asiya, and he tries in his own way to help.

The fires become the crucible of these fights. Nowzar angrily throws the wad of money that Abdul Hamid has given him toward the hot flames: the fight for him is not just about money. Abdul Hamid, obsessed with money and what it can buy, tries desperately and unsuccessfully to retrieve the paper money, but the fire is too hot. Only then does Nowzar realize he can use the money to buy tokens for Asiya and Saeed (the bangles and watch), and so he, too, tries to retrieve the money, also unsuccessfully. Later, when the bangles get thrown toward the fire, Asiya similarly scrambles for them.

The theme of mutual aid and its limits under the desperate circumstances of the impoverished working class and lumpen proletariat of south Tehran, of the many refugees from the war-torn south, continues in Kianoush Ayyari's 1993 film, *The Abbadanis*, a film more neorealistic than the wild and colorful *Beyond the Fire*. Bornia is the son of an illiterate war veteran who deals with the literate world and bureaucracy for his father by drawing pictures on food coupons—a cone for sugar, a hand for soap—and by skipping school to help his father deal with the police. When the family car is stolen, they turn to a friend, a petty thief, to help them find out if the local gang has the car. Bornia's family lives in an apartment and, although tight for money and dependent on ration coupons and on what the father's private car used as a taxi can make, is better off than their friend, the thief, whose hut has nothing but a couple of carpets and is built under a high-tension wire farm. The thief gets by, stealing anything he can—he is not evil, just a hard-bitten survivor—whereas Bornia's family members, not yet at that level, have not learned to steal and get caught when, in desperation, they try. Everyone in this under-class helps each other up to a point. At the conclusion of the journey through the netherworld of Tehran, Bornia's family finds the car in a police com-pound, crushed and stripped. They repair what they can, patching the car back together with the help of the thief, who comes up with various necessary parts, and with the help of a mechanic friend. The car resumes its taxi service lacking only a few cosmetic features like the rear window, now patched with plastic. Symbolically, young Bornia fashions a periscope mirror through which he can watch the world obliquely, sideways, behind, and upside down. In the technological icons of the film, an old movie projector is part of the circulation of broken mechanical devices, and the high-tension wires of the technological world pass over this lumpen world (just as the power lines for Johannesburg passed over Soweto in South Africa).

Ebrahim Hatamikia's 1999 film, *The Red Ribbon*, returns to the wilder, more colorful absurdist style of Ayyari's *Beyond the Fire*. With *The Red Ribbon*, Hatamikia continues the exploration of the aftereffects of the war that he began in *From Kharkhe to Rhein* (1992) and *The Glass Agency* (1997). (His 1992 film is about a group of war veterans who have traveled to Cologne for medical treatment. The protagonist, Saeed, had been blinded by chemical weapons when he gave his gas mask to a wounded friend during an attack. In Cologne he is visited by his sister, who lives there with her German husband and son. They have a bittersweet reunion of nostalgic memories.) In *The Red Ribbon* three characters are blocked by their own past traumas from living in the present and are caught in a love triangle of a gestural language that struggles to allow human affection to show through. A tribal woman, Mahboubeh, tries to return to her family's ruined compound. She has a "hysterical pregnancy" (after a while she pulls out a pillow) and is tortured by visions of her childhood family. A veteran, Davud, obsessively dedicated to clearing mines and marking mine-free areas with a red ribbon, is tortured by visions of his dead mates. The red ribbon becomes a metaphor for the mine-free areas of the psyche. An Afghan refugee who lives nearby in a small painted van in a tank cemetery is tortured by visions of his bride being shot.

These are isolated characters in a devastated landscape, like those of Samuel Beckett.[16] Deranged by their pasts, the characters must come to terms with each other. This imperative in turn forces them to deal at least a little with the figural phantasmagoria of their derangements. The film is set in the future, August 2010. It is about the ongoing effects of the war: the past is not behind us but interferes in the present and future. The opening begins with the sound of water, the mythic fountains of life, renewal. A turtle emerges from the water onto the land, shot through a fish-eye lens. The turtle is amphibious, the denizen of two worlds, land and sea, past and present; it is soft on the inside but with a hardened shell, like a human in a tank, like Davud, who, despite his surface gruffness, in his underground shelter carves scenes of his feelings and understandings, especially of Maboubeh as petrified woman; like the tank the three characters get to move out of a hole like a turtle emerging from the sea; like the Afghan Jomeh who says he will use the tank to open the road of life out of the valley of death and does so indirectly by bringing the three characters together.

On the soundtrack, there is drumming as the turtle marches across the desert, over rocks, with mesas in the background. A jeep comes down a road: turtle and jeep are on a collision course. The jeep brakes hard and just taps the head of the turtle, who stops, then determinedly marches on to the other side of the road. Meanwhile a young woman has climbed out of the jeep. She wears tribal dress, a burqa veil over her face, and carries a cardboard suitcase. She stands and stares at the landscape, which has two red ribbons forming parallel lines. She begins to hopscotch inside the red ribbons, trips, and her suitcase goes flying. It explodes when it hits the ground—it has tripped a mine. A male voice shouts at her to go away. She: who are you? He: go home. She: this is home. He: you came too soon. He tries to tell her it is a minefield. She ignores him and steps over a red ribbon. He yells at her to stop and throws a stone to show her: it sets off an explosion. He says he did not plant them, but that there is no place to live. She replies that she is cleverer than all you men and moves past his tent toward an old mud-brick-fortified ruin. Davud picks up the turtle and asks it, "Where did you find her?" Mahboubeh meanwhile comes to the locked door of the ruin, lifts her veil to gaze at her family home, smiles, climbs through the broken walls, finds an old swing, lies in it, and cries and sings.

That night a mole or rat startles her, and she chases it in a frenzy of fear, pursuing it down a hole with a broom handle. In this way, she uncovers a pipe, which turns out, after she pushes back dust, dirt, and a straw-mat covering, to be a tank's long gun barrel. Suddenly she screams again: her hand has been stung, a scorpion walks away. She holds her hand up and runs toward Davud's tent yelling for help. Scorpions and turtles, moles and buried tanks (with even a skull inside): out of these life must be renewed.

A few of Hatamikia's images rework themselves in Ali Shah-Hatami's *Shrapnels in Peace* (*Tarkesh-ha-ye Solh* [2001]): instead of carcasses of tanks, the carcass of a plane; instead of holes of refuge, spaces for scrap-metal collection and recycling. A woman emerges from behind the carcass of a plane in the desert. In a dreamlike long shot, she moves slowly toward the camera and descends into a hole under a sheet of metal. The starkness of her black chador against the bright sunlight and the darkness of the hole gives the scene an abstract quality. We initially wonder if it is a shelter she has made, but it turns out to be a large piece of the wing, which she climbs under in order to lift it, with difficulty, onto her head. Slowly she walks across the desert. We come to understand that impoverished people bring bits of metal to a welder who pays by weight. He cuts and recycles the metal in a hangarlike building.[17] Jomeh, a young boy, participates in this sweatshop harvesting of war debris. He attempts to lead a strike for higher wages, but the workers have no bargaining power. He needs money for his sister's dowry, and so goes to harvest scrap from a minefield, with predictable consequences.

Like *Beyond the Fire* and *The Red Ribbon*, what makes *Shrapnels in Peace* such a haunting film is its figural camerawork: the opening scene of the chadored woman lifting the piece of airplane wing; a later scene in which she arrives at the welder's shed and slips to her knees, exhausted; the scene of the workers lined up by the paymaster next to scales and a ledger in the industrial darkness of the welder's cavernous shed; the desert scene of the boy avoiding the military guards and making his way into the minefields to search for scrap metal. These carcasses, holes, recyclings of refuse, and fatigue all operate as dreamwork, as phantasmagoria of anxieties (endless labor, exhaustion, inadequate recompense, need driving one into dangerous terrain), as much as neorealist portraits of economic adversity, social inequality, and political oppression. *Beyond the Fire* and *The Red Ribbon* are driven by libidinal elements. The emotional, inarticulate struggle between the brothers, the paranoid fears of the traumatized threesome in *The Red Ribbon* and their efforts to relate on the emotional level if not on an articulate one are both the topic and the form. Storyline is less primary than acting out, following the repressions, projections, and secondary revisions while at the same time trying to make emotional connections.

Drunken Mules, Flapping Blackboards, Broken Lives: War's Aftermath in Kurdistan

The children were gunshy from having seen so much war:
when cameramen went behind the camera, and would shout 'light, camera, shoot,' they were scared. So . . . I tied a rope to my cameraman and soundman, and would pull on it to signal them.
—BAHMAN QOBADI, Boston, 1 October 2001

Any film is like a poem, it is not interesting just to repeat. And that is what Iranian cinema is doing, like poetry bringing out something different. . . . Film should depict reality and transform it. . . . Something happens in front of the camera, and it is the first moment it happens, new life takes shape in front of the camera.—SAMIRA MAKHMALBAF, in Meysam Makhmalbaf's *How Samira Made* The Blackboard

> War produces a kind of twilight, which like fog or
> moonlight often tends to make things seem grotesque.
> —CARL VON CLAUSEWITZ, *On War*

If revolutions often generate images of life turned upside down, the aftermath of war in devastated borderlands such as Kurdistan take on a grimmer surrealist quality of living in a sacrifice zone where, as Nassim's father's sister in Darius Mehrju'i's 2002 film *Bemani* says, "We are people who don't count. We live to suffer and die, and no one notices." Four narrative films and two documentaries do notice and attempt to call attention.

Bahman Qobadi's 2001 film, *The Time of the Drunken Horses (Zamman-i bara-ye masti-ye asb-ha)*, is about land that is sown with mines and about the lives of smuggling this imposes, intensified when seen through the lives of children. Qobadi's earlier documentary *Life in Fog* (1997), along with a series of shorts, prepared the ground. Samira Makhmalbaf's 2001 film, *The Blackboard*, is about the aftermath of the chemical bombing of the Iraqi town of Halabja by the Iraqi government in an effort to subdue the Kurds; it is a story about teachers who carry blackboards on their backs, seeking asylum in Iran and searching for paying pupils to teach. Their paths cross those of human mules, young boys carrying on their backs not blackboards but heavy packs of smuggled goods. Periodically both must run to hide from border guards and surveillance aircraft. The films' styles are quite different, but they are allied (Qobadi was one of the actors in Samira Makhmalbaf's film) and their content intersects (Qobadi focuses on the family life of one of the young human mules figured as a demographic population in *The Blackboard*). Both films focus on life-giving ties across deadly borders: trade, medical help, weddings, families divided by borders, and blocked end-of-life quests. Samira Makhmalbaf's brother Meysam made a riveting documentary, *How Samira Made* The Blackboard, partly in response to critics' suggestions that a woman could not have made the film, that it must really have been made by their father.

Bahman Qobadi's 2002 film, *Marooned in Iraq*, takes up *Beyond the Fire*'s black humor and deranged search for love and emotional connection; thematically, like *The Blackboard*, it is set in the aftermath of the chemical attack on Halabja. Darius Mehrju'i's *Bemani* (2002) turns to the theme of women's liberation, a major preoccupation for both female and male auteurs in the 1990s, and also experiments with braiding three stories together and with having various characters face the camera to be interviewed by the filmmaker, perhaps in an effort to break genre conventions and appeal to the audience directly. *Black Tape*, by Kurdistan-born Fariborz Kamkari, follows the devastation of the lives of Kurds who become migrants in Tehran.

Bahman Qobadi is a Kurd, and *The Time of the Drunken Horses* is about a village he has spent time in. His actors are villagers to whom the stories happened. Qobadi shot the film over two winters because it did not snow enough the first winter, so he had to borrow money from family and friends because the Farabi Foundation did not see any reason to let him reshoot. The production crew was his family. It was the first film for his cameraman, a talented photographer, and the visuals are spectacular and haunting. Qobadi screened the film for the villagers—the first film they had ever seen, there being only two cities in Kurdistan that still have cinemas. He himself had previous experience making short films, acting as an assistant for Abbas Kiarostami, and working as an actor in Samira Makhmalbaf's *The Blackboard*. He credits as influences Emir Kustarica for the energy in his films, Theo Angelopoulos for atmosphere, and especially the 1983 Turkish film *Yol* directed by Serif Goren and Yilmaz Guney, the latter also a Kurd. (I asked about Abbas Kiarostami. Qobadi waved off the question with the laugh line, "Everyone in the Iranian film industry is indebted to Kiarostami," followed by a somewhat disingenuous or rebellious-son denial, "but no there is no direct influence: he does many seconds long shots; I do short four- to five-second shots" [Boston Museum of Fine Arts, 2001].)

Because the land is mined and too dangerous to farm or run sheep and goats, villagers along the Iran-Iraq border are forced to sell land to buy pack animals with which they can engage in cross-border smuggling, itself a deadly enterprise in the mined borderlands. People are constantly being killed or maimed by either the mines or gunfire at the border. The really poor, who have no mules, donkeys, or horses, offer themselves as beasts of burden for the smugglers. The story of the film is about one such family, in which the father has been killed. His fourteen-year-old son, Ayub, and his older daughter, Rojneh try to take charge, with the uneven help of the father's brother. Their younger sister, Amineh, provides the narrative voice. There is also a toddler sister, Kolsum, and a sick, hunchbacked, and dwarf brother, Mehdi. The title comes from the practice of putting alcohol into the mules' and horses' drinking water to keep them warm and help them negotiate the rough terrain in the snow.

The film is a series of iconically composed shots and scenes: long, muddy trails up and down snowy hills (not unlike the signature shots of Kiarostami); hard-bitten men tying huge truck tires and packs of goods onto each side of their mules; an unexplained fight between mulers in the mud and cold that

Mule train
Mules and boy mules
Mule pack
(*The Time of the Drunken Horses*)

scares the Ayub to tears; the daily routines of the family of children, chopping wood, lighting the stove, and serving tea in their house, and packing boxes in the bazaar; Amineh filling her school notebook and requesting a new one; poignant efforts to protect the sick dwarf brother, carrying him, comforting him, getting him medicine. The need to pay for medicine (and school note-books for Amineh) is one of the factors that drives Ayub to enter the smug-gling trade, first with the help of a mule his uncle helps provide him, and then after the mule slips in a stream, as a human mule, who is often cheated of his pay. In the end he desperately tries to carry his brother over the border to get medical care.

The uncle arranges a marriage for Rojneh with a family on the other side of the border. She agrees because the bride-wealth promised can pay for a life-saving operation for Mehdi, and on the promise that her new family will also accept Mehdi so she can care for him. Mehdi is stuffed into a saddlebag and the wedding procession takes off, menfolk watching silently from the roofs. It is a sad little affair. The women kiss her goodbye. She rides a horse and wears a red, embroidered wedding dress, while Mehdi, her dowry goods, and her carpet are on a mule following behind. It snows. They are received by the groom's family waiting around a fire in a cold and desolate no-man's-land. Voices rise in argument: "What did you bring him for? Take him back!" The mother-in-law shouts, "I already have ten children. Instead of bride-wealth we will give a mule, okay?" They lead Rojneh away with clapping and a wedding song, leaving Mehdi behind. Ayub then tries to carry Mehdi over the border, but the caravan runs into gunfire. All run, shouting, "Ambush!" Mules slip and fall. Ayub's mule falls and its load comes off, but it is able to scramble up, and they make it to the border. They are alone when in the snow they come to a low barbed-wire fence, which they step over. The film ends on notes of clapping and the wedding song.

The film is part of the now-rich Iranian film tradition of viewing the world through the lives of children. Qobadi himself has done several mar-velous shorts with children, including *The Party*, which is about a girl who, left at home alone, tries to play hostess on a *gelim* in the alley outside her house, bringing out a samovar, cups and saucers, fruit and nuts. She interacts with neighboring age-mates, their mothers, and relatives as they pass by. The film includes some marvelous exchanges, using repetition, mimicking, and mirroring within a structure of play, as well as projecting a child's experience onto that of a grandfather. Similarly, *God's Fish* is a wonderful parable about two boys accused of stealing fish from the pond of the village mosque on Noruz, the Persian New Year. A Noruz custom is to buy a goldfish and take

Amineh, Mehdi, and Ayub
Accounts
Mehdi and muscleman
(*The Time of the Drunken Horses*)

it home for the first days of the new year, then release it in some water. Adults vouch for the boys that the plastic bag that held the pair of fish they had bought had broken and that they had put the fish in the pond to save them, returning later with another bag to recapture them. It becomes an allegory of the authoritarian rigidity of the old servant of the mosque, whose power and status is in question and who accuses them bitterly of stealing the mosque's fish; it is hard not to extend the allegory to the contemporary political situation: mullahs standing in front of mosques, accusing youth and those taking initiative in solving daily problems of violating the law and sacred space, even though witnesses attest to the virtue of the latter. There is also perhaps a historical reference to Samad Behrangi's famous story *The Little Black Fish*, a children's story from before the revolution urging liberation from conformity and blind obedience to tradition. Qobadi's twenty-eight-minute documentary, *Life in Fog*, was made in the same year (1997) as *The Party* and *God's Fish* and likewise participates in the rich tradition of Iranian films that use nonprofessional actors.

With regard to using nonprofessional actors, Abbas Kiarostami (Harvard Film Archives, 7 June 2000) comments, "Professional actors do exactly what you tell them: they repeat your mistakes. With non-professionals, if something is wrong, they recognize it, and you can correct what you are doing on the scene. . . . A poem from Rumi, I think, reflects the difficulties of working with non-professional actors: Film is like a game of polo, you are the ball, and I hit the ball with a stick to make it move; yet, I am the one who is following your movements." Qobadi, who partly trained as an assistant director and acted with Kiarostami, says something similar when asked about the making of *The Time of the Drunken Horses*, for which there was no script: "Filming in Kurdistan is so powerful, even if you just follow anyone for two hours, you will have a film. The screenplay belongs to the people, it is their lives. I lived in the first village and have seen everything you have seen. I just adapted it for the film format" (Boston Museum of Fine Arts, 1 October 2001). For instance, commenting on Amineh's request for fresh notebooks, Qobadi says, "When I went to make a film and asked a child that I would give him so much money to help find twenty children, he said, we don't want money, we want erasers, notebooks, and this is reflected in Ayub, who has seen he has lost his opportunity to study, but tries to make sure his sister can study" (ibid.). Furthermore, "The sequence where Ayub is carrying the little Mehdi and says 'I love you,' that was not scripted, it came out spontaneously. In the scene where Ayub and Amineh make up [after he cuffs her and shouts at her], I turned on the camera and we [the crew] left the room saying: go make up" (ibid.). There were some challenges, of course: "The children were gunshy from having seen so much war: when cameramen went behind the camera, and would shout 'light, camera, shoot', they were scared. So we tried to have natural conditions: I tied a rope to my cameraman and soundman, and would pull on it to signal them" (ibid.).

Life in Fog covers the same material as *The Time of the Drunken Horses*: when Rojneh carries Mehdi to the graveyard to cry over their parents' graves, and Ayub cuffs her for bringing Mehdi there in the cold; the school scene in which Ayub brings Amineh a fresh notebook (but this time not before we are treated to a boy reading out loud about identifying a donkey by its tracks); the boy on a mule; the workers' teahouse; the boy shocked by a fight between the men of the caravan; a panicked scene of disaster in which three mules fall off a cliff. Other scenes that end up in the narrative film are not yet here, including the wedding, the scenes of the market, the loading of donkeys in the mud. The beginning and the ending also are slightly different. In the documentary, the opening shot shows the five children sitting for a portrait, and they begin to talk about themselves: their mother died giving birth to Kolsun, their father died while smuggling when his mule fell on a mine. Heightening the poignancy, they tell us that Mehdi, the sick dwarf, is thirteen, only a year younger than Ayub, but the most dependent. The documentary's ending is more tragic: after the Ayub's mule falls and breaks its leg, it is found at the edge of a stream. Ayub pulls the guide rope but the mule will not budge. In desperation he tries to massage the injured hind leg. Two adult men come to his aid and lift him onto dry land. Suddenly he is no longer the man of the family, but after all a little boy who can be lifted up, who no longer can control what is about to happen. He cries as they check the leg: the mule cannot be saved. We see and hear the stream's rushing muddy water. The film ends with Ayub carrying a box on his back—now he is the mule. The fog of the title envelopes these laborers as they break trail through snow and mud, proceeding through the whistling of the wind, and perhaps the cries of wolves, into the fog. Although the dilemmas of these Kurds occur on the periphery and as an aftereffect of the war, fog provides a visual-semiotic and metaphoric link to the physical and psychological effect of war, as in the epigram from Clausewitz: "War produces a kind of twilight, which like fog or moonlight often tends to make things seem grotesque," and in Freud's essay "The Uncanny."

Samira Makhmalbaf's film *The Blackboard* is also set in the borderlands of Kurdistan. In her brother Meysam's documentary about the making of her film (to counter the critic's skepticism that a young woman could make such a polished film with rough, male, nonprofessional actors), she describes it as "about the homeless in Kurdistan in a land of dangerous mines, old men return after the war, it is a little like fish in the ocean returning to where they were born." As she speaks, we see a scene of a large group of men walking around a curve in a barren valley. "The situation is where having a little knowledge is a heavy burden, this knowledge is carried like the cross of Jesus. Knowledge can let you fly, but now, here, the knowledge doesn't let them fly, it is a burden." We watch Samira showing a man how to walk with weariness, carrying a blackboard on his back. "It looks so real, as if a documentary, but each scene is recreated. To make drinking water look real in front of a camera takes many hours of practice." We watch an actor drink water from a plastic bag. "The actors come in the morning eager, freshly showered, in clean clothes: they do not look like wandering homeless men, so we have to make them dirty." There is only one woman featured, but she opens the film with a song; of her Samira says, "She provides contrast. . . . Until we went to shoot I did not have a woman in mind, but then I saw a woman walking, and Meysam filmed her from behind [a village woman is shown walking wearily]; she was depressed and even people said she was insane after she lost her husband." We see Samira cajoling the woman, Manijeh. The actress did not know Kurdish: "She rehearsed some phrases, and we would record her, and do a sound check [the actress repeats the Kurdish word for *blackboard*] and then we would film [the actress shakes the toddler, 'Blackboard, blackboard, pee, pee.']. . . . I had the last scene in mind from the beginning: it is about the memory of chemical bombardments. But it wasn't possible to create the feeling. We had to wait until there was a fight, and then we ran after it, carrying our equipment. . . . We had to go three hours from the village to near the border, to be near to Halabja, to capture a spirit of energy and the terrible effects of war on children who have to deal with landmines." We see a man wailing, "He can't be dead! He was supposed to have died in our homeland."

Halabja was the Iraqi Kurdish town on which Saddam Hussein dropped chemical weapons on 16–19 March 1987, after first demolishing villages around the town and driving the rural population into the town. A joint force of Kurds and Iranian Revolutionary Guards had expelled Iraqi soldiers briefly. In response the Iraqi air force sprayed mustard, sarin, and tabun gases, and perhaps vx gas and the biological agent aflatoxin. Five thousand people died, thousands were injured, and refugees fled to the Iranian border. This was but one of some forty chemical assaults conducted by the Iraqi air force on Kurdish populations (Power 2001, 188–89) in a campaign that killed some 200,000 and displaced 1.5 million people (Urquhart 2002, 16).

In the film *The Blackboard* the old men who fled Halabja wish now to return home. One of these old men is unable to urinate (*shash-bandeh*), not unlike Rustam Mistry's brilliant image in *Swimming Lessons*: the immigrant to Canada who cannot defecate until he returns home to Bombay. In any case, the old man has an unmarried daughter with a little boy, who, inversely, needs to be taught when and where to urinate.

Opening hieroglyphs. The film opens with the woman's song, a brilliantly golden, sunlit valley and mountains. Seven or so men come around a curve in a road carrying blackboards on their shoulders like a flock of surreal black-birds. Two of the men talk about the paths they have taken in search of pupils. The group pauses as the wind whips up around a turn, turning their full Kurdish *shalvar*s (wide trousers) into flapping sails. One goes ahead to scout the terrain and gives a warning: they all turn and run back as the sound of a helicopter comes overhead. They squat close to the ground, holding their blackboards over their heads. A flock of blackbirds rises up off a high moun-tain peak, cawing. Someone calls the all clear, and they get up. A hand smears mud on a blackboard as camouflage. At a fork in the road, the two men part, one going uphill to seek out shepherds, the other down to a village.

Burdens of knowledge. Downhill, the village is a set piece of ironies. A peasant tosses wheat into the air to separate the chaff. He is uncommunica-tive. "Is there a school here?" asks the teacher. "I don't know." "Is there a teacher here?" "I don't know." But as the teacher turns to leave, the peasant lifts his face-mask against the dust, draws a cherished letter from his pocket, and asks the teacher to read it to him. The teacher, himself literate only in Persian, looks at it and says it is not in Persian. The peasant begs, "For the love of God, please read it." The teacher asks, "Is it in Arabic? Is it from Iraq? From your son?" The peasant replies, "I don't know if it is in Arabic, Turkish, or Kurdish. It is from my son." The presumed Kurdish of the letter is illegible between the warring national literacies of Iraqi Arabic, Iranian Persian, and Turkish; so, too, are the Kurds caught between Iran, Iraq, and Turkey. So the teacher pretends to read: your son says he is in good health and sends greet-ings to you, health to mother, his sister and brothers and uncles. "Does he have money?" asks the peasant. "I think he has a little." "How is he getting on in jail?" "Fine." "When will he be released?" "If it is God's will, he will be released." Each then returns to his own path: the teacher continues on his search; the peasant puts on his mask and returns to work. The absent son, absent literacy, absent labor force of young men, and absent young adults as transmitters between old and very young are all figured in this scene.

Mules and old men. Meanwhile, the other teacher proceeds uphill. He falls in with some young boys who are mules in the smuggling trade: they resist all his reasons for hiring him to teach them to read. He even asks a group of old men traveling together if they can read and if they want to learn; they answer no to both questions, more kindly saying, "We have nothing to eat, we are nomads, we are all lost and do not know how to go to Iran." Finally, they bargain with the teacher to use his blackboard as a stretcher to carry the old man who cannot walk any more. The old man wants to marry off his daughter so he can die. The teacher is offered the woman as a wife with no dowry. The teacher agrees to marry her and a ceremony is performed using the blackboard as a curtain (*pardeh*) between bride and groom until they have exchanged their vows. A piece of the blackboard also serves as a splint for the broken leg of one of the mule-boys who falls down a hill. In exchange for this bit of real help, one of the boys admits, "Yes, most of us can read, but we were taught by our mothers not to trust strangers" (thus they had denied interest in, ability for, or use for reading). The teacher tries, with little success, to teach his new wife the multiplication tables on the blackboard.

Borderland. Someone cries out a warning, and people hit the ground and crawl for cover. The teacher gives his new wife, son, and father-in-law cover under the blackboard. A flock of sheep pass by. The woman is panicky: is it a chemical bombardment? No, it is just rifle fire. They argue about where they are. They come to some barbed wire, and all kneel and pray. The teacher doesn't want to cross the border, so he has to divorce the wife, and the blackboard again comes into play as a curtain between them as the wedding bonds are ritually untied. But now the blackboard has become her property, and as she walks off carrying it on her back, it displays in white chalk what he had been trying to teach her: "I love you." She calls to her little boy as he is about to pick up a black metal object, presumably a mine (the audience takes in its breath), but then he lets it go and trots off after his mother. The film begins with a woman's solo song; it ends with a chorus of male voices.

At the "Cinema of Tomorrow" session at the Cannes Film Festival in May 2000, Samira spoke of the camera becoming like the pen, a light and decentralized technology, with quite radical implications: "Cinema has always been at the mercy of political power . . . and the concentration of the means of production. . . . Earlier in the twentieth century, because of the weight of the camera, the difficulty of operating it, and the need for technical support, this eye was cast like a heavy burden on the thoughts and emotions of the filmmaker. But today, following the digital revolution, I can very easily imagine a camera as light and small as a pair of eyeglasses." The literal image of the camera as a pen is one that her father, Mohsen Makhmalbaf, uses in his parodic *Testing Democracy* ("this film is dedicated to all who oppose it"), in which, during a scene of filmmaking on the beach, there is a comic set piece of the filmmakers trying to get a dark-skinned older man of Khish Island to take off his clothes, put on a sarong, and carry a door on his back. Is the door a reference to the blackboards? Is the comic scene a self-reflexive and good-natured reply to heavy-handed questions about oppressing nonprofessional actors either by not paying them sufficiently or by making them look foolish before an exoticizing urban gaze?

In "The Quadratic Aspect Relationship of Samira and I," a posting on his Web page, Mohsen Makhmalbaf comments on the blackboard as Sisyphus's stone: "All people carry the Sizif [Sisyphus] stone: the mother carries her child, children carry smuggled stuff, teachers carry blackboards. The blackboard sometimes is a stretcher, sometimes it is a wall between the relationship of a man and a woman" (Makhmalbaf n.d.).

The Blackboard and *The Time of the Drunken Horses* are part of a cinematic discourse that, while being imaginative, humorous, and serious, is also attentive to its own medium of invention and commentary. Two more such films on Kurdistan appeared in 2002. Qobadi's *Marooned in Iraq* stylistically picks up the wild emotional and comic intensity of Ayyari's *Beyond the Fire* and Hatamikia's *The Red Ribbon* (as well as Emir Kusterica's *Underground*, a favorite of Qobadi), while Darius Mehrju'i's *Bemani* pushes the generic envelope on three melodramatic tales, which he braids together as commentaries on one another, and experiments with the device of interviewing the characters in medias res, having them address the camera in explanation, desperation, and ethical dialogue. Insofar as the textuality of film, like that of writing, is a distanced form of communication, a graphics of absence in which characters cannot reply to audience responses or audiences to characters' corrections of their misapprehensions, perhaps this is a gesture toward a dialogic ethics. In any case, it draws attention to hybrid forms that combine documentary, through which filmmakers assert their view of the truth, usually in a sutured way that limits the viewer's ability to evaluate the documentary's selections and constructions, and narrative, which attempts to model more fully the complexity of competing pressures that devastate, redeem, and motivate ongoing lives.

Qobadi's *Marooned in Iraq* is set in the early 1990s. It was produced with funds earned from *The Time of the Drunken Horses* and employed friends and relatives as the actors. Sixty percent of it was filmed secretly inside Iraq. The film opens with the sounds of fighter planes and views of desert-brown mountains, blue sky, telephone wires, and a goggle-wearing motorcyclist looking up at the sky as Kurdish music wells up. Next we see people riding in a tractor-trailer, jabbering at each other: sit down, quiet, that poor man is crazy, the police have been tracking him for twenty-three years. The tractor-trailer stops for a weathered old man, Doc, and we discover that the motorcyclist, Barat, is seated on his motorcycle on the back of the trailer. The crazy Doc and the wild motorcyclist are sure signs that there is comedy and absurdity afoot in this war-torn borderland. Doc wants to know why Barat is on the tractor-trailer, and Barat replies that there are bandits about. Doc says there are no bandits, but he is going to the border to buy things up cheap from the refugees from Saddam's bombing ("God bless Saddam's father, I've made a lot of money!")—he's obviously one form of bandit himself. He asks Barat about his father, Mirza, and curses Hanareh for having left Mirza all alone.

The primary storyline follows an old musician, Mirza, and his two sons, Barat and Odeh, on a search for Hanareh, his former wife, mother of Barat and Odeh, and a symbol or soul of Kurdistan. (Hanareh [Kurdish, *hanar*; Persian, *anar*] means pomegranate. "Hanareh" is also the name of the Kurdish song that Mirza and his sons sing like an anthem and that audiences always request.) Twenty-three years before, after fighting with Mirza over her right to sing in public, Hanareh had run off to Iraq with Mirza's music partner, Sayyid. The search for Hanareh is a double theme of the struggles for the liberation of women and of the Kurds (and more pressingly of the continuation of these struggles in the aftereffects of the chemical attacks on the survivors of Halabja). Mirza is berated by character after character for having allowed his musical troupe to disband. "Who will now sing for the Kurds?" points to the centrality of cultural identity as carried through cultural forms such as music.

Barat and Odeh resist Mirza's sudden insistence that he must find Hanareh; they had been raised to believe that he had divorced her as a matter of honor, both because her public singing was dishonoring the family and because she had run away with Sayyid. But now they are told that in fact Mirza had never divorced her and that aiding her now in her time of need is a matter of honor. Twenty-three years puts the separation in the late 1960s or early 1970s, a time when Kurdish refugees and activists were being dispersed in cities throughout Iran to suppress the border fighting and tensions. Hanareh's singing might thus be a metaphor for open political activity: a forcible suppression on the Iranian side and a continued singing on the Iraqi side of the border, one that would lead in the aftermath of the Gulf War and Saddam Hussein's campaigns against Halabja and other Kurdish areas of the north to the present medical as well as political plight of Hanareh. When Mirza goes in search of Hanareh, he queries a woman his own age for the whereabouts of Hanareh or Sayyid's mother, who is rumored to have a letter from Hanareh asking him to come. This woman asks what he has told his sons, then tells him what he told them was a lie, to which he says he had no choice. She disagrees, pointing out that he is so well known among the Kurds that everyone knows his business. This is a refrain. First, there are the quack doctor's comments about Hanareh and Mirza in the opening scene on the tractor-trailer. Later, in the teahouse of a mule bazaar (shades of the teahouse in *The Time of the Drunken Horses*), other patrons taunt Mirza, saying that Hanareh sings and dances for homeless refugees and that even Saddam is under her charm. The teaman intervenes saying he, too, like other Kurdish refugees, has lost sons. But when Mirza asks if he has heard of Hanareh's whereabouts, the teaman says that he has but that he can no longer remember where he heard of her, because he has had to relocate the teahouse so often because of the bombing. The television behind the teaman drives home the plight of refugees lost amid entertainment distractions for first-world audiences, showing first a race-car event, then African refugees. A little later, a teacher says to Mirza, "Everyone knows you are looking for Hanareh," and it is intimated that the teacher knows more about her situation than he tells Mirza while directing him on the next stages of his quest. When he finds Sayyid's mother, herself living in a refugee tent, she says she does not have the letter, does not remember if she ever did, and then berates Mirza for having disbanded his music troupe, to which he replies that it was not his responsibility alone. "Who will now sing for the Kurds?" she insists. He replies, in a literalist irrelevancy, that there are many Kurds who sing.

In fact, Mirza attempts to teach a generation of young boys to play instruments and sing: his schoolhouse in Iran is under a propped-up metal container such as are used in long-distance trucking and as makeshift housing for devastated villages. One of his little pupils is pulled out from under the container by Barat and made to perform with a homemade lute constructed from a tin can, a stick, and wire. Mirza's sons are also singers, and they, too, search for means of transmitting their craft to the next generation. Odet, a curly-haired Marx Brothers type to Barat's cyclist persona, has seven wives and thirteen daughters, but no sons, and so asserts that he will not stop bothering women until he gets a son. Barat is unmarried and seeks a wife with all the incompetence of a bachelor. He pursues a young woman whose voice he hears singing and proposes marriage. He missteps, however, when in answer to her condition that he teach her to sing, he says she can only sing in the house in private, because he does not want to relive the family destruction his mother caused. When she turns away, he repents, but it is only later, when he finds her mourning the death of her brother and failing to find his corpse in a newly discovered mass grave, that his offer to join himself to her search begins to work. Meanwhile Odeh is offered the possibility of adopting two little boys in a refugee camp. But the main storyline follows Mirza's journey. When he finally traces Hanareh to a refugee camp inside Iraq, he discovers both that Sayyid had died wanting, and waiting for, Mirza to come to bury him and that Hanareh is also dead but has left a little girl for him to raise.

Scenes of pathos alternate with comic absurdity. The journey of Mirza with his two sons on Barat's motorcycle and sidecar is a peregrination through the Brueghelian landscape of war-torn Kurdistan. On the Iranian side is the village where Mirza teaches music. We see a visual ode, full of color and movement, to women wielding shovels, tossing up sand and dust with sieves, mashing mud with bare feet, and making bricks by hand. One of Odeh's wives admonishes him, saying that he had better not come back with a foreign woman in his obsession for a son. At a camp along the border, with snow-capped mountains and the barbed wire of the border in sight, Mirza sees the corrupt Doc administering to a sick child: "Injections cost eight dinars, shall I inject?" While in search of Mullah Qadir, who might have Hanareh's letter, Mirza and his sons see a man being dragged along the road tied to a motorcycle. It turns out to be Mullah Qadir, who is being prevented from conducting a wedding on the grounds that the woman is marrying without her father's consent. Mirza and his sons are forced at gunpoint to bury the mullah up to his neck so that he cannot go to the wedding. They end up playing for the wedding, but when the groom and his family arrive, the mullah's abductors start shooting. Mirza refuses to dig out the mullah until he coughs up the letter from Hanareh, which, however, he claims not to have. The police arrive and Mirza and his sons escape on their motorcycle and sidecar. But further down the road they are stopped by gunmen who strip them of everything, including the motorbike and Barat's gold teeth. They hitch a ride on a truck and pass two policemen stripped to their long johns by the thieves.

In the mule bazaar, familiar from *Life in Fog* and *The Time of the Drunken Mules*, Barat finds Doc selling drugs for AIDS—"the disease that affects mules, they are trying to kill our race of mules"—and it dawns on him that Doc might well have been the fence for the now disassembled motorcycle that he sees two young men carrying, and that they claim they bought fair and square.[18] The sounds of bombs and explosions make everyone duck for cover. ("Saddam is no joke, he will kill us all!" cries Doc.) We watch the familiar line of mules going up a valley in the snow (as in *The Time of the Drunken Mules*).

Two telling scenes of children follow. The first is of an open-air school class. As an airplane flies across the sky, the teacher tells the students that planes do two things: transport goods and bomb our houses. ("Hear that! That's someone's house.") A child asks the teacher if he has ever been in a plane: he hasn't but his brother has a friend whose nephew has. The other scene is a refugee camp for children. Barat and Odeh sing for the children. When Odeh tries to flirt with one of the young nurses, she admonishes him to teach his daughters to sing, but if he must have a son there are plenty here to adopt. (Both open-air classrooms and refugee camps also now appear in the films of Mohsen and Samira Makhmalbaf and have become new tropes and frames for exploration.)

The teacher and nurses warn Mirza that he must not take his sons into Iraq, because Saddam will press them into his army. So, while Odeh pursues the adoption and Barat follows his love, Mirza walks on alone. In Iraq he finds Sanooreh (frontier), the little girl Hanareh left for him, and he begins to carry her to Iran on his back. ("All people carry the Sizif [Sisyphus] stone: the mother carries her child, children carry smuggled stuff, teachers carry blackboards"—and an old man carries a girl who in terms of age should be his granddaughter.) As he leaves, we hear a woman's voice ask Hanareh, "Why did you not show your self? The poor man, after all, came so far to see you." She replies that she did not want him to see her in her disfigured state and with her destroyed vocal chords (from the Halabja chemical attack). We watch old Mirza carefully pick his way across the barbed wire in the white snow. The film ends with a shot of barbed wire against white snow.

An image of barbed wire, murmuring voices, and a wide-angle shot of a valley opens Darius Mehrju'i's *Bemani*. The barbed wire again represents both the border with Iraq and the imprisonment of women's lives in a patriarchal structure of desperation. The film mixes melodramatic realism with self-conscious interventions by the filmmaker that draw attention to the filmmaking. There are also gestures toward more liberating possibilities for women's lives. Vignettes of three women's lives are interbraided, and characters are periodically interviewed by the filmmaker as they face and talk to the camera. In one scene Bemani's father faces the camera and cries out his despair; after two stillbirths, he had named his surviving baby Bemani (remain) so that she would remain alive, and he is now devastated by her attempt to commit suicide by immolation. After years of war, of being bombed, of having everything destroyed, he was desperate to make ends meet, so marrying his daughter to a rich man was making the best of a tough life. But life has gotten even worse, as the women in the family now lament because no one will visit the family of a suicide.

The three vignettes are: first, Medina, a young divorcee, high-school graduate, and refugee from Iraq who makes her living as carpet weaver on the Iranian side of the border, lives with her mother under the suspicious eyes of her two brothers. The brothers kill her because they think she has violated their honor by being too friendly with a soldier who has paid her to weave a carpet and is beginning to court her. The second tale is of Bemani, who is increasingly unable to attend her high school because she must care for her sick mother. Her father is a desperately poor municipal sweeper and cleaner whose rent is three months in arrears. He accepts a marriage proposal from their landlord in exchange for three years' rent. (It is after running away from this marriage, learning that her shepherd boyfriend is gone, and being berated by her father for returning them to penury and debt that Bemani attempts to immolate herself.) The third tale is of a medical student, Naseema, who studies secretly because her father does not want her to go to medical school and mix with male doctors in corrupt hospitals. The father drags her out of her medical-school class and locks her in the basement, where she sets herself on fire.

Against these grim and pessimistic melodramas, there are counterimages, flashes of alternative lives and of different responses to the disasters that result from the tearing apart of family systems and misplaced patriarchal actions. Although Bemani often misses school, when she does go, we see girls playing power volleyball, and they joke about the headmistress' distress when a female photographer appeared. There is talk of the province not getting its fair share of government support for education and other services. The soundtrack then goes silent as we see the faces of the girls and women—an appeal to the audience.

Suddenly there are screams and schoolgirls yell to the camera and to Bemani that there is a decapitated head and a body with arms hanging out a car window: we see the bloodied face of Medina Saber, the Iraqi carpet weaver killed by her brothers as a matter of honor. Each brother faces the camera to answer the police (and filmmaker): by what right he had killed his sister? Had he actually witnessed any misconduct? The brothers are dismissive of the questions and are led off in handcuffs, the one in Kurdish or Luri wide trousers, the other in Arab white jelabyaa. The modern young soldier who would have been Medina's fiancé, who called her Delaram (my heart), provides a contrast to the brothers' obsession with avenging honor. At the funeral, the filmmaker asks the soldier, "Don't you want revenge?" He replies, "Revenge? For whom? For what? She won't return. Damn this life, I want to join her."

In the second vignette, about Bemani, two men face the camera. When the filmmaker asks Bemani's father how he will find the money to pay back rent when his rent is half his monthly salary, he responds, "God is great," with the smile of desperate desire to please a potential patron. It is a hieroglyph of prostration. His counterpart in the next generation is a hieroglyph of absurdity and surrealism in the sacrifice zone of life after war. He is a lively young shepherd who entertains Bemani when she comes to a spring to wash dishes (the pipes in her house being devoid of water): she looks up and laughs to see a goat wearing sunglasses. The shepherd then whips out a cell phone and pretends to speak into it, "Yes, St. Petersburg? You need dung? Yes, we have done all the international certifications of quality, yes ISO 2001." (Audience laughter.) He is a shepherd not from a primordial way of life, but as a marginal activity when there is no other work.[19] Later in the film he takes his turn facing the camera, answering the filmmaker's questions. His name, he says, is Morad Ali Panahi (*morad* means wish, *panha* means hidden). He cares for twenty sheep and seven goats. Does he own them? Don't be silly, he earns a salary. How much does he earn? He opens his palm and shows three nuts. Is this what he is happy doing? No, of course, not, but there is no other job, everyone is jobless. "Some day I'll leave and go somewhere. Where? I don't know. St. Petersburg or Tasmania." He tells Bemani he will go to the city and buy a car, and he mimes driving. She replies that everyone is jobless in the city, too, and that she cannot go because she has responsibilities for the household. When she returns home, her father hits her and accuses her of besmirching the family honor by talking to the shepherd, a reaction that resonates with that of Medina's brothers and of Naseema's father. As Naseema is taken by ambulance to a hospital that cares for severe burn cases, the filmmaker asks her father if his actions were worth it. He refuses to face the camera and, angered, walks away, "I have no answer, I don't want to talk to you!"

The vignettes are braided once more toward the end of the film. As Naseema speeds along the highway in the ambulance, we see in the fields passing by scenes of Medina and her soldier walking through the fields, along a stream, sharing a *sofreh* (tablecloth picnic) of bread and cheese. He asks her if she has a knife to cut the cheese. She says no, but she has an identification card, and she mimics the border guards asking her for her identification card, nationality, and so on. He says he hopes he was never so hard on refugees and asks if after he finishes his army service he may bring his mother to her house (to ask for her hand). We see Naseema later, helping to comfort other burned women, in this way taking up her medical aspirations. We see Bemani leave her father's house after her suicide attempt (and after laments of the other women in the house that no one will visit a house where someone attempted suicide) to visit a graveyard and shrine, where she meets Ali Ziai, the corpse washer. He faces the camera and asks the filmmaker if he is afraid; the filmmaker says no. Ali says, "No one visits, no one will drink water from my hand." On the wall in his little house he has painted crude drawings of airplanes and men running away: he was the only survivor of a strafing attack by Iraqi planes; he survived by irrationally running toward the planes rather than away, as the others did. Later he comes in while Bemani is looking at her disfigured face in a mirror; she does not cover up, and he does not flinch. He asks her to stay, and as they walk he picks a rose to give to her. (Audience applause.)

Shi'ite symbolism is evoked here and elsewhere in the film to designate deeper values in a corrupt world: the dead, as Ali Ziai, says are more faithful than the living; there is no place in this life for me, says the soldier; at the funeral of Medina, the women chant the name of the Third Imam, "Hossein, Hossein"; at the house of her old husband, Bemani faces the camera as the airplanes and gunfire sound. The airplanes and other references to the Iraq-Iran War are images of oppression and corruption in this world, braiding together narratives of the aftereffects of war, the moral discourse of Karbala, and the cri de coeur for women's rights in a modern world.

The searing film *Black Tape: A Tehran Diary (The Videotape Fariborz Kamkari Found in the Garbage)* traces the effects of the fighting in Kurdistan on the plight of refugees in Tehran, including girls abducted into prostitution and forced marriages. A number of earlier films have dealt with Kurdish and Afghan laborers on construction sites, in bazaars, and in various marginal sites. *Black Tape* is different in formal tactics and psychosexual traumatic content. Shot as if it were a found home videotape, its initial framing is one of domestic violence involving a successful older engineering contractor (and former military officer in the Iran-Iraq Kurdish border area) and his nineteen-year-old Kurdish wife (daughter of a Kurdish guerrilla leader). As in many domestic violence cases, she escapes and returns repeatedly. There is an ambiguous suggestion of an underlying sadomasochistic sexual relationship of seduction and (offscreen) violence. At the same time, there is a more serious duel: she is gathering "evidence" of his crimes (selling girls, imprisoning her, using corrupt business practices, cleansing refugee squats for his high-rise construction projects); meanwhile he is engaged in a Pygmalion civilizing scenario, turning a rough tribal beauty into a Tehran nouveau riche lady, using seduction and the degradation of her past as disciplining tactics. The frames of domestic violence, violence against the Kurds, and violence against the homeless war victims in Tehran become analogues of one another.

The husband, Parviz (Sergeant Turani), could be read as a figure warped by battle trauma (not in control of himself) and by the corruptions of the black economy, but also genuinely attracted to his young bride. Parviz is a Persian name, and in this perverted Pygmalion story, he is the figure of Persian civilization, dominating the Kurds (and other minorities). Turani might be a reference to the figures of evil in the *Shahnameh* story—the enemies of Iran in Turan, to the north, the direction of evil in the Zoroastrian ritual structure. In this reading, warfare and corruption become evils insidiously infiltrating the personhood of Parviz, rather than making him just an enigmatic or purely evil cardboard figure.

But Parviz is in a sense only a minor character in the filmic structure. Villains are structural motivators and commentators, but the real center of the film is the camera used as a weapon in the construction of evidence for future use in the war of justification and memory. It is a weapon of surveillance used for degradation by the husband and for evidence gathering by the wife, as well as for documentation of her increasingly imprisoned life. In the opening hieroglyph, the camera is being sold at a pawnshop by two women. They ask two hundred tomans but get only fifty. The camera is then resold to Parviz with the claim that it has a lens particularly good for unusual angle shots. It is thus a *used* camera, itself discounted and circulating in secondary economies (not high-end cameras used in television) for seduction, violence, power struggles, inscriptions of accounts of reality, undercover sleuthing, and panopticon means of intimidation.

The wife is an analogue of the camera: used, sold as a nine-year-old by a desperate father, raped, a trophy wife, an object of desire for sex and progeny, a means to power or control over others, and the eye of truth, the vehicle through which truth is inscribed. She is called Goli by her Iranian husband but yearns to hear her own language and name, Galavije. She longs for her family; on a foray out of the house she finds a younger sister, Shoukhan, and learns about her old father, ill with chest pains but without funds to see a doctor. She brings the old man to the house and tries to get Parviz to accept a Kalashnikov rifle as a gift from father-in-law to son-in-law. Parviz refuses, spirits the father away "to the hospital," and increasingly isolates his wife, cutting the phone line, removing the computer. He tells her he will provide for the father if she consents to bear a child; she refuses. She becomes pregnant, and he intensifies her isolation. These are not just the acts of a possessive husband but a deadly game of finding "the evidence" she has been collecting. He takes away her books, papers, and videotapes (she has hidden scenes of the Kurdish guerrilla struggles within children's cartoon videotapes).

The scenes of *Black Tape* (videotape is black, the story is black, the tape is found in the garbage, Kamakari identifies himself in the subtitle as a scavenger in the garbage) progress in an essentially five-act structure. First there is "Goli's" eighteenth birthday party, for which Parviz has bought the camera. He uses it to film the demeaning joking about her family and culture that his friends engage in. There is joking, for instance, about how her father, a guerrilla leader, was flushed out by Parviz's troops and had taken a bullet in the chest. When one of the party guests throws up on the floor, Goli refuses Parviz's request to get a cloth to wipe it up and tells the guests to lick it up themselves. They leave insulted, oblivious that they are the ones who have been insulting her and are complicit in her imprisonment.

The second act concerns the struggle over Galavije's bringing of her little sister and old father to the apartment and Parviz's "cleansing" of the squats, where they and their fellow refugees live, so that he can build new high-rise buildings. Parviz realizes that his effort to detach Goli from her family and Kurdish identity is failing. He recalls how he had once imprisoned her father and had married the daughter of his enemy (a perverse form of marriage alliances across enemy lines that royalty of yesteryear practiced, with similarly gifting and poisonous effects). She mourns that she has been imprisoned for ten years by Parviz and goes berserk when she finds that the squat is gone, that her newly restored contact with her family is once again lost, and that Parviz's promise to take care of her father in a hospital is a lie. Parviz hits her and yells back the Pygmalion theme, saying that she stank when he took her in and that she and her people are garbage (the garbage in which the videotape is found).

The climactic third act is Galavije's plea for help to Sohrab (in the *Shahnameh*, the offspring of one of these cross-enemy marriages). Sohrab is her patrilateral parallel cousin (*pesar amu*), was her childhood sweetheart, and is now a homeless refugee, working in a truck junkyard. Galavije cries that she has been waiting ten years for him to save her, and Sohrab goes into a spectacular raging lament of desperation: "Mrs. Engineer (living in the lap of luxury), you want me to save you?! I can't even save myself. You dream of my taking you to Kurdistan, but it is just like here: there is nothing but ruins (gesturing at the rows of junked trucks). You dream of our homeland, but what homeland? We fought and went into the mountains and what have we gained? I sleep with the dogs and prostitutes; everyone is dying of hunger. You are concerned your father is sick, so is everyone, and he even sold his daughters." Galavije responds in kind: "You think I'm having a nice time? Look at my arms, at these cigarette burns; you think it's fun to be raped as a little girl?"

Sohrab notices the camera. Let me see? Is this like the ones they use for television? He and an older Kurd begin to dance, beating the rhythm on a car and then on a portable bit of metal, dancing for the camera, a dance macabre, a dance of the slave laborers, a dance of the colonized for the camera. Again the camera serves as a commentary on the way television and documentary detach war and suffering and turn it into entertainment for others.

The fourth and fifth acts are the denouement. Parviz and Goli fight in the apartment with increasing degradation. She cowers under the table; he feeds her cold beans in a plate on the floor, as for a dog. He puts her camera on the floor and says it will watch her so that she does no damage to his child. She faces the camera and says to it that she will show him, then she takes a pair of scissors to her pregnant belly. He screams at her and rushes out for help. Sohrab shows up to say he has found Shoukhan; she urges Sohrab to run before Parviz's men return. Parviz has his men drag Sohrab off and yells that her sister is where she should be: in Satan's bazaar. A second struggle ensues sometime later. Goli proposes their special (sexual bondage) games, this time tying him up; she goes to put on something sexy and returns with the Kalashnikov. He breaks out of his chair, the gun goes off. She runs out, returns; he grabs her leg; he dies.

Galavije finds her way to a trucking agency, uses the camera to talk her way in as a television reporter, goes out among rows of shiny new long-distance container trucks, and finds Shoukhan locked with other girls in one of the containers. She and Shoukhan leave and make their way to an abortionist. Galavije dies as the woman attempts to remove the dead fetus. Little Shoukhan is sent out into the barren world alone.

While the repressed rage and trauma of war and economic devastation have been a constant theme in many Iranian films, *Black Tape* expresses it with a raw power that, thanks to its analogue structure of layered frames of violence, can easily be read as a further development of topics such as the shell shock in Mohsen Makhmalbaf's *Marriage of the Blessed*, the physical and moral legacies of Hatamikia's *The Glass Agency*, and the devastation of Samira Makhmalbaf's *The Blackboard* into a more pervasive, and at times perverse, pleasure in internalized psychopathology. One wonders if one is watching the birth of a new underground genre of what Mazyar Lotfalian has tagged "psycho-d(t)ra(u)ma."[20]

Limbs without Bodies:
War's Aftermath in Afghanistan

"All people are of limbs of one body," [says a poem of Sa'edi], but Afghanistan is "limbs of no body."—MOHSEN MAKHMALBAF, "Limbs of No Body: The World's Indifference to the Afghan Tragedy"

The car seat is an extraordinary seat. . . . The front window is like a cinema screen. The rear view mirror is like a small monitor through which you can see the world behind you. You can pick up a hitchhiker . . . to have an easy dialogue. . . . Two people in profile are easier to show communicating than two people face to face. You can have personal and heavy communications because the characters know that after a while they will get out. It is like a couch in a shrink's office: without staring, you can extract information. . . . Like a seat in the cinema, everything around you is moving. . . . Sound is more important than image. . . . Of the cube of life, on screen you see one dimension, the other five dimensions are added through sound. . . . Sound reminds the viewer that what one sees is not all that is happening. . . . Sound allows us to give volume to the film.
—ABBAS KIAROSTAMI, 7 June 2000, Harvard Film Archives

He . . . taught us how to use the camera to make art like a good writer uses a pen to make literature.—HASSAN YEKTAPANAH on Abbas Kiarostami

In 2001 filmic attention turned also to the eastern border of Iran, to Afghanistan, with four Iranian feature films—Hassan Yektapanah's *Jomeh*, Majid Majidi's *Baran*, Abolfazl Jalili's *Delaram*, Mohsen Makhmalbaf's *Safar-e Qandahar* (and the associated documentary *Afghan Alphabet* about the schooling of Afghan children in refugee camps in Iran)—and an Italian documentary *Jang (War): In the Land of the Mujaheddin*, which can function as a counterpoint to *Safar-e Qandahar*, a counterpoint of art and footage: one film giving space and stimulus for intellect, some black humor, and reflection; the other providing a reality check, emotion, and gravitas.[21] The first two films are about Afghans in Iran, about young men (rather than children), and follow in the traditions of Kiarostami. The third is about a fourteen year old and is a remarkable cinematic tone poem of orchestrated sounds and signs of the constant border-zone chess game between everyday survival and the extra-legalities of life near a war zone. It can be read as part of the emerging figuralism of 1990s Iranian cinema, quieter than *Beyond the Fire, Red Ribbon*, or *Marooned in Iraq*, but exploring adjacent emotional territories. *Safar-e Qandahar* and the Italian documentary *Jang* are about Afghanistan itself. Mohsen Makhmalbaf's film uses the abstract cinematic language of which he is a founding practitioner but that includes the lineage of *Beyond the Fire, Red Ribbons*, and *The Blackboard*, as well as his own *The Cyclist* and *The Peddler*.

In 2003 films directly about and shot in Afghanistan began to emerge from the Makhmalbaf Film House's initiative. Samira Makhmalbaf released *At Five in the Afternoon (Panj-e Asr)*, a film about generation conflict in post-Taliban Afghanistan between a pro-Taliban father and his daughter, who dreams of becoming a future president of Afghanistan. Fourteen-year-old Hannah Makhmalbaf released her second film, a documentary on the making of *Paj-e Asr*; a former Makhmalbaf associate (*Secret Ballot*), Babak Payami released *Silence Between Two Thoughts*, a film shot five kilometers from the Afghan border about life under a Hajji modeled on the Taliban's Mullah Omar; and the Afghan director Siddiq Barmak, a former fellow with the Makhmalbaf Film House, released his debut film, *Osama*. The techniques of *Osama* and *Silence Between Two Thoughts* include the close camera attention to hieroglyphic details that both focus semiotic attention and refer to other films in the cinematic discourse of Iran.

Cinema as Pen

Jomeh rewrites the undercurrents of boy meets girl. Hassan Yektapanah was trained through work on production crews and then as an assistant to the directors Tahmineh Milani, Jafar Panahi, Ebrahim Foruzesh, and Abbas Kiarostami. Of Kiarostami he says, "He not only taught me cinema but how to look at the world. He . . . taught us how to use the camera to make art like a good writer uses a pen to make literature." *Jomeh* explores currents under the apparently simple surface of an Afghan immigrant laborer's generic pursuit of an impossible love for an Iranian shopkeeper's daughter.

Jomeh works for an Iranian milk distributor. As he rides in the distributor's truck, they have time to talk. The youngster asks his boss why he is not married and receives a sharp reply, "Who do you think you are!" The question is diegetic, but it is also the existential question of this parable tale.

Jomeh tries to repair the damage with an apology and a joke, " Forgive me, but are Habib [a fellow Afghan worker] and I merely part of your herd of cows?" He gets the man to laugh. But in explaining himself, Jomeh again makes a faux pas by insisting that in Afghanistan if you are not married by age twenty, people begin to talk and say that you are over the hill, a comment his boss again takes personally, tolerating it but bemused by the boy's insistence. In turn the Iranian probes the sensitivities of his employee: why did he leave home? Was it a family dispute? Is he political? The boy replies that he had gotten involved with a widow twelve years his senior, which had put his mother and sisters in an awkward position.

Over the next few days, Jomeh maneuvers his boss into serving as a go-between to ask for the hand of a shopkeeper's daughter. He has been flirting, buying things to have an excuse to talk to her, and letting her know it. When her father replaces her in the shop, she lets Jomeh know of her interest by slamming the door from which she has been watching him. Jomeh's boss is clearly uncomfortable in the role he is being asked to play and tries gently to warn Jomeh that his request will be rejected. Jomeh will not be deterred, and when the rejection comes, we feel its harshness. The boss tries to find a way to break the news without being too quick or cruel. "Who do you think you are?" proves to be the classic class-, age-, ethnicity-, or other category-based rejection, even though the boss had not used it that way.

Car Seats, Construction Sites

A construction site provides the "car seat" for Majid Majidi's *Baran*. Baran (rain) is the title character's name, the name of the river of Kabul (thus alluding to Afghanistan), and a metaphor for the wet, cooling element of life. Baran tames the hot, dry, male temper of seventeen-year-old Lateef. Rain periodically douses the roiling ethnic and class conflicts of the construction site. The film thus operates on at least three levels. As a commentary on ethnic and social problems, it brings together illegal Afghan workers with three Iranian ethnic minorities (Lurs, Kurds, Azeris). The contractor or foreman, Memar (builder), is Azeri, as is Lateef. Memar plays the gruff mediator of demands from all sides. He hires and tries to protect illegal Afghan laborers, not only to satisfy his own interests—they are cheap, docile, good workers—but also out of compassion for people in need. As a love story, it explores the crossfire of monetary, familial, and ethnic demands. As a moral parable, it is a story of spiritual purity attained through selfless caring for others, a capacity that Baran seems to have innately but that Lateef must learn over time.

Construction site

A woman's touch: lunch sofreh

Recognition scene: Baran combs her hair in the mirror

(*Baran*)

At the beginning of the film, Lateef serves tea and prepares food for the workers with a cocky repartee that leads to many fights. One of the Afghan workers, Najaf, falls and breaks a leg. Najaf's friend Soltan shows up the following day with Najaf's young son, Rahmat, who proves too small and weak to carry heavy bags of cement. Memar's compassionate solution is to give Rahmat Lateef's job and to make Lateef a laborer. Lateef is furious and becomes further inflamed when he hears acclaim for the dramatic improvement in the food and tea service. He tries to sabotage Rahmat's work until one day he sees Rahmat combing her hair and realizes she is a girl dressed as a boy: Baran. He begins both to pursue her and to be protective of her. He now watches how she cultivates all life-forms around her: feeding the pigeons, putting plants in the tearoom, making food tasty and attractive, and building community (laying out a sofreh so everyone can eat lunch together, rather than just having her bring plates to them as they work). When the inspectors show up the second time, they see Baran bringing food to the construction site, and they confront her (Memar had sworn there were no Afghans working on the site, that all laborers were legal). She panics and runs. Lateef interferes in the chase, allowing her to escape. As a result, Memar has to get Lateef out of jail, pay a fine, and get rid of all his cheap, illegal Afghan labor.

Journey of Transformation

Lateef cannot bear Baran's absence and begins a journey to search for her, a journey as well of self-transformation in which he learns to emulate Baran's selflessness and care for others, first by observing, later by action. He asks Memar for a few days leave because, he claims, his sister is deathly ill. At a hotel that night, he observes an Afghan being turned away because he has no identity card. In a suburban village of Afghans, where he is looking for Baran, Lateef meets an enigmatic cobbler, a kind of Sufi figure, and visits a shrine where Afghans gather for communal events. Baran is there and sees him, but he apparently does not see her. The next day he locates her working in a stream with other women, trying to lift heavy boulders out of the stream. Distressed, he requests all of his accumulated back pay from Memar, begging and insisting until he gets it. Memar first protests that he has no money: he has had to fire all the Afghans, the architects have said walls are not straight and need to be redone before he will get his next payment; but in the end Lateef's laments about his sister's desperate illness raise Memar's compassion, and he relinquishes the money. Lateef gives this money to Soltan to give to Baran's father, Najaf. Soltan asks why Lateef himself will not give the

Parting: truck loaded for Afghanistan, Baran in chadri
Footprint filled with rain (*Baran*)

money directly to Najaf. Lateef says it would be embarrassing; he is learning
the principle of not embarrassing those one tries to help. They agree that
Soltan will take Lateef to meet Najaf the next day. But the next day, it is Najaf,
hopping with a cane, who comes to inform Lateef that Soltan has gone to
Afghanistan. Soltan had offered him some of the borrowed money, but Najaf
had refused the money, telling Soltan to use it to go to his sick family in
Afghanistan. Najaf gives Lateef a rolled-up message from Soltan, in which
Soltan swears by the Imams that he will repay Lateef's money. Lateef puts the
pledge in the stream and watches it float away.

Noticing next that Najaf's cane is not a very good aid, Lateef runs to the
bazaar and buys a pair of crutches. On the way back he tries to hitch a ride,
but cars will not stop, until he gets the idea that he should put himself on the

crutches. Immediately a car stops. But when he runs to the car without using the crutches, it speeds away. At Najaf's house, he overhears a conversation about a battle in Afghanistan in which Najaf's brother has been killed. He leaves the crutches outside the door, again exhibiting tact.

Next, he sees Baran again in the stream helping to drag out large tree debris. Powerless to help, he returns to the construction site in a state of depression. There he sees and overhears Najaf, empowered to have walked there on his new crutches, begging Memar for money without success. Lateef now makes a sacrifice even greater than giving away his year's wages: he goes to the bazaar to sell his identity card. Initially he fails to get a good price and is chased by thugs who intend to simply take his card, but he finally does get a stack of money. He takes the money to Najaf and tells him it is from Memar. Lateef is subsequently dismayed that the money is being used so Najaf can take his family back to Afghanistan. In a state of anguish he goes to the shrine, and there hears the sounds he heard when he first saw Baran.

In the final scene, Lateef helps Najaf load the truck, and with a serene expression is finally face-to-face with Baran. Through eye contact and proximity they silently exchange their love. Baran then covers herself in a chadri, but as she walks to the truck, a shoe comes off in the mud. Lateef gets on his knees, takes the shoe out of the mud, and Baran allows him to place it so she can slip her foot back into it. The truck takes her away. Left alone, Lateef stares at her footprint in the mud as rain fills it.

Car Seats, Car Repair:
Camera as Pen and the Cube of Sound

Sound reminds the viewer that what one sees is not all that is happening. Abolfazl Jalili's *Delaram* (2001) marks a shift to a younger protagonist and a more figural style. In the film a fourteen-year-old boy, Qaem, helps an older couple run a truck-stop teahouse and repair shop on the desert road near the Afghan-Iranian border. The film opens, not literally in the car seat, but with a close-up of Qaem riding in the back of a pickup (we see little of the passing desert). There is a shot of a flat tire, and then of Qaem's hands and frayed tennis shoes; we hear his still-young, girlish voice as he struggles to dislodge a large stone to place under the truck axle so the flat tire can be changed. (Although in response to a policeman's query later in the film, Qaem says that his name does not mean anything, that it is just a name, his name in fact possesses resonances with hide-and-seek, appropriate for an illegal alien, and with being a representative of a certain kind of moral legitimacy and strength.)[22]

Delaram is filmed as a profusion of close-ups, signifiers, and icons; it is ordered as serial repetitions or pointillist renderings. The film moves forward, after the introduction of place and characters, through the repetition of daily events that have their consequences: the flow of smuggled Afghan labor; the repeated visits by a jaded, not-too-motivated, and outwitted policeman; interactions with a young doctor and his pregnant teacher-wife who stirs up Qaem's desire for literacy and whose serendipitous picking up of schoolbooks lying in the road provide a potential clue to the policeman; the rousing of the old lady to get Qaem out of detention; a foiled sending of money to his sister in Afghanistan, along with demise of the boy's messenger; and the closing of the border, which cuts off the life of the truckstop and teahouse.[23] Orchestrated as a kind of cinematic tone poem, the sounds of war and the signs of local border defense and smuggling control register as only signs of worlds beyond the screen, beyond local control: gunfire and airplane sounds, uncertainty about rates and ease of Afghan and Iranian money exchanges, scarecrow-like sticks in the ground from which torn cloths hang, two finned bombs propped up on Y-shaped sticks as if they were lost road signs.

When toward the end of the film, the Delaram road is closed, the camera-pen writes with a figural concision, using as its alphabetic elements clasps, signifiers, icons, and sounds: across the turn-off from the main road onto the Delaram road are a row of stones and three traffic signs (two yellow triangles, each with a black, cautionary exclamation point, stand on either side of a red circle with a horizontal do-not-enter line); black truck exhaust drifts over the moon (a play on the Qur'anic and frequent cinematic image of the clouded-over moon, usually just with white clouds); artillery fire rumbles; the two old bombs on Y-shaped supports stand in the desert; the sound of airplanes is audible; another close-up of the three traffic signs appears. This sequence is soon followed by the "tautological" death of Khan, now that his livelihood has been shut off, his function ended. Qaem walks away with a small bedroll on his back, scattering black wrought-iron nails, like Khan's ashes, on the road; they reverberate metallically on the soundtrack. These are the nails we had just seen Khan earlier going by train to fetch, nails we had just seen on an anvil, glowing molten red and being hammered into shape by blacksmith's hands (again in close-up, there being no need to view the blacksmith's face or body or rest of the foundry). The nails have become Khan's coffin nails, handmade and rough.

As with the nails, the elements or alphabetic units of the camera-pen's writing have gained depth during the course of the film. The do-not-enter sign, for instance, is used as a target in marksmanship practice when the hunter teaches Qaem to shoot an ancient hammerlock rifle, signifying the local community's resistance to do-not-enter signs, as their lives are based on facilitating cross-border trade, whatever its legal status. Whenever the policeman comes to the cafe to inquire whether there are any illegal-alien Afghans around, Khan and his assistant always respond with fluent denials, even as Qaem stands there serving tea to the policeman. When the policeman becomes a little too intrusive, his tires are shot out on the road, and he is handcuffed, arms behind his back, so he is unable to flag down passing vehicles and must walk back to the truckstop to get help from Khan's crew. They repair and retrieve his car as if this were simply one of the many breakdowns they deal with daily.

When the policeman does stumble on a wedding between an Afghan man and an Iranian woman, the locals again parry his interrogations of illegality. The father of the bride claims the marriage is legal because he has agreed to it; when told that crossnational marriages themselves are illegal, he simply says he did not know but that it is now a fait accompli. When the policeman accuses Khan of deceit in having claimed that there were no Afghans around, Khan affects innocence, saying that the groom had been living in Iran for years and so is not an alien. When the policeman asks the groom how long he has lived in Iran and how he got there, the groom responds, with Qaem translating, that he had been resident two years and had arrived with official identification; asked why he married an Iranian girl when he cannot even speak to her in Persian, he says simply that he loves her (*dust-esh daram*). Outmaneuvered again, the policeman cannot do much, so he lets them go; a small but significant victory of everyday life against the distant decrees of state borders and rules.

Although not entirely devoid of narrative or dialogue, the film works primarily with the beauty of the desert and uses many series of small elements that both produce their own elaborations and reproduce the repetitions of everyday life: Qaem running; the men smoking opium or playing cards; the repair of various vehicles; Afghan men arriving by truck, doing ablutions at the pool, getting paid by Khan against their fingerprint signatures. A basic elaborating series, for instance, is the truckstop itself: at first we see it isolated in the desert; later we see it has three small trees; still later, from another angle, we see it against large trees blown by the wind (as danger to our protagonists increases); and finally we see it set alongside a whole row of trees (as we have become aware of the small desert village, comprising perhaps only a single row of cylindrical-roofed mud-brick houses, on whose outskirts the teahouse sits).

Another series sketches in one of the characters: the wife of Khan. She first appears as a face in the window, an old lady, perhaps infirm or immobile, watching the activity outside as cars or trucks pull in. Later she is more active, peeling potatoes. Still later we see that she has a crutch, and only much later that she not only has two crutches, but that she has only one leg. Two brilliant riffs on this series show that while she may be old and hobbled, she can be roused to vigorous action. A first close-up, when she and Qaem dismount from Khan's Toyota pickup truck, shows us three feet in slow motion: we see the old lady's single foot moving between the feet of her crutches, followed by the two feet of Qaem. The second, follow-through close-up comes when she sets off to free Qaem from the policeman's office, and harkens back to *Qaisar* and *Beyond the Fire*. A woman's shoe drops on the floor, the two feet of her crutches then appear, followed by her foot slipping into the shoe; crutches and foot swing into motion (the beat of a tambak drum is hardly necessary to evoke her determination to fight and win).

Another basic elaborating series are the motor vehicles we watch come and go: Khan's old Toyota pickup; a supplier's blue pickup; the doctor's Landrover; the policeman's old orange Mercedes 2002; the hunter's motorcycle; the larger truck that brings Afghan laborers from the border; the gasoline tankers, container trucks, flatbed trucks hauling pipes, and the dump truck with scrap metal. The motorcycle carries initially only its owner, the hunter, then a series of two riders—the hunter and Qaem, the hunter and Musa the mechanic, the hunter and the old lady—then sets of three, and at one point, eliciting audience laughter, even four. The motorcycle, like every other vehicle in this landscape, breaks down and is pulled back to the truck-stop by a rope attached to a passing motorcycle, whose owner carries a goat in each saddlebag. A truck overturned in a ditch off the road is similarly retrieved first with a rope pulled by Khan, the hunter, and Qaem, and then with a metal cable tied to the Toyota. Like the goats in the saddlebags, a touch of local color enlivens this scene as well: before righting and pulling out the overturned truck, the men rescue the driver and treat his injured arm, then play a game of cards, during which a squabble breaks out. Epithets of "Dirty Afghan!" and "Dirty Iranian!" are hurled back and forth in that border zone between play and enmity, agonism and antagonism.

Whereas motor vehicles are the local means of movement, enabling the social life of the truckstop/teahouse, legal and illegal trade, the railroad provides connection to more distant markets and supplies (Qaem rides in the freight car door, Khan in the passenger car). The distance is figured by close-ups of the wheels of the train as Qaem or Khan wait, as Qaem sees them from a crack in the freight door car, as Khan sits in a railcar seat: we do not see the passing scenery. Even more distant are the audible but never visible airplanes above.

Other kinds of trains also point to tangent worlds: lines of sheep seen across the desert, lines of military trucks pulling artillery pieces.[24] Artillery forms yet another visual and sonic series: the hunter has an ancient hammerlock rifle that must be cleaned and primed after each shot; single shots are heard from the border, one of which kills the man Qaem had entrusted with a packet for his sister; artillery fire is occasionally audible; the sounds of airplanes and the old finned bombs suggest fighter planes and bombers. The hunter uses the hammerlock rifle to shoot local game birds to eat, to teach Qaem in target practice at the do-not-enter sign, and to shoot out the tires of the policeman's old orange Mercedes 2002.

Delaram's cinematic tone-poem quality and its cinematic tactics participate in the figural traditions which Mohsen Makhmalbaf helped create, and its car-seat journeys deploy the imagery Abbas Kiarostami and Hassan Yektapanah charted to get at elusive psychological and soteriological interiorities of Afghans, of Iranians in relation to Afghans, and of everyone in relation to death. In Yektapanah's *Jomeh* the dialogue between Iranian employer and Afghan employee reflects Kiarostami's comments on car seats. In *Delaram* a parallel discussion occurs as a young doctor treats Qaem for an ear infection. Asked if he wants to return to Afghanistan, Qaem says no, his mother was killed by a bomb dropped from a plane, his father is fighting on the front against the Taliban, his sister is with a grandmother, and even if he misses her, it does not matter. These minimal revelations point beyond their immediate content to the state of being caught in an impossible position, a no man's land of the border, as does the iconic image following the death of the messenger as he attempts to run across the border: a hand drops the little packet into the barbed wire of the border fence

Cycling and Gambling against Death

Jomeh, *Baran*, and *Delaram*—all released in 2001—along with *The Peddler*, *The Cyclist*, and *A Taste of Cherry* register the travails of Afghan refugees in Iran and include Afghans in the sympathetic moral universe of Iran. These films are important vehicles for ethical reflection and add to a rich tradition of such reflections. But the Afghans and their problems are incidental vehicles for Iranian ethical self-reflection. It is not until the film *Safar-e Qandahar* that attention is turned to Afghanistan itself.

In the third part of *The Peddler* (birth, life, death), an underworld of illegal Afghan laborers in the netherworlds of the bazaars and coffeehouses of Tehran provides the context for a meditation on dignified death. Smugglers, who use the cover of selling second-hand clothes, decide to kill an Afghan who has seen too much and who shows signs of not remaining quiet. Imprisoned in a cell-like room, the Afghan contemplates various ways in which he might have escaped. In effect he dies repeatedly in his thoughts. Better, says Makhmalbaf, in what at the time he called an effort to forge an Islamic cinema, to act when it is still possible, and in a way that one can reflect back on with dignity, even at the risk of a quick death. In *A Taste of Cherry* the Afghan *talebeh* (seminary student) is one of three characters—a Kurdish peasant-boy soldier, the Afghan seminarian, and an Azeri taxidermist—to whom the protagonist offers money to bury him in a kind of game of Russian roulette in which only God knows if the suicide will be successful. The taleb invokes Islamic rules and refuses to help, contrasting with the older Azeri taxidermist who tries to draw the protagonist out and reengage him in life. Allegorically, the talebeh stands for the rigidity and lack of this-worldly pragmatism that characterizes fundamentalist Islam (the Afghan Taliban, the Iranian hard-liners).

The Cyclist begins a long-term concern of Makhmalbaf with Afghanistan itself. In part an homage to Vittorio da Sica's 1950 film *The Bicycle Thief*, it builds on an experience Makhmalbaf recalls from when he was ten years old. A Pakistani cyclist came to Khorasan Square in Tehran to raise money for flood victims by cycling in a circle for ten days without stopping. Initially people dismissed the act as a mere commercial scam, lumping the cyclist in with snake charmers, strongmen, and other street entertainers. (See the news photo of a stunt rider in Qandahar during the festivities of Eid-e Fitr 2001.)[25] Had not the cyclist done the same act, asked the cynics, for earthquake victims somewhere else? Was the money really for the victims or for the man himself? For ten-year-old Mohsen and his friends the most exciting parts were to see how the cyclist would relieve himself and to sneak in at night to verify the rumors that he secretly slept instead of cycling. They found his promoter asleep but the man himself slowly cycling all alone, "for God's eyes only." Crowds began growing by the fifth day. Even Queen Farah came to see and to give him a present. On the seventh day, he fell, and the rumor was that he died. Suddenly people began taking up collections for the flood victims. The man did not in fact die and was able to continue his efforts elsewhere.

In the film Makhmalbaf's memory is transmuted—abstracted, modified, delimited—into the story of an Afghan refugee trying to raise money for his wife's hospitalization. Learning that he had been a long-distance cyclist, a promoter offers to help him put on a week-long cycling to raise money. The site soon attracts a circus of onlookers, hawkers, gamblers, and con men setting up various sorts of wagers, men "holding the strings of others' fates in their hands." The original promoter, of course, runs off with the money. The week ends, but the cyclist keeps cycling in his circle, cycling, cycling, cycling. (The cyclists' little daughter is played by Samira Makhmalbaf.) The film can be read as a metaphor of the Sisyphean struggles to get help for this im-poverished neighbor of Iran in a cruel world of corruption and indifference.

Makhmalbaf recalls that originally he had wanted to end the story by having the cyclist complete the week, then, unable to walk in a straight line, walk in circles until he died. But Makhmalbaf's sponsors and producers, as well as the censoring authorities, considered this unacceptable ideological pessimism rather than aesthetically and visually satisfying closure.

With the 2001 film *Journey to Qandahar*, Makhmalbaf works out the figural aesthetics much more powerfully, attempting to use a cinematic language to make an affective as well as aesthetic intervention. *Qandahar* is a film, a place, and a moral, ethical, political site.

Qandahar, the Film

Like the music cassettes that circulate ahead of Bollywood film releases, word-of-mouth descriptions of some of the stunning surrealistic images of *Journey to Qandahar* (*Safar-e Qandahar*, English title: *Kandahar*) stirred up interest ahead of the film. The scene most talked of depicts men crippled by landmines hopping on crutches toward prosthetic limbs parachuting down from the sky, an image that functions as a signature logo of a land known to be one of, if not the most mined country in the world. In another scene, which takes place in a refugee camp in Iran, children are taught never to pick up a doll or teddy bear found in the desert lest it be a booby-trapped mine and blow off a limb. Another image discussed ahead of the film's release portrays a doctor examining a woman through a hole in a sheet, much like the memorable scene early in Salman Rushdie's *Midnight's Children*, but intensified here by the effort at a secret exchange in English hidden within a triangular communication in Persian between doctor and patient via the Afghan boy guide.²⁶ The doctor is a false-bearded African American who calls himself Tabib Sahib (doctor sir). The woman is a Canadian-Afghan journalist. The boy is a student who has been expelled from a religious school and who is also a skilled scavenger. A third kind of image circulating ahead of the film's release presents lines of people walking across the desert in colorful *chadris* (the head-to-toe veils of Afghanistan; Arabic: *burqa*). Indeed the most powerful of the chadri scenes comes at the end of the film, when men and women are hidden under these veils, and travelers to Qandahar, to Iran, or to a local wedding intermingle to avoid the interference of the Taliban authorities. In a fourth strong image or scene amputees wait at a Red Cross camp in the desert for the next shipment or airdrop of limbs. A man earnestly, persistently, insistently begs and badgers blond English and Scandinavian nurses for a prosthetic leg for his wife. Although they protest that the leg he wants was customized for someone else, he eventually persuades them to give it to him. He then (as one expects) immediately tries to sell it to the North Americans and, when that fails, carries it around on his shoulder as a future resource. A fifth image or scene is of men and boys with shovels along the road, creating, and for money removing, rubble and pothole barriers to traffic.

The Journey to Qandahar is both picaresque journey (the protagonist encounters a series of people who advance her understanding) and a diary spoken into a dictaphone. Stories of two real people provide pretexts. The character Nafas—an Afghan-Canadian journalist who attempts to get to Qandahar to save a suicidal sister left behind when she stepped on a mine and was unable to escape the country with Nafas—is based on the true story of Nilofer Pariza, who failed to get very far into Afghanistan in 1998, and whose story has now also been made into a Canadian Broadcasting Corporation documentary, *Return to Afghanistan* (2003), directed by herself and Paul Jay. The character of the doctor is played by Hassan Tantae'i, an African American who has been a journalist in Iran and spent some time in Afghanistan with the mujahideen in the fight against the Soviet Union. His other names or aliases are said to be Hassan Abdul Rahman, Daoud Salahuddin, and David Belfield. Belfield was the militant Muslim who assassinated anti-Khomeini dissident Ali Akbar Tabataba'i in Bethesda, Maryland, in July 1980 and then left for Iran to work for the state news agency.

Other real-life experiences also contribute to the fabric of the film. Makhmalbaf recalls in an interview that he talked to a British girl who worked with the International Red Cross making artificial legs and hands and who told

Parachuting prostheses
Running on crutches for prostheses
Arguing for a better prosthesis (*Safar-e Qandahar*)

him that she knew of no more satisfying job than to help a few hundred people walk. He speaks of his dismay, on visiting a refugee camp near Zabul to find extras, that people were not being fed regularly. He brought food and protested their deportation back to Afghanistan, a scene that in the film is left underdeveloped. He invoked the refugees' status as guests but was told that these guests, having been in Iran for twenty years, had outstayed their welcome. He notes that girls are taken hostage by smugglers who transport Afghans to labor sites in Tehran, which explains the shadowy Iranians who periodically show up at construction sites to take the earnings of the Afghan laborers until the smuggling fees (and interest) are repaid. He notes that many Afghans do not blend in with Iranians, as Pashtuns do with Pakistanis: Shi'a Hazaras in particular have Mongolian features (as do some Turkmen in northern Iran), which are distinctive, as is their Dari or Afghan Persian. These distinctive features also play significant roles in *Baran* and *Jomeh*.

The genres of picaresque journey and tape-recorded diary open the film to allegorical interpretations: is the suicidal sister, maimed by mines, a figure for Afghanistan, maimed and suicidal under Taliban oppression? The film opens with a striking image of an eclipse (a dark moon surrounded by the bright halo of the sun, "the last eclipse of the twentieth century"): does the searing sun over the desert represent divinity veiled, as well as, perhaps, a panopticon constructed of the self-disciplining fear that one is being watched by a network of Taliban eyes? Are the sun and moon, traditional icons of female beauty, eclipsed and veiled in black, the veiling briefly lifted to show a rainbow of color, only to be again eclipsed and veiled? Is this an intertextual reference to Samira Makhmalbaf's 1998 film *The Apple*, which is about an overprotective father who keeps his daughters locked up in the house, a metaphor, Mohsen has said, of Iran locked up as if in a cave, not allowed to even see the sun, and its liberation from that condition? The journalist speaks English into her dictaphone: is this because the filmmaker wants to address an international English-speaking audience, or is it a kind of self-centered obliviousness? (The sister may well understand English if from a well-educated bourgeois family, but would English be the first language of communication between Afghan sisters?) The tape recorder collects sounds, voices, and thoughts which the journalist calls "candles of hope" for her sister: is this self-serving, an allegory of the often irrelevant and insufficient aid sent from abroad, a dual-use therapeutic for her sister and material for her own journalistic career, or is it an intuition that she may not survive her journey but the message might still arrive? In the end it is her inability to get rid of this Western technology that puts her at risk when the Taliban search the veiled travelers; but it is taking such risk that makes her an active modern woman.[27]

Some of the allegory and visual metaphor are explicit. The veil, beard, and prosthesis are linked metaphors. The veil hides gender and identity, not just sexuality. The false beard hides the African American's face, identity, and his inability to grow a full beard. The veil and beard are thus prostheses functioning like the artificial legs: all three allow freer movement of the otherwise disabled. The names as well act as poetic shifters to an allegorical register: Nafas (breath, soul) is the exile returned from Canada, a journalist, a spirit journeying in a land of chaos, poverty, micro-economies of survival, fear, and shifting alliances of convenience. Khak (earth, land, dust) is the name of the boy who becomes her guide. He has been expelled from a fundamentalist theological school (*maktab, madrassa*), despite his mother's pleas to the mullah, principal of the school, that she is poor and needs to feed the boy. Expelled for failing to learn to read Arabic, he is perhaps the Afghan soil (*khak*) resistant to impositions from the outside, the pragmatic Muslim spirit of villagers resistant to Wahabbi puritanism. The man with the artificial leg on his shoulder tells Nafas to say his name is Hayat (life) if asked by the Taliban, that they should claim to be man and wife. Hayat and Nafas: life and soul. Khak and Nafas: earth and spirit, rooted place and cosmopolitan spirit; Adam (earth) and Eve (Hava), body and relational spirit. In a similar anonymizing, generalizing, allegorizing moment, Nafas asks who the groom of the wedding party is and is told: Mosaffer (traveler), that is, the traveler toward God, the seeker. These appellations—soul, earth, life, traveler—name not only the quests of the characters but also the plight of Afghanistan as a traumatized, fragmented, devastated society. Makhmalbaf uses two key poems to frame the fate of Afghans, one by Sa'di: "All people are of limbs of one body." However, writes Makhmalbaf (2001b), Afghanistan is "limbs of no body," a place of the world's indifference. The other poem is by a refugee.

> I came on foot,
> I'll leave on foot.
> The stranger who had no piggybank will leave
> And the child who had no dolls will leave.
> . . . . .
> I came on foot,
> I'll leave on foot.

The film is also structured by its music themes: mystical, pop, folk, funeral, Qur'anic chant, maternal lament, children's and wedding music. The opening eclipse is accompanied by a 'ud (lute) and a male voice singing a mystical lament. Eclipse/rainbow/eclipse. A veil is lifted to reveal the face of Nafas, and she answers the question "Who are you?" with "I am the bride's cousin." We share the aerial view with Nafas, flying over rugged, barren mountains in a helicopter. She explains her quest to the pilot while she also records her experiences into her tape recorder, which she tells the pilot is her "black box" in case they should crash. It is a Red Cross helicopter. They fly over white Red Cross tents next to a desert mud-brick peasant compound. Men on crutches run under them. Parachutes drop artificial legs, prostheses.

In the next movement, Iranian-Indian–style pop music accompanies scenes of a girls' school in a refugee camp on the Iranian side of the border. A male teacher says to Nafas that they will find a family to take her into Afghanistan and that she should say she is family, a wife or sister. He next counsels the schoolgirls in chadors that although there will be no school for them when they return to Afghanistan, that although they will have to stay home, they should not give up hope. One day, he tells them, the world will see your plight and will help, but if not, or until then, you should look at the expanse of the sky to escape the claustrophobia of being shut in. Meanwhile, a female teacher instructs the girls about land mines. Nafas remembers how her sister's legs were blown off as she approached a booby-trapped doll. The teacher holds up a doll and warns not to approach such temptations. Nafas, in her journalist voice, narrates that someone in Afghanistan is killed by a landmine every five minutes. As photographs are taken of the girls and their parents, Nafas muses about whether it is Afghan government or Afghan culture which imposes the veil on women. Each ethnic group has its name and image; only women, 50 percent of the population, have no name or image: they are only black-heads (siah-sar).

Siah-sar, black-heads. It is an interesting usage: Afghan chadris are not necessarily black, and Makhmalbaf makes great use of the rainbow of colors in lines of chadri-clad people. The term siah-sar points to Iran. Iranian chadors are primarily black. (A meaning of the opening symbols have been confirmed: eclipse, rainbow, eclipse.) The refugee camp official or teacher offers an old man money to take Nafas with his family and a United Nations flag for protection. He hands out three dollars to each chadored schoolgirl returning to Afghanistan. He offers the same to Nafas, who lifts her veil to show who she is, saying, "No thanks!" Eclipse, rainbow, eclipse.

As the music switches to graveyard laments, the three-wheeler truck that carries them into Afghanistan passes a village. They stop to let the driver and his assistant eat. Nafas impatiently urges them to move on. The old man remonstrates that she should not lift her veil every time she talks: "No man must see my wife's face." "I am not your wife." "What difference does that make to scandalmongers? My honor is at stake." The three wheeler gets under way again, with the womenfolk singing in the back, painting their fingernails, and using lipstick and mirrors under their chadris. Following this, the truck driver and an accomplice relieve the travelers of all their belongings, then drive off, tossing the UN flag back to the stranded family. The mystical music wells up again as the old man leads his four women and six girls back to the village, to the graveyard and laments.

The music turns to Qur'anic chanting. Boys in white turbans sit on the floor swaying and chanting over open Qur'ans. The mullah calls for silence and points at a boy: "What is a sword?" Answer: a sword executes God's order, cuts off a thief's hand. The mullah shouts, "Continue!" The chanting resumes, until again the mullah shouts, "Silence!" and points to a second boy: "What is a kaloshnikov?" Answer: "A semi-automatic with repeat action that kills the living and mutilates the dead." Mullah: not quite, try again. Boy: "A semi-automatic with repeat action that kills the living, destroys their flesh, and mutilates the flesh of those already dead." Mullah: "Continue!" To a third boy, "Why are you not moving?" Boy: "My back hurts." Mullah: "Recite." The boy mimes the chant but obviously does not know the words by heart and cannot read them either. Mullah: "You don't know it?" He asks a fourth boy to recite the verse, and he chants it exquisitely. The mullah gives the third boy, Khak, another chance, but the results are the same. He exits the school where the boy's mother pleads her son's case. The mullah is unmoved, "He does not learn and should be sent to Iran to work as a laborer." The mother laments about how Khak's father was killed by a land mine, but her son removes his turban and cloak, exchanging it for the street clothes of a new boy entering the school.

The funerary laments continue. The old man and his women are now riding on a donkey cart: "We are the dead, sing for us. We must turn back to Iran, there is nothing but famine and suffering in Afghanistan." At the grave-yard, Khak offers to chant the prayers for their dead. The old man throws the UN flag to Khak and asks if he will take Nafas to Qandahar. Khak bargains. He asks Nafas for fifty thousand Afghanis. She says she has only U.S. dollars, so he asks for fifty thousand dollars. She laughs and explains the exchange rate, offering him fifty dollars. He asks her to lift her veil so he knows there is no trick. Khak claims that he earns his living with his voice and that for another dollar he will demonstrate: the music now is a folk song. Nafas holds out her tape recorder to catch his singing and says to her sister, "I collect everything to give you hope. Can the young boys in Qandahar still sing in the alleyways, can the young girls listen and dream of love for these boys?" (What has happened to the rich traditions of song and folk culture under the regimes of the communists and now the Taliban?) Suddenly Khak directs Nafas to go in one direction while he detours to "look for things to sell." She panics and chases after him. Over a dune, she stumbles on him and shrieks in terror. He holds out a ring to her. The camera pulls back to show a skeleton. Khak says, "Look how beautiful. Do you want to buy it? It matches your eyes. Only five dollars."

Back in a village, Khak walks through a group of women washing laundry at a well, where he pulls up a bucket of water for Nafas to drink. She becomes ill but muses into the tape recorder, "I don't know if it is from the well water, the fear of the skeleton, or the violence I see everywhere." And she recalls the cockfight after their mother had died: "There were two circles of men surrounding the cockfights. You ran to the dolls and lost your legs." A flashback shows us Nafas as a little girl nicknamed Nafasgol (*gol*, "flower") acting as an intermediary for her mother with a doctor as he tries to diagnose the mother through a hole in the sheet. The scene is then repeated between Nafas and Tabib Saheb talking through Khak. The doctor gets her to dismiss Khak, though this proves not so easy.

Return to the mystical male vocal as Tabib Saheb tells the story of his quest, coming first to fight with the Afghans against the Russians, then with ethnic factions, with the Tajiks against the Pashtuns, then with the Pashtuns against the Tajiks. "When the Afghans won [against the Russians], then the fight over God began." One day seeing two sick children, a Tajik and a Pashtun, he continues, he realized the search for God was to help people heal their pain. He claims that even with no medical training "the basic knowledge of a Westerner is more than what these people know."

"Danger ahead!" Tabib Saheb quickly sketches out a strategy: if it is a guard, they should say they are man and wife. They exchange names, and he tries to think up names for their fictive children, Nafasgol for the girl, and . . . he cannot think of a boy's name, so she suggests Khak. He tries to memorize the name by repeating it over and over. If it is a thief, he will try to rush past. As they pass the man, they see he is holding out an artificial leg, so they give him a lift. He claims his wife's legs were blown off and that these temporary prostheses now need to be exchanged for permanent ones.

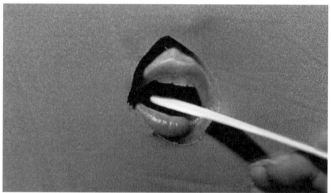

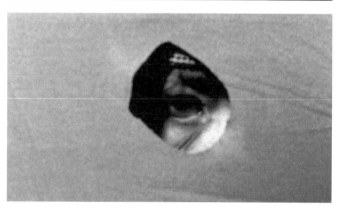

Doctoring through a hole in the sheet
Say "Ah!"
"Anemia!" (*Safar-e Qandahar*)

At the Red Cross camp a man with a hand blown off demands a new prosthetic one, but the two foreign nurses respond that they only have legs, to which, of course, he says, "Okay, give me legs." They try to get rid of him, but he is insistent, begs legs for his friend and, when that doesn't work, "for my mother." Finally, they give him a pair of temporary prosthetic legs, which he rejects: these are no good, give me real ones. Tabib Saheb and Nafas arrive, and in their search for someone to take her to Qandahar, they are directed after the man who has just taken the prostheses. Meanwhile, lively music wells up, the sound of children (hope?) is discernible, and the helicopter arrives: men on crutches hop toward the parachutes while the nurses radio the helicopter. Nafas and Tabib Saheb catch up with the man, who tries to sell them the prostheses he has just begged off the Red Cross, saying that they are his mother's but that she has never used them because she is bedridden. Tabib Saheb retorts he has his own legs, to which the man counters, "It is always good to have a spare pair, the roads are full of mines." Tabib Saheb says he cannot take Nafas to Qandahar himself because he has already been arrested there once. The man is also hesitant, saying he will be asked in Qandahar where he lost his hand; it was in fighting the Taliban. Tabib Saheb suggests he is a coward, and they finally settle on two hundred dollars.

While they wait for the man to collect his things, Nafas talks into her tape recorder, "I pass through the desert of dry poppies. . . . I bring you hope from people's dreams." She asks Tabib Saheb to say something into the tape recorder for her sister. Wedding music: women in a rainbow of colored chadris come toward them, singing and playing the tambourine. A figure in a yellow chadri comes up to them, lifts the veil, and grins: it is the one-armed man. As Nafas and the one-armed man move among the chadri-covered figures, he asks her to ask someone in the wedding party what the name of the groom is, introducing herself as a cousin of the bride. This is dangerous, and she nearly gives herself away. When she tries again, a woman begins to mutter that Nafas has first pretended to be a cousin of the bride and now of the groom. Nafas listens to what Tabib Saheb has recorded: "I am a man in search of eternal love, but always instead fall in love with a woman." Suddenly anxiety goes up, "Why are they going that way? They are going the wrong way!" A group separates, and a woman says, "I am taking my sons to Iran."

Black-clad men and two black-chadri–cloaked women from the Taliban stop and search the travelers. A book is found under one chadri, a stringed lute under another; these people are ordered to sit on the side. Hayat urgently whispers to Nafas to get rid of her tape recorder, but suddenly the search is over, and the Taliban say the rest may go, "congratulations on the wedding."

Taliban (women) seize contraband book (*Safar-e Qandahar*)

Nafas says into the tape recorder, "Although we escaped the jails, now I am captive in each of these presents recorded for you, dear sister." Eclipse.

Prescient literature and film, in different ways, operate across two different logics: the logic of the structure or unfolding or evolution of events; and the virtual structures of potentials, alternative possible lives, trajectories, and universes. *Qandahar* was made before the U.S. bombing campaign helped topple the Taliban from power in Afghanistan. It was, however, already a land littered with more landmines than any other, due to the war against the Soviet Union's occupation in the 1990s and to the subsequent civil strife abetted by proxy forces for Pakistan, Iran, the United States, and the Soviet Union. The micro-economies of petty bargaining, smuggling, and scavenging, and so on constitute at individual, local, regional, and transnational levels an assemblage of larger geopolitical forces, resistances, and strategic moves.

The stories of the Canadian-Afghan and the African American make of Qandahar a site of transnational crossings between North America (and Europe in the figures of the aide workers) and the Muslim world (Iran and Afghanistan). The filmmaker himself is also a former Islamic militant, as he has recalled and restaged in his 1996 film *Nun va Goldun* (Bread and Flowerpot), and more indirectly in the 1985 film *Boycott* (about being imprisoned). The three languages used in the film are transnational as well: the English spoken into the tape recorder, between doctor and patient, and to the film audience is the cosmopolitan language of journalism and human rights. Persian, in its standardized, bookish form, serves as the lingua franca of the film, rather than negotiating the various local dialects of Dari and Tajik (Afghan Persian), Uzbek (Turkic), or Pashto. Qur'anic Arabic, in the Islamic school from which Khak is expelled, as well as in the use of the word *burqa* for the chadri veil, stands for the fundamentalist, puritanical, transnational Islamist movements, rather than portraying the mullah as an Urdu-speaking Pakistani or a Saudi-dialect–speaking Arab.

Makhmalbaf says that Afghanistan in the 1990s became a country with no images: women were hidden in burqas or chadris; no television, painting, or photography was allowed; the few two-page newspapers had no photographs; all fourteen cinema houses were closed.[28] In a memoir of Kabul under the Taliban in the 1990s, Latifa, a daughter of a merchant and a gynecologist, echoes Makhmalbaf's point about a land without images of itself in the context of the plight of women. She writes about the efforts to run secret schools and to appeal to the West, and about the soaring rates of depression and physical illness under the Taliban. "The Taliban are trying to steal my face from me, to steal the faces of all women" (Latifa 2001).

Makhmalbaf's making of *The Cyclist* in 1986 involved experiences which reappear in *Qandahar*. He recalls coming on a "surreal gate in the desert not connected to anything, as in Salvador Dali's paintings" (2001a) and as in Parviz Kimiavi's 1973 *Moghul-ha*. "A group of bikers asked our bus driver to step down. They gave him a bag of money and got in the bus, and our driver and assistant drove off on the bikes. The bus and all in it, including us, had been sold. It happened every few miles" (2001a). A version of this scene, without the gate, occurs in *Qandahar*. In Afghanistan's smuggling economy, bullets were sold by the bag, "like beans," weighed on scales and exchanged. Drugs were a mainstay of this economy and of trade with Central Asia. Another real-life phenomenon influenced Makhmalbaf: the UN paid refugees twenty dollars to volunteer to return to Afghanistan, where they would be dropped off, make their way back to the border when they found no jobs, and get in line again for another twenty dollars. A version of this scenario occurs in *Qandahar* when the refugee camp official hands out three dollars to each girl returning to Afghanistan; the family with whom Nafas travels, of course, turns back after being robbed, leaving Nafas in the desert.

"A country of no images," also of no national identity and no national economy. Again talking of his experiences in the refugee camps, Makhmalbaf says that Pashtun and Hazara children would not play together; Tajiks and Hazaras would not attend Pashtun mosques; doctors had to see Pashtuns one day, Hazaras another; when Makhmalbaf tried to show movies to children, different ethnicities would not sit next to each other; even when he filmed extras, he had to use one or the other, not a mix. With regard to the nation's economy, Afghanistan's two largest exports in 2000 were opium (half a billion dollars) and natural gas ($300 million). War, however, provided its own economy, and Makhmalbaf notes that if one took away all the weapons, the young men, who joined the madrassehs and the militant cause because they were hungry, would simply swell the ranks of the refugees. With the option of military service, families could support at least their sons, while women and children went into the refugee camps.

Qandahar began an effort to help mobilize the kinds of affects and percepts that will allow Afghanistan again to have mobile images which can allow "limbs of no body" to find reattachment to the bodies of social futures. This filmic-artistic goal is different than those of war photojournalism. The latter help create an environment for realist politics, and occasionally for human rights, by mobilizing documentation and emotion.

As Samira Makhmalbaf says in a 2003 interview, "When an Iraqi filmmaker presents a work on what went on in Iraq in the past three decades, then I will be able to understand what kind of place Iraq has been and what it means to live as an Iraqi." The point is a crucial one and has to do with media machines and access to local cultures (not as unified entities but as sites of intersections of networks of meanings, dissensions, and agons): "Through Jim Jarmush's work I can understand a stranger's pleasure upon stepping out in Harlem, but not from CNN reports about it." Three films—her own 2003 film, *At Five in the Afternoon*, shot in Kabul with Afghan non-professional actors whose lives and dialogue provide much of the inspiration; the documentary film by Hannah Makhmalbaf, *Joy of Madness*, about the process of making Samira's film; and *Osama*, the first film made by the Afghan director Siddiq Barmak—begin to build upon Mohsen Makhmalbaf's effort to give Afghanistan back its own ability to produce images of itself and a broadening, rather than narrowing, variety of discourses about itself.

However, occasionally there are a few striking photographs that do more than the usual war photojournalism. One of these is of a U.S. soldier on horseback partaking in a game of buzkashi just after the expulsion of the Taliban from Kabul. Buzkashi is the national sport of Afghanistan. In the past it was, among other things, a site for rivalries between provinces in which much of the local, regional, and national politics of Afghanistan could be read (Azoy 1982, 2003). For the moment, it can serve to introduce the dilemmas of the struggle against the Taliban and of the role of international intervention and aid.

Locality and Documentary: Qandahar,
the Panshir Valley, and the Great Game (Oil, Drugs)

Turkestan, Afghanistan, Transcaspia, Persia. . . . To me, I confess,
they are pieces on a chessboard upon which is being played out a game
for the domination of the world.—LORD CURZON (1898), quoted
in Ahmed Rashid, *Taliban*

It has been fashionable to proclaim, or at least predict, a replay of
the "Great Game" in the Caucasus and Central Asia . . . fuelled and
lubricated by oil. . . . Our goal is to avoid that atavistic outcome. . . .
The Great Game which starred Kipling's Kim and Fraser's Flashman
was very much of the zero-sum variety.—STROBE TALBOT (1997),
quoted in Ahmed Rashid, *Taliban*

"Against all odds, we, meaning the free world and Afghans, halted
and checkmated Soviet expansionism a decade ago. But the embattled
people of my country did not savor the fruits of victory. Instead they
were thrust in a whirlwind of foreign intrigue, deception, great-
gamesmanship and internal strife.—AHMAD SHAH MASSOUD to
the U.S. Senate Committee on Foreign Relations (8 October 1998),
quoted in Michael Griffin, *Reaping the Whirlwind*

It's time for the Americans to play the game.
—GENERAL SAID MAIN TARIF, Northern Alliance, *Boston Globe*,
31 September 2001.

Qandahar, the film, has few, if any, markers of specific place. But Qandahar,
the *place*, has a rich history, geopolitics, and particularity. In 1969, when I
visited Qandahar, it was a place of wondrously skilled chess players and
entertaining transvestite singers, teahouses filled with music late into the
crisp desert nights, verdant gardens, and storied histories.

We put up in a wild hotel which featured a band, two singers, and two
colorfully made up female-impersonating hostesses, with an audience of
some two hundred stoned men. We went to a restaurant for dinner where we
found a group of respectable looking men playing chess: our collegiate chess
champion, Ben W., challenged one to a game and got beat twice in a row.
When we returned to the hotel, the band was still going strong: a sitar,
drums, tambourine, two harmoniums, a lute, and a lute-like cello. I tried to

record the music, but the batteries had run down while the B.s had used my recorder. Outside guys kept trying to sell us hashish: McG. was offered a thousand kilos shipped by air back to the States! The last song of the evening was a long epic sung by an old man with grand oratorical gestures. It all ended at 1 A.M. People then retired to eat in their rooms. (Fischer 1969, 49)

After the Taliban took power in Qandahar in 1994, hashish was banned. Opium production, on the other hand, was permitted on the grounds that it was not consumed by Afghans, only by foreign infidels, and, more pragmatically, because it rapidly became the primary source of revenue for warlords and the Taliban. Taxes collected on opium were called, by the Taliban, *zakat* (traditionally a religious tax of 2.5 percent of disposable income earmarked for the poor). The Tabliban's "zakat" was levied instead on trucks transporting opium and at a rate of 20 percent (Rashid 2000, 118).

Qandahar is located between the towns of Ghazni (on the road northeast to Kabul) and Bost, Qala Bost, and Lashgar-i Bazaar (off the road to Herat to the southwest). Ghazni, with a fabulous, Tibetan-like wood and mud brick citadel, hosts the grand tomb of Mahmud of Ghazni (r. 998–1030 C.E.), the creator of an empire that extended from Iran to the Punjab and a patron of the arts and culture. On the other side of Qandahar at Lashgar-i Bazaar and Qala Bost are the remains of the huge winter grounds of Mahmud the Great, vast walled spaces that could enclose his encamped cavalries, their mounts, and camp followers. With 15,000 horse-mounted troops, Mahmud raided India seventeen times, using the plunder to build a splendid capital in Ghazni that hosted, among others, the poet Firdausi (who dedicated the *Shahnameh* to Mahmud) and the great geographer al-Biruni (born in Khawrazm 973 C.E., died in Ghazni, 1048 C.E.). The great irrigation and river-control systems for the 700-mile-long Helmand River (rising in the Hindu Kush and emptying into the marshes of Sistan, the Hamum-i Helmand) were destroyed by Ghengiz Khan and Timur Khan in the thirteenth and fourteenth centuries.[29] That was history.

In the 1960s and 1970s Bost was the center of the Helmand River Irrigation Project and Helmand Valley Authority, the impressive but poorly executed USAID development project. Parts of Bost looked like a displaced California development, with California-style houses sporting American nameplates and cars in the driveways. The Helmand River Irrigation Project became a negative exemplar of salinization and the destruction of once arable land, due to the failure to line the irrigation canals, a not-infrequent, short-sighted, money-saving error of 1960s large-scale irrigation schemes. The project had

Ghazni city wall. *Photo by author.*

other problems as well (Fischer 1969, 48; Fischer 1980). In this period, before the Russian invasion, Afghanistan was somewhat able to play off the USSR and the United States for development projects and infrastructure: the paved road that circled three quarters of the country from Herat to Kabul to Mazar-i Sharif and Balkh was built partly by the Russians and partly by the Americans. (The quarter between Balkh and Herat remained unpaved, but it was graded and passable except in heavy rains, when hilly sections turn into slippery mud.) The Qandahar airport was built by the Americans in the 1970s and expanded and fortified by the Russians in the 1980s.

In the 1980s the Helmand Valley became a key opium-production region, under the control of Mullah Nassim Akhundzada, who under the Taliban served briefly as Afghanistan's deputy minister for defense and with whom U.S. Ambassador Robert Oakley negotiated a two-million-dollar aid package in exchange for suppression of opium and return of Stinger shoulder-carried rockets. When the United States failed to deliver, opium production resumed. Production increased markedly after the Taliban took control: opium production in Qandahar Province increased from 79 metric tons in 1995 to 120 metric tons in 1996. Poppy fields could be seen immediately outside Qandahar on land with irrigation systems repaired from the destruction wreaked by Soviet forces. Laboratories for processing the opium into heroin were established in Baluchistan and then in Afghanistan. Exports were smuggled out the Makran coast. The Pakistani Inter-Service Intelligence (ISI) is alleged to have turned to this industry to support its own adventures in Kashmir and India, as well as in Afghanistan when the United States cut off funding in 1994. It is said that not only was the richest area for irrigated poppy on lands developed by the USAID project in the 1960s but also that the varieties of poppy were no longer traditional but genetically enhanced, or so Pakistani newspapers speculated (Griffin 2001, 148; see also Rashid 2000, chap. 9). This was a multibillion dollar business: 1998 heroin exports from Afghanistan were estimated at three billion dollars; and the Afghan Transit Trade revenues, based on a free-trade agreement but fueling the black-market economy, generated another three billion dollars (Rashid 2000, 124, 189–94).

While the opium and heroin trades funded the Afghan civil wars and the Taliban in the 1990s, as well as much of the Pakistani state, the real regional game was, and is, over control of territory for future oil and gas pipelines. The Afghanistan War was one of the wars of this game that included Chechnya, Georgia/Abhazia, eastern Turkey/Kurdistan, and the Ferghana Valley. The emerging energy markets will be in China and India, so that the flow will be not only westward but also east and southward. Two oil consortia, led by the Argentine company Birdas and by the Texas-based Unocal, vied to build pipelines from Turkmenistan to the Pakistan coast. Birdas signed contracts in March 1995 to build an 875-mile pipeline from the Yashlar gas field in Turkmenistan via eastern Afghanistan to link to the Pakistani network centered in Sui, Pakistan's Baluchistan. Birdas initially offered to include Unocal in its consortium but later countered Unocal's aggressive competition by linking up with Ningarcho, a Saudi Arabian company with direct ties to Prince Turki, head of Saudi intelligence, and in 1997 sold a 60 percent share of its Latin American stakes to the U.S. oil company Amoco. Unocal, with Henry Kissinger as one of its consultants, signed contracts in October 1995 for a 1,050-mile pipeline from the Daulatabad gas field in Turkmenistan to the Pakistani coast in a consortium with Delta Oil of Saudi Arabia, Gazprom of Russia, and Turkmenrozgas of Turkmenistan. Unocal also hosted Taliban delegates in Sugarland (Houston) in 1997, set up a million-dollar training program in Qandahar, gave the University of Kansas Center for Afghan Studies $900,000 to train Afghans, and set up an office in Qandahar in April 1998. The bombing of the U.S. embassies in Kenya and Tanzania in August 1998 and the retaliatory missile strikes on al-Qaeda training camps in Afghanistan ended all negotiations with the Taliban, as did the downturn in oil prices, which caused Unocal to slash spending by 40 percent, to close offices also in Pakistan and Central Asia, and to withdraw from a Turkish pipeline project.

Qandahar stands in the midst of all this by virtue of the east-west truck routes from Herat to Kabul and from Pakistan to Central Asia (particularly while the Salang pass north of Kabul was closed by the destructive fighting between the Taliban and the Tajik forces under Ahmad Shah Massoud) and by virtue of being the seat of the Taliban and its leader Mullah Muhammad Omar. Said to have been founded by (and named after) Alexander the Great (Eskandar), but laid out anew in 1761 by Ahmad Shah Duranni (the Durrannis claim a genealogy that extends back to a Companion of the Prophet, Qais Abdul Rashid), Qandahar was badly damaged during the decade of struggles against the Russians, in which Mullah Omar, who was to emerge as the amir of the Taliban, lost his right eye. In 1996 Mullah Omar claimed charismatic leadership in a public ritual display of the Cloak of the Prophet, a relic kept in Qandahar's mosque of that name. Reconstruction of Qandahar did not really begin until 1997, when Osama bin Laden directed funding and Arab construction crews to repair the water and sewage systems, to build a new commercial center, a mosque, and housing complexes for the Taliban elite, to repair and fortify the airport, and to build other fortifications around the perimeters of the city (Bodansky 2001, 312–14).

Mullah Omar's fellow Taliban leaders also came from the ranks of the guerrilla wars against the Russians, used their wounds as badges of honor, and sported the religious title "Mullah." Born to landless peasants in a village near Qandahar, Mullah Omar lived for a while during the 1980s in Urozgan Province, became a village mullah in Maiwan village in Qandahar Province, and during the entire period of Taliban ascendancy and rule (1994–2001) lived in Qandahar, only rarely visiting Kabul, the country's capital. Taliban leaders widely adopted the title "Mullah," recalling the inflationary use of the title "Ayatullah" in the Iranian revolution. Mullah Mohammad Hassan Rehmani, the Taliban governor of Qandahar, who sported a wooden peg leg and refused offers of more elegant prosthetic legs, readily noted that Mullah Omar "has not too much religious knowledge," and he himself had little to do with religion before becoming the Taliban's number three official (Griffin 2001, 62). "Mullah" Borjan (Touran Abdul Rahman), the commander of the Taliban forces as they besieged Kabul in 1995 (and killed by a landmine during the siege), was a former Afghan army officer and a former member of the Harakat Party. "Mullah" Shah Sawar, the artillery commander north of Kabul, and General Mohammad Gilani, the Taliban air commander, were Khalq members of the army until 1992 (Rashid 2000, 62). Justice Minister

Mullah Nuraddin Turabi and Foreign Minister Mullah Mohammad Ghaus were one-eyed like Mullah Omar; the Taliban mayor of Kabul Abdul Majid, like Mullah Mohammad Hassan, also had a missing leg and fingers.

Taliban also outgrew its traditional usage. *Taliban* originally meant "theology students," and Rehmani and Mullah Omar spent some time in madrassas, as did thousands of their rank-and-file fighters. But in the 1980s, observes Michael Griffin, every mujahideen group fighting the Russians had its taliban, unmarried young men "with a tolerance for *shahadat* or martyrdom higher than their comrades" and who "maintained a distinct and separate identity during operations, even eating and sleeping apart" (2001, 55). These were the analogs of Athenian ephebes (Vidal-Naquet 1981).

From 1992 to 1994, following the withdrawal of the Soviets in 1989, Mohammad Shafeeq "Gul Agha" (Sir Flower) Shirzai (son of the Lion), a member of the Barakzai clan of Pashtuns, served as governor of Qandahar. He was the son of the late "Lion of Kandahar," a storied fighter against the Soviets who was assassinated by poisoning in the late 1980s. Under Gul Agha Shirzai, the province was divided between seven rival commanders and their militias, each of which set up checkpoints to tax convoys of weapons, drugs, goods, travelers, and others. The rivalries became so fierce that the province seemed a zone of lawlessness. The legend of the rise of the Taliban revolves around Mullah Omar and his colleagues as they avenged the excesses of warlord terror and established order and security. More important was the aid supplied by the Pakistani ISI in their efforts to streamline the road from Quetta to Turkmenistan and to reduce the numerous tolls to a single one under Taliban control (Rashid 2000, 27–28, 189).

In 2001, when the Taliban were driven from power, Gul Agha Shirzai returned from a seven-year exile in Quetta, where he had led the lucrative life of a merchant in the Afghan-transit trade economy. He returned with a force of some three thousand fighters, which rapidly grew to ten thousand. To regain and consolidate control, he made deals with various factions and opponents, and was eventually recognized by the new interim government under Hamid Karzai as governor not only of Qandahar (whose local control he shared with a commander Mullah Naqibullah) but also of the provinces of Helmand, Uruzgan, and Zabul. The process of making deals for power included the release of Mullah Nuraddin Turabi, author of many of the Taliban's repressive edicts, and of Sayed Tayyab Agha, the spokesman for Mullah Omar.

In one of the many ironies of history, Jack Creighton was a member of the Unocal board of directors during the period of negotiation with the Taliban and briefly served as the board's chairman during the first half of 2001.

In August 2001 Creighton became CEO of United Airlines. In September 2001 a United Airlines plane flew into the World Trade Center and another crashed in Pennsylvania, both with al-Qaeda hijackers at the controls (Scigliano 2001).

Run It Again in Documentary: Panshir Valley

Like Qandahar, which is both film and place, the Panshir Valley north of Kabul is the site of a documentary film, as well as a place with a long history and geopolitical locus on the road north from Kabul. The documentary *Panshir Valley* is about a frontline hospital established to care for civilian casualties of the war and of landmines; geography, sociology, and geopolitics are secondary to the story of the human tragedy of war. While Qandahar is primarily Pashtun, the Panshir Valley is primarily Tajik. Tajiks constitute about a quarter of Afghanistan's population and once constituted much of the educated bureaucratic and professional classes of Kabul and Herat. In the period of the documentary, the Panshir Valley was under the command of the forces of Ahmad Shah Massoud and President Buhuranuddin Rabbani, both of whom are interviewed in the film.

Jang (War): In the Land of the Mujaheddin (1998–2000)—directed by Italian documentary filmmakers Fabrizio Lazzaretti and Alberto Vendemmiati, produced and edited by Giuseppe Petitto—provides some images of Afghanistan that counterpoint those in Makhmalbaf's *Qandahar*. *Jang* chronicles the extraordinary saga of the Italian surgeon Gino Strada, who under the protection of Massoud built the frontline hospital for civilian minefield and war victims in the Panshir Valley. The hospital starts off with nothing. Operations are performed under a desk lamp. Only a single, primitive surgical saw is available for amputations. By the end of two years there are bright surgical lights, crisp green surgical scrubs, hospital pajamas for patients, whitewashed walls, and an eight-hundred tent encampment for refugees and patients. The film has the raw power that footage can bring, and there are strong scenes with Massoud and a sympathetic scene with Rabbani. The film presents many images of children and young people, as well as older people, with amputated legs and other wounds, and a number of these images have either visual or narrative power.

The film uses a repetition of images—tanks, rocket launchers, Kalashnikovs; children injured, with amputated legs; hospital operating scenes—to create a *M.A.S.H.*-like flow of emergency medicine. The filmmakers wanted to focus not on politics or war strategy but on the relationships of civilians, the tragedy that warfare brings to civilians. had they been allowed to film in southern Afghanistan, on the Pashtun-Taliban side of the frontlines, the filmmakers suspect, the picture would have been the same. This form of humanism fails to provide some of the geographic, cultural, and human specificities that provide greater texture and depth of understanding. At one point, very late in the film, Dr. Strada points out that 80 percent of the doctors and health-care workers are Kurds, and he suggests that Kurds have some linguistic, cultural, and religious affinities that allow them to work more effectively with the Afghans of northern Afghanistan. One would like to know more about the backgrounds of these people and indeed of Dr. Strada himself, of the English Nurse Rowland, and of the patients.

One of the more powerful and well-staged cameos is of a young woman hired by Nurse Rowland to be a front-door guard for the hospital, that is, to help search the women as they enter and to make them take off their veils, which are not allowed in the hospital. The young woman responds energetically: she only wears a head covering, she says, out of fear of the Taliban and were she in Iran, she probably would conform as well; but anywhere else, she says, "Why would you want to wear a tent on your head?" (The line provides one of the rare opportunities in the film for the audience to laugh.) Only much later in the film do we hear her talk about losing her legs, about how she cannot return to her earlier life, and about how lucky she feels to have a job in the hospital. As we absorb this new information, we watch her walk to her tent. There is a moment of disbelief, denial, or startling disconnect between her quite smooth walk and her words, until we see her sit and remove her two artificial legs. Later still, we see her watching a young man on crutches and only one leg.

Another powerful series of scenes follow a man who is wasted by melanoma and who is allowed to stay at the hospital as a terminal patient although his care requires fairly intensive nursing, which means fewer resources for the many other patients. In a striking scene soon after he enters the hospital, Nurse Rowland requests his permission to hire his wife to help clean the hospital; he furiously rejects this, until with many promises that she will be working with women, will not be treating patients, and will be segregated from men, and following entreaties for the economic benefit of his family, he finally agrees and is thanked for this permission. Somewhat later, no longer able to talk clearly (the melanoma has badly distorted his face), after much back-and-forth gesturing with hand and sounds, he gets his young son to find an apple by his bed, only then to offer it to the boy in an urgent token of offering and communication. When he dies, the family is shown wailing, allowing the audience to share grief for a "normal," if terrible, death amid all the deaths of war.

Less well developed, because done only as a short sequence, is a wonderful scene, etched in humor and bravado, of three young men singing in Afghan-ballad style about the war, their own roles, and the enemy. These songs open a small window on the cultural resources that Afghans bring to their suffering. More of this throughout the film could have been powerful. There are, however, some beautiful recitations of the call to prayer and Qur'anic verses; a brief interview with a Pakistani among the 270 prisoners of war who provides an unshaken fundamentalist insistence that everyone in the world must become Muslim; and sequences of dancing, wrestling, and buzkashi during the festivities of Noruz (Persian New Year, 21 March) in 1999 and 2000.

Somehow the power of the film's humanitarian cause is paid for by an erasure of the geopolitics that prevented the filmmakers (and the Italian surgeon) from filming on the other side of the battlefront (or from building a similar hospital there), despite their insistence that the horrors of war (and need for medical care) would be the same.

The Taliban Is Our Backwardness

This film is not only about Afghanistan but it could very well have happened in Iran. In today's environment in Afghanistan I was able to express myself easier. [I used] words that can't even be expressed in Iran today. . . . The Taliban is our backwardness.

In the past two years all of the planet earth's mass media have talked about my country's neighbors. So as an Iranian situated between the two tragedies of Afghanistan and Iraq, how could I have remained only a listener and an observer?—SAMIRA MAKHMALBAF interview, 2003

"We are not political; we are hungry; we want work!" So read the placards carried by a sea of blue-chadri-clad women demonstrating in Kabul, at the beginning of Siddiq Barmak's 2003 debut film, *Osama*. Taliban with machine guns on Toyota pickup trucks break up the demonstration, turning water cannon on the women and putting a few into a chicken coop wire cage on one of the trucks (on the soundtrack sounds of caged hens reinforce the point, as they do again in a later scene where hens and women are locked into a house).

How to intervene in cultural politics that are matters of life and death is one of the challenges that Iranian filmic discourse has taken on. In 2003 three films took up the venue of Afghanistan to return voices, faces, and images to that country. Samira Makhmalbaf and Babak Payami speak of their films (*At Five in the Afternoon; Silence Between Two Thoughts*) as also being figurations for the dilemmas of Iran (and for others more generally), while Barmak's film is the first from an Afghan auteur-director who speaks within an Iranian cinematic discourse inside Afghanistan. Samira Makhmalbaf notes, "Noqreh the actress in my film is the same age as myself. She has three children and since her husband had been missing since the American attack she was working as a teacher in a school to support her children. I had a hard time to convince her to play the role but now she loves the cinema and looks forward to acting in another movie. By playing in this film she helped Afghan women to overcome their fear of cinema" (S. Makhmalbaf 2003). Hannah Makhmalbaf's documentary about the making of the film shows us the extent to which Samira's claim (like Bahman Qobadi's similar description of *The Time of the Drunken Horses*) is accurate: "I chose the film's characters among ordinary people and got the film's details from their lives. I picked up much of the dialogue while searching for actors and locations and from what I heard from ordinary people in the streets or markets and re-enacted them in the film" (ibid.).

Panj-e Asr takes its title from a Garcia Lorca poem about the ubiquity of death in the bull ring, and is about the daughter of a pro-Taliban father, one of three girls who raised their hands when the teacher asked who wanted to be president of Afghanistan. The question makes the girl think about what such an ambition would take: she talks to a poet about poetics and politics; she defiantly slips out of the house without her school uniform so that she can attend class. (The theme of what such an ambition would take is also the subject of Rakhshan Bani-Etemad's documentary film *Ruzegar-e Ma* [Our Times, 2002], which follows several women, and one in particular, who try to run for president in the eighth Iranian presidential elections (2001); the subject of women demonstrating and being active in elections for their own interests is also the frame story in Bani-Ehtemad's narrative film *Zir Pust-e Shahr* [Under the Skin of the City, 2000]). *Panj-e Asr* is shot in post-Taliban Kabul amid the million or so refugees, many returnees from Pakistan. Finding no work, the girl's father drags his family off into the even more desperate and bleak rural areas. Samira tries not to demonize the Taliban father but to understand the motivations of both generations and the different situations of men and women. Samira says that originally she had the poet in the film change Lorca's poem about the death of a matador into a poem about the death of a cow (shades of Mehrju'i's *Gav*), but changed her mind in the final editing (S. Makhmalbaf 2003).

Siddiq Barmak's *Osama*, beautifully shot, with music by the Iranian composer Muhammad Reza Darvishi, uses a series of small details to work its magic and participate in the Iranian cinematic discourse. One of these details is a fantasy of the girl protagonist jumping rope while she is in a women's jail: she cannot really jump rope in jail, of course, so the fantasy is filmed as an overlay of the prison cell. It is a reference to Nelson Mandela's jumping rope and keeping fit while incarcerated on Robbens Island. The film begins, in fact, with a quote from Mandela written in white on a black screen: "I cannot forget but I can forgive." Another detail is the poignant image of a very small boy with a leg problem (shot from behind), slowly hobbling after the patients and staff who evacuate a hospital after it has been declared closed and a warning is sounded that the Taliban are arriving. It is an image of abandonment of the defenseless. A third detail is a reference to a scene in an early short by Kiarostami, where a boy tries to get by a watchdog in an alley. In Kiarostami's short it is an affectionate and amusing encounter: while the boy is momentarily terrified, there are no larger stakes. In *Osama*, the girl is afraid of a scruffy little dog who can barely bark, but even more of the Taliban following her. Her fear that the Taliban will unmask her impersonation of a boy (to work and move freely about in male spaces) overcomes her fear of the dog and she makes it past him. When the Taliban comes up to the same point in the alley and watches her run, the dog does not bark at him but whimpers and slinks away. It is a small moment of comic relief for the audience (which laughs) and a reference to the ill treatment of dogs, to Kiarostami, and perhaps to Hedayat's *sag-e velgard* (the abandoned dog).

As in Yektapanah's film *Jomeh*, a girl dresses as a boy, but while the ruse works in neither case, there are more devastating consequences in *Osama*. "Osama" is the name given to the girl by a protective boy who knows her secret; it also refers to Osama bin Laden: when boys are rounded up by the Taliban and herded off to who knows where, they speculate that they are being taken to prison or to fight for Osama bin Laden. In fact they are taken to be indoctrinated in a makeshift madrasseh in the magnificent ruins of the old fort of Kabul. The scene of rows of boys in white turbans bowing and reciting over open Qur'ans is much like the madrasseh scene in Mohsen Makhmalbaf's *Journey to Qandahar*, but added to this is now the rough play of boys in the recess period, particularly after they suspect Osama might be a girl, and the scene where an old mullah teaches the boys how to ritually wash their genitals in preparation for when they are old enough to have wet dreams. In the following recess she is forced by the boys to prove her masculinity by climbing the tree again; the two mullahs break up the crowd of frenzied boys shouting at her; they punish Osama by hanging her in a well, where she screams for her mother. When they pull her up, she drips blood down her legs; they then check her out and discover she is a girl.

The ordinary cruelty of boys and madrasseh discipline now turns into the cruelty of the Taliban system of justice. Before a crowd of men, a foreign journalist is accused of illegally filming the women's demonstration and is sentenced to death. A foreign nurse is accused of spreading obscenity and is sentenced to stoning. An older man in the crowd mutters angrily to his neighbor, "Where is the witness?" and the neighbor mutters back, "God knows!" The case of the girl who disguised herself as a boy is next. Before judgment can be pronounced, the old mullah drives up on a donkey cart, makes his way to the judge, and whispers; the judge then proclaims, "I forgive her. And because she is an orphan who has no one, I give her to this mullah as a wife." The mullah drives her off and locks her in with other wives (and hens). While they dress her and make her up for her night with her new husband, they lament how they were also forced into marriage with this old man. Both this film and Babak Payami's *Silence Between Two Thoughts* portray the sadism of locking women into rooms. In *Osama* only the Nelson Mandela image of jumping rope in prison holds out hope for a future.

The Iranian-Canadian filmmaker Babak Payami's *Silence Between Two Thoughts* was shot five kilometers from the Afghan border in eastern Iran. In an interview, he echoes Samira Makhmalbaf's comments about the Taliban being backwardness in Afghanistan, but goes on to say that one can find a Hajji in anyone's backyard; further, when President Bush cries "You are either for us or against us" and tries to impose "democracy" by military force, he too is a Taliban (Payami 2003). Payami lived in Afghanistan until his teens. The inspiration for the film came in Venice, he says, as he was preparing to premier his film *Secret Ballot*. He wanted to make a "Heart of Darkness" film about the search for Osama bin Laden, and in reading materials given him by Afghan refugees, he made a note to himself, "If you execute a virgin she will go to heaven, a convict must go to hell. Where is that written?" The "silence between two thoughts" is the long period between the dim-witted initial decision of the young village executioner to join the cause of Hajji, the Taliban warlord, who has taken control of the village (the decision of many villagers in the Qandahar region when the Taliban first brought order), and the realization that this authoritarian rule is bad news after the warlord kills the village muezzin. It is also the period between the stop of the execution of a girl (because, Hajji explains, if executed as a virgin she will go to heaven, and so, he says, her punishment will first involve her marriage to or deflowering by the executioner) and her release when the villagers finally chase the Taliban warlord out and turn on the executioner. Hajji is modeled on the Taliban Mullah Omar, Payami says, and while the story is set in Afghanistan, it could as easily be in Iran or in the United States. Payami says that while shooting the film, a local Iranian imam sent a warning that his female crew members should not be feeding male dogs. His film was seized. And at the airport he was told that "Hajji" had said he was not allowed to pass. Asked the name of this Hajji, the officials claimed not to know: just "Hajji." (The film was banned in Iran, and although now released in Europe and America, remains from Payami's point of view unfinished the way he would have liked.)

It's a Wrap: After-words, After-images, After-effects

Figure dwells in discourse like a phantasm while discourse dwells in the figure like a dream. . . . Seeing interferes with hearing and speaking, as desire interferes with understanding. Such at least is the Freudian algebra.—JEAN-FRANÇOIS LYOTARD, "The Dreamwork Does Not Think," in *The Lyotard Reader*

What we cannot reach flying, we must reach limping. . . . The Book tells us it is no sin to limp.—MAQAMAT OF AL-HARIRI, quoted in Sigmund Freud, *Beyond the Pleasure Principle*

Artworks recall the theologumenon that in the redeemed world, everything would be as it is and yet wholly other.
—THEODORE W. ADORNO, *Aesthetic Theory*

In her contribution to the film project *11'09'01*—a set of shorts by leading international filmmakers—Samira Makhmalbaf uses the familiar and still powerful device of the Iranian film tradition: the "telling scene" of a children's class. As in Qobadi's *Marooned in Iraq*, a teacher tries to explain to the children something of which they have no experience. The teacher wants them to observe a moment of silence for the victims of the attack on the New York World Trade Center towers. Because the children in the Afghan refugee camp in eastern Iran have never seen a skyscraper and do not quite understand the significance, the teacher takes them to the kiln of a nearby brickyard to contemplate what it might feel like if the tall chimney spewing out thick dark smoke were to fall on them.

The 9-minute 11-second short, appropriately titled *God, Construction, and Destruction*, opens with three hieroglyphs. An old man slowly walks away from a colorful gaggle of people into the desolate desert, hands behind his back, pulling on a rope, hauling up water from a deep-bore well in a bucket made of recycled tire rubber. It is an icon of Afghanistan, aged and reduced to basic human labor, a devastated land. But this is followed by children kneading the water and clay into mud, filling the wood brick forms, and carrying them to the kiln—a hieroglyph of a bright, lively, beautiful new generation told that "America wants to bomb Afghanistan; let us make a shelter." The camera then focuses on a little boy and girl of about four talking: if not quite a comic eiron-alazon pair, they nonetheless perform a theatrical narrator function for us innocents, as wise in their own way but happier and not yet as experienced as the children in Bahman Qobadi's *Time of the Drunken Horses*. The girl tells the boy (and us) that a man fell into the well and died, and a second one who went to help also fell and broke his leg. The boy repeats the story, but gets it wrong: two men died. No, corrects the girl: Chaman's father did not die, he only broke his leg.

With the stage thus set, an Iranian teacher (in her Iranian-style chador) intervenes to inject engagement with an adult moral world. She walks through the refugee camp gathering children, telling them that education is more important than making bricks: bricks will not protect against bombs, and she will give them books if they come to her class. As she walks through the crowded alleys of the camp, a voice-over tells us, "Three million refugees live in Iran," followed by the scorpion sting, "What happens to them will happen to you." Sacrifice zones, collateral damage. Under the shady arches of a ruin, she asks the rows of bright-eyed, chattering children, "Something very big and important happened yesterday; what was it?" The children are puzzled. The boy offers his latest news: "Two people fell in the well, two men died." The girl corrects him: "Two fell in. One died. One broke his leg." Adam and Eve, brother and sister, husband and wife, learning partners, getting it right iteratively. The teacher asks, "What else? Something really big." Another girl excitedly volunteers, "They buried Auntie in the ground up to her neck and stoned her." Repression of women is a major concern, but the teacher asks again, "I mean something really big, that affects the whole world, that could trigger World War III, that could make America drop an atom bomb. Two planes flew into the World Trade Center Towers in New York. What is a tower?" The children have no idea, so she takes them outside to look at the chimney to help them imagine and asks, "Who destroyed the towers?"

The boy answers: God. The girl corrects him: no, God does not destroy people, he creates them; God does not have planes. The teacher asks for a minute of silence for those killed in New York. The boy cannot keep still, the theological *bahs* (debate, learning dialectic) has not been finished: God creates people and then destroys them and creates them again. The girl: no, God is not so crazy. Another child, finding an excuse to speak: they are breaking the silence! Boy, still enthralled in the argument: God snaps his fingers like this, and people die; God does as he likes.

The teacher tries to maintain focus by telling them that a victim was buried in the rubble and called for help on his cell phone, do you know what a cell phone is? Recognizing that she is hopelessly invoking a parallel universe to which the children have no experiential connection, she shifts gear: because you didn't keep silent for a minute, we will stand under the chimney to think of how it might feel and think about all those buried by the collapse of a really tall tower. But, pipes up an irrepressive child, what do we do if we want to talk? The irrepressibility is part of the parable: what do Afghans (Iranians) do if they want to talk? The film ends with the murmuring of people, a sonic reminder of infinite commentary and of local worlds and practical logics.

Iranian cinema provides a new poesis, layered on the older stories and images of the Avesta, the Qur'an, *Shahnameh*, Rumi's Masnavi, Saedi and Hafez, miniature paintings, mural cloths (pardeh) used in oral storytelling, short stories, novels, and modern poetry. This poesis weaves back and forth between figure and discourse, quilting responses to circumstances that were not there before, shifting back and forth between temporalities of generic pattern, repetitions, and palimpsests, on the one hand, and catastrophic breaks and new terrains of challenge and action, on the other. The cinematic tour around Iran's war-affected borders has also traversed an evolving cinematic language. As the camera becomes smaller and lighter and easier to use, the possibilities of a digital cinematic pen and a "nomadic war machine" of filmic judgment and cultural critique promise escape from current censorship and funding constraints, allowing more polyphonic, participatory civil societies, with more paths around what Samira Makhmalbaf (2003) calls the "tidal mode of [information] transmission or what Jacques Derrida calls the autoimmune disease-like paradoxes of the teletechnologies. "Information transmission," suggests Samira Makhmalbaf, "resembles a wave. First 100 percent of news is on Afghanistan or Iraq, for example. Then they lower it and bring it to zero percent and when that happens we are supposed to accept that there's no problem in that region" (ibid.). The increasing technical capacities to foreground alternative dimensions of reality through sound, close-up, montage, serialism, and the like, as if in an n-dimensional virtual-reality cave, allow film to operate as artwork in Adorno's sense of providing redemptive cultural critique by presenting the world as it is and as wholly Other, modulating its possibilities, seeing the alternatives that are already embedded within, if only they can be accessed and set in motion. Thus, at times, films can function with the double logics of tapping into the unfolding structure of events and of invoking virtual alternative worlds, seeming thereby to have a kind of prescient foreknowledge, and a Möbius eternal return in a world of historical disruption and transformation. It is not surprising that film should become a new Persian medium with which to tell stories that connect old stories and new ones, reconstructing humanism amid worlds of violent change, and questioning the pieties of humanism by inscribing us as active viewers and interpreters within the apparatus of unfinished stories.

From the car seat and construction site (Kiarostami in *A Taste of Cherry*, Yektapanah in *Jomeh*, Majidi in *Baran*), abandoned boat or bus and repaired taxi or truck (Naderi in *The Runner*, Makhmalbaf in *The Peddler*, Ayyari in *Beyond the Fire* and *The Abadanis*, Jalili in *Delaram*), we are provided a purchase on multisited or multilocale transnational processes where local logics are disrupted by and attempt to repair what happens at other localities as parts of larger and often distant flows, relations, and structures. It is turtles all the way down: turtles and buried tanks, eclipses and veils, women on bicycles in black chadors chased by men on horseback, blackbirds and helicopters.

"What we cannot reach flying we must reach limping." Freud's invoking of al-Hariri has nothing to do with *Qandahar*, and yet *Qandahar*'s image of men on crutches running after helicopters dropping prostheses powers up both Freud's insight and the weaving back and forth of learning between East and West. The limp of Oedipus, Freud's master metaphor for self-knowledge, provides a clue to the Sphinx's riddle and thus to the salvation of the city from plague, corruption, and war, a metaphor that resonates across these historical and cultural horizons. How apt that in the aftermath of World War I and in rethinking some of the fundamental frameworks for psychoanalysis and the work of the figural, Freud should have found a literary tag for the intellectual challenges in an old Muslim source, as many in the international film circuits today turn to Iranian film as among the most innovative and interesting for exploring much more than a national cinema.

Coda Balancing Acts (After 9/11)

"The great difference between Cervantes's imagination and
our present realities is that although Don Quixote is constantly
feeding on his own illusions, he is also a humane, noble, and kind
person. . . . In our age when superpowers break out wars, only their
opponents suffer destructions, slaughters, and catastrophes."
— PRESIDENT KHATAMI, 30 October 2002, Madrid

Bala raftim, mast bud; pain amadim, dough bud;
   qeyseh-ye ma dorugh bud.
Bala raftim, dough bud; pain amadim, mast bud;
   qeyseh-ye ma rast bud.
[We went up, it was yogurt; we came down, it was
   dough; our story was a lie.
We went up, it was dough; we came down, it was
   yogurt; our story was right.]
— Nursery rhyme used as the ending for Ebrahim Hatamikia's
2002 film *Ertafae Past* (Low Heights)

Iran played a complicated role in the aftermath of the 2001 attack on the New
York World Trade Center towers. The people of Iran immediately turned out
in massive candle-light demonstrations of sympathy with Americans and
other victims from around the world (Lebanon, India, Grenada, El Salvador, Japan, China, Britain, Ireland, Germany, Australia, Canada, and so on).
Many Iranians have relatives in the United States, and despite the tense

relations between the governments of the two countries, there are considerable and deep bonds. Iran lent support to the United States drive to oust al-Qaeda and the Taliban from Afghanistan, perhaps calculating this was a way to increase its leverage in the eastern and central parts of Afghanistan. After the ousting of the Taliban, Iran began to nudge repatriation of the millions of refugees who had been housed in refugee camps along the border for years, as well as working in construction and other menial jobs in cities across Iran. Although it periodically provided refuge to some members of al-Qaeda and the Taliban in the aftermath of their ouster from Afghanistan, Iran turned some of these over to Saudi Arabia and other U.S. allies in a complicated political chess game. Similarly, while continuing to support Hezbullah guerrillas with money, arms, personnel, and rhetoric in Lebanon and Syria and in their cross-border attacks on Israel, Iran also helped the United States in the Persian Gulf enforce the UN embargo on Iraqi oil exports. It did so even while President George W. Bush called Iran part of an "axis of evil" and made bellicose statements about an imminent war on Iraq to force Iraq to give up all biological, chemical, and nuclear weapons of mass destruction, a war which Iran publicly opposed.

Rebalancing Unequal Relations

Iran's president Muhammad Khatami, on a state visit to Madrid drew attention to the new unbalanced forces in the world and the devastations that superpower war unleashes. Struggling domestically for a civil society against repressive and rigid conservative mullahs with a lock on many of the key institutions in Iran's divided Islamic republican constitutional structure, Khatami also found himself navigating dangerous international waters. Like many other commentators, he drew attention to the mirrored rhetoric of Osama bin Laden and George W. Bush, "a logic that on one side produces terror, and on the other in the guise of fighting terror creates the worst form of violence in the world" (30 October 2002, Madrid). Although Khatami's invocation of Don Quixote was partly propagandistic and self-interested, it is remarkable that he should have invoked not merely Don Quixote (after all he was in Spain) but a series of other European literary and humanist figures such as Dostoevsky, Turgeniev, Hobbes, Kafka, Orwell, and Proust, bringing the call, as it were, into the heart of Western culture. When he warned of the great difference between Cervantes's imagination and our present realities, he was drawing attention to telemediated war at a distance, which is increasingly devastating for civilians who are labeled regrettable "collateral damage." Hence he pleads, "those politicians who follow the path of Don Quixote in our age lack his ethical and emotional virtues."[1]

Perhaps the most profound of the deep bonds between Iran and America can be seen in the simple but powerful resonance of the metaphors that Seamus Heaney, the Irish poet who teaches at Harvard, uses in his meditation on September 11, images that arrive by way of the Roman poet Horace and by way of Greek and Iranian metaphors.

> . . . just now
> He [Jupiter] galloped his thunder cart and his horses
>
> Across a clear blue sky. It shook the earth
> And the clogged under-earth, the River Styx,
> The wandering streams, the Atlantic shore itself.
> Anything can happen, the tallest things
>
> Be overturned, those in high places daunted,
> Those overlooked regarded.
> . . . . .
> . . . nothing resettles right."[2]

Film, too, can create such poetic concision, evocation of multiple horizons, and exactitude through indirection.

Balancing Guns and Votes, Responsibilities and Lines of Flight, Freedom and Rules of Order

Three popular films of 2002 express the profound balancing acts that Iranians perform daily. Imagistic abstraction, dramaturgic alchemy, allegory, figuralism, and discursive displays provide both ethnographic clues for interpretive intelligence and abreactive spaces for emotional working out and working through. Babak Payami's *Secret Ballot*, Manijeh Hekmat's *Women's Prison*, and Ebrahim Hatamikia's *Low Heights* all take place in enclosed spaces (island, prison, airplane) that are microcosmic stages for the debates, conflicts, paradoxes, and tensions of Iranian society at large.

September 11 is referenced directly in Hatamikia's *Low Heights*. In one of the opening scenes, a television monitor in the Abadan airport replays footage of one of the hijacked airliners flying into the World Trade Center and causing an explosion and fire ball. We watch this passing televised reference just as the Abadan passengers are boarding a two-propeller plane which is about to be hijacked and explode in its own psychodrama. The film is a hilarious, yet tensely dramatic, comic remake, as it were, of Hatamikia's earlier thriller *The Glass Agency* (*Ajans Shishe-i*). Manijeh Hekmat's *Women's Prison*, by contrast, is less hysterical ("a psychoneurosis characterized by emotional excitability . . . due to autosuggestion, dissociation, or repressed emotion"), albeit more *hysterikos* (Greek, "of or pertaining to the womb"), representing a *hystera*-like transformation from sterile womb/prison to life-giving womb/birth.[3] Over the course of the two decades of the Islamic revolution, the prison is progressively filled with characters and life, as if it were a latter-day Brueghel that extended the canvas not only to movement but to the passage of time, from one generation to the next, and slowly opened to the outside.

Payami's *Secret Ballot*, based on an idea by Mohsen Makhmalbaf and foreshadowed in Makhmalbaf's *Testing Democracy* (2000), follows the comic exploits of an enthusiastic, chadored young woman who is out to get everyone to vote and a young male soldier, unwillingly seconded to be her escort, who believes that without him she will be taken advantage of by smugglers and who points out the various contradictions in her enthusiasm for democracy.[4] *Secret Ballot* is a satire about guns and votes as two alternative strategies for changing an agrarian, herding, and fishing society, each with its absurdities and reality checks. "She" is an urban, civilized woman, educated, idealistic, headstrong, naive. "He" is a law-and-order guy, sensitive to local honor codes, deviousness, and intricate, dancelike interactions. She, an election agent, is so single-minded that she will travel to the ends of the earth—to a smuggler's ship, to a cemetery—to hunt down potential voters. He, a dry-humored and unflappable soldier with a Turkish accent and down-to-earth Azeri pragmatism, is weaned from being reluctant to escort a woman ("My orders did not say the election agent would be a woman") to pointing out the flaws in her idealism ("These crooks would not listen to you without my gun"). She: "All citizens can vote if they are of legal age." He: "Smugglers too?" She: "Yes." He: "If they vote, I'll be out of a job." She: "It has nothing to do with that." They come to a lone traffic light in the middle of the desert, as pointless and ineffective as their mission, and he rubs the connection in by refusing to run the red light. She: "There are no cars, go on." He: "It is against the law; we cannot break the rules." She (exasperated): "It's the middle of the desert, rules mean nothing here." He: "You've spent all day defending the laws, now you want to break them?"

Even smugglers at sea should (not) vote
"If you vote, your sheep will be healthier" (*Secret Ballot*)

While the film is about the absurdity of democratic voting as the solution to problems everywhere—that is, even where people cannot read, do not know who the candidates are, are told by their husbands how to vote, and so on—yet she rightly admonishes the soldier, "Elections let people talk; guns shut them up." In her efforts to get people to vote, she promises an Arabic-speaking shepherd who doesn't understand her that there will be less disease among his animals if he exercises his right to vote and a fisherman that fishing conditions will improve. She tells a group of women, "You do not need permission to vote; if you women cannot read, I have photographs of all the candidates so you can choose." To which, of course, the women reply, "No photos of unknown men!" An elderly guard at the new solar-energy plant (which, pristine, guarded, and otherwise unused, the guard uses to make tea) says if he must vote, he will only vote for God. She admonishes him in good modernist fashion: "You have to decide your own fate." He replies, "Fate is preordained, written on one's forehead [*sarnevesht*]." She: "The candidates understand your needs and problems." He: "See the sun, it has not changed; the candidates on your list cannot even decide their own fate."

She has one day in which to accomplish her work, and she misses the motorboat which was to take her off the island. A large airplane lands and taxis across the screen right to left. She boards it with the ballot box, and it taxis for take-off from left to right, a nice absurdist touch. The scene returns to earth, to the opening scene of a bunk bed from which the soldier and his buddy guard the beach. Nothing has changed; everything has changed. As his buddy once again takes a nap on the lower bunk, which is shaded from the sun by the upper bunk, our soldier friend sits on a makeshift lookout plank. But the feeling-tone this time is that he is missing the excitement of the day, less guarding the beach than mulling over the world represented by the young woman, voting his secret ballot of desire beyond the practicalities, the manipulations from the guardians of the elections afar, and the daily border feuding between soldiers and smugglers. When at the end of the day, she had said, "I don't have your vote," he had replied, "I will vote for you." She: "I am not a candidate." He: "I thought it was a secret ballot." It is the same answer given by a family who had traveled to catch the election agent so they could vote and were disappointed that their candidate was not on the approved list, but decided to vote for their choice anyway. As they part ways, the soldier says to the young woman, "You can come back soon again to collect votes." The subtle (or not) erotic charge also expresses excitement about a sense of change, hope, future openness, and a new generation.

Although the spirit (ever-returning ghost, ideology, or hope) of democracy may be one of modernism, a seeming repetition, or catching up, as it were, of the struggles two centuries earlier for democracy in Europe and the United States, here the modernist moments are out of joint, producing similarities and differences, families of resemblance, different social growths in different cultural media, different balancing acts. But the reproduction of democracy in the United States also contains its families of resemblance, elections providing mandates for governance and elections understood to be manipulated (histories of elections captured by big business or by immigrant and labor machine politics, of popular-vote winners losing the election, of dead men voting and live voters disqualified). The excitement for democracy in *Secret Ballot*, however satirical and personified through the unconsummated passions of the young woman and the soldier, contrasts with voting in the American elections, which is felt by many to be stale or in hands other than those of the voters.[5] The struggles for democracy—for its specters, theatricals, passions, revelations, and voicings of popular will, intrigues and play of interests, its divided and self-checking powers, tolerance of differences, support for civil society, its negotiation among legacies and resources of many returning pasts, and its support for legal institutions to aspire beyond norms and sanctions toward justice—in both transnationally linked sites, Iran and America, are at once parallel, linked, and different.

Parachuting—of the ballot box in *Secret Ballot*, of prostheses in *Qandahar*—is an apt metaphor of the humanitarian and democratic ideologies that are parachuted in without organic grassroots and that provide the tools with which national and global forces and ideologies (including the humanitarian industry of nongovernmental organizations that mobilize expertise and funding globally) whether cynical or well-intentioned, can manipulate local worlds. Ballot boxes, in this sense, are also prostheses. The airplane is another such metaphor, simultaneously a deus ex machina dropping things from the sky; a dovelike symbol of flight, freedom, the soul; a womb of safe transport; and a potentially explosive nightmare.

In *The Glass Agency*, Ebrahim Hatamikia's 1997 film, an ex-commando leader takes hostage everyone in a travel agency to force the Fund for Disabled Soldiers to pay for a medical trip to England for one of his former men. Amid Hajji's brinkmanship of using imaginative threats while intending to do no harm, the hostages argue about how the injustices affecting the injured veteran and Hajji's effort at repair relate to the claims of the Iran-Iraq War in defense of the revolution, to the postwar society, and to their own rights to live their own (consumerist) lives. The tension is sustained not just by the dynamics of the potentially lethal standoff but by the fact that drama is not of good versus evil but of negotiation and compassion in a nexus of salutary goals complicated by passion, determination, idealism, and pragmatism.

In *Ertefae Past* (Low Heights) Hatamikia continues the debates about postwar society, about the constraints on opportunities in Iran, and about fantasies of escape, either to Dubai (where at least when one is ill and out of work, a welfare system will provide support) or, ideally (for the hipster Mehdi), to Los Angeles. This time the hostage-taker or hijacker is from Abadan, the father of a child disabled by cerebral palsy and of another child still in the womb—does one sense a resonance with Makhmalbaf's *The Peddler* and with Bahman Qobadi's *The Time of the Drunken Horses*?—who promises relatives and friends jobs with the French oil company Total and transports them by plane.[6] Once in the air, he attempts to hijack the plane and divert it to Dubai.

Ertefae Past begins and ends with familiar nursery rhymes, which situates the narrative as a fable or parable conveying complicated truths for better viewing and debate. A handicapped child, a figure of innocence, with a little prompting from an older cousin, faces us (the camera) and orients us with the nursery rhymes. Throughout the film, the father, Ghassem, is never far from this child, often holding him, using his child and pregnant wife rhetorically as evidence that he is not a wild man but is acting with desperate calculation. At one point, acknowledging the life-threatening risk in which he has placed all on the plane, he says, "My only assets in life have been my hands or my brain, and this time my only asset is my life." Indeed he has pulled off the hijacking in a bravura performance of ad hoc wit, without his gun, staging a rage during which he throws a pot of boiling water into the face of the sky marshal and seizes his gun. His pregnant wife, Narges, has been in on the plans for the hijacking but has also had reservations and tries to prevent her husband from carrying out the plans (she takes the gun from him in the Abadan airport, then claims to have left it behind), desperate to protect him and the family. At one of the turning points in the hijacking, when Ghassem is handcuffed, she dramatically defends him, saying that after the Iran-Iraq War, when there was nothing in Abadan, no water, no electricity, not even a single injection which might have cured their child, Ghassem had helped everyone.

Many of the characters on board are played for laughs. The plane's captain is a deep-voiced center of calm and reason throughout the chaos: he has lived abroad, and tries to counsel Ghassem. Tell me what you really want and I can help you, he says, for I've been abroad, but I did it legally and then could return, while you are burning all your bridges. The pilot's daughter, raised in Canada, speaks little Persian, and when the passengers first board the plane and Ghassem asks how long the flight to Bandar Abbas will be, the better to calculate when to stage the hijacking, the captain says if Ghassem can teach his daughter to speak Persian along the way, he will get them there faster. Narges has a set of Three Stooges–like brothers—Mehdi, the hipster; Hasan, the balding, about-to-be-married conservative; and Malek, the burly, bearded airhead—all of whom swing back and forth between their devotion to Ghassem and their inability to stand up to their mother. The old mother, with a lighted cigarette always in her hand, is a hilarious histrionic, defending and cowing her boys, berating Ghassem, begging forgiveness from the sky marshal, disarming Malek when he has the gun, and then being appalled that the second sky marshal simply takes it from her without first promising that her boys will not suffer. She claims to be fearless (while acting otherwise) since after eight years of having bombs drop on her head during the Iran-Iraq war, nothing further can impress her. Abolfazl Kuchezadeh ("alley born") plays the character, familiar on any Iranian working-class bus, who repeatedly calls out for prayer ("Let us pray for our safety") until another passenger protests, "Man, there's a time and a place for everything."

But amid the comedy are vignettes of real life. In a foreshadowing hieroglyph before the action of the film begins, we see Ghassem being driven in a taxi, slightly weaving along the highway because the left rear tire is flat almost down to the rim (the driver comments, "This car cannot handle it any more"), and Ghassem, ignoring the warning, looks at his various identity cards and one-by-one tosses them out the window, as a plane flies overhead. The vignettes of getting through customs, as well as the actions of the sky marshal in preventing the plane from landing in Dubai, drive home Ghassem's dard-e dell (pouring out one's heart's pain), "We are forced to migrate like our ancestors, but they were lucky that they could go freely, while we have to supply money, visas, and more and more."[7] Dubai repeatedly refuses permission to land. Ghassem, not trusting the pilot's communications in English, does a credible job of taking the radio and with some nervous stuttering forcefully demanding in Arabic to land. His game of wits with the pilots—he suspects them of playing for time, of double dealing—is checked for a moment when there is no answer and the co-pilot takes his time in pointing out that Ghassem did not push the transmit button when he spoke; so he does it again, stuttering even more the second time, being less forceful in his demand. The response again is a denial, so Ghassem points out that if the pilots do not do something they will all go into the soup, including the captain's daughter. They get Dubai to agree. But at the last moment, just as they are touching down, the sky marshal, having in the meantime been freed, forces the pilot at gunpoint to take off, despite the pilot's angry protests that they are running low on fuel. Ghassem and the other passengers suspect that the sky marshal's primary purpose is to prevent people from leaving Iran. Earlier, in trying to psychologically manipulate Ghassem, the sky marshal had warned that there were agreements with all neighboring countries to return hijackers. The marshal has been freed, because as Ghassem had initially assumed, there was a second marshal aboard but initially could not identify for sure because he was unarmed. A second gun was carried by the stewardess (in black chador, with gold stripes on her black sleeves), who nervously passed it to the second marshal, Ali Reza. Ali Reza is a chameleon, pretending to be a businessman who knows how to frisk passengers; later, when he tries to get close to Ghassem, he says he is a businessman whose business is a cover for the political opposition. He sits with Ghassem and says that the problem is that Dubai refuses permission to land, probably due to fear of Iran. But here's an idea, he continues: why not go to the heart of America in the Middle East—Ghassem just looks at him—Israel? The audience laughs, but Ghassem turns away in disgust, saying he is not political. Ali Reza calmly points out that what Ghassem has done will already bring world attention. Interspersed, of course, the comedy continues, with Mehdi asking who wants to go to America (and someone suggests Hawaii) and starting a list of all those who want to leave Iran with Ghassem: more than half the passengers sign up. Mehdi himself claims to have a serious reason, pulling up his shirt to reveal lash marks for having been caught drinking. In a flash of anger, he shouts, "You forget what they did to me! Thirty lashes for a drink! I'm not going back," then returns to the comic mode, saying, "I will write in my will that I want to be buried in Los Angeles [audience laughter]. All for Ghassem, clap." The clapping turns into singing, with Mehdi banging on the tea pot for percussion and Abolfazl beginning to dance.

Back and forth between comedy and seriousness, slapstick and reality, desire and prudence. A woman puts on a wig and shades, doffs her chador, and stands in brightly colored Western dress. Ghassem is shocked and admonishes her. She is abashed. Then she rallies, saying, "I make my own decisions!" But then she crumples and angrily puts her chador back on, throwing the wig at Ghassem. Ghassem admonishes her, "Don't forget we are Muslims." She sullenly retorts, "Then we had better go back to Iran." After the sky marshals seize control, they read out the list of names of those who had signed up with Ghassem under the earlier regime when he was in charge, but a girl points out that her father had never signed and the repressive regime of the sky marshals is also momentarily exposed as based on various false groundings. The old mother at one point challenges the first sky marshal, whose face had been scalded, "I can see in your eyes, you are driven by revenge." Ghassem had previously responded to this marshal's efforts to provoke him ("One who uses his wife and child as protection is not a man") by putting his face up to him and saying, "You are no angel, and I am no devil, so let us not oppose each other."

In the final struggle for control, Narges pulls out her gun to defend her husband and family, many are injured, and Narges herself goes into labor, just as the plane runs out of fuel and the right engine quits. A hieroglyphic image of the fist of the newborn fills the screen like a political statement, then it opens in playful stretching and closes again into a fist. The plane begins to shake violently like a butter churn as it begins to lose altitude. It comes to rest, with the passengers looking out and each seeing something different out the blood-streaked window. *Bala raftim, mast bud, pain amadim dough bud.* Dough is made by adding water to yogurt or to a solid yogurt extract. The plane had landed on what the pilot early in the flight had called the peacefulness of the Persian Gulf, in contrast with the dryness of the desert land. The dry yogurt extract is made with water into a refreshing drink; the dry land is made fertile with water; the newborn's fist glistens wetly.

Birth imagery is at the center of Manijeh Hekmat's *Women's Prison* as well. Just as there is a test of wills between Ghassem and the sky marshal and the captain, so, too, is there a test of will in *Women's Prison* between the warden, Sister Tahareh Yusefi, and the prisoner, Mitra Shakeri. During the seventeen years of her imprisonment, which span the years from the onset of the Iran-Iraq War to present, Mitra evolves into the maternal center of the prison-womb. She is in for murdering her stepfather who had manhandled her mother. While it may be too facile to see the mother as Iran manhandled by Iraq, and the daughter, Mitra, the goddess of light and contracts, a patroness angel of ancient Iran, as imprisoned by the war—the film after all is also about the gritty lives of poor, battered, and dispossessed women who have their own gangs, pecking orders, and violence—the prison-womb does work as a microcosm for Iran and its struggle to balance freedom and new rules of order.

On the night of bombing in the first part of the film, Mitra helps deliver a newborn child during a blackout. Seventeen years later that child reenters the prison as a young, street-smart, vivacious kid wearing a baseball cap with the bill fashionably over her neck, seemingly at home in the prison, playing pranks on one and all, especially the female wardens and male guards. Early on, when she is called to the office from the exercise yard, she blows a kiss to the male marksman on the walls, and he clicks his heels and salutes in return. She calls herself "Essie Goldfinger," for her wit and nimble pickpocket hands. The name she was given at birth—by Mitra in fact—was Sefideh (white, pure), Sefideh Panhai (secret, hidden). She is the free spirit of the next generation, curious about her mother, but grateful for not being too attached to the past. Essie/Sefideh contrasts with the figure of Shahar, a young woman who, by the middle of the film, is totally crushed psychologically.

The film opens as a genre prison film: a new warden arrives, tough, introducing new rules, cleaning up the riotous conditions, improving prison life, albeit with an iron hand. There are relatively few prisoners. As the new warden, Sister Tahareh (purity, as in the religious purity code) Yusefi (Joseph the administrator/vizier to the pharaoh), establishes her rule, she finds inmates with whom she can construct a modus vivendi, primarily Mitra, whom she has to break first. Yusefi, although college educated (as is Mitra), is said to have served on the battlefront in the war with Iraq; she admonishes the prisoners that things have changed in the world outside, with women serving on the front, while here in the prison they still haggle over "beans and meat." (Guns and butter: Iran indeed was being squeezed by the war into economic straits that the early days of the revolution had not anticipated.)

In the second period of the film, a decade later, and labeled a kind of (false) spring, the prison has, albeit with many slippages, begun to run smoothly: there is a sewing-machine worship, volleyball is available in the exercise yard, and the accommodations are clean and orderly, if a little over-crowded. There are executions, however, and in a poignant and excruciating scene, one of the women on the ward we are living with is informed that she will be executed in the morning; she spends the evening distributing her few belongings while the women sit and chant from the Qur'an and Arabic prayers. As she is led away in the morning, she collapses and is dragged off, leaving a trail of excrement, and a standing salute of silent women, behind. Not only are there executions, they are manifestly unfair, with lesser offend-ers executed while some of the worst offenders live like baronesses, oversee-ing local power structures of intimidation, violence, and sexual harassment. Sahar, the "only virgin left," as Mitra warns the warden, falls victim to one of these women, and although the warden gets the punishments right this time ("Everyone to solitary confinement except Mitra!"), it is too late: Sahar com-mits suicide.

The third period of the film is the return of Essie/Sefideh, whose mother, Goldaram (I have a flower) Bolboli (nightingale), had unleashed a shatter-ing/triumphal scream at her birth, not unlike Narges's scream in the falling plane of *Low Heights*. Seventeen years have passed, the warden is looking old and tired, and Mitra has transformed into a calm matriarch caring for the growing number of children in the prison, as well as for her fellow inmates. Indeed, the prison population in general has filled out to overflowing bustle. The warden complains by phone that she cannot continue accepting women, as there is no more room. A period is passing: there are intimations of a new warden to replace Yusefi, and in an ambiguous scene Yusefi takes down her packed suitcase and looks through it. Essie is released and tells Mitra over the phone that she is going to Dubai (shades again of *Low Heights*). Mitra for years has been told by Yusefi that she can be released for good behavior if she posts bond, but Mitra has repeatedly stated that she has no one waiting for her on the outside who can raise bail. Now she has someone, and she asks Essie to wait for her. We watch as Mitra signs out and is offered sweets. Yusefi offers her a coat (taken from her own suitcase?) in lieu of a chador and slowly walks her to the front gate. As the gates open, the two of them look at each other. Finally, Mitra walks out into the bright sunshine and busy traffic of Tehran streets, and the gates close, throwing dark shadows over the warden.

We are not sure what the future holds for Mitra or, for that matter, for Essie. But the images of Essie's many pranks linger. In one, she peeks into a meeting with perhaps the new incoming warden or higher-level female supervisor, steals some pieces of fruit from a tray being carried in, then takes the tray of tea out of the hands of a surprised servant and serves the female officials around the conference table. As she goes around the table she drops a piece of fruit, leans down to retrieve it, and knocks open a purse. She pushes items back into the purse and leaves, rushing to her cell to do a countdown with her mates: hearing an explosion and screams, she high-fives her friends. A bit later, she runs into the cell and tosses something in; a moment later the warden comes in barking "Hejab konid!" (cover up, put on your chadors or kerchiefs, that is, there's a man on the floor), followed by a big, rather dumb looking, male guard with a white bandage on his forehead. As Yusefi is about to order a search of the cell, Mitra calmly says, "If he is looking for his epaulette, I have it," and holds out an epaulette that Essie Goldfinger had lifted.

Somehow we have faith that together Mitra and Essie Goldfinger/Sefideh Panhai will make it: experience and youth, the farrah of mother and daughter, the genealogy of women directors of Iranian film, building visions of new worlds along with their brothers and fathers.

Balancing Social Theory, Film, and Ethnography

Both film and social theory, like film, arise from particular ethnographic and historical contexts. The films and short stories of the 1970s were the product of the intelligentsia, a particular fraction of the bourgeoisie, working out and articulating the particular generational, class, nationalist, and gender dilemmas of roots in traditional worlds and aspirations in modernist worlds. Similarly, the European social theories of the late nineteenth century and early twentieth century arise from particular generational experiences and differ from their successors of the late-twentieth and early-twenty-first century (Fischer 1999). Ghosts from the past haunt the present in both cases.

Film and stories do not directly mirror Iranian society but are fictive spaces that provide screens and virtual sets for cycling through potential alternative implications of social tensions, paradoxes, trade-offs, dilemmas, moral conflicts, ethical struggles, artistic mutational experiments that hybridize local and foreign, past and present, east and west, north and south, desire and prudence, repression and liberation, nightmare and dream, vision and sound-dance, superficial meaning and deep play, over-investment and under-investment. With the revolution, the genres and styles of 1970s moody, surrealist, filmmaking and writing were stilled and shown to be out of touch with the larger society. But the 1980s and 1990s picked up those filmic stylistic innovations, paid them tribute (*Once Upon a Time, Cinema*), retooled them, and proceeded anew. Film, again, is not a direct mirror not only because the metaphor is inherently generative—at minimum, mirrors reverse left and right; at an angle, they create varied refractions and perspectives; set in tubes at angles, they microscope and telescope, bringing the invisibly small and the invisibly far into sight—and capable of, as Makhmalbaf put it, changing the "realism" being constructed, but also because film is a collaborative object (writers, directors, cameramen, editors, actors, composers) with varied genealogies of style and reference and with circuits of dissemination interweaving within a tapestry of other visual, sound, informational, evocative, psychodynamic, and kinetic media. As with democracy (in *Secret Ballot*, in Florida), Iranian film in its domestic, diasporic, and international contexts of reception operates as a family of resemblances, weaving across strata of history and experience differently for different audiences.

Telemedia have emerged as powerful forces, and contemporary social theory must take account of them as thoroughly saturating the local, national, and transnational worlds in which everyone participates with differentiated, unequal, and stratified access. Thoughtful, historically effective, social action is impossible today if one is not media-savvy, knowing how to guage and prepare for the aftereffects of circulation and mutation. And yet, to engage in the deep cultural politics and the discursive structures that create the background assumptions on which politicians and others premise their actions, one cannot simply attempt to get one's message included in the dominant media streams. As Samira Makhmalbaf hints, "Through Jim Jarmush's work I can understand a stranger's pleasure upon stepping out in Harlem but not from CNN reports about it" (S. Makhmalbaf 2003). What auteur-film of the Iranian filmic discourse supplies is not the same as what ethnography supplies. In this book, I have tried to provide signpostings of the ethnographic context, from the different contexts in which Zoroastrian legendry is understood to the local contexts of film reception in Yazd or Abadan, to the social contexts of the intelligentsia in the 1970s and the filmmakers of the 1990s, and the transnational ones of the Iranian diasporic audiences in Los Angeles and Boston. In the aftereffects of war as seen through the Iranian figural and discursive cinewriting of the 1980s and 1990s, we can see both new modes of filmic judgment and cultural critique emerging from Iranian ethnographic contexts and profound commentaries, images, and hieroglyphics to think with—illuminating the devastations being unleashed in the contemporary world and the humanistic responses grounded in helping one another and in very deep layers of the Persian humanistic traditions.

Epilogue

Beyond "Mobile Armies of Metaphors":

Scheherazade Films the Games

The cover photograph of the young engineering student with the video-camera shows—projected onto her black chador from a spotlight inside the Fukuoka sports dome—the tricolored logo of the 2002 Sixth Annual Robo-Cup (robot soccer) games. Let this stand as an icon for a final set of reflections on mute dreams, blind owls, and dispersed knowledges; on the shifts beyond the "mobile army of metaphors" of Nietzsche and Hedayat to Mani-jeh Satrapi's comics and Samira Makhmalbaf's moving images; and on the democratic and aesthetic forces of cultural critique pressing against the asceticism of the fundamentalists (of Iran and of the United States) for an opening of the public sphere in both societies.[1]

> Mute Dreams and Just Gaming:
> Chess and Fables, RoboCup and Buzkashi
>
> 'Tis knowledge that doth make men live.—FIRDAUSI, *Shahnameh*

The Fukuoka games brought computer science teams to Japan from universities and a few corporations across the globe: a half dozen teams from Japan; five each from the United States and Germany; three from China; two from Sweden; one each from Singapore, New Zealand, India, Turkey, Italy, Portugal, Holland, Denmark, and France; and one collaborative team from Japan and Germany.[2] But the largest number of teams—seven—came from Iran, including one high-school team, Allameh Helli-Respina High School for the

Development of Exceptional Talents; a team from Sharif University, Iran's leading technical university; the Hanif Rescue Robot Team, composed of recent graduates from Sharif University; and one team each from Shahid Beheshti University, Isfahan University ("Persia"), Isfahan University of Technology ("IUT Flash"), and the Kavous-Javid Robotics Club. The Iranian teams took part in four of the six leagues: small- and midsized robots on wheels, disaster rescue robots on treads or on legs, and the simulation league, with two-dimensional flat and three-dimensional animation display, and a separate coaching-software competition. In 2004 Sharif University had sent an all-women's team, but in 2002 teams were co-ed. Only in the humanoid and Aibo leagues did Iran not enter teams.

The small-sized robots are the speediest and most fun to watch. One can see the advantages the different technologies offer. The Isfahan University of Technology, for instance, had six months earlier competed in the German Open and been beaten within three minutes by the technically superior Free University of Berlin robots. By the time they came to Fukuoka, the Iranian students had totally rebuilt their robots with omnidirectional wheels they had been given by the Free University and were among the teams with two overhead cameras for global vision (most teams still only had one overhead camera; only Cornell had three). This time their robots defended well but had no offensive kicking capabilities. It was heartrending to watch the little gizmos repeatedly deflect incoming German kicks, but when they retrieved the ball, it was as if they did not know how to kick, despite urging by the spectators. Still, their defensive game held off defeat for a full sixteen minutes.[3] With great optimism and enthusiasm, the students said they were more buoyed by their learning curve than disappointed by the loss. The highlight of the year's small-size robot matches was provided by Cornell's new dribbling bar, which enabled the robots to back up and maneuver without losing control of the ball in competition with the powerhouse teams from the Free University of Berlin, Queensland, and Carnegie-Mellon. Their lead scorer was a robot named Frodo.

RoboCup is not just games. A professional conference and a trade show of commercial robots (e.g., nursing, security, entertainment, toy, industrial, household, and cleaning robots) and educational, business, and research support tools occur in tandem with the games. RoboCup itself is intended to speed the development of new technologies: artificial intelligence, sensors, integrated circuits, graphics processing, communications, mechanisms, drive systems, power supplies, materials, including even biotechnology and nanotechnology. Hiroaki Kitano—the organizer of RoboCup and builder,

Iranian engineer at
sixth annual RoboCup
competition in Fukuoka,
Japan (2002). Photo by
author.

Buzkashi, painting by A. Batyr
(2002). From collection of the
author.

with Sony Corporation, of Pino, a partly open-source humanoid robot (in order to encourage collaborative development)—is a lead researcher in simulations of systems biology. The presumptive goal of RoboCup is to build robot teams that can beat human soccer teams by the year 2050. The rules are refreshed and upgraded each year to keep pace with the technological learning curve, to keep the games interesting, to ensure that technological development remains generic and not overly specialized for winning these particular games, and to force the pace of innovation. Each team is supposed to post its designs and techniques on the Web after the games so that others can learn, and the pace of technological innovation is stimulated.

For some teams, such as Cornell University, the games help teach undergraduates how to integrate different kinds of engineering into functional and innovative systems; each year the RoboCup, or integrated engineering, undergraduate course builds new small-size robots from scratch and tests them in the various competitions. Similarly, at Upsala, the big Swede Murphy, the world's largest humanoid robot (seven feet tall, weighing 140 kilograms, fully autonomous, powered by two twelve-volt motorcycle batteries, and with two laptop computers for a brain) is being built by a series of master's student teams as their term project. Each three months, a new team takes over. (On his way to Japan, Murphy lost his head in the airport in Amsterdam; the head, called "Murray," had to catch up with Murphy a day later.) For other teams, such as Carnegie Mellon, the robots are graduate-student research platforms: for instance, the algorithm for passing the ball in RoboCup also works for passing packets of bytes on a network; the minimal number of rules a multi-agent team needs to coordinate for a set of goals has uses in military communication (think helicopter squad) under conditions where one wants to broadcast a minimal number of signals (that might be monitored by an enemy) under time constraints and the need for precision (coordinated rescue or attack).

The successes and difficulties of the Iranian student teams provides an index of the diffusion and unevenness of global technologies. The students themselves are impressive for their quickness, their maturity, their English-language skills, their computer and Internet skills, and their ingenuity. An Iranian engineer and entrepreneur, Fereydun Taslimi, based in Atlanta, Georgia, who has not been back to Iran since the revolution, has been one of the leaders in setting up a foundation and organization in London and Atlanta to help Iranian student teams attend a variety of international competitions, not just RoboCup. One of the teams from Iran paid its bills in Japan with a credit card from a friend in New Jersey (credit cards do not exist in Iran). Aside from airfares, hotel costs, and fees in hard currency, among the challenges are the difficulties of getting components from the United States. Due to the U.S. embargo on trade with Iran, parts have to be bought from third parties (or be smuggled from Dubai) and so costs double or triple. Sharif University's mid-size robots were agile when they worked, but they had had trouble getting parts and little time to install and test them. A pneumatic component ordered three months earlier had arrived three days before the team left for Japan, and a camera only one day before they left. The teams have to build everything they can from scratch, which is good for learning, but slows them down. In 2001 Iranian teams prepared for the RoboCup competitions in Seattle, but the United States denied them visas. Still, it was a UCLA-trained computer-science graduate student, Jafar Adibi, who, going home to Iran, had popularized the idea of RoboCup, and the engineering professor-coaches are variously trained in the United States, England, Germany, and France. All the nuisances and obstacles aside, the primary problem is of a different order: the lack of technologically challenging jobs in Iran once these engineers graduate from school.

The RoboCup story is a contemporary fable that parallels the introduction of chess and the parables of Kalila and Dimma to the royal court of Nushiravan Adel as related in the *Shahnameh*. Chess and the fables came as substitutions for and teaching tools for war and dealing with adversity, both emotional and strategic, as means of developing the capacity for justice and the capacity for foresight beyond the next move. The book of fables grew, translated back and forth from oral to literate forms, memorized by Barzwi, who later recommitted them to writing, copied out by Bozorgmehr at the court of Nushiravan, translated into Arabic at the court of Mamun, into Persian at the Samanid court of Central Asia by Abu'l Fazl, and versified by Rudaki. Barzi had been sent to find the herb that brings the dead to life: " 'tis knowledge that doth make men live . . . Kalila is the herb, and understanding" (Firdausi 1010/1905, 7.427).

Among the greatest of such storytellers is, of course, Scheherezade, who tells a tale each night to the king Shariyar, or to her sister Duniyazad with the shah listening in. (Such triangles of indirect strategic control and maneuver between sovereign and subaltern storyteller is also the structure of the Ring of Gyges, the Greek myth of the origin of money, itself a means of control at a distance, and the similar story of Queen Esther at the Persian courts of Susa and Hamadan.) The stories of Scheherezade have resonated through the centuries. One of the notable recent versions is that of John Barth (1972), shaped as a commentary on the dilemmas of storytellers in the late twentieth century. That the textual versions of Scheherezade's stories have tended to

Fervor (Crowd from back, woman looking over her shoulder) (2000).
Gelatin silver print, 66 × 47 inches (167.6 × 119.4 cm.). © 2000
Shirin Neshat. *Photo by Larry Barns. Courtesy Barbara Gladstone.*

marginalize women is but a sign of the control of literacy by men, and one
can read between the lines, against the grain, for the erased female presences,
as Fadwa Malti-Douglas has brilliantly analyzed, a project that she and others
have begun to undertake for other literary classics and for the Qur'an and
hadith (Malti-Douglas 1991). Not only are there important women-warriors
in the medieval tales (Hanaway 1972), but in real-life Zoroastrian and Muslim
villages, the storytellers of work stories and shrine stories, which provide
insights into the world beyond and into the background social relations that
haunt everyday life, were women. Of these, I am most indebted to Banu Luti
of Nasrabad-e Yazd.

But just what is our contemporary Scheherezade filming, and why does

Offered Eyes (1993). RC
print and ink, 40 × 60 in.
© 1993 Shirin Neshat. *Photo
by Plauto. Courtesy Barbara
Gladstone.*

Rebellious Silence (1994).
B&W W RC print and ink,
11 × 14 in. © 1994 Shirin
Neshat. *Photo by Cynthia
Preston. Courtesy Barbara
Gladstone.*

Allegiance with Wakefulness (Women of Allah Series) (1994). B&W RC print and ink, 46¾ × 37⅛ in. © 1994 Shirin Neshat. Photo by Cynthia Preston. *Courtesy Barbara Gladstone.*

American soldier plays buzkashi. © 2001 AP/ World Wide Photos. Photo by Maxim Marmur.

she turn to the camera? Is the camera a third eye, one more of the female eyes that discipline local worlds, observing and registering from the openings in chadors and burqas, the space of both calligraphic writing upon the female body and the agentive calligraphic writing of the female in motion in the world, as in the haunting images of the photographer and video artist Shirin Neshat (1997, 1998, 1999a, 1999b, 2000, 2001; Neshat et al. 2002)? In the cover photograph, our engineer is recording her team, which is competing in the simulation league, in the Fukuoka sportsdome. Just as she, in the photograph, is a surface for projection and an agent of recording, so, too, is her video both a recording of the team's games and a tool for postmortem analysis for upgrades and software improvement. But the small screen insert at the bottom of the paperback cover montage—like a CNN split-screen report on the war, using a bluish noir filter as if deploying the filmic convention for signifying a different time frame or dream world—suggests another scene is being videographed: buzkashi, which, aside from chess, is the national sport of Afghanistan and Central Asia. Buzkashi in Afghanistan has, like soccer in Brazil, been tightly coupled to local and national political power games (Azoy 1982) and is also an image for the "Great Game" of competition between the Russian and British empires, today transmuted into the competition for Central Asian oil and gas. The insert is a painting by the Russian-Tajik painter A. Batyr, which I acquired in 2002 in Dushanbeh, where buzkashi remains important, especially at Noruz (New Year) celebrations. But the painting also evokes recent news photographs of young U.S. soldiers invited to saddle up and play buzkashi in the aftermath of the American war in Afghanistan to drive the Taliban from power ("it is time for the Americans to play the game"; *New York Times* 19 Dec. 2001, sec. A, p. 35).

Blind Owls and Jamshid's Cup:
2001: A Space Odyssey, the Freud-Nietzsche Couple

"And how could I bear to be a man if man were not also a poet [*Dichter*] and guesser of riddles and redeemer of accidents [*Erlöser des Zufalls*]?"—FRIEDRICH NIETZSCHE, *Thus Spoke Zarathustra*

"If we read the second half of Zarathustra's dream with attention to the images, figures and symbols that constitute its content . . . But if we read it with an eye to the cinematic form of its appearance . . ."
—ROBERT GOODING-WILLIAMS, *Zarathustra's Dionysian Modernism*

Das dialektische Bild malt den Traum nicht nach. (The dialectical image does not copy the dream in a painterly representation.) Die Ebne des Zeichens liegt von Menschen aus gesehen horizontal, die des Males vertikal. (The plane of the painting/sign is seen from the perspective of the human being, horizontal, that of the mark/painting, vertical.)
WALTER BENJAMIN, cited in Rainer Nägele, "Thinking Images"[4]

They say that when the Zoroastrian court of Yazdegird III fled before the invading Muslims, a number of the courtiers—perhaps even Yazdegird himself—continued across the Silk Road to the imperial court of China, and eventually a number of the royal objects came to be in Japan. In later times, the Parsis (Zoroastrians in India) built trading ships and plied opium and other trades between India and China, and small merchant communities with fire temples were established in various ports along the way. Hong Kong still has a small community. Similar mercantile outposts were established in Aden, Colombo, Madras, and Calcutta. The famed Parsi shipbuilders, the Wadias, built the HMS *Minden*, on which Francis Scott Key was detained by the British as they attacked Baltimore and on which he wrote the *Star Spangled Banner*. Nusserwangi Maneckji Wadia was among the first foreign donors to the East India Maritime Society Museum (now the Peabody Essex Museum) in Massachusetts. His portrait, by a Chinese artist, has hung in that museum since 1803.

In the other direction, Zoroastrian ideas via Manicheanism and, perhaps, the Mithra cult filtered into the Roman Empire and was absorbed into the mix that became Christianity and the various heterodoxies of Bogomils, Sarmatians, Albigensians, Cathars, Kudugers, Patarenes, Phundaites, Poplicanti, Ruekelers, and gnostics.[5] In the eighteenth century, the memory of Zarathustra revived in Europe, beginning perhaps with Thomas Hyde's collation at Oxford in 1700 of references to Zoroaster in Greek, Latin, Hebrew, and Arabic. In 1718 Bouchier of the East India Company brought a copy of the *Vendidad* from India and deposited it in the Bodelian Libary at Oxford. In 1730, when the composer Rameau was forbidden, on the grounds of blasphemy, to stage an opera about Samson, he wrote one about Zoroaster instead. In 1758 Abraham Hycacynthe Anquetil du Perron made his way to Surat, cajoling the Zoroastrian priests there and playing one off against another, to teach him Avestan. His translations of the Avesta (1771) were a sensation in Europe, albeit dismissed as nonsensical by no less than William Jones, who later, however, having become one of England's leading Sanskritists, would be impressed by the similarity of Avestan and Sanskrit. Mozart incorporated a variant memory of "Soastre" in his 1791 opera *The Magic Flute*. The 1850s and 1860s, the height of philological discussions of the relations between Sanskrit and Avestan, were the decades when Friedrich Nietzsche was training as a philologist. Nietzsche was an enthusiast of Ralph Waldo Emerson, who wrote both about the oversoul and Rustam and Sohrab. Matthew Arnold, in 1853, also wrote a version of the Sohrab and Rustam story that became very popular.

Nietzsche's *Also Sprach Zarathustra* (1883–1885) became one of the master texts of the late nineteenth century, both in German-speaking and other parts of Europe. Richard Strauss set it to music in 1896, subtitling his composition "Symphonic optimism in *fin de siècle* form, dedicated to the twentieth century."[6] Seventy years later, Stanley Kubrick would use the opening bars of Strauss's tone poem in the film *2001: A Space Odyssey* (1968), and it became an ubiquitous sound of late-twentieth-century popular culture. Strauss described his work as an effort to liberate man through laughter from his alienation from nature (Zoroaster laughs at birth, one of the many signs of his difference from ordinary children). In the tone poem's "Science Fugue," Strauss, preceding Schoenberg by fourteen years, used all twelve notes of the chromatic scale. Throughout, "the two remotest keys," C major (nature) and B major (humanity), alternate until at the end they are heard simultaneously. In a set of systematic associations, Strauss used D minor to characterize despair, B minor longing, A-flat major for the passion theme stated by the brass, and so on.[7] Kubrick's film, coinciding with the first moon landings, pioneered a front-projection system and a slit-scan machine that would become important to the film industry and its special effects visual technologies.[8] The film paid homage to the post–World War II, Cold War era, as well as to the nascent computer and robotic space age, in its use of Strauss's waltz *The Blue Danube* in association with the revolving space station, a visual nod to the revolving Ferris wheel in Vienna's Prater Gardens highlighted in Graham Greene and Alexander Korda's *The Third Man* (1949).[9]

The Ferris wheel is not inapt to Nietzsche's famous line from Zarathustra, "Man is a rope stretched between beast and superman—a rope over an abyss [*Abgrund*]," with regard to its carnival setting and to Zarathustra's many meditations on the circle, eternal return, the circling eagle with friendly coiled serpent around its neck, the ring (of the Zoroastrian saoshyant-redeemer), the parodies of Ecclesiastes 7.13, Neoplatonism, and Paul's account of the descent and ascent of Jesus;[10] it also aptly echoes Zarathustra's retort to the dwarf's cynical "everything straight lies, all truth is crooked, time itself is a circle" that the dwarf has not yet grasped the riddle of return to life and new creation. Mimicking the going-under and over-coming of the Ferris wheel, the tightrope walker falls in a dizzy whirl of arms and legs [*Wirbel von Armen und Beinen*], forced, like Oedipus, to confront a destiny he seeks to escape. Called Lamfuss (Lame One, Oedipus) by the jester who jumps over him, the tightrope walker prefigures, warn the gravediggers, Zarathustra's own death/failure. Kubrick's *2001: A Space Odyssey* has its own variant of the tightrope between beast and superman, moving from images of ape to man to, finally, star-child or Zoro-*aster*, playing on the false Greek etymology for the Iranian's name.

Zarathustra's mission is to find a way beyond all these naysayers, and this, in "On the Vision and the Riddle," is the message of the vivid dreamwork and rewinding of the reel of his childhood at the Gate of the Moment, where the roads to the eternities of the past and future converge, in one direction separated by the limen of only the blink of an eye (*Augenblick*), a vanishing point or a separation as minute as that of a phoneme from its others, in the other direction the two eternities as if circling back onto the same (eternity). ("For Zarathustra, the present moment is privileged in that it enables him to envision the whole of time as an eternally present moment" [Gooding-Williams 2001, 221]). It is here that Zarathustra poses his two riddles to the dwarf and suddenly hears a dog howling—in Zoroastrian funerary ritual, four-eyed dogs see into the next world, the world of ghosts and demons of impurity—and his thoughts race back to his childhood, reminding him of a scene when he heard a similar dog howling.

> And I saw him too, bristling, his head up, trembling in the stillest midnight when even dogs believe in ghosts. . . . [J]ust then the full moon, silent as death, passed over the house; just then it stood still, a round glow—still on the flat roof, as if on another's property—that was why the dog was terrified, for dogs believe in thieves and ghosts. . . . [T]here lay a man. . . . A young shepherd I saw, writhing, gagging, in spasms, his face distorted, and a heavy black snake hung out of his mouth. . . . My hands tore at the snake and tore in vain. . . . Then it cried out of me: "Bite! Bite its head off! Bite!" . . . You who are glad of riddles, guess me the riddle. . . . What did I see then in a parable. . . . [H]e bit with a good bite. . . . No longer shepherd, no longer human—one changed, radiant, laughing! . . . [N]o human laughter. (qtd. from Walter Kaufmann's translation, in Gooding-Williams 2001, 226)

The dreamwork is a structure of inversions: while the eagle soars high in the shadowless, actively shining midday sun, carrying the friendly, gold-colored serpent of discernment, master of disguise and metamorphosis; the black snake down under in the midnight of shadows and ghosts, in the stolen light of the moon, grabs the back of the throat of the prostrate, gagging, suffocating shepherd (Zarathustra). Zarathustra viscerally struggles for life, biting off the head of the snake, a figuration of self-transformation and awakening. He is no longer caught in the nightmare of retraumatizations, past experiences, and recurrences as are the human rabble merely going through the motions of life. Rewinding the reel of childhood to the beginning, he can begin anew, a "return to self."[11] In childlike creative play, he is one who laughs (again Zoroaster, like certain other prophets and culture heroes, is said to have been born laughing).

Apart from the parodies, allusions, symbolisms, and allegories, at issue in *Also Sprach Zarathustra* is a more fundamental question of whether sensory images not only provide a richer "language" than verbal, conceptual philosophies, but also provide means for self-renewal of healthy body and community. While this discussion traditionally included the use of the Olympian middle world of the arts—music-dance, painting-writing—to overcome the terrors of the world, paralleling the 'alam al-mithal interzone of images in Suhrawardi, nineteenth-century discussions increasingly focused on the physical exhaustion and neurasthenia produced by modernity, of the demonic powers of metaphor and poesis to pervert logic and passion, and thus of the physiological restorative possibilities of music and *Gesamtkunstwerke*. These form a context for Zarathustra's riddles, and as Gooding-Williams points out, "*Zarathustra*, if performed, would incorporate poetry, song and dance. . . . [It] is oriental myth, Wagnerian opera, spirited evangelism, and secular culture critique, yet never seems reducible to any one of these categories" (2001, 21–22). *Also Sprach Zarathustra* is also, Zarathustra says of himself, composed in a stammer: "Stammering is characterized by an opposition between a speaker's intentions and her involuntary repetition of words she has already spoken," a figure of the almost Freudian situation that "despite a speaker's intentions, her future is destined to repeat her past" (ibid., 22–23).

Does this recursive stammer, traditionally attributed to Moses and to poets, also become, over the course of the century after Nietzsche, a figure for the camera shutter and the serialism, jump cuts, repetitions, and montage editing characteristic of filmwork? Indeed, at one point in his reading of Zarathustra's dream "On the Vision and the Riddle," Gooding-Williams suddenly finds himself musing that if one reads it "with an eye to the cinematic form of its appearance" (ibid., 28) one gets a different result than if one reads it through a hermeneutics of its content.

Along with Goethe, Hölderlin, Hegel, and Wagner, Nietzsche is part of a tradition of discussion about the nature of tragedy and poesis and about the changing nature of representation, staging (*Darstellen*), imaging (*Vorstellen*), graphic or legible (re)construction, impartibility or communication (*Mitteilungen*), and production of a politically conscious body politic. Hölderlin's translations of Sophocles provided materials for considering how Greek tragedies constitute a dissection of myth into dramatic moments. The original unity of the world of myth—or, for Iran, of the Pishdadians—is broken into the heroic forms (Kayanians) of dissonance and separation. Tragedy is "the enactment of a general poetic necessity to disperse and disseminate all unity and totality into sequential moments" (Nägele 2002, 26). The law of succession (verbal strings, dynastic succession, sovereignty) is the law of poetics. The shattering of unities into humanly usable communication and dissemination—the biblical breaking of the tablets of God, the fragmentary revelations over twenty-three years to Muhammad recollected in the Qur'an in a sequence that differs from that of the heavenly *Umm al-Kitab* (see Fischer and Abedi 1990, 102–3, 464n11)—involves both transport (metaphor) and moments of presentist arrest (images, frames, Vorstellen). The German term *Mitteilbarkeit* contains this double meaning of division or shattering into parts and communication, and as the discussion has moved from the nineteenth-century music to twentieth-century film (Nietzsche to Benjamin and Deleuze), and from film to digital media, the nature of the communicative structures have increased their divisibility (*Teilbarkeit*) and thus their potentials for reconfiguring the sensorium and the body politic. Benjamin's vocabulary foregrounds this reconfigurable virtuality: translatability, recognizability, criticizability, reproducibility, legibility (McLaughlin 2002, 209).[12] It is this partibility, separability, differentiability that makes it a language of and for (models of and for) judgment (*Urteil*).

Iranian modernism tracks a similar course from Sayyid Mohammad Ali Jamalzadeh's pathbreaking short stories, which he wrote in simple colloquial language, to Hedayat's use of surrealism, Iranian New Wave and postrevolution filmmaking, and Iranian diaspora experimental video and performance arts. (Jamalzadeh justified his use of simple language with a couplet from the poet Farokhi, a contemporary of Firdausi [compare Nietzsche's *Zarathustra*]: Fasaneh gozasht kohan shod hadis Eskendar / Sokhan navar ke no-ra halavati ast digar [Old myths have worn out: the story of Alexander / Word strings which are new are henceforth sweeter]).[13] As Akbar Tajvidi wrote in an essay introducing a traveling exhibition of contemporary Iranian paintings, which toured the United States in 1962, "We too are living in the Century of Machinery, Speed, and the Atom" (Balaghi and Gumpert 2002, 21–22).

Nietzsche's *Zarathustra* is composed in a series of riddles, challenging one to move beyond "the three images of man which our modern age has set up . . . the man of Rousseau, the man of Goethe, and finally the man of Schopenhauer,"[14] none of which will bring redemption from the martyr-stake (*Marterholz*) of failure to transform embodied passion, modern culture, or to create new values. Not the "fire hound bellowing smoke and ashes like a volcanic mountain" of the modern revolutionary (the man of Rousseau), not the nourishing of self on all that is "great and memorable" (Goethe's Faust), not the annihilation of the worldly self and turning to the inner will-in-itself (Schopenhauer).[15] Zarathustra searches beyond the camel's burden of redeeming the past and beyond the lion's pretensions to create with pure will to the child's creation of the new out of a Dionysian revaluing of the earthly passions. Zarathustra sees three redemptions in the shibboleth "eternal recurrence": the bricoleur reuse of fragments of the past; reliance on the will to make something of the present; keeping open the possibilities for the future.

It is tempting to see the post-Nietzschean development of communicative structures in Iran (and elsewhere) as proleptic readings and possible or virtual solutions (*Erlösung*) to Zarathustra's riddles. The first redemption is that of the bricoleur who, Freudlike, works to make irrational chaos into rational ego control. Freud's version: "Wo das Es war, da wird Ich sein" [Where the it/id was, there I/ego shall be]. Nietzsche's version through Zarathustra: "To recreate [*umzuschaffen*] all 'it was' into a 'thus I willed it'—that alone should I call redemption [*Erlösung*]" (Nietzsche 1883–1885/1961, 251). This will to recreate is described in a passage that could have been thought by any Iranian lieutenant on the battlefield who carried Hedayat's *The Blind Owl* secreted in his pocket, or by any Iranian filmmaker (a Mohsen Makhmalbaf, perhaps, or an Ebrahim Hatimikia): "Verily my friends, I walk among men as among the fragments and limbs of men. . . . I find man in ruins and scattered as over a battlefield or a butcher field. And when my eyes flee from the now to the past, they always find the same. . . . I walk among men as among the fragments of the future—that future which I envisage. And this is all my poesis [*Dichten*] and striving, that I compose and carry together into one what is fragment and riddle and dreadful accident. And how could I bear to be a man if man were not also a poet and guesser of riddles and redeemer of accidents" (ibid., 250–51). The second would-be redemption, creation with pure will, but still under the ascetic ideals of renunciation of Dionysian life might be thought of as those—the Council of Guardians, the Komitehs and Pasdaran—who block elected parliaments, shut down newspapers, and enforce restrictive codes of dress and behavior. The lion-spirit of pure will is inefficacious (forcibly imposed, riddled with corruption, and the exercise of pure power without concern for changing grounds of legitimacy).

The third redemption, the one toward which Zarathustra works, is that of the yea-saying child, of the play of repetitions with differences. One might see it as a representation (Vorstellung) of the promises (and, for better or worse, realities) of the three great revolutions of the twentieth century: molecular biology, computer science, and film. All are operas of repetitions with differences, and thereby the creation of the new. In biology, repetition with a difference is a mutation or experimental system that generates surprises in a logic of displacement and increasingly allows us to engineer or assemble molecules that never before existed, allowing us not just to understand life but to write new life with biologicals. While Nietzsche could not know contemporary genomics or proteonomics, his Zarathustra speaks of man as "an experiment in whose body dwell the mistakes of millennia" (Gooding-Williams 2001, 206): "Alas much ignorance and error have become body within us. Not only the reason of millennia, but their madness too, breaks out in us" (Nietzsche 1883–1885/1961, 281). In computer science, repetition with a difference is the play of ones and zeros, the expansion of binary oppositions and complementary distributions, the pro-gramming, algorithms, and generation of complex infrastructures that no one individual can understand and that can both serve as prostheses for humans and also embed them in larger cybernetic or cyborg systems. And in film, repetition with a difference is both the speed of frames repeating and slightly changing to produce the sensation of motion, and also a new visual rhetoric, operating in the dimension of time (or *duree*), rearranging time with montage, frame, and shots, citations and allusions, hieroglyphs and figural movements—and thereby also rearranging judgment and perception.

It is not much of a stretch to see Iranian film as instantiating these shifts speculatively foreseen by Nietzsche's *Zarathustra* in his meditations on the ills of modernity. The age-old metaphor, and model, of the child as the site of not just renewal but of revaluation, creation of the different new, is one that Iranian postrevolutionary film has sometimes privileged through the works of Abbas Kiarostami, Beza'i's *Bashu*, Naderi's *The Runner*, and others, rather than the metaphor of the New Man that Soviet film projected, and that communist-era East European filmmakers such as Andrzej Wajda spent their energy critiquing.

The new generation in Iran—and in the diaspora—is beginning to produce dramatically new visions, weaving into the tightrope of life many new strands in film (Samira Makhmalbaf, Bahman Qobadi, Maziar Bahari) and in other media as well.

Dispersed Knowledges: Staging the Simorgh, Karbala, and Googoosh in New York

man nemidanam ghezavat chist
agar mikhanam ke jorm ast
man nemikhanam ke jorm ast
ke dar tan khosh sakht e in molk e ghadimi
ke ghadimi tar be tarikh ast
khandanam kay mitavanad jorm bashad
ke zartosht ba sorood in sarzamin ra kasht
ba sorood in sarzamin ra
man agar khandam baraye bachehayesh
baraye madaran e ghargh gerye
gerey ra avaz khaham kard
gerey ra avaz khaham kard
[I don't know what this judgment is
that if I sing it is a crime
I don't sing because it is a crime
that in this dry body of this ancient land
that is more ancient than history itself
when came my singing to be a crime
in the land Zarathustra sowed with song
with song sowed the land
If I sing it is for his children
for the mothers in tears
I will turn tears to song
I will turn tears to song]
—GOOGOOSH [FAEGHEH ATASHIN], *Zartosht*

2001–2002: As with RoboCup, Persian culture managed to slip in, through, and around the Bush Administration's embargo and harassment of cultural flows and exchanges:[16] pop-music star Googoosh sang in New York, Los

Angeles, and elsewhere; Shirin Neshat staged a video and performance, *Logic of the Birds*, an abstract interpretation of the story of the Simorgh in Attar's *Conference of the Birds*, starring the vocalist Sussan Deyhim, at the Kitchen in New York; and three taziyeh, passion plays of the events at Karbala, were staged in a tent at Lincoln Center by Muhammad Ghafuri with actors from villages near Isfahan, despite the fact that the Bush Administration refused visas to half the cast.[17] In a gesture of arbitrary harassment, the Bush Administration also refused visas to filmmakers Abbas Kiarostami and Bahman Qobadi: both had been to the States before and were invited to appear with their films at the Museum of Modern Art in New York and the Museum of Fine Arts in Boston. Nonetheless, there was a fair amount of individual movement back and forth between Iran and the United States, including three workshop meetings between the U.S. National Academy of Sciences, National Academy of Engineering, and Institute of Medicine and the Iranian Academies of Science.

Walter Benjamin spoke of film as having the functions of providing a second chance in learning to deal with the assaults of technological modernity and of providing means of learning and play in properly integrating the feedback between technologies, human sensorium, and body politic. Play is the repetitive iterability that is given license in ludic performance, the virtuality of possible futures that can be experimented with. Models of such mimetic "innervations" or rewirings of the nervous systems of both the individual body and the collective civic body include childhood, writing, advertising, dreaming, eros, and politics (Miriam Hansen 2002, 61; Taussig 1992). The child, as Benjamin reminds us, "plays at being not only a shopkeeper or teacher, but also a windmill and a train"; children practice inventive reception of a new world of things (Miriam Hansen 2002, 61). Advertising, like film, redramatizes one's relation to things and hits one between the eyes with things, "like a car growing to gigantic proportions careens at us out of a film screen" or billboard (qtd. in ibid., 64). The optical unconscious makes visible "another nature which speaks to the camera rather than to the eye," which through the fracturing, alienating techniques of the film editing, does "not merely depict a given world, but makes that world visible for the first time, produces it for the sensoria of a spectating collective, and opens up a new region of consciousness" (ibid., 68).

But the flow of images, as in nineteenth-century discussions about the daemonic transports of metaphor, needs to be arrested, formed into legibility, critiquability, and reconfigurability. Benjamin's notion of the image, Nägele reminds us, is "not the mimetically inflected painterly image, but a literalized graphic or rhetorical figure" that "hovers in a spectral sphere because it struggles to name something that is both living and dead" (2002, 9). The image, or Vorstellung, for Benjamin as for Hölderlin, "comes to a standstill at the *Stelle*, the place of its interruption; the rushing images, ideas, sensations coalesce in a figure to be read" (ibid., 29).

Two pieces of artwork—a watercolor and an engraving—served Benjamin as touchstones. Paul Klee's *Angelus Novus*, as has been much commented on, provided Benjamin with a "picture for meditation" of such a figure hovering in a spectral sphere of a *malakh* (Hebr. messenger-angel) with torah scrolls as his curly hair (the Talmudic angel, perhaps, who once he had sung his psalm to God evaporated into nothingness), and of the saturnine Owl of Minerva blown backward and unable to close its wings against the winds of the catastrophes of history (which found its way into the ninth thesis of Benjamin's 1940 "The Concept of History" in response to the Stalin-Hitler pact) (Miriam Hansen 2002, 174–75).

Albrecht Dürer's engraving *Melancholia I* (1514) provided a dialectical image at the tipping point between two epistemes: that of Dürer's own time between the Middle Ages and the Renaissance and that of Benjamin's time at the transition to our contemporary modernity; it inspired his reworking of melancholia as a representation (*Darstellung*) of the "technique of disclosure" (ibid., 181). Melancholia, once a disease of the humors, later a character type, came under the astrological and cosmological symbols of saturnine manic-depressive swings of mood between sublime exultation (Zarathustra's bliss in the noon sun at the Gate of the Moment) and despondency (the midnight of thieves and ghosts). Such saturnine extremes became the Renaissance and Romantic tropes of the winged genius, riding on the violence and power of the "ripping shifts of representations" of Hölderlin's poetics (ibid., 179). For Benjamin, in a world of remains and ruins after the flight of the gods, human beings are challenged to read the spectral relays between pasts and futures. This task of the translator is to make legible, critiqueable, reconfigurable naive historicisms and political legitimations or ideological readings of history, to show how their modes of presentation are constructed. For Benjamin, this meant also an investigation into the nervous system of the civic polity. Updating Zarathustra's (and Hedayat's) metaphor of the rabble as having suffered warlike ravages ("Verily my friends, I walk among men as among the fragments and limbs of men. . . . I find man in ruins and scattered as over a battlefield or a butcher field"), Benjamin reflected in 1928 on the effects of World War I on the planet's physical and social nervous systems: "Human multitudes, gases, electrical forces were hurled into the open country, high-frequency currents coursed through the landscape, . . . aerial space and ocean depths thundered with propellers, and everywhere sacrificial shafts were dug . . . for the first time on a planetary scale" (cited in Mark Hansen 2000, 254). To pay attention to the "technological-becoming" that man is always already undergoing is one of the functions of film, not just in its optical and theatrical presentation (Darstellung) but also in its "tactility" and play with the nervous system of the audience and in its potential for rewiring the members of the audience as members of the civic polity.

Melancholia is also a master Iranian trope, stemming from the same humoral, Galenic roots, taking on the same philosophical anxieties about gravitas and passion. It is figured most dramatically in the images of Ayatullah Ruhullah Khomeini, which always depict him as unsmiling (Fischer 1983; Fischer and Abedi 1990, 374, 376). But it also figures in popular commentaries on contrasts between Zoroastrian optimism and Shi'ite melancholic realism, as well as in Reza Shah's modernist campaign against a ritual calendar focused on mourning. The passion plays of the Karbala paradigm parallel Benjamin's account of the German baroque *Trauerspiel* (tragedy). They also have roots in the ancient Zoroastrian, or at least Central Asian, mourning for the hero Siyavush.[18] During the revolution, Khomeini played the Karbala paradigm like a liturgical organ of the civic body's nervous system; during the 1977–1979 revolutionary process, mourning was turned to active witnessing in the form of political demonstrations—one does not cry for Husain's death but witnesses to the truth of his message for social justice by actively engaging in making it come about. It was a mobilizing tool for mass demonstrations around the year. After the revolution, Khomeini tried to turn off activist passions. The smiling visage of President Khatami and his call for a more individuated and democratic polity is part of this struggle over representation in both the domestic and transnational public spheres.

Muhammad Ghaffuri's staging (Darstellung) of three traditional mourning plays (*shabih*, taziyeh, Trauerspiel, passion plays) for the death of Imam Husain at Karbala at Lincoln Center in 2002 provides a venue for asking questions about impartability (Mitteilung). What happens when religious ritual performances are transported to the New York stage? What happens for the actors beyond importing clothes, compact discs, videocassettes, electronics, other commodities, and newly made experiences on their return to Iran? Do these individuals and these things become now activated vectors in transnational capillaries? What recognizabilities and acknowlgeabilities can a New York audience bring to such performances, stripped of locality, context, familiarity, and political resonances? Are the passion (salvational, emotional), the theatrical power, or the philosophical registers (stoicism, determination to struggle for justice against all odds) translatable, and do they travel together or separately? (The extraordinary range of the singer-actors, their theatrical stage-presence, especially that of the children, and the power of their stylized movements and blocking were the subject of much audience comment and admiration. In Iran the passion aroused against Yezid, the villainous representative of injustice in the world leads, occasionally in fact and often in story, to enraged spectators beating the actor.) What was going on in the minds and emotions of the Iranians who live in America and had never seen a taziyeh (the diaspora generation born or raised in America; minorities who might not have had a chance or dared be present at a taziyeh in Iran; secularists or Muslims who, in Iran, had been opposed on moral and philosophical grounds to such wild Dionysian passions)?

How does such a performance at Lincoln Center compare to the circulation of pop-music star Googoosh in the great diasporic and transnational nodes of New York, Los Angeles, Houston, Washington, Toronto, and elsewhere? A young Iranian American who left Iran at age two, in attendance at New York Nassau Coliseum, made the analogy breezily: "The concert," she wrote in several venues, obviously savoring the line, "was more like a collective *rowzeh-khani* (preachment form framed by the story of Karbala and mourning), a tearful cleansing bash, sort of like an EST personal growth meeting with 12,000 people crying all at once" (Sabety 2001). She went on to make a somewhat less dismissive analysis of the appeal of this icon of pre-revolutionary Iran. Bahman Bagheri, who went to Houston's Compaq Center to see Googoosh, read Sabety's comment and replied, "I didn't see much crying" (2001). Both agreed, however, that nostalgic passion was intense. Googoosh was Iran's Shirley Temple and Madonna, working from childhood on as an actress and later as a pop singer. Sabety (2001) describes her music before the revolution as what today might be called transnational popular music, and it is that feature that makes it of interest for studies of the transnational circuits of media culture.

> Shamelessly pastiche and heavily synthesized and orchestrated. She sang happy songs in the Italian pop style of the sixties (Khalvat) and love songs in the style of French singer Mireille Mattiew and rock songs in English (like Carol King's "Its too late"). She had what was considered a modern sound and an extraordinary ability to accompany it with meaningful gestures.

Although she repeatedly and enthusiastically sang in other languages, her big hits were all in a modern, simple but poetic Farsi that bestowed a certain classiness to the female desire that she expressed. The orchestrated, synthesized Western-style music and the modern poetry (*shaer-e-now*) along with her gestures, which were at once bold and restrained, provided a new language within which female sexuality and desire could be expressed without fear of sinking into vulgarity.

Googoosh's current show as an act on the transnational circuit is better described by Bagheri (2001): a band of fifteen, including musicians from the United States, Cuba, and Venezuela, at a professional standard to which ethnic shows often do not rise ("Tehrangeles has been put on alert!"). But like Sabety, Bagheri was not impressed by the quality of the newer songs in comparison to those of the 1970s. He attributed this in part to Googoosh's musical director and lead guitarist, Babak Amini ("does not compose or arrange at the level of the Persian Pop masters of yesteryear such as Chesm Azar, Varoozhan or Shamaie-Zadeh"; ibid.). In part, the songs had to do with a current moment ("they are all sad and obviously very political"; ibid.), and Bagheri calls for a bit of reflexivity about the role that Googoosh plays in everyone's expectations: "people need to cut Googoosh some slack. All the talk about the politics involved with her tour and whether or not we should go to her concerts was totally out of place. We should not complicate this matter beyond what it really amounts to. Googoosh is just a popular singer who touches a soft spot in our hearts, because she was and still is so good at what she does and because she takes us back to our youth (for some of us back to our childhood)" (ibid.).

"Just a popular singer." If Ghaffuri's taziyehs are an opportunity to read a powerful religious and political ritual in transposed contexts (under the marquee of Walter Benjamin, in a tent at Lincoln Center), the North American concerts of Googoosh are an opportunity to read the workings of a popular-culture icon across historical horizons as well as across a diaspora circuit. Sabety (2001) traces the meaning of Googoosh's style for women in the 1970s and acknowledges that the repression of her singing voice for two decades has only increased its nostalgic power as a renewed symbol of resistance to the religious hard-liners in Tehran: "In these twenty years a quiet 'lipstick feminism' which Googoosh epitomizes has stubbornly resisted the regime. . . . The loudest applause comes when she utters her desire to give a concert, some day, in Iran." Sabety, Bagheri, and other commentators write of what Nietzsche might have called the dipping into the chaos of Dionysian passions (nostalgia, guilt, identification, pleasure; tears and laughter) to re-energize a joyous sense of will to life, one that works through Mitteilungen (impartability, communication), Urteil (judgment), and dispersion.

If Ghaffuri's taziyehs bring stagings from Iran to the United States, and if Googoosh's concerts are stagings that cannot yet happen in Iran, Shirin Neshat's work stages the diaspora itself across media, creating hypertexts or layered palimpsests of photography, calligraphy, bodies in calligraphic processions, video, performance, dance, vocalization, song, and poetic form. *Logic of the Birds*, staged at the Kitchen in New York and Union Chapel in London, is an abstract fusion of electronic music and vocal soundscapes performed live by Sussan Deyhim, choreographed with a thirty-person chorus, and cinematography by the filmmaker Ghasem Ebrahimian.[19] When the on-screen heroine walks into a lake and disappears under its surface, the electronic soundtrack and Deyhim, who is onstage, gurgle. It is often impossible to tell if the keening ululations and flights of vocalization are Deyhim or the synthesizers, as they blend in and out of one another. Deyhim's phenomenal voice and stage presence convince that the allegorical journey is momentous, even though its meaning is left enigmatic. Deyhim emerges onscreen walking through mud and fire, the rough, apocalyptic, coal-mine terrain of Pennsylvania, where it was actually shot, evoking the battle-scarred terrain and burning oilfields of the Iran-Iraq War. At another point, a circle of people surround a man, taunting and pushing, on the verge of riot. The travelers proceed across a Beckett-like, empty, desiccated, rugged landscape, themselves sometimes seeming more like the characters in a calligraphic writing of obscure import.

To the extent that the piece succeeds, we are now in the realm of figural form, legible and certainly im-part-able, albeit of somewhat inscrutable content beyond the dance of social forms and emotions. The hieroglyphs of Iranian cinema similarly draw on rich and deep legacies of ritual, parable, and *Bilderrede* (talking or thinking through images). These have now become, like other elements of Iranian culture, part of the transnational circuitry: Kiarostami in his car seat (*Taste of Cherry*) or running up the hill to get a clear cell-phone reception (*The Wind Will Carry Us*); Mohsen Makhmalbaf's prosthetic legs dropping from helicopters to landmine-damaged Afghans (*Safar-e Qandahar*); Beza'i's truck bearing Bashu north and the schoolbook that shows his schoolboy peers that he, too, is Iranian (*Bashu, the Little Stranger*); Hatimikia's glass houses and airplanes taken hostage in the cause of medical care (*Ajans Shishe* and *Low Heights*); Kiarostami's and Mohsen Makhmalbaf's cameras of judgment (*Close Up* and *Arusi Khuban*, respec-

tively); Samira Makhmalbaf's teachers using their blackboards as camouflage, stretchers, and ritual separators for marriage and divorce (*The Blackboard*); Qobadi's mules and singers looking for the pomegranate (hanareh)
of life (*The Time of the Drunken Horses* and *Marooned in Iraq*). Such everyday
material things—cars, cell phones, prostheses, schoolbooks, hostage-taking
and hostage-rescue strategies and weapons, blackboards, pomegranates—are
as important to defining, representing, and reconstructing the world today as
Adam Smith's pin factory, Karl Marx's textile mills, or Benjamin's Parisian
arcades and catacombs, Mississippi River levees, and cinema gymnasia of the
senses were in defining their times. These material things and their relations
and representations are important, not because they are ubiquitous elements
of global life, but rather because they hit us between the eyes "like a car
growing to gigantic proportions careens at us out of a film screen," shocking
us into thinking about the spectral relays that carry the changes in interpersonal relations and ethical challenges to which we need to stay emotionally
alive and ethically awake. The play of cinema works both on our nervous
systems and our brains, providing alternative configurations that can shatter
ideologies and technophysiological infrastructures, giving us another chance
to laugh and interact, comment, and reconstruct—to make mute dreams
speak (be legible), blind (backward flying) owls see (ahead), and dispersed
knowledges be recognized as the resources they are.

Notes

Acknowledgments

1   The foundation takes its name from the Latin word for evergreen holly or holm oak. It was founded and chaired by Olga "Holly" M. Davidson. Trustees include her husband, the Harvard classicist Gregory Nagy; and Muhammad Ja'far Mahallati, a former ambassador of the Islamic Republic of the United Nations (1987–89), a son of the leading Ayatullah of Shiraz before the revolution, holder of a B.S. degree from the University of Kansas (q.v. in Fischer and Abedi 1986), a M.S. from Oregon, the rank of Hojat-ul-Islam (as of 2000), and a Ph.D. candidate from the Islamic Institute at McGill University.

2   For the texts of these stories as told by the ladies of Yazd, see Fischer 1973.

Prelude

1   There are two main characters. One, in blinders, utters only nonverbal sounds. The other teaches, disciplines, directs, and tortures the first through a series of pedagogical, disciplinary, and sadomasochistic interactions. Insofar as dreaming is being mimed, both characters constitute the sleeper. Video images of these characters performing actions other than those being enacted onstage are projected on screens behind them. These filmed actions of the characters in other times, places, or actions are superimposed on images of crumpled newspapers, signifying perhaps stories crumpled, made nonlinear, fragmented, or folded back on themselves. At the front of the proscenium, a light metallic mesh further hems the characters in. A third figure, who sits to the side, below the proscenium, engages in a gestural language of hand and finger movements as if signing the meanings to the audience. The labile, prearticulate synesthesia of the three characters enacts a partial analog for the exercise of the senses—sensual, partially sentient—in the gymnasium of film.

2 See Lyotard 1979, Harvey 1990, Jameson 1991, Baudrillard 1994, Beck 1997/2000, Poster 2000, Castells 1996, Castells 1998.

3 Herodotus famously wrote of the Persian postal system in words that remain the creed for the U.S. Postal Service: "This is how the Persians arranged it: they saw that for as many days as the whole journey consists—there is nothing of human making that is quicker than this system of messengers—in, that many horses and men are stationed at intervals of a day's journey, one horse and one man assigned to each day. *Neither snow nor rain nor heat nor night holds back for the accomplishment of the course* that has been assigned to him, as quickly as he may" (*Histories* 8, 98; emphasis added).

4 See Fischer and Abedi 1990, chap. 6; Hanaway 1985. For color images, see also the coffee-table book by Chelkowski and Dabashi (2001).

5 One thinks of the Grimms in Germany, Yangit Kunio in Japan, Itzik Manger for Yiddish Poland, and Sadeq Hedayat in Iran. "In the West, Ernest Renan perceptively pointed out how France was made, not by shared memories, but by a shared amnesia, and he opposed the intrusion of ethnology in politics: will, not ethnography, was to be the basis of the state. . . . But in the eastern half of Europe, things were different. The Czechs, for instance, tried to buttress their own identity and existence by a medieval epic which was shown to be a forgery during the period when [Bronislaw] Malinowski was growing up. The Russians possess a similar piece of literature whose status continues to be disputed to this day. . . . There cannot be much serious doubt concerning the motives of his ahistoricism in anthropology" (Gellner 1988, 175).

6 On the gahambars, kheirats, pilgrimages, funerary memorials, and other communal rituals in the Yazd communities, see Fischer 1973, 1990; Boyce 1977.

7 Under the circumstances of continuous pressure from Muslim clerics and others to delegitimize all non-Islamic practices, and if possible to convert all to Islam, this rule of thumb was prudent. Even well-meaning Muslim individuals might come under pressure from the religiously mobilized Muslim activists, with negative results for the Zoroastrians. On this history, as well as the correlation between anti-minority riots in provincial Iran since the mid-nineteenth century and politics aimed at the national stage, see Fischer 1973.

Prologue

1 An outline of the ritual structure and chapter subtitles are provided as an aid or reference index on page 35.

2 A recent mystical interpretation of Zoroastrianism was developed by the so-called Ilm-i Khsnoom among the Gujurat and Bombay communities. Other forms of guru- or sufi master–based mysticism were developed by several migrants from Iran to India, from Meher Baba to Rashid Shahmardan, with followers primarily in India.

3 Shariati condemns the *Shahnameh* because, he says, it deals only with kings, not

with the people, with the one exception of the blacksmith Kaveh (*"Ari, Inchunin Bud, Baradar"* [Yes, That's How it Was, Brother]). Khomeini's use of the Firdausi line occurs in his 1943 book *Revealing the Secrets* (see Fischer 1980).

4 The Minneapolis-based actor and playwright Zaraawar Mistry has recently performed his own *Sohrab and Rustam*, this time about an old Parsi father in Bombay (Rustamji) and his son living in the United States. Mistry notes that Matthew Arnold wrote in relation to his own father and so put the son's name first, as did Mistry in commenting on the relation of the Zoroastrian New World diaspora to its Bombay and Iranian roots. Mistry's one-man play was showcased at the Asia Society in New York in November 2003.

5 On the zurkhaneh's sociological background, description of exercises, and texts, see Fischer 1973.

1. Yasna

1 Mary Boyce similarly noted single-priest performances of the yasna in Sharifabad by Dastur Khodadad, although in that case portions of the yasna were omitted (1977, 187).

2 Jivanji Jamshedi Modi, a Parsi high priest and anthropologist, as well as a frequent contributor to the Bombay Anthropological Society, wrote what remains the basic description of Zoroastrian rituals in English.

3 The contemporary Parsi high priest Dastur Firoze Kotwal, who in some respects follows in Modi's footsteps by contributing scholarly commentaries on the rituals, similarly deflected questions about definitive meanings when he was at Harvard. The ritual, he engagingly pointed out, is clear; theological superstructures remain to be recovered or constructed. On issues of marriage and funerary debates, by contrast, Kotwal has maintained conservative or even fundamentalist dogmas.

4 Rustam Shahzadi, a trained priest, but not a daily practicing one, was a leader of the Tehran community. Trained in Bombay, he was acknowledged as the most scholarly of the Iranian priests.

5 One of Mary Boyce's primary informants (Boyce 1977).

6 Boyce notes that there is a longstanding dispute among "Zoroastrian theologians" (*sic*) as to whether giving alms to unbelievers strengthened the forces of evil (and was therefore prohibited) or if it reduced the demon of poverty and hunger (and was therefore enjoined) (1977, 56). More likely than simple yes or no rules in the cases she invokes, there is an ethical principle involved: one does not feed Muslims if they come to mock or deprive (if their intent is evil); but one does not deny a poor person of good will just because he is not a Zoroastrian.

7 Dastur Khodadad was a delightful repository of folklore. Boyce (1977) describes, for instance, his belief that there is a cleft of God above the shrine of Banu Pars where heroes sleep until Resurrection and where if one prays, one's

sins will be forgiven; or again, she describes him going to the shrine of Pir-e Naraki when dreams so direct him.

8 Convened by William Darrow, then associate director of Harvard's Center for World Religions. Darrow and James Boyd also produced a video of the yasna procedure, together with Dastur Kotwal's explanations.

9 Boyce speculates that the original ritual was established to preserve some pre-Zoroastrian mantras (the Yasna Haptanhaiti, the seven chapters of Y. 35–42); the Gathas of Zoroaster, which enclose (precede and follow) them; and the three oldest short prayers, Ahuna Vairya, Yenhe Hatam, and Ashem Vohu. This original ritual unit is called Staota Yesnya. Then, in Achaemenian times, ritual additions were made equally before and after the Staota Yesnya, and in Sassanian times more additions were made including a second preparation of hom (Boyce 1979, 37, 75, 125).

10 This was done among Parsis as late as a century ago (Kotwal and Boyd 1982, 3).

11 While many Zoroastrians believe all of the Staota Yesnya, and even all of the Avesta to be the divinely inspired words of Zoroaster, Boyce attributes some of the mantras of the Staota Yesnya to pre-Zoroaster days, and Kotwal and Boyd point out suggestions in the Zoroastrian literature that some of the Gathas might have been mantras of Zoroaster's disciples living up to a hundred years after his death.

12 I find it striking that under similar circumstances of the destruction of a priestly temple tradition, Jewish scholars should have turned to a scriptural-interpretive medium rather than a ritual-based one. The content of much of the early rabbinic debate—for example, in compiling the Mishnah, as Jacob Neusner argues (1981)—may have been about ritual, but the form was interpretive debate. There is no comparable "talmudic" tradition in Zoroastrianism. What questioning of ritual exists in the Rivayats, for example, concerns how to conduct ritual behavior as a continuing practice. In the talmudic tradition the ritual praxis is secondary to the logic underlying both ritual and ethical practice. Thus the Jews continued to discuss the rules for a temple which no longer existed, while the Zoroastrians provide practically no information on the state cult but are instead concerned with those parts of the ritual which could be maintained in radically changed social circumstances.

13 Consider the battle of wits won by Yoishta against the sorcerer Akhtyar in Yasht 5.82. Yoishta is a descendant of the Turanian warrior Fryana, who became a follower of Zoroaster at the court of Vishtaspa (Y. 46.12). Johnson's work helps break through Mary Boyce's puzzled incomprehension of the workings of the Gathas of the *zaotar* (priest) Zoroaster. After noting their formal (eleven-syllable verses) parallels to the wisdom poetry of the Indian *hotar*, she says, "This *zaotar/hotar* poetry, with its predominantly instructive content, is extremely elaborate, the product evidently of a long and learned tradition; and it was intended plainly for the ears of those familiar with that tradition, who would be capable of understanding its highly artificial constructions and elucidating its meanings, despite a 'marked inclination to enigmatical obscurity'"

(Boyce 1975a, 9). The yashts parallel the Indian *udgatr* in their meters and characteristic eight-syllable line. The third of the "three main categories of formal ritual utterance" (ibid., 8) are the shorter mantras, a Vedic term now current in English.

14 The protective power of poetry and narrative, often under the protective, if also dangerous, influence of drugs or wine, is evoked by the writer Tim Parks with reference to the Vedic meter, the Homeric story, and Dante's *terza rima*. In imagery close to that of the Avesta, the Indian Vedic priest is said in the Taittirya Samhita, "So as not to be hurt . . . before coming near the fire, he wraps himself in the meters" (50). This advice, notes Parks, "is more practical than it may first appear. How did Dante pass through the Inferno after all, if not with ancient Rome's most able poet as his guide and the fiercely regular chime of the terza rima to keep things moving?" The ability of poetry and literature to allow us to speak about and yet protect us from the most painful of human experiences—to allow us to approach the divinity of insight, and yet protect us from the burning power of that insight, be it the hell fires of Dante or of existentialist Jean-Paul Sartre's *No Exit*—is encapsulated in the story toward the end of the Odyssey, "when Helen and Menelaus are safely, scandalously, back home and are surprised one evening by the arrival of Telemachus. All three are eager to talk about Troy. . . . But it is too painful. The young man's father, Odysseus, is missing, presumed dead. Helen and Menelaus would have to reflect on her betrayals, his weakness. So Helen leaves the room and returns with some drugged wine . . . a drug, Homer tells us, that would allow you to talk . . . which allows us to pass through the burning Troy and escape unscathed" and to relive "all that was most awful and exciting," and yet "to wake the following morning refreshed" (2001, 50).

15 In the Visperad ritual, the zot, reciting chapter 3 of the Visperad text, still asks if each of the other seven priests are present; and the raspi responds affirmatively. The seven are: (1) Havan, who prepared the haoma juice and placed the pestle in the water; (2) Atarvaksh, who kept the fire going; (3) Fravarta, who brought the date leaf as a girdle for the barsom; (4) Aberetar, who brought pure water from a well or stream; (5) Ashatar, who washed everything on the ritual table; (6) Rathvishkar, who washed the haoma juice with consecrated milk and distributed the haoma; (7) Sroshavarz, who superintended the ceremony and possibly heard confessions.

16 The story is told of Dastur Erachji Sorabji Meherjirana acting as zot when the chief priest of Navsari, Dastur Kekobadji Rustamji Dastur Meherjirana, entered (Kotwal and Boyd 1982, introduction).

17 In the Vendidad four kinds of esm-bui are mentioned: *urvacna* (sandalwood), *vohugaona* or olibanum (frankincense), *vohu keresti* or agar (a fragrant shrub), and *hadhanayata* (pomegranate). In modern times sandalwood is used for *aesma/esm*, and frankincense for *bui*. The trade in frankincense from south Arabia was a major one in ancient times. Herodotus (book 3:93) speaks of the great amounts of tribute in frankincense sent from Yemen to the Persian shah

Darius. The concern with fragrance is widespread in the contemporary Middle East. For a stunning structuralist account of the cultural codes of fragrance and spices in the Greek world, see Detienne 1972/1977.

18 Modi points out that *stareta*, the term for the zot's seat in the Visperad (11.2), means "things spread, carpet" (1922, 257).

19 See Windfuhr (1976) regarding the Chinese correlation, MacKenzie (1964) on the astrology of the Bundahishn, and more generally, Corbin (1960/1990).

20 Among Parsis, goat milk is used, although the text clearly indicates cow's milk. In nineteenth-century Pune, a priest tried to use cow's milk. The other priests were outraged and made him perform a purificatory bareshnum (Kotwal, class notes at Harvard, 15 February 1980).

21 Twenty-one twigs are used for the yasna, thirty-three for the Vendidad and Visperad. Yasna 25.3 specifies that the barsom is from a tree but does not say which tree. The *Dadistan* still speaks of the barsom as vegetable twigs. The word *barsom* (Av. *baresman*) is from the root *barez*, "to grow."

22 A detailed description of the paragna ritual is provided by Kotwal and Boyd (1982); see also Modi (1922). Modi divides the paragna into seven ceremonies, one for obtaining each of the items necessary for the yasna: barsom (originally a ceremony of cutting the twigs from the tree*)*; *aiwyaonghana* (date palm leaf*)*; *urvara* (pomegranate); *jivam* (milk*)*; *zaothra* (pure water); hair of the sacred bull; haoma. Almost all of the ritual of the yasna is performed during the paragna: it is a kind of abbreviated yasna. Modi suggest the paragna be seen as the preparation ceremony and the yasna as the consummation ceremony.

23 The following account can be followed visually in the video *A Zoroastrian Ritual: The Yasna*, produced by Jim Boyd and William Darrow with Dastur Kotwal, available from the Office of Instructional Services at Colorado State University.

24 Anything which becomes separated from the living body becomes part of the world of decay and pollution (the world of Ahriman): excreta, blood, semen, nail and hair clippings, spittle, and even exhaled breath.

25 The full form of exchange of baj between zot and raspi is for the zot to salute the raspi by touching his right hand to his forehead; the raspi replies with both hands to his forehead; and the zot again salutes with his right hand. On four of the sixteen exchanges during the yasna, the zot's opening gesture is dropped (chapters 7, 8, 26, and 65), and once there is no line for the raspi (chapter 15) (Boyce and Kotwal 1971).

26 "And they worshipped the sun toward the east . . . and lo, they put the branch to their nose" (Ezek. 8.16–17).

27 *Dron*, from Avestan *draonah*, "portion offered to the divine" (e.g., in Y. 33.8; Y.11.4). In Pahlavi, it refers specifically and only to the unleavened, wheaten ritual bread eaten with butter and ghee. Mary Boyce speculates that originally the priest tasted the animal offering at yasna 37 and only bread at yasna 8; and so, from yasna 8, *dron* was restricted to meaning only the bread. In Iran

the term *luwog* is used for the wafer, but *dron* is also used to distinguish the marked breads/wafers from the unmarked ones or frasast (Boyce and Kotwal 1971).

28 Insler's translation, "rapine of the bloody spear," stresses the rejection of warrior and simple aggressive uses of intoxicants by the text. His version provides more poetically subtle and philosophically sophisticated access to the meaning. Boyce's translation, by contrast, is more formulaic, emphasizing the personification of wrath as a demon imaged as a "savage ruffian." Boyce's translation and commentary tend to the Victorian in their insistence on anthropomorphic gods and demons, and she is quite precious in her (Christian) distinctions between amoral pagan ideas as opposed to ethical Zoroastrian ones. Her literalism however can remind of the formulaic rhythm of ritual language.

29 The biological effects of ephedra have been a matter of repeated attention by health authorities in recent years. Ephedra supplements are promoted as useful for both athletic performance and weight loss, but they have also been linked to heart attacks and strokes. This bipolar pattern is like other drugs, and the double meaning of the Greek term *pharmakon* as curative/poison, has been recently popularized again by Jacques Derrida's essay on "Plato's Pharmacy" (Derrida 1972). The bipolar effects of hom/soma are described in the myths. Contemporary accounts of ephedra are contested: the company Metabolife International, which produces ephedra supplements in the United States in 2002 gave the U.S. Food and Drug Administration copies of 13,000 adverse event reports, including three deaths, twenty heart attacks, and twenty-four strokes, based on "unverified telephone calls"; however, claims Metabolife, scientific studies show that "when used as directed by adults," its supplement is "safe and effective." The company is in favor of limiting sales to adults, strict monitoring of adverse events, and warning labels, but argues that proper use is safe. Meanwhile the U.S. armed services, National Collegiate Athletic Association, and National Football League have banned its use, and Canada, Germany, and the United Kingdom have banned its sale (Paul Recer, "Panel Urges Ban of Ephedra, Cites Numerous Health Risks." *Boston Globe* 9 October 2002, sec. A, p. 12).

30 Indra is one of three Indo-Iranian gods to be rejected by name in the Iranian tradition. (Nasatya and Sarva are the other two. Sarva becomes Rudra, a chief demon for Zoroastrianism.) In the Vedas, Indra is a royal god described in terms parallel to those used for Varuna. The difference is that Indra's rule is grounded in might, while Varuna's is grounded in law. Boyce sees this as an additional reason for why the ethical Zoroastrian tradition downgraded Indra but maintained Varuna under the name Apam Napat.

31 See Gershevitch 1974, a delightful sleuthing article in which this story is reconstructed and other points cited above are elaborated.

32 Mary Boyce takes literally that the god Haoma once received the jawbone, tongue, and left eye of sacrifices (1975a, 160) and that hence a bit of roasted

tongue is often still given to a dog at pilgrimage sacrifices. Boyce also thinks ephedra is a hallucinogen (ibid.).

33 Such legends are to be found in the Bundahishn, Denkart, and Zatspram. A valuable compendium is provided in Darrow (1981).

34 Boyce (1966) describes the rite as performed in Yazd villages: someone in a state of ritual purity milks a cow, catching the milk in a silver or copper bowl and adding two things from the vegetable kingdom: rose petals, leaves of wild marjoram (*zwizan*), or oleander fruits (*senjed*). A priest takes the milk to a stream, where he seats himself with the bowl in the left hand and a spoon in the right. He pours three spoonfuls (good words, good thoughts, good deeds) into the water, then begins reciting the *drin-i owzur* (*Ab Zohr*) while turning single spoonfuls into the water; this takes about half an hour, at the end of which the priest empties the bowl in three pourings, then immerses the bowl and spoon.

35 The legend of the sayoshants is not in the Gathas, as is to be expected if these are indeed compositions of Zoroaster. Yasht 13 is the source of the legend and even there only one sayoshant is mentioned. Two other names, however, also occur: Ushedar and Ushedarmab. Tradition appropriated all three as successive saviors.

36 There is, of course, a Jesus-like portrait of Zoroaster that has now been disseminated among Zoroastrians as an icon, set up in homes and other places. Western scholars (and the provenance of this icon would be interesting to trace) have been more personality-cult oriented than Zoroastrians. European scholars have proposed an array of characterizations ranging from the outrageous to the trivializing. Even Mary Boyce has insisted on reducing Zoroaster to one of his attributes—zaotar, zot, or priest—as if that somehow brings one closer to a lost historical realism. Her procedure of dismissing the miraculous as later accretion and retaining the nonmiraculous as historical fundament has the feel more of British rationalism than of a real historical methodology. This fits with note 29 on the difference between Insler's and Boyce's translations of the amshaspands, the former drawing on an appreciation of the literary or poetics less well developed in the latter.

37 See Shahbazi 1977. Alexander invaded Iran in 331 and ruled for seven years: 331 + 258 = 589 B.C.E. References to Alexander in dating usually meant the Seleucid era, established 1 Nissan 311 B.C.E. when Seleucus I entered Babylon. The Seleucid era was the first to date from a fixed year rather than simply in regnal years, and so it rapidly became the conventional common era. Thus, 311 + 258 = 569– 30 (the first three decades of Zoroaster's life) = 539 B.C.E. Oddities of the traditional speculations in the Bundahishn are the granting of Alexander a term twice that he actually ruled and the ignoring of Cyrus the Great, Darius, and Xerxes. For a possible explanation, see Shabazi.

38 Zoroaster is said to have lived halfway through the 1,200 year cosmic cycle. Some Greeks tried to date Zoroaster 6,000 years before Plato to make Plato a kind of second Zoroaster in the world-age system. The Bundahishn also provides a second schema according to which man appears in the seventh millen-

nium, Zahhak the Evil One rules in the eighth millennium, Fereydun over-throws Zahhak in the ninth millennium, Zoroaster's mission coincides with the tenth millennium, the first two saoshyants come in the eleventh and twelfth millennia, followed by the final saoshyant and the Restoration. According to this schema, the Abbasids fall close to the end of the tenth millennium.

39 See especially Henri Corbin's discussion of Suhrawardi's efforts to recapture the theosophy of ancient Iran (Corbin 1946, 1960/1990). Corbin traces this strand of theosophical speculation to the Shaikhis of the modern period.

2. Shahnameh

1 Both the *Darab Nameh* and the *Eskandar Nameh* are excellently summarized and analyzed in Hanaway 1970.

2 English translations unless otherwise marked are from Warner and Warner 1905.

3 An archetypical example is how Imam Ali defeated Amr ibn Abu Da'ud in the Battle of the Moat. Pointing to Amr's saddle straps, he suggested they had come undone. When Amr looked, 'Ali knocked him off his horse. Deceit in defense of Islam or the communal good is acknowledged as justified, just as metis was a quality valued in ancient Greece (Detienne and Vernant 1974).

4 When Ghazan died, his corpse was taken on horseback to Tabriz, followed by his women and courtiers; people came out of their houses, clad in sackcloth, with bare feet and bare heads—they put dust on their heads. Uljaytu had a coffin of gold, silver, and gems which lay in state on the throne to receive last homages by officials while subjects sat on the ground lamenting. The corpses of Amir Chupan and his son were slowly transported across Iran for internment at Karbala. Such scenes can be seen in the funerals portrayed in the *Shahnameh* miniatures.

5 Faridun finding out about his lineage; Zav discovered by Zal to be a descendant of Faridun; Darab's miraculous protection, which allowed him to become the rightful ruler; Ardeshir's concern with his descent; Jamshid's treasure discovered by Bahram Gur; Faridun testing his sons.

6 Rudabeh's mother attempting to prevent her union with Zal; Gulnar switching her favors from Ardavan to Ardeshir; Ardavan's daughter attempting to poison her husband, Ardeshir; Mahbud's wife unknowingly preparing poisoned food.

7 For other meiotic variants found in the Avestan texts, see the useful charts in Page 1977, the section entitled "Genealogies in the National Tradition."

8 See Mary Ellen Page's discussion (1977) of the corpus of the naqqal Ali Sana-khan. In Firdausi, by contrast, Esfandiar marries his sister.

9 Involved here is the unresolved debate about *khedvadatha* marriage, or next-of-kin marriage. The Greeks claimed that Iranians practiced such marriages, and Firdausi's account of Bahman's marriage to his daughter says that it was done in the spirit of the faith. *Khedvadatha* ("self giving") is highly praised in the

Zoroastrian texts, though the contexts there do not allow any definition of what this praiseworthy act might be. Some scholars are rather insistent that it refers to marriage of the next of kin (see, for example, Boyce 1975a; 1979). For a detailed analysis and refutation by a Parsi priest, see Sanjana 1888. Hopkins 1978 perhaps adds indirect support by suggesting that such marriages might have been widespread among Egyptian commoners, not just royalty. But there may also be an old confusion between mythic metaphors and marriage rules.

10 At first blush, one might think it would have been a more elegant device had Homa's child been Sasan rather than Darab (transcendence over time, or submerged and delayed transmission of royalty). However, given the ambivalence, if not hostility, still felt about the Sassanians, the linkage of Homa with the miracles of Alexander is in fact more apt.

11 Compare the meat-eating birds with cinnamon nests in the spice mythologies of the Greeks and their elaboration into a metaphorical series: phoenix, eagle, falcon, vulture (Detienne 1977, 19–35).

12 Bizhan and Gurgin go to Kurdistan to clear it of magical wild boars; after this they decide to chase girls across the Turanian border. The princess Manizha, daughter of Afrasiyab, smites the heart of Bizhan and smuggles him into the palace. He is caught and condemned to death. Piran intercedes, cautioning Afrasiyab about the grief caused when the last youthful Iranian hero, Siyavush, was killed by Turan. Bizhan is thus put into a pit, and Manizha is forced to beg food for him. Meanwhile Gurgin has been imprisoned by Kai Khosrow, who sees in a magic cup what has befallen Bizhan. Rustam, disguised as a merchant, is sent to free his grandson. Manizha comes to this merchant and asks why no word of Bizhan's fate has reached Iran and why no rescue has come. Rustam fears she will spoil his disguise and says he knows nothing of the ways of the court, but gives her food for her beloved and hides his ring in it. Bizhan recognizes the ring and tells Manizha to ask Rustam a question which will confirm his identity and alert Rustam that Manizha can be trusted. In the later tale, Esfandiar also disguises as a merchant, and the sequence of events is recounted in similar terms.

13 Marcia Maguire (1978) sees Rustam's gluttony as a vulgar anachronistic display, appropriate to a barbarian, heroic style. In Bahman's relative moderation she sees Zoroastrian temperance.

14 Maguire (ibid.) sees the countering as Esfandiar's fall into sin and hence the unraveling of his religious virtues and invulnerability: Rustam asks Esfandiar to invite him. Esfandiar cannot refuse but fails to issue the invitation. Rustam nonetheless shows up with retinue and rebukes Esfandiar: a pahlavan should not break promises. Esfandiar lies, saying that he had not wanted to trouble Rustam. This lie, plus the subsequent two insults to Rustam, seal his fate.

15 Maguire (ibid.) suggests that by appearing with retinue, Rustam was making a claim to being a semi-independent ruler. She credits Gushtasp's charge that Rustam was no longer so loyal a vassal. She suggests that during the campaign of vengeance against Siyavush, Rustam had served seven years as lord of Turan

without sending tribute (an interesting interpretation but not one that Fir-dausi's Kai Khosrow levels against Rustam). And she interprets the fight with Esfandiar as being in defense of his independence. Finally, she argues that in his response to the charges about his ancestry, he cites his mother's father, Mihrab, with pride because it gives him claim to royalty (again an interesting possibility in the narrative structure but not one that finds support in Firdausi, where Mihrab explicitly swears fealty to the Iranian crown).

16 The archetype of the latter, the *aghebat-e khair*, is Hurr, the general at Karbala who conspired to kill Imam Husain but at the last moment repented and switched sides to be martyred with Husain. The opposite, *aghebat-e shar*, is said by Khomeini partisans to be the judgment on the life of Ayatullah Muhammad-Kazem Shariatmadari, whose standing, and opposition to Khomeini, they tried to discredit.

17 The notion that Esfandiar represents the new religion and a new stage of ethical being is not original to Maguire: both Spiegel (1864) and the ninth-century Dinawari (d. 896) take the same stance. Nöldeke, while not adopting this inter-pretation, stresses the multiple doublets in the *Shahnameh* (Nöldeke 1979). But none of these earlier critics attempted a sustained analysis of the sort attempted in the present generation of scholars. The older generation tended to be more concerned to sift out what might be a fictionalized trace of historical events (see the excellent notes in the Warner and Warner translation).

18 The name Kubad literally means "threshold" (Warner and Warner 1905).

19 According to the Bundahishn, he is found floating in a river by the Pishdadian king Zav, who adopts him.

20 In the Vedas, Kavya Ushana installed the fire as high priest of mankind, led the heavenly cows to pasture, and wrought the iron club with which Indra slew the demon Vritra. In the Denkard, Kavi Usa had an ox to which all frontier disputes with Turan were put, before he was beguiled by the Turanians to slay the ox. In the Bundahishn he is the grandson of Kai Kubad.

21 In one of the oral versions described by Page (1977), Lohrasp's appointment initiates a feud between Zabul and Lohrasp. There is an elaboration of the flight of Afrasiyab before Kai Khosrow's victorious fourth campaign. He is taken prisoner by the ruler of Makran, who will not yield him up to Iran. Bizhan is sent to seize him but is imprisoned. Jahanbakhsh is sent next, then Rustam. Spells and charms are involved in the imprisonment of both Bizhan and Jahan-bakhsh. The simorgh says that only Lohrasp can break these spells. In exchange for his service, the sickly, ten-year-old Lohrasp demands the throne. Rustam strikes him for this, but Kai Khosrow yields. Bizhan is released. The army continues to pursue Afrasiyab, who in the meantime has been released by the daughter of the ruler of Makran.

22 Jamshid is a contraction of Yima + *khshaeta* (king).

23 In the Vedas Yima and Manu are twin sons of Vivasvat: Yima is a god, and Manu is the lawgiver to human beings.

24 Compare Claude Lévi-Strauss's account of structural forms that begin (like

phonemes in language) with binary oppositions (differences that make a difference), generating mediating thirds that, in turn, generate further and further oppositions and mediating thirds (Lévi-Strauss 1971/1981).

25 In the Denkard, Faridun first tries to cut off Zahhak's head, but this only multiplies the noxious creatures in the world. Ahura Mazda advises him to bind Zahhak instead and thereby constrain evil. In the Bundahishn and the Bahman Yasht, Zahhak will be slain at the end of time by Keresaspa, son of Thrita (the first to offer haoma). He is called Sama Keresaspa Narimanu. In the epic legends he becomes three personages: Sam (Rustam's father's father), Nariman (Rustam's father's father's father), and Faridun. Keresaspa is seduced by a demon of Ahriman (parika Knathaiti) to neglect the worship of fire. For this he is condemned to hell until Zoroaster intercedes, arguing that Keresaspa had slain the man and horse-swallowing serpent, Srovbar.

26 These lines, spoken to his father, describe what he intends to say to his brothers. The following lines are from his speech carrying out that intent.

27 Nectanebus II, king of Egypt and a magician, goes to Macedonia in disguise and sets up as a soothsayer. He is consulted by Olympias, wife of Philip, asking if Philip will divorce her. Nectanebus says yes, but he can help: she will bear a child by the two-horned Egyptian god Amen. By deciphering dreams, he reconciles Philip and Olympias. In the process he impersonates Amen and fathers Alexander.

28 Many of the Iranian accounts of Alexander (the *Shahnameh*, the *Darab Nameh*, the *Eskandar Nameh*, Dinavari, Tha'alebi, the *Hojmal al-Tavarikh*) say that Darab (Darius) sent Alexander's mother back to Macedonia because of her bad breath or bad odor and that there were efforts to cure her with herbs. Hence one folk etymology of Alexander is *al-i sandar* (a wood resin); other variants take it from the Greek word for *garlic* or the Latin for *shallot* (*ascalonium*). In a twelfth-century translation from Arabic to Latin of the Alexander stories, Aristotle teaches Alexander how to protect himself against poison damsels (reared on poison, who kill by kiss, touch, mingling perspiration, or intercourse). See Warner and Warner 6.19; Hanaway 1970, 55–65.

29 The poet Nizami makes Alexander a sage and traces his education, beginning with ethics, then proceeding to philosophy and prophecy. In India it is Alexander who is questioned by an old sage, rather than, as in Firdausi, Alexander questioning the sages. See Bacher 1871.

30 Warrior women are not infrequent as minor characters in the heroic literature. Gordafarid, daughter of Gozhdaham, challenges Sohrab, is unhorsed by him, and thus causes him to fall in love. Gordya, the sister of Bahram Chubin, and Jarira, the Turanian wife of Siyavush are other examples from the *Shahnameh*. Hanaway (1970) lists other examples from the *Qessa-i Hamza*, the *Firuz Shahnameh*, and the *Samak-i 'Ayyar*, noting as well the existence of a short epic about Banu Goshasp, the daughter of Rustam. *The Thousand and One Nights* also contains three tales about such women. These women, Hanaway concludes, are portrayed as a match for any but the greatest hero: they don armor,

wield swords, brandish clubs, ride chargers, engage in single combat, shout war cries loud enough to intimidate the enemy by their very volume. In the Turkish *Dede Korkut* cycle, as well, there are a number of warrior women, who there are portrayed not merely as a match for any but the greatest hero but as the only suitable match for male heroes.

31 See the text and notes in Warner and Warner (6.105–6) for variant interpretations of the story. They cite a parallel story in Hiuen Tsiang about two Buddhist monks: one is not admitted by the other. The refusal is made by sending a begging bowl full of water (fullness, depth, lucidity of the wisdom of his master). The visitor drops a needle into the bowl without causing any spillage; he is then admitted. This story is also central to the legends of the arrival of the Parsis in India: when they asked permission to settle, the local king refused by sending a full glass of milk; the Parsis added sugar.

32 Having saved one of Queen Kaidafa's sons in a ruse to gain her sympathy, Alexander with her collusion uses a second ruse to escape her second son. In the first ruse Alexander trades places with his courtier and pleads for the life of the first son, who has been taken prisoner. Alexander then travels to Kaidafa's court disguised as his own ambassador. Kaidafa recognizes him from a portrait on silk and warns him that her second son will not allow him to escape so easily. Alexander, maintaining his disguise as his own ambassador, pretends to hate Alexander and promises to deliver Alexander to this son alone without arms or protecting troops. He marches toward Iran with the second son's forces, then proceeds alone to entice the shah Alexander into the woods alone. He returns with troops and reveals his ruse: I kept my promise, I was in your hands defenseless.

33 Insofar as the Parthian names are preserved in the *Shahnameh*, they are assimilated into the Kayanian period. They appear at the court of Kai Kaus and serve as participants, counsel, and heroes through the rest of the dynasty. Gudarz, for instance, seems to be Gotaarzes II (mid-first century C.E.).

34 The theme of miraculous aid in accomplishing the drudgery of women's work is a basic premise of work stories used by women—Bibi Shah Pari, Moshekel Goshah, and Bibi Seshambeh, for example—to accompany and lighten such tasks as cleaning *nakhod* (chickpeas) at shrines (for full versions of these stories from Yazd, see Fischer 1973).

35 This, of course, is purely a folk etymology, one attached to the oasis town of Kerman along the southeastern border of Iran's central desert. Rulers of Kerman often did vie with those of Shiraz (Fars), as Haftwad did with Ardashir, but the *Shahnameh* places its Kerman at the edge of the sea.

36 Firdausi merely says that Rum pays a tribute of money, a thousand slaves, and brocade. Contemporary Persian wit ruefully elaborates that European colonial domination had already begun when Iran ostensibly defeated Emperor Valerian (Bazarnush) and took him prisoner. Shapur I agreed to free Valerian if the latter would build an irrigation dam. Valerian sent to Rome for a thousand slave girls. He then hired a thousand Iranians willing to work for one dinar a day. Each day

after work, the girls met the workers and charged one dinar for their attentions. In this way, with a revolving capital input of only one thousand dinars, Valerian managed to build a large dam and buy his freedom.

37 An omen reveals that Yazdegird is destined to die at the spring of Sav in Tus. Yazdegird refuses to go near the spring but gets a nosebleed that will not stop and can be cured only at the spring. Yazdegird finally goes to the spring, and the nosebleed is cured. A white horse emerges from the spring, is docile when the shah approaches, then whirls and kicks him to death and returns to the waters.

38 The high priest Ruzbeh opines, "Once in a month is intercourse enough," and worries that "dalliance with women marreth him, / He soon will be feeble as a ghost" (7.57).

39 Mordecai overhears a conspiracy between two courtiers to poison the king, saves the king, vindicating himself and asserting that Jewish distinctiveness is not inherently evil (sorcery). Warner and Warner point out that there seems to have been a conspiracy against Nushiravan by his brothers Kaus and Jam; since Jam is disqualified from the throne by a physical defect, they plot to put Jam's son on the throne.

40 Backgammon has been interpreted as a symbolic universe: black and white are day and night; the thirty pieces, the days of the month; each dice throw allegorized (the first is Uhrmuzd; the second the duality of heaven and earth; the third good words, good thoughts, good deeds; the fourth the four temperaments, and so on); and the markings on the dice the seven planets (the markings on opposing sides always add up to seven: 1 and 6; 2 and 5; 3 and 4).

41 The story "Moshkel Goshah" (Dispel Difficulties) contains a segment in which the heroine is imprisoned by the princess on charges of stealing a necklace which has actually been taken by a bird. This turn of events occurs because the heroine has forgotten to give chickpeas (tokens of help) to others as instructed by her father; the theme of mutual aid among human beings as a prerequisite for miraculous aid is basic to these work stories. When her oversight is corrected, the bird brings back the pearls of wisdom. In Firdausi's version the pearls also return, and Nushiravan recognizes the steadfastness of Bozorgmehr.

42 Rayy is said to have been a seat of Arsacid power. Bahram Chubin is of the Mihran clan, descended from Gurgin, the mischievous companion of Bizhan who caused Bizhan to be captured in Turan. Shapur of Rai, called by Kubad to defeat Sufarai, was also of this clan. Ruhham of Rai helped put Firuz on the throne. Bahram Chubin had three siblings: one, Gurdwi, remained loyal to Khosrow Parviz; another, Yalasina Mardanshah, was loyal to Bahram; the third, Gurdya, stayed with Bahram but sympathized with Khosrow.

43 This motif is central to the shrine legends of the Zoroastrians of Yazd, as well as several Muslim shrine legends (see Fischer 1973).

44 Khosrow Parviz has her narrate and act out how she held the battlefield. Though she had stuck by her brother, Bahram Chubin, in her advice to him she had always maintained that Khosrow Parviz was in the right. After Chubin's death, the Khan of China proposed to her; she fled and married Gushtaham. Later,

after Khosrow Parviz kills Bandwi for his part in blinding of Hormuzd, he convinces Gurdya to poison Gushtaham for his part.

45 The Cross was taken by the Persians in their capture of Jerusalem in 614 C.E.; it was returned by Kubad to Heraclitus in 628.

46 A reference to the gnostic doctrine that someone else was crucified in Jesus's place; hence Jesus laughs. Thus the Qur'an's claim: "They slew him not. . . . [T]hey had only his likeness."

47 In Nizami's *Khamseh* ("five" *masnavi*s, or long poems), Shirin is a niece of the reigning queen of Armenia, not a commoner as in Firdausi's text. There is also a love triangle: the second man is Farhad, the royal sculptor who initially serves as the king's go-between with Shirin but who falls in love with Shirin himself. Farhad is supposed to have carved the great stone relief at Taq-i Bustan, near Kirmanshah. Nizami's story is much richer and more polished than Firdausi's and is also turned to other parabolic ends. Chelkowski (1975) sees it as a slow education of Khosrow by the examples of Shirin and Farhad (who commits suicide when he hears that Shirin has died). And indeed, toward the beginning of the tale, Nizami has Khosrow Parviz envision Khosrow Nushiravan in a dream. Nushiravan tells his grandson that he will have happiness because he is willing to accept punishment and that he will receive four things: the horse Shabdiz, the throne Taqdis, the musician Barbad, and the love of Shirin.

48 Jahn, son of Barzin, is said to have created a throne for Faridun. Each shah to occupy the throne added on to it, until Alexander destroyed it. The shards were preserved by various nobles. Ardashir had another throne made. Khosrow Parviz had the original reconstructed with three rows of seats on the steps: one of rams heads for local chiefs, a higher one of lapis lazuli for warriors, and a turquoise one for the ministers; at the top was a carpet of gold with a map of the heavens and the heads of the kings. Barbad sings "Dadafrid" (Source of Justice), "Paikar-i Gurd" (Battle of the Brave), and "Sabz dar Sabz" (Green on Green).

49 He sends a letter to Guraz, the disloyal retainer, praising him for luring Caesar into a trap; Caesar intercepts the letter and refuses to participate.

50 The sixth-century *Khwaday namak* is a Sassanian source of systematized epic tales. The most important of the later Islamic historians here are Tabari (d. 310 A.H./923 C.E.), Yaqubi (d. 292 A.H./904 C.E.), Masudi (d. 345 A.H./965 C.E.), Dinavari (d. 281 A.H./895 C.E.), and Tha'alebi (d. 427 A.H./1035 C.E.).

51 Ritual idiom appears in images such as the worm slain by Ardashir Papakan with molten metal; the barsom invoked at critical or public junctures in the reigns of Shapur, Hormuzd, Khosrow Parviz, and Yazdegird III; the ox-headed mace of Bahram Gur; the cow which goes dry at bad thoughts of Bahram Gur; the breaking of the magic boundary by Firuz; and the saving of Khosrow Parviz by Sorush.

There are two Khosrows (Nushiravan and Parviz) who resonate with the earlier Kai Khosrow; two Uhrmazds or Hormuzds who are transition figures (Ardashir's grandson; the Hormuzd between Nushiravan and Khosrow Parviz); and two Kubads, both weak and manipulated by others.

Ardashir marries Ardavan's daughter, and Shapur I marries Mirak's daughter; both are intermarriages but within the factions of Iran. Similar is Khosrow Parviz's later marriage with Gurdya, although no future shah issues from that marriage. Nushiravan and Hormuzd marry Rum to sire heirs, as does Khosrow Parviz with Rum.

52 Muslim Iranians, and also many Zoroastrians, tell the story that when S'ad came to the tent of Rustam, he and his men were barefoot and kicked aside the rich Persian carpets that their feet might rest on the earth. The soldiers of Rustam stood with bowed heads before their superiors and saw the Arabs were egalitarian. Impressed, the soldiers began to throw off their submission and refused to fight. Iranians, however, also claim that the Caliph Omar cut up the gold carpets of the palaces in Ctesiphon, including the famed Spring Carpet of Khosrow, into little pieces to hand out as booty. Only 'Ali, the son-in-law of the Prophet and the First Imam, protested, but as usual too late and ineffectively. The parable meanings are often made explicit. The hubris and fall into decadence and oppression is not infrequently cited by Zoroastrians when they try to explain how a powerful empire could have been defeated by Arab tribesmen. The Iranian nationalist or civilizational story about the carpet of Khosrow is one of a crime against culture that only barbarian or rude Arab troops would do. Alternatively the story is a Shi'ite one: the destruction of the carpets were among the many signs of the illegitimacy and unworthiness of the caliphs, the usurpers of rule over the *umma* that legitimately belonged to the Twelve Imams.

Illuminationism

1 Having had an epiphanous dream about Aristotle, Suhrawardi counsels that those who have not achieved a certain level of mystical visionary experience should not attempt Aristotle's intuitive philosophy but should remain with the rational Peripatetic philosophy that constitutes the first two of his cycle of four philosophical texts. He further advises that before starting the intuitive philosophy one should prepare oneself with ascetic discipline, eliminating meat from the diet and detaching from the world.

2 Maimonides is said to have been influenced by Suhrawardi. Ziai (1990, 3–4) cites the work of Paul Fenton in particular.

3 Walbridge and Ziai (1999) point to Adhar Kaywan, a Parsi Zoroastrian priest, and to the production in India of the *Dasatir* and the *Dabistan al-madhahib*.

3. Awaiting the Revolution

1 Barkhorda made his fortune as a middleman in the weaving business, selling yarn and thread. His three sons became important in growing pistachios, importing Japanese goods, and dealing in Teheran real estate.

2   The literature on mass culture is considerable, but good introductions are the chapters on aesthetics in the books on the Frankfurt School (see Jay 1973; Held 1980). See also Rosenberg and White 1957, and Gans 1974.

3   Many writers might deny that they draw on popular culture, claiming instead to draw directly on older folk forms. Without much commercialized mass culture as a contrasting frame, the line between folk and popular forms becomes indistinct. An emerging mass culture did exist in Pahlavi Iran, particularly in music and to some extent in film. But one wonders to what extent writers drew on the vaudeville shows of Lalezar Avenue or from the *ruhowzi, taziyeh, bazi-nemayeshi*, and professional poetry-reciting traditions.

4   Compare Rabelais's use of carnivalization and grotesque realism of the lower classes to challenge the proprieties, pretentions, and individualism of bourgeois society (Bakhtin 1940).

5   See Richard Cottam's review of "Major Voices in Contemporary Persian Literature" (Hillmann 1980): "What they write bears the tenor of mildly despairing acquiescence. . . . Nor is there apparent any recognition of the depth of religious appeal to the Iranian mass" (Cottam 1981, 125). Michael Hillmann is even stronger in two later essays: "As for the influence of modern Persian literature upon Iranian society at large, it remains in a word negligible. . . . A third and important aspect of contemporary Persian literature is what appears to be politically nonrevolutionary orientation[s] of most Iranian modernist writers" (1981, 133, 135); "The purpose of this essay is to suggest why modernist Persian literature has not had to date a significant social impact" (1982b, 10).

6   An English translation by John Green and Ahmad Alizadeh is available (Al-i Ahmad 1982a).

7   On postmodernist fiction, see Barth 1967, Gass 1980, Klinkowitz 1975, Stevick 1973, Velie 1982. Young (1981) draws a distinction between literature that struggles to comprehend the nature of memory and history (which one might group with modernism) and literature that gives up that particular struggle and instead attempts to find some acceptable relation between the self and an apparently absurd universe (as can be found in the works of Walker Percy, John Barth, and other postmodernists).

8   For introductions to Persian literature, see Browne 1924, Kamshad 1966, Gelpke 1962, Rypka 1959, and more recently Hillmann 1980 and Ghanoonparvar 1979 (intro.).

9   There appear to have been two crests of activity. The first in the late nineteenth century is associated with Aref-e Qazvini, Mirzazadeh Eshqi, Malcolm Khan, Shaikh Ahmad Ruhi, Haj Zein-ul-Abedin Maraghe'i, and Fath Ali Akhundzadeh. The second comes with the work in the 1930s of Nima Yushij, particularly his poem "Ah Adamha," which poeticizes colloquial language instead of "Ey Adami(an)."

10   Hillmann (1982a) suggests a division of short-story writers into three generations. Jamalzadeh, Sadegh Hedayat, and Bozorg Alavi set the stage in the Reza Shah period (pre-1941). They were followed in the post–World War II period by

Beh'azin (Mahmud E'temadzadeh), Sadegh Chubak, Ebrahim Golestan, and Jalal Al-i Ahmad. The third generation, active in the 1960s and 1970s, includes Nader Ebrahimi, Hushang Golshiri, Gholam Hussein Sa'edi, and Samad Behrangi. This last generation also birthed the Persian novel, beginning with Ali Mohammad Afghani's 1961 *Showhar-i Ahu Khanum* (Ahu's Husband), Al-i Ahmad's 1961 *Nun va Qalam* (N and the Pen), Sadegh Chubak's 1966 *Sang-i Sabur* (Patient Stone), and Hushang Golshiri's 1969 *Shazdeh Ehtejab* (Prince Ehtejab).

11 In a Pakistani setting the dialectic between Zoroastrian and Muslim could be parochialized as the problem of a particular minority community, whereas in Iran this dialectic could not be so sanitized. While the revolutionary theme of the film is more directly tied to Pakistan, both themes can be read, and are most powerful if read, as more far-reaching metaphors. At issue in the first theme is not just a Zoroastrian minority but the partial claim traditional Islam has on contemporary Muslims. Similarly, revolutionary struggle is portrayed not as a specific political movement but as part of the cyclical struggle that affects generation on generation.

12 For instance, Fereydun M. Esfandiari's novel *Identity Card*, written in English, deals unsatisfactorily with corruption in the bureaucracy as experienced by an Iranian returning from abroad. Another, finer, novel by the same author, *Day of Sacrifice*, raises psychological questions about participation in political demonstrations. Jalal Al-i Ahmad's *School Principal* is like *Identity Card* in its stance of outrage at corruption, this time in the school system. Jamalzadeh, in his story "Persian Is Sugar" (1921), deals with problems of multilingualism and social status. Sadegh Hedayat's short story "Veramin Nights" (1933) perhaps comes closest to an account which probes more deeply at the tearing of the soul experienced by one who returns to Iran from the West.

Possibly the best novel in the Middle East which deals with East versus West in a fully artistic manner is the Sudanese novel by Tayeb Salih, *Season of Migration to the North* (1969). It is striking how similar in technique it is to both *Towers of Silence* and *The Blind Owl*.

13 See especially Hedayat's famous story, "Sag-i Velgard" (The Abandoned Dog, 1942), translated into English by Brian Spooner in Yarshater 1979.

14 There is no indication in the Qur'an that Mohammad ever said this. Nonetheless, Muslims widely think so. In fact, the one substantive reference to a dog (in the Sureh of the Cave [18.18]) is to a good dog, immortalized also in a verse by the Persian poet Sa'di. (Might Muslim antipathy to the dog have developed as a mark of rejection of pre-Islamic Iranian beliefs?)

15 There are now in English a number of critical reading aids for *The Blind Owl*: Kamshad 1966, Hillmann 1978, Bashiri 1974, Beard 1982, Lashgari 1982.

16 Al-i Ahmad, himself a well-known literary figure, stands in a somewhat self-contradictory relationship to Hedayat. His interpretation of Hedayat accords with the Marxist tendency to read artistic work as reflective merely of social conditions. His own fiction also suffers from this too-literal effort to make his

art comment on social conditions: *The School Principal* and *The Cursing of the Land* are more fictionalized social commentaries than pieces of artistry. Yet Al-i Ahmad was a translator of Gide, Camus, Sartre, and Dostoyevski, and his best piece of fiction, "The Letter N and the Pen" (1961a/1988), fits within both the stylistic and thematic discourses used by Hedayat and Dehlavi. It, too, uses a structure which suggests cyclical repetition and thus perennial issues; it, too, concerns the continued dialectical relation between idealism and corruption mediated via revolution. The story is framed by a prologue and an epilogue. In the prologue a falcon swoops down from the skies to designate a simple shepherd to succeed the late vizier (executed by having molten lead poured down his throat). The shepherd-vizier instructs his sons not to forget their rural origins, and when he himself is poisoned, the sons attempt to return to the village, but they have become so citified they cannot adjust. So they return to the city and run a school. In the epilogue one of the sons has become a poet-laureate, while the other runs the school. It is suggested that one of them is the proper author of the story. The story is of two scribes: one poor, self-reliant, steadfast in conviction, and the father of a schoolboy; the other childless, wealthier, and connected at court. These two scribes are caught up in a revolution led by the egalitarian Qalandaris. The new government after a short time collapses, and the Qalandaris flee to India, followed by the childless scribe. Much of the story turns around the differing character of the two scribes (self-reliant and principled versus social climbing) and how they relate to governments. A fragment in the epilogue suggests the story has been written by the principled scribe as a legacy for his son; that is, it is the principled, self-reliant, incorruptible one who passes on the torch of the sentient, human search.

17 Another variant, which Freud may also have drawn on, is the struggle of Goethe's Faust between his self-destructive Mephistophelean side and the embodiment of his beloved better self, Gretchen. The Greek myth of Eros and Psyche describes the devotion of the young man, Eros, to the soul, Psyche, the latter depicted as young and beautiful with wings of a bird or butterfly. Venus, mother of Eros, is at first jealous and subjects Psyche to life-threatening trials, including a trip to the underworld. Eventually Venus accepts Psyche, the lovers are wed before the gods, and Psyche is made immortal. Freud describes the effort of the "I" or ego to gain control over the "it" or id as a cultural achievement (*Kulturarbeit*) like the draining of the Zuyder Zee, an image he may well have taken from Goethe, whose Faust describes his greatest achievement in the struggle for understanding and gaining control over his self as having been able to reclaim some new land for cultivation—a play between cultivation of the self (*Bildung*) and creation of culture (*Kultur*), which go hand in hand. The depths, in either case, are chaotic, turbulent, and threatening. This psychic or soulful reading leads directly to the third aesthetic reading of *The Blind Owl* as both Kulturarbeit and Bildung (on Freud and these terms, see Bettelheim 1983).

18 The abbasi, a silver coin stamped under Shah Abbas Safavi, went out of circulation in 1806 but continued as a unit of mental calculation. The geran was

introduced by Fath Ali Shah Qajar (1797–1834) but was replaced by the rial under Reza Shah Pahlavi (1925–1941). Thus the first narration must be roughly between 1900 and 1930 (see Daniel 1978).

19 Bogle (1978) suggests a direct relation not only with Omar Khayyam's notion that starts are sinister but also with Khayyam's assertion that, of the pleasures of women and wine, the latter is preferable because it brings forgetfulness. Like Khayyam, Bogle suggests, Hedayat was disgusted with the people of his time and the dominance of Arabian Islam, and longed for the glories of pre-Islamic Iran. Hedayat published an analysis of Khayyam's quatrains, and there is certainly a resonance between the two authors: indeed, the figure of the woman in *The Blind Owl* refuses to allow the narrator to sink into forgetfulness. Note, however, that the image of the star is but one in a series of metaphors Muslim Iranians used for bad fate (Ahriman, in pre-Islamic times) so as not to have to blame God.

20 *The Blind Owl*, trans. D. N. Costello (reprint, New York: Grove Press, 1969), 9–10. Hereafter page references are to this Costello translation.

21 The water of Karbala (ab-i Karbala) is given to a dying man to speed up his fate for good or bad, so that he be spared unnecessary suffering. Thus, if he is dying the end comes more quickly, and if he is to recover then that, too, is hastened. It is an ambi-valent tool of *shefa* (cure) or *shafa* (death).

22 The cobra in Indian tradition may directly represent a life force rising through the chakras and out through the head in a very phallic manner (see Obeyesekere 1981).

23 With reference to the opening pages of the second narration, where the narrator says he does not know if he is in Nishapur or Balkh or Benares, translator D. P. Costello quotes Khayyam (48):

> Since life passes whether sweet or bitter,
> Since the soul must pass the lips, whether in Nishapur or in Balkh,
> Drink wine, for after you and I are gone many a moon
> Will pass from old to new, from new to old.

Benares is added in Hedayat's story: the city near where the Buddha achieved nirvana, and a center of Sivaism, where the great lingam temple was destroyed by Aurangzeb in in 1669. (See also Champagne, 1978).

24 The Owl of Minerva takes flight at dawn and, as Walter Benjamin put it, attempts to warn men of the destruction piling up in the past as she is blown by the winds of progress inexorably and blindly into the future.

25 André Breton labeled Hedayat's novella a masterpiece (Kamshad 1966, 178).

26 A brief history of the Barmakis revolt: Tahir (the two right hands [i.e., who could fight with either hand]) is said to have shaken hands with the Eighth Imam using his left hand, using the excuse that his right was reserved for fealty to the caliph Ma'mun (father-in-law to the son of the Eighth Imam). Tahir had helped put Ma'mun on the throne by killing Ma'mun's brother, Amin. Amin

had been a full-blooded Arab, while Ma'mun had a Persian mother. Ma'mun dispatched Tahir to Khorasan as a governor, sending along a slave girl to watch him. Shortly after reading a *khotbeh* (sermon at the Friday noon prayers) in his own name (a claim of sovereignty), Tahir died of poisoning, presumably at the hand of the slave girl. As the poison began to work on him, people urged him to lie down, but he refused, saying, "Even at death manhood is necessary." He died seated in the Buddha's cross-legged, lotus position.

Mazyar led a Persian revolt against the Arab caliphs. Babak started a syncretistic religion of Zoroastrianism and Mazdakism, called Khorram Din, which was to be the ideology of the insurgent movement. The third conspirator, Afshin, was to infiltrate the caliph's army, which he did; but at the crucial moment he betrayed the conspiracy, remaining loyal to the caliph.

One might add to the list an earlier revolt, that of Abu Muslim, which overthrew the Umayyids and established the Abassids. Abu Muslim was killed by the second Abbasid caliph, Mansur, because, according to Persian tradition, the Arabs did not trust anyone who was not one of them.

27 Khayyam writes,

> This jar was once a mournful lover too,
> Caught in the tangles of a loved one's hair;
> This handle that you see upon its neck
> Once, when a hand, caressed a loved one's throat.
> (quoted in Dashti 1971, 148)

28 On Rilke and Kafka as influences, see Hillmann 1978 and Bashiri 1974. Hedayat translated works by Kafka, Sartre, Arthur Schnitzler, and Chekhov. On parallel techniques and cognitive style in Strindberg, T. S. Eliot, and Canetti, see the passages cited in Bradbury and McFarlane 1976 (71–93).

29 Some twenty cultural customs or beliefs are used in *The Blind Owl*: (1) *hamshir*: those suckled together commit incest if they marry or have sex; (2) the thirteenth of Noruz is a time when one best vacates home and city; (3) the withdrawing of the soul at death can be as painful as extracting a rusty nail from a board or as smooth as using up the oil in a lamp; (4) stars are metaphors for the dubious side of fate; (5) owls are symbols of death and changes of fate; (6) the water of Karabala are healing; (7) dogs can see into the next world; (8) birds are symbols of the soul; (9) headless shadows are signs of impending death; (10) the last Wednesday of the year is a potent time; (11) following a funeral at least a few steps demonstrates forgiveness toward the deceased; (12) sneezing is a warning to postpone action; (13) coins (dhirhams and peshiz, gerans and abbasis) and types of cloth (Tus cloth) are chronological clues; (14) cypress trees are icons of vigor and youth; (15) historical sites (Suran Tiver, Mohammadiyya Square) and tags ("Bride of the World"); (16) Islamic tokens, such as mosques, muezzins, Qur'ans placed on corpses' chests, and Arabic as the only language in which to talk to God or to the dead; (17) Omar Khayyam

and his skeptical quatrains; (18) codes of honor and propriety; (19) miniature tableaux of old men and houris as images of this world and the next;
(20) snakes, jars, and ruins are all associated with ancient treasure.

30 See also Ghanoonparvar 1979 for an excellent analysis of Chubak's *The Patient
Stone*.

31 See Rehder 1970. *Rind* seems to first appear in the twelfth century and is in
popular usage by the thirteenth.

32 Halu says formally, "If you are ready to sprinkle the water of repentance on your
head, if you accept me as your servant, let us marry and live together." The
normal betrothal formulas are: "May our son be your slave," "May our daughter
be your slave," and "May both be slaves of Ali." These formulas are also used at
the birth of a child.

33 A number of delightful idioms and locutions are displayed with comic genius in
the script. For instance, when the rind asks him how business is, the diviner
responds with a double entendre: "God does not let an open mouth go hungry,"
which refers to the pious notion that God will provide but also implies "as long
as I can talk I can con suckers into departing with their money."

34 Included in the *Montakhab al-tavarikh* (Selections from Histories) by Mulla
Mohammad Hashem Sabesvari.

35 Compare this ritual with the Moroccan one described by Crapanzano (1983),
particularly the ambiguous play between becoming a man and remaining a
child.

36 *Namus* is a Greek word, a borrowing that no doubt goes back to classical times.

37 See the sermon preserved in Ali's *Nahj ul-Balagha* (Qibla 1972, 116–17) and the
discussion in Fischer 1980 (162, 267n4).

38 Shirin, a lovely Median princess, attracts the eye of the Persian commander
Khosrow. Shirin's fiancé, Farhad, saves Khosrow from an angry Median mob.
Khosrow and Farhad thus strike up a strong bond of friendship, neither realiz-
ing they love the same girl: Shirin and Farhad know that Khosrow is Persian but
not that he is governor of Media. Khosrow enjoys playing a game, demanding
that if he is not to take revenge on the rebellious Medes, Shirin must marry him.
He thinks that when she finds out that the lad she only knows as Khosrow is the
governor, she will be overjoyed. The Median queen agrees despite Shirin's tears.
Farhad in despair goes off to find his friend Khosrow. When he finds out who
Khosrow is, he demands to be sent far away to carve out the imperial tomb.
Khosrow, perplexed, agrees to whatever his friend demands. When he finds out
that he has stolen Farhad's sweetheart, he summons Farhad to marry her, but
Farhad dies of exhaustion and heartbreak before all can be set right, and Shirin
follows him.

In *Kuche Mardha* Ali defends his friend Hasan against a claim of blood
revenge, despite suspicions that Hasan might be guilty. Ali does this also despite
the fact that he has just stopped courting his beloved because Hasan intends to
marry her. When Hasan learns of Ali's love, however, he refuses to go through

with the marriage. Hasan is killed just as Ali learns definitively that Hasan is innocent.

39 The script has been published (Sa'edi 1350/1971) with pictures from the film. The script was a collaboration between Sa'edi and Darius Mehrju'i, with direction by Sohrab Shaid Sales (Naficy 1981). The story originally appeared in 1964 as the fifth story in Sa'edi's collection *Mourners of Bayal (Azadarani Bayal)*.

40 Just as in Mas'ud Kimia'i's film *Khak* (Land), land is the essence of the peasant.

41 The harvest is traditionally divided into five equal portions, one portion each going to the supplier of land, seed, water, animal power, and labor. This, of course, is a nominal formula, varying by area and crop. In Yazd water was so scarce and expensive to apply (via *qanats*, or underground water canals) that it was worth one-third to half of the crop.

42 The cow is a central metaphor of the beneficent vision of Zoroastrianism. In the *Shahnameh*, the cow, Birmaya, is instrumental in saving the life of the hero Fereydun and is therefore killed by the arch-tyrant Zahhak. In Zoroastrian ritual, symbols of ultimate purity are taken from a pure white bull.

Ala'i (1948) wrote about a cow donated to the peasants of Veramin by the Near East Foundation one day in 1947. The next day the cow was returned because the local *gav-band* (owner and renter of cows) objected to invasion of his economic turf. Ala'i used the story as a symbol of a fear psychosis, a fear of standing up for one's rights, and he commented on the then proposed first seven-year plan: "Such fear psychosis cannot be cured by American loans. The most precious export commodity the U.S. has to offer is not its money wealth, but its revolutionary society in which individuals take their chances, express opposition to authority when and if they want to, and feel no dread of punishment if their experiment fails" (147).

There is yet another story of a cow which becomes the focus of excessive veneration. In Tabriz it is said that a tomb thought to be that of the Twelfth Imam attracted a cow. People kissed the hooves of this cow, collected its dung as blessings, and dedicated lamps to it even after it died. Further, the people claimed that since Tabriz was the shrine town of the Twelfth Imam, it ought to be exempt from taxes and government control. The story is told as an example of the gullibility of Tabrizis in debates over whether the Babi movement could be considered antifeudal (Vardosbi n.d., 12–20).

43 A juvenile fish wants to explore the world. His family and friends turn against him, feeling he is rejecting their love, and they stigmatize him as a heretic. But, he cries, there must be a world beyond, another way of life than just swimming in this pond. He swims over the rapids, lands in another pool, and finds himself in another equally narrow-minded society, this time of tadpoles who find him ugly. The story's author, Samad Behrangi, died suddenly, the government claimed by drowning in the Aras River. His readers rather suspected that the story of the little fish was now his true life's story, that he had explored too far and so had been killed. The children's book was periodically banned.

44 The pop singer Daryush popularized the words, "Oh my sadness, Oh my companion, My nights are long" [*Ay gham-i man, Munes-i man, Shabha deraz-eh*]. There are many such poems.

There is a popular hadith: if God loves someone, He gives him pain that he not forget Him. Another hadith proclaims: the world is the prison of the believers and the paradise of the kaffirs. A third says: the people of disaster are the friends of God. The Qur'an says to call on God with tears and fear (6.63, 7.55, 7.205). The *Du'a Komail*, read each Thursday evening, is Ali's plea to God that if he is to be condemned to hell, he will be able to bear the fire but not the distance from God (the hell-fire being understood as life in this world). In the *Monajot-i Manzum,* another prayer of Ali, Ali cries that he is a great sinner, and he begs that God's mercy be greater. Both these prayers are in the collection *Mufati al-Jinan* (Keys to Heaven) (Qummi 1970). One interpretation of Husain's martyrdom suggests that it occurred so that believers might cry and go to heaven. (Husain Wa'iz Kashefi gives this explanation in his *Rawzat al-Shuhada* [Garden of the Martyrs], the most famous of the verse *rowzat*, or homiletic sermons framed with references to the martyrdom of Husain at Karbala [see Fischer 1980 for a description of this and the related taziyeh forms].) The cosmic tragedy, the grounding for all these tears, begins with the expulsion of Adam from Paradise. The tragedy at Karbala is called *mosibat* (from *esabeh,* an arrow's target); that is, it has connotations of something predestined. *Taziyaeh* and *azadari* (mourning) stem from *'aza* (telling a story about death). The object of these forms is to elicit tears and instill a mood of quiet determination even in the face of overwhelming injustice and odds.

45 For example, a well-known verse states, "The sadness of love came upon me and drove off my other sadnesses, A needle is needed to rid the foot of a thorn" [*Gham-e eshq amad o ghamha-yi digar bad bebord / Suzani bayad kazb pa bazard khari*].

46 A hadith of the Sixth Imam, Imam Jafar Sadeq, says: our Shi'ites are of three types: a group which eats because of us; a group like glass which shatters; and a group like red gold—the more they are put in the fire, the purer they become. The Seventh Imam, Musa Kazem (one who swallows his anger) is so titled because one day he lost his temper and was admonished with a Qur'anic verse; he immediately swallowed his anger. Ali, the First Imam, is the other central parable figure for *kazem-i gheys*; when 'Amr ibn Abu Da'ud spit in his face, Ali refused to kill him until his anger cooled, lest he slay the pagan hero out of anger rather than for Islam (see the story in Fischer 1980, 267n5); there is also a refrain of this motif in the story of Ali's death (ibid., 17). Moses is unique in the Qur'an as the prophet who spoke directly to God (hence he is called Kalimullah, and his followers, the Jews, when spoken of politely, are called Kalimi); Moses is introduced as one who not only underwent many trials but who was consumed by remorse and sadness for having killed the Egyptian to stop him from beating a slave. Noah is said to have cried for nine hundred years because his message was ignored. Muhammad is said to have smiled (*tabassom*) but not

to have laughed. Ali is said to have endured twenty-five years of watching the community err and ignore his guidance, a pain likened to having a thorn in his eye and a bone in his throat. Khomeini is almost never shown smiling (on Khomeini, see Fischer 1983).

47 Ali, for instance, does dard-e del into a well.

48 Rowzat are often used in this fashion; perhaps the most famous literary description of this is the opening of Jalal Al-i Ahmad's eulogy for Samad Behrangi (English translation in Al-i Ahmad 1982). On Iranian depression and sadness, see Good and Good 1982.

49 Contrast the portrayal of grief, for instance, in *Doroshkeh-chi* and the honor and revenge genre films.

50 Hedayat wrote up the folktale behind the patient stone; an English translation appears in Hillmann 1980.

51 Anushiravan Adel (Khosrow I, r. 531–579) reorganized the government, reformed the tax system, established the Jundishapur medical school, and brought chess from India. There is a famous folktale, which Chubak utilizes, of the jackass and the Bell of the Justice. Anushiravan is suspicious that for so long no one has rung the bell to ask for the king's justice. The prime minister, Bozorgmehr, says a jackass has rung it and has a claim against his master. The jackass, however, refuses to testify, saying his master is poor. Meanwhile the rabble rises up outside the palace. The jackass suggests the king should himself ring the bell to summon those loyal to the crown. The king tries, but finds the bell is but an empty hide.

4. Filmic Judgment and Cultural Critique

I thank Joao Biehl and Mazyar Lotfalian for commenting on drafts of this paper, for insights and suggestions, and for general encouragement.

1 For an analysis of these posters, see Fischer and Abedi 1990. That volume is organized into parts on oral, literate, and visual-media worlds.

2 Derrida plays on the German terms *Offenbarung* and *Offenbarkeit*, invoking primarily their theological and philosophical resonances, but the terms also raise questions, especially given the debate over religion in Iran, of religion, democracy, and the public sphere. The term used by Habermas is *Offentlichkeit* (1962/1989).

3 For an account of these debates, see Fischer 1980.

4 See now also the late 1990s documentary, *Divorce Iranian Style*, by Kim Longinotto and Ziba Mir-Hosseini, which, in documenting both the continuing struggles of Iranian women and their ability to speak for themselves forcefully and volubly, has as its most affecting moment the scene in which the six-year-old daughter of the clerical judge sits on his empty seat, puts a cap on her head to imitate his turban, and proceeds to pronounce all the reasons why she would refuse to marry, mimicking the discourse of the adults in the court.

5 Engineer Mehdi Bazargan used the contrast between peep show and cinema to signify Iranian knowledge of the West of the generation at the turn of the century, and of his own generation of the pre–World War II era educated in Europe and America. I am indebed to Mazyar Lotfalian for recovering this metaphorical useage for me [Mazyar Lotfalian, Technoscientific Imaginaries: Muslims and the Culture of Curiosity, Ph.D. dissertation, Rice University, 1999].

6 The documentary film *Rosie the Riveter* deals explicitly both with this push of women back into the home and with some of the film propaganda used to help effect it (Friedan 1963).

5. War Again

1 One need not be a Lacanian to unpack this idea, and indeed Žižek traces it also to Schelling: "(What we experience as) reality is always already symbolized, and the problem resides in the fact that symbolization ultimately always fails, that it never succeeds in fully 'covering' the real, that it always involves some unsettled, unredeemed symbolic debt. *This real (the part of reality that remains non-symbolized) returns in the guise of spectral apparitions.* Consequently, 'specter' is not to be confused with . . . [what] some sociologists [call] 'socially' constructed; the notions of specter and (symbolic) fiction are codependent in their very incompatibility (they are 'complementary' in the quantum-mechanical sense)" (Žižek 1994, 21).

2 Other film examples discussed in chapters 3, 4, 5, and the epilogue include the Nietzschean (or Hedayatian) ring of promise or circular-return relation between the vultures on the towers of silence and the newborn child in Dehlavi's *Towers of Silence* (fantasies of escape to New York, overcoming the past; psychological tuggings back down and physical inescapabilities of Pakistan); the simorgh and blind owl in Attar and Hedayat; the black crows and blackboards in Samira Makhmalbaf's *The Blackboard*; the fires, dreams, and nightmares of Khuzistan in Naderi's *The Runner*, and Beza'i's *Bashu*. On Moses and Khidr, see Fischer and Abedi 1990, 110–11.

3 A photographer tries to escape his assignment of going to the front, but because a road sign pointing to Karbala is turned around, instead of fleeing toward Tehran as he intends, he ends up coming closer and closer to the front, and eventually becomes a hero. Meanwhile, a young boy wants to be martyred at the front but is held back from merely sacrificing his life by men who say he must wait his turn for martyrdom. The photographer is thus a bit like Moses trying to ignore or flee God's calling, or Oedipus attempting to escape the Sphinx's cryptic warning.

4 One could argue that the strategic mistake was to abandon Afghanistan after the Russian withdrawal, leaving opium and heroin production to prepare the political economy grounds for the Taliban and allowing Islamic fundamentalists to network between Afghanistan, Pakistan, Saudi Arabia, Egypt, and the

Sudan, thus creating a viable headquarters for al-Qaeda, complete with recruiting links to Europe, the United States, Algeria, Indonesia, and Malaysia.

5 Virtual Reality Caves have been built at the University of Illinois, Champaign-Urbana, Illinois, and at Brown University, Providence, Rhode Island. They are rooms with active projection screens on five walls (3 side walls, floor, ceiling). The user puts on goggles and data gloves which track eye and hand movements so that one has a feeling of total immersion in a space that one can move through.

6 Sudhir Kakar (1980), in a lovely short paper on film in India, makes a useful distinction between the fantasy structure and function of popular Indian ("masala" or "Bollywood") film and the complexity of auteur film in India or elsewhere. This is not to say that fantasy may not be an important operator in auteur film as well, as 1970s psychoanalytic film theory suggested, but that for films such as the Iranian films discussed here, those are an insufficient set of questions to rest with—and, as I argue, these films do indeed perform other kinds of cultural critique.

7 Regarding speed and stress calculations, as well as their conversion into kinetic energy and placement on the structural loads of the buildings, Eric Lipton and James Glanz provide an overview of analyses by MIT engineers ("First Tower to Fall Was Hit at Higher Speed, Study Finds," *New York Times* 23 February 2002, sec. A, pp. 1, 9). On the collapse of the towers themselves, see James Glanz's, "Why Trade Center Towers Stood, Then Fell," *New York Times* 11 November (*http://www.nytimes.com/2001/11/11nyregion/11COLL.html*); also see the bibliography at *http://nynv.aiga.org/res_engineering.shtml*. On the forthcoming report of the Federal Emergency Management Agency and the American Society of Civil Engineers, see Glanz and Lipton's "Towers withstood Impact, But Fell to Fire, Report Says," *New York Times* 29 March 2002, sec. A. pp. 1, 14.

8 Among the most interesting of the developments of the war was the formation of a film unit within the Baseej forces called the Forty Witnesses (*chehel shahid*, beginning with forty camera lads), which sent high-school youths to the front with mainly Super-8 cameras. Naficy says most of this footage was never turned into finished films, and much of it is now stored in such poor conditions that the archive is rapidly deteriorating. At least two documentaries were composed from such footage, one on the 1982 Moharram campaign, one on the liberation of Khoramshahr. Naficy gives a figure of fifty-six fiction feature films made during the war (seventy-four by 1990, two years after the ceasefire). He provides no measure of the representations of the enemy, saying only that most concentrated "on military operations, while a few concerned themselves with the war's social and psychological toll" (2001b). Sohrabi (1994) claims that many of the films made at and near the warfront about soldiers in battle do not show the Iraqis. Varzi says, "I saw no documentation in [Shahid Morteza Avini's long-running documentary series] *Rivayat Fath* of Iraqi soldiers: they are only represented filmicly during the war as fiction" (2002, 137n267). She describes Avini's techniques as innovative and as reacting against earlier war-propaganda films:

Avini would leave cameras in villages until villagers and soldiers stopped paying attention, so that one could shoot naturalistically and have soldiers speak directly to the camera. In particular, Avini reacted against the presentation of Iraqis as cowering in the face of approaching heroic Iranians; he both intended to present a truer picture of the war and argued that portraying Iraqis as cowardly was counterproductive, as it falsely obviated the need for Iranians to prepare themselves for the toughness of battle. Although Varzi says that in 1983 the ministry of culture initiated a war-movies section at the Farabi Film Foundation and some seventy amateur film directors were trained there, Avini operated a Jahad-i Sazandegi's (Reconstruction Corps) film section of the Qanun Islami Filmsazi, which Varzi claims was a semi-independent, semigovernmental organization and so had more freedom of operation than had it been a fully governmental unit. Or perhaps these were the same: she says a number of key filmmakers, such as Mohsen Makhmalbaf and Ebrahim Hatamikia, got their start in the war-movies section and under Avini's Jihad-e Sazandegi. Avini's funding, she says, came from the Sepah-e Pasandaran and the Farabi Film Foundation. Avini's *Rivayat Fath* was a documentary series—filmed in Tehran and at the front, where it was also partially edited—which aired on Iranian television almost every night for the length of the eight-year war. This clearly is a series that would be rewarding to review in some detail.

9   The American-Kurdish director Jano Rosebiani's film *Jiyan* (Life) (2002), the first of a trilogy on Kurdistan, complements the Iranian films. It is the story of a Kurdish-American who returns to Halabja, after the 1988 chemical attack, to build an orphanage. At the January 2003 screening of *Jiyan* at the Boston Museum of Fine Arts, Rosebiani underscored the Kurds' sense of being unable to trust any of their surrounding states (Iraq, Iran, Turkey). He noted that the Iranian army had held Halabja briefly before the Iraqi chemical attack and withdrew before the attack because they suspected the Iraqis would use chemical warfare. Tragically, however, they were complicit in the tragedy by preventing many people from leaving the town, because, he alleges, they wanted the propaganda value of being able to film many dead bodies (Iranian army footage apparently exists). The Turkish director Yesim Ustaoglu, in her second feature, *Journey to the Sun* (1999), beautifully shot by Jacek Petrycki (Krystof Kieslowski's former director of photography), portrays the troubles of working-class Kurdish migrants in Istanbul and the devastation of villages in eastern Turkey.

10   Since 2001 there has been a limited (in content and subject matter) but growing number of documentaries about Afghanistan. These include Paul Jay and Nelofer Pazira's *Return to Afghanistan* (Canadian Broadcast Corporation, 2003). Nelofer Pazira is the Canadian-Afghan woman whose story forms a core of Makhmalbaf's *Journey to Qandahar*. Two widely circulated documentaries include Saira Shah's *Behind the Veil* (British Broadcasting Company, 2001), done with the help of RAWA (Revolutionary Association of Women of Afghanistan); and Stephen Cocklin's *Afghanistan Revealed* (National Geographic, 2002). Particularly noteworthy on international intervention is Marijke Jongbloed's *Smile*

and Wave (2003), which follows the Dutch contingent of the U.N. International Security and Assistance Force into Kabul, describing their increasing isolation, their desire to help but cultural limitations, and the daily frustrations on the ground. The Japanese documentary filmmaker Noriaki Tsuchimoto made three documentaries in the 1980s under the Russian occupation: *Traces* (1988, released 2003), *Kabul Diary* (1985, released 2003), and *Afghan Spring* (1990, made with the Afghan director Abdul Latif). In 2002 the Afghan-American Jawad Wassel almost completed a film, *Fire Dancer*, about returning to Afghanistan before he was murdered by one of his producers; it has been shown in unfinished form and is being finished by his crew and friends. In 2004 Frontline World produced two shorts with interesting footage. Brian Knappenberger's *A House for Haji Baba* has footage of the corrupt administration of the warlord governor Gul Agha Shirzai of Qandahar. Because the Americans are planning to repave the Qandahar-Kabul road, Gul Agha Shirzai has his armed men seize Haji Abdullah's stone quarry without compensation so he can sell gravel and cement. Sarah Chayes, a former NPR journalist who is working with a Karzai brother's foundation to rebuild a village damaged by Americans in the fighting against the Taliban near the airport, goes to Gul Agha's offices to demand the stone that she has contracted from Haji Abdullah. The camera follows the bureaucratic runaround that she is given. Rath Arun's *Starring Osama bin Laden* has footage of a street opera (*jatra*) in Calcutta, in which Osama bin Laden is shown as a heroic Robin Hood, while the White House is portrayed as villainous (shouting "let corpses of babies litter the street!" after the attack on the New York World Trade Center). A lurid poster shows President George W. Bush with horns and vampire teeth.

11 A variant of this is one theme portrayed in the relationship between nephew and uncle in Ramin Serry's 2002 film *Maryam*. The nephew comes from Iran to the United States to get a masters degree, sponsored by and having to live with his father's brother, who, he thinks, was responsible for the betrayal and death of his father.

12 Haruki Murakami muses about "closed circuit" worlds of terrorists: "What I write are stories in which the hero is looking for the right way in this world of chaos. That is my theme. At the same time I think there is another world that is underground. You can access this inner world in your mind. Most protagonists in my books live in both worlds—this realistic world and the underground world. If you are trained you can find the passage and come and go between the two worlds. It is easy to find an entrance into this closed circuit, but it is not easy to find an exit. Many gurus offer an entry into the circuit for free. But they don't offer a way out. . . . I think that is very much like what happened with those people who flew the planes into those buildings" (qtd. in Howard French, "Seeing a Clash of Social Networks: A Japanese Writer Analyzes Terrorists and Their Victims," *New York Times* 15 October 2001, sec. E, p. 5).

13 Pakistan went from having no heroin addicts in 1979 to having an estimated five million in 1999 (Rashid 2000, 122).

14 Compare the similar images in Spike Lee's *Do The Right Thing* and Mani Rathnam's *Bombay*.

15 The political satire, such as it is, in *Dog Day Afternoon* is about police brutality in the aftermath of the brutal uprising and suppression in Attica prison, and about the inability of working-class people to have access to expensive sex-change operations. Both of these elements emerge as motivations for Sonny (Al Pacino), the first for his ability to turn the crowd against the police, and the second for his need for money. In *The Glass Agency* the need for specialized surgery and the money to pay for it and for transportation emerge more integrally as the opening premises of the story. The opening street vignettes, perhaps, encapsulate the difference. In Hatamikia's film Hajji, caught in one of Tehran's notorious gridlock traffic jams, sees his army buddy and in a joyous gesture calls, waves, gets out of his car, clambers over cars in the way, and hugs him—an image of friendship valued over all social impediments. In Lumet's *Dog Day Afternoon* the conspirators talk to each other, clearly nervous, setting the scene for this as a tragicomedy of ordinary people (rather than a noir crime thriller), but otherwise establishing little resonance or meaning.

16 See also Asghar Farhadi's 2003 film *Raghs Dar Ghobar* (Dancing in the Dust), a beautifully done film about love, loneliness, and sacrifice that has elements of *Red Ribbon* and *Beyond the Fire*. A laconic old recluse, who makes his living from a battered old van catching snakes to extract venom for vaccines, and a verbose young man are propelled together into the desert by inverse tragic love stories; their stories and their interactions are choreographed like a Möbius strip or Escher painting. The opening hieroglyphs are of *zurkhaneh* (traditional gymnasia) *pahlavans* (champions) slaying dragons (snakes), as the tambak drums and music of the zurkhaneh epic poetry well up (a hand wipes the condensation from the window of a bus, revealing that it is passing by a statue of a pahlavan slaying a dragon; this image is followed immediately by the title of the film); on the bus the young man is entertaining a toddler, who shakes his rattle, its sound interdigitating with that of the chains and drums of the zurkhaneh.

17 Although portrayed here on the scavenger and artisanal level, scrap-metal recy-cling is also a global industry. Fifty thousand tons of scrap metal from the collapse of New York's World Trade Center towers was immediately bid for and purchased by Shanghai Bao Steel Group, which planned to turn it into steel plates, which would then perhaps be reused for office furniture and filing cabi-nets. Indian companies also bought up World Trade Center scraps at $120/ton in 33,000-ton shipments, three to Madras and a fourth to the port of Kandla (*http://www.cnn.com/2002/WORLD/asiapcf/east/0/23/china.wtcsteel/index/html*).

18 Shades of Graham Greene's *The Third Man* and the making of money in post–World War II Vienna by selling diluted penicillin.

19 I am reminded of the story of two "peasants" trying to learn how to grow

potatoes in the Pamir region of Tajikistan who both, father and son, turned out to have been photographers in St. Petersburg before the collapse of the Soviet Union and the civil war in Tajikistan (story from the anthropologist William O. Beeman, personal communication).

20 Personal communication. Kamkari is a member of a young new generation of filmmakers outside the mainstream, sometimes having to smuggle their films out of the country.

21 *Afghan Alphabet*, done with a digital camera, looks at the problem of Afghan girls who do not attend school despite no longer being under Taliban rule. Makhmalbaf is particularly impressed with a girl at a UNICEF school who refuses to put off her burqa, who he says is "more afraid of the horrifying god the Taliban have created than of the Taliban" (2001b).

22 Qaem Alizadeh is the actual name of the young actor, and in the film, when the policeman in charge of tracking down illegal aliens asks him what the name means, the boy says that it has no meaning. The implication at that point in the film is that it is an alien name. *Qaem-mushak*, however, is the Persian name for the game hide-and-seek. *Qaem-magam*, moreover, is a title meaning something like viceroy, the representative of a ruler, and it implies strength from the Arabic root for perpendicular, as in a pillar of strength. Qaem-magams were typically sent from the center of power to govern in the provinces, thus owing their loyalty to the center, albeit often marrying with locals to bind them to the center. The family of a well-known reform prime minister is Qaemmagami, one of whom served as postmaster of Yazd when I first lived there. In the film, then, the name could work as the name of an illegal alien (hide-and-seek) who perseveres through the provincial adversity and chaos around him; and thus represents a structural phenomenon far more robust than a single character.

23 Seeing the schoolbook at the teahouse, the policeman asks Khan, with mild sarcasm, if he is learning to read. Khan, without missing a beat, says it is a book left by a trucker.

24 There is also an animal series: cows, sheep, goat kids, dogs. It pays homage not only to the traditional use of these animals as signs of life buffeted by conditions beyond their control, but also to more individualized awareness and consciousness, as when a dog barks a warning that the policeman is arriving or when another dog looks around before tasting the water of the pool. The image of goat kids who can't get out of a cavelike opening in a circular, yurtlike pen that is half underground and half aboveground is juxtaposed to that of the half-clandestine wedding taking place in a half-underground yurt covered with dirt for insulation and camouflage—an amusing analogy that brings a chuckle from the audience.

25 Gregory Bull's Associated Press photo in the *New York Times* (23 February 2002, sec. A, p. 8) is not of a bicycle but of a motorcycle. Stunt rider Kahlil Ahmed is caught at nearly right angles to the verticle on the circular wood slat wall of the performance pit. Still, the scene is familiar with men crowded around the

perimeter looking down at him, the shadows of their fellows from across the circle forms a second tier of onlookers projected onto the wall he is spinning around on.

26 In the margin of my copy of *Midnight's Children* I had noted, "Compare Khomeini's fatwa that women may not go to male gynecologists, but if it is absolutely necessary the gynecologists must look only indirectly via a mirror." A cartoon in an anti-Khomeini newspaper shows a woman, feet in stirrups, and the doctor looking in a mirror, captioned "Say 'ah.'" For a memoir of life under the Taliban in Kabul by the daughter of a woman gynecologist, see Latifa 2001.

27 In *Once Upon a Time, Cinema*, Makhmalbaf's female figure of the future, Attieh, is passive, the muse to which the filmmaker swears not to forget the promise of the cinema, technology, change; here the female figure of the future, Nafas, is active, taking risks, using technology, strategizing with and against oppressive instruments such as the veil. I'm indebted for this lovely contrast to Mazyar Lotfalian.

28 The mujahideen made a few propaganda films after the Russian retreat, mainly of Afghans fighting in desert terrain. In Russia two films took as their subject the memories of Russian soldiers. (In the United States *Rambo* did little to help audiences see Afghanistan.)

29 "Ghazni," writes Babur, "is a truly miserable place. Why kings who hold Hindustan and Khurasan would ever make such a wretched place their capital has always been a source of amazement to me. In Sultan Mahmud's time, there were three or four dams. A large one—forty or fifty yards high and approximately three hundred yards long—was constructed by him on the Ghazni River three leagues upriver to the north of Ghazni. A reservoir was created behind it, and the waterways to the fields were opened according to need. When Ala'uddin Jahansoz Ghuri [r. 1149–61] gained control of this province, he wrecked the dam, torched the tomb of Sultan Mahmud and those of many of his sons, and destroyed and burned the city of Ghazni. . . . But the year I conquered Hindustan [in 1526], I sent money with Khwaja Kalan to repair it" (in Thackston 1996, *The Baburnama*, 164). He does allow that there are "few places that have such fat game as Ghazni" (168).

Balancing Acts

1 See the news reports by Elaine Sciolino in the *New York Times*, in the Iran Press Service archives, and those of IranMania.com, all on 30 October 2002.

2 "Horace and Thunder" (after Horace, *Odes*, book 1, 34), read at and broadside printed for Seamus Heaney's reading at the Massachusetts Institute of Technology on 17 October 2002.

> Anything can happen. You know how Jupiter
> Will mostly wait for clouds to gather head

Before he hurls the lightning? Well, just now
He galloped his thunder cart and his horses

Across a clear blue sky. It shook the earth
And the clogged under-earth, the River Styx,
The wandering streams, the Atlantic shore itself.
Anything can happen, the tallest things

Be overturned, those in high places daunted,
Those overlooked regarded. Stropped-beak Fortune
Swoops, making the air gasp, tearing the crest off one,
Dropping it like a dripping crown on the next.

Ground gives. The heaven's weight
Lifts up off Atlas like a kettle lid.
Capstones shift, nothing resettles right,
Telluric ash and fire-spores boil away.

3 From *Weber's New Collegiate Dictionary*, 2nd ed. (Springfield, Mass.: G. C. Merriam, 1958), 409.

4 The forty-minute short *Testing Democracy*, directed by Makhmalbaf and Shahobuddin Faorkhyar, was produced in tandem with another short by Darius Mehrju'i, both being parts of a larger project called "Tales of an Island" (Kharg and Khish islands). In the penultimate scene of *Testing Democracy* a speed boat arrives painted with the message "The ballot box is coming" and a parachute with a box wrapped in white and a woman in a black chador descends into the sea along the beach. Makhmalbaf, as a character in the film, asks the woman if they need their identity cards, and she responds that they need not identity cards but their original birth certificates! Okay, the filmmaker and crew reply, we will go to Teheran. They wish her well ("Moafaq bashid!" [Be successful!]), and the film then runs backward so that she rises back up into the sky.

5 The presidential elections of 2000 generated offers from many nations to send election observers to the United States (to Florida in particular) as the United States had previously done to other nations. The widespread voting irregularities (of machine malfunction or mal-use; of voters turned away from the polls; of ad hoc official decisions about how results were counted and reported), the statistically tied vote, the swirling campaign-finance–reform controversies, controversies about the role of the press and how television-media formats omitted all but the most slogan-ridden and superficial discussion of policies, and the see-sawing decisions of the Florida and Federal Supreme Courts (which split along party lines, despite the fact that courts are supposed to be above partisan politics) left many feeling that the election was not decided by the voters who cast ballots, even though no allegations were made that the ballots themselves were not secret.

6 In all three films, fathers (or elder brothers) are driven to desperate action when the means to care for handicapped children run out, itself a sign of their

economic cul-de-sacs. In both *The Peddler* and *Low Heights* the arrival of yet another new child, the hope for an undamaged new life, precipitates the parents' actions.

7 The reference here is unclear, but Iran has a long history of peasants migrating to India when there were cyclical famines; and for Abadanis and others along the Persian Gulf coast there was fairly free migration back and forth across the Gulf when economic conditions worsened in one place or the other.

Epilogue

1 "What then is truth? A mobile army of metaphors, metonyms, and anthropomorphisms—in short, a sum of human relations, which have been enhanced, transposed, and embellished poetically and rhetorically, and which after long use seem firm, canonical, and obligatory to a people: truths are illusions about which one has forgotten that this is what they are; metaphors which are worn out and without sensuous power; coins which have lost their pictures and now matter only as metal, no longer as coins" (Nietzsche 1873/1954).

2 These are my approximate counts by institutions: if a university sent teams to more than one league competition, I have counted that still as one team. There's no virtue here in the numbers, except my delighted surprise to find so many Iranian teams. Philips sent a team of midsize robots, developed by engineers as a hobby on their free time (friendly, large men happily costumed in intimidating black overalls to add psychological terror to their robots' impressively strong kicking power), and is thinking of teaming up with a university to develop a humanoid robot. Sony and Honda were the other two major corporations represented. Sony is a longtime sponsor and developer with Hiroaki Kitano of the Pino humanoid. Honda in 2002, amid much careful choreography, hype, and secrecy, showcased its hardcased humanoid Asimo, also deployed throughout Japan at Honda dealerships with giveaway soft dolls and plastic models.

3 Whenever a team scores 10–0, it is declared the winner. By then, one can see which of the technologies has created a clear advantage.

4 Cited in Nägele (2002, 23–24) from Walter Bejamin's letters to Gretel Adorno and Gershom Scholem: "Painterly representation appears on the vertical surface (as in the shape of a tree that has been cut vertically), the graphic sign or design appears on the horizontal surface (as the rings on the tree on the horizontal surface of the trunk. Condensed to the opposition of *Zeichen* (sign) and *Mal* (mark, stigma, birthmark, from which is derived malen = to paint), Benjamin [writes to Scholem]: 'The plane of the sign (*Zeichen*) is—seen from the perspective of man—horizontal, that of the mark (*Mal*) vertical.'"

5 Saramatians, an Iranian group, are to this day proudly counted as ancestors of the Polish nobility. Bosnians trace themselves to the Bogomils; it is said that some six-hundred-seventy nomads, comprising Bulgars or Huns and Iranians,

led by Khan Asparuch, defeated Constantine IV and founded the first Bulgarian Empire. It was only in 1867 that the last clan of Bogomils converted to Islam in Herzegovina. The Cathars were forced to wear a yellow cross of heresy, were crushed in 1244, and were the object of Roman Catholic inquisitors for the next century. They believed in the two powers of Good and Evil, and were strict vegetarians. Although a Mithra cult spread through the Roman Empire, with temples as far away as London, the iconography and the cult, with its slaying of the bull, were quite different from that of Persia.

6 The following notes on Richard Strauss are taken from Wilhelm 1984/1989 (72). Gustav Mahler and Friedrich Delius also set *Zarathustra* to music.

7 In *Also Sprach Zarathustra* Strauss associates D-flat major with ceremony; A minor with destiny; E minor with disgust; E-flat minor with death; C minor with heroic defiance; F-sharp minor with anguish; E major with erotic exuberance; G major with childlike naïveté.

8 Kubrick and Arthur C. Clarke began collaborating in 1964, shooting began in December 1965, the film was released in 1968. In March 1965 the Russian astronaut Aleksei Leonov was the first man to "walk" in space, followed in June by American Ed White. *Mariner IV* flew within six thousand miles of Mars that same month, sending back pictures. In 1967 first a Russian, then an American unmanned spacecraft landed on the moon.

9 See the collection of reviews and reminiscences, *The Making of* 2001: A Space Odyssey, selected by Stephanie Schwam (New York: Modern Library, 2000), for a reminder of the mixed reactions to the early showings of the film, and the mix of homages to the past, present and future of the 1950s and 1960s. See particularly Thomas Willis's observation that there is no music of the future in the film, but that film is one of the technologies of sampling that "is insuring the survival of the fittest" among popular sounds. Also see Renata Adler's cataloging of the features stemming from a sensibility that is "intellectual fifties child": chess-games, body-building, camp bunk beds, Egyptian mummies, time games, World War II movie "bomb bay doors open," and the final slab closing in "begins to resemble a fifties candy bar." Simon Garfinkle's notes on the state of computer, artificial intelligence, and voice-recognition technologies thirty years later in 2001 are particularly useful.

10 Note that the circling eagle is wrapped by a serpent as opposed to grasping a serpent in its talons as a predator would to prey.

The symbol of Zoroastrianism, popularized in recent times from ancient Achaemenid reliefs, is of the *faravahar* or fravashi, the winged disc and spread eagle, the symbol of the divine light or grace of royal sovereignty (farr). The winged disc is a motif common to ancient Egypt and Mesopotamia for divine kingship or divine favor on a king. In Egypt the winged sun disc denoted the hawk-god Horus incarnate in pharaoh. The Zoroastrian symbol is popularly said to represent, in the image of two streamers from the central disc, the choice between good and evil, and, in the three tiers of the wings, "good words, good thoughts, good deeds"; the left hand of the bearded figure of the soul holds the ring of promise of the right path and salvation, while the right hand gestures to the path of righteousness; and the disc itself represents eternity (like the snake that chases its own tail).

Regarding Ecclesiastes, see Gooding-Williams 2001: "The proposition 'God is a thought that makes crooked all that is straight' (*Gott ist ein Gendanke, der macht alles Gerade krumm*) clearly resounds the perspective of Ecclesiastes 7:13 ('Consider the work of God for who can make that straight, which he hath made crooked' [*Siehe an die Werke Gottes, denn wer kann das schlect machen! das er kurmmet*]) and indirectly invokes a vision of time that, elsewhere in Ecclesiastes (1:9–10), captures the imprisoning circularity of God's work: 'The thing that hath been, it is that which shall be . . . there is no new thing under the sun' " (196).

11 A phrase associated with Ali Shariati in Iran. Heidegger (1937/1984, 212) connects *der Genesende* (the Convalescent) with Greek *neomai, nostos* (to head for home, to turn to what defines oneself).

12 McLaughlin cites Benjamin: " 'In exchange for the immediacy of the [divine] name that was damaged by [the Fall], a new immediacy arises: the magic of judgment [Urteil],' " then himself comments, "if the Fall is a judgment (Urteil) consigning all communication (Mitteilung) to impurity and mediateness . . . then Mitteilung becomes the virtual site of Urteil" (2002, 213–14).

13 "I have grown weary of the poets, old and new; superficial they all seem to me, and shallow seas. Their thoughts have not penetrated deeply enough; therefore their feelings did not touch bottom." (Nietzsche 1883–1885/1961, 240).

14 "The Education of Schopenhauer" (Nietzsche 1874/1983, 46–47; qtd. in Gooding-Williams 2001, 190).

15 As if addressing the hard-liner mullahs holding on to power in Iran today, Nietzsche's Zarathustra recommends: "Admit it! Whenever your [revolutionary] noise and smoke were gone, very little had happened. . . . This counsel, however, I give to kings and churches and everything that is weak with age and weak with virtue: let yourselves be overthrown—so that you may return to life, and virtue return to you" (Nietzsche 1883–1885/1961, 243). The theme of martyrdom remains as relevant to the mobilization of the Karbala paradigm in Iran as it was for the European discussions of sacrifice as part of the poesis of tragedy and for Benjamin's sharp distinction between Greek tragedy and the mourning of baroque passion plays.

16 Although relations between the United States and Iran have been suspended since the revolution, under the Clinton Administration cultural exchanges were encouraged. This was reversed by the Bush Administration.

17 Sussan Deyhim is known, among other things, for her spectacular renditions of lyrics by Rumi and Hafez; see her compact disc *Madman of God* (2000, Crammed Discs, Belgium).

18 It would be interesting to explore the discussions of mythic sacrifice versus baroque mourning and Promethean sacrifice versus the biblical Fall (see Fenves 2002 on Benjamin's interventions), using both the trope contexts of Siyavush

and Husain and the contemporary political uses of martyrdom in mobilizing village boys as Baseej (irregular forces) in the Iran-Iraq War and among suicide bombers in Palestine, against which the Palestinian poet Muhammad Darwish has recently composed poems, pleading "The martyr teaches me, makes clear to me, warns me. . . . No role for me was left in the language" (*Under Siege* [Ramallah, 2002; Hebrew trans. Jerusalem: Andalus 2003]).

19 For an account of his film *The Suitors* (1988), see Fischer and Abedi 1990 (256–58).

Bibliography

Abbas, Ackbar. 1992. "Review of Gilles Deleuze's *Cinema 1, 2*." *Discourse* 14, no. 3.

Abdoh, Salar. 2000. *The Poet Game*. New York: Picador.

Adorno, Theodor W. 1970/1997. *Aesthetic Theory*. Edited by Gretel Adorno and Rolf Tiedemann. Translated by Robert Hullot-Kentor. Minneapolis: University of Minnesota Press.

Ala'i, H. 1948. "How Not to Develop a Backward Country." *Fortune* 38, no. 2: 76–77, 145–57.

Albright, Charlotte F. 1976. "The Azerbaijani 'Ashiq and his Performance of a Dastan." *Iranian Studies* 4: 220–47.

A'li, Abulfazl, ed. 1985. *The Graphic Art of the Islamic Revolution*. Tehran: Publications Division of the Art Bureau of the Islamic Propagation Organization.

Al-i Ahmad, Jalal. 1958/1974. *The School Principal*. Translated by John K. Newton. Minneapolis: Bibliotheca Islamica.

——. 1961a/1988. *By the Pen (Nun va al-qalam)*. Translated by Mohammad R. Ghanoonparvar. Austin, Texas: Center for Middle East Studies.

——. 1961b/1982. *Gharbzadegi (Weststruckness)*. Translated by John Green and Ahmad Alizadeh. Lexington, Kentucky: Mazda Publishers.

——. 1967. *Nifrin-i Zamin (The Cursing of the Land)*. Tehran: Intisharat-i Nil.

——. 1978. "The Hedayat of The Blind Owl." In *Hedayat's "The Blind Owl" Forty Years After*, edited by Michael Hillmann. Austin, Tex.: Center for Middle East Studies.

——. 1982. *Iranian Society: An Anthology of Writings*. Edited by Michael C. Hillmann. Lexington, Ky.: Mazda Publishers.

Aminrazavi, Mehdi. 1993. "The Significance of Suhrawardi's Persian Sufi Writings in the Philosophy of Illumination." In *Classical Persian Sufism: From Its Origins to Rumi*, edited by Leonard Lewisohn. London: Khaniqah Nimatullah Publications.

——. 1997. *Suhrawardi and the School of Illumination*. Richmond, Surrey: Curzon Press.

Appadurai, Arjun, Frank J. Korom, and Margaret A. Mills. 1991. *Gender, Genre, and*

Power in South Asian Expressive Traditions. Philadelphia: University of Pennsylvania Press.

Arberry, A. J. 1964. *The Koran Interpreted.* London: Oxford University Press.

Azoy, G. Whitney. 1982. *Buzkashi: Game and Power in Afghanistan.* Philadelphia: University of Pennsylvania Press. 2d ed. Prospect Heights, Ill.: Waveland Press, 2003.

Bacher, Wilhelm. 1871. *Nizami's Leben und Werke und der Zweite Theil des Nizamischen Alexandersbuches.* Leipzig: Englemann.

Bagheri, Bahman. 2000. "Houston, We Have a Diva!" *Iranian* (26 Sept.). http://www.iranian.com/Features/2000/September/Houston/index.html.

Bakhtin, Mikhail. 1940. *Rabelais and His World.* Boston: Massachusetts Institute of Technology Press.

———. 1981 *The Dialogic Imagination.* Austin: University of Texas Press.

Balaghi, Shiva, and Lynn Gumpert. 2002. *Picturing Iran: Art, Society, and Revolution.* New York: I. B. Tauris.

Baraheni, Reza. 1977. *The Crowned Cannibals: Writings on Repression in Iran.* New York: Vintage Books.

Barth, John 1967. "The Literature of Exhaustion." *Atlantic Monthly* 220 (August).

———. 1972. "Dunyazadiad." In *Chimera.* New York: Random House.

Bashiri, Iraj. 1974. *Hedayat's Ivory Tower.* Minneapolis: Manor House.

Bateson, Mary Catherine, Jerome W. Clinton, J. Barkev M. Kassarjian, Hassan Safari, and Mehdi Soraya. 1977. "Safa-yi Batin: A Study of the Interrelations of a Set of Iranian Ideal Character Types." In *Psychological Dimensions of Near Eastern Studies*, edited by L. Carl Brown and Norman Itzkowitz. Princeton, N.J.: Darwin Press.

Baudrillard, Jean. 1981/1994. *Simulacra and Simulation.* Translated by Sheila Faria Glaser. Ann Arbor: University of Michigan Press.

Beard, Michael. 1982. "The Hierarchy of the Arts in Buf-e Kur." *Iranian Studies* 15, nos. 1–4: 53–68.

Beck, Ulrich. 1986/1992. *Risk Society: Towards a New Modernity.* Translated by Mark Ritter. London: Sage.

———. 1997. *What Is Globalization?* London: Blackwell.

Beeman, William O. 1986. *Language, Status, and Power in Iran.* Bloomington: Indiana University Press.

Behrangi, Samad. 1976. *"The Little Black Fish" and Other Modern Persian Stories.* Translated by Mary Hooglund and Eric Hooglund. Washington: Three Continents.

Benjamin, Walter. 1928/1979. "A Short History of Photography." *One Way Street and Other Writings.* London: New Left Books.

———. 1969. *Illuminations.* Edited by Hannah Arendt. Translated by Henry Zohn. New York: Schocken.

Bertels, Eugeni Eduardovich, et al. 1960–1971. *Shahname: Kriticheskii tekst.* Vols. 1–9. Leningrad: Institut Vostolrovedeniia.

Bettelheim, Bruno. 1983. *Freud and Man's Soul.* New York: Knopf.

al-Biruni, Muhammad ibn Ahmad. 1879/1969. *The Chronology of Ancient Nations*. Edited and translated by C. Edward Sachau. London: Curzon.

Blackburn, Stuart. 1988. *Singing of Birth and Death: Texts in Performance*. Philadelphia: University of Pennsylvania Press.

Blackburn, Stuart, Peter Calus, Joyce Flueckiger, and Susan Wadley, eds. 1989. *Oral Epics in India*. Berkeley: University of California Press.

Bodansky, Yossef. 2001. *Bin Laden: The Man Who Declared War on America*. New York: Random House.

Bogle, L. 1978. "The Khayyamic Influence in 'The Blind Owl.' " In *Hedayat's "The Blind Owl" Forty Years After*, edited by Michael Hillmann. Austin, Tex.: Center for Middle East Studies.

Boyce, Mary. 1955. "Zariadres and Zarer." *Bulletin of the School of Oriental and African Studies* 17: 463–77.

——. 1957. "The Parthian Gosan and the Iranian Minstrel Tradition." *Journal of the Royal Asiatic Society* 18: 10–45.

——. 1966. "Atash-zohr and Ab-zohr." *Journal of the Royal Asiatic Society* 27: 100–118.

——. 1970a. "Haoma, Priest of the Sacrifice." In *W. B. Henning Memorial Volume*, edited by Mary Boyce and Ilya Gershevitch. London: Lund, Humphries.

——. 1970b. "Zoroaster the Priest." *Bulletin of the School of Oriental and African Studies* 33, no. 1: 22–28.

——. 1975a. *A History of Zoroastrianism*. Leiden: E. J. Brill.

——. 1975b. "On Mithra, Lord of Fire." In *Monumentum H. S. Nyberg. Acta Iranica* 1: 69–76.

——. 1977. *A Persian Zoroastrian Stronghold*. Oxford: Clarendon Press.

——. 1979. *Zoroastrians: Their Religious Beliefs and Practices*. London: Routledge, Kegan, and Paul.

Boyce, Mary, and Firoze Kotwal. 1971. "Zoroastrian 'baj' and 'dron.' " *Bulletin of the School of Oriental and African Studies* 34, nos. 1–2: 56–73, 298–313.

Bradbury, Malcolm, and James McFarlane, eds. 1976. *Modernism: 1890–1930*. New York: Penguin.

Browne, Edward Granville. 1924. *A Literary History of Persia*. Cambridge: Cambridge University Press.

Castells, Manuel. 1996. *The Rise of the Network Society*. Vol. 1 of *The Information Age.* Malden, Mass.: Blackwell.

——. 1997. *The Power of Identity*. Vol. 2 of *The Information Age*. Malden, Mass.: Blackwell.

——. 1998. *End of Millennium*. Vol. 3 of *The Information Age*. Malden, Mass.: Blackwell.

Caton, Steven. 1990. *"Peaks of Yemen I Summon": Poetry as Cultural Practice in a North Yemeni Tribe.* Berkeley: University of California Press.

Chadwick, Nora K., and Victor Zhirmunsky. 1969. *Oral Epics of Central Asia*. London: Cambridge University Press.

Chelkowski, Peter. 1975. *Mirror of the Invisible World: Tales from the Khamseh of Nizami*. New York: Metropolitan Museum of Art.

Chelkowski, Peter J., and Hamid Dabashi. 1999. *Staging a Revolution: The Art of Persuasion in the Islamic Republic of Iran*. New York: New York University Press.

Champagne, D. C. 1978. "Hindu imagery in 'The Blind Owl.'" In *Hedayat's "The Blind Owl" Forty Years After*, edited by Michael C. Hillmann. Austin, Tex.: Center for Middle East Studies.

Clausewitz, Carl von. 1984. On War. Princeton: Princeton University Press.

Corbin, Henri. 1946. *Les Motifs Zoroastriens dans la Philosophie de Sohrawardi, Shaykh ol-Ishraq*. Tehran: Editions du Courrier.

——. 1960/1990. *Spiritual Body and Celestial Earth: From Mazdean Iran to Shi'ite Iran*. Translated by Nancy Pearson. London: Tauris.

Cottam, Richard. 1981. "Review of Michael Hillmann (ed.), *Major Voices in Contemporary Persian Literature*." *Iranian Studies* 14, nos. 1–2: 123–26.

Crapanzano, Vincent. 1983. "Rites of Return: Circumcision in Morocco." In *The Psychoanalytic Study of Society*, edited by Werner Muensterberger and L. Bryce Boyer. Vol. 9. New York: Psychohistory.

Dabashi, Hamid. 2001. *Close Up: Iranian Cinema Past, Present, and Future*. London: Verso.

Daniel, E. 1978. "History as a Theme of 'The Blind Owl.'" In *Hedayat's "The Blind Owl" Forty Years After*, edited by Michael Hillmann. Austin, Tex.: Center for Middle East Studies.

Darrow, William R. 1981. The Zoroaster Legend: Its Historical and Religious Significance. Ph.D. diss., Harvard University.

Dashti, Ali. 1971. *In Search of Omar Khayyam*. Translated by L. P. Elwell-Sutton. New York: Columbia University Press.

Davidson, Olga. 1994. *Poet and Hero in the Persian Book of Kings*. Ithaca, N.Y.: Cornell University Press.

Davis, Dick. 1992. *Epic and Seduction: The Case of Ferdowsi's Shahnameh*. Washington: Mage.

——. 2002. *Pantheia's Children: Hellenistic Novels and Medieval Persian Romances*. New York: Bibliotheca Persica Press.

Dawes, James. 2002. *The Language of War*. Cambridge: Harvard University Press.

Deleuze, Gilles. 1983. *Cinema I: The Movement-Image*. Translated by Hugh Tomlinson and Barbara Habberjam. Minneapolis: University of Minnesota Press.

——. 1985. *Cinema II: The Time-Image*. Translated by Hugh Tomlinson and Robert Galeta. Minneapolis: University of Minnesota Press.

Deleuze, Gilles, and Felix Guattari. 1980/1987. *A Thousand Plateaus: Capitalism and Schizophrenia*. Translated by Brian Massumi. Minneapolis: University of Minnesota Press.

DeMan, Paul. 1971. *Blindness and Insight: Essays in the Rhetoric of Contemporary Criticism*. New York: Oxford University Press.

——. 1979. *Allegories of Reading: Figural Language in Rousseau, Nietzsche, Rilke, and Proust*. New Haven, Conn.: Yale University Press.

Derrida, Jacques. 1967. *Of Grammatology*. Baltimore, Md.: Johns Hopkins University Press.

———. 1972/1981. *Dissemination*. English translation by Barbara Johnson. Chicago: University of Chicago Press.

———. 1982/1988. *The Ear of the Other: Otobiography, Transference, Translation: Texts and Discussions with Jacques Derrida*. English edition edited by Christie McDonald; translation by Peggy Kamuf from the French edition edited by Claude Levesque and Christie McDonald. 2d ed. University of Nebraska Press.

———. 1996/1998. "Faith and Knowledge: The Two Sources of 'Religion' at the Limits of Reason Alone." Edited and translated by Samuel Weber. In *Religion*, edited by Jacques Derrida and Gianni Vattimo, 1–78. Stanford: Stanford University Press.

———. 2001. "Above All, No Journalists!" In *Religion and Media*, edited by Hent de Vries and Samuel Weber, 56–93. Stanford: Stanford University Press.

Detienne, Marcel. 1972/1977. *The Gardens of Adonis: Spices in Greek Mythology*. Edited and translated by Janet Lloyd. Atlantic Highlands, N.J.: Humanities.

Detienne, Marcel, and Jean-Pierre Vernant. 1978. *Cunning Intelligence in Greek Culture and Society*. Atlantic Highlands, N.J.: Humanities.

Durkheim, Emile. 1912/1915. *The Elementary Forms of Religious Life*. Translated by Joseph Ward Swain. New York: Macmillan.

Esfandiari, Fereydun M. 1959. *Day of Sacrifice*. New York: Random House.

———. 1966. *Identity Card*. New York: Grove.

Fabian, Johannes. 1983. *Time and the Other*. New York: Columbia University Press.

Fanon, Frantz. 1961/1968. *The Wretched of the Earth*. New York: Grove.

Fenves, Peter. 2002. "Tragedy and Prophecy in Benjamin's *Origin of the German Mourning Play*." In *Benjamin's Ghosts*, edited by Gerhard Richter. Stanford: Stanford University Press.

Firdausi. 1905. *The Shahnama of Firdausi Done into English by Arthur George Warner and Edmund Warner*. London: K. Paul, Trench, Trübner.

Fischer, Michael M. J. 1969. Fieldnotes: Trip to Afghanistan. Ms.

———. 1973. "Zoroastrian Iran between Myth and Praxis." Ph.D. diss., University of Chicago.

———. 1980. *Iran: From Religious Dispute to Revolution*. Cambridge: Harvard University Press. 2d ed., with new introduction. Madison: University of Wisconsin Press, 2003.

———. 1982. "Islam and the Revolt of the Petite Bourgeoisie." *Daedalus* 111, no. 1: 101–25.

———. 1983. "Imam Khomeini: Four Ways of Understanding." In *Voices of Resurgent Islam*, edited by John Esposito. New York: Oxford University Press.

———. 1990. "Bombay Talkies, the Word and the World: Salman Rushdie's Satanic Verses." *Cultural Anthropology* 5, no. 2.

———. 1995a. "Film as Ethnography and as Cultural Critique in the Late Twentieth Century." In *Shared Differences: Multicultural Media and Practical Pedagogy*, edited by Diane Carson and Lester Friedman. Urbana: University of Illinois Press.

———. 1995b. "Starting Over: How, What, and for Whom Does One Write about Refugees? The Poetics and Politics of Refugee Film as Ethnographic Access in a

Media-Saturated World." In *Mistrusting Refugees*, edited by E. Valentine Daniel and John Chr. Knudsen. Berkeley: University of California Press.

———. 1997. "Filming Poland: The Ethnographic (Documentary, Narrative) Films of Maria Zmarz-Koczanowicz." In *Cultural Production in Perilous States: Editing Events, Documenting Change*, vol. 4 of *Late Editions: Cultural Studies for the End of the Century*, edited by George Marcus, 91–150. Chicago: University of Chicago Press.

———. 1998. "Filmic Judgment and Cultural Critique: Film in Revolutionary Iran and Postcommunist Poland." In *Recent Trends in Anthropological Theory and Ethnography*, edited by Dimitra Gefou-Madianou. Athens, Greece: Ellinika Grammata.

———. 1999. "Emergent Forms of Life: Anthropologies of Post- and Late Modernities. *Annual Reviews of Anthropology* 28: 455–78.

Fischer, Michael M. J., and Mehdi Abedi. 1990. *Debating Muslims: Cultural Dialogues in Postmodernity and Tradition*. Madison: University of Wisconsin Press.

Fischer, Michael M. J., and Thomas J. Barfield. 1980. "Khuzistan and Helmand." In *The Social Impact of Development on Ethnic Minorities: Iran, Afghanistan, Sudan, Brazil* (with D. Maybury-Lewis, J. Clay, R. Huntington, B. Pajackowski). Cambridge, Mass.: Cultural Survival.

Forbes, Jill, and Michael Kelly, ed. 1995. *French Cultural Studies*. New York: Oxford University Press.

Foucault, Michel. 1971. *The Order of Things*. New York: Pantheon Books.

———. 1979. *Power, Truth, Strategy*. Edited by Meaghan Morris and Paul Patton. Sydney: Feral Publications.

Freud, Sigmund. 1913/1923. *The Interpretation of Dreams*. 3d ed. Translated by Abraham Arden Brill. New York: Macmillan.

———. 1925/1953. "The Uncanny." In *The Standard Edition of the Complete Psychological Works of Sigmund Freud*, edited by James Strachey, 17:217–56. London: Hogarth Press.

———. 1915/1953. "Thoughts for the Times of War and Death." In *The Standard Edition of the Complete Psychological Works of Sigmund Freud*, edited by James Strachey, vol. 14. London: Hogarth Press.

———. 1919. *Beyond the Pleasure Principle*. Translated by James Strachey. New York: Norton, 1959.

Friedan, Betty. 1963. *The Feminine Mystique*. New York: Norton.

Gadamer, Hans Georg. 1975. *Truth and Method*. Edited and translated by Garret Barden and John Cumming. New York: Seabury.

Gans, Herbert J. 1974. *Popular Culture and High Culture: An Analysis and Evaluation of Taste*. New York: Basic Books.

Gass, William H. 1980. *Fiction and the Figures of Life*. Boston: David R. Godine.

Gellner, Ernest. 1988. "The Zeno of Cracow." In *Malinowski between Two Worlds*, edited by Roy Ellen, Ernest Gellner, Grzyna Kubica, and Janusz Mucha. Cambridge: Cambridge University Press.

Gelpke, Rudolph. 1962. *Die Iranische Prosaliteratur im 20. Jahrhundert*. Wiesbaden: Otto Harrasowitz.

Gershevitch, Ilya. 1953. "Iranian Literature." In *Literature of the East*, edited by E. B. Ceadel, 50–73. London: John Murray.

——. 1959. *The Avestan Hymn to Mithra*. Cambridge: Cambridge University Press.

——. 1974. "An Iranist's View of the Soma Controversy." In *Mémorial Jean de Menasce*, edited by Philippe Gignoux and Ahmad Tafazzoli. Louvaine: Orientaliste.

Ghanoonparvar, Mohammad R. 1976. "Jalal Al-i Ahmad's *The Cursing of the Land*: A Plot Summary." *Literature East and West* 20, nos. 1–4: 240–44.

——. 1979. "Sadeq Chubak's *The Patient Stone*." Ph.D. diss., University of Texas at Austin.

Goffman, Erving. 1959. *The Presentation of Self in Everyday Life*. New York: Doubleday.

——. 1961. *Asylums*. New York: Doubleday.

Good, Bryon, and MaryJo DelVecchio Good. 1982. "The Interpretation of Iranian Depressive Illness and Dysphoric Affect." Paper presented to the American Anthropological Association, Washington.

Gooding-Williams, Robert. 2001. *Zarathustra's Dionysian Modernism*. Stanford: Stanford University Press.

Goody, Jack. 1977. *The Domestication of the Savage Mind*. London: Cambridge University Press.

Grabar, Oleg, and Sheila Blair. 1980. *Epic Images and Contemporary History: The Illustrations of the Great Mongol* Shahnameh. Chicago: University of Chicago Press.

Griffin, Michael. 2001. *Reaping the Whirlwind: The Taliban Movement in Afghanistan*. London: Pluto.

Habermas, Jürgen. 1962/1989. *The Structural Transformation of the Public Sphere*. Cambridge: Massachusetts Institute of Technology Press.

Ha'iri Yazdi, Mahdi. 1973. "A Treatise on Knowledge by Presence." Ph.D. diss., University of Toronto.

Hanaway, William. 1970. "Persian Popular Romances before the Safavid Period." Ph.D. diss., Columbia University. Ann Arbor, Michigan.: University Microfilms.

——. 1985. "The Symbolism of the Persian Revolutionary Posters." In *Iran since the Revolution*, edited by Barry Rosen. New York: Columbia University Press.

Hansen, Mark. 2000. *Embodying Technesis: Technology beyond Writing*. Ann Arbor: University of Michigan Press.

Hansen, Miriam. 2002. "Benjamin and Cinema: Not a One Way Street." In *Benjamin's Ghosts*, edited by Gerhard Richter, 41–73. Stanford: Stanford University Press.

Hanssen, Beatrice. 2002. "Portrait of Melancholy (Benjamin, Warburg, Panofsky)." In *Benjamin's Ghosts*, edited by Gerhard Richter, 169–90. Stanford: Stanford University Press.

Harvey, David. 1989. *The Condition of Postmodernity: An Enquiry into the Origins of Cultural Change*. Cambridge, Mass: Blackwell.

Havelock, Eric. 1986. *The Muse Learns to Write*. New Haven, Conn.: Yale University Press.

Hedayat, Sadegh. 1930. *Zinda Bi-gur* (*Buried Alive*: 8 short stories). Tehran.

———. 1931. "Saya-hi Mughul" (Mongol Shadow). In Sadegh Hedayat, Bozorg Alavi, and Shin-l Partwa. *Aniran* (*Non-Iranian*). Tehran.

———. 1932a. *Seh Qatre Khun* (*Three Drops of Blood*: 11 short stories). Tehran.

———. 1932b. "Dash Akol." In *Seh Qatre Khun*.

———. 1933a. *Saya Rushan* (*Chiaroscuro*: 7 short stories). Tehran.

———. 1933b. "Shab-ha-yi Veramin" (The Nights of Veramin). In *Saya Rushan*. Tehran.

———. 1933c. "Akharin Labkhand" (The Last Smile). In *Saya Rushan*.

———. 1933d. *Nayrangistan* (*Persian Folktales*). Tehran.

———. 1937/1957. *Buf-I Kur* (*The Blind Owl*). Translated by D. P. Costello. London: John Calder.

———. 1941. "Sang-I Sabur" (The Patient Stone). *Musiqi*, nos. 6–7.

———. 1942. *Sag-I Vilgard* (*Abandoned Dog*: 8 short stories). Tehran.

———. 1947/1979. *Tup-I Murvari* (*The Pearl Cannon*). Tehran.

———. 1953. *Karnama-yi Ardeshir Papakan* (*The Book of the Deeds of Ardashir Papakan*) *and Zand-i Vuhuman yasn* (*Commentary on the Vohuman Hymn*). Tehran.

Heidegger, Martin. 1937/1984. *Nietzsche*. Vol. 2. *The Eternal Recurrence of the Same*. Translated by David Farrell Krell. New York: Harper and Row.

Held, David. 1980. *Introduction to Critical Theory: Horkheimer to Habermas*. Berkeley: University of California Press.

Herodotus. 1996. *The Histories*. Edited and translated by Aubrey De Selincourt. New York: Penguin.

Higgins, Kathleen. 1987. *Nietzsche's Zarathustra*. Philadelphia: Temple University Press.

Hillmann, Michael, ed. 1976. *Major Voices in Contemporary Persian Literature. Literature East and West* 20, nos. 1–4: 1–351.

———. 1981. "Revolution, Islam, and Contemporary Persian Literature." In *Iran: Essays on a Revolution in the Making*, edited by Ahmad Jabbari. Lexington, Kent.: Mazda Publishers.

———, ed. 1982a. *Literature and Society in Iran. Iranian Studies* 15, nos. 1–4: 1–260.

———. 1982b. "The Modernist Trend in Persian Literature and Its Social Impact." *Iranian Studies* 15, nos. 1–4: 7–29.

———, ed. 1978. *Hedayat's "The Blind Owl" Forty Years After*. Austin, Tex.: Center for Middle East Studies.

———, ed. 1985. *Sociology of Iranian Writers. Iranian Studies* 18, nos. 2–4: 131–460.

Hopkins, Keith. 1978. *Conquerors and Slaves*. Cambridge: Cambridge University Press.

Hunt, Eva. 1977. *The Transformation of the Hummingbird: Cultural Roots of a Zinecantecan Mythical Poem*. Ithaca, N.Y.: Cornell University Press.

Huntington, Samuel. 1996. *The Clash of Civilizations and the Remaking of World Order*: New York: Simon and Schuster.

Ignatieff, Michael. 2002. "Barbarians at the Gate?" *New York Review of Books* 49, no. 3: 4–6.

Insler, Stanley. 1975. *The Gathas of Zoroaster*. Leiden: E. J. Brill.

"International Film." 1999. *Iranian Film Quarterly* 6, no. 3.

Issa, R. and Sheila Witaker, ed. 1999. *Life and Art: The New Iranian Cinema*. London: National Film Theater.

Jamalzadeh, Mohammad 'Ali. 1921/1976. "Persian Is Sugar." Translated by Seyed Manoochehr Moosawi. In *Major Voices in Contemporary Persian Literature*, edited by Michael Hillmann. *Literature East and West* 20, nos. 1–4: 13–20.

Jameson, Fredric. 1991. *Postmodernism: Or, The Cultural Logic of Late Capitalism*. Durham, N.C.: Duke University Press.

Jay, Martin. 1973. *The Dialectical Imagination*. Boston: Little, Brown.

Jelavich, Peter. 1982. "Popular Dimensions of Modernist Elite Culture: The Case of Theater in Fin-de-siecle Munich." In *Modern European Intellectual History*, edited by Dominick LaCapra and Steven L. Kaplan. Ithaca, N.Y.: Cornell University Press.

Joyce, James. 1939. *Finnegan's Wake*. London: Faber and Faber.

Kakar, Sudhir. 1980. "The Ties that Bind: Family Relationships in the Mythology of Hindi Cinema." Special Issue on Indian Popular Cinema, edited by Pradip Krishen. *India International Centre Quarterly* 8, no. 1: 11–21.

Kamshad, Hassan. 1966. *Modern Persian Prose Literature*. Cambridge: Cambridge University Press.

Kashefi, Husayn (d. 1504). 1970. *Rawzat al-Shuhada*. Tehran: Kitabfurushi-i Islamiyah.

Khomeini, S. Ruhullah Musavi. 1363Q/1943. *Kasbif-i asrar* (Revealing the Secrets). Qum.

——. 1391Q/1971. *Hukumat-i Islami: Wilayat-I Faqih*. Najaf.

Klinkowitz, Jerome. 1975. *Literary Disruptions: The Making of a Post-Contemporary American Fiction*. Urbana: University of Illinois Press.

Kotwal, Firoze M., and James W. Boyd. 1982. *A Guide to the Zoroastrian Religion: A Nineteenth Century Catechism by Dastur Erachji Sohrabji Meherjirana with Modern Commentary*. Chico, Calif.: Scholars Press.

Kreyenbroek, G. 1985. *Sraosa in the Zoroastrian Tradition*. Leiden: E. J. Brill.

Labov, William. 1966. *The Social Stratification of English in New York City*. Washington: Center for Applied Linguistics.

——. 1973. *Sociolinguistic Patterns*. Philadelphia: University of Pennsylvania Press.

Lant, Antonia. 1991. *Blackout: Reinventing Women for Wartime British Cinema*. Princeton, N.J.: Princeton University Press.

Laroui, Abdallah. 1976. *The Crisis of the Arab Intellectual: Traditionalism or Historicism?* Translated by Diarmid Cammell. Berkeley: University of California Press.

Lashgari, Deirdre. 1982. "Absurdity and Creation in the Work of Sadeq Hedayat." *Iranian Studies* 15, nos. 1–4: 31–52.

Latifa, with Shekeba Hachemi. 2001. *My Forbidden Face: Growing Up under the Taliban*. Translated by Linda Coverdale. New York: Hyperion.

Lévi-Strauss, Claude. 1966. *La Pensée Sauvage/The Savage Mind*. London: Weiden-feld and Nicolson.

——. 1971/1981. *The Naked Man*. Translated by John Weightman and Doreen Weightman. New York: Harper and Row.

Lord, Albert. 1949. "The Singer of Tales: A Study of the Processes of Composition of Yugoslav, Greek and Germanic Oral Poetry." Ph.D. diss., Harvard University, Cambridge, Massachusetts.

Lotfalian, Mazyar. 1999. "Technoscientific Identities: Muslims and the Culture of Curiosity." Ph.D. diss., Rice University, Department of Anthropology.

Lutgendorf, Philip. 1991. *The Life of a Text: Performing the Ramacaritmanas of Tulsidas*. Berkeley: University of California Press.

Lyons, Malcolm. 1995. *The Arabian Epic: Heroic and Oral Storytelling*. Cambridge: Cambridge University Press.

Lyotard, Jean-François. 1971. *Discours, Figure*. Paris: Klincksieck.

——. 1979. *The Postmodern Condition: A Report on Knowledge*. Minneapolis: University of Minnesota Press.

——. 1989. "The Dreamwork Does Not Think." In *The Lyotard Reader*, edited by Andrew Benjamin, 19–35. Cambridge, Mass.: Basil Blackwell.

Maguire, Marcia. 1974. "The Haft Khvan of Rustam and Isfandiyar." In *Studies in Art and Literature of the Near East: In honor of Richard Ettinghausen*, edited by Peter J. Chelkowski, 137–47. New York: New York University Press.

——. 1978. *Rustam and Isfandiar in the* Shahnameh. Ann Arbor, Mich.: University Microfilms International.

Mair, Victor. 1988. *Painting and Performance: Chinese Picture Recitation and Its Indian Genesis*. Honolulu: University of Hawaii Press.

Makhmalbaf, Mohsen. 1987. "Interview on *The Peddler*." Translated by Naghmeh Sohrabi. In *Gong-e Khabdideh*. Tehran: Nashr-i Ney.

——. 1990. "Realism in the Whole of Realism: On the Pretext of Reviewing Abbas Kiarostami's *Close Up*." Translated by Naghmeh Sohrabi. In *Gong-e Khabdideh*. Tehran: Nashr-i Ney.

——. 1995. *Gong-e Khabdideh*. Tehran: Nashr-i Ney.

——. 2001a. "Interview with Jahanbakhsh Nouraei." *Film International Quarterly* (May).

——. 2001b. "Limbs of No Body: The World's Indifference to the Afghan Tragedy." *Iranian* (20 June).

——. 2002. "The Condemned." *Guardian* (11 January).

——. n.d. "A Dialog on Violence and Tenderness, Love and Death, Cinema and Poetry between Werner Herzog and Mohsen Makhmalbaf." *http://www.makhmalbaffilmhouse.com*.

Makhmalbaf, Samira. 2003. "An Interview for the Movie 'At Five in the Afternoon' in the Cannes Film Festival." *http://www.makhmalbaf.com*.

Malandra, William W. 1971. "The Fravashi Yasht: Introduction, Text Translation, and Commentary." Ph.D. diss., University of Pennsylvania.

Malti-Douglas, Fadwa. 1991. *Women's Body, Women's Word: Gender and Discourse in Arabo-Islamic Writing*. Princeton, N.J.: Princeton University Press.

Mannoni, Octave. 1950/1956. *Prospero and Caliban: The Psychology of Colonization*. New York: Praeger.

May, Lary. 1980. *Screening Out the Past: The Birth of Mass Culture and the Motion Picture Industry*. New York: Oxford University Press.

McLaughlin, Kevin. 2002. "Virtual Paris: Benjamin's Arcades Project." In *Benjamin's Ghosts*, edited by Gerhard Richter, 204–25. Stanford: Stanford University Press.

McLuhan, Marshall, and Quentin Fiore. 1967. *The Medium Is the Message*. New York: Random House.

Meeker, Michael. 1979. *Literature and Violence in North Arabia*. New York: Cambridge University Press.

Mehrjirana, Dastur Erachji Sohrabji. 1982. *A Guide to the Zoroastrian Religion: A Nineteeth Century Catechism with Modern Commentary* by Dastur Firoze M. Kotwal and James W. Boyd. Chico, Calif.: Scholars.

Memmi, Albert. 1957/1965. *The Colonizer and the Colonized*. New York: Orion.

Meskoub, Shahrokh. 1342/1964. *Moqaddama'i bar Rostam o Esfandiyar*. Tehran.

Milani, Farzaneh. 1982. "Writers' Association of Iran: A Journey through Disillusionment." Paper presented to the Middle East Studies Association, Philadelphia, Pennsylvania.

Mills, Margaret A. 1991. *Rhetorics and Politics in Afghan Traditional Storytelling*. Philadelphia: University of Pennsylvania Press.

Mistry, Rustam. 1989. *"Swimming Lessons" and Other Stories from Firozha Baag*. Boston: Houghton Mifflin.

Mistry, Zaraawar. 2003. *Sohrab and Rustam*. Play script (photocopy), 20 pp.

Modi, Jivanji Jamshedi. 1922. *The Religious Ceremonies and Customs of the Parsees*. Bombay: J. B. Karanji Sons.

Murakami, Haruki. 2001. *Underground*. New York: Vintage.

Nabokov, Vladimir. 1951. *Speak, Memory*. New York: Harper.

Naficy, Hamid. 1981 "Cinema as a Political Instrument." In *Continuity and Change in Modern Iran*, edited by Michael E. Bonine and Nikki R. Keddie. Albany: State University of New York Press.

———. 1992. "Islamicizing Film Culture in Iran." In *Iran: Political Culture in the Islamic Republic*, edited by Samih K. Farsoun and Mehrdad Mashayekhi. London: Routledge.

———. 1993. *The Making of Exile Cultures: Iranian Television in Los Angeles*. Minneapolis: University of Minnesota Press.

———. 1994. "Veiled Vision/Powerful Presence: Women in Post-Revolutionary Iranian Cinema." In *In the Eye of the Storm: Women in Post-Revolutionary Iran*, edited by Mahnaz Afkhami and Erika Friedl. Syracuse, N.Y.: Syracuse University Press.

———. 2001a. *An Accented Cinema: Exilic and Diasporic Filmmaking*. Princeton, N.J.: Princeton University Press.

——. 2001b. "Iranian Cinema." In *Companion Encyclopedia to Middle Eastern and North African Film*, edited by Oliver Leaman. London: Routledge.

Nägele, Rainer. 2002. "Thinking Images." In *Benjamin's Ghosts*, edited by Gerhard Richter, 23–40. Stanford: Stanford University Press.

Nagy, Gregory. 1994. Foreword to *Poet and Hero in the Persian Book of Kings*, by Olga M. Davidson. Ithaca, N.Y.: Cornell University Press.

Nasr, S. Hussein. 1964. *Three Muslim Sages: Avicenna, Surawardi, Ibn Arabi*. Cambridge: Harvard University Press.

Neshat, Shirin. 1997. *Women of Allah*. Turin: Marco Noire Editore.

Neshat, Shirin, dir. 1998. *Turbulence*.

——. 1999a. 1999. *Rapture*.

——. 1999b. 1999. *Soliloquy*.

——. 2000. *Fervor*.

——. 2001. *Pulse and Passage*.

Neshat, Shirin, Sussan Deyhim, Ghasem Ebrahimian, and Shoja Azari. 2002. *The Logic of the Birds*. Performance with video.

Neusner, Jacob. 1981. *Judaism, the Evidence of the Mishnah*. Chicago: University of Chicago Press.

Nietzsche, Friedrich. 1872/1967. *The Birth of Tragedy*. Translated by Walter Kaufmann. New York: Random House.

——. 1873/1954. "On Truth and Lie in an Extra Moral Sense." In *The Portable Nietzsche*. Translated by Walther Kaufmann. New York: Random House.

——. 1874/1983. "Schopenhauer as Educator." In *Untimely Meditations*. Translated by R. J. Hollingdale. Cambridge: Cambridge University Press.

——. 1883–1885/1961. *Thus Spoke Zarathustra*. Translated by R. J. Hollingdale. New York: Penguin.

Nöldeke, Theodor. 1896/1927. *The Iranian National Epic, or,* The Shahnameh. Edited and translated by Leonid Bogdanov. Bombay: J. K. R. Cama Institute. Reprint, Philadelphia: Porcupine, 1979.

Obeysekere, Gananath. 1981. *Medusa's Hair: An Essay on Personal Symbols and Religious Experience*. Chicago: University of Chicago Press.

Ong, Walter. 1982. *Orality and Literacy: The Technologizing of the Word*. New York: Methuen.

Page, Mary Ellen. 1977. "Naqqali and Ferdowsi: Creativity in the Iranian National Tradition." Ph.D. diss., University of Pennsylvania. Ann Arbor: University Microfilms International.

Parks, Tim. 2001. *Hell and Back: Selected Essays*. London: Seeker and Warburg.

Parry, Milman. 1930–1932. *Studies in the Epic Technique of Oral Verse-Making*. *Harvard Studies in Classical Philology* part 1: 41 (1930): 73–147; part 2: 43 (1932): 1–50.

Payami, Babak. 2003. "Interview with David Walsh." www.wsws.org/articles/2003/sep.2003/paya-s24.shtml.

Peacock, James. 1968. *Rites of Modernization: Symbolic and Social Aspects of Indonesian Proletarian Drama*. Chicago: University of Chicago Press.

Poster, Mark. 1990. *The Mode of Information*. Cambridge, U.K.: Polity.

———. 2001. *What's the Matter with the Internet*. Minneapolis: University of Minnesota Press.

Power, Samantha. 2001. *"A Problem from Hell": America and the Age of Genocide*. New York: Basic Books.

Powers, Richard. 2000. *Plowing the Dark*. New York: Farrar, Straus, Giroux.

Pour-e-Davoud, Ibrahim. 1927. *Introduction to the Holy Gathas*, E.T. D.J. Irani. Bombay.

Qibla, M. J. H. S. 1972. *Nahj ul-Balagha*. Karachi.

Qobadi, Bahman. 2001. Question and Answers, Museum of Fine Arts, Boston. 1 October.

Qummi, 'Abbas ibn Muhammad Rida. 1970. *Mufati al-Jinau*. N.p.

Rahman, Fazlur. 1975. *The Philosophy of Mulla Sadra (Sadr al-Din al-Shirazi)*. Albany: State University of New York.

Rashid, Ahmed. 2000. *Taliban*. New Haven, Conn.: Yale University Press.

Rehder, R. McC. 1970. "Hafez: An Introduction." Ph.D. diss., Princeton University.

Richter, Gerhard. 2002. *Benjamin's Ghosts*. Stanford: Stanford University Press.

Ricoeur, Paul. 1975. "Biblical Hermeneutics." *Semeia*.

Ridgeon, Lloyd. 2000. "Makhmalbaf's Broken Mirror: The Socio-Political Significance of Modern Iranian Cinema." Durham, England: University of Durham, Centre for Middle East Studies, Middle East Paper, no. 64. 40 pp.

Rodowick, D. N. 2001. *Reading the Figural: Or, Philosophy after the New Media*. Durham, N.C.: Duke University Press.

Rosenberg, Bernard, and David Manning White, eds. 1957. *Mass Culture: The Popular Arts in America*. Glencoe, Ill.: Free.

Rushdie, Salman. 1980. *Midnight's Children*. New York: Alfred A. Knopf.

Russian General Staff. 2002. *The Soviet-Afghan War*. Translated and edited by Lester W. Grau and Michael A. Gress. Lawrence: University of Kansas Press.

Rypka, J. 1959. *Iranische Literaturgeschichte*. Leipzig.

Sabety, Setareh. 2001. "Googoosh on Tour: Decoding a Popular Phenomenon." *Journal of the University of Michigan International Institute* (winter). *http://www.iranian.com/Opinion/2001/May/Googoosh/index.html*.

Sa'edi, G. H. 1350/1971–1972. *Gav: A Story for a Film*. Tehran: Agah Publications.

Saeed-Vafa, Mehrnaz, and Jonathan Rosenbaum. 2003. *Abbas Kiarostami*. Urbana: University of Illinois Press.

Salih, Taleb. 1969. *Season of Migration to the North*. London: Heinemann Educational Books.

Sanjana, Darab Dastur Peshotan. 1888. *Next-of-kin Marriages in Old Iran*. London: Trübner.

Sanjana, Peshotan Bahramji, and Darab Peshotan Sanjana, trans. *Dinkard*. 1928. Bombay: Daftar Ashkara Press.

Satrapi, Marjaneh. 2003. *Persepolis: The Story of a Childhood*. New York: Pantheon.

Shahbazi, A. Shapur. 1977. "The 'Traditional' Date of Zoroaster Explained." *Bulletin of the School of Oriental and African Studies* 40, no. 1: 25–35.

Shariati, Ali. 1391Q/1971. *Are, inchuninbud, baradar* (Yes, That's How It Was, Brother). Tehran: Wusainiyya Ershad.

———. 1978. *Hajj*. Translated by Somayyah and Yaser. Bedford, Ohio: Free Islamic Literatures.

———. 1979. *On the Sociology of Islam*. Translated by Hamid Algar. Berkeley, Calif.: Mizan Press.

Simpson, Marian Shreve. 1979. *The Illustration of an Epic: The Earliest Shahnama Manuscripts*. New York: Garland.

Slyomovics, Susan. 1987. *The Merchant of Art: An Egyptian Hilali Oral Epic Poet in Performance*. Berkeley: University of California Press.

Sohrabi, Naghmeh. 1995. Weapons of Propaganda, Weapons of War: Iranian Wartime Rhetoric 1980–1988. Bachelor's thesis, Massachusetts Institute of Technology.

Sontag, Susan. 1977. *On Photography*. New York: Farrar, Straus and Giroux.

Sophocles. 1949. *Oedipus at Colonus*. English and Greek. Cambridge: Bowes and Bowes.

Sorlin, Pierre. 1991. *European Cinema, European Societies, 1939–1990*. London: Routledge.

Southgate, Minoo. 1974. "Fate in Firdawsi's Rustam va Suhrab." In *Studies in Art and Literature of the Near East: In Honor of Richard Ettinghausen*, edited by Peter J. Chelkowski. New York: New York University Press.

Sterritt, David. 2000. "Taste of Kiarostami." www.senseofcinema.com/contents/00/9/kiarostami.html.

Stevick, P. 1973. "Scheherezade Runs Out of Plots, Goes On Talking; the King, Puzzled, Listens: An Essay on the New Fiction." *Triquarterly* 26.

Strabo. 1960. *Geography*. Edited and translated by Horace Leonard Jones. London: Heinemann.

Suhrawardi, Shihab al-Din Abu al Futh Yahha ibn Habash ibu Amirak. 1186/1999. *The Philosophy of Illumination*. Translated by John Walbridge and Hossein Ziai. Provo, Utah: Brigham Young University Press.

Suhrawardi, Shihabuddin Yahya. 1982. "The Language of the Ants"; "The Simurgh's Shrill Cry"; *Treatise on Birds*. In *The Mystical and Visionary Treatises of ShihabuddinYahaya Suhrawardi*. Translated by Wheeler M. Thackston. London: Octagon.

Taussig, Michael. 1992. *The Nervous System*. New York: Routledge.

———. 1993. *Mimesis and Alterity: A Particular History of the Senses*. New York: Routledge.

Taylor, Mark. 1999. *The Picture in Question: Mark Tansey and the Ends of Representation*. Chicago: University of Chicago Press.

Thackston, Wheeler M. 1982. *The Mystical and Visionary Treatises of Shihbuddin Yahya Suhrawardi*. London: Octagon.

———. 1996. *The Baburnama: Memories of Babur, Prince and Emperor*. Washington: Smithsonian Institution Press.

———, ed. and trans. 1999. *The Philosphical Allegories and Mystical Treatises of Shihabuddin Yahya Suhrawardi*. Costa Mesa, Calif.: Mazda Publishers.

Urquhart, Brian. 2002. "The Prospect of War." *New York Review of Books* (19 December).

Vardosbi, A. Z. n.d. *A Short Criticism of [Feshahi's] "Last Feudal Movement in Medieval Times."* Teheran: Moassesseh Khadamat-i Farhang-i Reza.

Varzi, Roxanne. 2002. "Visionary Terrains of Post Revolution Iran: War, Youth, Culture, Media and Public Space." Ph.D. diss., Columbia University.

Velie, Alan R. 1982. "Gerald Vizenor: Post-Modern Fiction." In *Four American Indian Literary Masters*, edited by Alan R. Velie. Norman: University of Oklahoma Press.

Vidal-Naquet, Pierre. 1981/1986. "The Black Hunter and the Origin of the Athenian Ephebia." In *The Black Hunter: Forms of Thought and Forms of Society in the Greek World*. English translation by Andrew Szegedy-Maszk. Baltimore: Johns Hopkins University Press.

Virilio, Paul. 1989. *War and Cinema: The Logistics of Perception*. London: Verso.

Vries, Hent de. 2001. "In Media Res: Global Religion, Public Spheres, and the Task of Contemporary Comparative Religious Studies." In *Religion and Media*, edited by Hent de Vries and Samuel Weber, 3–42. Stanford: Stanford University Press.

———. 2002. *Religion and Violence: Philosophical Perspectives from Kant to Derrida*. Baltimore: Johns Hopkins University Press.

Vries, Hent de, and Samuel Weber, eds. 1998. *Violence, Identity and Self-Determination*. Stanford: Stanford University Press.

Walbridge, John. 1992a. "The Political Thought of Qutb al-Din al-Shirazi." In *The Political Aspects of Islamic Philosophy: Essays in Honor of Muhsin Mahdi*, edited by Charles Butterworth. Cambridge: Harvard University Press.

———. 1992b. *The Science of Mystic Lights: Qutb al-Din Shirazi and the Illuminationist Tradition in Islamic Philosophy*. Cambridge: Harvard University Press.

———. 2000. *The Leaven of the Ancients: Suhrawardi and the Heritage of the Greeks*. Albany: State University of New York Press.

Walbridge, John, and Hossein Ziai. 1999. "Translators' Introduction." In *The Philosophy of Illumination: A New Critical Edition of the Text of Hikmat al-ishr'aq*, edited by John Walbridge. Provo, Utah: Brigham Young University Press.

Waldman, Marilyn. 1980. *Toward a Theory of Historical Narrative: A Case Study in Perso-Islamicate Historiography*. Columbus: Ohio State University.

Warner, Arthur George, and Edmund Warner. 1905. *The Shahnama of Firdausi Done into English*. London: K. Paul, Trench, Trübner.

Wasserstrom, Steven M. 1999. *Religion after Religion: Gershom Scholem, Mircea Eliade, and Henry Corban at Eranos*. Princeton, N.J.: Princeton University Press.

Wasson, R. Gordon. 1968. *Soma: Divine Mushroom of Immortality*. The Hague: Mouton.

Weber, Samuel. 2001. "Religion, Repetition, Media." In *Religion and Media*, edited by Hent de Vries and Samuel Weber, 43–55. Stanford: Stanford University Press.

Wilhelm, Kurt. 1984/1989. *Richard Strauss: An Intimate Portrait*. New York: Rizzoli.

Windfuhr, Gernot. 1976. "Vohu Manah: A Key to the Zoroastrian Word Formula." In *Michigan Studies in Honor of George G. Cameron*, edited by Louis L. Orlin, 269–310. Ann Arbor, Mich.: Department of Near Eastern Studies.

Würzer, Wilhelm. 1999. *Filming Judgment*. New York: Columbia University Press.

Yarshater, Ehsan, ed. 1979. *Sadeq Hedayat: An Anthology*. Boulder, Colo.: Westview.

Young, Thomas Daniel. 1981. *The Past in the Present: A Thematic Study of Modern Southern Fiction*. Baton Rouge: Louisiana State University Press.

Zend-Avesta: Sacred Books of the East. Part I: *The Vendidad*, English trans. J. Darmsteter, 1895, *Sacred Books of the East*, vol. 4; Part II: *The Sirozahs, Yashts and Nyayesh*, English trans. J. Darmesteter, 1883, *Sacred Books of the East*, vol. 23; Part III: *The Yasna, Visparad, Afrinagan, Gahs, and Miscellaneous Fragments*, English trans. L. H. Mills, 1887, *Sacred Books of the East*, vol. 31; *Bundahishn*, English trans. E. W. West, 1901, *Sacred Books of the East*, vol. 5. Oxford: Clarendon Press.

Ziai, Hossein. 1990. *Knowledge and Illumination: A Study of Suhrawardi's Hikmat al-Ishraw*. Brown Judaic Studies, no. 97. Atlanta, Ga.: Scholars Press.

———. 1992. "The Source and Nature of Authority: A Study of al-Suhrawardi's Illuminationist Political Doctrine." In *The Political Aspects of Islamic Philosophy: Essays in Honor of Muhsin Mahdi*, edited by Charles Butterworth. Cambridge: Harvard University Press.

Žižek, Slavoj. 1991. *Looking Awry: An Introduction to Jacques Lacan through Popular Cinema*. Cambridge: Massachusetts Institute of Technology Press.

———. 1994. "Introduction: The Specter of Ideology." In *Mapping Ideology*. New York: Verso.

Index

This index privileges Persian proper names that remain in contemporary use, so that they can be easily tracked to their legendary sources and to key theoretical threads or categories (class, economics, interpretive transposition, intersignification, metaphors, narrative devices, parables, social divisions). Theoretical threads remain exemplary and suggestive rather than exhaustive, and the reader is invited to seek out further examples and connections in the text.

NOTE: **bold** = topic subcategories; SEMI-BOLD SMALL CAPITALS = descriptive, folkloric, or thematic subcategories; ***bold italic*** = film categories and themes

Abbasids, 415nn26

Abraham and the fire, 146

Abu Muslim, 415n26

Abu Sa'id (r. 1316–1335), intrigues in miniatures, 73

adab literature, 108

Adorno, Theodore, 245, 264, 351, 354

Afghanistan, 12, 265

—PLACES: GHAZNI, 340, 341, 426n29; HELMAND VALLEY: opium, 341, USAID Irrigation Project, 340; KABUL, 337, 348, 349, 426n26; PANSHIR VALLEY, 268, 345; QANDAHAR (KANDAHAR), 268, 339, 343–44, Governor "Gul Agha" (Mohmmad Shafeeq Shirzai), 344, 423n10, Mosque of the Cloak of the Prophet, 343; ZABUL PROVINCE, 344

—**economy**: oil and gas pipleine competitions, 342, opium, 340–41 —**ethnicities**, 337, Barakzai clan of Pashtuns, 344, Pashtuns, 269, Tajiks, 345

—***films***, 314–53, country without images, 337; ***documentaries:*** *Afghanistan Revealed* (Cocklin), 422n10, *Afghan Spring* (Tsuchimoto), 423n10, *Behind the Veil* (Shah), 422n10, *A House for Haji Baba* (Knappenberger), 423n10, *Jang* (War): *In the Land of the Mujaheddin*, 268, 314, 345, *Kabul Diary* (Tsuchimoto), 423n10, *Return to Afghanistan* (Pariza and Jay), 327, 422n10, *Smile and Wave* (Jongbloed), 422n10; ***narrative films***: *Fire Dancer* (Wassel), 423n10, *Osama* (Barmak), 315, 338, 347, 349, 350

—**political leaders**: Karzai, 344; Massoud, 339, 343, 345; Rabbani, 345 —**war**: ballads, 347; Karzai relief foundation, 423n10; medical aid, 346; refugees in Iran, 268, 314, refugees returning to Afghanistan, 348; U.S.

—**political leaders** (*cont.*)
negotiations to buy back Stinger missiles, 341

—**women**: demonstrations, 348, stealing my face, 337

Afrasiyab (Frangrasyan), 9, 74, 75, 82, 83, 84, 85, 87, 96, 99, 103, 405n21; death, 87

afrinigan, 52

Afshin, 415n26

Ahriman (Angra Mainyu), 46, 52, 57, 81, 86, 87, 88, 110, 137, 172, 178, 406n25; binding of, 54; kills primal human being, 76, 99; swallows Tahmuras, 99; seduces Zahhak, 100

Ahsa'i, Shaikh Ahmad (founder of Shaikhis), 137

Ahuna Vairya, 41, 42, 52; assures passage over Chinvat Bridge, 42; dispels demons, 40, 52, 58; worth a hundred other prayers, 42

Ahura Mazda (Ohrmazd, Spenta Maiynu), 27, 30, 31, 43–44, 47, 48, 54, 57, 137, 138, 172; advises binding of Zahhak, 406n25; "Lord of Memory" or Wisdom, 48; as zot, 30, 63, 138

Airyema Ishyo (Y.3), against sickness, use on Judgment Day, 51

Akhavan Sales, Mehdi, 167

Alavi, Bozorg, 199, 218, 411n10

alchemy, 138, 145

Aleppo, 135, 143

Alexander the Great, 17, 22, 66, 73, 77, 96, 112, 114, 115, 130, 343, 402n37, 404n10, 407n32; DESTROYS FARIDUN'S THRONE, 409n48; EXEMPLAR of good and bad kings, 108; FOLK ETYMOLOGIES, 406n28; SAVED BY WOMAN-WARRIOR ALTER EGO (Buran Dokht), 110; AS SECOND ESFANDIAR, 108, knowledge superior to brawn, 109, heroic qualities lost as converts people to Islam, 110; SIRED BY: Darab, 109, 114, Nectanebus II,

406n27; WIT AND WISDOM, 108, 109, 406n29, in test with Kaid, 111, 145; WORLD PEREGINATION, 109, builds wall against Gog and Magog, 109, liberates Arabia and installs Quraish (tribe of Muhammad), 109

Al-i Ahmad, Jalal, 168, 181, 412nn10, 12, and 16, 419n48; on communist party, 164; on fascism, 163; on Hollywood, 163; on mechanical age as two-headed disease, 163

amshaspands (aspects of divinity, creation), 23, 32, 33, 43, 60, 131, 133; gender balance, 63; lozum arrangement, 50, 64, seating arrangement, 63; oldest usage, 47; as poesis of the moral order, 63: correspondence with Platonic Ideas (Suhrawardi), 137, correspondence with elements and months, 65

—ARMAITI (AMARATAT) identified with Neoplatonist *sophia* (wisdom), q.v., and musk, 138

—BAHMAN (VOHU MANU) fathered by Ashura Mazda via his daughter Armaiti, 64; visionary, strategic, flexible understanding as opposed to Asha's ruthless judgment, 64

—HAURVATAT AND AMERATAT as predicates of completion and eternity, 63

Anahita, 54, 110, 115, 138

animals, 145, 281–82, 425n24

—ANTS, FLIES, INSECTS, 131, 138, 174, 179, 182

—BIRDS, 135–36, 146, 172, 219, 286, 415n29; blackbirds, 301; doves/pigeons, 278, 282; eagles, 380, 381, 429n10; falcons, 134, 412n16; feather quills, 173, 178, 179; hoopoes, 131, 136; owls, 131, 183, 193, 196, 414n24, 415n29; and pearls (Moshkel Goshah, Noshiravan), 408n41; in tree of life, 171; vultures, 169, 170, 171, 174, 175, 177, 182, 402n2

—CAMELS, 384

—COWS, 40, 43, 64, 116, 135, 253, 255, 289, 349; Birmaya, 103, 417n42; bulls of heaven, 43, 50, 417n42, seed of, 57, seven white bull tail hairs used in yasna, 32; the Cow's Lament (Y.29), 44; cow that goes dry at Bahram Gur's bad thoughts, 409n51; Mashd Hasan's cow (Gav), 211; metaphor of beneficent vision, 417n42; milk of, 41, 42, 52, gives Peshotan immortality, 44, as khwarrah of Zoroaster, 46

—CREATURES OF AHRIMAN, 178

—DOGS, 177, 179; abandoned (sag-e velgard), 349, 412n13; four-eyed dog and sag-did, 170, 181, 190, 214, 381; najes (impure), 174; in the Qur'an, 412n14

—FISH, 214, 298, 300, 417n43

—HORSES: in Avesta and Plato, 20, 43, 44; Shabdiz, 409n47; in Shahnameh: -asp in names, 48, Rakhash (Rustam's steed), 97; in Suhrawardi, 136; white horse from the waters kicks Yazdegird III to death, 408n37

—JACKASSES, 419n51

—LIONS, 384

—MOLES, 291

—SALAMANDERS, 145, 146, chameleon, 171, 178, lizards, 171, 178

—scorpions, 145, 291

—SNAKES AND DRAGONS, 145, 380, 382, 424n16; cobra, 187, 188, 193, 198, 414n22; Srovbar, 406n25; and treasure, 416n29; two serpents from Zahhak's shoulders, 101, 104

—turtles, 169, 173, 179, 253, 290, 291

—WOLVES, 98; -gorg in Turanian names, 97

Anushiravan. See Nushiravan Adel

Apam Napat, 48–49

Arabs, Arabia: Iraj, q.v., 105; Quraish liberated by Alexander, 111; Zahhak, 97

Ardabil, 86

Ardashir, 71, 72, 108, 114, 403n5, 409n51; legitimacy of, 112

Ardavan, 112, 113, 114

Aristotle: achieves mystical state of Jabarsa (Suhrawardi), 138; Islamic Aristotelians and Peripatetics ('ilm-i mashsha'i), 133, 134, 139, 410n1 (see also Ibn Sina); teacher of Alexander, 108, 111, 406n28

Arjasp, 80, 81, 93, 103

Armenia, 409n47

Arnold, Mathew, 22, 380, 397n4

art, 183–84, 196; alienation and representation, 197; appearance and illusion (Schein/Erscheinung, maya), 197; breaking of story repetition, 166, 188, 242, 266; dance, 185, 187, 188, 197, 313; écriture versus idolatry, 245; interzone of archetypes (mundus imaginalis, 'alam al-mithal, al-khayal, Olympian middle world), 134, 136, 137, 143, 197, 382; post-Holocaust ethical dilemma (Adorno, Celan, Levinas), 245, 264. See also image; painting; literary genres; orality

Ashem Vohu (threefold mantra of asha/truth), 38, 40–41, 42, 54, 176

Ashkanians (Parthians), 17, 22, 77, 109

Attar, Farid-ud-din, 130, 132, 134, 387, 420n2

audiences, 157, 159, 208, 329

Avesta, 21, 170, 176, 180, 348; canon (330 C.E.), 52, 71, 78

Babak (Papak, Ardavan's vassal whose dream identifies Sasan line), 112, 114, 415n26

Babel, 111

Babur, 426n29

Baghdad, 72, 103. See also Ctesiphon

Bahman (sixth Kayanian shah), 93, 94, 106, 114, 404n1; khedvedatha marriage of, 77, 92, 96, 403n9

Bahman (Vohu Manu, one of the amshaspands), 63, 64, 138; Bahman Yasht, 406n25; result of khedvedatha next-of-kin marriage, 64

Bahram Chubin, 124–126, 127; of royal Arsacid lineage, 124, 125, 408n42

Bahram Gur, 113, 114, 115–117, 403n5; and parables of wise rule, 115–16

Bahram Varjovand, 137

Baraheni, Reza, 84

Barbad (singer at court of Khosrow Parviz), 126, 409n48

bareshnum (nine-day purification), 30; and jailing of Zoroaster, 62

Barmakis, 196, 414n26

barsom, 27, 32, 35–37, 52–54; Barsom Yasht, 35; at meals of higher social estates, 35–36; parallels with Vedic *kusha* and Roman *flamines*, 36; in *Shahnameh*, 115, 120, 124, 125, 409n51; sign of Zorastrianism, 35; tying and loosening of, 41, 52, 54; variation by ritual, 400n21; and vegetable creation, 36

Barth, John, 184

Barthes, Roland, 168, 199, 203

Barzwi (bringer of fables of Kalila and Dimma), 122, 374

Bayhaqi (historian, Ghaznavid advisor), 108

Bazargan, Mehdi, 420n5

Bazarnush (general of Rum), and parable of colonialism, 9, 115, 130, 407n36

Behrangi, Samad, 214, 298

Benjamin, Walter, 224, 226, 231, 262, 263, 379, 383, 387, 388, 393, 428n4, 430nn12 and 13

Bible: on breaking of the tablets, 383; on Persians, 36

Bilal, 225

bin Laden, Osama, 266, 343, 359; *Starring Osama bin Laden* (Rath Arun), 423n10

Birdas (Argentine oil company), 342

al-Biruni, 59

Bizhan, 86, 93, 405n21, 408n42; ascent to heaven like Kai Khosrow, 96; inherits Siyavush's armor, 96; and Manizha, 87, 404n12; rescue by Rustam, 87

Blind Owl, 4, 156, 167, 180–99, 240, 255; explores the arts (dance and music, painting and writing), 197

Borujerdi, Ayatullah Sayyid Husain, 160

Bozorgmehr (vizier, "Great Light"), 112, 118, 123, 130, 133, 374, 407n41, 419n51; and chess, 9; in miniatures, 73

Brecht, Bertolt, 199, 263

Breton, André, 414n25

Buddha and Buddhists, 196, 414n23

Bundahishn, 32, 63, 81, 402nn33, 37, and 38, 405nn19 and 20, 406n25

Buran Dokht (Alexander's wife, Dara's daughter), 110; Anahita figure, 110

Bush, George W., 265

Buyids, 71

buzkashi, 338, 347, 372, 377, 378

Camus, Albert, 163, 164, 413n16

Central Asia: post-Soviet Tajikistan, 425n19

Cervantes, Miguel de, 355, 356, 357

Chaplin, Charlie, 199, 203

China, 105, 111, 115, 116, 120, 124, 127, 267, 379; as energy market, 342; scrap metal recycling in, 424n17

Chinese and Zoroastrian cosmological parallels, 31, 400n19

Chinvat Bridge, 42, 138

Christians: demand for return of the Cross, 126, 127, 409n45; heterodoxies of, 379; rejection of barsom as pagan, 125; and teletechnological media, 223–25

Chubak, Sadeq, 199, 218, 270, 412n10, 416n30, 419n51; *The Patient Stone*, 219–20

circumcision, 204, 205, 207, 416n35

class: army, 241; bassej, 246, 264, 275,

276, 280; bazaaris, 162, 239, 250; bourgeoisie, 152, 160, 161; bureaucratic elite, 158; class-linked writing and reception, 217–18; class-stratified cultural politics, 246; indignities of, 285; intelligentsia, q.v.; laborers, 243, 244; lumpenproletariat, 289, 290; and marginal economies, 273; and poverty, 238, 277; professionals, 241; refugee squatters, 312; and social estate, 156, 157; villagers, 154, 162, 202; and voyeurism, 252, 256

Clausewitz, Karl von, 299

coffeehouse, 24

Corbin, Henri, 24, 137, 138

courtship and modesty rules, 204, 205, 206

Ctesiphon, 115, 127, 410n52. *See also* Baghdad

culture

—**concepts of**, 151–55; historicist bourgeois culture, 161; local culture as intersection, 338; mass, folk, and popular culture, 161, 411nn2 and 3

—**criteria for dynamic theory of**, 155; conflicting background assumptions available for world-historical productivity, 225; cross-cultural conversations, 153; discursive competition (Kulturkampf) among social classes and intelligentsias, 153, 155, 161, 165, 218, 237, 246

—**cultural critique**, 11, 74–75; film as, 231, 370 (*see also* film); modernist, 165; past historical horizons as critique of present: Firdausi and Shahnameh, 71, 76, 77, 79, Hedayat, Barmaki, and other Persian revolts against Islam, 195–96; Shariati's Alavi Shi'ism, 195; surrealism as, q.v.

Dabistan al-madhahib, 410n2

Dadistan, 42, 400n21

Dahaka. *See* Zahhak

Dakiki, 71–72

Dante and *terza rima* in the *Inferno*, 399n14

Dara, 92, 109–110, 114

Darab (Darius), 77, 92, 99, 109, 114, 403n5, 404n10, 406n28; as baby set afloat (*dar ab*), 107

Darwish, Muhammad, 430–31n18

Dasatir, 410n2

death, dignified, 325

deep play, in *Close Up*, 229

Deleuze, Gilles, 5, 11, 232–33, 261, 262, 263, 265

Denkart, 58, 59, 60, 402n33, 405n20, 406n25

Derrida, Jacques, 11, 199, 223, 224–25, 246, 353

Dinavari, 406n28, 409n50

discourses: competing modernist and religious idioms in, 155, 157; as lexicon of images in writing and film, 157; and symbol systems, 155

Dostoyevski, Fodor, 356, 413n16

Dubai, 361, 363, 366, 372

Dugdav (Zoroaster's mother), 46–47, 59, 60

Dürer, Albrecht, 388

Durkheim, Emile, on science and religion, 223

Ecclesiastes, 430n10

economy: agricultural harvest division, 417n41; and illegal workers, 316, 325; opium, 338, 340; recycling, 287, 291; global industry in scrap metal, 424n17; smuggling, 299, 321, 329, 337, 358; strikes and demonstrations, 292, 348; war as employment, 338. *See also* oil enclave economy

egalitarianism, 145; futuwwat, 145; Qalandaris, 413n16

Egypt, 406n27, 429n10; next-of-kin marriages, 404n10

Eisenstein, Sergey, 233, 263

Elias, 111

Emerson, Ralph Waldo, 380

emotion, 157; mourning, 154; struggle to liberate the self from contradictory claims of the past, 156, 175

ephedra, 401n29. See also *hom*

epics: *Darab Nameh*, 66, 110, 403n1, 406n28; *Eskandar Nameh*, 66, 403n1, 406n28; *Firuz Shahnameh*, 406n30; *Khwaday namak*, 409n50; *Qessa-i Hamza*, 406n30; *Samak-i Ayyar*, 406n30; *Shahnameh*, q.v.; *Vis-o-Rus*, 71; *Zariadres and Zarer*, 71

"Esfandarmaz" (Suhrawardi's interworld of archetypes), 137

Esfandiar "Ruintan" ("the bronzed bodied"), 21, 47, 62, 77, 81, 92, 93, 103, 105, 106, 109, 112, 404n12; bronzed in Firdausi, with pomegranate in Avesta, 79; champion of new faith, 79–80; flawed hero, 79; and Gushtasp, 80, 84, 94, 95; and Rustam, 79, 88–90, 94, 136, 404n14; trials of, 96–98

Esfandiari, Fereydun M., 412n11

eternal return: cycles of nature, 169, 380, 420n2; recycling, 177; in Suhrawardi, 145

ethical discourse, 6, 11, 226, 228

—art: as call for response across cultures, 2; after Holocaust, 245; images as demonic versus visionary, 144

—character types (*aubash, dash, darvish, javanmard, rind*), 200, 208, 210, 416n31; *adam-e sangin/sabok* (person of gravitas/lightweight), *nush/nishkhand* (foolish/philosophical grin or smile), 215; exemplars of anger or rage control (Ali, Khomeini, Moses, Muhammad, Noah), 216; naïf (*Aghaye Halu*), 199–202; and otherworldly refuge in poetic reverie, 203; tempered by water and fire (*adam-e ab o atesh dideh*), 216

—commentary traditions, 11; humanist logics, 153, 286, humanitarianism and geopolitics, 347; morals police and pragmatic wit, 285; parables of good rule (see also *kwarrah*); repetition and difference as second chance (free will), 175

—interactional codes: in experiments with egalitarianism, 116, 118; of friendship, honor, and purity, 207, 209, 120, 211, 252, 308, 332, 415n38; of heroism transformed, 209; of interior purity and exterior pragmatism (batin/zaher, anderun/birun, darvishi/ta'arof), 270

—mythic versus parable logic, 248; good and evil, in Indo-Iranian ritual idiom, 130, as parts of triadic structure, 102, in *Qaisar* and *Shahnameh*, 209; mutual aid limits, 289, mutuality in women's work stories, 407n41

—stoicism, 157, 285

—voyeurism, 252

ethnic minorities, 308, 316, 325; Afghan, 240–41; Azeri, 240–41; Kurd, 240–41

Falsafi, Shaikh Muhammad-Taqi, 160

Fanon, Frantz, 162, 168

Farhad and Shirin, 409n47

Fariborz (son of Kai Kaus), 85, 86

Faridun, 59, 67, 68, 73, 75, 76, 78, 105, 106, 126; 403n5; descent from Jamshid, 103; overthrow of Zahhak, 103, 406n25; parallels with Kayanians, 106; role in three-generation unit, 103; throne destroyed by Alexander, reconstructed by Khosrow Parviz, 409n48

Farimarz, 96

Farokhzad, Farough, 252, 254, 256

farr, 429n10. See also *khwarrah*

Farrokhi (poet), 166, 383

Farud (half brother of Kai Khosrow), as tragic figure, 86

film: agitation against, 159, 236; censorship of, 227, 241–42; democracy and, 267; Farabi Film Foundation, 294; genealogies of, 249; New Wave, 2, 10, 160, 167, 211, 222, 247; post-revolution generations, 270; problems of production and audience, 226–27, 228, 294; revolution restaged in, 258; struggle for control of, 237; war film units and production, 222, 234–46, 247, 421n8

—*camera:* distortions of cinematic restagings, 281; as productive of something new, 292; as self-reflexive device, 257–58, 275, 278, 279; as weapon, 311

—*cinematic writing,* 228, 271, 280, 302, 303, 314, 384; analogic layering (of domestic, ethnic, urban violence), 311; as ethnographic writing machine, 231, 234; experience of viewing versus analytic review, 194; figural, 4, 5, 10, 11, 263, 265, 266, 286, 292, 324; Islamic, 239; poetic, 242; serial, 322–23; structuralist, 278

—*filmic cultural critique:* **comparative perspective**, 225–26, 231: contesting and negotiating Islam, 258, counter-images and alternative responses, 308, tolerance for ethnic diversity, 267; **ethical dilemmas** staged, 226: abandonment of child you cannot care for, 238, conditions of aiding another, 240, second wives, 240; **failures of the social revolution**, 275; **medium of cultural negotiations:** over the local and global, 235, 238, from peep show (exoticism) to close-up, 231; **work of interruption**, 233, 266: staging circuits of desire, orders of representation, powers of the false (*odklamanie*), 232, 233, 257, 262

—*filmic discourse,* 247–48, 257–58, 270

—*filmic judgment:* **alternative court of appeal**, 226, 229–30: facing the camera, 293, 307, 308, 309, 310, modulating common sense and popular culture, 235, reconstructing public spheres, 235; **prosthetic and gymnasium of multi-sensory scanning,** 231–32, 233, 263, 387: change in perception and judgment over the twentieth century, 230–31, 232–33; experience of viewing versus analytic review, 194, mute dreams and optical unconscious, 387; **surveillance cameras**, 285, 286

—*filmic social functions:* creation of national publics, 234; cross-linguistic reach, 258; detachment from local worlds, 223, 232; future-oriented cognitive work, 233; turning war into entertainment, 313; working through trauma, 234

—*genres: ab-gushti*, 160, 247; documentaries, 266, 303, 312; eiron-alazon comedy (wit/fool, sophisticate/naïf), 200, 352, 362; family comedy, 203; melodrama, 266, 281, 303, 308; psycho-drama, 281, 358, psycho-d(t)ra(u)ma, 314; spaghetti western, 286

—*inability to forget,* 278

—*names in,* 311, 320, 330, 365–66; Qaem, 425n22. *See also under* intersignification

—*sound,* 226, 262, 281, 314, 315, 353; film as tone-poem, 321; music, 331, 332, 333, 334

—*tropes in:* **car seats and picaresque journeys**, 314, 315, 318–20, 324, 327, 329, 354, 360, 392; **construction sites and things unfinished**, 241, 310, 315, 329, 354, 359; **children as renewal and revaluation,** 180, 243, 244–45, 247, 384, 385: classrooms, 305, 307, 331, 351, girls passing as boys, 318, 349, madrassehs, 330, 349, 350, nursery rhymes as signal of parable or fable,

—*tropes in* (*cont.*)
355, 362, 365, sick children as motivation for fathers, 361, 427n6; **enclosed spaces** (island, prison, airplane) as microcosm, 357; **parachuting** (aid, democracy), 361; **refugee camps**, 305, 307, 326, 329, 351, 352; **sacrifice zones**, 352

—*voyeurism and ethics of filmmaking,* 252, 256, 258

—*war and:* derangement of populations for war, 232, 251; World Wars I and II, 234, 264

—*women in,* 266, 348, 311, 426n27

filmography by country: **Afghanistan**, q.v.; **Balkans**, 228, Kustarica, 294, 303; **China:** Fifth Generation, 2; **Eastern Europe**, 257; **France: New Wave**, 2, 262, 264, 265; **Germany: New Cinema**, 262, 264; **Greece**: Angelopoulos, 294; **India**, 229, 326, *Bombay* (Rathnam), 424n14; **Italy: neorealism**, 2, 257, 262, 264, *The Bicycle Thief* (da Sica), 325, *Jang: In the Land of the Mujaheddin* (Lazzaretti and Vendemmiati), 268, 314; **Kurdistan:** *Jiyan* (Rosebiani), 422n9, *Yol*, 294, *see also* under filmography by director: Kamkari, Qobadi; **Poland**, 262, Wajda, 386; **Turkey**, *Journey to the Sun* (Ustaoglu), 422n9; **United States,** 2, 266, *Dog Day Afternoon* (Lumet), 250, 285, 424n15, *Do the Right Thing* (Lee), 424n14, *Psycho* (Hitchcock), 238, *Rosie the Riveter*, 420n6, *The Third Man* (Korda), 380, *2001: A Space Odyssey* (Kubrick), 380, 381, 429nn8 and 9

filmography by director (Iran): Avini 247, 421–22n8; Ayyari 267, 271, 286, 289, 290, 354; Babak, 267; Bahari, 386; Bani-Etemad, 250, 348; Barmak, 267; Beza'i, 247, 267, 271, 385, 392; Darvish, 281, 282; Davudnezad, 250; De-

hlavi, 154, 168, 181, 182, 194, 420n2; Farhad, 424n16; Foruszesh, 315; Hatamikia, 251, 267, 271, 281, 290, 303, 313, 355, 357, 358, 361, 384, 392, 420n8, 424n16; Hekmat, 357, 358, 365; Jalili, 258, 268, 310, 314, 320, 354; Kamkari, 267, 294, 310 Karimi, 203; Kiarostami, 1, 229, 240–43, 247, 248, 249, 252, 258, 259, 260, 262, 268, 271, 285, 314, 315, 324, 349, 354, 385, 387, 392; Kimia'i, 208, 417n40; Kimiavi, 10, 220, 237, 248; Majidi, 260, 268, 314, 316, 354; Makhmalbaf, Hana, 268, 338, 348; Makhmalbaf, Meysam, 267, 293; Makhmalbaf, Mohsen, 1, 2, 12, 229, 238–40, 247, 248, 252, 258, 259, 260, 261, 264, 265, 268, 271, 273, 288, 302, 303, 307, 313, 314, 324, 329, 330, 349, 354, 358, 361, 368, 384, 385, 392, 420n8, 425n21, 426n27, 427n4; Makhmalbaf, Samira, 259, 260, 267, 268, 292, 293, 299–300, 302, 307, 313, 329, 338, 347, 348, 349, 350, 351, 353, 368, 370, 386, 391, 420n2; Mehrju'i, 5, 160, 240, 247, 249, 264, 267, 270, 288, 293, 303, 307, 417, 426n4; Meshkini, 267; Milani, 315; Mir Hosseini, 419n4; Motaleb, 210; Naderi, 247, 267, 271, 354; Panahi, 267, 285, 315; Payami, 348, 350, 351, 357, 358; Qobadi, 267, 271, 292, 296, 303, 348, 351, 352, 361, 386, 387, 391; Sales, 417; Serry, 423n11; Shah-Hatami, 271, 291; Sina'i, 267, 280, 282; Tabrizi, 261; Yektapaneh, 268, 314, 324, 349, 354

filmography by title: *The Abadanis,* 267, 289–90, 354; *Afghan Alphabet*, 268, 314, 425n21; *Agha-ye Halu* (Mr. Gullible), 10, 167, 199–202; *And Life Goes On,* 248, 249, *The Apple,* 329; *At Five in the Afternoon,* 315, 338, 348; *Baran,* 268, 314, 316–318, 324, 329, 354; *Bashu,* 234–35, 258, 267, 271, 272, 288, 420n2;

Bemani, 267, 293, 303; *Beyond the Fire*, 267, 271, 286–89, 290, 292, 293, 303, 315, 323, 354, 424n5; *Blackboard*, 3, 267, 293, 299–303, 310, 420n2; *Black Tape: A Tehran Diary (The Videotape Fariborz Kamkari Found in the Garbage)*, 267, 294, 310–14; *Blue-Veiled*, 250–51; *Boycott*, 247, 258; *Bread and Vase*, 247; *Close Up*, 3, 229, 257, 258, 260: psychodrama, 229, social critique, 229, Islamic court, 230; *Crimson and Gold*, 267, 285; *The Cyclist*, 268, 315, 324, 325, 326, 337; *Dayareh Mina* (The Cycle), 167; *Delbaram*, 268, 314, 320–24, 354; *Divorce Iranian Style*, 419n4; *Diyar-e Ashegan* (Land of Lovers), 276; *Droshky-chi* (The Droshky Driver), 10, 203–6, 419n49; *From Kharkhe to Rhein*, 290; *Gav* (The Cow), 5, 10, 154, 157, 160, 167, 211–17, 236, 249, 264, 270, 288; *The Glass Agency*, 251–52, 265, 281, 290, 310, 358, 361, 392, 424n15; *God, Construction, and Destruction*, 352; *God's Fish*, 296, 298; *Harmonica*, 272; *How Samira Made* The Blackboard, 267, 293; *In the Alleys of Love*, 267, 280–81, 282; *Jomeh*, 268, 314, 324, 329; *Joy of Madness*, 337; *Kimia*, 281, 282; *Kuche Mardha* (Alley of Men), 416n38; *Leila*, 240, 258; *Leila Is With Me*, 261; *Life in Fog*, 267, 293, 298, 299, 306; *Low Heights*, 267, 355, 357–58, 361–64, 392, 428n6; *Marooned in Iraq*, 267, 293, 303, 315, 351, 393; *Marriage of the Blessed*, 3, 238, 247, 248, 252, 258, 264, 267, 273–80, 313, 392; *Maryam*, 423n11; *Miadgah-i Hashem* (The Meeting Place of Hashem), 210; *Moghul-ha* (The Mongols), 10, 167, 220, 237–38, 248, 337; *Niaz* (Need), 250, 251, 257, 258; *Once Upon a Time, Cinema*, 247, 248–49, 257, 258, 368, 426n27; *Osama*, 268; *Panj-e Asr*, 268; *The Party*, 296, 298; *The Peddler*, 238–40, 247, 248, 258, 268, 288, 315, 324, 325, 354, 361, 428n7; *Qaisar* (Caesar), 10, 167, 207–210, 287, 288, 323; *Raghs Dar Ghobar* (Dancing in the Dust), 424n15; *Red Ribbon*, 3, 267, 268, 271, 290–92, 303, 315, 424n15; *Requiem*, 272; *Rivayat Fath*, 421–22n8; *The Runner*, 267, 271, 273, 286, 288, 354, 420n2; *Ruzegar-e Ma* (Our Times), 348; *Safar-e Qandahar* (Journey to Kandahar), 2, 12, 259, 265, 268, 314, 315, 326–38, 354, 392; *Secret Ballot*, 315, 350, 357, 358–61; *Shazdeh Ehtejab* (Prince Ehtejab), 167, 411–12n10; *Showhar-i Ahu Khanum* (Ahu's Husband), 167, 412n10; *Shrapnels in Peace*, 2, 271, 291, 292; *Silence Between Two Thoughts*, 268, 315, 348, 350; *Suitors*, 431n19; *Taaraaj*, 276; *Tangsir*, 167, 271, 272; *A Taste of Cherry*, 240–44, 258, 268, 324, 325, 354, 392; *Testing Democracy*, 303, 358, 427n4; *Through the Olive Tree*, 258; *Time of the Drunken Horses*, 3, 267, 294–99, 303, 305, 306, 307, 348, 352, 361, 393; *Time of Innocence*, 258; *A Time of Love*, 247, 258; *Towers of Silence*, q.v.; *A True Story*, 258; *Waiting*, 272; *Where Is My Friend's House?* 249; *The Wind Will Carry Us*, 252–57, 260, 392; *Women's Prison*, 357, 358, 365–67; *Zir Pust-e Shahr* (Under the Skin of the City), 348

Firangiz (mother of Kai Khosrow), 85

Firdausi, 6, 7, 8, 18, 21, 22, 35, 36, 66, 67, 68, 69, 71, 77, 79, 83, 99, 109, 112, 123, 124, 147, 156, 166, 207, 248, 370, 383, 406n36; collector and versifier, 68; dictates to 'Ali Dilam and takes reciter Abu Dulaf, 68; double-edged text on royal power, 119; patrons, 69–70; transforms myths of creation into genealogies, 76, 99, 107 fire. *See under* metaphor and symbols

fire temples: Azargashasp, 87, 120; Noubahar, 196

Firuz (Seventeenth Sassanian shah), 123, 409n51

folklore, ethnography, literature, modernism, and nationalism, 4, 10, 181, 396n5

Foucault, Michel, 263

fraavahar (fravashi), 429

fragrances, 399–400n17

Frashaoshtra (disciple of Zoroaster), 54

Freud, Sigmund, 7, 183, 262, 264, 299, 351, 384, 413n17

funerary rites, 204, 255, 256, 257, 308, 332; in *Gav*, 212–13; towers of silence (*dakhmeh*), 171; Zoroastrian *sag-did*, 170, 177

gahambars (seasonal feasts), 26–27, 61, 65, 396n6

Gaiumart (Kayomars), 76, 77, 78, 99, 100, 106, 138

games, 118; backgammon (*takht-e nard*), 118, 121, 408n40; buzkashi, q.v.; cards, 323; chess, 118, 120, 121–23, 339, 374; cockfight, 333; the Great Game (Central Asia, oil), 339, 342, 378; polo, 84; riddles, 111, 119, 123, 145, 382, 384

García Lorca, Federico, 348

Gathas, 3, 8, 18, 28, 43–45, 49–51; "I shall Speak" (Y. 44), 49; "This I ask Thee" (Y. 44), 49; ordering by metrical form, 28; "To What Land Shall I Flee" (Y.45), 49; "To You the Soul of the Cow Lamented" (Y. 29), 44; "wedding sermon" Gatha (Y.53), 51; "With Hands Outstretched" (Y.28), 43

getig-menog (*guiti-minoo*, materialspiritual), 30, 57. See also *gha'ib*

Ghafuri, Muhammad, 387, 389, 392

gha'ib (unseen worlds, connections, relations), 141, 144, 253, 261, 309. See also *getig-menog*

gharbzadegi ("West-struckness"), 163

Ghaznavids, 68, 108. *See also* Mahmud of Ghazni

Ghengiz Khan, 74, 340

Ghiyath al-Din, 72, 73

Giv, 85, 88

Goethe, Johann Wolfgang von, 384, 413n17

Gog and Magog (Yajuj and Majuj), 109, 111

Golshiri, Hushang, 412n10

Googoosh (Faegheh Atashin), 386, 390, 391

Greeks, 3, 17, 20, 93, 131; **epics** (*Iliad* and *Odyssey*), 17, 399n14; **Indian parallels**, 20, 28; *namus*, 207, 416n36; **on the Persians**: Herodotus, 396n3, 399n17, Peripatetic philosophers, 133, 134, 138, 139, 141, 410n1, Strabo 36, Xanthos of Lydia, 59; **pharmakon/hom/soma**, 401n29, elixirs (drugs, wine), 399n14; spice mythologies, 404n11; **Sophocles**, 196–97; **Stoic and Zoroastrian golden rule**, 65. See also Alexander the Great; Aristotle; Hellenism; Plato; Seleucids

Greene, Graham, 380, 424n18

Gudarz (Gotaarzes II), 407n33;

Gushtasp, 77, 80, 81, 84, 88, 89, 92, 93, 101, 106, 109, 404n15; in Avesta versus *Shahnameh*, 95; endangering son (in series: Harun al-Rashid, Shah Abbas Safavi, Nadir Shah, Fath Ali Shah), 80; errors of, 101; trials of, 91, 96, 98, 101

Gypsies, 117

Hafez, 75, 200, 227, 248, 353, 430n17

al-Hakim, Tawfiq, 155, 165

Harun al-Rashhid, 62, 80; compared to Gushtasp, 80; and cypress of Zoroaster, 62

Heaney, Seamus, 357, 426n2

Hedayat, Sadeq, 4, 5, 10, 156, 157, 159,

162, 167, 180–99, 218, 240, 246, 255, 349, 370, 383, 384, 411n10, 412nn12, 13, and 16, 415n28, 420n2; "Akharin Labkhand" (The Last Smile), 196; *The Blind Owl*, q.v.; "Dash Akol," 196; "Sayeh-ye Moghul" (Shades of the Moghuls), 196; use of Persian revolts against Islam, 195

Hellenism, 68, 71

hieroglyphs, 2, 263, 301, 352, 363, 424n16; of abjection, 309; of fratricide and modernization, 288; of mutual help, 248; of secondary economies and surveillance-resistance agons, 311

Hieun Tsiang, 407n31

Hinduism, 190, 196; Kali-Parvati, 185, 188; Shaivite lingam-temple dancer, 185

Hölderlin, Friedrich, 383, 388

hom (haoma), 32, 34, 38, 42–43, 44, 138; **hypothesized original identity**: fly agaric, ephedra, 38–40, 401n29; **ingredients of elixir**: hom twigs, milk, pomegranate twig, zohr), 42; **first preparers**, 40; **frawahar of Zoroaster** represented by, 46; **uses**: healing the world of deceit and ruin, 50–51; health and blessing soul of the dead, 27, 55; immobilizing evil, 39, 87, 89; victory in war, 55; wit and vision, 38; **ritual traces** (personified in *Shahnameh*, reigns of Bahman, Gushtasp, Kai Khosrow), 107, 406n25; **white haoma of immortality**, 138; *Hom Yasht*, 38, 40

Hom (hermit, personified hom), instrumental in capacitating Afrasiyab, 87, 99

Homa (Humai), 23, 77, 80, 91, 92, 96, 99, 114, 116, 404n10

Horace, 357, 426n2

Hormuzd (twenty-first Sassanian shah), 123–25

Hulagu, 74

Hurqalya, 137

Husain, Taha, 165

Hushang, 76, 78, 99, 106

Hussein, Saddam, 306

Husserl, Edmund, 140

Ibn Sina (Avicenna), 138, 139, 141

icons, 321: barbed wire, 307, 324; camera as nomadic war-machine, 238, 239; cell phone, 253; darvish, 238; footprint, 319, 320; guillotine-microwave tower executing film-maker/film canister, 238, 249; hole-in-the-sheet medical exam, 326, 333, 334; intercom buzzer on iron gate in the desert, 238, 337; moon clouding over, eclipse, 241, 331; prostheses dropping from the sky, 326, 328, 334; ruins, 238; shadows, 240; shoe, 209, 287, 323; tree of life, 241, 249, 253; zig-zag road, 241, 248

Il-khanids, 68, 70, 72, 74, 75

illness, 285

illuminationism (*hikmat-i israqi*), 21, 24, 133–47, 156 (*see also* Kermani, Mir Damad, Mullah Sadra, Shaikhis, Shirazi, Suhrawardi); Aristotelian metaphysics of being substituted by metaphysics of light, 138; harmonics of cycles, correspondences, tropisms towards spiritual light, 137; harmonization of Shi'ism, Zoroastrian, Neoplatonic, Ptolomaic schemes, 137; image manipulation, demonic power of illuminationist sages (*khaliq al-baraya*), 144; interlanguage between epistemology of self, rationally grounded metaphysics, and political-religious institutional legitimation, 138–39; inversion of Zoroastrian and Vedic imagery, 146; purification of the soul for higher spheres, 137

Imams (Family of the Prophet): assassination of Fifth, Sixth, and Sev-

Imams (*cont.*)
enth Imams by Barmakis, 196; marriage with Iranian royal family, 63, 128
—**Imam 'Ali** (First Imam), 75, 142, 209, 227; animal tries to block his death (like Esfandiar), 81; cunning of, 403n3; dard-e del, 419nn46 and 47; ineffectual against Omar's cutting up of Persian carpets, 410n52, 416n37; *kazem-i gheys* (model of swallowing anger), 418n44; prayers of, 418n44
—**Imam Husain** (Third Imam), 75, 85, 279, 310, 418n44; marries daughter of Yazdigird III, 63, 128, 246, 431n18
—**Imam Jafar Sadeq** (Sixth Imam), 203, 276, 418n44
—**Imam Musa "Kazem"** (Seventh Imam, "who swallows his anger"), 418n44
—**Imam Reza** (Eighth Imam), 283, 414n26; grave at site of Zoroaster's cypress, 62
—**Imam Zaman** (occulted Twelfth Imam), 137, 141, 142, 143, 417n42
India (Hind): Alexander in, 110, 111, 147; backgammon and chess, 121–22; Benares, 414n23; Calcutta, 167; energy market, 342; Kalila and Dimma, 122; migrations from Iran, 428n7; scrap metal recycling, 424n17; Upanishads, 20, 29; Vedas, q.v.
Indra, 401n30
intelligentsia, 157, 236; enlightened (*roshan fekran*), 153; liminal stratum of, 153, 156, 160, 161, 162, 164; Writers' Association of Iran, 164
interpretation by transposition: **inversion:** countercosmogony (Chubak), 219, by Islam of Zoroastrian metaphors: dog, 174, 412n14, insects, 178, by mysticism of Zoroastrian and Vedic metaphors, 29, 146, 178; **juxtaposition:** meaningful association,

169, 179, 181; **merging or splitting of male and female**, 76, 182, 185; **montage**: reconfiguring fragments of the past, 169, 180; **repetition:** redundancy as meaning specification, 179, as second chance (free will, *différance*), 175, 179, 180, 196
intersignification, 79
—**child and alley dog,** in Kiarostami and Barmak's *Osama*, 349
—**egalitarianism**: anarchistic failure under Bahram Gur and Kubad/Mazdak), 117, 118; attractive Islamic ideal, 128, 130, of Qalandaris, 413n16
—**Esfandiar**: and Alexander, 10; and Ali, 81
—**foreign alliances producing heros** (Alexander, Esfandiar, Kai Khosrow, Manuchehr, Rustam, Siyavush, Sohrab), 95, 96; evil not necessarily passed down through evil in maternal line (Shirin, Rudabeh), 126
—**good rulership** (Alexander, Ardashir, Bahman, Kai Khosrow, Nushiravan), 99, 108, 118
—**hubris of rulership** (loss of *khwarrah*, revolt, fear of hubris): Jamshid, Kai Kaus, Kai Khosrow, Khosrow Parviz, Naudar, Yazdegird III, 95, 100, 142
—**names in films**, 255; Husain (in *Crimson, Gold*), 285; Panha (in *Bemani*), 309; Turani (in *Black Tape*), 311; *Osama*, 349
—**Oedipus inverted** as topos and psychology (Baraheni's "crowned cannibals," Gushtasp and Esfandiar, Rustam and Sohrab, Sam and Zal, Siyavush and Kai Kaus), 84, 95
—**pahlevan-shah relation**, 92, 93, 95, 123; Bahram Chubin and Rustam, 125; Rustam and Esfandiar, 87, 88–91, 404n12; Rustam and Sufari, 117; Rustam and Zal, 92

—shoe or sandal (*Beyond the Fire, Delbaram, Qaisar*), 287, 323

—three-generation units, 92–94, 99, 103, 123–27

—transformations among myth, archetype, parable, 100, 103; Man-uchehr, prefiguring Kai Khosrow and Nushiravan Adel, 105, 118; Zahhak as archetype for three errors of Kai Kaus and Gushtasp and for trials of Rustam, Esfandiar, Gushtasp, and Rustam, 100; Zuran-Mahbud and Haman-Mordecai, 119–20; *see also* Hom, Kereshaspa

—trials of Rustam, Esfandiar, Gushtasp, 96–98, progressive learning from trial to trial, 97

Ionesco, Eugene, 163, 164

Iraj, 76, 78, 79, 103, 105, 106

Iran

—places: AZERBAIJAN: Tabriz, 417n42; FARS: Shiraz, 72, 77, 407n35; GILAN: *Bashu*, 234; KERMAN: Hafwad and the Worm, 112, 406n35; KHORASAN, 128, 415, Balkh, 196, 414n23, Marv, 128, Mashhad, 62, 212, 283, Nishapur, 414n23, Tus, 62; KHUZISTAN, 267, Abadan, 209, 237, 272, 282, 357, 428n7, Ahwaz, 267, 286, Bushire, 271, Khoramshahr, 267, films: 234, 267, 271–92; KURDISTAN, 404n12, films about, 267, 292–314, origin legend of Kurds (*Shahnameh*), 103; RAYY, 186, 187, 191, 408n42, shrine of Shah Ab-dol Azim, 186; TEHRAN, 199–203, 238, 240, 250, 289, Imam Jafar Sadeq's hadith about, 203; YAZD, 8, 12, 26, 157–60, 417n41, cinemas, 159, 236, shrines, 128, 398n7; Zabul, 329

—computer science teams in, 370

—refugees in, 352: from Afghanistan, 307, 324, from Iraq, 308, 309

Iraq: Halabja, 293, 300, 304, 307, 422n9; Saddam Hussein, 267, 304, 306, 307

Islam: cultural armor, 163; hegemony and resistance: in Hedayat's work, 195, marriage alliance of Husain and Yazdigird III, 128, revolts of Afshin, Babak, Barmakis, Mazyar, Tahir "Zulyaminein," 195, in *Shahnameh*, 71, 76, 77, 78, 195: hadith to interpret *Shahnameh*, 75, quip by naqqal (Is-lam based on Prophet's disposition, Khadijeh's wealth, Ali's sword), 75; modernist movements, 165, "Alavi" versus "Safavi" Islam, 195, transna-tional fundamentalisms, 337, Pakistani, 347, Wahhabi, 330; pros-elytizing and loss of heroism (Es-fandiar, Alexander), 110

Ismailis, 74, 135

Jabarsa and Jabalqa (emerald cities, mystical states), 138

Jamalzadeh, Mohammad Ali, 165, 166, 383, 411n10, 412n12

Jamaspa, cup of (ability to see into the future), 47, 49, 62, 90, 133

Jamshid (Yima, q.v., and *khshaetra*, "king"), 67, 76, 78, 91, 95, 99, 105, 133, 403n5, 405n22; builds Var, 99; *jam-e Jamshid* (cup of Jamshid), 144; loses *khwarrah*, 99, 100

Japan: robotics, 12, 370, 371; Sassanian objects, 379

Jerusalem, 238

Jesus: not slain, laugher of, 409n46

Jews (Kalimi, followers of Musa Ka-limullah): Passover haggadah, 245; Purim doublet to Bozorgmehr para-ble on just rule, 119, 408n39; *targums* similar to Pazend glosses, 71; temple-talmud transformation, contrast with Zoroastrianism, 398n12

Jones, William, 379

Joyce, James, 217

justice, 118

Juvaini, 'Ala' al-Din 'Ata-Malik, 75;

Juvaini (*cont.*)
  Tarikh-i Jahangusha (History of the
    World Conqueror), 69, 74, 237

Kafka, Franz, 198, 356, 415n28
Kaid, king in India, 110–111, 113, 145
Kaidafa, queen of Andalusia, 111, 407n32
Kai Kaus (Kavya Ushana, Kavi Usa), 67,
  75, 82, 83, 84, 85, 86, 92, 94, 95, 97,
  100, 103, 106, 406n33; three errors of,
  95, 100, 101
Kai Khosrow (Haorsravah), 75, 84, 85,
  92, 93, 94, 95, 100, 106, 131, 133; **fifth
  of *Shahnameh* devoted to**, 85; **ritual
  functions**: ascends to heaven, 88, 99,
  demonstrates *khwarrah*, 86, inherits
  jam-e Jamshid, 133, 404n12, invoked
  in Avestan prayer, 88, purifies earth,
  abdicates, withdraws to read Avesta,
  85–86, 93; **royal functions**: four military campaigns, 85–87, 98; wit and
  wisdom in riddling joust with Afrasiyab, 85
Kai Kubad, 91, 92; Kubad (meaning
  "threshold"), 405n18
Kalila and Dimma: Kalila as drug that
  makes the dead speak, 122; parables
  of, 122, 374
Kant, Immanuel, 134, 140
Karbala, 75, 85, 227, 238, 246, 250, 251,
  257, 310, 389, 405n16, 418n46, 430n15
Kasoya Lake (in which final saoshyant
  will be born), 58
Kasravi, Ahmad, 165
Kaveh, 103, 397
Kayanians, 17, 23, 79, 86, 91, 93, 99; genealogy of, 92
Keresaspa (Sama Keresaspa Narimanu):
  becomes three in legends (Sam, Nari-
  man, Faridun), 406n25; offspring of
  Thrita (first to offer haoma) and
  slayer of Zahhak, 406n25
Kermani, Muhammad Karim Khan
  (Qajar prince, Shaikhi), 137

Khadijeh (wife of Muhammad), 75
Khamene'i, Ali, 248
Khanjast (Lake Urumiah), site of Afrasiyab's capture, 87
Khatami, Muhmmad, 248, 270, 355, 356
Khayam, Omar, 191, 197, 414nn19 and
  23, 415nn27 and 29
khedvadatha (next-of-kin marriage),
  403n9
Khizr, 111, 137
Khomeini, Ayatullah Ruhollah, 6, 21,
  133, 141, 225, 238, 247, 248, 275, 276,
  327, 419n46, 426n26
Khosrow/Kirsa Nushiravan. *See*
  Nushiravan Adel
Khosrow Parviz, 114, 123, 125, 408n42,
  44, 409n51; and barsom, 36; claim to
  be a god among men, 95; formal
  charges against and his defense, 127;
  reconstruction of Faridun's throne,
  409n48; and Shirin, 9, 127, 130, as
  ambiguous marriage alliance parable
  in Firdausi, as love story in Nizami,
  126
kingship: and religion, 95. See also
  khwarrah; legitimacy
Kitano, Hiroaki, 371
knowledge over brawn, 109
Kubad (nineteenth Sassanian king),
  117–118
Kubad aka Shirwi (twenty-third Sassanian king), 123; insurrection and
  claims Shirin, 127
Kurds: doctors in Afghanistan, 346; migrants in Istanbul, 422n9
kusti (sacred thread), 30; of date leaves,
  36; device for binding evil, 108; as
  peyvand in funeral, 171; represented
  by Rustam's lasso, Esfandiar's chain,
  Homa's kamerband, 108
kwarrah (divinely blessed sovereignty,
  Middle Persian: *farr*) : hubris and
  loss of, 95, 107, 133, 141: Jamshid, 81,
  92, 95, 107, Kai Kaus, 107, Kai

Khosrow, 86, 92, 107, 133; as royalty accompanying Mithra across the sky, 49; of Zoroaster, 46. See also *ta'allah*

Lacan, Jacques, 233, 260
language, 147; etymological-metaphorical revelation of, 147; structuralism in, 405n24; vulgarity and asceticism in, 147
Laroui, Abdullah, 159, 168
legitimacy, 68, 72, 112, 141, 142; imamat, hikmat, hokumat, farrah, 133; just kings (*padshahan*) versus tyrants (*mutaghalliban*), 108; threatening aspects of charismatic philosopher-kings, 135. See also *kwarrah*
Levinas, Emmanuel, 224, 225
Lévi-Strauss, Claude, 405n24
literary genres: essay, 168; mathnawi, ghazal, hikayat, 134; memoirs, 169; modern poetry, 166–67; novels, 412nn 10 and 12; short story, 170, 180, 410n10, 412n12
Lohrasp, 80, 81, 88, 92, 93, 106, 109, 405n21
Los Angeles, 361, 364, 369, 387
love stories, 316; Bizhan and Manizha, 87, 404n12; Khosrow and Shirin, 9, 126–27, 130; about sadness of love, 418n45; *sag-e velgard* and lover of Iran, 183
Lyotard, Jean-François, 11, 244, 262, 351

Mah Afrid (slave, bears posthumous daughter to Iraj), 105
Mahallati, Muhammad Ja'far, 395
Mahfuz, Naqib, 155, 165
Mahmud of Ghazni, 7, 18, 68, 70, 167, 340, 426n29
Maimonides, 134, 410n2
Malcolm X, 225
Ma'mun, Caliph, 122, 374, 414–15n26; Persian mother of, 414–15n26
Mandeans, 137
Mani, 115

Manicheanism, 379
Manizha and Bizhan, 87, 404n12
Mannoni, Octave, 168
mantras. See *Ahuna Vairya; Airyema Ishyo; Airyema Ishyo; Yinhe Hatam*
Manuchehr, 76, 78, 81, 96, 103, 105, 106
Mariyam (wife of Khosrow Parviz, poisoned by Shirin), 126
marriage alliances and consequences, 9, 95, 96, 113, 312, 410n51; table of, 96
Marx, Karl, 161, 393
masculinity, 205, 207, 209–11
Mashya-Mashyoi, 78, 100
Masudi, 409n50
Mazandaran, 93, 101
Mazdak, 117–18, 123
Mazyar, 415n26
Medes, 416n38
media: local cultures versus media machines, 338; messianic space and small media, 225; orality, literacy, and electronic media, 227–38; theories, 9–10, 12; virtual reality CAVE, 421n5
Memi, Albert, 168
Merleau-Ponty, Maurice, 140
Mesoamerica, 22
Mesopotamia, 429n10
metaphors and symbols, 20–21, 29, 44, 152, 370, 383, 428n1
—AIRPLANES: bombing and transport, 307, 324; deus ex machina, explosive missile, symbol of escape (dove), womb, 361
—ALCHEMY AND METALS, 138
—ANIMALS, q.v.: swift steeds of good thought, 43, 44; chariot races as symposia (Vedic *sadhamada*), 20; language of the birds, 145; birds on the tree of life, 171
—AROMAS and ability to see into the future, 471
—BIRTH, 365
—BLACKBOARD, as Sisyphus's stone, 303, 307

—BOTANY AND PLANTS (Amaratat), 50, 65, 138; **cherry** blossoms (other world) versus a taste of cherry (this world), 241, 243; **mandrake**, 185, 188, 193; **pomegranates,** 278, 304, Esfandiar and invulnerability, 32, 42, 47, 79; **trees**: cypress and date palms as youth, immortality (Chaldean, Assyrian, Egyptian, Hebraic, Greco-Roman parallels), 36, 62, 171, 178, 182, 185, 415n29; cypress of Zoroaster cut down by Harun al-Rashid, 62; Gaokarana (cosmic tree), 62; tree in Kiarostami, 241; tree of vegetation and the Simorgh, 81; Tuba tree of Paradise, 136

—BLOOD AND INK, 172, 173, 177, 179, 182

—COLORS, black and white as binary structuring, not simple signs, 176–77

—COSMIC DIRECTIONS, 31–32, 34, 137

—DANCE: **breaking cycle of rebirth and repetition**, 185, 188, Shiva, 197, writing as, 187; **danse macabre**, 187, 313, of colonized slave labor, 313

—DEATHS: burial alive: in Hedayat's work, 440, in *The Peddler*, 239, in *A Taste of Cherry*, 243; femur floating downstream (*The Wind Will Carry Us*), 260; phantasmagoric life, 243, 244

—FIRE, LIGHT, AND SUN (*atash, khorshid, mihr, nur, khwarrah, tawali/lawa'ib*), 184; **fires of war**, 273; **Mihr** Niyayesh ("Hymn to **Mithra/Mihr**, Sun/Light"), 49, recited three times a day with the **Khorshid** Niyayesh ("Hymn to the Sun"), 48; Mithra, god of covenants, ordeal by fire, 48; Mithra accompanied across the sky by royal *kwarrah*, 49; *nur* **(light) doctrines** (divine, incandescent, light of lights [*nur al-anwar*]): of the 124,000 prophets and twelve Imams, 133, 140, 143, 144, intensities of divine luminousness and degrees of consciousness, 141; **ordeal by fire**: Abraham, 146, Dante protected by terza rima, 399n14, life in this world as (Ali in *Do'ah Komeil*), 418n44, Qur'anic hellfires (Ayeh Julud, in Sureh 4.55), 174, salamander, 145; **sacred fires**, 139, *Atash Niyayash* ("Hymn to the Fire," Y.62), 52–53, created by purifying ordinary fires, 31, sacrificial offerings (sandalwood, frankincense, fat), 31, 53, like "swift-driving charioteer," 53, symbol of *menog*, 30; **sun:** flares (*tawali*) and rays (*lawa'ib*) as *sakina/shekhina*, 136, sun and cave, 329, sun and moon, 329; **tropes of light:** used by European Enlightenment, 140, by Illuminationists, q.v., and by Suhrawardi, q.v.; *see also* ethical discourses; films: names

—JUMPING ROPE IN JAIL (Mandela, *Osama*), 349

—LAUGHTER, 185, 188, 193, 194; of Jesus, 409n46; of Khomeini, 419n46; kinds, 215; nish-khand (ironic philosophical smile of Muhammad), 215, 418n46; nush-khand (foolish grin) of adam-e sabok (lightweight), 215; of Silenus, 196

—LOVER-BELOVED, 147; of Iran, 182; and jar, 197, 415n27; and treasure, 186, 416n29

—MIRRORS: eyes as accusatory mirrors, pain of transcendental knowledge, 182, 188; rearview mirrors as memory, 175, 182; still water, polished armor, as access to third world of archetypes (*'alam al-mithal*), 136; and windows, 187; **moon and stars** (dead, reflected light), 173, 179, moon eclipse, clouded over, 321, 331, stars and sinister fate, 184, 414n19, and sun, 329; **pastoral metaphors of mutuality:** draft oxen of truth (man and God yoked), 50; in yasna and Gathas, 56

—pharmakon (shefa/shafa), 414n21; see also *hom*

—Pygmalion, 312

—rain-filled footprint, 260, 319, 320

—reinterpretation of pre-Islamic metaphors, 133, 135

—rusty nail attachment to life, 190, 415n29

—squats in abandoned bus or boat, 273, 288

—transports (airplanes, boats, cars, motorcycles, planes, trains), 273, 324

—typewriters, 276, 280

—veiling, 331

—water: *ab-i Karbala* (water of Karbala), 187, 414n21, 415n29, *ab-i towbeh* (water of repentance), 201, *ab zohr* (consecrated water), 32, 42, 44, 52, *Ab Zohr* (Libation to the Waters), 53–54; 402n34; Anahita, 54, 110, 115, 138; Arpat Napat, 48–49, 54; Daiti river's four branches, symbols of spread of Zoroastrianism, 60; Lake Khanjast (Urumiah), locus of Afrasiyab's death, 88; running water or quantity of water as purifying, 177; stream separating this world and the next, 185; Vouruskasha Sea (cosmic sea), 62, 138

—weddings hidden in cave, goats penned, 425n24

—wine, 185, 210, 414n19; and juice of life, 187; see also *hom*

—women, 184; carriers of repression and renewal, 177, 182; cross-gender personification, 185

—yogurt, 365

Mir Damad, 135

Mistry, Zaraawar, 397n4

Mithra (god of covenants, of the morning): benevolent judge, 48, 65; cult of, 379

Mitra-Varuna (paradigmatic binary unit, e.g., night-day, left-right, breathing in-out), 48. *See also* Varuna

modernity and modernisms, 2, 10

Mongols, 72, 74; *Moghul-ha* (The Mongols), q.v.

Mosadeq, Mohammad, 165

Moses (Musa Kalimullah, "who speaks to God"), 261, 382, 418n46, 420 nn2 and 3

Motahheri, Morteza, 277

Mozart, Wolfgang Amadeus, 3, 22

Muhammad, 142; foreseen in Nushiravan's dream, 113, 123

Mullah Sadra, 135, 144

music, 281, 282, 305; Afghan war ballads, 347; Armstrong's "St. James Infirmary" (*A Taste of Cherry*), 242; by Cole, (*The Runner*), 273; by Darvishi, 12, 349; by Dehlim, 12, 387, 392, 403n17; song intensifies divine spark, 147; Zoroastrian themes, 379, in Mozart, 380, in Richard Strauss, 380; zurkhaneh drum and chain percussion, 209, 288, 290

mythemes: **bad breath**, odor, poisonous kiss, 109, 406n28; **battle scenes** as tests of prudence, 98; **creation** by "meiosis," 76; **cycles** of nature (babies, vultures), 169; **demon slaying** as royal legitimation, 112; **failure to burn** (Ibrahim, Zoroaster), 59; **food**, 100; **fountain of youth**, 111; **heroes**: explosure as babies (Moses, Oedipus, Romulus and Remus, Zoroaster), 59, flaws, 79, miraculous swords, chains, etc., passed to heirs, 103; **hubris** (e.g., Jamshid), 95; **king-warrior** (shah-pahlavan) pair in Indo-European myth, 123; **laughing at birth as prophetic sign** (Moses, Zoroaster), 59; **purification by molten metal**, 111, 409n51; **sons lost or killed**, 95; **three-**

mythemes (*cont.*)

generation units (loss and regaining of legitimacy), 92, 93, 94, 99, 103, 106, 107, 113

Nabokov, Vladimir, 164, 170, 203
Naderpour, Nader, 211
Nadir Shah, 80
Nahid (daughter of Caesar, wife of Gushtasp), 80
Nariman, 406n25
narrative and intersignifying structures, 5, 18
narrative devices, 383; **agons**: banquets for testing Bozorgmehr, 118, banquets for warriors, 77; battles of wit, 109, 363, testing of the sage, 111; battle scenes (see mythemes); cycles of feuds (Iran, Turan, Rum); *dard-e del*, 182, 363; **disguise**: girl as boy, 318, 349 (*see also* warrior-woman), king as merchant, 112; **doublets**, 130: Alexander and Esfandiar, 108–109; Alexander and Shapur, 115, three Khosrows (Kai, Noshiravan, Parviz), q.v., twins, 187, two Kaids (India, Andalusia), 111, two Kubads and two Hormuzds (Urmazds), 409n51; **funerals and mourning**, 73, 169, 403n4, 418n44, 419nn 47 and 48; **genealogies** versus meiotic-myth, 77, 99; **male sacrifice** of love for friendship, 416n38; **marriage alliances**, 95, 96, 130, 169, flawed marriage, 182, incestuous marriage, 188; **melodrama versus psychodrama**, 280, 281; **mythemes transformed into parables**, 130
naqqals (reciters), 24, 75, 77, 80; Meskoub on, 79;
Nasir al-Din Tusi, 74
nationalism: four sites in use of Shahnameh, 69; language of Shahnameh as, 72

Naudar, 100
neoplatonism, 133, 134, 137, 380
Neshat, Shirin, 375–78, 387
New York, 172, 176, 387, 389; attack on World Trade Center (9/11/01), 351, 352, 355, 357, 421n7
Nietzsche, Friedrich, 3, 8, 22, 161, 180, 196, 370, 378, 420n2, 428n1; *Also Sprach Zarathustra*, 380–85
Nizami, 75, 126, 130, 406n29, 409n47
Noah, 77
Noruz, 185, 189, 227, 251, 296, 415n29
novelists: Abdoh (*The Poet Game*), 270; Chubak, q.v.; Efandiari (*Day of Sacrifice*), 270; Hamid, 270; Mistry (*Swimming Lessons*), 301; Powers (*Plowing the Dark*), 262; Rushdie (*Midnight's Children*), 326
Nushiravan Adel (Kisra/Khosrow, "the Restorer," "the Just"), 9, 18, 30, 73, 95, 113, 117–23, 374, 407nn39 and 41, 409n47, 419n51; defends Zoroastrianism against Mazdak, 118; as final Kai Khosrow, 118

Oedipus, 381, 420n3
oil enclave economy, 287; gas flares, 286, 288, National Iranian Oil Company, 286, 287; oil fields in Iran-Iraq war, 392
Omar (caliph), 71, 410n52
opium, 342. *See also* Afghanistan
orality and literacy, 7, 11, 12, 227 280; epics, 4, 8; Kalila and Dimma, 122; rituals, 4

pahlavans (athletes, heros, champions), 24. *See also* Bahram Chubin; Rustam; Sufarai
Pahlavi (Pazend, Zend Avesta), 71
Pahlavi period, 165, 181, 414n18
painting, 183, 186, 353, 428n4; contrast with film, 280; Dali, 337; MINIATURES, 73, 185, 195, 353, 416n29, Behzad, 252, old man and houri tab-

leau, 195–96; posters, 222; Tansey, 233; wall painting, 310

Pakistan, 169, 267, 268; Baluchistan and the Makran Coast, 342; drug addicts in, 423n13; Inter-Service Intelligence (ISI), 342, 344; Karachi, 172, 176; Kashmir and India, 342; and Abdul Ghaffar Khan, 269; Quetta, 344

parables (masal), 7, 8, 9, 18, 75, 106, 130, 227

—ADDING VALUE WITHOUT DISTURB-ING FULL BOWL: Alexander, 111; Buddhist monks, 407n31; Parsis, 407n31

—BALANCED GRIEF, death and life (Gav), 215

—BAZARNUSH AND COLONIALISM, 407n36

—CAIN AND ABEL, 287, 288

—CHOOSING DEATH over fear of death (*The Peddler*), 239

—CHOOSING GOOD FOSTERAGE (*The Peddler*), 238

—GOD'S FISH AND AUTHORITARIAN-ISM, 298

—ILLEGITIMACY AND UNWORTHINESS OF OMAR (cutting up Spring Carpet of Khosrow), 410n52

—JUST GROUNDS FOR BURYING Pashang or heretic in a Muslim cemetery, 75

—KHIZR AND MOSES, 261

—KHOSROW AND SHIRIN, q.v., as parable of ambiguous marriage alliances, 126

—LAUGHTER OF JESUS, 409n46

—RUSTAM AND SA'AD IBN WAQQAS (uncivilized Arabs, inegalitarian Persians), 130; egalitarianism as positive and negative, 116, 118, 410n52

—SELFLESS CARE FOR OTHERS (*Baran*), 316

—WISDOM OVER BRAWN, 270

Parsis, 145, 379, 407n31

Parthians, 71, 108; names assimilated by Shahnameh into Kayanians, 407n33

Pashang (son of Tur, grandson of Iraj, father of Afrasiyab), 105; wish to be buried in Iran not honored, 75

Persian Empire, 3, 4, 59

Peshotan, 47, 62, 81

Pessayani, Attila, 1

photojournalism, 338

Piran, 84, 85, 86, 98

Pishdadians, 17, 23, 76, 79, 86, 99, 100; genealogy, 78

Plato, 131, 133, 134; Plato as second Zoroaster in cosmic cycle, 402n38; Platonic Forms, 140

poesis and performative achievement of vision, 5, 19–20, 25, 145, 147; in film, 242; revelatory of etymological-metaphorical and grammatical structure of language, 147

poetry, 147, 399n14; competitive symposia or nsadhamada, 28; modern Persian, 166–67, 411n9; terza rima, 399n14

political pundits: Huntington, 261; Ignatieff, 262; realist, 262

Poruchista (Zoroaster's daughter), 51

posters, 3, 13, 225

Pour-e Davoud, Ibrahim, 22

propaganda posters, identifying Zahhak and Hitler, 102, 104

psychology: **being eaten up from the inside**, 240; **burial alive**: in Hedayat, 440, in *The Peddler*, 239, in *A Taste of Cherry*, 243; **depression under the Taliban**, 37; **desire versus forgetfulness**, 414n19; **emotional control:** grief and mourning, 214–15, models for swallowing anger (Ali, Musa Kazem), 418n46, through teasing, 216; **Eros and Psyche**, 183, 413n17; **Faust**, 413n17; **fear psychosis**, 417n42; **introversion and narcissism**, 181; **mechanical culture** (*The Peddler*), 238; **memory**, 169, 180; **repression**, 177, and repetition, 169, 180, 182, 188;

psychology (*cont.*)

    oedipal, 54, 84, 95, 169, 182–83; **psychodrama of dignity and self esteem** (*Close Up, Crimson and Gold*), 229, 285–86; **sadness (melancholia)**, 211, 214, 218, 388, 418n44: genres: *dard-e del* (pain of the heart), 182, 216, 286, *taziya, azadari* (mourning), 418n46, *zaban-e hal* (finding words for a state of philosophical awareness), 216; regret (Moses, Noah), 418n46; sadness as a patient stone (*sang-e sabur*), 216; sadness of love, 418n46; **shell shock and war trauma**, 264, 290, 313; **stoicism**, 285; **suicide**, 180, 240, 241, 308, 310, 329; **youth and demonstrations**, 412n13, Freud, q.v., Rivers, 264

purity code, 20, 174, 178

Purushasp (Zoroaster's father), 46–47

al-Qaeda, 266, 267, 268, 342, 345, 355, 402n4

Qajar, Fath Ali Shah, 80, 414n18

Qum, 157, 160; cinema, 160; television, 160

Qur'an, 13, 75, 77, 141, 146, 332, 348, 366, 383; on corpse's chest, 415n29; distinctive features, 228; as *sang-e sabur*, 216; Sureh 4.55 (*Ayeh Julud*, "The Skins Verse"), 174; Surehs 6.63, 7.55, and 7.205 (call on God with tears and fear), 418n44; Sureh 18.18 (The Cave), 412n14; Sureh 28.76 ("God loves not those who are joyous"), 211; Sureh 54.1 ("The hour of Judgment . . . moon cleft asunder"), 164; Sureh 96.1–5 (earliest revelation, "taught by the pen"), 228; transcript (*mushaf*), 227, 228

qutb (pole of the age, whose presence keeps the world from ruin), 143

rabble, 388

Rakhsh (Rustam's horse), 97

Rashid al-Din, 73, 74

realism, 261

reincarnation, 144

religion (*deen, iman, mazhab, dawa*): and calls to response and responsibility, 226; countervailing traditions, 261

revolution, incapacities of, 169

revolutions in Iran: **artistic**, 166; **constitutional (1905–11)**, 166, euphoria of, 181; **Islamic (1977–79)**, 163, call for adelat (justice), 142, 226, and film, 246, 281, play on Khomeini as Imam Zaman, 143, slogans, 276

ritual, 18–20; circumcision, 205, 207; gestural language and structure of, 5, 19; and myth, 19; Shi'ite mourning genres: rawzeh, dasteh, sineh zani, 279, 281; traces in *Shahnameh*, 409n51; transformed into narrative, 9, 110; travel, 363; in weddings: *Marooned in Iraq*, 306, *Marriage of the Blessed*, 279, *Safar-e Qandahar*, 335, *Time of the Drunken Horses*, 296

Rivayats, 55, 298n12

Rizmihr (son of Sufarai), 117

robots, 12, 370–71, 373–74, 380, 428n2

Roshanak (Roxanne), 92, 109, 111

Rousseau, Jean-Jacques, 384

Rudabeh (mother of Rustam), 78, 81

Rudaki (poet), 122, 219, 374

Rum (Rome, Greece, Byzantium, the West), 80, 93, 94, 95, 111, 115, 116, 125, 127

Rumi, 134, 200, 227, 248, 261, 298, 430n17

Rushdie, Salman, 12; *Midnight's Children*, 426n26

Russia, 268; Gazprom, 342

Rustam, 78, 86, 92, 93, 95, 100,103, 105, 112, 117, 404n15, 405n21, 406n25; as champion of the old faith, 79; coffin of, 73; and Esfandiar, 79, 81, 88–90, 144, 404n14, in Suhrawardi, 136; gluttony of, 404n13; occult powers, 144; rescue of Bizhan, 87, 404n12; and Sohrab, 9, 22, 82–83, 94, 380, 397n4; sword compared to Ali's, 75; **trials of**, 96–98, in Akhavan Sales, 167, table of, 98

Rustam (commander of Yazdegird III's army), 127

Sa'ad ibn Waqqas, 9, 128, 130
Sabeans, 137
Sa'di, 74, 75, 248, 330, 353, 412n14
Sa'edi, Gholam Husain, 5, 160, 162, 211, 214, 236, 412n10, 417n39
Safavi, Shah Abbas, 80, 413n18
Saladin, 135, 143
Salih, Tayeb, 154, 412n12
Salm, 76, 78, 79, 105
Sam, 74, 78, 81, 100, 103, 406n25
Samanghan (between Iran and Turan), 95; princess of, mother of Sohrab, 95
Samanids, 18, 70, 71; and translation of Kalila and Dimma, 122, 374
Saramatians, 379, 428n5
Sartre, Jean-Paul, 163, 164, 413n16, 415n28
Sassanians, 17, 22, 77, 99, 109, 112, 145, 404n10; codification of the yasna, 27; **in the *Shahnameh***, q.v.: charged with being usurpers, 125, climax and decline of an age, 130, genealogy, 114
Satrapi, Manijeh, 370
Saudi Arabia: Delta Oil, 342; Nigarcho, 342; Prince Turki, 342
sayaoshants (redeemers), 42–43, 50, 58, 138; one in Yasht, 13; legend of three, 402n35. *See also* Bahram Varjovand
Scheherezade, 144, 242, 370, 374, 378
Schelling, Friedrich Wilhelm Joseph von, 420n1
Schopenhauer, Arthur, 384
Scythians, 76
Seleucids, 402n37
Seljuks, 74

Shahnameh, 4, 7–9, 17–18, 21, 66–130, 156, 209, 227, 252, 255, 270, 311, 312, 353, 374, 396n3
—COLLECTION OF LEGENDS, 71, oral versus written transmission, 7–8, 68, 73; variants by tumar, manuscript, dictations, and naqqal, 69, 73
—CONTRASTS WITH AVESTA, 66–67, 92, 405n20
—CRITIQUE, USE AS, 74, 75; *see also* intersignification; legitimacy; narrative devices; parables
—ETHOS: Islamicizing changes, 76, 77; martial heroism and cunning wit, 68; tragic sensibility, 67, 78; wariness against fanaticism, 79
—FEUDS: between ancients and moderns (Rustam-Esfandiar, Zoroastrians-Islam); 103; cycles of conflict with Turan (Tur, Afrasiyab, Arjasp), 103; cycles of conflict with the West (Alexander, Arabs and Greco-Roman-Byzantines, Caesar, Vologeses, Zahhak), 103; between good and evil (Ahura Mazda and Ahriman, Iran and Zahhak, men and demons), 79; tri-polar world (Salm-Iran-Tur), 76, 79, 105
—LANGUAGE, 72, 166
—MANUSCRIPTS AND MINIATURES, 70, 72–74, 101; Bayhangsir (c. 1425), 71; DeMotte (c. 1335), 72; Il-Khanid (Inju court, Shiraz, c. 1330–1352), 72, 73; in British World War II propaganda posters, 102, 104
—MYTHIC VERSUS PARABLE LOGIC, 67, 76, 106; ritual traces, 9, 23, 35, 36, 107, 108, 110, 130, 409n51; see also barsom; mythemes; parables
—TREATMENT OF DYNASTIES: **attention**: Kai Khosrow takes up a fifth of Firdausi's epic, 108; naqqals treat mainly first third of *Shahnameh*, 77, 79; only three of twenty-nine Sas-

—TREATMENT OF DYNASTIES: (*cont.*)
sians dealt with in depth, 109; **genre:**
Pishdadians as mythic age, genealogization of creation and culture heroes,
archetypes and basic feuds (see feuds
above) for later epic stories, 17, 79, 86,
93, 99, 100, 103; *Kayanians* as heroic
and prophetic age, struggle of ancients
and moderns (Rustam versus Esfandiar, Zoroastrianism versus Islam,
Arab Islam and Persian Islam), 17, 79;
Ashkanians and Alexander as epic romance, powers of wit and wisdom,
feuds with the West, 23, 103, 108; *Sassanians* as decline of heroic age, moral
parables of fallible humans, good
rulership, importance of wisdom over
brawn, 18, 112–13; **scholars:** Bertels, 69;
Grabar and Blair, 69, 73; Hanaway, 110,
406n28; Maguire, 90–91, 96, 404nn13–
15; Meskhoub, 79, 90, 94–95, 106;
Nöldeke, 70, 71, 405n17; Page, 69,
403n6, 405n21; Simpson, 69, 73–74;
Spiegel, 405n17; Warner and Warner,
406n28, 407n39
Shaikhis, 137
Shapur I, 95, 406n36
Shapur II ('Zul Aktaf), 113, 115
Shariati, Ali, 6, 21, 162, 163, 164, 168, 195,
277, 288, 396n3, 430n11; polemics
against "Safavid Islam," 195
Shariatmadari, Ayatullah S.
Muhammad-Kazem, 225
Shem, 111
Shi'ism: competing rhetorics and dis-
courses within, 155; cues, 283; sym-
bolism, 310
Shirazi, Qubt al-Din, 142
Shirin ("sweet"): death of, 127; and
Farhad, 210, 409n47, 416n38; and
Khosrow Parviz, parable of bowl of
blood and wine, 126; niece of queen
of Armenia, 409n47; poisons Mar-
iyam to become chief wife, 126

short stories: three generations, 411n10
sibling rivalries, 86
Simorgh, 77, 81, 90, 100, 103, 129, 130,
131, 135, 136, 138, 145, 146, 387, 405n20
Siyamak, 78, 99
Siyavush, 84–85, 92, 93, 94, 95, 96, 103,
106, 404n15, 430n18; compared with
Joseph and Potiphar's wife, 84;
mourning for, as archetype for
mourning Imam Husain, 85; and
Sohrab, 95
social divisions: **class:** gentry (dehqans)
69, 71, slaves, 70; **ethnicities:** Greeks,
Persians, Turks, Semites, Romans, 68,
Hazaras and Pushtuns, 337–38, Pushtuns and Tajiks, 345, sultanat (Persian
bureaucracy) versus sepahsalari
(Turkic military command), 77,
Turkic Ghaznavids and Mongol
Ilkhanids, 68; **religious:** Zoroastrian and Islamic, 67, 68, 76, 77, 78,
169–80, 259, 236
social theory: Gellner, on European
folklore and nationalism, 396n5;
Hunt, on pantheistic transformational systems, 22–23; Lévi-Strauss,
on ritual, 19; Weber, on religion and
imperium, 3
Sohrab, 74, 84, 93, 94; and Rustam, 9,
22, 82–83, 380; and Siyavush, 95; unhorsed by woman-warrior Gordafrid, 406n30
Sontag, Susan, 151
sophia (wisdom), identified with Armaiti (daughter of Yahweh, craftswoman of creation), 138
Sorush (Srosh), 27, 30, 37, 51, 53–54, 60,
103, 111, 125, 409n51; consecration of
bread to, 37; Srosh Yasht, 51–52
sovereignty. See *khwarrah*; legitimacy;
ta'allah
stammering: attributed to Moses, 382;
in cinema, 382; in Nietzsche, 382
stoicism, 157

Strauss, Richard, 380, 429n6,n7

Sudabeh, 84, 95

Sufarai, 117, 408n42

Suhrawardi, 21, 24, 131–147; allegorical tales, 135, *Treatise on Birds*, 145; analysis of self (I-ness), 134, 139–40; ascetic practice of self-knowledge, 134, 139, 140; eternal return, 144; knowledge by presence and experience, 134, 139; life history, 135; recovery of ancient Zoroastrian wisdom, 133; relation of rationalism (*hikmat bathiyya*) and intuitionism (*hikmat dhawquiyya*), 134, 135; relation of three forms of cognition (logic, sense impressions, innate ideas or direct apprehension), 140

surrealism, 152, 153–154, 157, 162, 168, 169, 178, 181, 194, 195, 213, 218, 246

Tabari, 95, 409n50

Tahmina, 83

Tahmuras ("binder of divs," brother of Jamshid), 76, 78, 99; and Ahriman, 99

Taq-i Bustan, 409n47

ta'allah (to become God, transgressive term for illuminationist philosophy, sovereignty belongs to one who is *mut'allih*, divinized), 143

Taliban, 266, 267, 339, 340, 341, 347, 355, 425n21, 426n26; leaders, 343–44; negotiations with Unocal, 342

Tantae'i, Hassan (aka Hassan Abdul Rahman, Doud Salahuddin, David Belfield), assassin of Ali Akbar Tababa'i), 327

Taslimi, Fereydun, 373

Taslimi, Susan, 272

taziyeh ("mourning," passion plays), 12, 387, 389, 390

television, 12, 141, 160, 200, 220, 246, 266, 305, 313, 357

teletechnologies: cell phones, 266; tele-

mediated war, 356; videocameras, 266, virtual reality cave, 354

terrorism in 1990s–2001, 269, 270, 423n12

Tha'alebi, 409n50

Thousand and One Nights, 144, 406n30

Thraetaona (slayer of Dahaka/Zahhak), 40

Timur, 71

Tiradates (Zoroastrian priest, brother of Parthian king Vologeses I), 71

Towers of Silence, 154, 156, 168–180, 181, 194; intertwining of Zoroastrian and Muslim, 169, surrealist techniques, 181

tragedy, melancholia, philosophical sadness, 67, 78, 153, 157, 219, 383

Tuba tree of Paradise, 136

Tur, 76, 79, 103, 105

Turan, Turanians, 31, 62, 77, 86, 93, 94, 95, 98, 99, 106, 117, 311; mystical boundary, 116; signified by wolf suffix -gorg, 97

Turkey, 147

Turkmenistan oil, 342

Tus (son of Naudar), 78, 86

Uighur, 74

Uljaytu, 73, 403n4

Ummayids, 415n26

Union of Soviet Socialist Republics (USSR), 268; former Soviet Union and the Great Game for oil in Central Asia and the Caucusus, 342

United Nations: paying refugees to return to Afghanistan, 337; peacekeeping troops, 423n10

United States

—RELATIONS WITH Afghanistan, 402n4; **pre-2001**: negotiation by Ambassador Robert Oakley, 341; involvement of **oil companies:** Amoco and Unocal, 342, and Creighton (Unocal board, later ceo of United Airlines

—RELATIONS, AFGHANISTAN (*cont.*)
during 9/11/01), 344–45, host Taliban
in Houston, 342, and Kissinger, 342,
and University of Kansas Center for
Afghan Studies, 342; and USAID: irrigation project (Helmand), 340, road
building (1960s), 341; **post-2001:** attack
on Taliban and al-Qaeda, 265, 266–67,
268, soldiers playing buzkashi, 338
—RELATIONS WITH IRAN: cultural exchanges, 430n16; political cooperation and agon, 356
—TARGETED: embassies in Kenya and
Tanzania, 342; New York World
Trade Center (9/11/01), 351, 352, 355,
357, 421n7
Upanishads, 29, 146, 178
Urumiah (Lake Khanjast), site of Afrasiyab's capture, 87

Var: and Bahram Varjovand, 137, 138;
built underground in preparation for
resurrection by Jamshid/Yima and
besieged by Afrasiyab, 32, 99, 107
Varuna (husband or son of the waters,
Apam Napat), punitive judge, 48,
401n30
Vedas, 20, 28, 29, 32, 36,137, 146, 178,
399n14, 405n20,23; *bráhmans* (mind-
enhancing poetic puzzles) versus
brahmodya (standardized disputa-
tions), 29; **cognate Vedic/Avestan
ritual forms**: *hotar/zaotar* priest,
399n13, *kusha/barsom*, 36, *mantra*
(Av. *mathra*), 20, protection of poetry against pain (*Taittirya Samhita*),
399n14, *sadhamada* (poetic contests),
20, 28–29, *udgatr/yasht* (hymn),
399n13, yagna/yasna worship and
sacrifice, 29, 137; **shared Vedic/
Avestan metaphors, similes, and
symbols**: *agni* (fire), 28, chariots and
horses, 29, cow, 29, sun and moon,
29, Vac/Var, 28–29, 32, 43

Valerian, 407–8n36
Vendidad, 56, 67, 379
Virilio, Paul, 232
Vishtaspa (Gushtasp, q.v.), 27, 49, 60;
conversion and four wishes, 47
vision: seeing with eyes and two bor-
rowed eyes, 242; four-eyed dog or
ghayeb, 242
Visperad, 399n15
Vologeses I (Valkash), 71
Vourukasha (cosmic sea), 53, 88, 107

war: chemical weapons, 290, 293, 300;
minefields, 291, 292, 294, 300; **veterans:** *see under* filmography by title:
*The Abadanis, Crimson and Gold,
The Glass Agency, Marriage of the
Blessed*
wit and wisdom (*sophia*, q.v.) in a
world of the unseen (*gha'ib*), 141,
142–43, 144, 253, 261; binding of
Zahhak/Ahriman better than illusory effort to cut off head, 406n25;
parables of wise and legitimate rule,
112, 115–16; sages, viziers,
philosopher-kings, Imams, 134,
hakim ilahi (divine sage), 143; wit
over brawn, 118, 130, 270, 362. *See also*
Bozorgmehr; Elias; Khizr; Maimonides; Sohrush
women
—**film directors**: Bani-Etemad, 250,
348; Hekmat (*Women's Prison*), 357;
Jongbloed (*Smile and Wave*), 422n10;
Makhmalbaf, Hana, 268, 338, 348;
Makhmalbaf, Samira, 259,260, 267,
268, 292, 293, 299–300, 302, 307, 313,
329, 338, 347, 348, 349, 350, 351, 353,
368, 370, 38t, 391, 420n2; Meshkini
(*The Day I Became a Woman*), 267;
Milani, 315; Mir Hosseini (*Divorce
Iranian Style*), 419n4; Pariza (*Return
to Afghanistan*, with Paul Jay),
422n10; Shah (*Behind the Veil*),

422n10; Ustaoglu, 422n9;
— in *Shahnameh*: Baghdad Khatun, 73;
Bibi Shahbanu, 128; Ferangiz, 85;
Gulnar, 73; Homa (Humai), 80, 92;
Khadijeh, 75; Manizha, 87, 404n12;
Rudabeh, 81; Rushanak, q.v.,
Sudabeh, 84; Tahmina, 81
—**women-warriors**, 110, 113, 126, 375,
406n30; Banu Goshasp (daughter of
Rustam), 406n30; Gordafrid un-
horses and marries Sohrab, 406n30;
Gurdya, 126, 406n30, 408n42,
409n44; Jarira (wife of Siyavush),
406n30
—**work stories**, 112, 123, 375, 407n34,
408n41
world pereginations, 109; Alexander
(for knowledge), 109; Esfandiar (for
conversion), 109; Kai Khosrow (for
royal legitimation), 109

Yaqubi, 409n50
yashts, 28
yasna, 18, 19, 21, 22, 25–65; chants in
Avestan in full voice, in Pazand sotto
voce, 28, ringing, 42–43, 52; **codification, stability, changes**, 27, 398n9,
archaic epithet Varuna for Ahura
Mazda, 48, eight priests once required, now two, 27, 30, 40, 399n15,
offering of fat to the fire, 27, 45–56,
references to four social estates, 42,
references to five political levels, 42,
references to Rayy as center of the
realm, 42; **contest of poesis and wit**,
28–29, 398n13; **cosmic creation rite**,
27, 57–58; **dramatic dialogues**, 38,
40, 43, 44, 54, 59, zot-raspi dialogue,
37; **dron (luwog)**, 32, 33, 37, 400n27,
dron ritual as linkage between zot
and patron of the ritual, 37; **gestural
vocabulary**, 55; **hom ritual**, 38–41,
42, 45–47, production of hom (q.v.)
using the bulls of heaven (forces of

the amshaspands, q.v.), 43, 50, seed
of bulls, 57, *waras tashte* (seven bull
tail hairs), 32; **mnemonic for legends
of Zoroaster**, 28, 47, reenacting creation of Zoroaster, 46–47; **paragna
preparatory rite**, 32–33, 400n22;
schematic structure 35; Yasna Haptanhaiti (worship of seven chapters,
without ritual), 47
Yazdegird III, 18, 35, 113, 114, 127–128;
abandoned courts to sue the sovereign, 142; daughter Bibi Shahbanu
marries Imam Husain, 128; kicked to
death by white horse from the waters, 408n37
Yemen, 93, 101, 103, 111
Yima, 32, 40, 59, 137, 138, 405n23
Yinhe Hatam, 42, 52

Zabul: province in Afghanistan, 344;
town in Iran, 329
Zabul, House of (Rustam, Sam, Zal),
76, 77, 92, 405n21; end of, 96;
Scythian epic, 76
Zahhak (Dahaka), 21, 22, 40, 68, 76, 77,
78, 81, 101; **bound** (by Tahmuras,
Faridun, and Homa), 108, 406n25; **as
dragon/Arab**, 97, rules from
Baghdad, 103; **Hitler as**, 102, 103;
thrice led astray by Ahriman (ar-
chetype for errors of Kai Kaus and
Gushtasp, and for trials of Esfandiar,
Gushtasp, and Rustam), 100
Zakaraya, 77
Zal, 81, 92, 100, 103, 129, 403n5; appoints
Zav king, 73; and Rudabeh, 73, 403n6
Zardosht Nameh (thirteenth century),
58, 60
Zarir, 80
Zatspram, 58, 60, 402n33
Zav, 73, 403n5, 405n19
Žižek, Slavoj, 232, 260, 420n1
Zoroaster, 18, 27, 28, 42, 43, 54, 58–62,
80, 88, 93, 406n25; **in Europe**, 379;

Zoroaster (*cont.*)

　　prophetic career: birth, 60, 138, 382; creation, 46–47; dates, 58–59, 402n37; death, 62, 80; failings as missionary, 25, 57; followers as ten mares (-aspa) and a camel (-ushtra), 49; and *hom*, 34, 40; journeys, 61; locations, 58; trials, 60; **revaluation**: in Kermani assimilated to decline of seven empires and occultation/ resurrection of the Twelfth Imam (Bahram Varjovand), 137, in *Shahnameh* assimilated to bad rule of Gushtasp, 95, in Tabari assimilated to bad rule of Sassanians, 95; steel chain of, used by Esfandiar, 97, 103

Zoroastrianism, 12, 20, 396n2, ***behdin*** **("good religion/vision")**, 43

—CULTURAL RESONANCES: European, 3, 379; Mozart, 3, 22; Nietzsche, q.v.; in popular Persian language, 6, 21

—ETHOS: honesty and purity, 22; optimism, 20, 22, 175; **mutuality**: *fravashi* (*farawahar*) symbol, 429n10; between God and man, 38, 43, 50; between human beings, 51, *paiwand* (physical linkage) and *baj* (exchange of blessings), 34, 400n25; between husband and wife, 51; ritual and worldly action as yoked or mirror images, 64

—MYSTICAL INTERPRETATIONS, 20; Ilm-i Khsnoom, 396n2; Meher Baba, 396n2; Rashid Shahmardan, 396n2; see also Corbin; illuminationism; Kermani; Shaikhis; Suhrawardi

—PRESSURES: to be monotheistic (Christian), 23; to have a single prophet (Muslim), 58

—PRIESTS, 8, 26; Dastur Erachji Sorabji Meherjirana, 399n16; Dastur Kekobadji Rustamji Dastur Mehrjirana, 399n16; Dastur Khodadad-i Shahriar Nerosangi, 26, 397n7; Dastur Manuchehr Homji-Mehr, 8; Dastur Mehreban-i Mobed Siavush, 8, 26, 27; Dastur Rustam Shahzadi, 8, 26, 397n4; eight priest roles for yasna, 399n15; Kotwal, 8, 26, 27, 397, 397n3; Modi, 8, 26, 397n2, 400n22

—RITUAL GESTURES: alternating percussion (smiting devils) and cessation of ritual action (to concentrate on beneficient vision, mantras), 47; directions, 311; exchanging baj, 35; tying and loosening the kusti, 36

—SCHOLARS: Anquetil du Perron, 379; Boyce, 48, 397nn1, 3, and 6, 398nn9 and 13, 400n25, 401nn27, 28, 30, and 32, 402nn34 and 36; Boyd, 398n8, 399n16, 400n23; Darrow, 58, 398n8, 400n23, 402n33; Gershevitch, 38, 39, 401n31; Hyde, 379; Insler, 29, 401n28, 402n36; Kotwal, 397, 397n3, 399n16, 400n25, 401n27; Modi, 26, 397n2; Windfuhr, 50, 64, 400n19

zurkhaneh, 24, 209, 397n5, 424n16

MICHAEL M. J. FISCHER is professor of anthropology and science and technology studies at the Massachusetts Institute of Technology and lecturer in the Department of Social Medicine at Harvard Medical School. He is the author of *Emergent Forms of Life and the Anthropological Voice* (Duke University Press) and *Iran: From Religious Dispute to Revolution* and coauthor of *Debating Muslims: Cultural Dialogues in Postmodernity and Tradition* and *Anthropology as Cultural Critique: An Experimental Moment in the Human Sciences.*

Library of Congress Cataloging-in-Publication Data

Fischer, Michael M. J., 1946–
Mute dreams, blind owls, and dispersed knowledges : Persian poesis in
the transnational circuitry / Michael M. J. Fischer.
p. cm.
Includes bibliographical references and index.
ISBN 0-8223-3285-X (cloth : alk. paper) — ISBN 0-8223-3298-1 (pbk. : alk. paper)
1. Motion pictures—Iran—History. 2. Iran—Civilization. I. Title.
PN1993.5.I846E57 2004
791.43′0955—dc22   2004006055